PEARSON ALWAYS LEARNING

Seán Duffy • Timothy Dansdill • Jill Shahverdian • Aileen Dever

The Individual in the Community

Seventh Edition

Front cover image courtesy of John Hassett.

Previously published as:
The Individual in the Community, Second Edition
by Sean Duffy
Copyright © 2006, 2005
Published by Kendall/Hunt Publishing Company
Dubuque, Iowa 52002

Pearson Learning Solutions, 501 Boylston Street, Suite 900, Boston, MA 02116
A Pearson Education Company
www.pearsoned.com

Printed in the United States of America

2 3 4 5 6 7 8 9 10 V0ZN 18 17 16 15 14 13

000200010271764956

MM/SK

ISBN 10: 1-269-31666-4
ISBN 13: 978-1-269-31666-8

For You

Call For Entries for 2014 Textbook Cover Design

Are you a student who is currently enrolled in or completed the QU Seminar Program?

Do you have an idea for a cover for the 2014 Edition of QU101's ***The Individual in the Community?***

We will consider photographs, drawings, collage, sculpture, diagrams, and typographic designs. The cover design may be in full color or black and white.

Deadline for submissions is January 1, 2014. The **winner** will receive a copy of the book and a $50 Visa Gift Card. The artist's name and credit will be printed in the book.

Photos submitted as TIFF files, scanned at 300 dpi at 9 x 12 or larger
Photos taken with a 4.8 (or higher) megapixel camera at its highest setting
Logos from drawing programs saved as vector-based files (i.e. .EPS or AI)
Logos saved as 1200 dpi bitmaps

All artwork needs to be original. The publisher will ask you to fill out a form granting permission to use the work. Any recognizable faces in the image will be required to sign a model release. The artist retains the rights to use the image. The decision of the judges is final.

Send your idea in the form of a tiff to quseminars@quinnipiac.edu with the words "Cover Design Contest" in the subject line.

The release form will need to be filled out by the student whose cover image is selected.

PEARSON
Custom Publishing

501 Boylston Street, Suite 900
Boston, Massachusetts 02116
[617] 671-2000

A Pearson Education Company

Please return this form to the attention of your editor

Reproduction Rights

I grant my permission to Pearson Custom Publishing for reproduction rights of my (Artwork), (Photograph), (Article), (Essay) titled:

____

This permission is solely for inclusion in the following project at:

____
School

______________________________ ______________________________
Title of Book or Project Professor(s) or Author(s)

The credit line for this work should read:
[Author: please add to manuscript if required.]

____

I grant permission for this and future print and electronic editions.

______________________________ ______________________________
Signature Date

____
Print Name

____
Address

____

____

______________________________ Title ID

CONTENTS

INTRODUCTION

"I see you're reading the Introduction to the QU 101 book."

"Yes."

"If you have any questions about QU 101, I can help. I'm a Peer Catalyst."

"What's that?"

"I'm a sophomore who took QU 101 last year. I liked the class so much that I'm collaborating with the QU 101 professor I had last fall. I give the professor insights from a student's perspective about course activities and assignments. I also help the students taking the class now as they adjust to college and show them why this course is so important."

"Thank you."

Why are you taking this course called QU 101—The Individual in the Community? The answer perhaps lies in a circle around a flickering fire in a cold, dark cavern hall thousands of years ago. The people gathered around that fire were our human ancestors. A sense of community and kinship was developing among them along with the critical evolution of language (Time-Life 9). Professor Daniel C. Dennet affirms that there was "no step more uplifting, more momentous in the history of mind design, than the invention of language. When *homo sapiens* became the beneficiary of this invention, the species stepped into a slingshot that has launched it far beyond all other earthly species in the power to look ahead and reflect" (Calvin 80).

As these early humans communicated in the warmth and security of their campfires, perhaps they wondered about the circles in the sky, the shimmering sun during the day and the silvery moon at night. Little could they have known that their descendants would invent telescopes to the sun and spaceships to the moon. Professor David Lewis-Williams underscores that "a crucial threshold in human evolution was between two kinds of consciousness, not merely between moderate and advanced intelligence. Neanderthals were able to borrow only certain activities from their new *Homo sapiens* neighbors not because they were hopelessly bemired in animality and stupidity but because they lacked a particular kind of consciousness" (285). Living only in the here-and-now, Neanderthals "were unable to enter into long-term planning, categorize generations and human relationships in order to initiate complex kinship and political systems, and speak of and construct mental 'scenes' of past and future times" (Lewis-Williams 285). By contrast, our ancient ancestors were dream-weavers. The howling beasts kept at bay with their blazing bonfires and their bellies full, these creative predecessors of ours likely told stories in their caves or huts, reenacted hunting scenes, danced, and made music with flutes carved from mammoth ivory (Desdemaines-Hugon 193). Having food, fire, and the freedom to live outside the eternity of a single moment permitted these early humans to reflect upon themselves, their world, and a possible Afterlife as they realized with dawning awareness and deepening anguish that time passes—and they do too (Lewis-Williams 80).

Our human forebears left soul-stirring evidence of their quest for meaning as they attempted to understand themselves and the world full of mystery they inhabited. Art thousands of years old bejewels caves on the five continents (Saura Ramos 15-16). According to anthropologist Christine Desdemaines-Hugon, Cro-Magnon cave art "went well beyond simple aesthetics or literal representation, to embody and explain its makers' view of the world and their place in it" (xi). In our mind's eye we see these prehistoric artists entering subterranean galleries carrying pine torches and grease-filled stone lamps containing mossy sprigs set afire and sputtering. With heart-quickening wonder we observe finger marks that "bring us directly into contact with the reality of a person's touch, a hand, a human being, alive, breathing, thinking, creating, not just some anonymous *Homo sapiens*" (Christine Desdemaines-Hugon 118).

It is noteworthy that even at a time when survival would have seemed uppermost in their minds, these early humans did not only concentrate on making specialized weapons and tools. Nor did they merely teach their children to hunt and gather food. Remarkably, as we've seen, they showed future generations how to grind up pigment from minerals to produce paint with which they left their impressions on stone walls sometimes hidden in almost inaccessible places (Saura Ramos 81). As Professor David Lewis-Williams shares:

> To my way of thinking, there is no greater archaeological enigma than the subterranean art of Upper Palaeolithic western Europe. Anyone who has crouched and crawled underground along a narrow, absolutely dark passage for more than a kilometre, slid along mud banks and waded through dark lakes and hidden rivers to be confronted, at the end of such a hazardous journey, by a painting of an extinct woolly mammoth or a powerful, hunched bison will never be quite the same again. Muddied and exhausted, the explorer will be gazing at the limitless *terra incognita* of the human mind. (11)

Our human precursors also carved statuettes and all sorts of *objets d'art* and jewelry from stone, ivory, amber, and antler (Christine Desdemaines-Hugon 75-76). Engaged in these ostensibly "useless" activities they were likely learning to survive better and to apply their brains to solve problems in new and inventive ways. Many kinds of knowledge and modes of thinking were clearly important to them.

These predecessors of ours also engaged in complex social interactions in their budding communities. In fact, Christine Desdemaines-Hugon explains that "even personal objects were subject to rules and traditions as far as their decoration was concerned, thus revealing, in turn, the existence of strong societal conventions" (xvi). Professor David Lewis-Williams highlights that human beings "lived in history-making communities, and that means there were social tensions and conflicts. How did individuals in Upper Palaeolithic communities challenge or subvert 'traditional' social relations and socially sanctioned art? If the hierarchy of a community was questioned, did that challenge show itself in cave art?" (268–269) The answers to these intriguing questions may be eternally lost among the cold, dark shadows deep within these caves. But we can affirm that the origins and epic story of all humans began in Africa six million years ago (Desdemaines-Hugon xiv-xv). *Homo sapiens* then "migrated to the European continent approximately 40,000 years ago, on their way encountering widely scattered indigenous Neanderthal populations" (Desdemaines-Hugon 71). Thus they not only helped to hold torches in decorated caves but also embarked on a momentous journey together displaying a capacity for cooperation.

Student: "I've read a few paragraphs of this QU 101 text and still have no idea what on earth this course is about."

Peer Catalyst: "What are you reading about now?"

Student: "About some migration of humans out of Africa."

Peer Catalyst: "Let's fast forward, okay? After all the violent events of recent memory, the ethnic cleansing in Bosnia, the genocide in Rwanda, the tragedy of September 11th, 2001 and the wars that followed, maybe the continuation of our species doesn't just depend on cold reason and competitiveness but also on cooperation and compassion. Among many interesting topics in QU 101 you'll be talking about how communities of all kinds are formed and sustained."

Student: "I guess we do need to cooperate if we're going to move ahead constructively as a society."

Peer Catalyst: "When you think of the international students here, it's amazing. We get along with them, they get along with us, and they all get along with each other. I think we at Quinnipiac could teach the world a thing or two. Maybe because we're living and learning together, we're choosing to see our commonalities rather than our differences."

Student: "Come to think of it, that is a powerful example of collaboration. I guess I'll go back to reading. Thanks."

From caves to modern-day cafeterias and cafés, some of the greatest innovations in all fields of endeavor have come from people sitting around and actively discussing their ideas in circles. In QU 101, you will be exploring a wide range of topics and perspectives related to identity and community and also sharing your own insights as you grapple with some of society's most persistent and urgent problems. Contribute freely in these conversation communities; all those in the circle possess equal status. Such focused, reasoned exchanges around a ghostly bonfire are important for your intellectual growth as you learn to express your ideas publically in a clear, coherent, and logical manner. At the same time you will be acquiring skills to prepare you to work effectively with large and small groups as you take on both leadership and collaborative roles. You will further develop your proficiency in critical thinking in the realm of writing with plenty of systematic practice in examining evidence and supporting your assertions using a variety of academic experiences including the readings contained in this text, films, class discussions, and attending community involvement activities.

Student: "What sorts of community activities do we attend in QU 101?"
Peer Catalyst: "Well, the idea is for you to become better acquainted with the university community and all of the opportunities available to you. Typically these activities include the Involvement Fair at the beginning of the semester where you get a chance to learn about all of the amazing clubs and organizations on campus. Your professor may also suggest you hike up Sleeping Giant as a class, attend a sporting event, a musical or theatrical performance, a lecture – we have all kinds of really interesting people come to campus including Nobel Laureates and many famous, fascinating people."
Student: "Thanks. And—we don't sit in rows in QU 101?"
Peer Catalyst: "No. Your professor will ask you to put your desks in a circle for class. In my section sometimes we sat in a big circle and other times a group of us were in a small circle within the big circle—actually my professor got pretty creative with the circles! The truth is sitting in a circle helps to build a sense of community. And anyway when you think about it, a circle more closely resembles what happens in meetings in a professional setting."
Student: "I guess it gives the class a greater sense of community because you're looking into people's eyes rather than at the backs of their heads."
Peer Catalyst: "True."

Professor Andrew P. Mills affirms that "a college education equips people with the tools for self-examination that renders them able to make informed and intelligent choices about the direction of their own lives" (145). Antonio Machado (1878–1939), the Spanish poet and teacher tells us, too, that *"son tus huellas/el camino, y nada más;/ caminante, no hay camino,/se hace camino al andar"/* our footprints/ are the path, and nothing more;/ traveler, there is no path, you make a path by walking (203). The interdisciplinarity and integration of fundamental questions about the formation of individual identity in QU 101 helps to illumine more brightly the many paths you may choose as you begin your life's journey. You may believe you are on one path but you could find yourself quite unexpectedly confronted by other intriguing possibilities and prospects. You will be asked to reflect with increasing thoughtfulness in QU 101 about the person you are and who you want to become. As part of this self-evaluative process, you will need to consider what you truly care about, what you are good at and what you love to do. Although it is important to conquer academic weaknesses, it is essential when you think about a career to identify your strengths and concentrate on those. In this way you will find the most suitable profession for you. In QU 101 you will also discuss your Personal Success Plan (PSP) that will help you to understand the importance of goals and continuing to assess those goals. Interestingly, one of the possible meanings of Quinnipiac that derives from the Native-American word *quinnuppinuk* is "a turning point" or "to make a change in the direction of travel". Like the rivers that flow beside our university, your life is fluid and rich with potential as you ponder the opportunities before you.

Student: "I wish I knew what I wanted to major in. My roommates all know and it worries me that I don't."

Peer Catalyst: "QU 101 will actually help with that as you think about your own identity and interests and try to clarify what you'd like to do."

Student: "I'm just afraid that I'll choose the wrong major and end up stuck in a job that I don't like."

Peer Catalyst: "That's why it's so crucial to choose a major in something that you find interesting and you're good at so you'll wind up in a position related to what you like to do and feel confident about doing it. Think of the president of Quinnipiac, John Lahey. He has his bachelor's, master's, and doctoral degrees in philosophy. Imagine all of the interesting twists and turns his career must have taken for him to become president of a university. But he's still teaching philosophy, doing what he loves, and his background probably also helps him in leading Quinnipiac."

Student: "I wonder if he always knew he wanted to be a philosopher or if that realization came from a course he took as an undergraduate?"

Peer Catalyst: "You can ask him, you know."

Student: "I can?"

Peer Catalyst: "Yes. The President's door is always open to students."

As the first of the three university seminars, QU 101 provides a firm foundation for students to explore their roles and responsibilities as engaged members of the campus and also their local communities. You will then widen your outlook to include the national and global communities in QU 201 and QU 301.

Student: "Do you mind if I ask, what's a seminar?"

Peer Catalyst: "A seminar means the professor won't be up front lecturing but rather guiding discussion with you and your classmates taking the lead in exploring issues and expanding on important ideas. In other words, you can't just sit around and be passive. You and the other students ARE the class. You have to contribute your thoughts in connection with the topics for each day. The key words in a seminar course are 'active participation'."

Student: "I'm nervous about QU 101 with all the talking you have to do."

Peer Catalyst: "I can understand. I'm kind of shy myself. But I kept getting so absorbed in what we were discussing that I actually forgot to be nervous. Something you never even thought you'd be interested in and there you are, listening and talking. QU 101 was one of my all-time favorite classes."

Student: "I can see you really like QU 101."

Peer Catalyst: "Well, I'm back for a second go-around as a Peer Catalyst. A piece of advice—always do the assignments. You don't want to be left out of the conversation. It's important to do your share to be completely part of the group."

Student: "Thanks."

Peer Catalyst: "Also – another word to the wise. It's key that you do your own work. Quinnipiac takes integrity and honesty very seriously. For any formal paper you write be sure you do it yourself and include the proper citations. If you need help with citing or writing or academic support in any of your classes, we have a wonderful Learning Commons located in the Arnold Bernhard Library. The Learning Commons is for students who want to improve their academic skills and also for those who want to excel."

Student: "I appreciate the advice."

Peer Catalyst: "You'll also find helpful advice about getting the most out of college in Andrew Mills' article in your text, 'What's So Good About a College Education?' In the Appendix, too, there are some useful ideas for succeeding in college."

Recurrent themes in QU 101 include a commitment to life-long learning and the creation of a strong sense of community which are expressions of core values at this university. Integral components of this inclusive education are diversity awareness and sensitivity which are fully explored. One way students can learn about various kinds of communities is through volunteering which Quinnipiac University supports in tangible ways.

Student: "So service is pretty big here."

Peer Catalyst: "Yes! Every spring we have something called the Big Event in which students, staff, and faculty do volunteer work in Hamden, New Haven, and surrounding towns for non-profit organizations. Quinnipiac students are always looking for ways to lend a helping hand to people in need in the community. Volunteerism is a topic that comes up quite a bit in QU 101 because so many students get involved."

Student: "That's good to know."

As you learn about different kinds of communities, you will observe the tensions and conflicts that can arise between individuals and society. In QU 101 students read about those who possessed the courage of their convictions to stand against an unfair status quo continued merely out of convenience or tradition. Students comprehend that injustice exists and when we tell ourselves that it will always exist or that everyone engages in dishonest acts, we give in to complacency instead of striving for meaningful change in ourselves and others. We realize that by endeavoring to be the best versions of ourselves, we teach through example. Furthermore, in this course you will see that as a democracy we honor the idea of 'unity' in the community but also respect and understand the value of disagreement and different points of view. As author Colin Tudge reminds, history "is largely the story of relationships. Nations interact with other nations; species with other species. The other creatures that have occupied our planet this past 50 million years or so helped to shape our evolution—we evolved in part to cope with them—and we, in our turn, have influenced them" (25). The hope is that we can come together in ways that affirm regard and respect for all which are fundamental principles Quinnipiac imbues in its students.

You'll come to find that Quinnipiac University stands out as a glittering jewel nestled at the foothills of Sleeping Giant Mountain with its emphasis on the importance of a liberal education over merely a vocational one. General education, which includes the QU seminar series, enables students to see more clearly and broadly thus enhancing and enriching experiences throughout life. Professor Martha C. Nussbaum states:

> Unlike all other nations, we ask a higher education to contribute a general preparation for citizenship, not just a specialized preparation for a career. To a greater degree than all other nations, we have tried to extend the benefits of this education to all citizens, whatever their class, race, sex, ethnicity, or religion. We hope to draw citizens toward one another by complex mutual understanding and individual self-scrutiny, building a democratic culture that is truly deliberative and reflective, rather than simply the collision of unexamined preferences. And we hope in this way to justify and perpetuate our nation's claim to be a valuable member of a world community of nations that must increasingly learn how to understand, respect, and communicate, if our common human problems are to be constructively addressed. (294)

Considering Quinnipiac's dedication to a broad education, it is not surprising that our library is named for Arnold Bernhard who created Value Line in 1931 and built it into one of the largest independent advisory services in the United States as well as a foremost money management organization in the world. A plaque in the foyer explains further why he deserves this honor:

Arnold Bernhard (1901–1987)

Dedication, discipline, imagination, courage, integrity, dignity

Arnold Bernhard became known as the Dean of Wall Street. He was the founder, publisher, and editor of the Value-line Investment Survey and the Value-line Family of Mutual Funds. He was a first generation American. As a young man he was an eclectic achiever, classical pianist, Latin scholar, linguist, and theatrical critic. Arnold Bernhard –

A life-long lover of the arts and humanities.

He was a visionary who brought to Wall Street a unique combination of creativity, drive, and intellectual honesty.

Arnold Bernhard's life was one of exceptional achievement in which he cultivated a breadth and depth of knowledge and interests. Similarly, QU 101 exemplifies a multifaceted and multi-purpose approach to learning. Andrew P. Mills maintains: "A college education does not, as most people believe, prepare you to do *something*. Rather, it prepares you to do *anything*" (147). With its mind-opening range of topics, QU 101 inspires higher order thinking that is both reflective and analytical. Students are introduced to the ideas of well-known activists, authors, and thinkers. The course additionally seeks to improve the quality of students' thinking in speaking and writing with regard to clarity, expression, logic, and fairness. In other words, students are taught not only to see the superficial flash and shine as on the surface of a river but to delve deeper in order to understand more completely all that lies beneath.

To accomplish its broad educational objectives, QU 101 employs pedagogical methods common to all sections that include:

a. Annotation—refers to students' own personal comments and reactions to what the author of a text is saying. Through your annotations in pen or pencil in the margins of this text, it is hoped that you will become more thoughtful in your readings and more responsive during class discussions. It is useful to consider the readings in light of the six course questions that appear below as you ponder such themes as individual identity, community, and the conflict that can sometimes arise between the two.

Student: "Can I ask you, what exactly is annotation? Is it like paraphrasing?"

Peer Catalyst: "No, annotation is different than just paraphrasing or summarizing. Annotations are your own notes and responses to what an author is saying. I usually underline or highlight a passage or quote in a reading that I think is important. Then I write in the margin how it connects with a course question and/or to another reading, a film, a current event, a community event I attended or even something from my own life. In this way I'm actually responding to some of the greatest thinkers in the history of humanity. The annotations also help you participate better in class discussions and write your papers because you have all these notes you've taken. Going forward, too, in your professional life, using the annotation method for reports will allow you to speak with confidence and knowledge as you'll be able to reference your points quickly and form coherent arguments. At that future meeting table, you'll be facing colleagues, looking them in the eye, speaking up intelligently and showing yourself to be a hard-working, conscientious member of the team."

Student: "Thanks."

b. Dialectics—refers to a focused conversation between two or more people with opposing points of view. This format often involves tension in an attempt to get at the truth by means of reasoned discussion. Thus dialectics entails the exchange of logical arguments and counterarguments that can result in changes in perspective. Socrates would use questions to analyze the ideas of other people to showcase contradictions and inconsistencies. In these cross-examinations, he would draw out the consequences of their statements about such abstract ideas as courage, virtue, justice or wisdom with questions like, 'What do you mean?' and 'How do you know?' Socrates fundamentally saw himself as "an intellectual midwife, whose questioning delivers the thoughts of others into the light of day" (Gottlieb 15).

Student: "Could you explain dialectics to me? I'm not sure I quite get it."

Peer Catalyst: "How about if we try out a Socratic dialectic? Let me ask you, what is morality?"

Student: "Doing what's right."

Peer Catalyst: "How do you know if something is right?"

Student: "Something is right if you're obeying the law. Something is not right if it's illegal."

Peer Catalyst: "Lying under oath is illegal and it's not right. But what if your mother asks you if you washed your hands before dinner and you lie and say 'yes'. That's not illegal, but is it 'doing what's right', to use your words?"

Student: "It's not illegal to lie in this situation, but it's not right, either."

Peer Catalyst: "So do you still think morality equals legality?"

Student: "I guess not. Something can be legal, but still immoral."

Peer Catalyst: "I think morality is something that's legal AND something your conscience is okay with."

Student: "But people have different standards, don't they? What one person's conscience is okay with, another person's conscience may not be okay with. Can morality be defined using a universal standard?"

Peer Catalyst: "You're a quick learner! You can see how we could go back and forth on this for a while. So by using the dialectical method, a person often comes to see the gray in a belief or concept they'd seen before as only black and white."

c. Thematic triangulation—refers to making connections and applying concepts from three separate sources or aspects of the course in order to develop your own ideas or theories. Frequently a thematic triangulation begins with the professor asking students to examine two readings with discussion and reflection occurring both in and out of class. Next a third text or film or community activity is introduced and discussed in class. Students can then develop a thematic triangulation in a paper, for example, in which they reference the three sources and develop their particular ideas and assumptions about them.

Student: "Can I ask, what's the point of a thematic triangulation?"

Peer Catalyst: "Doing thematic triangulations helps us to understand or look at ideas in new ways. Often in thematic triangulations I find myself making references to my own personal experiences as a way of clarifying or reinforcing my ideas. Sometimes keeping a journal is helpful as you develop your thoughts. Some professors actually require us to reflect on readings and ideas by writing in journals."

d. Writing to Learn—refers to short pieces of writing that help students think through important concepts or ideas related to the course.

Student: "What exactly is Writing to Learn?"

Peer Catalyst: "Writing to Learns (or WTLs) are assigned by your professor to help you clarify key ideas from the readings or other aspects of the class. Some are done in class and some are done outside class. In QU 101 you'll be doing both formal and informal kinds of writing. The WTLs tend to be informal writing."

The ample margins in your text are designed to provide you with space to annotate as you personally react and respond to the readings. The blank pages at the end of each reading allow you to take notes from class discussions, reflect and triangulate, and generally put on paper thoughts that occur to you. On the back flap of your textbook you'll find a detachable bookmark on which are printed the six course questions for easy reference. As you read, annotate using these questions as your guide. You will be continually filtering the course content through these six questions. Your professor will center the class on the questions and will ask you to examine the readings and other course material in light of them on an ongoing basis. These questions are vital, eternal and without easy or absolute answers. As you will see, perennial themes naturally flow from these questions that include:

1. What defines and locates an individual?
2. How is individual identity formed and sustained?
3. What defines and locates a community?
4. How is a sense of community formed and sustained?
5. How do individuals deal with tensions and conflicts between personal interests and community interests?
6. How do perceptions of individual difference and diversity affect community?

As you consider the questions, you'll be practicing specific learning proficiencies including oral and written communication, critical and creative thinking, social intelligence (an ability to work effectively with others), diversity awareness and sensitivity, and responsible citizenship. All of these proficiencies will help you in college, in your career(s), and in your own lives.

This text is divided into three sections: The Individual, The Community, and The Individual in the Community. Under each heading there are readings required of all sections of QU 101 so that you have this commonality of experience. Then there are selections for further reading which your professor (and probably you) will uniquely determine for your QU 101 class. Some professors on the first day give their students a syllabus that contains the entire semester mapped out while others prefer to distribute the syllabus in two week increments for the sake of flexibility. There will be professors who use blogs to jumpstart conversations before class and some who write a question on the board for students to answer in their journals. In other words, no two sections of QU 101 will be exactly alike in how they proceed during the semester but there will be considerable commonality in what is covered. In this way, you will be able to continue intellectual discussions outside of class with all students who have taken the course.

The first required reading includes chapters two and three of *A Vindication of the Rights of Woman* published in 1792 by the British writer Mary Wollstonecraft (1759–1797). This is her best-known book in which she boldly proclaims that women should have equality with men (Franklin ix). Wollstonecraft contends that if they had access to better educational opportunities, women would live more fulfilled, creative lives. Through sheer determination, Wollstonecraft educated herself by studying books at home (Franklin 6). Her ideas were influenced by the democratic principles of the French Revolution and her own personal experiences (Langan 40). Reading Mary Wollstonecraft in her original prose means her writing will appear very antiquated to you. Although her expressions are indeed old-fashioned, her ideas are not. They are compelling and continue to speak profoundly about the strength of the human spirit. In discussing Wollstonecraft's chapters, do not limit your discussion merely to blaming males for oppressing females. Look far deeper to examine the societal structures in the past (and present) that would keep any group of people subjugated, demoralized, and unable to fulfill the potential that would grant greater meaning to their lives.

Student: "I see that the first reading is by Mary Wollstonecraft. I know her daughter was Mary Wollstonecraft Shelley who wrote Frankenstein."
Peer Catalyst: "Yes! That's right!"

Next under the section The Individual you will be reading parts one and three from the book *In the Name of Identity* by the sociologist and author Amin Maalouf (1949–). If the experience of being born a woman in Wollstonecraft's time would appear to be different than the experience of being born a woman today, Maalouf adds another dimension and perspective to our consideration in his thorough exploration of identity: "To be born a girl is not the same in Kabul as it is in Oslo: the condition of being a woman, like every other factor in a person's identity, is experienced differently in the two places" (23). Maalouf further affirms that an "individual's identity is made up of a number of elements" (10). Maalouf himself represents a fascinating amalgamation of identities as he was born in Lebanon, speaks Arabic as his native tongue, is Christian, and resides today in Paris. Continually Maalouf highlights the importance of embracing our multiple identities. He also demonstrates how identity becomes particularly problematical when it is perceived as threatened in some way. Maalouf's thoughts will be essential as you seek to understand yourself better and the reasons why people may react as they do.

Student: "I notice that on the back of this bookmark is a quote from Amin Maalouf."
Peer Catalyst: "It comes from his book In the Name of Identity."
Student: "It says how each of us has a 'vertical heritage' and a 'horizontal heritage'."

Peer Catalyst: "The vertical one comes down to us from our ancestors, our religious communities and traditions. Our horizontal heritage comes to us through our contemporaries and the time period in which we live. As you do the readings, keep that bookmark close at hand. Connect the course questions with topics and issues presented in the readings as they relate to identity, community and the tensions and conflicts between them. You'll find that the course questions are often intertwined and ideas and issues overlap from one question to another as you group the readings."

Peer Catalyst: "Thanks."

Peer Catalyst: "You'll soon see why this course is so great! You get to express your ideas and opinions and everyone's interested in what you have to say."

The Community comes next and begins with selected passages of a masterpiece of political philosophy entitled *The Social Contract* (1762) by the French philosopher Jean-Jacques Rousseau (1712–1778). Like Mary Wollstonecraft, he was self-educated. His ideas profoundly influenced the events leading to the French Revolution and the Founding Fathers of this nation (Damrosch 1). In *The Social Contract* Rousseau shares his views regarding government and the rights of citizens. He believes that human beings are innately good but are corrupted by society as can be observed through their behavior. Rousseau envisioned a society in which people might freely renounce their natural rights to yield to the "general will" which would be for the common good of all. Essentially the social contract is an attempt to answer why people should obey the state or government that limits their individual freedom.

Student: "I'm reading about Rousseau now. Without laws I guess we could do whatever we wanted."

Peer Catalyst: "That's true. You wouldn't need to pay taxes or even obey police officers."

Student: "But on the other hand, I guess, people could do whatever they wanted to me, too."

Peer Catalyst: "Exactly."

People agree to live under the rule of law because of the benefits they gain. They give up some freedoms but get others in return such as walking the streets in safety. Philosopher Stephen Law puts it succinctly when he says: "This is the contract: the state may command the citizen as long as he or she is protected by laws" (165). Professor Leo Damrosch asserts the following regarding Rousseau:

> He invented a whole new way of thinking about the social contract and about the sovereign. Whereas previous writers thought of the contract as a historical event, Rousseau's innovation was to see it as unconnected with history. He understood it to mean an implicit

> understanding that exists continuously, here and now, as the shared commitment without which no system of any kind can be legitimate. And whereas previous writers referred to the king as the sovereign, a ruler whose subjects were literally "subjected" to him, Rousseau insisted that the people as a whole were the sovereign. This meant that whatever ruler they might have was simply a civil servant, and that there was no conceptual difference between monarchies and republics. The royal absolutism of France, the constitutional monarchy of England, and the republic of Geneva all had executives responsible for carrying out the will of a sovereign people. If today we hold these truths to be self-evident, it is in large part because we are heirs of Rousseau. (346–347)

Rousseau's premise "that each individual is legally and morally the equal of every other" (Damrosch 347) was considered radical in his time. Centuries later human beings are still struggling with this concept as you will see in this course.

Following Jean-Jacques Rousseau in The Community section is Neil DeGrasse Tyson (1958–), an African-American astronomer and currently the director of the Hayden Planetarium in New York City. Included are the preface and chapters 14, 15, and 16 of his co-authored book *Origins: Fourteen Billion Years of Cosmic Evolution*. As with Rousseau, Tyson significantly reminds that each of us on this planet is part of a far bigger picture. He gives the example of the Polish astronomer Nicolaus Copernicus (1473–1543) who discredited the prevailing theory of his day that the earth was the center of all creation (230). Certainly it is within the realm of possibility that other intergalactic communities exist. If this is true "astrobiologists can already assert with confidence that life elsewhere in the universe, intelligent or otherwise, will surely look at least as exotic as some of Earth's own life forms, and quite probably more so" (232). Tyson affirms:

> Each new way of knowing heralds a new window on the universe—a new detector to add to our growing list of nonbiological senses. Whenever this happens, we achieve a new level of cosmic enlightenment, as though we were evolving into supersentient beings. Who could have imagined that our quest to decode the mysteries of the universe, armed with a myriad of artificial senses, would grant us insight into ourselves? We embark on this quest not from a simple desire but from a mandate of our species to search for our place in the cosmos. (294–295)

It is incumbent upon us to interact with other members of society in ways that produce peaceful and prosperous lives. If we are not alone in the universe perhaps in the future we will need to work together with yet undiscovered species from distant planets.

To take us to the last required reading under The Individual in the Community section, we come finally to Plato (427?–347? B.C.) An ancient Greek philosopher and teacher, Plato holds a preeminent position in the history of Western culture. Under a grove of trees on the outskirts of Athens, Plato would bring people together to discuss philosophy, mathematics and astronomy. This gathering of intellects became known as the Academy, which some consider to have been the first university (Williams 3–4). In his writings, Plato used a literary form called a 'dialogue', which is a conversation between two or more people. Plato's dialogues were mainly concerned with philosophical ideas. His own teacher, the Greek philosopher Socrates (c. 470–399 B.C.), appears frequently in his early dialogues, and they are considered the most reliable and important insight into Socrates' life and teachings (Williams 2). In the later dialogues, such as *The Republic,* Plato uses Socrates as his spokesperson rather than depicting him in a more literal way. According to philosopher Bernard Williams, "Socrates is the inspiration of the dialogues in more than one way. He himself wrote nothing, and indeed claimed to know nothing, devoting himself, it seems, to engaging people in conversations in which he questioned their most basic beliefs and showed that they had no basis for them" (2). This method, which we now call 'the Socratic method', is described in several of Plato's dialogues, and many of them display it in action. But Socrates' influence on Plato was not only due to his method of teaching. Socrates' life, and more particularly his death, left Plato with some of his deepest concerns. In turn, Plato explored many of these concerns by making them the central themes of his dialogues. It is understandable why Socrates' death had such a profound effect on Plato. Socrates was tried by the Athenian courts in 399 B.C. and executed on charges of, among other things, 'corrupting the youth'.

Throughout his trial, Socrates was also portrayed as disrupting and challenging the status quo in other ways. Before Socrates, Greek philosophy had concentrated on the nature and origin of the universe. But Socrates thought it was imperative to consider moral problems and how human beings should best live their lives. Athenians accused him of not believing in the gods of the state and for introducing new divine powers. It is perhaps significant to remember, however, that five years before Socrates' trial, Athens had suffered defeat in a twenty-seven-year war with Sparta in 404 B.C. (Gottlieb 10–11). According to author Anthony Gottlieb, "During the long war with Sparta, Athenians had grown increasingly nervous about the home front. It was felt that intellectuals were weakening Athenian society by undermining its traditional views and values. Well might a man who captivated idle youths with his questioning about justice have aroused suspicion" (11). If we return for a moment to the ideas of Amin Maalouf, Socrates' unorthodox ways may have appeared to Athenian citizens as a challenge to the legitimacy of their democratic state and thus a threat to the very identity of traditional Athenians. Socrates was convicted and sentenced to death by drinking hemlock, a poison the Athenians used for their death penalty. Socrates could have escaped the prison where he was being held, but he felt duty-bound to accept the decision of the court. Anthony Gottlieb states that "Socrates made it clear that although you must disobey the laws if they are unjust, you must nevertheless submit to punishment if caught, which is exactly what he himself did when he was condemned. Some friends gave him the chance to escape prison and flee Athens before execution; one of Plato's early dialogues, the Crito, deals with this episode and gives Socrates' reasons for rejecting the offer" (52–53). Socrates' death starkly raised a range of questions for Plato: "what the evil was in a political order that could do this; how it was that Socrates' presence had not made his fellow citizens (including some of his associates) better people; and how much it mattered—whether in the end it mattered at all—that Socrates' life was lost, granted that his character was uncorrupted" (Williams 2).

The main question in *The Republic* is 'What is justice?' You will repeatedly ponder the answer to that question in this course too. One of the most thought-provoking parts of Plato's *The Republic* describes Socrates inviting his student Glaucon to imagine a subterranean cave with a long entrance that reaches upwards to the light. The fettered prisoners in the cave can only see the shadows of statues and other items men are carrying across that entrance. With no idea of what the world is like beyond their cave, the prisoners believe that they are gazing upon reality. If one of the prisoners, who is supposed to represent a philosopher, were to break free of the chains and manage to make it to the light streaming behind the source of the shadows, and then go back to inform the prisoners that what they see is not real but merely shadows, the escapee would not be believed.

This course, in great part, is a legacy bequeathed by Socrates, who persistently emphasized how important it was to replace vague opinions with logical ideas and to live with a clear purpose. Plato gives everyone good advice when he quotes Socrates as saying that the unexamined life is not worth living. Remember that knowledge is always but one, fragile generation away from being lost to darkness. The clear recognition of the kind of knowledge that is important means having the wisdom and insight that leads ultimately to endurance and success. The wide range of readings and experiences in QU 101 are precisely designed to enlighten and help you to understand why it is essential to tend that flame delicately dancing among the shadows in the cave.

The voices in this text issue from those who wish to share their understanding of life and the human condition. As you read, become consciously self-reflective. How would you have reacted in a similar situation? What are your thoughts about the author's assertions? How are the ideas presented relevant to your life? What values are represented and do they embody ethics you also admire and adhere to? Why or why not? Is there something missing in the perspective presented? If so, what? What is the author's purpose in presenting this particular point of view? Think, too, on the life paths of the people who wrote these works and about where you are going.

Your own life is unfurling. You are part of something big that spans from the Stone Age to the Space Age. This course is an important stop along your journey to an examined life worth living well. Perhaps the essence of QU 101—The Individual in the Community is most beautifully and poignantly expressed by Margaret Mead (1901-1978) the U.S. anthropologist: "Never doubt that a small group of thoughtful, committed citizens can change the world; indeed, it is the only thing that ever has" (Lutkehaus 4).

Student: "I think I'm going to like QU 101 and learn a lot. Thanks for your help."

Peer Catalyst: "Welcome to the circle of Quinnipiac University."

Aileen Dever
Quinnipiac University
March 2013

WORKS CITED

Calvin, William H. *A Brief History of the Mind.* New York: Oxford UP, 2004. Print.

Damrosch, Leo. *Rousseau: Restless Genius.* New York: Houghton Mifflin, 2005. Print.

Desdemaines-Hugon, Christine. *Stepping Stones, A Journey through the Ice Age Caves of Dordogne.* New Haven, Yale UP, 2010. Print.

Franklin, Caroline. *Mary Wollstonecraft: A Literary Life.* New York: Palgrave Macmillan, 2004. Print.

Gottlieb, Anthony. *Socrates.* New York: Routledge, 1999. Print.

"History + Vision." Quinnipiac University, 2012. Web. 1 March 2013.

Langan, Jeffrey. *The Influence of the French Revolution on the Lives and Thought of John Adams, Thomas Jefferson, Edmund Burke, Mary Wollstonecraft, Immanuel Kant, and Pius IV: The End of Conservatism.* New York: Edwin Mellen P, 2012. Print.

Law, Stephen. *Philosophy.* London: DK, 2007. Print.

Lewis-Williams, David. *The Mind in the Cave.* New York: Thames & Hudson, 2002. Print.

Lutkehaus, Nancy C. Margaret Mead: *The Making of an American Icon.* Princeton, NJ: Princeton UP, 2008. Print.

Machado, Antonio. *Obras, poesía y prosa.* Buenos Aires: Losada, 1964. Print.

Maalouf, Amin. *In the Name of Identity.* New York: Penguin, 2000. Print.

Mills, Andrew P. "What's So Good About a College Education?" *The Individual in the Community.* Ed. Jill Shahverdian. 6th ed. Boston: Pearson, 2012. Print.

Nussbaum, Martha C. *Cultivating Humanity.* Cambridge, MA: Harvard UP, 1997. Print.

Plato. *Apology, Crito, and Phaedo of Socrates.* Project Gutenberg. Web. 14 March 2013.

Saura Ramos, Pedro A. *The Cave of Altamira.* New York: Harry N. Abrams, 1998. Print.

Time-Life Books. *The First Men.* New York: Time, 1973. Print.

Tudge, Colin. *The Time Before History.* New York: Scribner, 1996. Print.

Tyson, Neil DeGrasse. *Origins: Fourteen Billion Years of Cosmic Evolution.* New York: W.W. Norton, 2004. Print.

Williams, Bernard. *Plato: The Invention of Philosophy.* New York: Routledge, 1999. Print.

IN APPRECIATION

Thank you to the original ten faculty members who designed and taught the very first sections of QU 101: **Cheryl Barnard**, **Crystal Brian**, **Eric Bronson**, **Deborah Clark**, **Ray Foery**, **Jill Martin**, **Scott McLean**, **Bruce Saulnier**, **Robert Smart**, and **Alison Stratton**. What we do today is a testament and a tribute to what you did before.

A debt of gratitude is also owed to **Seán Duffy** as Chair of the curriculum committee that envisaged and created the QU Seminar Series and who subsequently served as the first Director of University Curriculum.

Thank you to the faculty who have fulfilled the role of QU 101 Course Leaders: **Carrie Bulger**, 2006-2007; **Eric Bronson**, 2007-2009; and **Timothy Dansdill**, 2009-2012.

Special acknowledgement goes to the QU 101 Advisory Board who gave so unstintingly of their time: **Lori Amann-Chetcuti** for her truly exceptional devotion to QU 101. All of the opening quotations for each section were selected by her as well as numerous readings. She also carefully edited Martha Nussbaum's chapter for our purposes; **Seán Duffy** for his steadfast, dedicated presence in QU 101; **Bernard N. Grindel** for compiling the common reading requirements in this text, supplying the Appendix, and for his remarkable ability to analyze and synthesize; **Linda Lindroth** for her artist's eye in designing the stunning cover with the photograph provided by **John Hassett**, for her idea of a cover contest for next year, and for several new contributions to the present version of the Reader; **Betsy Rosenblum** for her enthusiasm, very helpful insights, and balanced perspectives; **David Vance** for his expertise in philosophy that enabled him to answer the call from faculty to include less severely excerpted selections; and, of course, thank you to **Jill Shahverdian** who was always there when we needed her with a holistic view of the seminar series. Each of you is an educator extraordinaire.

A special tip of the hat to many who generously provide guidance and support to QU 101 on an ongoing basis in your various professional capacities: **Diane Ariza**, Associate Vice President for Academic Affairs & Chief Diversity Officer; **Mohammed Bey**, Director for Multicultural Education; **Daniel W. Brown**, Assistant Dean of Student Affairs/Director, Student Center & Campus Life; **Vincent C. Contrucci**, Director of Community Service; **Jennifer Crane**, Associate Director of Residential Life; **Andrew Delohery**, Associate Vice President of Retention and Student Success; **Peter Gallay**, Academic Technology Multimedia Producer; **Edward J. Gillen**, Director of Academic Assessment & Research; **Gary Pandolfi**, Instructional Technologist; **Paul Pasquaretta**, Director of Research & Writing Institute; and **Joanne Robertson**, Associate Director of Transfer Admissions.

A sincere thank you to all of the outstanding professionals who teach QU 101. You speak to the hearts and minds of our students who continue to choose this university as their enduring *alma mater*. There are particular professors who stand out for their creativity and consistent contributions to bring the best education possible to our students and even take the time to provide faculty development. They are: **Lori Amann-Chetcuti, Stephen Balkaran, David Clarke, Kathy Cooke, Jennifer Crane, Nicki M. Dakis-Gallagher, Seán Duffy, Christina Engelsgaard, Bernard N. Grindel, Anne Harrigan, Mark Hoffman, Suzanne Hudd, Kanicka Ingram, Sharon Jenkins, Richard Kamins, Joan Krieger, Linda Lindroth, Michelle Madsen-Bibeau, James F. Malerba, Signian McGeary, Jill McKeon, Scott McLean, Michael Medina, Brian Noell, Sigrid Nystrom, Fred Raudat, Lyneene Richardson, Joanne Robertson, Betsy Rosenblum, Jennifer Sacco, Shannon Sousa, Anita Visentin-Perito, Jaime Ullinger, David Vance**, and **Thomas M. Williams**. Your dedication is truly humbling.

A special tribute to our cherished colleague **Kenneth McGeary** (1944–2013), husband of **Signian McGreary**, for his devoted service of 45 years to Quinnipiac University as a Professor of Biology and in the QU seminars. I came to see that Ken was a great man because he always did his best.

Recognition is due to those who served as POD Leaders, giving so kindly of their time to help our new faculty members: **Lori Amann-Chetcuti, Kathy Cooke, Seán Duffy, Ray Foery, Bruce Franklin, Bernard Grindel, Mark Hoffman, Sharon Jenkins, Linda Lindroth, Charles Naden, Sigrid Nystrom, Betsy Rosenblum, Anita Perito-Visentin.**

Heartfelt gratitude to **Niraida Soto** for her invaluable assistance in the day-to-day (smooth) running of QU 101.

Thank you to my department chair, **Ronald Quirk**, who reduced my teaching load to three courses so I could continue one more semester as QU 101 Course Leader.

Thank you to Peer Catalyst Mentor **Rachael S. Wolensky** for her marvelous presentation to faculty on 'Discussion in QU 101'. Thank you to **Mark Hoffman**, too, for lending one of his 'Peer Catalysts' for the Introduction to this Reader.

Thank you for the magnificent insights and suggestions provided by **Anat Biletzki, Cecilia Dalzell, Maria Dever, Mark Gius, Mark Hoffman, Suzanne Hudd, Edward J. Kavanagh, Sandy O'Hare, Ben Page, Robert Smart, Andri Smith,** and **Zoe Weil**. Particular gratitude goes to **Suzanne Hudd** as our wonderful WAC/WID consultant.

Thank you very much to **Tim Dansdill** for crucially lending a sense of mission to QU 101, for increasing the overall rigor of the course, and establishing the common pedagogical methods which, we can now say, are tried and true.

Special words of appreciation go to **Ewa Callahan** and **Ray Foery**, my companions in course leadership.

Thank you also to Jill **Shahverdian** for her indefatigable efforts on behalf of students and faculty, her vision and leadership, her incredible organizational skills and ideas that inspire us all.

Thank you to our fantastic representative at Pearson, **Deb O'Connell**, who responds to emails with lightning speed. I am also very grateful to **Michelle Morgan**, our Associate Project Manager, for her helpfulness and meticulous attention to detail.

Most especially, thank you to our students who give us so many reasons to greet each day with hope.

THE INDIVIDUAL

"A graduation ceremony is an event where the commencement speaker tells thousands of students dressed in identical caps and gowns that 'individuality' is the key to success."

Robert Orben (1927–), Author, Comedian, Speechwriter

"The smallest minority on earth is the individual. Those who deny individual rights cannot claim to be defenders of minorities."

Ayn Rand (1905–1982), Author, Philosopher

REQUIRED READINGS

"It's always 'Sit,' 'Stay,' 'Heel'—never 'Think,' 'Innovate,' 'Be yourself.' "

Courtesy of Pat Steiner/The New Yorker Collection.

THE PREVAILING OPINION OF A SEXUAL CHARACTER DISCUSSED
Mary Wollstonecraft

(1759–1797)

Mary Wollstonecraft was a British writer best known for her groundbreaking book A Vindication of the Rights of Woman *(1792) in which she declared that women should have equality with men.*

To account for, and excuse the tyranny of man, many ingenious arguments have been brought forward to prove, that the two sexes, in the acquirement of virtue, ought to aim at attaining a very different character: or, to speak explicitly, women are not allowed to have sufficient strength of mind to acquire what really deserves the name of virtue. Yet it should seem, allowing them to have souls, that there is but one way appointed by Providence to lead *mankind* to either virtue or happiness. 1

If then women are not a swarm of ephemeron triflers, why should they be kept in ignorance under the specious name of innocence? Men complain, and with reason, of the follies and caprices of our sex, when they do not keenly satirize our headstrong passions and grovelling vices. Behold, I should answer, the natural effect of ignorance! The mind will ever be unstable that has only prejudices to rest on, and the current will run with destructive fury when there are no barriers to break its force. Women are told from their infancy, and taught by the example of their mothers, that a little knowledge of human weakness, justly termed cunning, softness of temper, *outward* obedience, and a scrupulous attention to a puerile kind of propriety, will obtain for them the protection of man; and should they be beautiful, every thing else is needless, for, at least, twenty years of their lives. 2

Thus Milton describes our first frail mother; though when he tells us that women are formed for softness and sweet attractive grace, I cannot comprehend his meaning, unless, in the true Mahometan strain, he meant to deprive us of souls, and insinuate that we were beings only designed by sweet attractive grace, and docile blind obedience, to gratify the senses of man when he can no longer soar on the wing of contemplation. 3

How grossly do they insult us who thus advise us only to render ourselves gentle, domestic brutes! For instance, the winning softness so warmly, and frequently, recommended, that governs by obeying. What childish expressions, and how insignificant is the being—can it be an immortal one? who will condescend to govern by such sinister methods! 'Certainly, says Lord Bacon, 'man is of kin to the beasts by his body; and if he be not of kin to God by his spirit, he is a base and ignoble creature!' Men, indeed, appear to me to act in a very unphilosophical manner when they try to secure the good conduct of women by attempting to keep them always in a state of childhood. 4

Rousseau was more consistent when he wished to stop the progress of reason in both sexes, for if men eat of the tree of knowledge, women will come in for a taste; but, from the imperfect cultivation which their understandings now receive, they only attain a knowledge of evil.

Children, I grant, should be innocent; but when the epithet is applied to men, or women, it is but a civil term for weakness. For if it be allowed that women were destined by Providence to acquire human virtues, and by the exercise of their understanding, that stability of character which is the firmest ground to rest our future hopes upon, they must be permitted to turn to the fountain of light, and not forced to shape their course by the twinkling of a mere satellite. Milton, I grant, was of a very different opinion; for he only bends to the indefeasible right of beauty, though it would be difficult to render two passages which I now mean to contrast, consistent. But into similar inconsistencies are great men often led by their senses.

'To whom thus Eve with *perfect beauty* adorn'd,
My Author and Disposer, what thou bidst
Unargued I obey; so God ordains;
God is *thy law, thou mine:* to know no more
5 Is Woman's *happiest* knowledge and her *praise.*'

6 These are exactly the arguments that I have used to children; but I have added, your reason is now gaining strength, and, till it arrives at some degree of maturity, you must look up to me for advice—then you ought to *think,* and only rely on God.

Yet in the following lines Milton seems to coincide with me; when he makes Adam thus expostulate with his Maker.

'Hast thou not made me here thy substitute,
And these inferior far beneath me set?
Among *unequals* what society
Can sort, what harmony or true delight?
Which must be mutual, in proportion due
Giv'n and receiv'd; but in *disparity*
The one intense, the other still remiss
Tedious alike: of *fellowship* I speak
Such as I seek, fit to participate
7 All rational delight—

8 In treating, therefore, of the manners of women, let us, disregarding sensual arguments, trace what we should endeavour to make them in order to co-operate, if the expression be not too bold, with the supreme Being.

9 By individual education, I mean, for the sense of the word is not precisely defined, such an attention to a child as will slowly sharpen the senses, form the temper, regulate the passions, as they begin to ferment, and set the understanding to work before the body arrives at maturity; so that the man may only have to proceed, not to begin, the important task of learning to think and reason.

To prevent any misconstruction, I must add, that I do not believe that a 10
private education can work the wonders which some sanguine writers have attributed to it. Men and women must be educated, in a great degree, by the opinions and manners of the society they live in. In every age there has been a stream of popular opinion that has carried all before it, and given a family character, as it were, to the century. It may then fairly be inferred, that, till society be differently constituted, much cannot be expected from education. It is, however, sufficient for my present purpose to assert, that whatever effect circumstances have on the abilities, every being may become virtuous by the exercise of its own reason; for if but one being was created with vicious inclinations, that is positively bad, what can save us from atheism? or if we worship a God, is not that God a devil?

Consequently, the most perfect education, in my opinion, is such an exer- 11
cise of the understanding as is best calculated to strengthen the body and form the heart. Or, in other words, to enable the individual to attain such habits of virtue as will render it independent. In fact, it is a farce to call any being virtuous whose virtues do not result from the exercise of its own reason. This was Rousseau's opinion respecting men. I extend it to women, and confidently assert that they have been drawn out of their sphere by false refinement, and not by an endeavour to acquire masculine qualities. Still the regal homage which they receive is so intoxicating, that till the manners of the times are changed, and formed on more reasonable principles, it may be impossible to convince them that the illegitimate power which they obtain, by degrading themselves, is a curse, and that they must return to nature and equality, if they wish to secure the placid satisfaction that unsophisticated affections impart. But for this epoch we must wait—wait, perhaps, till kings and nobles, enlightened by reason, and, preferring the real dignity of man to childish state, throw off their gaudy hereditary trappings: and if then women do not resign the arbitrary power of beauty—they will prove that they have *less* mind than man.

I may be accused of arrogance; still I must declare, what I firmly believe, 12
that all the writers who have written on the subject of female education and manners, from Rousseau to Dr. Gregory, have contributed to render women more artificial, weak characters, than they would otherwise have been; and, consequently, more useless members of society. I might have expressed this conviction in a lower key; but I am afraid it would have been the whine of affectation, and not the faithful expression of my feelings; of the clear result, which experience and reflection have led me to draw. When I come to that division of the subject, I shall advert to the passages that I more particularly disapprove of, in the works of the authors I have just alluded to; but it is first necessary to observe, that my objection extends to the whole purport of those books, which tend, in my opinion, to degrade one half of the human species, and render women pleasing at the expense of every solid virtue.

13 Though, to reason on Rousseau's ground, if man did attain a degree of perfection of mind when his body arrived at maturity, it might be proper, in order to make a man and his wife *one,* that she should rely entirely on his understanding; and the graceful ivy, clasping the oak that supported it, would form a whole in which strength and beauty would be equally conspicuous. But, alas! husbands, as well as their helpmates, are often only overgrown children; nay, thanks to early debauchery, scarcely men in their outward form—and if the blind lead the blind, one need not come from heaven to tell us the consequence.

14 Many are the causes that, in the present corrupt state of society, contribute to enslave women by cramping their understandings and sharpening their senses. One, perhaps, that silently does more mischief than all the rest, is their disregard of order.

15 To do every thing in an orderly manner, is a most important precept, which women, who, generally speaking, receive only a disorderly kind of education, seldom attend to with that degree of exactness, that men, who from their infancy are broken into method, observe. This negligent kind of guess-work, for what other epithet can be used to point out the random exertions of a sort of instinctive common sense, never brought to the test of reason? prevents their generalizing matters of fact—so they do to-day what they did yesterday, merely because they did it yesterday.

16 This contempt of the understanding in early life has more baneful consequences than is commonly supposed; for the little knowledge which women of strong minds attain, is, from various circumstances, of a more desultory kind than the knowledge of men, and it is acquired more by sheer observations on real life, than from comparing what has been individually observed with the results of experience generalized by speculation. Led by their dependent situation and domestic employments more into society, what they learn is rather by snatches; and as learning is with them, in general, only a secondary thing, they do not pursue any one branch with that persevering ardour necessary to give vigour to the faculties, and clearness to the judgment. In the present state of society, a little learning is required to support the character of a gentleman; and boys are obliged to submit to a few years of discipline. But in the education of women, the cultivation of the understanding is always subordinate to the acquirement of some corporeal accomplishment; even when enervated by confinement and false notions of modesty, the body is prevented from attaining that grace and beauty which relaxed half-formed limbs never exhibit. Besides, in youth their faculties are not brought forward by emulation; and having no serious scientific study, if they have natural sagacity it is turned too soon on life and manners. They dwell on effects, and modifications, without tracing them back to causes; and complicated rules to adjust behaviour, are a weak substitute for simple principles.

17 As a proof that education gives this appearance of weakness to females, we may instance the example of military men, who are, like them, sent into the world before their minds have been stored with knowledge or fortified

by principles. The consequences are similar; soldiers acquire a little superficial knowledge, snatched from the muddy current of conversation, and, from continually mixing with society, they gain, what is termed a knowledge of the world; and this acquaintance with manners and customs has frequently been confounded with a knowledge of the human heart. But can the crude fruit of casual observation, never brought to the test of judgment, formed by comparing speculation and experience, deserve such a distinction? Soldiers, as well as women, practise the minor virtues with punctilious politeness. Where is then the sexual difference, when the education has been the same? All the difference that I can discern, arises from the superior advantage of liberty, which enables the former to see more of life.

It is wandering from my present subject, perhaps, to make a political 18
remark; but, as it was produced naturally by the train of my reflections, I shall not pass it silently over.

Standing armies can never consist of resolute, robust men; they may be 19
well disciplined machines, but they will seldom contain men under the influence of strong passions, or with very vigorous faculties. And as for any depth of understanding, I will venture to affirm, that it is as rarely to be found in the army as amongst women; and the cause, I maintain, is the same. It may be further observed, that officers are also particularly attentive to their persons, fond of dancing, crowded rooms, adventures, and ridicule.[1] Like the *fair* sex, the business of their lives is gallantry—They were taught to please, and they only live to please. Yet they do not lose their rank in the distinction of sexes, for they are still reckoned superior to women, though in what their superiority consists, beyond what I have just mentioned, it is difficult to discover.

The great misfortune is this, that they both acquire manners before morals, 20
and a knowledge of life before they have, from reflection, any acquaintance with the grand ideal outline of human nature. The consequence is natural; satisfied with common nature, they become a prey to prejudices, and taking all their opinions on credit, they blindly submit to authority. So that, if they have any sense, it is a kind of instinctive glance, that catches proportions, and decides with respect to manners; but fails when arguments are to be pursued below the surface, or opinions analyzed.

May not the same remark be applied to women? Nay, the argument may 21
be carried still further, for they are both thrown out of a useful station by the unnatural distinctions established in civilized life. Riches and hereditary honours have made cyphers of women to give consequence to the numerical figure; and idleness has produced a mixture of gallantry and despotism into society, which leads the very men who are the slaves of their mistresses to tyrannize over their sisters, wives, and daughters. This is only keeping them in rank

[1]Why should women be censured with petulent acrimony, because they seem to have a passion for a scarlet coat? Has not education placed them more on a level with soldiers than any other class of men?

and file, it is true. Strengthen the female mind by enlarging it, and there will be an end to blind obedience; but, as blind obedience is ever sought for by power, tyrants and sensualists are in the right when they endeavour to keep women in the dark, because the former only want slaves, and the latter a plaything. The sensualist, indeed, has been the most dangerous of tyrants, and women have been duped by their lovers, as princes by their ministers, whilst dreaming that they reigned over them.

22 I now principally allude to Rousseau, for his character of Sophia is, undoubtedly a captivating one, though it appears to me grossly unnatural; however, it is not the superstructure, but the foundation of her character, the principles on which her education was built, that I mean to attack; nay, warmly as I admire the genius of that able writer, whose opinions I shall often have occasion to cite, indignation always takes place of admiration, and the rigid frown of insulted virtue effaces the smile of complacency, which his eloquent periods are wont to raise, when I read his voluptuous reveries. Is this the man, who, in his ardour for virtue, would banish all the soft arts of peace, and almost carry us back to Spartan discipline? Is this the man who delights to paint the useful struggles of passion, the triumphs of good dispositions, and the heroic flights which carry the glowing soul out of itself?—How are these mighty sentiments lowered when he describes the pretty foot and enticing airs of his little favourite! But, for the present I wave the subject, and, instead of severely reprehending the transient effusions of overweening sensibility, I shall only observe, that whoever has cast a benevolent eye on society, must often have been gratified by the sight of humble mutual love, not dignified by sentiment, nor strengthened by a union in intellectual pursuits. The domestic trifles of the day have afforded matter for cheerful converse, and innocent caresses have softened toils which did not require great exercise of mind or stretch of thought: yet, has not the sight of this moderate felicity excited more tenderness than respect? An emotion similar to what we feel when children are playing, or animals sporting,[2] whilst the contemplation of the noble struggles of suffering merit has raised admiration, and carried our thoughts to that world where sensation will give place to reason.

23 Women are, therefore, to be considered either as moral beings, or so weak that they must be entirely subjected to the superior faculties of men.

24 Let us examine this question. Rousseau declares that a woman should never, for a moment, feel herself independent, that she should be governed by fear to exercise her *natural* cunning, and made a coquetish slave in order to render her a more alluring object of desire, a *sweeter* companion to man, whenever he chooses to relax himself. He carries the arguments, which he pretends to

---

[2]Similar feelings has Milton's pleasing picture of paradisiacal happiness ever raised in my mind; yet, instead of envying the lovely pair, I have, with conscious dignity, or Satanic pride, turned to hell for sublimer objects. In the same style, when viewing some noble monument of human art, I have traced the emanation of the Deity in the order I admired, till, descending from that giddy height, I have caught myself contemplating the grandest of all human sights;—for fancy quickly placed, in some solitary recess, an outcast of fortune, rising superior to passion and discontent.

draw from the indications of nature, still further, and insinuates that truth and fortitude, the corner stones of all human virtue, should be cultivated with certain restrictions, because, with respect to the female character, obedience is the grand lesson which ought to be impressed with unrelenting rigour.

What nonsense! when will a great man arise with sufficient strength of mind 25
to puff away the fumes which pride and sensuality have thus spread over the subject! If women are by nature inferior to men, their virtues must be the same in quality, if not in degree, or virtue is a relative idea; consequently, their conduct should be founded on the same principles, and have the same aim.

Connected with man as daughters, wives, and mothers, their moral char- 26
acter may be estimated by their manner of fulfilling those simple duties; but the end, the grand end of their exertions should be to unfold their own faculties and acquire the dignity of conscious virtue. They may try to render their road pleasant; but ought never to forget, in common with man, that life yields not the felicity which can satisfy an immortal soul. I do not mean to insinuate, that either sex should be so lost in abstract reflections or distant views, as to forget the affections and duties that lie before them, and are, in truth, the means appointed to produce the fruit of life; on the contrary, I would warmly recommend them, even while I assert, that they afford most satisfaction when they are considered in their true subordinate light.

Probably the prevailing opinion, that woman was created for man, may 27
have taken its rise from Moses's poetical story; yet as very few, it is presumed, who have bestowed any serious thought on the subject, ever supposed that Eve was, literally speaking, one of Adam's ribs, the deduction must be allowed to fall to the ground; or, only be so far admitted as it proves that man, from the remotest antiquity, found it convenient to exert his strength to subjugate his companion, and his invention to shew that she ought to have her neck bent under the yoke; because she, as well as the brute creation, was created to do his pleasure.

Let it not be concluded that I wish to invert the order of things; I have 28
already granted, that, from the constitution of their bodies, men seem to be designed by Providence to attain a greater degree of virtue. I speak collectively of the whole sex; but I see not the shadow of a reason to conclude that their virtues should differ in respect to their nature. In fact, how can they, if virtue has only one eternal standard? I must therefore, if I reason consequentially, as strenuously maintain that they have the same simple direction, as that there is a God.

It follows then that cunning should not be opposed to wisdom, little 29
cares to great exertions, or insipid softness, varnished over with the name of gentleness, to that fortitude which grand views alone can inspire.

I shall be told that woman would then lose many of her peculiar graces, and the opinion of a well known poet might be quoted to refute my unqualified assertion. For Pope has said, in the name of the whole male sex,

'Yet ne'er so sure our passion to create,
As when she touch'd the brink of all we hate.' 30

31 In what light this sally places men and women, I shall leave to the judicious to determine; meanwhile I shall content myself with observing, that I cannot discover why, unless they are mortal, females should always be degraded by being made subservient to love or lust.

32 To speak disrespectfully of love is, I know, high treason against sentiment and fine feelings; but I wish to speak the simple language of truth, and rather to address the head than the heart. To endeavour to reason love out of the world, would be to out Quixote Cervantes, and equally offend against common sense; but an endeavour to restrain this tumultuous passion, and to prove that it should not be allowed to dethrone superior powers, or to usurp the sceptre which the understanding should very coolly wield, appears less wild.

33 Youth is the season for love in both sexes; but in those days of thoughtless enjoyment provision should be made for the more important years of life, when reflection takes place of sensation. But Rousseau, and most of the male writers who have followed his steps, have warmly inculcated that the whole tendency of female education ought to be directed to one point:—to render them pleasing.

34 Let me reason with the supporters of this opinion who have any knowledge of human nature, do they imagine that marriage can eradicate the habitude of life? The woman who has only been taught to please will soon find that her charms are oblique sunbeams, and that they cannot have much effect on her husband's heart when they are seen every day, when the summer is passed and gone. Will she then have sufficient native energy to look into herself for comfort, and cultivate her dormant faculties? or, is it not more rational to expect that she will try to please other men; and, in the emotions raised by the expectation of new conquests, endeavour to forget the mortification her love or pride has received? When the husband ceases to be a lover—and the time will inevitably come, her desire of pleasing will then grow languid, or become a spring of bitterness; and love, perhaps, the most evanescent of all passions, gives place to jealousy or vanity.

35 I now speak of women who are restrained by principle or prejudice; such women, though they would shrink from an intrigue with real abhorrence, yet, nevertheless, wish to be convinced by the homage of gallantry that they are cruelly neglected by their husbands; or, days and weeks are spent in dreaming of the happiness enjoyed by congenial souls, till the health is undermined and the spirits broken by discontent. How then can the great art of pleasing be such a necessary study; it is only useful to a mistress; the chaste wife, and serious mother, should only consider her power to please as the polish of her virtues, and the affection of her husband as one of the comforts that render her task less difficult and her life happier.—But, whether she be loved or neglected, her first wish should be to make herself respectable, and not to rely for all her happiness on a being subject to like infirmities with herself.

36 The amiable Dr. Gregory fell into a similar error. I respect his heart; but entirely disapprove of his celebrated Legacy to his Daughters.

He advises them to cultivate a fondness for dress, because a fondness for 37
dress, he asserts, is natural to them. I am unable to comprehend what either
he or Rousseau mean, when they frequently use this indefinite term. If they
told us that in a pre-existent state the soul was fond of dress, and brought this
inclination with it into a new body, I should listen to them with a half smile,
as I often do when I hear a rant about innate elegance.—But if he only meant
to say that the exercise of the faculties will produce this fondness—I deny it.—
It is not natural; but arises, like false ambition in men, from a love of power.

Dr. Gregory goes much further; he actually recommends dissimulation, 38
and advises an innocent girl to give the lie to her feelings, and not dance
with spirit, when gaiety of heart would make her feet eloquent without making her gestures immodest. In the name of truth and common sense, why
should not one woman acknowledge that she can take more exercise than
another? or, in other words, that she has a sound constitution; and why, to
damp innocent vivacity, is she darkly to be told that men will draw conclusions which she little thinks of? Let the libertine draw what inference he pleases;
but, I hope, that no sensible mother will restrain the natural frankness of youth
by instilling such indecent cautions. Out of the abundance of the heart the
mouth speaketh; and a wiser than Solomon hath said, that the heart should
be made clean, and not trivial ceremonies observed, which it is not very difficult to fulfil with scrupulous exactness when vice reigns in the heart.

Women ought to endeavour to purify their heart; but can they do so when 39
their uncultivated understandings make them entirely dependent on their senses
for employment and amusement, when no noble pursuit sets them above the
little vanities of the day, or enables them to curb the wild emotions that agi-
tate a reed over which every passing breeze has power? To gain the affections
of a virtuous man is affectation necessary? Nature has given woman a weaker
frame than man; but, to ensure her husband's affections, must a wife, who by
the exercise of her mind and body whilst she was discharging the duties of a
daughter, wife, and mother, has allowed her constitution to retain its natural
strength, and her nerves a healthy tone, is she, I say, to condescend to use art
and feign a sickly delicacy in order to secure her husband's affection? Weakness
may excite tenderness, and gratify the arrogant pride of man; but the lordly
caresses of a protector will not gratify a noble mind that pants for, and deserves
to be respected. Fondness is a poor substitute for friendship!

In a seraglio, I grant, that all these arts are necessary; the epicure must have 40
his palate tickled, or he will sink into apathy; but have women so little ambition as to be satisfied with such a condition? Can they supinely dream life
away in the lap of pleasure, or the languor of weariness, rather than assert their
claim to pursue reasonable pleasures and render themselves conspicuous by
practising the virtues which dignify mankind? Surely she has not an immortal soul who can loiter life away merely employed to adorn her person, that
she may amuse the languid hours, and soften the cares of a fellow-creature
who is willing to be enlivened by her smiles and tricks, when the serious
business of life is over.

41 Besides, the woman who strengthens her body and exercises her mind will, by managing her family and practising various virtues, become the friend, and not the humble dependent of her husband, and if she deserves his regard by possessing such substantial qualities, she will not find it necessary to conceal her affection, nor to pretend to an unnatural coldness of constitution to excite her husband's passions. In fact, if we revert to history, we shall find that the women who have distinguished themselves have neither been the most beautiful nor the most gentle of their sex.

42 Nature, or, to speak with strict propriety, God, has made all things right; but man has sought him out many inventions to mar the work. I now allude to that part of Dr. Gregory's treatise, where he advises a wife never to let her husband know the extent of her sensibility or affection. Voluptuous precaution, and as ineffectual as absurd.—Love, from its very nature, must be transitory. To seek for a secret that would render it constant, would be as wild a search as for the philosopher's stone, or the grand panacea; and the discovery would be equally useless, or rather pernicious, to mankind. The most holy band of society is friendship. It has been well said, by a shrewd satirist, "that rare as true love is, true friendship is still rarer."

43 This is an obvious truth, and the cause not lying deep, will not elude a slight glance of inquiry.

44 Love, the common passion, in which chance and sensation take place of choice and reason, is, in some degree, felt by the mass of mankind; for it is not necessary to speak, at present, of the emotions that rise above or sink below love. This passion, naturally increased by suspense and difficulties, draws the mind out of its accustomed state, and exalts the affections; but the security of marriage, allowing the fever of love to subside, a healthy temperature is thought insipid, only by those who have not sufficient intellect to substitute the calm tenderness of friendship, the confidence of respect, instead of blind admiration, and the sensual emotions of fondness.

45 This is, must be, the course of nature:—friendship or indifference inevitably succeeds love.—And this constitution seems perfectly to harmonize with the system of government which prevails in the moral world. Passions are spurs to action, and open the mind; but they sink into mere appetites, become a personal and momentary gratification, when the object is gained, and the satisfied mind rests in enjoyment. The man who had some virtue whilst he was struggling for a crown, often becomes a voluptuous tyrant when it graces his brow; and, when the lover is not lost in the husband, the dotard, a prey to childish caprices, and fond jealousies, neglects the serious duties of life, and the caresses which should excite confidence in his children are lavished on the overgrown child, his wife.

46 In order to fulfil the duties of life, and to be able to pursue with vigour the various employments which form the moral character, a master and mistress of a family ought not to continue to love each other with passion. I mean to say, that they ought not to indulge those emotions which disturb the order of society, and engross the thoughts that should be otherwise employed. The

mind that has never been engrossed by one object wants vigour—if it can long be so, it is weak.

A mistaken education, a narrow, uncultivated mind, and many sexual prej- 47
udices, tend to make women more constant than men; but, for the present, I shall not touch on this branch of the subject. I will go still further, and advance, without dreaming of a paradox, that an unhappy marriage is often very advantageous to a family, and that the neglected wife is, in general, the best mother. And this would almost always be the consequence if the female mind were more enlarged: for, it seems to be the common dispensation of Providence, that what we gain in present enjoyment should be deducted from the treasure of life, experience; and that when we are gathering the flowers of the day and revelling in pleasure, the solid fruit of toil and wisdom should not be caught at the same time. The way lies before us, we must turn to the right or left; and he who will pass life away in bounding from one pleasure to another, must not complain if he neither acquires wisdom nor respectability of character.

Supposing, for a moment, that the soul is not immortal, and that man was 48
only created for the present scene,—I think we should have reason to complain that love, infantine fondness, ever grew insipid and pallid upon the sense. Let us eat, drink, and love, for to-morrow we die, would be, in fact, the language of reason, the morality of life; and who but a fool would part with a reality for a fleeting shadow? But, if awed by observing the improvable powers of the mind, we disdain to confine our wishes or thoughts to such a comparatively mean field of action; that only appears grand and important, as it is connected with a boundless prospect and sublime hopes, what necessity is there for falsehood in conduct, and why must the sacred majesty of truth be violated to detain a deceitful good that saps the very foundation of virtue? Why must the female mind be tainted by coquetish arts to gratify the sensualist, and prevent love from subsiding into friendship, or compassionate tenderness, when there are not qualities on which friendship can be built? Let the honest heart shew itself, and *reason* teach passion to submit to necessity; or, let the dignified pursuit of virtue and knowledge raise the mind above those emotions which rather imbitter than sweeten the cup of life, when they are not restrained within due bounds.

I do not mean to allude to the romantic passion, which is the concomi- 49
tant of genius.—Who can clip its wing? But that grand passion not proportioned to the puny enjoyments of life, is only true to the sentiment, and feeds on itself. The passions which have been celebrated for their durability have always been unfortunate. They have acquired strength by absence and constitutional melancholy.—The fancy has hovered round a form of beauty dimly seen—but familiarity might have turned admiration into disgust; or, at least, into indifference, and allowed the imagination leisure to start fresh game. With perfect propriety, according to this view of things, does Rousseau make the mistress of his soul, Eloisa, love St. Preux, when life was fading before her; but this is no proof of the immortality of the passion.

50 Of the same complexion is Dr. Gregory's advice respecting delicacy of sentiment, which he advises a woman not to acquire, if she has determined to marry. This determination, however, perfectly consistent with his former advice, he calls *indelicate,* and earnestly persuades his daughters to conceal it, though it may govern their conduct: as if it were indelicate to have the common appetites of human nature.

51 Noble morality! and consistent with the cautious prudence of a little soul that cannot extend its views beyond the present minute division of existence. If all the faculties of woman's mind are only to be cultivated as they respect her dependence on man; if, when she obtains a husband she has arrived at her goal, and meanly proud is satisfied with such a paltry crown, let her grovel contentedly, scarcely raised by her employments above the animal kingdom; but, if she is struggling for the prize of her high calling, let her cultivate her understanding without stopping to consider what character the husband may have whom she is destined to marry. Let her only determine, without being too anxious about present happiness, to acquire the qualities that ennoble a rational being, and a rough inelegant husband may shock her taste without destroying her peace of mind. She will not model her soul to suit the frailties of her companion, but to bear with them: his character may be a trial, but not an impediment to virtue.

52 If Dr. Gregory confined his remark to romantic expectations of constant love and congenial feelings, he should have recollected that experience will banish what advice can never make us cease to wish for, when the imagination is kept alive at the expense of reason.

53 I own it frequently happens that women who have fostered a romantic unnatural delicacy of feeling, waste their[3] lives in *imagining* how happy they should have been with a husband who could love them with a fervid increasing affection every day, and all day. But they might as well pine married as single—and would not be a jot more unhappy with a bad husband than longing for a good one. That a proper education; or, to speak with more precision, a well stored mind, would enable a woman to support a single life with dignity, I grant; but that she should avoid cultivating her taste, lest her husband should occasionally shock it, is quitting a substance for a shadow. To say the truth, I do not know of what use is an improved taste, if the individual is not rendered more independent of the casualties of life; if new sources of enjoyment, only dependent on the solitary operations of the mind, are not opened. People of taste, married or single, without distinction, will ever be disgusted by various things that touch not less observing minds. On this conclusion the argument must not be allowed to hinge; but in the whole sum of enjoyment is taste to be denominated a blessing?

54 The question is, whether it procures most pain or pleasure? The answer will decide the propriety of Dr. Gregory's advice, and shew how absurd and

[3]For example, the herd of novelists.

tyrannic it is thus to lay down a system of slavery; or to attempt to educate moral beings by any other rules than those deduced from pure reason, which apply to the whole species.

Gentleness of manners, forbearance and long-suffering, are such amiable 55
Godlike qualities, that in sublime poetic strains the Deity has been invested with them; and, perhaps, no representation of his goodness so strongly fastens on the human affections as those that represent him abundant in mercy and willing to pardon. Gentleness, considered in this point of view, bears on its front all the characteristics of grandeur, combined with the winning graces of condescension; but what a different aspect it assumes when it is the submissive demeanour of dependence, the support of weakness that loves, because it wants protection; and is forbearing, because it must silently endure injuries; smiling under the lash at which it dare not snarl. Abject as this picture appears, it is the portrait of an accomplished woman, according to the received opinion of female excellence, separated by specious reasoners from human excellence. Or, they[4] kindly restore the rib, and make one moral being of a man and woman; not forgetting to give her all the 'submissive charms.'

How women are to exist in that state where there is to be neither marry- 56
ing nor giving in marriage, we are not told.—For though moralists have agreed that the tenor of life seems to prove that *man* is prepared by various circumstances for a future state, they constantly concur in advising *woman* only to provide for the present. Gentleness, docility, and a spaniel-like affection are, on this ground, consistently recommended as the cardinal virtues of the sex; and, disregarding the arbitrary economy of nature, one writer has declared that it is masculine for a woman to be melancholy. She was created to be the toy of man, his rattle, and it must jingle in his ears whenever, dismissing reason, he chooses to be amused.

To recommend gentleness, indeed, on a broad basis is strictly philosoph- 57
ical. A frail being should labour to be gentle. But when forbearance confounds right and wrong, it ceases to be a virtue; and, however convenient it may be found in a companion—that companion will ever be considered as an inferior, and only inspire a vapid tenderness, which easily degenerates into contempt. Still, if advice could really make a being gentle, whose natural disposition admitted not of such a fine polish, something towards the advancement of order would be attained; but if, as might quickly be demonstrated, only affectation be produced by this indiscriminate counsel, which throws a stumbling-block in the way of gradual improvement, and true melioration of temper, the sex is not much benefited by sacrificing solid virtues to the attainment of superficial graces, though for a few years they may procure the individuals regal sway.

As a philosopher, I read with indignation the plausible epithets which men 58
use to soften their insults; and, as a moralist, I ask what is meant by such heterogeneous associations, as fair defects, amiable weaknesses, &c.? If there

[4]Vide Rousseau, and Swedenborg.

is but one criterion of morals, but one archetype for man, women appear to be suspended by destiny, according to the vulgar tale of Mahomet's coffin; they have neither the unerring instinct of brutes, nor are allowed to fix the eye of reason on a perfect model. They were made to be loved, and must not aim at respect, lest they should be hunted out of society as masculine.

59 But to view the subject in another point of view. Do passive indolent women make the best wives? Confining our discussion to the present moment of existence, let us see how such weak creatures perform their part? Do the women, who, by the attainment of a few superficial accomplishments, have strengthened the prevailing prejudice, merely contribute to the happiness of their husbands? Do they display their charms merely to amuse them? And have women, who have early imbibed notions of passive obedience, sufficient character to manage a family or educate children? So far from it, that, after surveying the history of woman, I cannot help agreeing with the severest satirist, considering the sex as the weakest as well as the most oppressed half of the species. What does history disclose but marks of inferiority, and how few women have emancipated themselves from the galling yoke of sovereign man?—So few, that the exceptions remind me of an ingenious conjecture respecting Newton: that he was probably a being of superior order, accidentally caged in a human body. In the same style, I have been led to imagine that the few extraordinary women who have rushed in eccentrical directions out of the orbit prescribed to their sex, were *male* spirited, confined by mistake in a female frame. But if it be not philosophical to think of sex when the soul is mentioned, the inferiority must depend on the organs; or the heavenly fire, which is to ferment the clay, is not given in equal portions.

60 But avoiding, as I have hitherto done, any direct comparison of the two sexes collectively, or frankly acknowledging the inferiority of woman, according to the present appearance of things, I shall only insist that men have increased that inferiority till women are almost sunk below the standard of rational creatures. Let their faculties have room to unfold, and their virtues to gain strength, and then determine where the whole sex must stand in the intellectual scale. Yet let it be remembered, that for a small number of distinguished women I do not ask a place.

61 It is difficult for us purblind mortals to say to what height human discoveries and improvements may arrive when the gloom of despotism subsides, which makes us stumble at every step; but, when morality shall be settled on a more solid basis, then, without being gifted with a prophetic spirit, I will venture to predict that woman will be either the friend or slave of man. We shall not, as at present, doubt whether she is a moral agent, or the link which unites man with brutes. But, should it then appear, that like the brutes they were principally created for the use of man, he will let them patiently bite the bridle, and not mock them with empty praise; or, should their rationality be proved, he will not impede their improvement merely to gratify his sensual appetites. He will not, with all the graces of rhetoric, advise them to submit implicitly their understanding to the guidance of man. He will not, when he treats of

the education of women, assert that they ought never to have the free use of reason, nor would he recommend cunning and dissimulation to beings who are acquiring, in like manner as himself, the virtues of humanity.

Surely there can be but one rule of right, if morality has an eternal foun- 62
dation, and whoever sacrifices virtue, strictly so called, to present convenience, or whose *duty* it is to act in such a manner, lives only for the passing day, and cannot be an accountable creature.

The poet then should have dropped his sneer when he says,

"If weak women go astray,"

"The stars are more in fault than they."

For that they are bound by the adamantine chain of destiny is most certain, 63
if it be proved that they are never to exercise their own reason, never to be independent, never to rise above opinion, or to feel the dignity of a rational will that only bows to God, and often forgets that the universe contains any being but itself and the model of perfection to which its ardent gaze is turned, to adore attributes that, softened into virtues, may be imitated in kind, though the degree overwhelms the enraptured mind.

If, I say, for I would not impress by declamation when Reason offers her 64
sober light, if they are really capable of acting like rational creatures, let them not be treated like slaves; or, like the brutes who are dependent on the reason of man, when they associate with him; but cultivate their minds, give them the salutary, sublime curb of principle, and let them attain conscious dignity by feeling themselves only dependent on God. Teach them, in common with man, to submit to necessity, instead of giving, to render them more pleasing, a sex to morals.

Further, should experience prove that they cannot attain the same degree 65
of strength of mind, perseverence, and fortitude, let their virtues be the same in kind, though they may vainly struggle for the same degree; and the superiority of man will be equally clear, if not clearer; and truth, as it is a simple principle, which admits of no modification, would be common to both. Nay, the order of society as it is at present regulated would not be inverted, for woman would then only have the rank that reason assigned her, and arts could not be practised to bring the balance even, much less to turn it.

These may be termed Utopian dreams.—Thanks to that Being who 66
impressed them on my soul, and gave me sufficient strength of mind to dare to exert my own reason, till, becoming dependent only on him for the support of my virtue, I view, with indignation, the mistaken notions that enslave my sex.

I love man as my fellow; but his scepter, real, or usurped, extends not to 67
me, unless the reason of an individual demands my homage; and even then the submission is to reason, and not to man. In fact, the conduct of an accountable being must be regulated by the operations of its own reason; or on what foundation rests the throne of God?

It appears to me necessary to dwell on these obvious truths, because females 68
have been insulated, as it were; and, while they have been stripped of the

virtues that should clothe humanity, they have been decked with artificial graces that enable them to exercise a short-lived tyranny. Love, in their bosoms, taking place of every nobler passion, their sole ambition is to be fair, to raise emotion instead of inspiring respect; and this ignoble desire, like the servility in absolute monarchies, destroys all strength of character. Liberty is the mother of virtue, and if women are, by their very constitution, slaves, and not allowed to breathe the sharp invigorating air of freedom, they must ever languish like exotics, and be reckoned beautiful flaws in nature;—let it also be remembered, that they are the only flaw.

69 As to the argument respecting the subjection in which the sex has ever been held, it retorts on man. The many have always been enthralled by the few; and monsters, who scarcely have shewn any discernment of human excellence, have tyrannized over thousands of their fellow creatures. Why have men of superior endowments submitted to such degradation? For, is it not universally acknowledged that kings, viewed collectively, have ever been inferior, in abilities and virtue, to the same number of men taken from the common mass of mankind—yet, have they not, and are they not still treated with a degree of reverence that is an insult to reason; China is not the only country where a living man has been made a God. *Men* have submitted to superior strength to enjoy with impunity the pleasure of the moment—*women* have only done the same, and therefore till it is proved that the courtier, who servilely resigns the birthright of a man, is not a moral agent, it cannot be demonstrated that woman is essentially inferior to man because she has always been subjugated.

70 Brutal force has hitherto governed the world, and that the science of politics is in its infancy, is evident from philosophers scrupling to give the knowledge most useful to man that determinate distinction.

71 I shall not pursue this argument any further than to establish an obvious inference, that as sound politics diffuse liberty, mankind, including woman, will become more wise and virtuous.

Challenging
Dictionary in hand

As you read, see if you can list the ideas Wollstonecraft is arguing against and so construct a picture of her social world.

(white, rich)
Narrow, priviledged arena of women's lives

¶ 3
eurocentric Negative allusions to Islam ¶ 58 Mahomet's coffin

¶ 69 Ref. to China

p. 9 What comparison does she make between ♀ and soldiers?
agree, disagree?

Outline her argument here including digressions

Doesn't end here →

NOTES

THE SAME SUBJECT CONTINUED
Mary Wollstonecraft

Bodily strength from being the distinction of heroes is now sunk into such 1
unmerited contempt, that men, as well as women, seem to think it unnecessary: the latter, as it takes from their feminine graces, and from that lovely weakness, the source of their undue power; and the former, because it appears inimical to the character of a gentleman.

That they have both, by departing from one extreme run into another, 2
may easily be proved; but first it may be proper to observe, that a vulgar error has obtained a degree of credit, which has given force to a false conclusion, in which an effect has been mistaken for a cause.

People of genius have, very frequently impaired their constitutions by study 3
or careless inattention to their health, and the violence of their passions bearing a proportion to the vigour of their intellects, the sword's destroying the scabbard has become almost proverbial, and superficial observers have inferred from thence, that men of genius have commonly weak, or, to use a more fashionable phrase, delicate constitutions. Yet the contrary, I believe, will appear to be the fact; for, on diligent inquiry, I find that strength of mind has, in most cases, been accompanied by superior strength of body,—natural soundness of constitution,—not that robust tone of nerves and vigour of muscles, which arise from bodily labour, when the mind is quiescent, or only directs the hands.

Dr. Priestley has remarked, in the preface to his biographical chart, that 4
the majority of great men have lived beyond forty-five. And, considering the thoughtless manner in which they have lavished their strength, when investigating a favourite science they have wasted the lamp of life, forgetful of the midnight hour; or, when lost in poetic dreams, fancy has peopled the scene, and the soul has been disturbed, till it shook the constitution, by the passions that meditation had raised; whose objects, the baseless fabric of a vision, faded before the exhausted eye, they must have had iron frames. Shakespeare never grasped the airy dagger with a nerveless hand, nor did Milton tremble when he led Satan far from the confines of his dreary prison.—These were not the ravings of imbecility, the sickly effusions of distempered brains; but the exuberance of fancy, that 'in a fine phrenzy' wandering, was not continually reminded of its material shackles.

I am aware that this argument would carry me further than it may be 5
supposed I wish to go; but I follow truth, and, still adhering to my first position, I will allow that bodily strength seems to give man a natural superiority over woman; and this is the only solid basis on which the superiority of the sex can be built. But I still insist, that not only the virtue, but the *knowledge* of the two sexes should be the same in nature, if not in degree, and that women, considered not only as moral, but rational creatures, ought to endeavour to acquire human virtues (or perfections) by the *same* means as men,

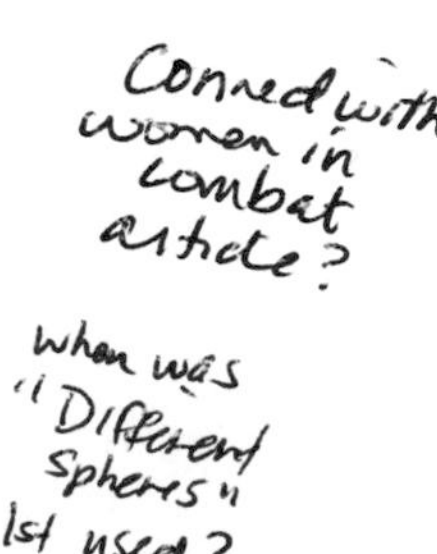

instead of being educated like a fanciful kind of *half* being—one of Rousseau's wild chimeras.[1]

6 But, if strength of body be, with some shew of reason, the boast of men, why are women so infatuated as to be proud of a defect? Rousseau has furnished them with a plausible excuse, which could only have occurred to a man, whose imagination had been allowed to run wild, and refine on the impressions made by exquisite senses;—that they might, forsooth, have a pretext for yielding to a natural appetite without violating a romantic species of modesty, which gratifies the pride and libertinism of man.

7 Women, deluded by these sentiments, sometimes boast of their weakness, cunningly obtaining power by playing on the *weakness* of men; and they may well glory in their illicit sway, for, like Turkish bashaws, they have more real power than their masters: but virtue is sacrificed to temporary gratifications, and the respectability of life to the triumph of an hour.

8 Women, as well as despots, have now, perhaps, more power than they would have if the world, divided and subdivided into kingdoms and families, was gov-

---

[1]'Researches into abstract and speculative truths, the principles and axioms of sciences, in short, every thing which tends to generalize our ideas, is not the proper province of women; their studies should be relative to point of practice; it belongs to them to apply those principles which men have discovered; and it is their part to make observations, which direct men to the establishment of general principles. All the ideas of women, which have not the immediate tendency to points of duty, should be directed to the study of men, and to the attainment of those agreeable accomplishments which have taste for their object; for as to works of genius, they are beyond their capacity; neither have they sufficient precision or power of attention to succeed in sciences which require accuracy: and as to physical knowledge, it belongs to those only who are most active, most inquisitive; who comprehend the greatest variety of objects: in short, it belongs to those who have the strongest powers, and who exercise them most, to judge of the relations between sensible beings and the laws of nature. A woman who is naturally weak, and does not carry her ideas to any great extent, knows how to judge and make a proper estimate of those movements which she sets to work, in order to aid her weakness; and these movements are the passions of men. The mechanism she employs is much more powerful than ours; for all her levers move the human heart. She must have the skill to incline us to do every thing which her sex will not enable her to do of herself, and which is necessary or agreeable to her; therefore she ought to study the mind of man thoroughly, not the mind of man in general, abstracted, but the dispositions of those men to whom she is subject, either by the laws of her country or by the force of opinion. She should learn to penetrate into their real sentiments from their conversation, their actions, their looks, and gestures. She should also have the art, by her own conversation, actions, looks, and gestures, to communicate those sentiments which are agreeable to them, without seeming to intend it. Men will argue more philosophically about the human heart; but women will read the heart of man better than they. It belongs to women, if I may be allowed the expression, to form an experimental morality, and to reduce the study of man to a system. Women have most wit, men have most genius; women observe, men reason: from the concurrence of both we derive the clearest light and the most perfect knowledge, which the human mind is, of itself, capable of attaining. In one word, from hence we acquire the most intimate acquaintance, both with ourselves and others, of which our nature is capable; and it is thus that art has a constant tendency to perfect those endowments which nature has bestowed.—The world is the book of women.'—*Rousseau's Emilius.* I hope my readers still remember the comparison, which I have brought forward, between women and officers.

erned by laws deduced from the exercise of reason; but in obtaining it, to carry on the comparison, their character is degraded, and licentiousness spread through the whole aggregate of society. The many become pedestal to the few. I, therefore, will venture to assert, that till women are more rationally educated, the progress of human virtue and improvement in knowledge must receive continual checks. And if it be granted that woman was not created merely to gratify the appetite of man, nor to be the upper servant, who provides his meals and takes care of his linen, it must follow, that the first care of those mothers or fathers, who really attend to the education of females, should be, if not to strengthen the body, at least, not to destroy the constitution by mistaken notions of beauty and female excellence; nor should girls ever be allowed to imbibe the pernicious notion that a defect can, by any chemical process of reasoning, become an excellence. In this respect, I am happy to find, that the author of one of the most instructive books, that our country has produced for children, coincides with me in opinion; I shall quote his pertinent remarks to give the force of his respectable authority to reason.[2]

But should it be proved that woman is naturally weaker than man, from 9
whence does it follow that it is natural for her to labour to become still weaker than nature intended her to be? Arguments of this cast are an insult to common sense, and savour passion. The *divine right* of husbands, like the divine right of kings, may, it is to be hoped, in this enlightened age, be contested without danger, and, though conviction may not silence many boisterous disputants, yet when any prevailing prejudice is attacked, the wise will consider, and leave the narrow-minded to rail with thoughtless vehemence at innovation.

[2]A respectable old man gives the following sensible account of the method he pursued when educating his daughter. 'I endeavoured to give both to her mind and body a degree of vigour, which is seldom found in the female sex. As soon as she was sufficiently advanced in strength to be capable of the lighter labours of husbandry and gardening, I employed her as my constant companion. Selene, for that was her name, soon acquired a dexterity in all these rustic employments, which I considered with equal pleasure and admiration. If women are in general feeble both in body and mind, it arises less from nature than from education. We encourage a vicious indolence and inactivity, which we falsely call delicacy; instead of hardening their minds by the severer principles of reason and philosophy, we breed them to useless arts, which terminate in vanity and sensuality. In most of the countries which I had visited, they are taught nothing of an higher nature than a few modulations of the voice, or useless postures of the body; their time is consumed in sloth or trifles, and trifles become the only pursuits capable of interesting them. We seem to forget, that it is upon the qualities of the female sex that our own domestic comforts and the education of our children must depend. And what are the comforts or the education which a race of beings, corrupted from their infancy, and unacquainted with all the duties of life, are fitted to bestow? To touch a musical instrument with useless skill, to exhibit their natural or affected graces to the eyes of indolent and debauched young men, to dissipate their husband's patrimony in riotous and unnecessary expenses, these are the only arts cultivated by women in most of the polished nations I had seen. And the consequences are uniformly such as may be expected to proceed from such polluted sources, private and public servitude. 'But Selene's education was regulated by different views, and conducted upon severer principles; if that can be called severity which opens the mind to a sense of moral and religious duties, and most effectually arms it against the inevitable evils of life.'—*Mr. Day's Sanford and Merton,* Vol. III.

10 The mother, who wishes to give true dignity of character to her daughter, must, regardless of the sneers of ignorance, proceed on a plan diametrically opposite to that which Rousseau has recommended with all the deluding charms of eloquence and philosophical sophistry: for his eloquence renders absurdities plausible, and his dogmatic conclusions puzzle, without convincing, those who have not ability to refute them.

11 Throughout the whole animal kingdom every young creature requires almost continual exercise, and the infancy of children, conformable to this intimation, should be passed in harmless gambols, that exercise the feet and hands, without requiring very minute direction from the head, or the constant attention of a nurse. In fact, the care necessary for self-preservation is the first natural exercise of the understanding, as little inventions to amuse the present moment unfold the imagination. But these wise designs of nature are counteracted by mistaken fondness or blind zeal. The child is not left a moment to its own direction, particularly a girl, and thus rendered dependent—dependence is called natural.

12 To preserve personal beauty, woman's glory! the limbs and faculties are cramped with worse than Chinese bands, and the sedentary life which they are condemned to live, whilst boys frolic in the open air, weakens the muscles and relaxes the nerves.—As for Rousseau's remarks, which have since been echoed by several writers, that they have naturally, that is from their birth, independent of education, a fondness for dolls, dressing, and talking—they are so puerile as not to merit a serious refutation. That a girl, condemned to sit for hours together listening to the idle chat of weak nurses, or to attend at her mother's toilet, will endeavour to join the conversation, is, indeed, very natural; and that she will imitate her mother or aunts, and amuse herself by adorning her lifeless doll, as they do in dressing her, poor innocent babe! is undoubtedly a most natural consequence. For men of the greatest abilities have seldom had sufficient strength to rise above the surrounding atmosphere; and, if the page of genius has always been blurred by the prejudices of the age, some allowance should be made for a sex, who like kings, always see things through a false medium.

13 In this manner may the fondness for dress, conspicuous in women, be easily accounted for, without supposing it the result of a desire to please the sex on which they are dependent. The absurdity, in short, of supposing that a girl is naturally a coquette, and that a desire connected with the impulse of nature to propagate the species, should appear even before an improper education has, by heating the imagination, called it forth prematurely, is so unphilosophical, that such a sagacious observer as Rousseau would not have adopted it, if he had not been accustomed to make reason give way to his desire of singularity, and truth to a favourite paradox.

14 Yet thus to give a sex to mind was not very consistent with the principles of a man who argued so warmly, and so well, for the immortality of the soul.—But what a weak barrier is truth when it stands in the way of an hypothesis! Rousseau respected—almost adored virtue—and yet he allowed himself to love with sensual fondness. His imagination constantly prepared inflammable fewel

for his inflammable senses; but, in order to reconcile his respect for self-denial, fortitude, and those heroic virtues, which a mind like his could not coolly admire, he labours to invert the law of nature, and broaches a doctrine pregnant with mischief and derogatory to the character of supreme wisdom.

15 His ridiculous stories, which tend to prove that girls are *naturally* attentive to their persons, without laying any stress on daily example, are below contempt.—And that a little miss should have such a correct taste as to neglect the pleasing amusement of making O's, merely because she perceived that it was an ungraceful attitude, should be selected with the anecdotes of the learned pig.[3]

16 I have, probably, had an opportunity of observing more girls in their infancy than J. J. Rousseau.—I can recollect my own feelings, and I have looked steadily around me; yet, so far from coinciding with him in opinion respecting the first dawn of the female character, I will venture to affirm, that a girl, whose spirits have not been damped by inactivity, or innocence tainted by false shame, will always be a romp, and the doll will never excite attention unless confinement allows her no alternative. Girls and boys, in short, would play harmlessly together, if the distinction of sex was not inculcated long before nature makes any difference.—I will go further, and affirm, as an indisputable fact, that most of the women, in the circle of my observation, who have acted like rational creatures, or shewn any vigour of intellect, have accidentally been allowed to run wild—as some of the elegant formers of the fair sex would insinuate.

17 The baneful consequences which flow from inattention to health during infancy, and youth, extend further than is supposed—dependence of body naturally produces dependence of mind; and how can she be a good wife or mother, the greater part of whose time is employed to guard against or endure sickness? Nor can it be expected that a woman will resolutely endeavour to strengthen her constitution and abstain from enervating indulgencies, if artificial notions of beauty, and false descriptions of sensibility, have been early entangled with her motives of action. Most men are sometimes obliged to bear with bodily inconveniences, and to endure, occasionally, the inclemency of the elements; but genteel women are, literally speaking, slaves to their bodies, and glory in their subjection.

18 I once knew a weak woman of fashion, who was more than commonly proud of her delicacy and sensibility. She thought a distinguishing taste and puny appetite the height of all human perfection, and acted accordingly.—I have seen this weak sophisticated being neglect all the duties of life, yet recline

[3]'I once knew a young person who learned to write before she learned to read, and began to write with her needle before she could use a pen. At first, indeed, she took it into her head to make no other letter than the O: this letter she was constantly making of all sizes, and always the wrong way. Unluckily, one day, as she was intent on this employment, she happened to see herself in the looking-glass; when, taking a dislike to the constrained attitude in which she sat while writing, she threw away her pen, like another Pallas, and determined against making the O any more. Her brother was also equally averse to writing: it was the confinement, however, and not the constrained attitude, that most disgusted him.'—*Rousseau's Emilius.*

with self-complacency on a sofa, and boast of her want of appetite as a proof of delicacy that extended to, or, perhaps, arose from, her exquisite sensibility: for it is difficult to render intelligible such ridiculous jargon.—Yet, at the moment, I have seen her insult a worthy old gentlewoman, whom unexpected misfortunes had made dependent on her ostentatious bounty, and who, in better days, had claims on her gratitude. Is it possible that a human creature could have become such a weak and depraved being, if, like the Sybarites, dissolved in luxury, every thing like virtue had not been worn away, or never impressed by precept, a poor substitute, it is true, for cultivation of mind, though it serves as a fence against vice?

19 Such a woman is not a more irrational monster than some of the Roman emperors, who were depraved by lawless power. Yet, since kings have been more under the restraint of law, and the curb, however weak, of honour, the records of history are not filled with such unnatural instances of folly and cruelty, nor does the despotism that kills virtue and genius in the bud, hover over Europe with that destructive blast which desolates Turky, and renders the men, as well as the soil, unfruitful.

20 Women are every where in this deplorable state; for, in order to preserve their innocence, as ignorance is courteously termed, truth is hidden from them, and they are made to assume an artificial character before their faculties have acquired any strength. Taught from their infancy that beauty is woman's sceptre, the mind shapes itself to the body, and, roaming round its gilt cage, only seeks to adore its prison. Men have various employments and pursuits which engage their attention, and give a character to the opening mind; but women, confined to one, and having their thoughts constantly directed to the most insignificant part of themselves, seldom extend their views beyond the triumph of the hour. But was their understanding once emancipated from the slavery to which the pride and sensuality of man and their short-sighted desire, like that of dominion in tyrants, of present sway, has subjected them, we should probably read of their weaknesses with surprise. I must be allowed to pursue the argument a little farther.

21 Perhaps, if the existence of an evil being was allowed, who, in the allegorical language of scripture, went about seeking whom he should devour, he could not more effectually degrade the human character than by giving a man absolute power.

22 This argument branches into various ramifications.—Birth, riches, and every extrinsic advantage that exalt a man above his fellows, without any mental exertion, sink him in reality below them. In proportion to his weakness, he is played upon by designing men, till the bloated monster has lost all traces of humanity. And that tribes of men, like flocks of sheep, should quietly follow such a leader, is a solecism that only a desire of present enjoyment and narrowness of understanding can solve. Educated in slavish dependence, and enervated by luxury and sloth, where shall we find men who will stand forth to assert the rights of man;—or claim the privilege of moral beings, who should have but one road to excellence? Slavery to monarchs and ministers, which

the world will be long in freeing itself from, and whose deadly grasp stop the progress of the human mind, is not yet abolished.

Let not men then in the pride of power, use the same arguments that tyran- 23
nic kings and venal ministers have used, and fallaciously assert that woman ought to be subjected because she has always been so.—But, when man, governed by reasonable laws, enjoys his natural freedom, let him despise woman, if she do not share it with him; and till that glorious period arrives, in descanting on the folly of the sex, let him not overlook his own.

Women, it is true, obtaining power by unjust means, by practising or 24
fostering vice, evidently lose the rank which reason would assign them, and they become either abject slaves or capricious tyrants. They lose all simplicity, all dignity of mind, in acquiring power, and act as men are observed to act when they have been exalted by the same means.

It is time to effect a revolution in female manners—time to restore to them 25
their lost dignity—and make them, as a part of the human species, labour by reforming themselves to reform the world. It is time to separate unchangeable morals from local manners.—If men be demi-gods—why let us serve them! And if the dignity of the female soul be as disputable as that of animals—if their reason does not afford sufficient light to direct their conduct whilst unerring instinct is denied—they are surely of all creatures the most miserable! and, bent beneath the iron hand of destiny, must submit to be a *fair defect* in creation. But to justify the ways of Providence respecting them, by pointing out some irrefragable reason for thus making such a large portion of mankind accountable and not accountable, would puzzle the subtilest casuist.

The only solid foundation for morality appears to be the character of the 26
supreme Being; the harmony of which arises from a balance of attributes;—and, to speak with reverence, one attribute seems to imply the *necessity* of another. He must be just, because he is wise, he must be good, because he is omnipotent. For to exalt one attribute at the expense of another equally noble and necessary, bears the stamp of the warped reason of man—the homage of passion. Man, accustomed to bow down to power in his savage state, can seldom divest himself of this barbarous prejudice, even when civilization determines how much superior mental is to bodily strength; and his reason is clouded by these crude opinions, even when he thinks of the Deity. His omnipotence is made to swallow up, or preside over his other attributes, and those mortals are supposed to limit his power irreverently, who think that it must be regulated by his wisdom.

I disclaim that specious humility which, after investigating nature, stops 27
at the author.—The High and Lofty One, who inhabiteth eternity, doubtless possesses many attributes of which we can form no conception; but reason tells me that they cannot clash with those I adore—and I am compelled to listen to her voice.

It seems natural for man to search for excellence, and either to trace it in 28
the object that he worships, or blindly to invest it with perfection, as a garment. But what good effect can the latter mode of worship have on the moral

conduct of a rational being? He bends to power; he adores a dark cloud, which may open a bright prospect to him, or burst in angry, lawless fury, on his devoted head—he knows not why. And, supposing that the Deity acts from the vague impulse of an undirected will, man must also follow his own, or act according to rules, deduced from principles which he disclaims as irreverent. Into this dilemma have both enthusiasts and cooler thinkers fallen, when they laboured to free men from the wholesome restraints which a just conception of the character of God imposes.

29 It is not impious thus to scan the attributes of the Almighty: in fact, who can avoid it that exercises his faculties? For to love God as the fountain of wisdom, goodness, and power, appears to be the only worship useful to a being who wishes to acquire either virtue or knowledge. A blind unsettled affection may, like human passions, occupy the mind and warm the heart, whilst, to do justice, love mercy, and walk humbly with our God, is forgotten. I shall pursue this subject still further, when I consider religion in a light opposite to that recommended by Dr. Gregory, who treats it as a matter of sentiment or taste.

30 To return from this apparent digression. It were to be wished that women would cherish an affection for their husbands, founded on the same principle that devotion ought to rest upon. No other firm base is there under heaven—for let them beware of the fallacious light of sentiment; too often used as a softer phrase for sensuality. It follows then, I think, that from their infancy women should either be shut up like eastern princes, or educated in such a manner as to be able to think and act for themselves.

31 Why do men halt between two opinions, and expect impossibilities? Why do they expect virtue from a slave, from a being whom the constitution of civil society has rendered weak, if not vicious?

32 Still I know that it will require a considerable length of time to eradicate the firmly rooted prejudices which sensualists have planted; it will also require some time to convince women that they act contrary to their real interest on an enlarged scale, when they cherish or affect weakness under the name of delicacy, and to convince the world that the poisoned source of female vices and follies, if it be necessary, in compliance with custom, to use synonymous terms in a lax sense, has been the sensual homage paid to beauty:—to beauty of features; for it has been shrewdly observed by a German writer, that a pretty woman, as an object of desire, is generally allowed to be so by men of all descriptions; whilst a fine woman, who inspires more sublime emotions by displaying intellectual beauty, may be overlooked or observed with indifference, by those men who find their happiness in the gratification of their appetites. I foresee an obvious retort—whilst man remains such an imperfect being as he appears hitherto to have been, he will, more or less, be the slave of his appetites; and those women obtaining most power who gratify a predominant one, the sex is degraded by a physical, if not by a moral necessity.

33 This objection has, I grant, some force; but while such a sublime precept exists, as, 'be pure as your heavenly Father is pure;' it would seem that the virtues of man are not limited by the Being who alone could limit them; and that he may press forward without considering whether he steps out of his

sphere by indulging such a noble ambition. To the wild billows it has been said, 'thus far shalt thou go, and no further; and here shall thy proud waves be stayed.' Vainly then do they beat and foam, restrained by the power that confines the struggling planets in their orbits, matter yields to the great governing Spirit.—But an immortal soul, not restrained by mechanical laws and struggling to free itself from the shackles of matter, contributes to, instead of disturbing, the order of creation, when, co-operating with the Father of spirits, it tries to govern itself by the invariable rule that, in a degree, before which our imagination faints, the universe is regulated.

Besides, if women are educated for dependence; that is, to act according to the 34
will of another fallible being, and submit, right or wrong, to power, where are we to stop? Are they to be considered as vicegerents allowed to reign over a small domain, and answerable for their conduct to a higher tribunal, liable to error?

It will not be difficult to prove that such delegates will act like men sub- 35
jected by fear, and make their children and servants endure their tyrannical oppression. As they submit without reason, they will, having no fixed rules to square their conduct by, be kind, or cruel, just as the whim of the moment directs; and we ought not to wonder if sometimes, galled by their heavy yoke, they take a malignant pleasure in resting it on weaker shoulders.

But, supposing a woman, trained up to obedience, be married to a sensi- 36
ble man, who directs her judgment without making her feel the servility of her subjection, to act with as much propriety by this reflected light as can be expected when reason is taken at second hand, yet she cannot ensure the life of her protector; he may die and leave her with a large family.

A double duty devolves on her; to educate them in the character of both 37
father and mother; to form their principles and secure their property. But, alas! she has never thought, much less acted for herself. She has only learned to please[4] men, to depend gracefully on them; yet, encumbered with children, how is she to obtain another protector—a husband to supply the place of

[4]'In the union of the sexes, both pursue one common object, but not in the same manner. From their diversity in this particular, arises the first determinate difference between the moral relations of each. The one should be active and strong, the other passive and weak: it is necessary the one should have both the power and the will, and that the other should make little resistance. 'This principle being established, it follows that woman is expressly formed to please the man: if the obligation be reciprocal also, and the man ought to please in his turn, it is not so immediately necessary: his great merit is in his power, and he pleases merely because he is strong. This, I must confess, is not one of the refined maxims of love; it is, however, one of the laws of nature, prior to love itself. 'If woman be formed to please and be subjected to man it is her place, doubtless, to render herself agreeable to him, instead of challenging his passion. The violence of his desires depends on her charms; it is by means of these she should urge him to the exertion of those powers which nature hath given him. The most successful method of exciting them, is, to render such exertion necessary by their resistance; as, in that case, self-love is added to desire, and the one triumphs in the victory which the other obliged to acquire. Hence arise the various modes of attack and defence between the sexes; the boldness of one sex and the timidity of the other; and, in a word, that bashfulness and modesty with which nature hath armed the weak, in order to subdue the strong.'—*Rousseau's Emilius.* I shall make no other comment on this ingenius passage, than just to observe, that it is the philosophy of lasciviousness.

reason? A rational man, for we are not treading on romantic ground, though he may think her a pleasing docile creature, will not choose to marry a *family* for love, when the world contains many more pretty creatures. What is then to become of her? She either falls an easy prey to some mean fortune-hunter, who defrauds her children of their paternal inheritance, and renders her miserable; or becomes the victim of discontent and blind indulgence. Unable to educate her sons, or impress them with respect; for it is not a play on words to assert, that people are never respected, though filling an important station, who are not respectable; she pines under the anguish of unavailing impotent regret. The serpent's tooth enters into her very soul, and the vices of licentious youth bring her with sorrow, if not with poverty also, to the grave.

38 This is not an overcharged picture; on the contrary, it is a very possible case, and something similar must have fallen under every attentive eye.

39 I have, however, taken it for granted, that she was well-disposed, though experience shews, that the blind may as easily be led into a ditch as along the beaten road. But supposing no very improbable conjecture, that a being only taught to please must still find her happiness in pleasing;—what an example of folly, not to say vice, will she be to her innocent daughters! The mother will be lost in the coquette, and instead of making friends of her daughters, view them with eyes askance, for they are rivals—rivals more cruel than any other, because they invite a comparison, and drive her from the throne of beauty, who has never thought of a seat on the bench of reason.

40 It does not require a lively pencil, or the discriminating outline of a caricature, to sketch the domestic miseries and petty vices which such a mistress of a family diffuses. Still she only acts as a woman ought to act, brought up according to Rousseau's system. She can never be reproached for being masculine, or turning out of her sphere; nay, she may observe another of his grand rules, and cautiously preserving her reputation free from spot, be reckoned a good kind of woman. Yet in what respect can she be termed good? She abstains, it is true, without any great struggle, from committing gross crimes; but how does she fulfil her duties? Duties!—in truth she has enough to think of to adorn her body and nurse a weak constitution.

41 With respect to religion, she never presumed to judge for herself; but conformed, as a dependent creature should, to the ceremonies of the church which she was brought up in, piously believing that wiser heads than her own have settled that business:—and not to doubt is her point of perfection. She therefore pays her tythe of mint and cummin—and thanks her God that she is not as other women are. These are the blessed effects of a good education! These the virtues of man's help-mate![5]

[5]'O how lovely,' exclaims Rousseau, speaking of Sophia, 'is her ignorance! Happy is he who is destined to instruct her! She will never pretend to be the tutor of her husband, but will be content to be his pupil. Far from attempting to subject him to her taste, she will accommodate herself to his. She will be more estimable to him, than if she was learned: he will have a pleasure in instructing her.'—*Rousseau's Emilius.* I shall content myself with simply asking, how friendship can subsist, when love expires, between the master and his pupil.

I must relieve myself by drawing a different picture. 42

Let fancy now present a woman with a tolerable understanding, for I do 43
not wish to leave the line of mediocrity, whose constitution, strengthened by exercise, has allowed her body to acquire its full vigour; her mind, at the same time, gradually expanding itself to comprehend the moral duties of life, and in what human virtue and dignity consist.

Formed thus by the discharge of the relative duties of her station, she mar- 44
ries from affection, without losing sight of prudence, and looking beyond matrimonial felicity, she secures her husband's respect before it is necessary to exert mean arts to please him and feed a dying flame, which nature doomed to expire when the object became familiar, when friendship and forbearance take place of a more ardent affection.—This is the natural death of love, and domestic peace is not destroyed by struggles to prevent its extinction. I also suppose the husband to be virtuous; or she is still more in want of independent principles.

Fate, however, breaks this tie.—She is left a widow, perhaps, without a suf- 45
ficient provision; but she is not desolate! The pang of nature is felt; but after time has softened sorrow into melancholy resignation, her heart turns to her children with redoubled fondness, and anxious to provide for them, affection gives a sacred heroic cast to her maternal duties. She thinks that not only the eye sees her virtuous efforts from whom all her comfort now must flow, and whose approbation is life; but her imagination, a little abstracted and exalted by grief, dwells on the fond hope that the eyes which her trembling hand closed, may still see how she subdues every wayward passion to fulfil the double duty of being the father as well as the mother of her children. Raised to heroism by misfortunes, she represses the first faint dawning of a natural inclination, before it ripens into love, and in the bloom of life forgets her sex—forgets the pleasure of an awakening passion, which might again have been inspired and returned. She no longer thinks of pleasing, and conscious dignity prevents her from priding herself on account of the praise which her conduct demands. Her children have her love, and her brightest hopes are beyond the grave, where her imagination often strays.

I think I see her surrounded by her children, reaping the reward of her 46
care. The intelligent eye meets hers, whilst health and innocence smile on their chubby cheeks, and as they grow up the cares of life are lessened by their grateful attention. She lives to see the virtues which she endeavoured to plant on principles fixed into habits, to see her children attain a strength of character sufficient to enable them to endure adversity without forgetting their mother's example.

The task of life thus fulfilled, she calmly waits for the sleep of death, and 47
rising from the grave, may say—Behold, thou gavest me a talent—and here are five talents.

I wish to sum up what I have said in a few words, for I here throw down 48
my gauntlet, and deny the existence of sexual virtues, not excepting modesty. For man and woman, truth, if I understand the meaning of the word, must be the same; yet the fanciful female character, so prettily drawn by

poets and novelists, demanding the sacrifice of truth and sincerity, virtue becomes a relative idea, having no other foundation than utility, and of that utility men pretend arbitrarily to judge, shaping it to their own convenience.

49 Women, I allow, may have different duties to fulfil; but they are *human* duties, and the principles that should regulate the discharge of them, I sturdily maintain, must be the same.

50 To become respectable, the exercise of their understanding is necessary, there is no other foundation for independence of character; I mean explicitly to say that they must only bow to the authority of reason, instead of being the *modest* slaves of opinion.

51 In the superior ranks of life how seldom do we meet with a man of superior abilities, or even common acquirements? The reason appears to me clear, the state they are born in was an unnatural one. The human character has ever been formed by the employments the individual, or class, pursues; and if the faculties are not sharpened by necessity, they must remain obtuse. The argument may fairly be extended to women; for, seldom occupied by serious business, the pursuit of pleasure gives that insignificancy to their character which renders the society of the *great* so insipid. The same want of firmness, produced by a similar cause, forces them both to fly from themselves to noisy pleasures, and artificial passions, till vanity takes place of every social affection, and the characteristics of humanity can scarcely be discerned. Such are the blessings of civil governments, as they are at present organized, that wealth and female softness equally tend to debase mankind, and are produced by the same cause; but allowing women to be rational creatures, they should be incited to acquire virtues which they may call their own, for how can a rational being be ennobled by any thing that is not obtained by its *own* exertions?

NOTES

NOTES

SELECTIONS FROM *IN THE NAME OF IDENTITY*
Amin Maalouf

(1949–   )

Amin Maalouf is an acclaimed Lebanese-born French writer whose works have been translated into more than twenty languages. In 1993 he was honored with the highest literary award in France, the Prix Goncourt. More recently he received the Prince of Asturias Award for Letters in 2010 and in 2011 was elected to the Académie française.

Introduction

How many times, since I left Lebanon in 1976 to live in France, have people asked me, with the best intentions in the world, whether I felt "more French" or "more Lebanese"? And I always give the same answer: "Both!" I say that not in the interests of fairness or balance, but because any other answer would be a lie. What makes me myself rather than anyone else is the very fact that I am poised between two countries, two or three languages and several cultural traditions. It is precisely this that defines my identity. Would I exist more authentically if I cut off a part of myself?

To those who ask the question, I patiently explain that I was born in Lebanon and lived there until I was 27; that Arabic is my mother tongue; that it was in Arabic translation that I first read Dumas and Dickens and *Gulliver's Travels;* and that it was in my native village, the village of my ancestors, that I experienced the pleasures of childhood and heard some of the stories that were later to inspire my novels. How could I forget all that? How could I cast it aside? On the other hand, I have lived for 22 years on the soil of France; I drink her water and wine; every day my hands touch her ancient stones; I write my books in her language; never again will she be a foreign country to me.

So am I half French and half Lebanese? Of course not. Identity can't be compartmentalised. You can't divide it up into halves or thirds or any other separate segments. I haven't got several identities: I've got just one, made up of many components in a mixture that is unique to me, just as other people's identity is unique to them as individuals.

Sometimes, after I've been giving a detailed account of exactly why I lay claim to all my affiliations, someone comes and pats me on the shoulder and says "Of course, of course—but what do you really feel, deep down inside?"

For a long time I found this oft-repeated question amusing, but it no longer makes me smile. It seems to reflect a view of humanity which, though it is widespread, is also in my opinion dangerous. It presupposes that "deep down inside" everyone there is just one affiliation that really matters, a kind of "fundamental truth" about each individual, an "essence" determined once and

Reprinted from *In the Name of Identity* (2000), Arcade Publishing.

for all at birth, never to change thereafter. As if the rest, all the rest—a person's whole journey through time as a free agent; the beliefs he acquires in the course of that journey; his own individual tastes, sensibilities and affinities; in short his life itself—counted for nothing. And when, as happens so often nowadays, our contemporaries are exhorted to "assert their identity," they are meant to seek within themselves that same alleged fundamental allegiance, which is often religious, national, racial or ethnic, and having located it they are supposed to flaunt it proudly in the face of others.

Anyone who claims a more complex identity is marginalised. But a young man born in France of Algerian parents clearly carries within him two different allegiances or "belongings," and he ought to be allowed to use both. For the sake of argument I refer to two "belongings," but in fact such a youth's personality is made up of many more ingredients. Within him, French, European and other western influences mingle with Arab, Berber, African, Muslim and other sources, whether with regard to language, beliefs, family relationships or to tastes in cooking and the arts. This represents an enriching and fertile experience if the young man in question feels free to live it fully—if he is encouraged to accept it in all its diversity. But it can be traumatic if whenever he claims to be French other people look on him as a traitor or renegade, and if every time he emphasises his ties with Algeria and its history, culture and religion he meets with incomprehension, mistrust or even outright hostility.

The situation is even more difficult on the other side of the Rhine. I'm thinking of the case of a Turk who might have been born near Frankfurt 30 years ago and who has always lived in Germany. He speaks and writes German better than the language of his ancestors. Yet for the society of his adopted country he isn't a German, while for that of his origins he is no longer completely a Turk. Common sense dictates that he should be able to claim both allegiances. But at present neither the law nor people's attitudes allows him to accept his composite identity tranquilly.

I have quoted the first examples that came to mind, but I could have used many others. For instance, that of someone born in Belgrade of a Serbian mother and a Croatian father. That of a Hutu woman married to a Tutsi, or vice versa. Or that of an American with a black father and a Jewish mother.

It may be said that these are special cases. I don't agree. The handful of people I've cited are not the only ones with a complex identity. Every individual is a meeting ground for many different allegiances, and sometimes these loyalties conflict with one another and confront the person who harbours them with difficult choices. In some cases the situation is obvious at a glance; others need to be looked at more closely.

Is there any citizen of present-day Europe who doesn't sense a kind of tug-of-war, an inevitably ever-increasing conflict between on the one hand his affiliation to an ancient country like France, Spain, Denmark or England, and, on the other, his allegiance to the continental entity that is in the process of forming? And there are many dedicated "Europeans," from the Basque country to Scotland, who at the same time feel a strong and fundamental attachment to a particular region and its people, its history and its language. Can anyone in the United States even today assess his place in society without reference to his earlier connections, whether they be African, Hispanic, Irish, Jewish, Italian, Polish or other?

That said, I'm prepared to admit that the first examples I cited are to a certain extent special. All the people concerned in them are arenas for allegiances currently in violent conflict with one another: they live in a sort of frontier zone criss-crossed by ethnic, religious and other fault lines. But by virtue of this situation—peculiar rather than privileged—they have a special role to play in forging links, eliminating misunderstandings, making some parties more reasonable and others less belligerent, smoothing out difficulties, seeking compromise. Their role is to act as bridges, go-betweens, mediators between the various communities and cultures. And that is precisely why their dilemma is so significant: if they themselves cannot sustain their multiple allegiances, if they are continually being pressed to take sides or ordered to stay within their own tribe, then all of us have reason to be uneasy about the way the world is going.

I talk of their being "pressed" and "ordered"—but by whom? Not just by fanatics and xenophobes of all kinds, but also by you and me, by each and all of us. And we do so precisely because of habits of thought and expression deeply rooted in us all; because of a narrow, exclusive, bigoted, simplistic attitude that reduces identity in all its many aspects to one single affiliation, and one that is proclaimed in anger.

I feel like shouting aloud that this is how murderers are made—it's a recipe for massacres! That may sound somewhat extreme, but in the pages that follow I shall try to explain what I mean.

My Identity, My Allegiances

1

A life spent writing has taught me to be wary of words. Those that seem clearest are often the most treacherous. "Identity" is one of those false friends. We all think we know what the word means and go on trusting it, even when it's slyly starting to say the opposite.

Far be it from me to want to keep on redefining the idea of identity. It has been the fundamental question of philosophy from Socrates's "Know thyself!" through countless other masters down to Freud. To approach it anew today would call for more qualifications than I possess and for very much greater temerity. The task I set myself is more modest. I want to try to understand why so many people commit crimes nowadays in the name of religious, ethnic, national or some other kind of identity. Has it always been like this since time immemorial, or is the present era influenced by hitherto unknown factors? Sometimes what I say may seem rather simplistic. If so it's because I want to set my argument out as calmly, patiently and fairly as possible, without resorting to jargon or unwarranted shortcuts.

What's known as an identity card carries the holder's family name, given name, date and place of birth, photograph, a list of certain physical features, the holder's signature and sometimes also his fingerprints—a whole array of details designed to prove without a shadow of doubt or confusion that the bearer of the document is so-and-so, and that amongst all the millions of other human beings there isn't one—not even his double or his twin brother—for whom he could be mistaken.

My identity is what prevents me from being identical to anybody else.

Defined in this way the word identity reflects a fairly precise idea—one which in theory should not give rise to confusion. Do we really need lengthy arguments to prove that there are not and cannot be two identical individuals? Even if in the near future someone manages, as we fear they may, to "clone" human beings, the clones would at best be identical only at the time of their "birth"; as soon as they started to live they would start being different.

Each individual's identity is made up of a number of elements, and these are clearly not restricted to the particulars set down in official records. Of course, for the great majority these factors include allegiance to a religious tradition; to a nationality—sometimes two; to a profession, an institution, or a particular social milieu. But the list is much longer than that; it is virtually unlimited. A person may feel a more or less strong attachment to a province, a village, a neighbourhood, a clan, a professional team or one connected with sport, a group of friends, a union, a company, a parish, a community of people with the same passions, the same sexual preferences, the same physical handicaps, or who have to deal with the same kind of pollution or other nuisance.

Of course, not all these allegiances are equally strong, at least at any given moment. But none is entirely insignificant, either. All are components of personality—we might almost call them "genes of the soul" so long as we remember that most of them are not innate.

While each of these elements may be found separately in many individuals, the same combination of them is never encountered in different people, and it's this that gives every individual richness and value and makes each human being unique and irreplaceable.

It can happen that some incident, a fortunate or unfortunate accident, even a chance encounter, influences our sense of identity more strongly than any ancient affiliation. Take the case of a Serbian man and a Muslim woman who met 20 years ago in a café in Sarajevo, fell in love and got married. They can never perceive their identity in the same way as does a couple that is entirely Serbian or entirely Muslim; their view of religion and mother country will never again be what it was before. Both partners will always carry within them the ties their parents handed down at birth, but these ties will henceforth be perceived differently and accorded a different importance.

Let us stay in Sarajevo and carry out an imaginary survey there. Let us observe a man of about 50 whom we see in the street.

In 1980 or thereabouts he might have said proudly and without hesitation, "I'm a Yugoslavian!" Questioned more closely, he could have said he was a citizen of the Federal Republic of Bosnia-Herzegovina, and, incidentally, that he came from a traditionally Muslim family.

If you had met the same man twelve years later, when the war was at its height, he might have answered automatically and emphatically, "I'm a Muslim!" He might even have grown the statutory beard. He would quickly have added that he was a Bosnian, and he would not have been pleased to be reminded of how proudly he once called himself a Yugoslavian.

If he was stopped and questioned now, he would say first of all that he was a Bosnian, then that he was a Muslim. He'd tell you he was just on his way to the mosque, but he'd also want you to know that his country is part of Europe and that he hopes it will one day be a member of the Union.

How will this same person want to define himself if we meet him in the same place 20 years hence? Which of his affiliations will he put first? The European? The Islamic? The Bosnian? Something else again? The Balkan connection, perhaps?

I shan't risk trying to predict. All these factors are part of his identity. He was born to a family that was traditionally Muslim; the language he speaks links him to the Southern Slavs, who were once joined together in a single state, but are so no longer; he lives on land which belonged sometimes to the Ottoman and sometimes to the Austrian Empire, and which played a part in the major dramas of European history. In every era one or other of his affiliations swelled up, so to speak, in such a way as to eclipse all the others and to appear to represent his whole identity. In the course of his life he'll have heard all kinds of fables. He'll have been told he was a proletarian pure and simple. Or a Yugoslavian through and through. Or, more recently, a Muslim. For a few difficult months he'll even have been made to think he had more in common with the inhabitants of Kabul than with those of Trieste!

In every age there have been people who considered that an individual had one overriding affiliation so much more important in every circumstance to all others that it might legitimately be called his "identity." For some it was the nation, for others religion or class. But one has only to look at the various conflicts being fought out all over the world today to realise that no one allegiance has absolute supremacy. Where people feel their faith is threatened, it is their religious affiliation that seems to reflect their whole identity. But if their mother tongue or their ethnic group is in danger, then they fight ferociously against their own co-religionists. Both the Turks and the Kurds are Muslims, though they speak different languages; but does that make the war between them any less bloody? Hutus and Tutsis alike are Catholics, and they speak the same language, but has that stopped them slaughtering one another? Czechs and Slovaks are all Catholics too, but does that help them live together?

I cite all these examples to underline the fact that while there is always a certain hierarchy among the elements that go to make up individual identities, that hierarchy is not immutable; it changes with time, and in so doing brings about fundamental changes in behaviour.

one affiliation eclipsing others

Moreover, the ties that count in people's lives are not always the allegedly major allegiances arising out of language, complexion, nationality, class or religion. Take the case of an Italian homosexual in the days of fascism. I imagine that for the man himself that particular aspect of his personality had up till then been important, but not more so than his professional activity, his political choices or his religious beliefs. But suddenly state repression swoops down on him and he feels threatened with humiliation, deportation or death. It's the recollection of certain books I've read and films I've seen that leads me to choose this example. This man, who a few years earlier was a patriot, perhaps even a nationalist, was no longer able to exult at the sight of the Italian army marching by; he may even have come to wish for its defeat. Because of the persecution to which he was subjected, his sexual preferences came to outweigh his other affiliations, among them even the nationalism which at that time was at its height. Only after the war, in a more tolerant Italy, would our man have felt entirely Italian once more.

The identity a person lays claim to is often based, in reverse, on that of his enemy. An Irish Catholic differentiates himself from Englishmen in the first place in terms of religion, but vis-à-vis the monarchy he will declare himself a republican; and while he may not know much Gaelic, at least he will speak his own form of English. A Catholic leader who spoke with an Oxford accent might seem almost a traitor.

One could find dozens of other examples to show how complex is the mechanism of identity: a complexity sometimes benign, but sometimes tragic. I shall quote various instances in the pages that follow, some briefly and others in more detail. Most of them relate to the region I myself come from—the Middle East, the Mediterranean, the Arab world, and first and foremost Lebanon. For that is a country where you are constantly having to question yourself about your affiliations, your origins, your relationships with others, and your possible place in the sun or in the shade.

2

I sometimes find myself "examining my identity" as other people examine their conscience. As you may imagine, my object is not to discover within myself some "essential" allegiance in which I may recognise myself. Rather the opposite: I scour my memory to find as many ingredients of my identity as I can. I then assemble and arrange them. I don't deny any of them.

I come from a family which originated in the southern part of the Arab world and which for centuries lived in the mountains of Lebanon. More recently, by a series of migrations, it has spread out to various other parts of the world, from Egypt to Brazil and from Cuba to Australia. It takes pride in having always been at once Arab and Christian, and this probably since the second or third century AD—that is, long before the rise of Islam and even before the West was converted to Christianity.

The fact of simultaneously being Christian and having as my mother tongue Arabic, the holy language of Islam, is one of the basic paradoxes that have shaped my own identity. Speaking Arabic creates bonds between me and all those who use it every day in their prayers, though most of them by far don't know it as well as I do. If you are in central Asia and meet an elderly scholar outside a Timuride *medersa,* you need only address him in Arabic for him to feel at ease. Then he will speak to you from the heart, as he'd never risk doing in Russian or English.

This language is common to us all—to him, to me and to more than a billion others. On the other hand, my being a Christian—regardless of whether I am so out of deep religious conviction or merely for sociological reasons—also creates a significant link between me and the two billion or so other Christians in the world. There are many things in which I differ from every Christian, every Arab and every Muslim, but between me and each of them there is also an undeniable kinship, in one case religious and intellectual and in the other linguistic and cultural.

That said, the fact of being at once an Arab and a Christian puts one in a very special situation: it makes you a member of a minority—a situation not always easy to accept. It marks a person deeply and permanently. I cannot deny that it has played a decisive part in most of the decisions I have had to make in the course of my own life, including my decision to write this book.

Thus, when I think about either of these two components of my identity separately, I feel close either through language or through religion to a good half of the human race. But when I take the same two elements together, I find myself face to face with my own specificity.

I could say the same thing about other ties. I share the fact that I'm French with 60 million or so others; the fact that I'm Lebanese with between eight and ten million, if you include the diaspora; but with how many do I share the fact that I'm both French and Lebanese? With a few thousand, at most.

Every one of my allegiances links me to a large number of people. But the more ties I have the rarer and more particular my own identity becomes.

If I went into my origins in more detail I'd have to say I was born into what is known as the Melchite or Greek Catholic community, which recognises the authority of the Pope while retaining some Byzantine rites. Seen from a distance, this affiliation is no more than a detail, a curiosity; but seen from close to, it is a defining aspect of my identity. In a country like Lebanon, where the more powerful communities have fought for a long time for their territory and their share of power, members of very small minorities like mine have seldom taken up arms, and have been the first to go into exile. Personally, I always declined to get involved in a war that struck me as absurd and suicidal; but this judgemental attitude, this distant way of looking at things, this refusal to fight, are not unconnected with the fact that I belong to a marginalised community.

So I am a Melchite. But if anyone ever bothered to look my name up in the administrative records—which in Lebanon, as you may imagine, classify people in terms of their religious persuasion—they would find me mentioned not among the Melchites, but in the register of Protestants. Why? It would take too long to explain. All I need say here is that in our family there were two rival family traditions, and that throughout my childhood I was a witness to this tug-of-war. A witness, and sometimes even the bone of contention too. If I was sent to the French school run by the Jesuit fathers it was because my mother, a determined Catholic, wanted to remove me from the Protestant influence prevailing at that time in my father's family, where the children were traditionally sent to British or American schools. It was because of this conflict that I came to speak French, and it was because I spoke French that during the war in Lebanon I went to live in Paris rather than in New York, Vancouver or London. It was for this reason, too, that when I started to write I wrote in French.

Shall I set out even more details about my identity? Shall I mention my Turkish grandmother, or her husband, who was a Maronite Christian from Egypt? Or my other grandfather, who died long before I was born and who I am told was a poet, a freethinker, perhaps a freemason, and in any case violently anti-clerical? Shall I go back as far as the great-great-great-uncle who was the first person to translate Molière into Arabic and to have his translation staged in 1848 in an Ottoman theatre?

No, there's no need to go on. I'll merely ask: how many of my fellow men share with me all the different elements that have shaped my identity and determined the main outlines of my life? Very few. Perhaps none at all. And that is what I want to emphasise: through each one of my affiliations, taken separately, I possess a certain kinship with a large number of my fellow human beings; but because of all these allegiances, taken together, I possess my own identity, completely different from any other.

Question #2

I scarcely need exaggerate at all to say that I have some affiliations in common with every other human being. Yet no one else in the world has all or even most of the same allegiances as I do. Out of all the dozens of elements I can put forward, a mere handful would be enough to demonstrate my own particular identity, different from that of anybody else, even my own father or son.

I hesitated a long time before writing the pages that lead up to this one. Should I really start the book by describing my own situation at such length?

On the one hand, I wanted to use the example with which I was most familiar to show how, by adducing a few affiliations, one could simultaneously declare one's ties with one's fellow human beings and assert one's own uniqueness. On the other hand, I was well aware that the more one analyses a special case the more one risks being told that it *is* only a special case.

But in the end I took the plunge, in the belief that any person of goodwill trying to carry out his or her own "examination of identity" would soon, like me, discover that that identity is a special case. Mankind itself is made up of special cases. Life is a creator of differences. No "reproduction" is ever identical. Every individual without exception possesses a composite identity. He need only ask himself a few questions to uncover forgotten divergences and unsuspected ramifications, and to see that he is complex, unique and irreplaceable.

That is precisely what characterises each individual identity: it is complex, unique and irreplaceable, not to be confused with any other. If I emphasise this point it's because of the attitude, still widespread but in my view highly pernicious, which maintains that all anyone need do to proclaim his identity is simply say he's an Arab, or French, or black, or a Serb, or a Muslim, or a Jew. Anyone who sets out, as I have done, a number of affiliations, is immediately accused of wanting to "dissolve" his identity in a kind of undifferentiated and colourless soup. And yet what I'm trying to say is exactly the opposite: not that all human beings are the same, but that each one is different. No doubt a Serb is different from a Croat, but every Serb is also different from every other Serb, and every Croat is different from every other Croat. And if a Lebanese Christian is different from a Lebanese Muslim, I don't know any two Lebanese Christians who are identical, nor any two Muslims, any more than there are anywhere in the world two Frenchmen, two Africans, two Arabs or two Jews who are identical. People are not interchangeable, and often in the same family, whether it be Rwandan, Irish, Lebanese, Algerian or Bosnian, we find, between two brothers who have lived in the same environment, apparently small differences which make them act in diametrically opposite ways in matters relating to politics, religion and everyday life. These differences may even turn one of the brothers into a killer, and the other into a man of dialogue and conciliation.

Few would object explicitly to what I've been saying. Yet we all behave as if it were not true. Taking the line of least resistance, we lump the most different people together under the same heading. Taking the line of least resistance, we ascribe to them collective crimes, collective acts and opinions. "The Serbs have massacred . . .," "The English have devastated . . .," "The Jews have confiscated . . .," "The Blacks have torched . . .," "The Arabs refuse. . . ." We blithely express sweeping judgements on whole peoples, calling them "hardworking" and "ingenious," or "lazy," "touchy," "sly," "proud," or "obstinate." And sometimes this ends in bloodshed.

I know it is not realistic to expect all our contemporaries to change overnight the way they express themselves. But I think it is important for each of us to become aware that our words are not innocent and without consequence: they may help to perpetuate prejudices which history has shown to be perverse and deadly.

For it is often the way we look at other people that imprisons them within their own narrowest allegiances. And it is also the way we look at them that may set them free.

3

Identity isn't given once and for all: it is built up and changes throughout a person's lifetime. This has been pointed out in numerous books and amply explained, but it is still worth emphasising again: not many of the elements that go to make up our identity are already in us at birth. A few physical characteristics of course—sex, colour and so on. And even at this point not

everything is innate. Although, obviously, social environment doesn't determine sex, it does determine its significance. To be born a girl is not the same in Kabul as it is in Oslo: the condition of being a woman, like every other factor in a person's identity, is experienced differently in two places.

The same could be said of colour. To be born black is a different matter according to whether you come into the world in New York, Lagos, Pretoria or Luanda. One might almost say that, from the point of view of identity, we're not even talking about the same colour in the different places. For an infant who first sees the light of day in Nigeria, the operative factor as regards his identity is not whether he is black rather than white, but whether he is Yoruba, say, rather than Hausa. In South Africa, whether a person is black or white is still a significant element in his identity, but at least equally meaningful is his ethnic affiliation, whether Zulu, Xhosa or something else. In the United States it's of no consequence whether you have a Yoruba rather than a Hausa ancestor: it's chiefly among the whites—the Italians, the English, the Irish and the rest—that ethnic origin has a determining effect on identity. Moreover, someone with both whites and blacks among his ancestors would be regarded as "black" in the United States, whereas in South Africa or Angola he would be considered as "of mixed race."

Why is the idea of mixed race taken into account in some countries and not in others? Why is ethnic affiliation a determining factor in some societies but not in the rest? One could put forward various more or less convincing answers to both questions. But that is not what concerns me at this stage. I mention these examples only to underline the fact that even colour and sex are not "absolute" ingredients of identity. That being so, all the other ingredients are even more relative.

To gauge what is really innate among the ingredients that go to make up identity, we may make use of a mental exercise which is extremely revealing. Imagine an infant removed immediately from its place of birth and set down in a different environment. Then compare the various "identities" the child might acquire in its new context, the battles it would now have to fight and those it would be spared. Needless to say, the child would have no recollection of his original religion, or of his country or language. And might he not one day find himself fighting to the death against those who ought to have been his nearest and dearest?

What determines a person's affiliation to a given group is essentially the influence of others: the influence of those about him—relatives, fellow-countrymen, co-religionists—who try to make him one of them; together with the influence of those on the other side, who do their best to exclude him. Each one of us has to make his way while choosing between the paths that are urged upon him and those that are forbidden or strewn with obstacles. He is not himself from the outset; nor does he just "grow aware" of what he is; he *becomes* what he is. He doesn't merely grow aware of his identity; he acquires it step by step.

The apprenticeship starts very soon, in early childhood. Deliberately or otherwise, those around him mould him, shape him, instil into him family beliefs, rituals, attitudes and conventions, together of course with his native language and also certain fears, aspirations, prejudices and grudges, not forgetting various feelings of affiliation and non-affiliation, belonging and not belonging.

And soon, at home, at school and in the next street, he will suffer his first knocks. By their words and by their looks, other people will make him feel he is poor, or lame, short or lanky, swarthy or too fair, circumcised or uncircumcised, or an orphan; those innumerable differences, major and minor, that define every personality and shape each individual's behaviour, opinions, fears and ambitions. Such factors may act as formative influences, but they can also cause permanent injuries.

It is these wounds that at every stage in life determine not only men's attitudes towards their affiliations but also the hierarchy that decides the relative importance of these ties. When someone has been bullied because of his religion, humiliated or mocked because of the colour of his skin, his accent or his shabby cloths, he will never forget it. Up till now I have stressed the fact that identity is made up of a number of allegiances. But it is just as necessary to emphasise that identity is also singular, something that we experience as a complete whole. A person's identity is not an assemblage of separate affiliations, nor a kind of loose patchwork; it is like a pattern drawn on a tightly stretched parchment. Touch just one part of it, just one allegiance, and the whole person will react, the whole drum will sound.

People often see themselves in terms of whichever one of their allegiances is most under attack. And sometimes, when a person doesn't have the strength to defend that allegiance, he hides it. Then it remains buried deep down in the dark, awaiting its revenge. But whether he accepts or conceals it, proclaims it discreetly or flaunts it, it is with that allegiance that the person concerned identifies. And then, whether it relates to colour, religion, language or class, it invades the person's whole identity. Other people who share the same allegiance sympathise; they all gather together, join forces, encourage one another, challenge "the other side." For them, "asserting their identity" inevitably becomes an act of courage, of liberation.

In the midst of any community that has been wounded, agitators naturally arise. Whether they are hot-heads or cool schemers, their intransigent speeches act as balm to their audience's wounds. They say one shouldn't beg others for respect: respect is a due and must be forced from those who would withhold it. They promise victory or vengeance, they inflame men's minds, sometimes they use extreme methods that some of their brothers may merely have dreamed of in secret. The scene is now set and the war can begin. Whatever happens "the others" will have deserved it. "We" can remember quite clearly "all they have made us suffer" since time immemorial: all the crimes, all the extortion, all the humiliations and fears, complete with names and dates and statistics.

I have lived in a country at war, in a neighbourhood being shelled from a nearby part of the same city. I have spent a night or two in a basement being used as an air-raid shelter, together with my young wife, who was pregnant, and my little son. From outside came the noise of explosions; inside, people exchanged rumours of imminent attack and stories about whole families being put to the sword. So I know very well that fear might make anyone take to crime. If, instead of mere rumours, there had been a real massacre in the neighbourhood where I lived, would I have remained calm and collected? If, instead of spending just a couple of days in that shelter, I had had to stay there for a month, would I have refused to take a gun if it had been put in my hand?

I prefer not to ask myself such questions too often. I had the good luck not to be put to the test; to emerge from the ordeal with my family unharmed, with my hands clean and with a clear conscience. But I speak of "good luck" because things could have turned out very differently if I'd been 16 instead of 26 when the war began in Lebanon. Or if I'd lost someone I loved. Or if I'd belonged to a different social class, or a different community.

After each new ethnic massacre we ask ourselves, quite rightly, how human beings can perpetrate such atrocities. Certain excesses seem incomprehensible; the logic behind them indecipherable. So we talk of murderous folly, of blood-thirsty ancestral or hereditary madness. In a way, we are right to talk of madness. When an otherwise normal man is transformed overnight into a killer, that is indeed insanity. But when there are thousands, millions of killers; when this phenomenon occurs in one country after another, in different cultures, among the faithful of all religions and among unbelievers alike, it's no longer enough to talk of madness. What we conveniently call "murderous folly" is the propensity of our fellow–creatures to turn into butchers when they suspect that their "tribe" is being threatened. The emotions of fear or insecurity don't always obey rational considerations. They may be exaggerated or even paranoid; but once a whole population is afraid, we are dealing with the reality of the fear rather than the reality of the threat.

I don't think any particular affiliation, be it ethnic, religious, national or anything else, predisposes anyone to murder. We have only to review the events of the last few years to see that any human community that feels humiliated or fears for its existence will tend to produce killers. And these killers will commit the most dreadful atrocities in the belief that they are right to do so and deserve the admiration of their fellows in this world and bliss in the next. There is a Mr. Hyde inside each one of us. What we have to do is prevent the conditions occurring that will bring the monster forth.

I shall not venture to propose a universal explanation of all the massacres, still less to suggest a miracle cure. I no more believe in simplistic solutions than I do in simplistic identities. The world is a complex machine that can't be dismantled with a screwdriver. But that shouldn't prevent us from observing, from trying to understand, from discussing, and sometimes suggesting a subject for reflection.

The theme that runs like a thread through the tapestry of this book might be formulated as follows: if the men of all countries, of all conditions and faiths can so easily be transformed into butchers, if fanatics of all kinds manage so easily to pass themselves off as defenders of identity, it's because the "tribal" concept of identity still prevalent all over the world facilitates such a distortion. It's a concept inherited from the conflicts of the past, and many of us would reject it if we examined it more closely. But we cling to it through habit, from lack of imagination or resignation, thus inadvertently contributing to the tragedies by which, tomorrow, we shall be genuinely shocked.

4

From the very beginning of this book I have been speaking of murderous or mortal identities. Identities that kill. The expression doesn't strike me as inappropriate insofar as the idea I'm challenging—the notion that reduces identity to one single affiliation—encourages people to adopt an attitude that is partial, sectarian, intolerant, domineering, sometimes suicidal, and frequently even changes them into killers or supporters of killers. Their view of the world is biased and distorted. Those who belong to the same community as we do are "ours," we like to think ourselves concerned about what happens to them, but we also allow ourselves to tyrannise over them: if they are thought to be "lukewarm" we denounce them, intimidate them, punish them as "traitors" and "renegades." As for the others, those on the opposite side, we never try to put ourselves in their place, we take good care not to ask ourselves whether on some point or other they might not be entirely in the wrong, and we won't let our hearts be softened by their complaints, their sufferings or the injustices that have been inflicted on them. The only thing that counts is the point of view of "our" side; a point of view that is often that of the most militant, the most demagogic and the most fanatical members of the community.

On the other hand, when one sees one's own identity as made up of a number of allegiances, some linked to an ethnic past and others not, some linked to a religious tradition and others not; when one observes in oneself, in one's origins and in the course one's life has taken, a number of different confluences and contributions, of different mixtures and influences, some of them quite subtle or even incompatible with one another; then one enters into a different relationship both with other people and with one's own "tribe." It's no longer just a question of "them" and "us": two armies in battle order preparing for the next confrontation, the next revenge match. From then on there are people on "our" side with whom I ultimately have little in common, while on "their" side there are some to whom I might feel very close.

But to return to the earlier state of mind, it's easy to imagine how it can drive people to the worst kind of extremities: if they feel that "others" represent a threat to their own ethnic group or religion or nation, anything they might do to ward off that danger seems to them entirely legitimate. Even when they commit massacres they are convinced they are merely doing what is necessary to save the lives of their nearest and dearest. And as this attitude is shared by those around them, the butchers often have a clear conscience and are amazed to hear themselves described as criminals. How can they be criminals when all they are doing is protecting their aged mothers, their brothers and sisters and children?

The feeling that they are fighting for the survival of their own loved ones and are supported by their prayers; the belief that if not in the present instance at least over the long term they can claim to be acting in legitimate self-defence: these characteristics are common to all those who in recent years, throughout the world, from Rwanda to former Yugoslavia, have committed the most abominable crimes.

We are not talking about isolated examples. The world is full of whole communities that are wounded—either enduring present persecution or still overshadowed by the memory of former sufferings—and who dream of exacting revenge. We cannot remain unmoved by their martyrdom; we can only sympathise with their desire to speak their own language freely, to practise their own religion without fear, and to preserve their own traditions. But compassion sometimes tends towards complaisance: those who have suffered from colonialist arrogance, racism and xenophobia are forgiven for excesses they themselves have committed because of their own nationalistic arrogance, their own racism and xenophobia. This attitude means we turn a blind eye to the fate of their victims, at least until rivers of blood have been shed.

The fact is, it's difficult to say where legitimate affirmation of identity ends and encroachment on the rights of others begins. Did I not say that the word identity was a "false friend"? It starts by reflecting a perfectly permissible aspiration, then before we know where we are it has become an instrument of war. The transition from one meaning to the other is imperceptible, almost natural, and sometimes we all just go along with it. We are denouncing an injustice, we are defending the rights of a suffering people—then the next day we find ourselves accomplices in a massacre.

All the massacres that have taken place in recent years, like most of the bloody wars, have been linked to complex and long-standing "cases" of identity. Sometimes the victims are forever desperately the same; sometimes the situation is reversed and the victimisers of yesterday become victims of today; or vice versa. Such words themselves, it must be said, are meaningful only to outside observers; for people directly involved in conflicts arising out of identity, for those who have suffered and been afraid, nothing else exists except "them" and "us," the insult and the atonement. "We" are necessarily and by definition innocent victims; "they" are necessarily guilty and have long been so, regardless of what they may be enduring at present.

And when we, the outside observers, go in for this game and cast one community in the role of the sheep and another in that of the wolf, what we are unwittingly doing is granting the former community impunity in advance for its crimes. In recent conflicts some factions have even committed atrocities against their own people, knowing that international opinion would automatically lay the blame on their opponents.

This first type of complacency carries with it another, equally unfortunate form, whereby, at each new massacre arising out of identity, the eternal sceptics immediately declare that things have been the same since the dawn of history, and that it would be naive and self-deluding to hope they might change. Ethnic massacres are sometimes treated, consciously or otherwise, like collective crimes of passion, regrettable but comprehensible, and anyway inevitable because they are "inherent in human nature."

The *laisser-tuer* attitude has already done great harm, and the realism invoked to justify it is in my opinion a misnomer. Unfortunately the "tribal" notion of identity is still the one most commonly accepted everywhere, not only amongst fanatics. But many ideas that have been commonly accepted for centuries are no longer admissible today, among them the "natural" ascendancy of men over women, the hierarchy between races, and even, closer to home, apartheid and the various other kinds of segregation. Torture, too, was for a long time regarded as a "normal" element in the execution of justice. For centuries, slavery seemed like a fact of life, and great minds of the past took care not to call it into question.

Then new ideas gradually managed to establish themselves: that every man had rights that must be defined and respected; that women should have the same rights as men; that nature too deserved to be protected; that the whole human race has interests in common in more and more areas—the environment, peace, international exchanges, the battle against the great scourges of disease and natural disaster; that others might and even should interfere in the internal affairs of countries where fundamental human rights are abused. And so on.

In other words, ideas that have hitherto prevailed throughout history are not necessarily those that ought to prevail in times to come. When new facts emerge we need to reconsider our attitudes and habits. Sometimes, when such facts emerge too rapidly, our mental attitudes can't keep up with them and we find ourselves trying to fight fires by pouring oil on them.

But in the age of globalisation and of the ever-accelerating intermingling of elements in which we are all caught up, a new concept of identity is needed and needed urgently. We cannot be satisfied with forcing billions of bewildered human beings to choose between excessive assertion of their identity and the loss of their identity altogether, between fundamentalism and disintegration. But that is the logical consequence of the prevailing attitude on the subject. If our contemporaries are not encouraged to accept their multiple affiliations and allegiances; if they cannot reconcile their need for identity with an open and unprejudiced tolerance of other cultures; if they feel they have to choose between denial of the self and denial of the other—then we shall be bringing into being legions of the lost and hordes of bloodthirsty madmen.

But let us return for a moment to some examples I quoted at the beginning of this book. A man with a Serbian mother and a Croatian father, and who manages to accept his dual affiliation, will never take part in any form of ethnic "cleansing." A man with a Hutu mother and a Tutsi father, if he can accept the two "tributaries" that brought him into the world, will never be a party to butchery or genocide. And neither the Franco-Algerian lad, nor the young man of mixed German and Turkish origin whom I mentioned earlier, will ever be on the side of the fanatics if they succeed in living peacefully in the context of their own complex identity.

Here again it would be a mistake to see such examples as extreme or unusual. Wherever there are groups of human beings living side by side who differ from one another in religion, colour, language, ethnic origin or nationality; wherever there are tensions, more or less longstanding, more or less violent, between immigrants and local populations, Blacks and Whites, Catholics and Protestants, Jews and Arabs, Hindus and Sikhs, Lithuanians and Russians, Serbs and Albanians, Greeks and Turks, English-speaking and French-speaking Canadians, Flemings and Walloons, Chinese and Malays—yes, wherever there is a divided society, there are men and women bearing within them contradictory allegiances, people who live on the frontier between opposed communities, and whose very being might be said to be traversed by ethnic or religious or other fault lines.

We are not dealing with a handful of marginal people. There are thousands, millions of such men and women, and there will be more and more of them. They are frontier-dwellers by birth, or through the changes and chances of life, or by deliberate choice, and they can influence events and affect their course one way or the other. Those who can accept their diversity fully will hand on the torch between communities and cultures, will be a kind of mortar joining together and strengthening the societies in which they live. On the other hand, those who cannot accept their own diversity may be among the most virulent of those prepared to kill for the sake of identity, attacking those who embody that part of themselves which they would like to see forgotten. History contains many examples of such self-hatred.

5

No doubt I speak like a migrant and a member of a minority. But I think what I say reflects a sensibility that is more and more widely shared by our contemporaries. Isn't it a characteristic of the age we live in that it has made everyone in a way a migrant and a member of a minority? We all have to live in a universe bearing little resemblance to the place where we were born: we must all learn other languages, other modes of speech, other codes; and we all have the feeling that our own identity, as we have conceived of it since we were children, is threatened.

Many have left their native land, and many, though they haven't left it, can no longer recognise it. This may be partly due to the natural homesickness that is a permanent feature of the human soul; but it is also caused by an accelerated process of evolution which has made us travel further in 30 years than people used to go in many generations.

So to be a migrant no longer means merely belonging to a category of people who have been forced out of their native habitat; it has acquired a more general significance. The status of migrant itself is the first victim of a "tribal" notion of identity. If only one affiliation matters, if a choice absolutely has to be made, a migrant finds himself split and torn, condemned to betray either his country of origin or his country of adoption, and whichever course he follows the consequent betrayal is bound to cause him lasting bitterness and anger.

Before becoming an immigrant one is a migrant, an émigré. Before coming to one country one has had to leave another. And a person's feeling's about the country he has left are never simple. If you have gone away, it is because there are things you have rejected—repression, insecurity, poverty, lack of opportunity. But this rejection is often accompanied by a sense of guilt. You are angry with yourself for abandoning loved ones, or the house you grew up in, or countless pleasant memories. And some ties linger on: those of language, religion, music; those with your companions in exile; those celebrated special holidays; those connected with cooking and food.

Similarly, one's feelings towards one's country of adoption are also ambiguous. If you have come here it's because you hope for a better life for yourself and your family. But this expectation is tinged with apprehension about the unknown—the more so because you are at a disadvantage in various ways, afraid of being rejected or humiliated, and on the look-out for signs of contempt, sarcasm or pity.

One's first reflex is not to flaunt one's difference but to try to pass unnoticed. The secret dream of most migrants is to be taken for "natives." Their first temptation is to imitate their hosts, and sometimes they succeed in doing so. But more often they fail. They haven't got the right accent, the right shade of skin, the right first name, the right family name or the proper papers, so they are soon found out. A lot of them know it's no use even trying, and out of pride or bravado make themselves out to be more different than they really are. And needless to say some go even further, and their frustration turns into violent contestation.

If I dwell on the migrant's state of mind it is not only because his dilemma is familiar to me personally. It is also because in this connection, more than in others, tensions arising out of identity can lead to the most lethal aberrations.

In the many countries where a native population with its own local culture lives side by side with another, more recently arrived population with different traditions, tensions arise that not only influence the behaviour of individuals but also affect the atmosphere prevailing in society as a whole and have an impact on political debate. This makes it all the more necessary to take a calm and judicious view of these highly emotional questions.

Wisdom is a view from on high, from the narrow path between two precipices, two extreme ideas. In the matter of immigration, the first of these extreme ideas is that which regards the host country as a blank sheet of paper on which everyone can write whatever he pleases, or, worse, as a wasteland where everyone can set up house with all his own impedimenta without making any changes in his habits or behaviour. The other extreme idea sees the host country as a page already written and printed, a land where the laws, values, beliefs and other human and cultural characteristics have been fixed once and for all, and where all that immigrants can do is conform to them.

Both notions strike me as equally unrealistic, sterile and harmful. Have I caricatured them? Unfortunately, I think not. Even if I had, caricature can serve a useful purpose if it helps people see how absurd an attitude can be if pushed to merely logical conclusions. Some will go on clinging to their own notions, but men of good sense will take a step towards the self-evident common ground: the fact that a host country is neither a tabula rasa, nor a fait accompli, but a page in the process of being written.

Its history must be respected. And when I say history I speak as a lover of History with a capital H. For me, it is not synonymous with empty nostalgia or indiscriminate worship of the past. On the contrary, it stands for all that has been built up over the centuries: memory, symbols, institutions, language, works of art, and all the other things to which one may legitimately be attached. At the same time, everyone will admit that a country's future cannot be a mere continuation of its history. It would be terrible for any country to have more reverence for its past than for its future. While that future should be constructed in a certain spirit of continuity it should also incorporate profound changes, together with significant contributions from elsewhere, as was the case in all the great eras of the past.

Have I merely been listing self-evident truths with which everybody agrees? Perhaps. But if tensions still exist and are even getting worse, it must be because those truths are neither self-evident enough nor really generally accepted. What I am trying to prise out of these often confused considerations is not an intellectual consensus but a code of conduct, or at least a kind of safety barrier for everyone to use.

I insist on the fact that it is for everyone. My approach constantly calls for reciprocity, and this out of a concern for both fairness and efficiency. It's in this spirit that I would first say to the one party: "The more you steep yourself in the culture of the host country the more you will be able to steep yourself in your own"; and then, to the other party: "The more an immigrant feels that his own culture is respected, the more open he will be to the culture of the host country."

I set out the two equations in the same breath because they support one another, inseparable as the two parts of a ladder. Or, more prosaically, like clauses in a contract. For that is what we are really talking about—a moral contract, the elements of which need to be defined in each case to which it is applied: what, in the culture of a host country, is the minimum equipment that everyone is supposed to possess, and what may legitimately be challenged or rejected? The same question may be asked about the immigrants' own original culture: which parts of it deserve to be transmitted like a valuable dowry to the country of adoption, and which—which habits? which practices?—ought to be left behind at the door?

Such questions need to be asked, and everyone should make an effort to consider each one separately, even if the answers arrived at will never be entirely satisfactory. I live in France, but I wouldn't venture to list those parts of her heritage that ought to be adopted by anyone who wanted to live there. Everything I might suggest, whether a republican principle, an aspect of the French way of life, an outstanding person or a significant place—yes, everything I proposed, without exception, could justifiably be challenged. But it would be wrong to conclude from this that everything may be rejected out of hand. A fact may be vague, elusive and variable, but that doesn't mean it doesn't exist.

Again, the key word is reciprocity. If I try to belong to my country of adoption, if I now regard it as my own country and consider it part of me and myself part of it, and if I act accordingly, then I have the right to criticise every aspect of it. Similarly, if it respects me, if it recognises what I bring to it and regards me and my characteristics as now being part of itself, then it has the right to reject aspects of my culture that might be incompatible with its own way of life or with the spirit of its own institutions.

But the right to criticise someone else has to be won, deserved. If, in general, you treat another with hostility or contempt, your slightest adverse remark, whether justified or not, will be seen as a sign of aggression, much more likely to make him obstinate and unapproachable than to persuade him to change for the better.

Conversely, if you show someone friendship, sympathy and consideration, not merely superficially but in a manner that is sincere and felt to be so, then you may allow yourself to criticise, with some hope of being heard, things about him that you regard as open to objection.

Am I thinking of controversies like that which has arisen in various countries over the "Islamic veil"? These are not my main concern. But I am sure problems of that kind would be resolved more easily if relations with immigrants were approached in a different spirit. When someone feels that his language is despised, his religion ridiculed and his culture disparaged, he is likely to react by flaunting the signs of his difference. When someone feels he has a place in the country where he has chosen to live, then he will behave in quite another manner.

To approach someone else convincingly you must do so with open arms and head held high, and your arms can't be open unless your head *is* held high. If, every time you do approach another you feel you are betraying both your own people and yourself, your advances are doomed to failure. If I study someone else's language but he doesn't respect mine, to go on speaking his tongue ceases to be a token of amity and becomes an act of servitude and submission.

But to go back for a moment to the wearing of the veil, I don't doubt that this is an example of reactionary, backward-looking behaviour. I could explain at length why I take this attitude—because of my own convictions, and in the light not only of certain episodes in the history of the Arab-Muslim world but also of the long battle for emancipation being fought by the women there. But lengthy explanations would be pointless That is not the real question. The real question isn't whether we are dealing with a conflict between ancient and modern, but why, in the course of human history, modernity is sometimes rejected: why it isn't always seen as progress and as a welcome development.

In any consideration of identity that question is essential, nowadays more than ever. And in this respect the Arab world is a very instructive example.

The Age Of Global Tribes

1

Of course "in the air" is not a very rigorous expression. I use it to suggest the diffuse and elusive phenomenon that at certain moments in history makes a lot of people start to emphasise one element of their identity rather than the rest. Thus, at present, it is common for a person to stress his or her religious allegiance and regard it as the central factor in his or her identity. This attitude is probably less widespread now than it was 300 years ago, but it is undoubtedly more general than it was 50 years ago.

I could have spoken of intellectual environment or emotional climate—both of them terms scarcely less vague than "in the air." But whatever expressions one decides to employ, it's the real questions underlying them that matter: what is it that currently makes men and women all over the world, from every kind of background, rediscover and feel impelled to assert in various ways their religious affiliation, when the same people, only a few years earlier, would spontaneously have chosen to put forward quite different allegiances? What makes a Muslim in Yugoslavia suddenly stop calling himself a Yugoslav and proclaim himself first and foremost a Muslim? What causes a Jewish worker in Russia who all his life has regarded himself as a proletarian, suddenly begin to see himself as a Jew? How does it happen that the proud affirmation of subscribing to some religion, which might once have appeared unseemly, now strikes people in so many countries at the same time as quite natural and permissible?

It is a complex phenomenon with no single satisfactory explanation. Nonetheless, it is clear that a decisive role was played in its development by the decline, followed by the collapse, of the communist world. It is more than a century since Marxism promised to establish a new worldwide society from which the notion of God would be banished. The failure of this project not only on the economic and political, but also on the moral and intellectual planes, has resulted in the rehabilitation of beliefs that Marxism itself wanted to consign to the dustbins of history. From Poland to Afghanistan, religion, that spiritual refuge and buttress of identity, was an obvious rallying point for all who were fighting communism. So the defeat of Marx and Lenin has been perceived as the revenge of religions at least as much as the victory of capitalism, liberalism and the West.

But this is not the only operative factor behind the "rise" of religion in the last quarter of the twentieth century. While the terminal crisis of communism has weighed heavily on intellectual and political debate, and will continue to do so, many things would be incomprehensible if other factors were not taken into account, notably the other so-called "crisis" affecting the West.

This has to be considered as something quite different from the crisis of communism. It would be pointless to deny that in the long battle between the two sides there has been a winner and a loser. But nor can it be gainsaid that the western model, despite its triumph and the fact that its influence is spreading over every continent, sees itself as a model in crisis, unable to resolve the problems of poverty in its own cities, incapable of attacking unemployment, delinquency, drugs and many other scourges. It is one of our age's most disconcerting paradoxes that the most attractive model of society, the one that has overcome all the others, has deeply-felt doubts about itself.

Let us for a moment put ourselves in the place of a young man of 19 who has just entered a university in the Arab world. In the past he might have been attracted by an organisation with Marxist tendencies that would have been sympathetic to his existential difficulties and initiated him, in its own way, into the debate about ideas. Or else he might have joined some nationalist group that would have flattered his need for identity and perhaps spoken to him of renaissance and modernisation. But now Marxism has lost its attraction and Arab nationalism, annexed by regimes that are authoritarian, incompetent and corrupt, has lost much of its credibility. So it is not impossible that the young man we are thinking of will be fascinated by the West, by its way of life and its scientific and technological achievements. But that fascination would probably have little impact on his actions, since there is no political organisation of any consequence that embodies the model he admires. Those who aspire to the "Western Paradise" often have no alternative but emigration. Unless they belong to one of the privileged "castes" who do their best to reproduce aspects of the coveted model in their own homes. But all those who are not born with a limousine at their disposal, all those who want to shake up the established order or are revolted by corruption, state despotism, inequality, unemployment and lack of opportunity, all who have difficulty finding a place in a fast-changing world—all these are tempted by Islamism. In it they find satisfaction for their need for identity, for affiliation to a group, for spirituality, for a simple interpretation of too-complex realities and for action and revolt.

I can't help feeling deeply uneasy as I point out the circumstances that lead young people in the Muslim world to enrol in religious movements. This is because, in the conflict between the Islamists and the rulers who oppose them, I find myself unable to identify with either side. I am unmoved by the utterances of radical Islamists not only because as a Christian I feel excluded, but also because I cannot accept that any religious faction, even if it is in the majority, has the right to lay down the law for the population as a whole. In my view the tyranny of a majority is no better morally than the tyranny of a minority. Moreover, I believe profoundly not just in equality, between men and women alike, but also in liberty in matters of faith and in the freedom of every individual to live as he chooses; and I distrust any doctrine that tries to challenge such fundamental values.

That said, I must add that I disapprove just as strongly of the despotic powers against which the Islamists are fighting, and I decline to applaud the outrages such regimes perpetrate on the pretext that they constitute a lesser evil. The people themselves deserve something better than a lesser evil or any sort of makeshift. What they need are genuine solutions, which can only be those of genuine democracy and modernity—by which I mean a complete modernity freely granted, not an eviscerated one imposed by force. And it seems to me that by taking a fresh look at the idea of identity we might help find a way that leads out of the present impasse and towards human liberty.

I now end this digression and return to what is "in the air." And also to say that if the rise of the religious factor can be explained partly by the discomfiture of communism, partly by the impasse in which various Third World societies find themselves, and partly by the crisis affecting the western model, the scope and tone of the phenomenon cannot be understood except with reference, in particular, to the spectacular progress made recently in the field of communications and, in general, to what is usually called globalisation.

In a text published in 1973, the British historian Arnold Toynbee explained that the history of the human race had consisted of three successive phases.

During the first, which corresponds to prehistory, communications were extremely slow, but knowledge advanced even more painfully, so that every new development had time to spread everywhere before another came along. Thus all human societies evolved roughly in parallel with one another and had many characteristics in common.

In the second period, knowledge developed at a much faster rate than the means of disseminating it, so that in every field human societies grew more and more different from one another. This phase lasted for several thousand years, which corresponds to what we call History.

Then, quite recently, a third period has begun, in which although knowledge certainly advances more and more rapidly, the dissemination of knowledge progresses even faster, with the result that human societies are likely to become less and less differentiated from one another.

We could spend some time discussing the validity of this theory, which I have in any case presented in very simplified terms. However, I put it forward not as a basis for argument but rather as an appealing and intellectually stimulating insight into the situation we see around us today.

It is obvious that the current universal, ever more intense and apparently uncontrollable interchange of images and ideas will bring about a profound and, in terms of the history of civilisation, very swift transformation in our knowledge, perceptions and behaviour. Moreover, it will probably have an equally fundamental effect on our vision of ourselves, our allegiances and our identity. Extrapolating Toynbee's hypothesis slightly, we might say that everything human societies have done through the ages to mark differences and establish frontiers between them is due to come under pressures aimed at reducing those differences and abolishing those frontiers.

But the unprecedented metamorphosis taking place before our very eyes, like some endless but ever-accelerating fireworks display, brings with it certain shocks. We all accept many things offered by the world around us just because they seem either advantageous or inevitable. But each one of us has known what it is to jib when he feels that some significant factor in his identity is being threatened, whether it be his language, his religion, the symbolic elements, in his culture, or his independence. So we are living in an age of both harmonisation and dissonance. Never have men had so many things in common—knowledge, points of reference, images, words, instruments and tools of all kinds. But this only increases their desire to assert their differences.

All this is plain to the naked eye. The ever-increasing speed of globalisation undoubtedly reinforces, by way of reaction, people's need for identity. And because of the existential anguish that accompanies such sudden changes it also strengthens their need for spirituality. But only religious allegiance meets, or at least seeks to meet, both these needs.

I have mentioned the word "reaction," but I should point out that it alone cannot account for the phenomenon as a whole. True, we may call it reaction, in every sense of the word, when a group of people, frightened by change, seeks refuge in the values and symbols of a time-honoured tradition. But it seems to me that there is something more than mere reaction in the current rise of religious sentiment: perhaps an attempt at a synthesis between the need for identity and the desire for universality. I see the religious communities as global tribes: tribes because of their stress on identity, global because of the way they blithely reach across frontiers. For some people, to subscribe to a faith that transcends national, regional and social affiliations is a way of proclaiming their own universality. In a way, belonging to a faith community is the most global and universal kind of particularism—or perhaps rather the most tangible, the most "natural," the most deep-rooted.

Whatever the right term for it may be, the important thing is to note that, as it manifests itself today, the feeling of belonging to a religious community is not merely a return to the past. We are witnessing not the dawn, but the twilight of the age of nationalities. We are also living through not the dawn but the dusk of internationalism too, at least in its "proletarian" form. So the sense of belonging first and foremost to a religion cannot just be brushed aside as a fleeting historical moment, soon to be left behind. For the question has to be asked: left behind for what? For a new era of nations? That seems to me neither likely nor even desirable. In any case, the sense of belonging to a common "Church" is nowadays the most efficient factor for binding together varieties of nationalism, even those that call themselves secular. This is as true of the Turks as of the Russians, Greeks, Poles and Israelis, and for many other groups who wouldn't care to admit it.

So what will religious affiliation be replaced by? What other allegiance will be able to make it "obsolete," as it once seemed to be before?

2

At this stage of my argument a clarification is necessary if I am to avoid serious misunderstanding. When I speak of leaving religious allegiance behind I am not trying to say that religion itself should become a thing of the past. For me, religion will never be consigned to the storeroom of history either by science, by doctrine of some other kind or by any political regime. The further science progresses the more man is bound to ponder the purpose of his own existence. The God of "how" will become hazy one day, but the God of "why" will never die. Perhaps a thousand years hence we won't have the same religions as now, but I can't imagine the world without any kind of religion at all.

I hasten to add that in my view the need for spirituality doesn't have to express itself through participation in a religious community. We are concerned here with two fundamental aspirations, both of which are in differing degrees natural and permissible, but which we must be careful to distinguish. On the one hand there is the desire for a vision of the world that transcends our own existence with its sufferings and disappointments, and gives a meaning—even if only an illusory one—to life and death. On the other hand there is the need, felt by every individual, to feel part of a community which accepts and recognises him and within which he can be understood easily.

I dream not of a world where religion no longer has any place but of one where the need for spirituality will no longer be associated with the need to belong. A world in which a man, while remaining attached to his beliefs, to a faith, or to moral values that may or may not be inspired by scripture, will no longer feel the need to enrol himself among his co-religionists. A world in which religion will no longer serve to bind together warring ethnic groups. It is not enough now to separate Church and State: what has to do with religion must be kept apart from what has to do with identity. And if we want that amalgam to stop feeding fanaticism, terror and ethnic wars, we must find other ways of satisfying the need for identity.

This brings me back to my original question: what can be done today to replace affiliation to a religious community?

The difficulty, as suggested in the previous pages, is that such an affiliation seems now to be the ultimate allegiance, the least ephemeral, the most deep-rooted, the only one capable of fulfilling so many of man's essential needs.

It also looks as if it cannot be permanently supplanted by other traditional allegiances, whether to nation, ethnic group, race or even class; these all turn out to be narrower, more restrictive and scarcely less lethal. If affiliation to a "global tribe" is to be left behind, it can only be for a much wider allegiance, with a fuller vision of humanity.

Of course, you say. But which? What "wider allegiance"? What "vision of humanity"? A glance round the world is enough to show that there is no new affiliation capable of counterbalancing the powerful visceral allegiances that have demonstrated throughout the course of history their ability to arouse armies of followers. Moreover, any would-be global vision provokes mistrust among our contemporaries, either because it strikes them as naive or because it seems to threaten their identity.

Mistrust is undoubtedly one of the keywords of our age. Mistrust of ideologies, of dreams of a better future, of politics, science, reason and modernity. Of the idea of progress. Of practically everything we could believe in throughout the twentieth century—a century of great achievements, without any precedent ever, but also a century of unforgivable crimes and blighted hopes. Mistrust, too, of anything that presents itself as global, worldwide or planetary.

Only a few years ago many people would have been ready to see the idea of a worldwide allegiance as being in some way the natural culmination of human history. Thus an inhabitant of Turin, having been first a Piedmontese and then an Italian, would become next a European and thereafter a citizen of the world. I am simplifying greatly, but the notion of an irreversible progress towards ever-wider affiliations did not seem far-fetched then. Through a series of regional regroupings the human race itself would ultimately become the supreme group. There were even very attractive theories concerning the two rival systems, the capitalist and the communist, which would gradually converge, the former becoming ever more social, the latter ever less interventionist, until they finally fused into one. Similarly it was predicted that religions would eventually all come together in one great cosy syncretism.

We know now that history never follows the path we predict. This is not because history is by nature erratic, unfathomable or indecipherable, or because human reason cannot comprehend it. It is precisely because history is not just what men make of it but rather the sum of all their individual and collective acts, all their words, communications, confrontations, sufferings, hatreds and affinities. The more numerous and free the humans who make history, the more complex and difficult to understand is the total result of all their actions, and the less amenable to simplistic explanations.

History is continually advancing along an infinite number of paths. Does some meaning nevertheless emerge? Until we reach "The End"—if *that* means anything—we shall probably never know.

Will the future be that of our hopes or that of our nightmares? Will it consist of freedom or slavery? Will science ultimately be the means of our redemption or the instrument of our destruction? Will we have been inspired assistants of a Creator or no more than mere sorcerers' apprentices? Are we moving towards a better world or towards "the best of all possible worlds"?

And, to begin with, what do the coming decades have in store for us? A "war of civilisations" or the peace of the "global village"?

I firmly believe that the future is not written down anywhere. The future will be what we make it.

"But what about fate?" some will ask, alluding to the fact that I'm an oriental. My usual reply is that fate is to man as the wind is to a sailing boat. The helmsman cannot decide the direction or the force of the wind, but he can manipulate his own sails. And that can make an enormous difference. The same wind that may kill a mariner who is inexperienced, rash or merely unlucky will bring another safe to harbour.

Almost the same can be said of the "wind" of globalisation that is now sweeping the world. It would be absurd to try to stop it, but if we navigate skilfully, steering a steady course and avoiding reefs, we can reach haven safe and sound.

But the marine metaphor is too limited. I want to express myself more clearly. There is no point in asking ourselves whether the great technological progress that has been accelerating in recent years and that has profoundly changed our lives, especially in the field of communications and access to knowledge, is a good thing or a bad thing as far as we are concerned. It isn't the subject of a referendum. It's a fact. But the way it affects our future depends largely upon ourselves.

Some people might be tempted to reject it all out of hand, taking refuge in their "identity" and anathematising in one and the same breath globalisation, the hegemony of the West and the intolerable United States. Others, conversely, would be ready to accept everything, to swallow it all so indiscriminately that they end up not knowing where they are, where they are going or what the world is coming to! The two attitudes are diametrically opposite, but both end up in resignation. Both of them—the bitter and the cloying, the surly and the silly—are based on the premise that the world moves forward like a train on its rails and that nothing can make it alter its course.

I think differently. It seems to me that the wind of globalisation, while it certainly could lead us to disaster, could also lead us to success. While the new means of communication that all too swiftly bring us close to one another may bring us by way of reaction to stress our differences, they also make us aware of our common fate. This makes me think that current developments might in the long run favour the emergence of a new approach to the idea of identity. Identity would then be seen as the sum of all our allegiances, and within it, allegiance to the human community itself would become increasingly important, until one day it would become the chief allegiance, though without destroying our many individual affiliations. Of course I wouldn't go as far as to say that the wind of globalisation *must* blow us in that direction, but it seems to me it makes such an attitude less difficult to imagine. And, at the same time, necessary.

3

"Men are more the sons of their time than of their fathers," wrote the historian Marc Bloch. The maxim has probably always been true, but never more so than now. There is no need to insist further on how, in the last few decades, things have been moving ever faster. Which of our contemporaries has not sometimes felt he has witnessed in a couple of years changes that in the past would have been spread over a century? The oldest among us even have to make an effort to recall what their outlook was like in their childhood, and to do so they have to set aside the habits they have acquired since, together with new products and tools they cannot now do without. As for the young, they often haven't the slightest idea what their grandparents' way of life was like, let alone that of earlier generations.

In fact, we are all infinitely closer to our contemporaries than to our ancestors. Would it be an exaggeration to say I have much more in common with a random passerby in a street in Prague or Seoul or San Francisco than with my own great-grandfather? And this not only as regards appearance, clothes, behaviour, way of life, work, habitat and the objects that surround us, but also as regards moral concepts and habits of thought.

The same applies to belief. We may call ourselves Christians—or Muslims, Jews, Buddhists or Hindus—but our vision of both this world and the next no longer bears much resemblance to that of our "co-religionists" who lived 500 years ago. For the great majority of them, Hell was as real a place as Asia Minor or Abyssinia, complete with cloven-hoofed devils thrusting sinners into eternal fire, as in apocalyptic paintings. Practically no one thinks like that now. The example I chose was extreme, but the observation itself applies equally well to all our ideas in every field. Many types of behaviour that are perfectly acceptable to a believer today would have struck his "co-religionists" in the past as inconceivable. I put the word in quotes because the religion practised by our ancestors was not the same as ours. If we had lived among them and behaved as we do nowadays we would have been stoned in the street, thrown into prison or burned at the stake for impiety, debauchery, heresy or witchcraft.

In short, each one of us has two heritages, a "vertical" one that comes to us from our ancestors, our religious community and our popular traditions, and a "horizontal" one transmitted to us by our contemporaries and by the age we live in. It seems to me that the latter is the more influential of the two, and that it becomes more so every day. Yet this fact is not reflected in our perception of ourselves, and the inheritance we invoke most frequently is the vertical one.

This is an essential point with regard to current concepts of identity. On the one hand there is what we are in reality and what we are becoming as a result of cultural globalisation: that is to say, beings woven out of many-coloured threads, who share most of their points of reference, their ways of behaving and their beliefs with the vast community of their contemporaries. And on the other hand there is what we think we are and what we claim to be: that is to say, members of one community rather than another, adherents of one faith rather than another. I do not deny the importance of our religious, national or other affiliations. I do not question the often decisive influence of our vertical heritage. But it is necessary at this point in time to draw attention to the gulf that exists between what we are and what we think we are.

To tell the truth, if we assert our differences so fiercely it is precisely because we are less and less different from one another. Because, in spite of our conflicts and our age-old enmities, each day that goes by reduces our differences and increases our likenesses a little bit more.

I seem to be glad of this. But should one rejoice to see people growing more and more like one another? Are we heading for an insipid world where we may soon speak only one language, where everyone shares the same bunch of minimal beliefs, and where everyone watches the same American TV soaps, munching the same sandwiches?

Caricature aside, the question needs to be seriously addressed. We are living in a very bewildering age, in which many of our fellow-creatures see globalisation not as a great and enriching amalgam with advantages for all, but as a standardisation and an impoverishment, a threat that the individual needs to fight against in order to preserve his own culture, identity and values.

These may be merely rear-guard actions, but in present circumstances we must have the humility to admit we don't really know. We may not always find what we expect in the dustbins of history. In any case, if so many people see globalisation as a threat it is only natural that we should examine it more closely.

Those who feel themselves to be in danger may of course be influenced in part by the fear of change that is as old as mankind itself. But there are other, more current anxieties which I'd hesitate to dismiss as irrelevant. For globalisation draws us simultaneously towards two contrasting results, one welcome and the other not: i.e., universality and uniformity. The two tracks seem so alike and are so closely intermingled it's as if there were only one. You might almost wonder if one isn't just the presentable face of the other.

But for my part I'm sure there are two separate tracks, however much and however closely they intertwine. It would be over-optimistic to try to unravel the whole skein at once, but we might well attempt to tease out a thread or two.

4

The basic postulate of universality is that there exist inherent rights to human dignity that no one may deny to his fellow creatures, whether on the grounds of religion, colour, nationality or sex, or on any other consideration. This means, among other things, that any attack on the fundamental rights of men and women in the name of some tradition—religious or other—is contrary to the spirit of universality. There cannot be on the one hand an overall, general charter of human rights and on the other hand special and particular charters for Muslims, Jews, Christians, Africans, Asians and the rest.

Few people would agree with this in principle. But in practice many behave as if they didn't really believe it. For example, no western government scrutinises human rights in Africa or the Arab world as closely as it does in Poland or Cuba. This attitude claims to be motivated by respect, but in my view it is really based on contempt. If you respect someone and respect his history it's because you believe he belongs to the same human race as you do, not to some inferior version.

I don't wish to dwell on this question, which calls for lengthy argument in its own right. But I refer to it in passing because it plays an essential part in the notion of universality, which would be meaningless if it didn't presuppose that there are values that concern the whole human race without exception. And these values come before all else. Traditions deserve to be respected only insofar as they are respectable—that is, exactly insofar as they themselves respect the fundamental rights of men and women. To follow traditions or to obey laws that are discriminatory is to despise their victims. Every country and every doctrine has at certain times in its history produced behaviour which, with the evolution of mental attitudes, has come to be regarded as incompatible with human dignity. Such practices cannot be wiped out by a stroke of the pen, but that doesn't exempt us from denouncing them and doing our best to make them things of the past.

Everything that has to do with fundamental rights—the right to live as a full citizen on the soil of one's fathers, free of persecution or discrimination; the right to live with dignity anywhere; the right to choose one's life and loves and beliefs freely, while respecting the freedom of others; the right of free access to knowledge, health and a decent and honourable life—none of this, and the list is not exhaustive, may be denied to our fellow human beings on the pretext of preserving a belief, an ancestral practice or a tradition. In this area we should tend towards universality, and even, if necessary, towards uniformity, because humanity, while it is also multiple, is primarily one.

What then about the individuality of each civilisation? Of course it has to be respected, but differently and with lucidity.

At the same time as we fight for the universality of values it is imperative that we fight against the impoverishment of standardisation; against hegemony, whether ideological, political, economic or operating in the media; against foolish conformism; against everything that stifles the full variety of linguistic, artistic and intellectual expression. Against everything that makes for a monotonous and puerile world. A battle in defence of certain practices and cultural traditions, but one that is clear-sighted, rigorous, discriminating, not over-sensitive, not unduly timorous, always open to the future.

A great tide of different images, sounds, ideas and products submerges the whole planet, bringing every day new changes to our tastes, hopes, habits, life style and view of the world, and also to ourselves. This extraordinary ferment often brings forth contradictions. For example, we now see the familiar American fast food signs on the main streets of Paris, Moscow, Shanghai and Prague. But it is also true that on every continent we encounter more and more different kinds of cooking, not only Italian, French, Chinese and Indian, which have been exported for a long time now, but also Japanese, Indonesian, Korean, Mexican, Moroccan and Lebanese.

For some people that is a mere detail. But for me it is very revealing. It shows what the great mingling of cultures may mean in terms of everyday life. It also reflects people's different reactions. Many see this phenomenon merely as proof of some young people's fascination with American ways. I am not in favour of laisser-faire, and I admire those who stand up for themselves. It's permissible and sometimes necessary to fight to preserve the traditional character of a street, a neighbourhood, or a certain quality of life. But that shouldn't prevent us from seeing the picture as a whole.

That fact that all over the world you can now eat not only the local food but also, if you choose, try out other culinary traditions, not excluding those of the United States; the fact that the British might like mint sauce with their curry, that the French sometimes order a couscous instead of a stew, or that an inhabitant of Minsk, after decades of dullness, fancies a hamburger with ketchup—none of this irritates or bothers me. On the contrary, I'd like every culinary tradition to be enjoyed all over the world, whether it comes from Szechuan, Aleppo, Champagne, Apulia, Hanover or Milwaukee.

What I have said of cuisine could be extended to many other aspects of everyday culture. Music, for example. Here again, an extraordinary proliferation is taking place. The news from Algeria is often appalling, but from the same country there also emanates inventive music of many kinds, disseminated by young people who express themselves in Arabic, French or Kabyle. Some of them have stayed at home, despite everything, while others have gone abroad, taking with them, in them, and bearing witness to, the truth of a people and the soul of a culture.

Their journey cannot fail to remind us of the older, more massive trajectory of the Africans once taken as slaves to the Americas. Today their music, whether issuing from Louisiana or from the West Indies, has spread all over the world and become part of the musical and emotional heritage of us all. That is globalisation too. Never in the past have human beings had the technical means of listening at will to so many kinds of music—all those voices, whether from Cameroon, Spain, Egypt, Argentina, Brazil and Cape Verde, or from Liverpool, Memphis, Brussels and Naples. Never before have so many people been able to play, compose, sing—and be heard.

5

Though I stress what seems to me to be one of the advantages of globalisation, a genuine example of universality, I don't wish to ignore the unease of those who see the present upsurge of new music as much less significant than the growing predominance of English-speaking influence in popular song. This anxiety exists in many other fields—in some sectors of the international media, for instance, and in the cinema, where the influence of Hollywood is clearly overwhelming.

I've spoken of unease, but that is too vague a word to encompass the wide range of reactions involved. A French café owner annoyed at hearing so few French songs on the radio has nothing in common—except perhaps mistrust of global culture in its present form—with a fanatical preacher who calls satellite dishes satanic dishes because he regards them as transmitters of the siren voices of the West. Personally, I am worried, simultaneously but not equally, by both anxieties. I don't want the Arab world to look backwards and rage against modernity; but nor do I want France to enter the new millennium hesitant and unsure of herself.

But as I've said before, although the worries people have about globalisation sometimes strike me as excessive, I don't consider them unfounded.

They are of two kinds. I shall refer to the first kind more briefly than it deserves, because treating it fully would call for more space than is available here. It consists of the idea that the present ferment, rather than leading to a great enrichment, a multiplication of the means of expression and the diversification of opinion, instead conduce to the opposite—to impoverishment. According to this point of view, the current free outpouring of musical expression will ultimately result in no more than sugary, mawkish "wallpaper," and the extraordinary effervescence of ideas will produce only a simplistic conformism, an intellectual lowest common denominator. So much so that everyone, with the exception of a few eccentrics, will soon end up reading (if they read anything at all) the same stereotyped novels, listening to the same vague mass-produced tunes, and watching films all made according to the same recipes—in short, swallowing the same formless pap of sounds, images and beliefs.

The prospect facing the news media might be considered equally frustrating. Sometimes it's thought that with so many newspapers and radio and television channels likely to be available we shall have access to an infinite variety of opinions. Then the reverse seems to be true: the transmitters are so powerful that they merely amplify the currently prevailing opinion, drowning out any other point of view. And admittedly, the flood of words and images doesn't always encourage a spirit of criticism.

Are we then to conclude that a ferment such as we are witnessing at present, instead of favouring cultural diversity really leads, by virtue of some insidious law, to uniformity? The risk undoubtedly exists: we catch a glimpse of it in the tyranny of ratings and the excesses of political correctness. But it's a risk inherent in any democratic system. And though we may fear the worst if we were to rely passively on the power of numbers, disaster is not inevitable if we make good use of the means of expression at our disposal and are able to see through the simplistic reality of figures to the complex reality of human beings.

For it need hardly be said that, despite certain appearances, we live not in the age of the masses but in that of the individual. From this point of view, humanity, having skirted some of the worst dangers in its history during the course of the twentieth century, has emerged rather better than was expected.

Although world population has almost quadrupled in a hundred years it seems to me that on the whole everyone is now more conscious than in the past of his individuality, more aware of his rights, if probably slightly less so of his duties, and more concerned with his place in society, his health, his well-being, his body, his personal future, the powers at his disposal, and his identity—however he may interpret this notion. I also think that each one of us, if he can learn to make use of the unprecedented tools now within his reach, can exercise a significant influence both on his contemporaries and on future generations. On condition that he has something to say to them. On condition too that he is inventive, for the new realities don't come to us with instructions attached.

Above all, on condition that he doesn't cringe at home, abjuring the cruel world.

Such timidity would be equally fruitless with regard to the second anxiety aroused by globalisation: standardisation not through mediocrity but through hegemony. This worry is more widespread and is the source not only of countless tensions but also of many bloody conflicts.

It may be expressed as follows: is globalisation just another word for Americanisation? Won't its main result be to impose on the whole world one language; one economic, political and social system; one way of life; one scale of values—those of the United States of America? According to some people, the whole phenomenon of globalisation is nothing but a masquerade, a camouflage, a Trojan horse concealing an attempt at domination.

But for a rational observer it is absurd to suppose that technological progress and moral evolution might be wholly subject to a remote control exercised by one great power or a coalition of great powers. On the other hand, we might well ask ourselves whether globalisation will not at least favour the predominance of one civilisation or the hegemony of one power. That would entail two serious dangers, the first being the gradual disappearance of some languages, traditions and cultures, and the second being the adoption by cultures that are threatened of increasingly radical or suicidal attitudes.

The risks of hegemony are real. It is even euphemistic to speak of mere risks. There can be no doubt that over the centuries Western civilisation has acquired a privileged status vis-à-vis the others—those of Asia, Africa, pre-Colombian America and Eastern Europe—which have become increasingly marginalised and profoundly influenced, not to say remodelled, by the Christian West. Nor can it be denied that with the collapse of the Soviet Union the Western developed countries have managed to establish the absolute pre-eminence of their own economic and political system, which is in the process of becoming the norm for the whole world.

rly, it is superfluous to cite examples of how, since the end of the the United States, now the only genuine superpower, has come to precedented influence over the entire planet. This influence man- in a variety of ways: sometimes through deliberate action, to set- gional conflict, to destabilise an enemy or to subvert a rival's eco- cy; but sometimes also involuntarily, through the force and attraction of the model it offers. Millions of men and women from every other kind of culture are tempted to imitate the Americans—to eat or dress, to speak or sing as they do, or as they are supposed to do.

It seems to me worth recalling these facts before posing the questions that arise from them. For example, to what extent is the global culture, as it develops daily, essentially Western or even specifically American? From that question others follow. What is going to become of all the other cultures? What will happen to all the different languages we speak today? Will they just be reduced to local dialects, doomed sooner or later to disappear? And what will be the atmosphere in which globalisation takes place in coming decades, if it emerges as more and more destructive not only of cultures, languages, rituals, beliefs and traditions, but also of identities? If all of us were asked to deny our own selves in order to attain modernity as it is defined now and will be defined in future, would not conservatism and atavism, not to mention violence, be an increasingly general reaction?

NOTES

FOR FURTHER READING

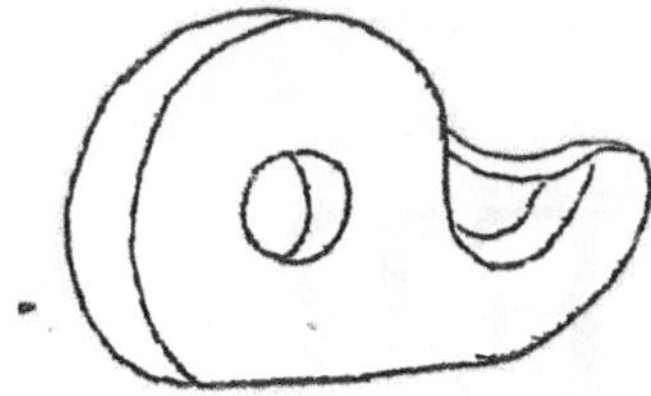

S. GROSS

"I don't care if she is a tape dispenser. I love her."

Courtesy of Sam Gross/The New Yorker Collection.

THE UNKNOWN CITIZEN
W. H. Auden

(1907–1973)

W. H. Auden was an English-born poet celebrated for the remarkable range of his works. In 1948 he was awarded the Pulitzer Prize for his book-length poem The Age of Anxiety.

(To JS/07 M 378 This Marble Monument Is Erected by the State)

He was found by the Bureau of Statistics to be
One against whom there was no official complaint,
And all the reports on his conduct agree
That, in the modern sense of an old-fashioned word, he was a saint,
For in everything he did he served the Greater Community.
Except for the War till the day he retired
He worked in a factory and never got fired,
But satisfied his employers, Fudge Motors Inc.
Yet he wasn't a scab or odd in his views,
For his Union reports that he paid his dues,
(Our report on his Union shows it was sound)
And our Social Psychology workers found
That he was popular with his mates and liked a drink.
The Press are convinced that he bought a paper every day
And that his reactions to advertisements were normal in every way.
Policies taken out in his name prove that he was fully insured,
And his Health-card shows he was once in hospital but left it cured.
Both Producers Research and High-Grade Living declare
He was fully sensible to the advantages of the Installment Plan
And had everything necessary to the Modern Man,
A phonograph, a radio, a car and a frigidaire.
Our researchers into Public Opinion are content
That he held the proper opinions for the time of year;
When there was peace, he was for peace: when there was war, he went.
He was married and added five children to the population,
Which our Eugenist says was the right number for a parent of his generation.
And our teachers report that he never interfered with their education.
Was he free? Was he happy? The question is absurd:
Had anything been wrong, we should certainly have heard.

Reprinted from *Collected Poems* (1976), Random House, Inc.

NOTES

HOPE, SAVED ON A LAPTOP

Dan Barry

Since joining The New York Times *in 1995, Dan Barry has been nominated twice for the Pulitzer Prize. He has also worked for the* Journal Inquirer *in Manchester, CT and for* The Providence Journal, *sharing a George Polk Award and a Pulitzer Prize. He has written three books including* Bottom of the 33rd: Hope, Redemption, and Baseball's Longest Game, *for which he received the 2012 PEN/ESPN Award for Literary Sports Writing.*

For a long time, Ann Nelson's laptop computer remained dark.

It had been returned to her family in North Dakota, along with the other belongings she left behind in that great city 1,750 miles to the east. She was 30, lively, working near the very top of the World Trade Center, and—you already know.

In the small town of Stanley, halfway between Minot and Williston, a fog thick enough to blur time's passing enveloped the Nelson home. Amid the many tributes to Ann, amid the grieving and the absence, it became hard to remember just when and how the laptop wound up in the basement of the one-story bank that the family owned.

There the laptop sat, for years, tucked away from sight in a black case. It was a Dell Inspiron 8000, bought shortly before Ann called home that day in early 2001 to say she had gotten a job as a bond trader at Cantor Fitzgerald—in New York! Soon she was living near the corner of Thompson and Spring, and working in an office 104 stories in the air.

Ann's parents, Jenette and Gary Nelson, say the laptop remained unopened because they are not computer savvy. But it was more than that, Mrs. Nelson admits. "To tell you the truth, it was just too painful."

Three summers ago, during an art class Mrs. Nelson was teaching in that basement, a couple of students showed her how to use the computer. After the class, she says, "I just left it there."

Who knows why never becomes someday, and someday becomes today. One day last fall—"when I got to feeling stronger," she says—Mrs. Nelson finally opened her daughter's computer. She pushed its power button and started by looking at the photographs stored in its memory.

Soon Mrs. Nelson was learning how to play the computer's games, including solitaire and hearts. These distractions both relaxed her and reminded her of the games she used to play with Ann. Somehow, this little black machine made Ann seem present, there beside her.

Reprinted by permission from the *New York Times*, May 17, 2006.

Getting lost in the computer became part of Mrs. Nelson's after-work ritual, though she never bothered to open a file that said "Top 100"; probably some music, she figured. Then, two months ago and who knows why, click.

What she found was a catalog of goals, humanly incomplete: a list that reflected a young woman's commitment to the serious, to the frivolous, to all of life. That night, Mr. and Mrs. Nelson sat down with the list, and were with their daughter again.

1. Be healthy/ healthful. 2. Be a good friend. 3. Keep secrets. 4. Keep in touch with people I love and that love me. 5. Make a quilt.

Mrs. Nelson used to sew all the time, until it simply became too hard to guide a needle properly with a joyous little girl frolicking in her lap. Then, when Ann grew older, mother and daughter decided to sew a tablecloth.

"I don't think we ever finished," Mrs. Nelson says, laughing. "She had to be doing 100 things at a time, and consequently some of them didn't get finished."

As for this goal of making a quilt, she adds, "I'm sure that I would probably have been deeply involved in this process."

6. Nepal. 7. Buy a home in North Dakota. 8. Get a graduate degree. 9. Learn a foreign language. 10. Kilimanjaro. 11. Never be ashamed of who I am.

"Ann was in many environments where being a girl from North Dakota may not have been the most sophisticated label to wear," Mrs. Nelson says, recalling that her daughter had traveled to China and to Peru, and had worked in the high-powered environments of Chicago and New York.

Even so, Ann always conveyed pride in who she was, who her parents were and where they came from—though never in a boastful way. "It's an important point about her personality," her mother says.

12. Be a person to be proud of. 13. Always keep improving. 14. Read every day. 15. Be informed. 16. Knit a sweater. 17. Scuba-dive in the Barrier Reef. 18. Volunteer for a charity. 19. Learn to cook.

By her late 20's, Ann had actually become a fairly decent cook. Still, her mother laughs in recalling late-night calls, like the one that began: "Mom, what's drawn butter?"

20. Learn about art. 21. Get my C.F.A. 22. Grand Canyon. 23. Helicopter-ski with my dad.

Then Ann Nelson's list repeats a number.

23. Spend more time with my family. 24. Remember birthdays!!!!

Birthdays loomed large in Ann's life. She would celebrate her birthday not for a day, but for a week—in part because her father's birthday came the very next day, in part because she was proud to have been born on Norwegian Independence Day—which is May 17, today.

"Ann would have been 35," says Mr. Nelson, who turns 65 tomorrow.

25. Appreciate money, but don't worship it. 26. Learn how to use a computer. 27. Visit the New York Public Library. 28. Maine. 29. Learn to write. 30. Walk—exercise but also see the world firsthand. 31. Learn about other cultures. 32. Be a good listener. 33. Take time for friends. 34. Kayak. 35. Drink water. 36. Learn about wine.

Ann was supposed to attend a wine class the evening of Sept. 11, in keeping with Nos. 13, 19, 31, 36—the whole list, really.

After 36, there is a 37, but it is blank.

Mr. Nelson reads the list as an inventory of his daughter's values. "You don't see any Corvettes in the garage or any of those material things you might expect from someone that age," he says. "She recognized that you appreciate a few things and kind of live your life wisely."

Mrs. Nelson interprets the list as another way in which Ann seems to communicate with her when she is most in need. So, just about every day in a small North Dakota town, halfway between Minot and Williston, the screen of a laptop computer goes from darkness to light.

NOTES

QUIET
Susan Cain

A U.S. writer, lecturer, and corporate attorney, Susan Cain's book Quiet: The Power of Introverts in a World That Can't Stop Talking *has become a best-seller. She is a graduate of Princeton and Harvard Law School.*

Introduction

The North and South of Temperament

Montgomery, Alabama. December 1, 1955. Early evening. A public bus pulls to a stop and a sensibly dressed woman in her forties gets on. She carries herself erectly, despite having spent the day bent over an ironing board in a dingy basement tailor shop at the Montgomery Fair department store. Her feet are swollen, her shoulders ache. She sits in the first row of the Colored section and watches quietly as the bus fills with riders. Until the driver orders her to give her seat to a white passenger.

The woman utters a single word that ignites one of the most important civil rights protests of the twentieth century, one word that helps America find its better self.

The word is "No."

The driver threatens to have her arrested.

"You may do that," says Rosa Parks.

A police officer arrives. He asks Parks why she won't move.

"Why do you all push us around?" she answers simply.

"I don't know," he says. "But the law is the law, and you're under arrest."

On the afternoon of her trial and conviction for disorderly conduct, the Montgomery Improvement Association holds a rally for Parks at the Holt Street Baptist Church, in the poorest section of town. Five thousand gather to support Parks's lonely act of courage. They squeeze inside the church until its pews can hold no more. The rest wait patiently outside, listening through loudspeakers. The Reverend Martin Luther King Jr. addresses the crowd. "There comes a time that people get tired of being trampled over by the iron feet of oppression," he tells them. "There comes a time when people get tired of being pushed out of the glittering sunlight of life's July and left standing amidst the piercing chill of an Alpine November."

He praises Parks's bravery and hugs her. She stands silently, her mere presence enough to galvanize the crowd. The association launches a citywide bus boycott that lasts 381 days. The people trudge miles to work. They carpool with strangers. They change the course of American history.

Reprinted from *Quiet: The Power of Introverts in a World that Can't Stop Talking* (2012), Crown Books, a division of Random House, Inc.

I had always imagined Rosa Parks as a stately woman with a bold temperament, someone who could easily stand up to a busload of glowering passengers. But when she died in 2005 at the age of ninety-two, the flood of obituaries recalled her as soft-spoken, sweet, and small in stature. They said she was "timid and shy" but had "the courage of a lion." They were full of phrases like "radical humility" and "quiet fortitude." What does it mean to be quiet *and* have fortitude? these descriptions asked implicitly. How could you be shy *and* courageous?

Parks herself seemed aware of this paradox, calling her autobiography *Quiet Strength*—a title that challenges us to question our assumptions. Why *shouldn't* quiet be strong? And what else can quiet do that we don't give it credit for?

Our lives are shaped as profoundly by personality as by gender or race. And the single most important aspect of personality—the "north and south of temperament," as one scientist puts it—is where we fall on the introvert-extrovert spectrum. Our place on this continuum influences our choice of friends and mates, and how we make conversation, resolve differences, and show love. It affects the careers we choose and whether or not we succeed at them. It governs how likely we are to exercise, commit adultery, function well without sleep, learn from our mistakes, place big bets in the stock market, delay gratification, be a good leader, and ask "what if."* It's reflected in our brain pathways, neurotransmitters, and remote corners of our nervous systems. Today introversion and extroversion are two of the most exhaustively researched subjects in personality psychology, arousing the curiosity of hundreds of scientists.

These researchers have made exciting discoveries aided by the latest technology, but they're part of a long and storied tradition. Poets and philosophers have been thinking about introverts and extroverts since the dawn of recorded time. Both personality types appear in the Bible and in the writings of Greek and Roman physicians, and some evolutionary psychologists say that the history of these types reaches back even farther than that: the animal kingdom also boasts "introverts" and "extroverts," as we'll see, from fruit flies to pumpkinseed fish to rhesus monkeys. As with other complementary pairings—masculinity and femininity, East and West, liberal and conservative—humanity would be unrecognizable, and vastly diminished, without both personality styles.

Take the partnership of Rosa Parks and Martin Luther King Jr.: a formidable orator refusing to give up his seat on a segregated bus wouldn't have had the same effect as a modest woman who'd clearly prefer to keep silent but for the exigencies of the situation. And Parks didn't have the stuff to thrill a crowd

*Answer key; exercise: extroverts; commit adultery: extroverts; function well without sleep: introverts; learn from our mistakes: introverts; place big bets: extroverts; delay gratification: introverts; be a good leader: in some cases introverts, in other cases extroverts, depending on the type of leadership called for; ask "what if": introverts.

if she'd tried to stand up and announce that she had a dream. But with King's help, she didn't have to.

Yet today we make room for a remarkably narrow range of personality styles. We're told that to be great is to be bold, to be happy is to be sociable. We see ourselves as a nation of extroverts—which means that we've lost sight of who we really are. Depending on which study you consult, one third to one half of Americans are introverts—in other words, *one out of every two or three people you know.* (Given that the United States is among the most extroverted of nations, the number must be at least as high in other parts of the world.) If you're not an introvert yourself, you are surely raising, managing, married to, or coupled with one.

If these statistics surprise you, that's probably because so many people pretend to be extroverts. Closet introverts pass undetected on playgrounds, in high school locker rooms, and in the corridors of corporate America. Some fool even themselves, until some life event—a layoff, an empty nest, an inheritance that frees them to spend time as they like—jolts them into taking stock of their true natures. You have only to raise the subject of this book with your friends and acquaintances to find that the most unlikely people consider themselves introverts.

It makes sense that so many introverts hide even from themselves. We live with a value system that I call the Extrovert Ideal—the omnipresent belief that the ideal self is gregarious, alpha, and comfortable in the spotlight. The archetypal extrovert prefers action to contemplation, risk-taking to heed-taking, certainty to doubt. He favors quick decisions, even at the risk of being wrong. She works well in teams and socializes in groups. We like to think that we value individuality, but all too often we admire one *type* of individual—the kind who's comfortable "putting himself out there." Sure, we allow technologically gifted loners who launch companies in garages to have any personality they please, but they are the exceptions, not the rule, and our tolerance extends mainly to those who get fabulously wealthy or hold the promise of doing so.

Introversion—along with its cousins sensitivity, seriousness, and shyness—is now a second-class personality trait, somewhere between a disappointment and a pathology. Introverts living under the Extrovert Ideal are like women in a man's world, discounted because of a trait that goes to the core of who they are. Extroversion is an enormously appealing personality style, but we've turned it into an oppressive standard to which most of us feel we must conform.

The Extrovert Ideal has been documented in many studies, though this research has never been grouped under a single name. Talkative people, for example, are rated as smarter, better-looking, more interesting, and more desirable as friends. Velocity of speech counts as well as volume: we rank fast talkers as more competent and likable than slow ones. The same dynamics apply in groups, where research shows that the voluble are considered smarter than the reticent—even though there's zero correlation between the gift of gab and good ideas. Even the word *introvert* is stigmatized—one informal study, by psychologist Laurie Helgoe, found that introverts described their own physical appearance in vivid language ("green-blue eyes," "exotic," "high cheekbones"), but when asked to describe generic introverts they drew a bland and distasteful picture ("ungainly," "neutral colors," "skin problems").

But we make a grave mistake to embrace the Extrovert Ideal so unthinkingly. Some of our greatest ideas, art, and inventions—from the theory of evolution to van Gogh's sunflowers to the personal computer—came from quiet and cerebral people who knew how to tune in to their inner worlds and the treasures to be found there. Without introverts, the world would be devoid of:

the theory of gravity
the theory of relativity
W. B. Yeats's "The Second Coming"
Chopin's nocturnes
Proust's *In Search of Lost Time*
Peter Pan
Orwell's *Nineteen Eighty Four* and *Animal Farm*
The Cat in the Hat
Charlie Brown
Schindler's List, E.T., and *Close Encounters of the Third Kind*
Google
Harry Potter*

As the science journalist Winifred Gallagher writes: "The glory of the disposition that stops to consider stimuli rather than rushing to engage with them is its long association with intellectual and artistic achievement. Neither $E=mc^2$ nor *Paradise Lost* was dashed off by a party animal." Even in less obviously introverted occupations, like finance, politics, and activism, some of the greatest leaps forward were made by introverts. In this book we'll see how figures like Eleanor Roosevelt, Al Gore, Warren Buffett, Gandhi—and Rosa Parks—achieved what they did not in spite of but *because* of their introversion.

Yet, as *Quiet* will explore, many of the most important institutions of contemporary life are designed for those who enjoy group projects and high levels of stimulation. As children, our classroom desks are increasingly arranged in pods, the better to foster group learning, and research suggests that the vast majority of teachers believe that the ideal student is an extrovert. We watch TV shows whose protagonists are not the "children next door," like the Cindy Bradys and Beaver Cleavers of yesteryear, but rock stars and webcast hostesses with outsized personalities, like Hannah Montana and Carly Shay of *iCarly.* Even Sid the Science Kid, a PBS-sponsored role model for the preschool set, kicks off each school day by performing dance moves with his pals. ("Check out my moves! I'm a rock star!")

---

*Sir Isaac Newton, Albert Einstein, W. B. Yeats, Frederic Chopin, Marcel Proust, J. M. Barrie, George Orwell, Theodor Geisel (Dr. Seuss), Charles Schulz, Steven Spielberg, Larry Page, J.K. Rowling.

As adults, many of us work for organizations that insist we work in teams, in offices without walls, for supervisors who value "people skills" above all. To advance our careers, we're expected to promote ourselves unabashedly. The scientists whose research gets funded often have confident, perhaps overconfident, personalities. The artists whose work adorns the walls of contemporary museums strike impressive poses at gallery openings. The authors whose books get published—once accepted as a reclusive breed—are now vetted by publicists to make sure they're talk-show ready. (You wouldn't be reading this book if I hadn't convinced my publisher that I was enough of a pseudo-extrovert to promote it.)

If you're an introvert, you also know that the bias against quiet can cause deep psychic pain. As a child you might have overheard your parents apologize for your shyness. ("Why can't you be more like the Kennedy boys?" the Camelot-besotted parents of one man I interviewed repeatedly asked him.) Or at school you might have been prodded to come "out of your shell"—that noxious expression which fails to appreciate that some animals naturally carry shelter everywhere they go, and that some humans are just the same. "All the comments from childhood still ring in my ears, that I was lazy, stupid, slow, boring," writes a member of an e-mail list called Introvert Retreat. "By the time I was old enough to figure out that I was simply introverted, it was a part of my being, the assumption that there is something inherently wrong with me. I wish I could find that little vestige of doubt and remove it."

Now that you're an adult, you might still feel a pang of guilt when you decline a dinner invitation in favor of a good book. Or maybe you like to eat alone in restaurants and could do without the pitying looks from fellow diners. Or you're told that you're "in your head too much," a phrase that's often deployed against the quiet and cerebral.

Of course, there's another word for such people: thinkers.

I have seen firsthand how difficult it is for introverts to take stock of their own talents, and how powerful it is when finally they do. For more than ten years I trained people of all stripes—corporate lawyers and college students, hedge-fund managers and married couples—in negotiation skills. Of course, we covered the basics: how to prepare for a negotiation, when to make the first offer, and what to do when the other person says "take it or leave it." But I also helped clients figure out their natural personalities and how to make the most of them.

My very first client was a young woman named Laura. She was a Wall Street lawyer, but a quiet and daydreamy one who dreaded the spotlight and disliked aggression. She had managed somehow to make it through the crucible of Harvard Law School—a place where classes are conducted in huge, gladiatorial amphitheaters, and where she once got so nervous that she threw up on the way to class. Now that she was in the real world, she wasn't sure she could represent her clients as forcefully as they expected.

For the first three years on the job, Laura was so junior that she never had to test this premise. But one day the senior lawyer she'd been working with went on vacation, leaving her in charge of an important negotiation. The client was a South American manufacturing company that was about to default on a bank loan and hoped to renegotiate its terms; a syndicate of bankers that owned the endangered loan sat on the other side of the negotiating table.

Laura would have preferred to hide under said table, but she was accustomed to fighting such impulses. Gamely but nervously, she took her spot in the lead chair, flanked by her clients: general counsel on one side and senior financial officer on the other. These happened to be Laura's favorite clients: gracious and soft-spoken, very different from the master-of-the-universe types her firm usually represented. In the past, Laura had taken the general counsel to a Yankees game and the financial officer shopping for a handbag for her sister. But now these cozy outings—just the kind of socializing Laura enjoyed—seemed a world away. Across the table sat nine disgruntled investment bankers in tailored suits and expensive shoes, accompanied by their lawyer, a square-jawed woman with a hearty manner. Clearly not the self-doubting type, this woman launched into an impressive speech on how Laura's clients would be lucky simply to accept the bankers' terms. It was, she said, a very magnanimous offer.

Everyone waited for Laura to reply, but she couldn't think of anything to say. So she just sat there. Blinking. All eyes on her. Her clients shifting uneasily in their seats. Her thoughts running in a familiar loop: *I'm too quiet for this kind of thing, too unassuming, too cerebral.* She imagined the person who would be better equipped to save the day: someone bold, smooth, ready to pound the table. In middle school this person, unlike Laura, would have been called "outgoing," the highest accolade her seventh-grade classmates knew, higher even than "pretty," for a girl, or "athletic," for a guy. Laura promised herself that she only had to make it through the day. Tomorrow she would go look for another career.

Then she remembered what I'd told her again and again: she was an introvert, and as such she had unique powers in negotiation—perhaps less obvious but no less formidable. She'd probably prepared more than everyone else. She had a quiet but firm speaking style. She rarely spoke without thinking. Being mild-mannered, she could take strong, even aggressive, positions while coming across as perfectly reasonable. And she tended to ask questions—lots of them—and actually listen to the answers, which, no matter what your personality, is crucial to strong negotiation.

So Laura finally started doing what came naturally.

"Let's go back a step. What are your numbers based on?" she asked.

"What if we structured the loan this way, do you think it might work?"

"That way?"

"Some other way?"

At first her questions were tentative. She picked up steam as she went along, posing them more forcefully and making it clear that she'd done her homework and wouldn't concede the facts. But she also stayed true to her own style, never raising her voice or losing her decorum. Every time the bankers made an assertion that seemed unbudgeable, Laura tried to be constructive. "Are you saying that's the only way to go? What if we took a different approach?"

Eventually her simple queries shifted the mood in the room, just as the negotiation textbooks say they will. The bankers stopped speechifying and dominance-posing, activities for which Laura felt hopelessly ill-equipped, and they started having an actual conversation.

More discussion. Still no agreement. One of the bankers revved up again, throwing his papers down and storming out of the room. Laura ignored this display, mostly because she didn't know what else to do. Later on someone told her that at that pivotal moment she'd played a good game of something called "negotiation jujitsu"; but she knew that she was just doing what you learn to do naturally as a quiet person in a loudmouth world.

Finally the two sides struck a deal. The bankers left the building, Laura's favorite clients headed for the airport, and Laura went home, curled up with a book, and tried to forget the day's tensions.

But the next morning, the lead lawyer for the bankers—the vigorous woman with the strong jaw—called to offer her a job. "I've never seen anyone so nice and so rough at the same time," she said. And the day after that, the lead banker called Laura, asking if her law firm would represent *his* company in the future. "We need someone who can help us put deals together without letting ego get in the way," he said.

By sticking to her own gentle way of doing things, Laura had reeled in new business for her firm and a job offer for herself. Raising her voice and pounding the table was unnecessary.

Today Laura understands that her introversion is an essential part of who she is, and she embraces her reflective nature. The loop inside her head that accused her of being too quiet and unassuming plays much less often. Laura knows that she can hold her own when she needs to.

What exactly do I mean when I say that Laura is an *introvert?* When I started writing this book, the first thing I wanted to find out was precisely how researchers define introversion and extroversion. I knew that in 1921 the influential psychologist Carl Jung had published a bombshell of a book, *Psychological Types,* popularizing the terms *introvert* and *extrovert* as the central building blocks of personality. Introverts are drawn to the inner world of thought and feeling, said Jung, extroverts to the external life of people and activities. Introverts focus on the meaning they make of the events swirling around them; extroverts plunge into the events themselves. Introverts recharge their batteries by being alone; extroverts need to recharge when they don't socialize enough. If you've ever taken a Myers-Briggs personality test, which is based on Jung's thinking and used by the majority of universities and Fortune 100 companies, then you may already be familiar with these ideas.

But what do contemporary researchers have to say? I soon discovered that there is no all-purpose definition of introversion or extroversion; these are not unitary categories, like "curly-haired" or "sixteen-year-old," in which everyone can agree on who qualifies for inclusion. For example, adherents of the Big Five school of personality psychology (which argues that human personality can be boiled down to five primary traits) define introversion not in terms of a rich inner life but as a lack of qualities such as assertiveness and sociability. There are almost as many definitions of *introvert* and *extrovert* as there are personality psychologists, who spend a great deal of time arguing over which meaning is most accurate. Some think that Jung's ideas are outdated; others swear that he's the only one who got it right.

Still, today's psychologists tend to agree on several important points: for example, that introverts and extroverts differ in the level of outside stimulation that they need to function well. Introverts feel "just right" with less stimulation, as when they sip wine with a close friend, solve a crossword puzzle, or read a book. Extroverts enjoy the extra bang that comes from activities like meeting new people, skiing slippery slopes, and cranking up the stereo. "Other people are very arousing," says the personality psychologist David Winter, explaining why your typical introvert would rather spend her vacation reading on the beach than partying on a cruise ship. "They arouse threat, fear, flight, and love. A hundred people are very stimulating compared to a hundred books or a hundred grains of sand."

Many psychologists would also agree that introverts and extroverts work differently. Extroverts tend to tackle assignments quickly. They make fast (sometimes rash) decisions, and are comfortable multitasking and risk-taking. They enjoy "the thrill of the chase" for rewards like money and status.

Introverts often work more slowly and deliberately. They like to focus on one task at a time and can have mighty powers of concentration. They're relatively immune to the lures of wealth and fame.

Our personalities also shape our social styles. Extroverts are the people who will add life to your dinner party and laugh generously at your jokes. They tend to be assertive, dominant, and in great need of company. Extroverts think out loud and on their feet; they prefer talking to listening, rarely find themselves at a loss for words, and occasionally blurt out things they never meant to say. They're comfortable with conflict, but not with solitude.

Introverts, in contrast, may have strong social skills and enjoy parties and business meetings, but after a while wish they were home in their pajamas. They prefer to devote their social energies to close friends, colleagues, and family. They listen more than they talk, think before they speak, and often feel as if they express themselves better in writing than in conversation. They tend to dislike conflict. Many have a horror of small talk, but enjoy deep discussions.

A few things introverts are not: The word *introvert* is not a synonym for hermit or misanthrope. Introverts *can* be these things, but most are perfectly friendly. One of the most humane phrases in the English language—"Only connect!"— was written by the distinctly introverted E. M. Forster in a novel exploring the question of how to achieve "human love at its height."

Nor are introverts necessarily shy. Shyness is the fear of social disapproval or humiliation, while introversion is a preference for environments that are not overstimulating. Shyness is inherently painful; introversion is not. One reason that people confuse the two concepts is that they sometimes overlap (though psychologists debate to what degree). Some psychologists map the two tendencies on vertical and horizontal axes, with the introvert-extrovert spectrum on the horizontal axis, and the anxious-stable spectrum on the vertical. With this model, you end up with four quadrants of personality types: calm extroverts, anxious (or impulsive) extroverts, calm introverts, and anxious introverts. In other words, you can be a shy extrovert, like Barbra Streisand, who has a larger-than-life personality and paralyzing stage fright; or a non-shy introvert, like Bill Gates, who by all accounts keeps to himself but is unfazed by the opinions of others.

good definition

You can also, of course, be both shy *and* an introvert: T. S. Eliot was a famously private soul who wrote in "The Waste Land" that he could "show you fear in a handful of dust." Many shy people turn inward, partly as a refuge from the socializing that causes them such anxiety. And many introverts are shy, partly as a result of receiving the message that there's something wrong with their preference for reflection, and partly because their physiologies, as we'll see, compel them to withdraw from high-stimulation environments.

But for all their differences, shyness and introversion have in common something profound. The mental state of a shy extrovert sitting quietly in a business meeting may be very different from that of a calm introvert—the shy person is afraid to speak up, while the introvert is simply overstimulated—but to the outside world, the two appear to be the same. This can give both types insight into how our reverence for alpha status blinds us to things that are good and smart and wise. For very different reasons, shy and introverted people might choose to spend their days in behind-the-scenes pursuits like inventing, or researching, or holding the hands of the gravely ill—or in leadership positions they execute with quiet competence. These are not alpha roles, but the people who play them are role models all the same.

If you're still not sure where you fall on the introvert-extrovert spectrum, you can assess yourself here. Answer each question "true" or "false," choosing the answer that applies to you more often than not.*

1. ___ I prefer one-on-one conversations to group activities.
2. ___ I often prefer to express myself in writing.
3. ___ I enjoy solitude.
4. ___ I seem to care less than my peers about wealth, fame, and status.

*This is an informal quiz, not a scientifically validated personality test. The questions were formulated based on characteristics of introversion often accepted by contemporary researchers.

5. ___ I dislike small talk, but I enjoy talking in depth about topics that matter to me.
6. ___ People tell me that I'm a good listener.
7. ___ I'm not a big risk-taker.
8. ___ I enjoy work that allows me to "dive in" with few interruptions.
9. ___ I like to celebrate birthdays on a small scale, with only one or two close friends or family members.
10. ___ People describe me as "soft-spoken" or "mellow."
11. ___ I prefer not to show or discuss my work with others until it's finished.
12. ___ I dislike conflict.
13. ___ I do my best work on my own.
14. ___ I tend to think before I speak.
15. ___ I feel drained after being out and about, even if I've enjoyed myself.
16. ___ I often let calls go through to voice mail.
17. ___ If I had to choose, I'd prefer a weekend with absolutely nothing to do to one with too many things scheduled.
18. ___ I don't enjoy multitasking.
19. ___ I can concentrate easily.
20. ___ In classroom situations, I prefer lectures to seminars.

The more often you answered "true," the more introverted you probably are. If you found yourself with a roughly equal number of "true" and "false" answers, then you may be an ambivert—yes, there really is such a word.

But even if you answered every single question as an introvert or extrovert, that doesn't mean that your behavior is predictable across all circumstances. We can't say that every introvert is a bookworm or every extrovert wears lampshades at parties any more than we can say that every woman is a natural consensus-builder and every man loves contact sports. As Jung felicitously put it, "There is no such thing as a pure extrovert or a pure introvert. Such a man would be in the lunatic asylum."

This is partly because we are all gloriously complex individuals, but also because there are so many different *kinds* of introverts and extroverts. Introversion and extroversion interact with our other personality traits and personal histories, producing wildly different kinds of people. So if you're an artistic American guy whose father wished you'd try out for the football team like your rough-and-tumble brothers, you'll be a very different kind of introvert from, say, a Finnish businesswoman whose parents were lighthouse keepers. (Finland is a famously introverted nation. Finnish joke: How can you tell if a Finn likes you? He's staring at your shoes instead of his own.)

Many introverts are also "highly sensitive," which sounds poetic, but is actually a technical term in psychology. If you are a sensitive sort, then you're more apt than the average person to feel pleasantly overwhelmed by Beethoven's

"Moonlight Sonata" or a well-turned phrase or an act of extraordinary kindness. You may be quicker than others to feel sickened by violence and ugliness, and you likely have a very strong conscience. When you were a child you were probably called "shy," and to this day feel nervous when you're being evaluated, for example when giving a speech or on a first date. Later we'll examine why this seemingly unrelated collection of attributes tends to belong to the same person and why this person is often introverted. (No one knows exactly how many introverts are highly sensitive, but we know that 70 percent of sensitives are introverts, and the other 30 percent tend to report needing a lot of "down time.")

All of this complexity means that not everything you read in *Quiet* will apply to you, even if you consider yourself a true-blue introvert. For one thing, we'll spend some time talking about shyness and sensitivity, while you might have neither of these traits. That's OK. Take what applies to you, and use the rest to improve your relationships with others.

Having said all this, in *Quiet* we'll try not to get too hung up on definitions. Strictly defining terms is vital for researchers whose studies depend on pinpointing exactly where introversion stops and other traits, like shyness, start. But in *Quiet* we'll concern ourselves more with the *fruit* of that research. Today's psychologists, joined by neuroscientists with their brain-scanning machines, have unearthed illuminating insights that are changing the way we see the world—and ourselves. They are answering questions such as: Why are some people talkative while others measure their words? Why do some people burrow into their work and others organize office birthday parties? Why are some people comfortable wielding authority while others prefer neither to lead nor to be led? *Can* introverts be leaders? Is our cultural preference for extroversion in the natural order of things, or is it socially determined? From an evolutionary perspective, introversion must have survived as a personality trait for a reason—so what might the reason be? If you're an introvert, should you devote your energies to activities that come naturally, or should you stretch yourself, as Laura did that day at the negotiation table?

The answers might surprise you.

If there is only one insight you take away from this book, though, I hope it's a newfound sense of entitlement to be yourself. I can vouch personally for the life-transforming effects of this outlook. Remember that first client I told you about, the one I called Laura in order to protect her identity?

That was a story about me. I was my own first client.

NOTES

BLINDSIDED
LIFTING A LIFE ABOVE ILLNESS: A RELUCTANT MEMOIR
Richard M. Cohen

(1948–)

Richard M. Cohen is a three-time Emmy award-winning journalist.

Preface

Sometimes it seems I daydream for a living. I sit in my office on the far west side of Manhattan, trying to write but gazing out over treetops and highways to barges pushing laboriously against the current, struggling up the Hudson River. I know how that feels. The long push is relentless, and nobody has it easy. What a haul life is.

For most of any day, my face is pressed to the computer screen, my back arched and aching, stiff from sitting hour after hour in that tortured position. I assume this awkward pose because I am legally blind and must go cheek to cheek with the screen just to see it clearly enough to work.

The river traffic I casually watch moves in exquisite detail only in my mind's eye. Little detail comes clear in the distance. And that is just the beginning. Limbs that no longer function well, appendages gone numb, turn life's little tasks into an arduous exercise. A gut gone goofy only adds to the chaos.

Strange as it sounds, I do love my life. An imaginative writer could not invent it. My journey wandered off the beaten path long ago. I am a journalist, a recovering network television news producer, who has found more satisfying fare in writing and teaching and doing odd jobs, a day's work for a day's pay.

I am a family man, husband to a lovely and funny woman, a loose cannon named Meredith. Anyone who watches *The View* knows her well. Meredith is the one all the way to the left on your screen. Meredith Vieira is a star rising. But the woman is liable to say just about anything. Life in the home territories is interesting.

I am the father of three gorgeous children with their own view of the world. Ben, Gabe, and Lily are forces to be reckoned with. I reckon they give us gray hair and keep us young. There is a powerful circumstance with which all of us must reckon, however. My health sucks, a condition that has become everybody's problem. Illness is a family affair.

For thirty years, I have done battle with multiple sclerosis (MS). The disease touches everything I do and affects my body from head to toe. Chronic illness occupies a lowly position in the hierarchy of suffering but takes a toll. By the end of the millennium, I was suddenly clashing with another fierce adversary. Twice in one year, firefights with colon cancer erupted, further compromising the quality of my life.

Reprinted from *Blindsided: Lifting a Life Above Illness* (2004), HarperCollins Publishers.

I have become a magnet for trouble, an aficionado of living on the edge, a most dangerous place for any individual to hang out. The experience has taught me extraordinary lessons about living. Once, I did not know the verb *cope.* Now I know it all too well.

When, fresh out of college, I arrived in Washington, D.C., on a clear spring day more than three decades ago, warm breezes buoyed my feelings of well-being and expectations of a limitless future. Within three years, just as my career as a television journalist was ascending in the historic hurricane of Watergate, I was engulfed in my own, very personal storm. Illness came calling when I was twenty-five years of age, and it has never left.

The once unhampered trek toward a bright horizon has become a shaky walk across moving terrain. The landscape and contours of life have shifted. I have passed from newsrooms through operating rooms to a more reflective existence. The large events of the world, the trembling earth that preoccupies the journalist, have given way to the struggle to sustain a small life.

My thirty-year effort to salvage that life, to wrest it from the clutches of sickness, has been a search for control and the perspective to adjust. Survival skills have been honed, forged in one of life's hottest furnaces. What I have learned is that I am stronger and more resilient than ever I imagined. My dysfunctional vision and impaired body are testaments to the damage MS can inflict. Colon cancer has left me with a gut I could not sell at a used car lot, no money down. But as my body weakens, my spirit grows strong and occasionally soars.

I am not just a collection of muscles and nerves, the wiring that has short-circuited my dreams. Who I am, my very identity rests in my head. It is from that fortress, my command post, that my being takes shape. Citizens of sickness, those who suffer from their own assaults on body and spirit, know disappointment. Ours is a common siege. The battle to control our heads is every bit as important as combating the attacks on our bodies.

Is this your experience?

The psychological war with illness is fought on two fronts, on the battlefield of the mind and in the depths of the heart. Emotional strength must be learned. I am a better person for that struggle. Attitude is a weapon of choice, endlessly worked. The positive impulse must struggle to survive in a troubled mind. I skirmish with myself, in an effort to shield my eyes from the harsh sight of the diminished person I believe I see looking out from the mirror.

Self-pity is poison. There is no time. I need a future and refuse to become a victim. Too often we become oblivious to our own prisons, taking the bars and high walls for granted. Sometimes we construct them ourselves, and the barbed wire goes up even higher. Too many of the limitations placed on us are an extension of our own timidity.

My weary sighs frequently come with a shrug and the soft statement, "I could write a book." And so, I have. This is my reluctant memoir, a self-conscious stab at an important subject. These pages are not about suffering.

That would be tedious. This book is about surviving and flourishing, rising above fear and self-doubt and, of course, anger. Meredith and the children must wear the scars of these epic battles.

And this book is not about sickness but about the search for emotional health. This is not *the* answer, only *an* answer. Coping is a personal art. There is no element of science in coping, no formula or objective standard for measuring proficiency. Coping is measured against only how you want to live and what you think works. I write no prescriptions and do not presume to offer guidance to others. I am just a guy with a fragile grip on my own life, peering through the fog that rolled in during a dream long ago and does not clear away.

I am learning to cope, certainly the toughest course in my continuing education. And the seminar is never over. For me, coping must be relearned every day. Adjusting is not taught at any famous university and will never be advertised on a matchbook cover. Learning to live with adversity is instinctive and self-taught. It is the stuff of life.

So welcome to my world, where I carry around dreams, a few diseases, and the determination to live life my way. This book is my daily conversation with myself. I am happy to share it with you. Life is good. I am happy. My family is intact. My sense of humor flourishes. These pages chronicle the struggles in that exotic place just north of the neck. At the moment, my attitude checks out well. Get back to me tomorrow. I do believe I am winning.

Richard M. Cohen
September 2003

Married 1986

AARP article – snob couldn't see them

NOTES

FREE TO CHOOSE: A PERSONAL STATEMENT

Milton and Rose Friedman

Recipient of the 1976 Nobel Prize for Economics, Milton Friedman (1912–2006) was a distinguished author, presidential advisor, and professor. In 2002 he was awarded the Medal of Freedom. Economist Rose Friedman was an important collaborator with her husband. They wrote three major books together. She was also a professor at the University of Chicago Law School.

Introduction

Ever since the first settlement of Europeans in the New World America has been a magnet for people seeking adventure, fleeing from tyranny, or simply trying to make a better life for themselves and their children.

An initial trickle swelled after the American Revolution and the establishment of the United States of America and became a flood in the nineteenth century, when millions of people streamed across the Atlantic, and a smaller number across the Pacific, driven by misery and tyranny, and attracted by the promise of freedom and affluence.

When they arrived, they did not find streets paved with gold; they did not find an easy life. They did find freedom and an opportunity to make the most of their talents. Through hard work, ingenuity, thrift, and luck, most of them succeeded in realizing enough of their hopes and dreams to encourage friends and relatives to join them.

The story of the United States is the story of an economic miracle and a political miracle that was made possible by the translation into practice of two sets of ideas—both, by a curious coincidence, formulated in documents published in the same year, 1776.

One set of ideas was embodied in *The Wealth of Nations*, the masterpiece that established the Scotsman Adam Smith as the father of modern economics. It analyzed the way in which a market system could combine the freedom of individuals to pursue their own objectives with the extensive cooperation and collaboration needed in the economic field to produce our food, our clothing, our housing. Adam Smith's key insight was that both parties to an exchange can benefit and that, *so long as cooperation is strictly voluntary,* no exchange will take place unless both parties do benefit. No external force, no coercion, no violation of freedom is necessary to produce cooperation among individuals all of whom can benefit. That is why, as Adam Smith put it, an individual who "intends only his own gain" is "led by an invisible hand to promote an end which was no part of his intention. Nor is it always the

Reprinted from *Free to Choose: A Personal Statement* (1980), by permission of Houghton Mifflin Harcourt Publishing Company.

worse for the society that it was no part of it. By pursuing his own interest he frequently promotes that of the society more effectually than when he really intends to promote it. I have never known much good done by those who affected to trade for the public good."[1]

The second set of ideas was embodied in the Declaration of Independence, drafted by Thomas Jefferson to express the general sense of his fellow countrymen. It proclaimed a new nation, the first in history established on the principle that every person is entitled to pursue his own values: "We hold these truths to be self-evident, that all men are created equal, that they are endowed by their Creator with certain unalienable Rights; that among these are Life, Liberty, and the pursuit of Happiness."

Or, as stated in more extreme and unqualified form nearly a century later by John Stuart Mill,

> The sole end for which mankind are warranted, individually or collectively, in interfering with the liberty of action of any of their number, is self protection. . . . [T]he only purpose for which power can be rightfully exercised over any member of a civilized community, against his will, is to prevent harm to others. His own good, either physical or moral, is not a sufficient warrant. . . . The only part of the conduct of any one, for which he is amenable to society, is that which concerns others. In the part which merely concerns himself, his independence is, of right, absolute. Over himself, over his own body and mind, the individual is sovereign.[2]

Much of the history of the United States revolves about the attempt to translate the principles of the Declaration of Independence into practice—from the struggle over slavery, finally settled by a bloody civil war, to the subsequent attempt to promote equality of opportunity, to the more recent attempt to achieve equality of results.

Economic freedom is an essential requisite for political freedom. By enabling people to cooperate with one another without coercion or central direction, it reduces the area over which political power is exercised. In addition, by dispersing power, the free market provides an offset to whatever concentration of political power may arise. The combination of economic and political *power* in the same hands is a sure recipe for tyranny.

The combination of economic and political *freedom* produced a golden age in both Great Britain and the United States in the nineteenth century. The United States prospered even more than Britain. It started with a clean slate: fewer vestiges of class and status; fewer government restraints; a more fertile field for energy, drive, and innovation; and an empty continent to conquer.

The fecundity of freedom is demonstrated most dramatically and clearly in agriculture. When the Declaration of Independence was enacted, fewer than 3 million persons of European and African origin (i.e., omitting the native

Indians) occupied a narrow fringe along the eastern coast. Agriculture was the main economic activity. It took nineteen out of twenty workers to feed the country's inhabitants and provide a surplus for export in exchange for foreign goods. Today it takes fewer than one out of twenty workers to feed the 220 million inhabitants and provide a surplus that makes the United States the largest single exporter of food in the world.

What produced this miracle? Clearly not central direction by government—nations like Russia and its satellites, mainland China, Yugoslavia, and India that today rely on central direction employ from one-quarter to one-half of their workers in agriculture, yet frequently rely on U.S. agriculture to avoid mass starvation. During most of the period of rapid agricultural expansion in the United States the government played a negligible role. Land was made available—but it was land that had been unproductive before. After the middle of the nineteenth century land-grant colleges were established, and they disseminated information and technology through governmentally financed extension services. Unquestionably, however, the main source of the agricultural revolution was private initiative operating in a free market open to all—the shame of slavery only excepted. And the most rapid growth came after slavery was abolished. The millions of immigrants from all over the world were free to work for themselves, as independent farmers or businessmen, or to work for others, at terms mutually agreed. They were free to experiment with new techniques—at their risk if the experiment failed, and to their profit if it succeeded. They got little assistance from government. Even more important, they encountered little interference from government.

Government started playing a major role in agriculture during and after the Great Depression of the 1930s. It acted primarily to restrict output in order to keep prices artificially high.

The growth of agricultural productivity depended on the accompanying industrial revolution that freedom stimulated. Thence came the new machines that revolutionized agriculture. Conversely, the industrial revolution depended on the availability of the manpower released by the agricultural revolution. Industry and agriculture marched hand in hand.

Smith and Jefferson alike had seen concentrated government power as a great danger to the ordinary man; they saw the protection of the citizen against the tyranny of government as the perpetual need. That was the aim of the Virginia Declaration of Rights (1776) and the United States Bill of Rights (1791); the purpose of the separation of powers in the U.S. Constitution; the moving force behind the changes in the British legal structure from the issuance of the Magna Carta in the thirteenth century to the end of the nineteenth century. To Smith and Jefferson, government's role was as an umpire, not a participant. Jefferson's ideal, as he expressed it in his first inaugural address (1801), was "[a] wise and frugal government, which shall restrain men from injuring one another, which shall leave them otherwise free to regulate their own pursuits of industry and improvement."

Ironically, the very success of economic and political freedom reduced its appeal to later thinkers. The narrowly limited government of the late nineteenth century possessed little concentrated power that endangered the ordinary man. The other side of that coin was that it possessed little power that would enable good people to do good. And in an imperfect world there were still many evils. Indeed, the very progress of society made the residual evils seem all the more objectionable. As always, people took the favorable developments for granted. They forgot the danger to freedom from a strong government. Instead, they were attracted by the good that a stronger government could achieve—if only government power were in the "right" hands.

These ideas began to influence government policy in Great Britain by the beginning of the twentieth century. They gained increasing acceptance among intellectuals in the United States but had little effect on government policy until the Great Depression of the early 1930s. As we show in Chapter 3, the depression was produced by a failure of government in one area—money—where it had exercised authority ever since the beginning of the Republic. However, government's responsibility for the depression was not recognized—either then or now. Instead, the depression was widely interpreted as a failure of free market capitalism. That myth led the public to join the intellectuals in a changed view of the relative responsibilities of individuals and government. Emphasis on the responsibility of the individual for his own fate was replaced by emphasis on the individual as a pawn buffeted by forces beyond his control. The view that government's role is to serve as an umpire to prevent individuals from coercing one another was replaced by the view that government's role is to serve as a parent charged with the duty of coercing some to aid others.

These views have dominated developments in the United States during the past half-century. They have led to a growth in government at all levels, as well as to a transfer of power from local government and local control to central government and central control. The government has increasingly undertaken the task of taking from some to give to others in the name of security and equality. One government policy after another has been set up to "regulate" our "pursuits of industry and improvement," standing Jefferson's dictum on its head (Chapter 7).

These developments have been produced by good intentions with a major assist from self-interest. Even the strongest supporters of the welfare and paternal state agree that the results have been disappointing. In the government sphere, as in the market, there seems to be an invisible hand, but it operates in precisely the opposite direction from Adam Smith's: an individual who intends only to serve the public interest by fostering government intervention is "led by an invisible hand to promote" private interests, "which was no part of his intention." That conclusion is driven home again and again as we examine, in the chapters that follow, the several areas in which government power has been exercised—whether to achieve security (Chapter 4) or equality (Chapter 5), to promote education (Chapter 6), to protect the consumer (Chapter 7) or the worker (Chapter 8), or to avoid inflation and promote employment (Chapter 9).

So far, in Adam Smith's words, "the uniform, constant, and uninterrupted effort of every man to better his condition, the principle from which public and national, as well as private opulence is originally derived," has been "powerful enough to maintain the natural progress of things toward improvement, in spite both of the extravagance of governments and of the greatest errors of administration. Like the unknown principle of animal life, it frequently restores health and vigour to the constitution, in spite, not only of the disease, but of the absurd prescriptions of the doctor."[3] So far, that is, Adam Smith's invisible hand has been powerful enough to overcome the deadening effects of the invisible hand that operates in the political sphere.

The experience of recent years—slowing growth and declining productivity—raises a doubt whether private ingenuity can continue to overcome the deadening effects of government control if we continue to grant ever more power to government, to authorize a "new class" of civil servants to spend ever larger fractions of our income supposedly on our behalf. Sooner or later—and perhaps sooner than many of us expect—an ever bigger government would destroy both the prosperity that we owe to the free market and the human freedom proclaimed so eloquently in the Declaration of Independence.

We have not yet reached the point of no return. We are still free as a people to choose whether we shall continue speeding down the "road to serfdom," as Friedrich Hayek entitled his profound and influential book, or whether we shall set tighter limits on government and rely more heavily on voluntary cooperation among free individuals to achieve our several objectives. Will our golden age come to an end in a relapse into the tyranny and misery that has always been, and remains today, the state of most of mankind? Or shall we have the wisdom, the foresight, and the courage to change our course, to learn from experience, and to benefit from a "rebirth of freedom"?

If we are to make that choice wisely, we must understand the fundamental principles of our system, both the economic principles of Adam Smith, which explain how it is that a complex, organized, smoothly running system can develop and flourish without central direction, how coordination can be achieved without coercion (Chapter 1); and the political principles expressed by Thomas Jefferson (Chapter 5). We must understand why it is that attempts to replace cooperation by central direction are capable of doing so much harm (Chapter 2). We must understand also the intimate connection between political freedom and economic freedom.

Fortunately, the tide is turning. In the United States, in Great Britain, the countries of Western Europe, and in many other countries around the world, there is growing recognition of the dangers of big government, growing dissatisfaction with the policies that have been followed. This shift is being reflected not only in opinion, but also in the political sphere. It is becoming politically profitable for our representatives to sing a different tune—and perhaps even to act differently. We are experiencing another major change in public opinion. We have the opportunity to nudge the change in opinion toward greater reliance on individual initiative and voluntary cooperation, rather than toward the other extreme of total collectivism.

In our final chapter, we explore why it is that in a supposedly democratic political system special interests prevail over the general interest. We explore what we can do to correct the defect in our system that accounts for that result, how we can limit government while enabling it to perform its essential functions of defending the nation from foreign enemies, protecting each of us from coercion by our fellow citizens, adjudicating our disputes, and enabling us to agree on the rules that we shall follow.

The Power of the Market

Every day each of us uses innumerable goods and services—to eat, to wear, to shelter us from the elements, or simply to enjoy. We take it for granted that they will be available when we want to buy them. We never stop to think how many people have played a part in one way or another in providing those goods and services. We never ask ourselves how it is that the corner grocery store—or nowadays, supermarket—has the items on its shelves that we want to buy, how it is that most of us are able to earn the money to buy those goods.

It is natural to assume that someone must give orders to make sure that the "right" products are produced in the "right" amounts and available at the "right" places. That is one method of coordinating the activities of a large number of people—the method of the army. The general gives orders to the colonel, the colonel to the major, the major to the lieutenant, the lieutenant to the sergeant, and the sergeant to the private.

But that command method can be the exclusive or even principal method of organization only in a very small group. Not even the most autocratic head of a family can control every act of other family members entirely by order. No sizable army can really be run entirely by command. The general cannot conceivably have the information necessary to direct every movement of the lowliest private. At every step in the chain of command, the soldier, whether officer or private, must have discretion to take into account information about specific circumstances that his commanding officer could not have. Commands must be supplemented by voluntary cooperation—a less obvious and more subtle, but far more fundamental, technique of coordinating the activities of large numbers of people.

Russia is the standard example of a large economy that is supposed to be organized by command—a centrally planned economy. But that is more fiction than fact. At every level of the economy, voluntary cooperation enters to supplement central planning or to offset its rigidities—sometimes legally, sometimes illegally.[1]

In agriculture, full-time workers on government farms are permitted to grow food and raise animals on small private plots in their spare time for their own use or to sell in relatively free markets. These plots account for less than 1 percent of the agricultural land in the country, yet they are said to provide nearly a third of total farm output in the Soviet Union (are "said to" because it is likely that some products of government farms are clandestinely marketed as if from private plots).

In the labor market individuals are seldom ordered to work at specific jobs; there is little actual direction of labor in this sense. Rather, wages are offered for various jobs, and individuals apply for them—much as in capitalist countries. Once hired, they may subsequently be fired or may leave for jobs they prefer. Numerous restrictions affect who may work where, and, of course, the laws prohibit anyone from setting up as an employer—although numerous clandestine workshops serve the extensive black market. Allocation of workers on a large scale primarily by compulsion is just not feasible; and neither, apparently, is complete suppression of private entrepreneurial activity.

The attractiveness of different jobs in the Soviet Union often depends on the opportunities they offer for extralegal or illegal moonlighting. A resident of Moscow whose household equipment fails may have to wait months to have it repaired if he calls the state repair office. Instead, he may hire a moonlighter—very likely someone who works for the state repair office. The householder gets his equipment repaired promptly; the moonlighter gets some extra income. Both are happy.

These voluntary market elements flourish despite their inconsistency with official Marxist ideology because the cost of eliminating them would be too high. Private plots could be forbidden—but the famines of the 1930s are a stark reminder of the cost. The Soviet economy is hardly a model of efficiency now. Without the voluntary elements it would operate at an even lower level of effectiveness. Recent experience in Cambodia tragically illustrates the cost of trying to do without the market entirely.

Just as no society operates entirely on the command principle, so none operates entirely through voluntary cooperation. Every society has some command elements. These take many forms. They may be as straightforward as military conscription or forbidding the purchase and sale of heroin or cyclamates or court orders to named defendants to desist from or perform specified actions. Or, at the other extreme, they may be as subtle as imposing a heavy tax on cigarettes to discourage smoking—a hint, if not a command, by some of us to others of us.

It makes a vast difference what the mix is—whether voluntary exchange is primarily a clandestine activity that flourishes because of the rigidities of a dominant command element, or whether voluntary exchange is the dominant principle of organization, supplemented to a smaller or larger extent by command elements. Clandestine voluntary exchange may prevent a command economy from collapsing, may enable it to creak along and even achieve some progress. It can do little to undermine the tyranny on which a predominantly command economy rests. A predominantly voluntary exchange economy, on the other hand, has within it the potential to promote both prosperity and human freedom. It may not achieve its potential in either respect, but we know of no society that has ever achieved prosperity and freedom unless voluntary exchange has been its dominant principle of organization. We hasten to add that voluntary exchange is not a sufficient condition for prosperity and freedom. That, at least, is the lesson of history to date. Many societies organized predominantly by voluntary exchange have not achieved either prosperity or freedom, though they have achieved a far greater measure of both than authoritarian societies. But voluntary exchange is a necessary condition for both prosperity and freedom.

Cooperation Through Voluntary Exchange

A delightful story called "I, Pencil: My Family Tree as Told to Leonard E. Read"[2] dramatizes vividly how voluntary exchange enables millions of people to cooperate with one another. Mr. Read, in the voice of the "Lead Pencil—the ordinary wooden pencil familiar to all boys and girls and adults who can read and write," starts his story with the fantastic statement that *"not a single person . . . knows how to make me."* Then he proceeds to tell about all the things that go into the making of a pencil. First, the wood comes from a tree, "a cedar of straight grain that grows in Northern California and Oregon." To cut down the tree and cart the logs to the railroad siding requires "saws and trucks and rope and . . . countless other gear." Many persons and numberless skills are involved in their fabrication: in "the mining of ore, the making of steel and its refinement into saws, axes, motors; the growing of hemp and bringing it through all the stages to heavy and strong rope; the logging camps with their beds and mess halls, . . . untold thousands of persons had a hand in every cup of coffee the loggers drink!"

And so Mr. Read goes on to the bringing of the logs to the mill, the millwork involved in converting the logs to slats, and the transportation of the slats from California to Wilkes-Barre, where the particular pencil that tells the story was manufactured. And so far we have only the outside wood of the pencil. The "lead" center is not really lead at all. It starts as graphite mined in Ceylon. After many complicated processes it ends up as the lead in the center of the pencil.

The bit of metal—the ferrule—near the top of the pencil is brass. "Think of all the persons," he says, "who mine zinc and copper and those who have the skills to make shiny sheet brass from these products of nature."

What we call the eraser is known in the trade as "the plug." It is thought to be rubber. But Mr. Read tells us the rubber is only for binding purposes. The erasing is actually done by "Factice," a rubberlike product made by reacting rape seed oil from the Dutch East Indies (now Indonesia) with sulfur chloride.

After all of this, says the pencil, "Does anyone wish to challenge my earlier assertion that no single person on the face of this earth knows how to make me?"

None of the thousands of persons involved in producing the pencil performed his task because he wanted a pencil. Some among them never saw a pencil and would not know what it is for. Each saw his work as a way to get the goods and services he wanted—goods and services we produced in order to get the pencil we wanted. Every time we go to the store and buy a pencil, we are exchanging a little bit of our services for the infinitesimal amount of services that each of the thousands contributed toward producing the pencil.

It is even more astounding that the pencil was ever produced. No one sitting in a central office gave orders to these thousands of people. No military police enforced the orders that were not given. These people live in many lands, speak different languages, practice different religions, may even hate one another—yet none of these differences prevented them from cooperating to produce a pencil. How did it happen? Adam Smith gave us the answer two hundred years ago.

The Role of Prices

The key insight of Adam Smith's *Wealth of Nations* is misleadingly simple: if an exchange between two parties is voluntary, it will not take place unless both believe they will benefit from it. Most economic fallacies derive from the neglect of this simple insight, from the tendency to assume that there is a fixed pie, that one party can gain only at the expense of another.

This key insight is obvious for a simple exchange between two individuals. It is far more difficult to understand how it can enable people living all over the world to cooperate to promote their separate interests.

The price system is the mechanism that performs this task without central direction, without requiring people to speak to one another or to like one another. When you buy your pencil or your daily bread, you don't know whether the pencil was made or the wheat was grown by a white man or a black man, by a Chinese or an Indian. As a result, the price system enables people to cooperate peacefully in one phase of their life while each one goes about his own business in respect of everything else.

Adam Smith's flash of genius was his recognition that the prices that emerged from voluntary transactions between buyers and sellers—for short, in a free market—could coordinate the activity of millions of people, each seeking his own interest, in such a way as to make everyone better off. It was a startling idea then, and it remains one today, that economic order can emerge as the unintended consequence of the actions of many people, each seeking his own interest.

The price system works so well, so efficiently, that we are not aware of it most of the time. We never realize how well it functions until it is prevented from functioning, and even then we seldom recognize the source of the trouble.

The long gasoline lines that suddenly emerged in 1974 after the OPEC oil embargo, and again in the spring and summer of 1979 after the revolution in Iran, are a striking recent example. On both occasions there was a sharp disturbance in the supply of crude oil from abroad. But that did not lead to gasoline lines in Germany or Japan, which are wholly dependent on imported oil. It led to long gasoline lines in the United States, even though we produce much of our own oil, for one reason and one reason only: because legislation, administered by a government agency, did not permit the price system to function. Prices in some areas were kept by command below the level that would have equated the amount of gasoline available at the gas stations to the amount consumers wanted to buy at that price. Supplies were allocated to different areas of the country by command, rather than in response to the pressures of demand as reflected in price. The result was surpluses in some areas and shortages plus long gasoline lines in others. The smooth operation of the price system—which for many decades had assured every consumer that he could buy gasoline at any of a large number of service stations at his convenience and with a minimal wait—was replaced by bureaucratic improvisation.

Prices perform three functions in organizing economic activity: first, they transmit information; second, they provide an incentive to adopt those methods of production that are least costly and thereby use available resources for the most highly valued purposes; third, they determine who gets how much of the product—the distribution of income. These three functions are closely interrelated.

Transmission of Information

Suppose that, for whatever reason, there is an increased demand for lead pencils—perhaps because a baby boom increases school enrollment. Retail stores will find that they are selling more pencils. They will order more pencils from their wholesalers. The wholesalers will order more pencils from the manufacturers. The manufacturers will order more wood, more brass, more graphite—all the varied products used to make a pencil. In order to induce their suppliers to produce more of these items, they will have to offer higher prices for them. The higher prices will induce the suppliers to increase their work force to be able to meet the higher demand. To get more workers they will have to offer higher wages or better working conditions. In this way ripples spread out over ever widening circles, transmitting the information to people all over the world that there is a greater demand for pencils—or, to be more precise, for some product they are engaged in producing, for reasons they may not and need not know.

The price system transmits only the important information and only to the people who need to know. The producers of wood, for example, do not have to know whether the demand for pencils has gone up because of a baby boom or because 14,000 more government forms have to be filled out in pencil. They don't even have to know that the demand for pencils has gone up. They need to know only that someone is willing to pay more for wood and that the higher price is likely to last long enough to make it worthwhile to satisfy the demand. Both items of information are provided by market prices—the first by the current price, the second by the price offered for future delivery.

A major problem in transmitting information efficiently is to make sure that everyone who can use the information gets it without clogging the "in" baskets of those who have no use for it. The price system automatically solves this problem. The people who transmit the information have an incentive to search out the people who can use it and they are in a position to do so. People who can use the information have an incentive to get it and they are in a position to do so. The pencil manufacturer is in touch with people selling the wood he uses. He is always trying to find additional suppliers who can offer him a better product or a lower price. Similarly, the producer of wood is in touch with his customers and is always trying to find new ones. On the other hand, people who are not currently engaged in these activities and are not considering them as future activities have no interest in the price of wood and will ignore it.

The transmission of information through prices is enormously facilitated these days by organized markets and by specialized communication facilities. It is a fascinating exercise to look through the price quotations published daily in, say, the *Wall Street Journal*, not to mention the numerous more specialized trade publications. These prices mirror almost instantly what is happening all over the world. There is a revolution in some remote country that is a major producer of copper, or there is a disruption of copper production for some other reason. The current price of copper will shoot up at once. To find out how long knowledgeable people expect the supplies of copper to be affected, you need merely examine the prices for future delivery on the same page.

Few readers even of the *Wall Street Journal* are interested in more than a few of the prices quoted. They can readily ignore the rest. The *Wall Street Journal* does not provide this information out of altruism or because it recognizes how important it is for the operation of the economy. Rather, it is led to provide this information by the very price system whose functioning it facilitates. It has found that it can achieve a larger or a more profitable circulation by publishing these prices—information transmitted to it by a different set of prices.

Prices not only transmit information from the ultimate buyers to retailers, wholesalers, manufacturers, and owners of resources; they also transmit information the other way. Suppose that a forest fire or strike reduces the availability of wood. The price of wood will go up. That will tell the manufacturer of pencils that it will pay him to use less wood, and it will not pay him to produce as many pencils as before unless he can sell them for a higher price. The smaller production of pencils will enable the retailer to charge a higher price, and the higher price will inform the final user that it will pay him to wear his pencil down to a shorter stub before he discards it, or shift to a mechanical pencil. Again, he doesn't need to know why the pencil has become more expensive, only that it has.

Anything that prevents prices from expressing freely the conditions of demand or supply interferes with the transmission of accurate information. Private monopoly—control over a particular commodity by one producer or a cartel of producers—is one example. That does not prevent the transmission of information through the price system, but it does distort the information transmitted. The quadrupling of the price of oil in 1973 by the oil cartel transmitted very important information. However, the information it transmitted did not reflect a sudden reduction in the supply of crude oil, or a sudden discovery of new technical knowledge about future supplies of oil, or anything else of a physical or technical character bearing on the relative availability of oil and other sources of energy. It simply transmitted the information that a group of countries had succeeded in organizing a price-fixing and market-sharing arrangement.

Price controls on oil and other forms of energy by the U.S. government in their turn prevented information about the effect of the OPEC cartel from being transmitted accurately to users of petroleum. The result both strengthened the OPEC cartel, by preventing a higher price from leading U.S. consumers to economize on the use of oil, and required the introduction of major command elements in the United States in order to allocate the scarce supply (by a Department of Energy spending in 1979 about $10 billion and employing 20,000 people).

Important as private distortions of the price system are, these days the government is the major source of interference with a free market system—through tariffs and other restraints on international trade, domestic action fixing or affecting individual prices, including wages (see Chapter 2), government regulation of specific industries (see Chapter 7), monetary and fiscal policies producing erratic inflation (see Chapter 9), and numerous other channels.

One of the major adverse effects of erratic inflation is the introduction of static, as it were, into the transmission of information through prices. If the price of wood goes up, for example, producers of wood cannot know whether that is because inflation is raising all prices or because wood is now in greater demand or lower supply relative to other products than it was before the price hike. The information that is important for the organization of production is primarily about *relative* prices—the price of one item compared with the price of another. High inflation, and particularly highly variable inflation, drowns that information in meaningless static.

Incentives

The effective transmission of accurate information is wasted unless the relevant people have an incentive to act, and act correctly, on the basis of that information. It does no good for the producer of wood to be told that the demand for wood has gone up unless he has some incentive to react to the higher price of wood by producing more wood. One of the beauties of a free price system is that the prices that bring the information also provide both an incentive to react to the information and the means to do so.

This function of prices is intimately connected with the third function—determining the distribution of income—and cannot be explained without bringing that function into the account. The producer's income—what he gets for his activities—is determined by the difference between the amount he receives from the sale of his output and the amount he spends in order to produce it. He balances the one against the other and produces an output such that producing a little more would add as much to his costs as to his receipts. A higher price shifts this margin.

In general, the more he produces, the higher the cost of producing still more. He must resort to wood in less accessible or otherwise less favorable locations; he must hire less skilled workers or pay higher wages to attract skilled workers from other pursuits. But now the higher price enables him to bear these higher costs and so provides both the incentive to increase output and the means to do so.

Prices also provide an incentive to act on information not only about the demand for output but also about the most efficient way to produce a product. Suppose one kind of wood becomes scarcer and therefore more expensive than another. The pencil manufacturer gets that information through a rise in the price of the first kind of wood. Because his income, too, is determined by the difference between sales receipts and costs, he has an incentive to economize on that kind of wood. To take a different example, whether it is less costly for loggers to use a chain saw or handsaw depends on the price of the chain saw and the handsaw, the amount of labor required with each, and the wages of different kinds of labor. The enterprise doing the logging has an incentive to acquire the relevant technical knowledge and to combine it with the information transmitted by prices in order to minimize costs.

Or take a more fanciful case that illustrates the subtlety of the price system. The rise in the price of oil engineered by the OPEC cartel in 1973 altered slightly the balance in favor of the handsaw by raising the cost of operating a chain saw. If that seems far-fetched, consider the effect on the use of diesel-powered versus gasoline-powered trucks to haul logs out of the forests and to the sawmill.

To carry this example one step further, the higher price of oil, insofar as it was permitted to occur, raised the cost of products that used more oil relative to products that used less. Consumers had an incentive to shift from the one to the other. The most obvious examples are shifts from large cars to small ones and from heating by oil to heating by coal or wood. To go much further afield to more remote effects: insofar as the relative price of wood was raised by the higher cost of producing it or by the greater demand for wood as a substitute source of energy, the resulting higher price of lead pencils gave consumers an incentive to economize on pencils! And so on in infinite variety.

We have discussed the incentive effect so far in terms of producers and consumers. But it also operates with respect to workers and owners of other productive resources. A higher demand for wood will tend to produce a higher wage for loggers. This is a signal that labor of that type is in greater demand than before. The higher wage gives workers an incentive to act on that information.

Some workers who were indifferent about being loggers or doing something else may now choose to become loggers. More young people entering the labor market may become loggers. Here, too, interference by government, through minimum wages, for example, or by trade unions, through restricting entry, may distort the information transmitted or may prevent individuals from freely acting on that information (see Chapter 8).

Information about prices—whether it be wages in different activities, the rent of land, or the return to capital from different uses—is not the only information that is relevant in deciding how to use a particular resource. It may not even be the most important information, particularly about how to use one's own labor. That decision depends in addition on one's own interests and capacities—what the great economist Alfred Marshall called the whole of the advantages and disadvantages of an occupation, monetary and nonmonetary. Satisfaction in a job may compensate for low wages. On the other hand, higher wages may compensate for a disagreeable job.

Distribution of Income

The income each person gets through the market is determined, as we have seen, by the difference between his receipts from the sale of goods and services and the costs he incurs in producing those goods and services. The receipts consist predominantly of direct payments for the productive resources we own—payments for labor or the use of land or buildings or other capital. The case of the entrepreneur—like the manufacturer of pencils—is different in form but not in substance. His income, too, depends on how much of each productive resource he owns and on the price that the market sets on the services of those resources, though in his case the major productive resource he owns may be the capacity to organize an enterprise, coordinate the resources it uses, assume risks, and so on. He may also own some of the other productive resources used in the enterprise, in which case part of his income is derived from the market price for their services. Similarly, the existence of the modern corporation does not alter matters. We speak loosely of the "corporation's income" or of "business" having an income. That is figurative language. The corporation is an intermediary between its owners—the stockholders—and the resources other than the stockholders' capital, the services of which it purchases. Only people have incomes and they derive them through the market from the resources they own, whether these be in the form of corporate stock, or of bonds, or of land, or of their personal capacity.

In countries like the United States the major productive resource is personal productive capacity—what economists call "human capital." Something like three-quarters of all income generated in the United States through market transactions takes the form of the compensation of employees (wages and salaries plus supplements), and about half the rest takes the form of the income of proprietors of farms and nonfarm enterprises, which is a mixture of payment for personal services and for owned capital.

The accumulation of physical capital—of factories, mines, office buildings, shopping centers; highways, railroads, airports, cars, trucks, planes, ships; dams, refineries, power plants; houses, refrigerators, washing machines, and so on and on in endless variety—has played an essential role in economic growth. Without that accumulation the kind of economic growth that we have enjoyed could never have occurred. Without the maintenance of inherited capital the gains made by one generation would be dissipated by the next.

But the accumulation of human capital—in the form of increased knowledge and skills and improved health and longevity—has also played an essential role. And the two have reinforced one another. The physical capital enabled people to be far more productive by providing them with the tools to work with. And the capacity of people to invent new forms of physical capital, to learn how to use and get the most out of physical capital, and to organize the use of both physical and human capital on a larger and larger scale enabled the physical capital to be more productive. Both physical and human capital must be cared for and replaced. That is even more difficult and costly for human than for physical capital—a major reason why the return to human capital has risen so much more rapidly than the return to physical capital.

The amount of each kind of resource each of us owns is partly the result of chance, partly of choice by ourselves or others. Chance determines our genes and through them affects our physical and mental capacities. Chance determines the kind of family and cultural environment into which we are born and as a result our opportunities to develop our physical and mental capacity. Chance determines also other resources we may inherit from our parents or other benefactors. Chance may destroy or enhance the resources we start with. But choice also plays an important role. Our decisions about how to use our resources, whether to work hard or take it easy, to enter one occupation or another, to engage in one venture or another, to save or spend—these may determine whether we dissipate our resources or improve and add to them. Similar decisions by our parents, by other benefactors, by millions of people who may have no direct connection with us will affect our inheritance.

The price that the market sets on the services of our resources is similarly affected by a bewildering mixture of chance and choice. Frank Sinatra's voice was highly valued in twentieth-century United States. Would it have been highly valued in twentieth-century India, if he had happened to be born and to live there? Skill as a hunter and trapper had a high value in eighteenth- and nineteenth-century America, a much lower value in twentieth-century America. Skill as a baseball player brought much higher returns than skill as a basketball player in the 1920s; the reverse is true in the 1970s. These are all matters involving chance and choice—in these examples, mostly the choices made by consumers of services that determine the relative market prices of different items. But the price we receive for the services of our resources through the market also depends on our own choices—where we choose to settle, how we choose to use those resources, to whom we choose to sell their services, and so on.

In every society, however it is organized, there is always dissatisfaction with the distribution of income. All of us find it hard to understand why we should receive less than others who seem no more deserving—or why we should be receiving more than so many others whose needs seem as great and whose deserts seem no less. The farther fields always look greener—so we blame the existing system. In a command system envy and dissatisfaction are directed at the rulers. In a free market system they are directed at the market.

One result has been an attempt to separate this function of the price system—distributing income—from its other functions—transmitting information and providing incentives. Much government activity during recent decades in the United States and other countries that rely predominantly on the market has been directed at altering the distribution of income generated by the market in order to produce a different and more equal distribution of income. There is a strong current of opinion pressing for still further steps in this direction. We discuss this movement at greater length in Chapter 5.

However we might wish it otherwise, it simply is not possible to use prices to transmit information and provide an incentive to act on that information without using prices also to affect, even if not completely determine, the distribution of income. If what a person gets does not depend on the price he receives for the services of his resources, what incentive does he have to seek out information on prices or to act on the basis of that information? If Red Adair's income would be the same whether or not he performs the dangerous task of capping a runaway oil well, why should he undertake the dangerous task? He might do so once, for the excitement. But would he make it his major activity? If your income will be the same whether you work hard or not, why should you work hard? Why should you make the effort to search out the buyer who values most highly what you have to sell if you will not get any benefit from doing so? If there is no reward for accumulating capital, why should anyone postpone to a later date what he could enjoy now? Why save? How would the existing physical capital ever have been built up by the voluntary restraint of individuals? If there is no reward for maintaining capital, why should people not dissipate any capital which they have either accumulated or inherited? If prices are prevented from affecting the distribution of income, they cannot be used for other purposes. The only alternative is command. Some authority would have to decide who should produce what and how much. Some authority would have to decide who should sweep the streets and who manage the factory, who should be the policeman and who the physician.

The intimate connection among the three functions of the price system has manifested itself in a different way in the communist countries. Their whole ideology centers on the alleged exploitation of labor under capitalism and the associated superiority of a society based on Marx's dictum: "to each according to his needs, from each according to his ability." But the inability to run a pure command economy has made it impossible for them to separate income completely from prices.

For physical resources—land, buildings, and the like—they have been able to go farthest by making them the property of the government. But even here the effect is a lack of incentive to maintain and improve the physical capital. When everybody owns something, nobody owns it, and nobody has a direct interest in maintaining or improving its condition. That is why buildings in the Soviet Union—like public housing in the United States—look decrepit within a year or two of their construction, why machines in government factories break down and are continuously in need of repair, why citizens must resort to the black market for maintaining the capital that they have for their personal use.

For human resources the communist governments have not been able to go as far as with physical resources, though they have tried to. Even they have had to permit people to own themselves to some extent and to let them make their own decisions, and have had to let prices affect and guide those decisions and determine the income received. They have, of course, distorted those prices, prevented them from being free market prices, but they have been unable to eliminate market forces.

The obvious inefficiencies that have resulted from the command system have led to much discussion by planners in socialist countries—Russia, Czechoslovakia, Hungary, China—of the possibility of making greater use of the market in organizing production. At a conference of economists from East and West, we once heard a brilliant talk by a Hungarian Marxist economist. He had rediscovered for himself Adam Smith's invisible hand—a remarkable if somewhat redundant intellectual achievement. He tried, however, to improve on it in order to use the price system to transmit information and organize production efficiently but not to distribute income. Needless to say, he failed in theory, as the communist countries have failed in practice.

A Broader View

Adam Smith's "invisible hand" is generally regarded as referring to purchases or sales of goods or services for money. But economic activity is by no means the only area of human life in which a complex and sophisticated structure arises as an unintended consequence of a large number of individuals cooperating while each pursues his own interests.

Consider, for example, language. It is a complex structure that is continually changing and developing. It has a well-defined order, yet no central body planned it. No one decided what words should be admitted into the language, what the rules of grammar should be, which words should be adjectives, which nouns. The French Academy does try to control changes in the French language, but that was a late development. It was established long after French was already a highly structured language and it mainly serves to put the seal of approval on changes over which it has no control. There have been few similar bodies for other languages.

How did language develop? In much the same way as an economic order develops through the market—out of the voluntary interaction of individuals, in this case seeking to trade ideas or information or gossip rather than goods and services with one another. One or another meaning was attributed to a word, or words were added as the need arose. Grammatical usages developed and were later codified into rules. Two parties who want to communicate with one another both benefit from coming to a common agreement about the words they use. As a wider and wider circle of people find it advantageous to communicate with one another, a common usage spreads and is codified in dictionaries. At no point is there any coercion, any central planner who has power to command, though in more recent times government school systems have played an important role in standardizing usage.

Another example is scientific knowledge. The structure of disciplines—physics, chemistry, meteorology, philosophy, humanities, sociology, economics—was not the product of a deliberate decision by anyone. Like Topsy, it "just growed." It did so because scholars found it convenient. It is not fixed, but changes as different needs develop.

Within any discipline the growth of the subject strictly parallels the economic marketplace. Scholars cooperate with one another because they find it mutually beneficial. They accept from one another's work what they find useful. They exchange their findings—by verbal communication, by circulating unpublished papers, by publishing in journals and books. Cooperation is worldwide, just as in the economic market. The esteem or approval of fellow scholars serves very much the same function that monetary reward does in the economic market. The desire to earn that esteem, to have their work accepted by their peers, leads scholars to direct their activities in scientifically efficient directions. The whole becomes greater than the sum of its parts, as one scholar builds on another's work. His work in turn becomes the basis for further development. Modern physics is as much a product of a free market in ideas as a modern automobile is a product of a free market in goods. Here again, developments have been much influenced, particularly recently, by government involvement, which has affected both the resources available and the kinds of knowledge that have been in demand. Yet government has played a secondary role. Indeed, one of the ironies of the situation is that many scholars who have strongly favored government central planning of economic activity have recognized very clearly the danger to scientific progress that would be imposed by central government planning of science, the danger of having priorities imposed from above rather than emerging spontaneously from the gropings and explorations of individual scientists.

A society's values, its culture, its social conventions—all these develop in the same way, through voluntary exchange, spontaneous cooperation, the evolution of a complex structure through trial and error, acceptance and rejection. No monarch ever decreed that the kind of music that is enjoyed by residents of Calcutta, for example, should differ radically from the kind enjoyed by residents of Vienna. These widely different musical cultures developed without anyone's "planning" them that way, through a kind of social evolution paralleling biological evolution—though, of course, individual sovereigns or even elected governments may have affected the direction of social evolution by sponsoring one or another musician or type of music, just as wealthy private individuals did.

The structures produced by voluntary exchange, whether they be language or scientific discoveries or musical styles or economic systems, develop a life of their own. They are capable of taking many different forms under different circumstances. Voluntary exchange can produce uniformity in some respects combined with diversity in others. It is a subtle process whose general principles of operation can fairly readily be grasped but whose detailed results can seldom be foreseen.

These examples may suggest not only the wide scope for voluntary exchange but also the broad meaning that must be attached to the concept of "self-interest." Narrow preoccupation with the economic market has led to a narrow interpretation of self-interest as myopic selfishness, as exclusive concern with immediate material rewards. Economics has been berated for allegedly drawing far-reaching conclusions from a wholly unrealistic "economic man" who is little more than a calculating machine, responding only to monetary stimuli. That is a great mistake. Self-interest is not myopic selfishness. It is whatever it is that interests the participants, whatever they value, whatever goals they pursue. The scientist seeking to advance the frontiers of his discipline, the missionary seeking to convert infidels to the true faith, the philanthropist seeking to bring comfort to the needy—all are pursuing their interests, as they see them, as they judge them by their own values.

The Role of Government

Where does government enter into the picture? To some extent government is a form of voluntary cooperation, a way in which people choose to achieve some of their objectives through governmental entities because they believe that is the most effective means of achieving them.

The clearest example is local government under conditions where people are free to choose where to live. You may decide to live in one community rather than another partly on the basis of the kind of services its government offers. If it engages in activities you object to or are unwilling to pay for, and these more than balance the activities you favor and are willing to pay for, you can vote with your feet by moving elsewhere. There is competition, limited but real, so long as there are available alternatives.

But government is more than that. It is also the agency that is widely regarded as having a monopoly on the legitimate use of force or the threat of force as the means through which some of us can legitimately impose restraints through force upon others of us. The role of government in that more basic sense has changed drastically over time in most societies and has differed widely among societies at any given time. Much of the rest of this book deals with how its role has changed in the United States in recent decades, and what the effects of its activities have been.

In this initial sketch we want to consider a very different question. In a society whose participants desire to achieve the greatest possible freedom to choose as individuals, as families, as members of voluntary groups, as citizens of an organized government, what role should be assigned to government?

It is not easy to improve on the answer that Adam Smith gave to this question two hundred years ago:

> All systems either of preference or of restraint, therefore, being thus completely taken away, the obvious and simple system of natural liberty establishes itself of its own accord. Every man, as long as he does not violate the laws of justice, is left perfectly free to pursue his own interest his own way, and to bring both his industry and capital into competition with those of any other man, or order of men. The sovereign is completely discharged from a duty, in the attempting to perform which he must always be exposed to innumerable delusions, and for the proper performance of which no human wisdom or knowledge could ever be sufficient; the duty of superintending the industry of private people, and of directing it towards the employments most suitable to the interest of the society. According to the system of natural liberty, the sovereign has only three duties to attend to; three duties of great importance, indeed, but plain and intelligible to common understandings: first, the duty of protecting the society from the violence and invasion of other independent societies; secondly, the duty of protecting, as far as possible, every member of the society from the injustice or oppression of every other member of it, or the duty of establishing an exact administration of justice; and, thirdly, the duty of erecting and maintaining certain public works and certain public institutions, which it can never be for the interest of any individual, or small number of individuals, to erect and maintain; because the profit could never repay the expence to any individual or small number of individuals, though it may frequently do much more than repay it to a great society.[3]

The first two duties are clear and straightforward: the protection of individuals in the society from coercion whether it comes from outside or from their fellow citizens. Unless there is such protection, we are not really free to choose. The armed robber's "Your money or your life" offers me a choice, but no one would describe it as a free choice or the subsequent exchange as voluntary.

Of course, as we shall see repeatedly throughout this book, it is one thing to state the purpose that an institution, particularly a governmental institution, "ought" to serve; it is quite another to describe the purposes the institution actually serves. The intentions of the persons responsible for setting up the institution and of the persons who operate it often differ sharply. Equally important, the results achieved often differ widely from those intended.

Military and police forces are required to prevent coercion from without and within. They do not always succeed and the power they possess is sometimes used for very different purposes. A major problem in achieving and preserving a free society is precisely how to assure that coercive powers granted to government in order to preserve freedom are limited to that function and are kept from becoming a threat to freedom. The founders of our country wrestled with that problem in drawing up the Constitution. We have tended to neglect it.

Adam Smith's second duty goes beyond the narrow police function of protecting people from physical coercion; it includes "an exact administration of justice." No voluntary exchange that is at all complicated or extends over any considerable period of time can be free from ambiguity. There is not enough fine print in the world to specify in advance every contingency that might arise and to describe precisely the obligations of the various parties to the exchange in each case. There must be some way to mediate disputes. Such mediation itself can be voluntary and need not involve government. In the United States today, most disagreements that arise in connection with commercial contracts are settled by resort to private arbitrators chosen by a procedure specified in advance. In response to this demand an extensive private judicial system has grown up. But the court of last resort is provided by the governmental judicial system.

This role of government also includes facilitating voluntary exchanges by adopting general rules—the rules of the economic and social game that the citizens of a free society play. The most obvious example is the meaning to be attached to private property. I own a house. Are you "trespassing" on my private property if you fly your private airplane ten feet over my roof? One thousand feet? Thirty thousand feet? There is nothing "natural" about where my property rights end and yours begin. The major way that society has come to agree on the rules of property is through the growth of common law, though more recently legislation has played an increasing role.

Adam Smith's third duty raises the most troublesome issues. He himself regarded it as having a narrow application. It has since been used to justify an extremely wide range of government activities. In our view it describes a valid duty of a government directed to preserving and strengthening a free society; but it can also be interpreted to justify unlimited extensions of government power.

The valid element arises because of the cost of producing some goods or services through strictly voluntary exchanges. To take one simple example suggested directly by Smith's description of the third duty: city streets and general-access highways could be provided by private voluntary exchange, the costs being paid for by charging tolls. But the costs of collecting the tolls would often be very large compared to the cost of building and maintaining the streets or highways. This is a "public work" that it might not "be for the interest of any individual . . . to erect and maintain . . . though it" might be worthwhile for "a great society."

A more subtle example involves effects on "third parties," people who are not parties to the particular exchange—the classic "smoke nuisance" case. Your furnace pours forth sooty smoke that dirties a third party's shirt collar. You have unintentionally imposed costs on a third party. He would be willing to let you dirty his collar for a price—but it is simply not feasible for you to identify all of the people whom you affect or for them to discover who has dirtied their collars and to require you to indemnify them individually or reach individual agreements with them.

The effect of your actions on third parties may be to confer benefits rather than impose costs. You landscape your house beautifully, and all passersby enjoy the sight. They would be willing to pay something for the privilege but it is not feasible to charge them for looking at your lovely flowers.

To lapse into technical jargon, there is a "market failure" because of "external" or "neighborhood" effects for which it is not feasible (i.e., would cost too much) to compensate or charge the people affected; third parties have had involuntary exchanges imposed on them.

Almost everything we do has some third-party effects, however small and however remote. In consequence, Adam Smith's third duty may at first blush appear to justify almost any proposed government measure. But there is a fallacy. Government measures also have third-party effects. "Government failure" no less than "market failure" arises from "external" or "neighborhood" effects. And if such effects are important for a market transaction, they are likely also to be important for government measures intended to correct the "market failure." The primary source of significant third-party effects of private actions is the difficulty of identifying the external costs or benefits. When it is easy to identify who is hurt or who is benefited, and by how much, it is fairly straightforward to replace involuntary by voluntary exchange, or at least to require individual compensation. If your car hits someone else's because of your negligence, you can be made to pay him for damages even though the exchange was involuntary. If it were easy to know whose collars were going to be dirtied, it would be possible for you to compensate the people affected, or alternatively, for them to pay you to pour out less smoke.

If it is difficult for private parties to identify who imposes costs or benefits on whom, it is difficult for government to do so. As a result a government attempt to rectify the situation may very well end up making matters worse rather than better—imposing costs on innocent third parties or conferring benefits on lucky bystanders. To finance its activities it must collect taxes, which themselves affect what the taxpayers do—still another third-party effect. In addition, every accretion of government power for whatever purpose increases the danger that government, instead of serving the great majority of its citizens, will become a means whereby some of its citizens can take advantage of others. Every government measure bears, as it were, a smokestack on its back.

Voluntary arrangements can allow for third-party effects to a much greater extent than may at first appear. To take a trivial example, tipping at restaurants is a social custom that leads you to assure better service for people you may not know or ever meet and, in return, be assured better service by the actions of still another group of anonymous third parties. Nonetheless, third-party effects of private actions do occur that are sufficiently important to justify government action. The lesson to be drawn from the misuse of Smith's third duty is not that government intervention is never justified, but rather that the burden of proof should be on its proponents. We should develop the practice of examining both the benefits and the costs of proposed government interventions and require a very clear balance of benefits over costs before adopting them. This course of action is recommended not only by the difficulty of assessing the hidden costs of government intervention but also by another consideration. Experience shows that once government undertakes an activity, it is seldom terminated. The activity may not live up to expectation but that is more likely to lead to its expansion, to its being granted a larger budget, than to its curtailment or abolition.

A fourth duty of government that Adam Smith did not explicitly mention is the duty to protect members of the community who cannot be regarded as "responsible" individuals. Like Adam Smith's third duty, this one, too, is susceptible of great abuse. Yet it cannot be avoided.

Freedom is a tenable objective only for responsible individuals. We do not believe in freedom for madmen or children. We must somehow draw a line between responsible individuals and others, yet doing so introduces a fundamental ambiguity into our ultimate objective of freedom. We cannot categorically reject paternalism for those whom we consider as not responsible.

For children we assign responsibility in the first instance to parents. The family, rather than the individual, has always been and remains today the basic building block of our society, though its hold has clearly been weakening—one of the most unfortunate consequences of the growth of government paternalism. Yet the assignment of responsibility for children to their parents is largely a matter of expediency rather than principle. We believe, and with good reason, that parents have more interest in their children than anyone else and can be relied on to protect them and to assure their development into responsible adults. However, we do not believe in the right of the parents to do whatever they will with their children—to beat them, murder them, or sell them into slavery. Children are responsible individuals in embryo. They have ultimate rights of their own and are not simply the playthings of their parents.

Adam Smith's three duties, or our four duties of government, are indeed "of great importance," but they are far less "plain and intelligible to common understandings" than he supposed. Though we cannot decide the desirability or undesirability of any actual or proposed government intervention by mechanical reference to one or another of them, they provide a set of principles that we can use in casting up a balance sheet of pros and cons. Even on the loosest interpretation, they rule out much existing government intervention—all those "systems either of preference or of restraint" that Adam Smith fought against, that were subsequently destroyed, but have since reappeared in the form of today's tariffs, governmentally fixed prices and wages, restrictions on entry into various occupations, and numerous other departures from his "simple system of natural liberty." (Many of these are discussed in later chapters.)

Limited Government in Practice

In today's world big government seems pervasive. We may well ask whether there exist any contemporaneous examples of societies that rely primarily on voluntary exchange through the market to organize their economic activity and in which government is limited to our four duties.

Perhaps the best example is Hong Kong—a speck of land next to mainland China containing less than 400 square miles with a population of roughly 4.5 million people. The density of population is almost unbelievable—14 times as many people per square mile as in Japan, 185 times as many as in the United States. Yet they enjoy one of the highest standards of living in all of Asia—second only to Japan and perhaps Singapore.

Hong Kong has no tariffs or other restraints on international trade (except for a few "voluntary" restraints imposed by the United States and some other major countries). It has no government direction of economic activity, no minimum wage laws, no fixing of prices. The residents are free to buy from whom they want, to sell to whom they want, to invest however they want, to hire whom they want, to work for whom they want.

Government plays an important role that is limited primarily to our four duties interpreted rather narrowly. It enforces law and order, provides a means for formulating the rules of conduct, adjudicates disputes, facilitates transportation and communication, and supervises the issuance of currency. It has provided public housing for arriving refugees from China. Though government spending has grown as the economy has grown, it remains among the lowest in the world as a fraction of the income of the people. As a result, low taxes preserve incentives. Businessmen can reap the benefits of their success but must also bear the costs of their mistakes.

It is somewhat ironic that Hong Kong, a Crown colony of Great Britain, should be the modern exemplar of free markets and limited government. The British officials who govern it have enabled Hong Kong to flourish by following policies radically at variance with the welfare state policies that have been adopted by the mother country.

Though Hong Kong is an excellent current example, it is by no means the most important example of limited government and free market societies in practice. For this we must go back in time to the nineteenth century. One example, Japan in the first thirty years after the Meiji Restoration in 1867, we leave for Chapter 2.

Two other examples are Great Britain and the United States. Adam Smith's *Wealth of Nations* was one of the early blows in the battle to end government restrictions on industry and trade. The final victory in that battle came seventy years later, in 1846, with the repeal of the so-called Corn Laws—laws that imposed tariffs and other restrictions on the importation of wheat and other grains, referred to collectively as "corn." That ushered in three-quarters of a century of complete free trade lasting until the outbreak of World War I and completed a transition that had begun decades earlier to a highly limited government, one that left every resident of Britain, in Adam Smith's words quoted earlier, "perfectly free to pursue his own interest his own way, and to bring both his industry and capital into competition with those of any other man, or order of men."

Economic growth was rapid. The standard of life of the ordinary citizen improved dramatically—making all the more visible the remaining areas of poverty and misery portrayed so movingly by Dickens and other contemporary novelists. Population increased along with the standard of life. Britain grew in power and influence around the world. All this while government spending fell as a fraction of national income—from close to one-quarter of the national income early in the nineteenth century to about one-tenth of national income at the time of Queen Victoria's Jubilee in 1897, when Britain was at the very apex of its power and glory.

The United States is another striking example. There were tariffs, justified by Alexander Hamilton in his famous *Report on Manufactures* in which he attempted—with a decided lack of success—to refute Adam Smith's arguments in favor of free trade. But they were modest, by modern standards, and few other government restrictions impeded free trade at home or abroad. Until after World War I immigration was almost completely free (there were restrictions on immigration from the Orient). As the Statue of Liberty inscription has it:

Give me your tired, your poor,
Your huddled masses yearning to breathe free,
The wretched refuse of your teeming shore.
Send these, the homeless, tempest-tossed to me:
I lift my lamp beside the golden door.

They came by the millions, and by the millions they were absorbed. They prospered because they were left to their own devices.

A myth has grown up about the United States that paints the nineteenth century as the era of the robber baron, of rugged, unrestrained individualism. Heartless monopoly capitalists allegedly exploited the poor, encouraged immigration, and then fleeced the immigrants unmercifully. Wall Street is pictured as conning Main Street, as bleeding the sturdy farmers in the Middle West, who survived despite the widespread distress and misery inflicted on them.

The reality was very different. Immigrants kept coming. The early ones might have been fooled, but it is inconceivable that millions kept coming to the United States decade after decade to be exploited. They came because the hopes of those who had preceded them were largely realized. The streets of New York were not paved with gold, but hard work, thrift, and enterprise brought rewards that were not even imaginable in the Old World. The newcomers spread from east to west. As they spread, cities sprang up, ever more land was brought into cultivation. The country grew more prosperous and more productive, and the immigrants shared in the prosperity.

If farmers were exploited, why did their number increase? The prices of farm products did decline. But that was a sign of success, not of failure, reflecting the development of machinery, the bringing under cultivation of more land, and improvements in communication, all of which led to a rapid growth in farm output. The final proof is that the price of farmland rose steadily—hardly a sign that farming was a depressed industry!

The charge of heartlessness, epitomized in the remark that William H. Vanderbilt, a railroad tycoon, is said to have made to an inquiring reporter, "The public be damned," is belied by the flowering of charitable activity in the United States in the nineteenth century. Privately financed schools and colleges multiplied; foreign missionary activity exploded; nonprofit private hospitals, orphanages, and numerous other institutions sprang up like weeds. Almost every charitable or public service organization, from the Society for the Prevention of Cruelty to Animals to the YMCA and YWCA, from the Indian Rights Association to the Salvation Army, dates from that period. Voluntary cooperation is no less effective in organizing charitable activity than in organizing production for profit.

The charitable activity was matched by a burst of cultural activity—art museums, opera houses, symphonies, museums, public libraries arose in big cities and frontier towns alike.

The size of government spending is one measure of government's role. Major wars aside, government spending from 1800 to 1929 did not exceed about 12 percent of the national income. Two-thirds of that was spent by state and local governments, mostly for schools and roads. As late as 1928, federal government spending amounted to about 3 percent of the national income.

The success of the United States is often attributed to its generous natural resources and wide open spaces. They certainly played a part—but then, if they were crucial, what explains the success of nineteenth-century Great Britain and Japan or twentieth-century Hong Kong?

It is often maintained that while a let-alone, limited government policy was feasible in sparsely settled nineteenth-century America, government must play a far larger, indeed dominant, role in a modern urbanized and industrial society. One hour in Hong Kong will dispose of that view.

Our society is what we make it. We can shape our institutions. Physical and human characteristics limit the alternatives available to us. But none prevents us, if we will, from building a society that relies primarily on voluntary cooperation to organize both economic and other activity, a society that preserves and expands human freedom, that keeps government in its place, keeping it our servant and not letting it become our master.

NOTES

INDIVIDUAL AND SOCIAL NARCISSISM
Erich Fromm

(1900–1980)

Erich Fromm was a German-born psychoanalyst and social philosopher who believed that most human behavior is a learned response to social conditions.

One of the most fruitful and far-reaching of Freud's discoveries is his concept of narcissism. Freud himself considered it to be one of his most important findings, and employed it for the understanding of such distinct phenomena as psychosis ("narcissistic neurosis"), love, castration fear, jealousy, sadism, and also for the understanding of mass phenomena, such as the readiness of the suppressed classes to be loyal to their rulers. In this chapter I want to continue along Freud's line of thought and examine the role of narcissism for the understanding of nationalism, national hatred, and the psychological motivations for destructiveness and war . . .

. . . What is the development of narcissism in the "normal" person? Freud sketched the main lines of this development, and the following paragraph is a short summary of his findings.

The fetus in the womb still lives in a state of absolute narcissism. "By being born", says Freud, "we have made the step from an absolutely self-sufficient narcissism to the perception of a changing external world and the beginning of the discovery of objects,"[1] It takes months before the infant can even perceive objects outside as such, as being part of the "not me." By many blows to the child's narcissism, his ever increasing acquaintance with the outside world and its laws, thus of "necessity," man develops his original narcissism into "object love." But, says Freud, "a human being remains to some extent narcissistic even after he has found external objects for his libido."[2] Indeed, the development of the individual can be defined in Freud's term as the evolution from absolute narcissism to a capacity for objective reasoning and object love, a capacity, however, which does not transcend definite limitations. The "normal," "mature" person is one whose narcissism has been reduced to the socially accepted minimum without ever disappearing completely. Freud's observation is confirmed by everyday experience. It seems that in most people one can find a narcissistic core which is not accessible and which defies any attempt at complete dissolution.

Those not sufficiently acquainted with Freud's technical language will probably not obtain a distinct idea of the reality and power of narcissism, unless some more concrete description of the phenomenon is forthcoming. This I shall try to give in the following pages. Before I do so, however, I wish to clarify something about the terminology. Freud's views on narcissism are based

Reprinted from *The Heart of Man: Its Genius for Good and Evil* (1964), American Mental Health Foundation, Inc.

on his concept of sexual libido. As I have already indicated, this mechanistic libido concept proved more to block than to further the development of the concept of narcissism. I believe that the possibilities of bringing it to its full fruition are much greater if one uses a concept of psychic energy which is not identical with the energy of the *sexual* drive. This was done by Jung; it even found some initial recognition in Freud's idea of desexualized libido. But although nonsexual psychic energy differs from Freud's libido it is, like libido an *energy* concept; it deals with psychic forces, visible only through their manifestations, which have a certain intensity and a certain direction. This energy binds, unifies and holds together the individual within himself as well as the individual in his relationship to the world outside. Even if one does not agree with Freud in his earlier view that aside from the drive for survival, the energy of the sexual instinct (libido) is the only important motive power for human conduct, and if one uses instead a general concept of psychic energy, the difference is not as great as many who think in dogmatic terms are prone to believe. The essential point on which any theory or therapy which could be called psychoanalysis depends, is the *dynamic* concept of human behavior; that is, the assumption that highly charged forces motivate behavior, and that behavior can be understood and predicted only by understanding these forces. This dynamic concept of human behavior is the center of Freud's system. How these forces are theoretically conceived, whether in terms of a mechanistic-materialistic philosophy or in terms of humanistic realism, is an important question but one which is secondary to the central issue of the dynamic interpretation of human behavior.

Let us begin our description of narcissism with two extreme examples: the "primary narcissism" of the newborn infant, and the narcissism of the insane person. The infant is not yet related to the outside world (in Freudian terminology his libido has not yet cathexed outside objects). Another way of putting it is to say that the outside world does not exist for the infant, and this to such a degree that it is not able to distinguish between the "I" and the "not I". We might also say that the infant is not "interested" (inter-esse = "to be in") in the world outside. The only reality that exists for the infant is itself: its body, its physical sensations of cold and warmth, thirst, need for sleep and bodily contact.

The insane person is in a situation not essentially different from that of the infant. But while for the infant the world outside has *not yet emerged* as real, for the insane person it *has ceased* to be real. In the case of hallucinations, for instance, the senses have lost their function of registering outside events—they register subjective experience in categories of sensory response to objects outside. In the paranoid delusion the same mechanism operates. Fear or suspicion, for instance, which are subjective emotions, become objectified in such a way that the paranoid person is convinced that others are conspiring against him; this is precisely the difference to the neurotic person: the latter may be constantly afraid of being hated, persecuted, etc., but he still knows that this is what he *fears*. For the paranoid person the fear has been transformed into a fact.

A particular instance of narcissism which lies on the borderline between sanity and insanity can be found in some men who have reached an extraordinary degree of power. The Egyptian pharaohs, the Roman Caesars, the Borgias, Hitler, Stalin, Trujillo—they all show certain similar features. They have attained absolute power: their word is the ultimate judgment of everything, including life and death; there seems to be no limit to their capacity to do what they want. They are gods, limited only by illness, age and death. They try to find a solution to the problem of human existence by the desperate attempt to transcend the limitation of human existence. They try to pretend that there is no limit to their lust and to their power, so they sleep with countless women, they kill numberless men, they build castles everywhere, they "want the moon", they "want the impossible."[3] This is madness, even though it is an attempt to solve the problem of existence by pretending that one is not human. It is a madness which tends to grow in the lifetime of the afflicted person. The more he tries to be god, the more he isolates himself from the human race; this isolation makes him more frightened, everybody becomes his enemy, and in order to stand the resulting fright he has to increase his power, his ruthlessness, and his narcissism. This Caesarian madness would be nothing but plain insanity were it not for one factor: by his power Caesar has bent reality to his narcissistic fantasies. He has forced everybody to agree that he is god, the most powerful and the wisest of men—hence his own megalomania seems to be a reasonable feeling. On the other hand, many will hate him, try to overthrow and kill him—hence his pathological suspicions are also backed by a nucleus of reality. As a result he does not feel disconnected from reality—hence he can keep a modicum of sanity, even though in a precarious state.

Psychosis is a state of absolute narcissism, one in which the person has broken all connection with reality outside, and has made his own person the substitute for reality. He is entirely filled with himself, he has become "god and the world" to himself. It is precisely this insight by which Freud for the first time opened the way to the dynamic understanding of the nature of psychosis.

However, for those who are not familiar with psychosis it is necessary to give a picture of narcissism as it is found in neurotic or "normal" persons. One of the most elementary examples of narcissism can be found in the average person's attitude toward his own body. Most people like their own body, their face, their figure, and when asked whether they would want to change with another perhaps more handsome person, very definitely say no. Even more telling is the fact that most people do not mind at all the sight or smell of their own feces (in fact, some like them), while they have a definite aversion for those of other people. Quite obviously there is no aesthetic or other judgment involved here; the same thing which when connected with one's own body is pleasant, is unpleasant when connected with somebody else's . . .

. . . Let us look at two phenomena which are apparently extremely different, and yet both of which are narcissistic. A woman spends many hours every day before the mirror to fix her hair and face. It is not simply that she is vain. She is obsessed with her body and her beauty, and her body is the only important reality she knows. She comes perhaps nearest to the Greek legend which speaks of Narcissus, a beautiful lad who rejected the love of the nymph Echo, who died of a broken heart. Nemesis punished him by making him fall in love with the reflection of his own image in the water of the lake; in self-admiration he fell into the lake and died. The Greek legend indicates clearly that this kind of "self-love" is a curse, and that in its extreme form it ends in self-destruction.[4] Another woman (and it could well be the same one some years later) suffers from hypochondriasis. She is also constantly preoccupied with her body although not in the sense of making it beautiful, but in fearing illness. Why the positive, or the negative, image is chosen has, of course, its reasons; however, we need not deal with these here. What matters is that behind both phenomena lies the same preoccupation with oneself, with little interest left for the outside world.

. . . How does one recognize the narcissistic person? There is one type which is easily recognized. That is the kind of person who shows all the signs of self-satisfaction; one can see that when he says some trivial words he feels as if he has said something of great importance. He usually does not listen to what others say, nor is he really interested. (If he is clever, he will try to hide this fact by asking questions and making it a point to seem interested.) One can also recognize the narcissistic person by his sensitivity to any kind of criticism. This sensitivity can be expressed by denying the validity of any criticism, or by reacting with anger or depression. In many instances the narcissistic orientation may be hidden behind an attitude of modesty and humility; in fact, it is not rare for a person's narcissistic orientation to take his humility as the object of his self-admiration. Whatever the different manifestations of narcissism are, a lack of genuine interest in the outside world is common to all forms of narcissism.[5]

Sometimes the narcissistic person can also be recognized by his facial expression. Often we find a kind of glow or smile, which gives the impression of smugness to some, of beatific, trusting, childlikeness to others. Often the narcissism, especially in its most extreme forms, manifests itself in a peculiar glitter in the eyes, taken by some as a symptom of half-saintliness, by others of half-craziness. Many very narcissistic persons talk incessantly—often at a meal, where they forget to eat and thus make everyone else wait. Company or food are less important than their "ego."

The narcissistic person has not even necessarily taken his whole person as the object of his narcissism. Often he has cathexed a partial aspect of his personality with his narcissism; for instance, his honor, his intelligence, his physical prowess, his wit, his good looks (sometimes even narrowed down to such details as his hair or his nose). Sometimes his narcissism refers to qualities about which normally a person would not be proud, such as his capacity to be afraid and thus to foretell danger. "He" becomes identified with a partial aspect of himself. If we ask who "he" is, the proper answer would be that "he" is his brain, his fame, his wealth, his penis, his conscience, and so on. All the idols of the various religions represent so many partial aspects of man. In the narcissistic person the object of his narcissism is any one of these partial qualities which constitute for him his self. The one whose self is represented by his property can take very well a threat to his dignity, but a threat to his property is like a threat to his life. On the other hand, for the one whose self is represented by his intelligence, the fact of having said something stupid is so painful that it may result in a mood of serious depression. However, the more intense the narcissism is, the less will the narcissistic person accept the fact of failure on his side, or any legitimate criticism from others. He will just feel outraged by the insulting behavior of the other person, or believe that the other person is too insensitive, uneducated, etc., to have proper judgment. (I think, in this connection, of a brilliant, yet highly narcissistic man who, when confronted with the results of a Rorschach test he had taken and which fell short of the ideal picture he had of himself, said, "I am sorry for the psychologist who did this test: he must be very paranoid.")

We must now mention one other factor which complicates the phenomenon of narcissism. Just as the narcissistic person has made his "self-image" the object of his narcissistic attachment, he does the same with everything connected with him. *His* ideas, *his* knowledge, *his* house, but also people in *his* "sphere of interest" become objects of his narcissistic attachment. As Freud pointed out, the most frequent example is probably the narcissistic attachment to one's children. Many parents believe that their own children are the most beautiful, intelligent, etc., in comparison with other children. It seems that the younger the children are, the more intense is this narcissistic bias. The parents' love, and especially the mother's love for the infant, is to a considerable extent love for the infant as an extension of oneself. Adult love between man and woman also has often a narcissistic quality. The man who is in love with a woman may transfer his narcissism to her once she has become "his." He admires and worships her for qualities which he has conferred upon her; precisely because of her being part of him, she becomes the bearer of extraordinary qualities. Such a man will often also think that all things he possesses are extraordinarily wonderful, and he will be "in love" with them.

Narcissism is a passion the intensity of which in many individuals can only be compared with sexual desire and the desire to stay alive. In fact, many times it proves to be stronger than either. Even in the average individual in whom it does not reach such intensity, there remains a narcissistic core which appears to be almost indestructible. This being so we might suspect that like sex and survival, the narcissistic passion also has an important *biological function.* Once we raise this question the answer comes readily. How could the individual survive unless his bodily needs, his interests, his desires, were charged with much energy? Biologically, from the standpoint of survival, man must attribute to himself an importance far above what he gives to anybody else. If he did not do so, from where would he take the energy and interest to defend himself against other, to work for his subsistence, to fight for his survival, to press his claims against those of others? Without narcissism he might be a saint—but do saints have a high survival rate? What from a spiritual standpoint would be most desirable—absence of narcissism—would be most dangerous from the mundane standpoint of survival. Speaking teleologically, we can say that nature had to endow man with a great amount of narcissism to enable him to do what is necessary for survival. This is true especially because nature has not endowed man with well-developed instincts such as the animal has. The animal has no "problems" of survival in the sense that its built-in instinctive nature takes care of survival in such a way that the animal does not have to consider or decide whether or not it wants to make an effort. In man the instinctive apparatus has lost most of its efficacy—hence narcissism assumes a very necessary biological function.

However, once we recognize that narcissism fulfills an important biological function, we are confronted with another question. Does not extreme narcissism have the function of making man indifferent to others, incapable of giving second place to his own needs when this is necessary for co-operation with others? Does not narcissism make man asocial and, in fact, when it reaches an extreme degree, insane? There can be no doubt that extreme individual narcissism would be a severe obstacle to all social life. But if this is so, narcissism must be said to be in *conflict* with the principle of survival, for the individual can survive only if he organizes himself in groups; hardly anyone would be able to protect himself all alone against the dangers of nature, nor would he be able to do many kinds of work which can only be done in groups.

We arrive then at the paradoxical result that narcissism is necessary for survival, and at the same time that it is a threat to survival. The solution of this paradox lies in two directions. One is that *optimal* rather than *maximal* narcissism serves survival: that is to say, the biologically necessary degree of narcissism is reduced to the degree of narcissism that is compatible with social co-operation. The other lies in the fact that individual narcissism is transformed into group narcissism, that the clan, nation, religion, race, etc., become the objects of narcissistic passion instead of the individual. Thus, narcissistic energy is maintained but used in the interests of the survival of the group rather than for the survival of the individual . . .

. . . There is, however, still another solution to the threat to narcissism which is more satisfactory to the individual, although more dangerous to others. This solution consists in the attempt to transform reality in such a way as to make it conform, to some extent, with his narcissistic self-image. An example of this is the narcissistic inventor who believes he has invented a *perpetuum mobile,* and who in the process has made a minor discovery of some significance. A more important solution consists in getting the consensus of one other person, and, if possible, in obtaining the consensus of millions. The former case is that of a *folie à deux* (some marriages and friendships rest on this basis), while the latter is that of public figures who prevent the open outbreak of their potential psychosis by gaining the acclaim and consensus of millions of people. The best-known example for this latter case is Hitler. Here was an extremely narcissistic person who probably could have suffered a manifest psychosis had he not succeeded in making millions believe in his won self-image, take his grandiose fantasies regarding the millennium of the

"Third Reich" seriously, and even transforming reality in such a way that it seemed proved to his followers that he was right. (After he had failed he had to kill himself since otherwise the collapse of his narcissist image would have been truly unbearable.)

There are other examples in history of megalomaniac leaders who "cured" their narcissism by transforming the world to fit it; such people must also try to destroy all critics, since they cannot tolerate the threat which the voice of sanity constitutes for them. From Caligula and Nero to Stalin and Hitler we see that their need to find believers, to transform reality so that it fits their narcissism, and to destroy all critics, is so intense and so desperate precisely because it is an attempt to prevent the outbreak of insanity. Paradoxically, the element of insanity in such leaders makes them also successful. It gives them that certainty and freedom from doubt which is so impressive to the average person. Needless to say, this need to change the world and to win others to share in one's ideas and delusions requires also talents and gifts which the average person, psychotic or nonpsychotic, lacks.

In discussing the pathology of narcissism it is important to distinguish between two forms of narcissism—one *benign,* the other *malignant.* In the benign form, the object of narcissism is the result of a person's effort. Thus, for instance, a person may have a narcissistic pride in his work as a carpenter, as a scientist, or as a farmer. Inasmuch as the object of his narcissism is something he has to work for, his exclusive interest in what is *his* work and *his* achievement is constantly balanced by his interest in the process of work itself, and the material he is working with. The dynamics of this benign narcissism thus are self-checking. The energy which propels the work is, to a large extent, of a narcissistic nature, but the very fact that the work itself makes it necessary to be related to reality, constantly curbs the narcissism and keeps it within bounds. This mechanism may explain why we find so many narcissistic people who are at the same time highly creative.

In the case of malignant narcissism, the object of narcissism is not anything the person does or produces, but something he *has,* for instance, his body, his looks, his health, his wealth, etc. The malignant nature of this type of narcissism lies in the fact that it lacks the corrective element which we find in the benign form. If I am "great" because of some quality I *have,* and not because of something I *achieve,* I do not need to be related to anybody or anything; I need not make any effort. In maintaining the picture of my greatness I remove myself more and more from reality and I have to increase the narcissistic charge in order to be better protected from the danger that my narcissistically inflated ego might be revealed as the product of my empty imagination. Malignant narcissism, thus, is not self-limiting, and in consequence it is crudely solipsistic as well as xenophobic. One who has learned to achieve cannot help acknowledging that others have achieved similar things in similar ways—even if his narcissism may persuade him that his own achievement is greater than that of others. One who has achieved nothing will find it difficult to appreciate the achievements of others, and thus he will be forced to isolate himself increasingly in narcissistic splendor.

We have so far described the dynamics of individual narcissism: the phenomenon, its biological function, and its pathology. This description ought to enable us now to understand the phenomenon of *social narcissism* and the role it plays as a source of violence and war.

The central point of the following discussion is the phenomenon of the transformation of personal into group narcissism. We can start with an observation about the sociological function of group narcissism which parallels the biological function of individual narcissism. From the standpoint of any organized group which wants to survive, it is important that the group be invested by its members with narcissistic energy. The survival of a group depends to some extent on the fact that its members consider its importance as great as or greater than that of their own lives, and furthermore that they believe in the righteousness, or even superiority, of their group as compared with others. Without such narcissistic cathexis of the group, the energy necessary for serving the group, or even making severe sacrifices for it, would be greatly diminished.

In the dynamics of group narcissism we find phenomena similar to those we discussed already in connection with individual narcissism. Here too we can distinguish between benign and malignant forms of narcissism. If the object of group narcissism is an achievement, the same dialectical process takes place which we discussed above. The very need to achieve something creative makes it necessary to leave the closed circle of group solipsism and to be interested in the object it wants to achieve. (If the achievement which a group seeks is conquest, the beneficial effect of truly productive effort will of course be largely absent.) If, on the other hand, group narcissism has as its object the group as it is, its splendor, its past achievements, the physique of its members, then the countertendencies mentioned above will not develop and the narcissistic orientation and subsequent dangers will steadily increase. In reality, of course, both elements are often blended.

There is another sociological function of group narcissism which has not been discussed so far. A society which lacks the means to provide adequately for the majority of its members, or a large proportion of them, must provide these members with a narcissistic satisfaction of the malignant type if it wants to prevent dissatisfaction among them. For those who are economically and culturally poor, narcissistic pride in belonging to the group is the only—and often a very effective—source of satisfaction. Precisely because life is not "interesting" to them, and does not offer them possibilities for developing interests, they may develop an extreme form of narcissism. Good examples of this phenomenon in recent years are the racial narcissism which existed in Hitler's Germany, and which is found in the American South today. In both instances the core of the racial superiority feeling was, and still is, the lower middle class; this backward class, which in Germany as well as in the American South has been economically and culturally deprived, without any realistic hope of changing its situation (because they are the remnants of an older and dying form of society) has only one satisfaction: the inflated image of itself as the most admirable group in the world, and of being superior to another racial group that is singled out as inferior. The member of such a backward group feels: "Even though I am poor and uncultured I am somebody important because I belong to the most admirable group in the world—I am white"; or, "I am an Aryan."

Group narcissism is less easy to recognize than individual narcissism. Assuming a person tells others, "I (and my family) are the most admirable people in the world; we alone are clean, intelligent, good, decent; all others are dirty, stupid, dishonest and irresponsible," most people would think him crude, unbalanced, or even insane. If, however, a fanatical speaker addresses a mass audience, substituting the nation (or race, religion, political party, etc.) for the "I" and "my family," he will be praised and admired by many for his love of country, love of God, etc. Other nations and religions, however, will resent such a speech for the obvious reason that they are held in contempt. *Within* the favored group, however, everybody's personal narcissism is flattered and the fact that millions of people agree with the statements makes them appear as reasonable. (What the majority of people consider to be "reasonable" is that about which there is agreement, if not among all, at least among a substantial number of people; "reasonable," for most people, has nothing to do with reason, but with consensus.) Inasmuch as the group as a whole requires group narcissism for its survival, it will further narcissistic attitudes and confer upon them the qualification of being particularly virtuous.

The group to which the narcissistic attitude is extended has varied in structure and size throughout history. In the primitive tribe or clan it may comprise only a few hundred members; here the individual is not yet an "individual" but is still united to the blood group by "primary bonds"[6] which have not yet been broken. The narcissistic involvement with the clan is thus strengthened by the fact that its members emotionally have still no existence of their own outside of the clan.

In the development of the human race we find an ever increasing range of socialization; the original small group based on blood affinity gives way to ever larger groups based on a common language, a common social order, a common faith. The larger size of the group does not necessarily mean that the pathological qualities of narcissism are reduced. As was remarked earlier, the group narcissism of the "whites" or the "Aryans" is as malignant as the extreme narcissism of a single person can be. Yet in general we find that in the process of socialization which leads to the formation of larger groups, the need for cooperation with many other and different people not connected among themselves by ties of blood, tends to counteract the narcissistic charge within the group. The same holds true in another respect, which we have discussed in connection with benign individual narcissism: Inasmuch as the large group (nation, state, or religion) makes it an object of its narcissistic pride to achieve something valuable in the fields of material, intellectual, or artistic production, the very process of work in such fields tends to lessen the narcissistic charge. The history of the Roman Catholic Church is one of many examples of the peculiar mixture of narcissism and the counteracting forces within a large group. The elements counteracting narcissism within the Catholic Church are, first of all, the concept of the universality of man and of a "catholic" religion which is no longer the religion of one particular tribe or nation. Second, the idea of personal humility which follows from the idea of God and the denial of idols. The existence of God implies that no man can be God, that no individual can be omniscient or omnipotent. It thus sets a definite limit to man's narcissistic self-idolatry. But at the same time the Church has nourished an intense narcissism; believing that the Church is the only chance of salvation and that the Pope is the Vicar of Christ, its members were able to develop an intense narcissism inasmuch as they were members of such an extraordinary institution. The same occurred in relation to God; while the omniscience and omnipotence of God should have led to man's humility, often the individual identified himself with God and thus developed an extraordinary degree of narcissism in this process of identification.

This same ambiguity between a narcissistic or an antinarcissistic function has occurred in all the other great religions, for example, in Buddhism, Judaism, Islam, and Protestantism. I have mentioned the Catholic religion not only because it is a well-known example, but mainly because the Roman Catholic religion was the basis both for humanism and for violent and fanatical religious narcissism at one and the same historical period: the fifteenth and sixteenth centuries. The humanists within the Church and those outside spoke in the name of a humanism which was the fountainhead of Christianity . . .

. . . Looking back to the religious hatred of the sixteenth and seventeenth centuries, its irrationalities are clear. Both sides spoke in the name of God, of Christ, of love, and they differed only in points which, if compared with the general principles, were of secondary importance. Yet they hated each other, and each was passionately convinced that humanity ended at the frontiers of his own religious faith. The essence of this over-estimation of ones' own position and the hate for all who differ from it is narcissism. "We" are admirable; "they" are despicable. "We are good; "they" are evil. Any criticism of one's own doctrine is a vicious and unbearable attack; criticism of the others' position is a well-meant attempt to help them to return to the truth.

From the Renaissance onward, the two great contradictory forces, group narcissism and humanism, have each developed in its own way. Unfortunately the development of group narcissism has vastly outstripped that of humanism. While it seemed possible in the late Middle Ages and at the time of the Renaissance that Europe was prepared for the emergence of a political and religious humanism, this promise failed to materialize. New forms of group narcissism emerged, and dominated the following centuries. This group narcissism assumed manifold forms: religious, national, racial, political. Protestants against Catholics, French against Germans, whites against blacks, Aryans against non-Aryans, Communists against capitalists; different as the contents are, psychologically we deal with the same narcissistic phenomenon and its resulting fanaticism and destructiveness.[7]

While group narcissism grew, its counterpart—humanism—also developed. In the eighteenth and nineteenth centuries—from Spinoza, Leibniz, Rousseau, Herder, Kant, to Goethe and Marx—the thought developed that mankind is one, that each individual carries within himself all of humanity, that there must be no privileged groups claiming that their privileges are based in their intrinsic superiority . . .

. . . As a reaction to this threat to humanity, a renaissance of humanism can be observed today in all countries and among the representatives of diverse ideologies; there are radical humanists among Catholic and Protestant theologians, among socialist and nonsocialist philosophers. Whether the danger of total destruction, the ideas of the neohumanists and the bonds created between all men by the new means of communication will be sufficient to stop the effects of group narcissism is a question which may determine the fate of mankind . . .

ENDNOTES

1. Freud, *Group Psychology* (Standard Edition), Vol. XVIII, p. 130.
2. Freud, *Totem and Taboo* (Standard Edition), Vol. XIII, p. 89.
3. Camus, in his drama *Caligula,* has portrayed this madness of power most accurately.
4. Cf. my discussion of self-love in *Man for Himself.* I try to show there that true love for self is not different from love for others; that "self-love" in the sense of egoistic, narcissistic love is to be found in those who can love neither others nor themselves.
5. Sometimes it is not easy to distinguish between the vain, narcissistic person and one with a low self-evaluation; the latter often is in need of praise and admiration, not because he is not interested in anyone else, but because of his self-doubts and low self-evaluation. There is another important distinction which is also not always easy to make: that between narcissism and egotism. Intense narcissism implies an inability to experience reality in its fullness; intense egotism implies to have little concern, love or sympathy for others but it does not necessarily imply the overevaluation of one's subjective processes. In other words the extreme egotist is not necessarily extremely narcissistic; selfishness is not necessarily blindness to objective reality.
6. Cf. the discussion of primary bonds in E. Fromm, *Escape From Freedom* (New York: Holt, Rinehart & Winston, 1941).
7. There are other more harmless forms of group narcissism directed toward small groups like lodges, small religious sects, "the old school tie," etc. While the degree of narcissism in these cases may not be less than in chose of the larger groups, the narcissism is less dangerous simply because the groups involved have little power, and hence little capacity to cause harm.

NOTES

INVICTUS
William Ernest Henley

(1849–1903)

William Ernest Henley was an English poet, editor, and critic. At age twelve he was diagnosed with tubercular arthritis that resulted in the amputation of one of his legs below the knee. While recuperating, he began writing poems, including "Invictus." He was a good friend of author Robert Louis Stevenson, who supposedly based his Treasure Island *character John Long Silver partly on Henley.*

Out of the night that covers me,
Black as the Pit from pole to pole,
I thank whatever gods may be
For my unconquerable soul.

In the fell clutch of circumstance
I have not winced nor cried aloud.
Under the bludgeonings of chance
My head is bloody, but unbowed.

Beyond this place of wrath and tears
Looms but the Horror of the shade,
And yet the menace of the years
Finds, and shall find, me unafraid.

It matters not how strait the gate,
How charged with punishments the scroll.
I am the master of my fate:
I am the captain of my soul.

NOTES

Are there certain horizontal or vertical heritages that make people more prone to narcissism?

CONQUERING SELF-CENTEREDNESS
The Reverend Martin Luther King, Jr.

(1929–1968)

An African-American Baptist minister, Martin Luther King, Jr. was the principal leader of the civil rights movement in the United States in the 1950s and 1960s. His eloquent speaking style and determined demands for social justice earned him international renown and the support of millions of blacks and whites in this country. Though he was often the target of violence himself, he continued to lead nonviolent civil rights demonstrations for which he won the 1964 Nobel Peace Prize. While organizing the Poor People's Campaign, he traveled to Memphis to take part in a black garbage workers' strike. He was shot and killed there by the white, escaped convict, James Earl Ray.

Sermon Delivered at Dexter Avenue Baptist Church

[11 August 1957]
Montgomery, Ala.

I want to continue the series of sermons this morning that I started several weeks ago. The series dealing with problems of personality integration. This morning our subject is: "Conquering Self-Centeredness." . . . . An individual has not begun to live until he can rise above the narrow horizons of his particular individualistic concerns to the broader concerns of all humanity. And this is one of the big problems of life; that so many people never quite get to the point of rising above self. And so they end up the tragic victims of self-centeredness. They end up the victims of distorted and disrupted personality.

Life has its beginning and its maturity comes into being when an individual rises above self to something greater. Few individuals learn this. And so they go through life merely existing and never living. Now you see signs all along in your everyday life with individuals who are the victims of self-centeredness. They are the people who live an eternal "I." They do not have the capacity to project the "I" into the "Thou." They do not have the mental equipment for an eternal, dangerous and sometimes costly altruism. They live a life of perpetual egotism. And they are the victims all around of the egocentric predicament. They start out, the minute you talk with them, talking about what they can do, what they have done. They're the people who will tell you, before you talk with them five minutes, where they have been and who they know. They're the people who can tell you in a few seconds, how many degrees they have and where they went to school and how much money they have. We meet these people every day. And so this is not a foreign subject. It is not something far off. It is a problem that meets us in everyday life. We meet it in ourselves, we meet in other selves: the problem of self-centeredness.

Now, we can say to a certain extent that persons in this situation are persons who have really never grown up. They are still children, at a point. For you see, a child is inevitably, necessarily egocentric. He is a bundle of his own sensations, clamoring to be cared for. And, to be sure, he has his own social context. He belongs to his mother but he cares for her only because he wants to be fed and protected. He does not care for his mother for her sake but he cares for his mother for his own sake. And so a child is inevitably egocentric, inevitably self-centered. And that is why Dr. Burnham says that during the first six or seven years of development, the ego is dominant within the child. And both in behavior and in attitudes, a child is a victim of self-centeredness. This is a part of the early development of a little child. When people become mature, they are to rise above this. I look at my little daughter every day and she wants certain things and when she wants them, she wants them. And she almost cries out, "I want what I want when I want it." She is not concerned about what I think about it or what Mrs. King thinks about it. She wants it. She's a child and that's very natural and normal for a child. She is inevitably self-centered because she's a child.

But when one matures, when one rises above the early years of childhood, he begins to love people for their own sake. He turns himself to higher loyalties. He gives himself to something outside of himself. He gives himself to causes that he lives for and sometimes will even die for. He comes to the point that now he can rise above his individualistic concerns . . . And so you see people who are apparently selfish; it isn't merely an ethical issue but it is a psychological issue. They are the victims of arrested development and they are still children. They haven't grown up. And like a modern novelist says about one of his characters, "Edith is a little country, bounded on the east and the west, on the north and the south, by Edith." And so many people are little countries, bounded all around by themselves and they never quite get out of themselves. And these are the persons who are victimized with arrested development.

Now the consequences, the disruptive effects of such self-centeredness, such egocentric desires are tragic. And we see these every day. At first, it leads to frustration and disillusionment and unhappiness at many points. For usually when people are self-centered, they are self-centered because they are seeking attention, they want to be admired and this is the way they set out to do it. But in the process, because of their self-centeredness, they are not admired; they are mawkish and people don't want to be bothered with them. And so the very thing they seek, they never get. And they end up frustrated and unhappy and disillusioned.

I'm sure you have seen people in life who are so desirous of gaining attention that if they cannot have and gain attention through normal channels, through normal social channels, they will gain it through anti-social means. There are those people who are so desirous of gaining attention that if everybody says, "Yes," they automatically say, "No," in order to be seen and to be heard. They are so self-centered that they must gain attention and they must be seen in order to survive. They want to be admired and in their quest for admiration, they don't gain it and in their failure to gain it, they become frustrated and bewildered and disillusioned.

Also, it leads to extreme sensitiveness. The individual who is self-centered, the individual who is egocentric ends up being very sensitive, a very touchy person. And that is one of the tragic effects of a self-centered attitude, that it leads to a very sensitive and touchy response toward the universe. These are the people you have to handle with kid gloves because they are touchy, they are sensitive. And they are sensitive because they are self-centered. They are too absorbed in self and anything gets them off, anything makes them angry. Anything makes them feel that people are looking over them because of a tragic self-centeredness. That even leads to the point that the individual is not capable of facing trouble and the hard moments of life. One can become so self-centered, so egocentric that when the hard and difficult moments of life come, he cannot face them because he's too centered in himself. These are the people who cannot face disappointment. These are the people who cannot face being defeated. These are the people who cannot face being criticized. These are the people who cannot face these many experiences of life which inevitably come because they are too centered in themselves. In time, somebody criticizes them, time somebody says something about them that they don't like too well, time they are disappointed, time they are defeated, even in a little game, they end up broken-hearted. They can't stand up under it because they are centered in self.

Then, finally, it can become so morbid that it rises to ominous proportions and leads to a tragic sense of persecution. There are persons who come to the point that they are so self-centered that they end up with a persecution complex and the end result is insanity. They end up thinking that the universe stands against them, that everybody is against them. They are turning around within themselves. They are little solar systems within themselves and they can't see beyond that. As a result of their failure to get out of self, they end up with a persecution complex and sometimes madness and insanity. These are some of the effects of self-centeredness.

Now one will inevitably raise the question: How then do we conquer self-centeredness? How do we get away from this thing that we call self-centeredness? How can we live in this universe with a balance and with a type of perspective that keeps us going smoothly and we are not too absorbed in self? How do we do it? Let me make two or three suggestions and I can assure you that these suggestions will not at all solve the problem. For you will have to solve it, in many points, for yourself. But at least these things, I hope, will give you some guidance.

I think one of the best ways to face this problem of self-centeredness is to discover some cause and some purpose, some loyalty outside of yourself and give yourself to that something. The best way to handle it is not to suppress the ego but to extend the ego into objectively meaningful channels. And so many people are unhappy because they aren't doing anything. They're self-centered because they aren't doing anything. They haven't given themselves to anything and they just move around in their little circles. One of the ways to rise above this self-centeredness is to move away from self and objectify yourself in something outside of yourself. Find some great cause and some great purpose, some loyalty to which you can give yourself and become so absorbed in that something that you give your life to it. Men and women have done this throughout all of the generations. And they have found that necessary ego satisfaction that life presents and that one desires through projecting self in something outside of self. As I said, you don't solve the problem by trying to trample over the ego altogether. That doesn't solve the problem. For you will always have the ego and the ego has certain desires, certain desires for significance. The three great psychoanalysts of this age, of this century pointed out that there are certain basic desires that human beings have and that they long for and that they seek at any cost. And so for Freud the basic desire was to be loved. Jung would say that the basic desire is to be secure. But then Adler comes along and says the basic desire of human nature is to feel important and a sense of significance. And I think of all of those certainly all are significant, but the one that Adler mentions is probably even more significant than any: that all human beings have a desire to belong and to feel significant and important.

And the way to solve this problem is not to drown out the ego but to find your sense of importance in something outside of the self. And you are then able to live because you have given your life to something outside and something that is meaningful, objectified. You rise above this self-absorption to something outside. We look through history. We see that biography's a running commentary of this. . . . We see an Albert Schweitzer who looks at men in dark Africa who have been the victims of colonialism and imperialism and there he gives his life to that. He objectifies himself in this great cause. . . .

This is the way to go through life with a balance, with the proper perspective because you've given yourself to something greater than self. Sometimes it's friends, sometimes it's family, sometimes it's a great cause, it's a great loyalty but give yourself to that something and life becomes meaningful. I've seen people who discovered a great meaning in their jobs and they became so absorbed in that that they didn't have time to become self-centered. They loved their job. . . . And the great prayer that anyone could pray at that point is: "O God, help me to love my job as this individual loves his or hers. O God, help me to give myself to my work and to my job and to my allegiance as this individual does." And this is the way out. And I think this is what [*Ralph Waldo*] Emerson meant when he said: "O, see how the masses of men worry themselves into nameless graves, while here and there, some great unselfish soul forgets himself into immortality." And this becomes a point of balance when you can forget yourself into immortality. You're not so absorbed in self, but you are absorbed in something beyond self.

And there is another way to rise above self-centeredness and that is by having the proper inner attitude toward your position or toward your status in life or whatever it is. You conquer self-centeredness by coming to the point of seeing that you are where you are today because somebody helped you to get there. And so many people, you see, live a self-centered, egocentric life because they have the attitude that they are responsible for everything and for their position in life. For everything they do in life, they feel, somehow, that they are responsible and solely responsible for it.

An individual gets away from this type of self-centeredness when he pauses enough to see that no matter what he does in life, he does that because somebody helped him to do it. And he then gains the type of perspective and the type of balance which keeps him from becoming self-centered. He comes to see that somebody stands in the background, often doing a little job in a big way, making it possible for him to do what he's doing. Can you believe that? That no matter where you stand, no manner how much popularity you have, no matter how much education you have, no matter how much money you have, you have it because somebody in this universe helped you to get it. And when you see that, you can't be arrogant, you can't be supercilious. You discover that you have your position because of the events of history and because of individuals in the background making it possible for you to stand there.

Would you allow me to share a personal experience with you this morning? And I say it only because I think it has bearing on this message. One of the problems that I have to face and even fight every day is this problem of self-centeredness. This tendency that can so easily come to my life now that I'm something special, that I'm something important. Living over the past year, I can hardly go into any city or any town in this nation where I'm not lavished with hospitality by peoples of all races and of all creeds. I can hardly go anywhere to speak in this nation where hundreds and thousands of people are not turned away because of lack of space. And then after speaking, I often have to be rushed out to get away from the crowd rushing for autographs. I can hardly walk the street in any city of this nation where I'm not confronted with people running up the street, "Isn't this Reverend King of Alabama?" Living under this it's easy, it's a dangerous tendency that I will come to feel that I'm something special, that I stand somewhere in this universe because of my ingenuity and that I'm important, that I can walk around life with a type of arrogance because of an importance that I have. . . . And one of the prayers that I pray to God everyday is: . . . . "O God, help me to see that where I stand today, I stand because others helped me to stand there and because the forces of history projected me there. And this moment would have come in history even if M. L. King had never been born." And when we come to see that, we stand with a humility. This is the prayer I pray to God every day, "Lord help me to see M. L. King as M. L. King in his true perspective." Because if I don't see that, I will become the biggest fool in America. . . .

. . . We never get anywhere in this world without the forces of history and individual persons in the background helping us to get there. . . .

. . . And only by seeing this can we rise out. If you have the privilege of a fine education, well, you have it because somebody made it possible. If you have the privilege to gain wealth and a bit of the world's goods, well, you have it because somebody made it possible. So don't boast, don't be arrogant. You, at that moment, rise out of your self-centeredness to the type of living that makes you an integrated personality. . . .

You know, Greek mythology used to talk about the goddess of Nemesis and this was one of the functions of the goddess of Nemesis. The goddess of Nemesis kept everything on a common level. If you got too low, beat down and you didn't feel that you were quite up to par, you felt a sense of inadequacy and a sense of inferiority, this goddess would pull you up. And then, if you got too high for yourself you felt too highly of yourself, you felt too exalted, this goddess would do what the older people used to say, "Pull you a buttonhole lower." And everything was kept on a common level. And there needs to be something in your life of a goddess of Nemesis which pulls you down when you get too high and pulls you up when you feel the sense of inadequacy and that is what religion at its best does. It keeps you to the point that you don't feel like you are too low and you don't feel like you are too high but you'll maintain that type of balance. . . .

And I'm so glad that the new science did something to dampen our arrogant spirits. For a long time, man felt that he was the center of the universe and all of his science had given him that. All of the days in the past he came up under what was known as the geocentric theory: the earth was the center of the universe and everything revolved around the earth. Then came Copernicus and Galileo and others said that the sun is the center, the heliocentric theory came into being. And that reminded us somehow that we are dependent on something. We are not just at the center of this universe. . . .

And I'm so glad that the new science came into being to dampen our arrogance. It says to us that our earthly planet is a dependent planet. It is a small planet in the orbits of this universe. The sun is the center of this universe, that man must look beyond himself to discover his significance. . . .

. . . . And when you take this attitude, you go into the room of your life and take down the mirrors because you cannot any longer see yourself. But the mirrors somehow are transformed into windows and you look out into the objective world and see that you are what you are because of somebody else. . . . He who seeks to find his ego will lose it. But he who loses his ego in some great cause, some great purpose, some great ideal, some great loyalty, he who discovers, somehow, that he stands where he stands because of the forces of history and because of other individuals. . . . And this is the way, it seems to me, to the integrated personality.

NOTES

NOTES

OUR FAVORITE "F-WORD": THE MISCONCEPTIONS OF FEMINISM IN UNI AND MAINSTREAM CULTURE

Beth Larson and Lara Orlandic

Beth Larson and Lara Orlandic are students at the University Laboratory High School, or Uni, which is on the campus of the University of Illinois in Urbana, Illinois.

When someone mentions the word "feminism," the first thoughts that come to our minds are about the brave women involved in the Women's Liberation Movement during the 60s and 70s. These women fought to give the women of our generation many rights that we take for granted. We can only begin to describe the political and social impacts that this movement has on our lives today.

If our generation is truly grateful for everything that these women have accomplished, why do so few young women wish to identify themselves as feminists?

Over the years, we have witnessed many instances in which the word "feminist" was used with negative connotations. As advocates for gender equality, we ask ourselves: how has such an inspirational term transformed into a derogatory insult? The answer lies in the history of the word, and in what it means to be a feminist in America.

The term "feminism" originated from the French word *féminisme,* first used in 1837 by the French philosopher Charles Fourier. Fourier wanted to improve the status of women in society, but he did not advocate equality between the sexes. The first English definition of "feminism" appeared in the Oxford English Dictionary in 1895: "advocacy of the rights of women (based on the theory of equality of the sexes)."

As the waves of the Women's Liberation Movement passed in the nineteenth and twentieth centuries, feminism began to assume the meaning with which it is associated in present-day American society: "the theory of political, economic, and social equality of the sexes," according to the Merriam-Webster Dictionary.

Although feminism has a clear definition in the dictionary, the term has a variety of interpretations. To some people, it may mean that women should have the right to choose whichever lifestyle they please. Others may interpret it to mean that women and men should be considered equals in all aspects.

"Feminism . . . basically means that you believe men and women deserve equal rights, equal treatment, to be afforded the same amount of respect—expectations that they are equally human beings and therefore deserve the same rights," said Gender Studies teacher Suzanne Linder.

Reprinted by permission from the *Online Gargoyle*, November 29, 2011.

As usual with controversial topics, feminism has been widely misinterpreted throughout history.

"The feminist agenda is not about equal rights for women," said Pat Robertson, a television evangelist and former Baptist minister during his GOP convention speech in 1992. "It is about a socialist, anti-family political movement that encourages women to leave their husbands, kill their children, practice witchcraft, destroy capitalism, and become lesbians."

Although most misinterpretations of feminism are not so radical, many have degraded feminists or might have discouraged women from joining the feminist movement. In 2004, the conservative political commentator Rush Limbaugh popularized the term "feminazi," arguing that feminists' views towards abortion are comparable to atrocities committed by the Nazis.

"When you associate someone with the Nazis or with Stalin or with Satan, you immediately cut out any possibility of an intelligent conversation," English teacher Elizabeth Majerus said. She explained that using such insults limits the exchange of productive conversation and causes people to resort to mindlessly "throwing words" and yelling at one another.

Perhaps these public denouncements of feminism are part of the reason our generation has misinterpreted feminism as a negative term. We have seen many Uni students, boys and girls alike, openly ridicule feminists, claiming that men and women are equal in our society, so feminists must be complaining for no reason. In addition, we have heard an increasing number of people argue that feminists wish to elevate women above men in society.

First of all, the idea that women are superior to men is definitely not a part of feminist ideology.

"I think that the root that relates to women, fem, is used because women are the ones, historically, who have had to fight to be recognized as of equal dignity and standing value as men, but it doesn't mean that women are superior in anyway," said Social Studies teacher Janet Morford.

Looking at how people's opinions toward feminism have changed over time helps us understand how these incorrect notions came about.

"When I . . . was in high school, feminism was a big radical cause," English teacher Steve Rayburn explained. "You know burning bras and stuff like that—fighting for equal treatment. I think it had maybe a more positive connotation then, in general, than it does now. I think it had more respect. I think now, in the past ten years, fifteen years it has become a much more pejorative term than I think it was when I was younger."

Rayburn added that this change in people's views toward feminism was caused by the "conservative backlash" against liberal issues, which emerged after the counterculture movement of the 1970s. Counterculture introduced an influx of liberal ideas and issues, which triggered an adverse reaction by conservatives. Thus people's viewpoints became increasingly polarized.

People also tend to attack an idea because it is easier than discussing the issue and understanding someone else's point of view.

"If you're a person who is willing to say 'I recognize injustice in the world,' people are going to come back at you and belittle you," Linder commented. "Rather than having to deal with the injustices you've pointed out, rather than having to deal with the fact that perhaps our institutions are constructed in such a way that some people have an easier time than other people, it's much easier to say 'you're a feminazi' and dismiss that, or 'you're queer I'm going to dismiss that, so you're a freak and I don't have to listen to your critique of society.'"

One popular way of dismissing the present-day feminist movement is the common misconception that men and women are "equal enough" in our society.

"Things have just gotten so much better for women. It's very easy for women to take feminism for granted, and there are a lot of benefits and privileges that we as women living in 2011 enjoy that came as a result of hard fights," Majerus said. "And now, and any time there is a big social change and things get better, it's easy to start taking for granted the sacrifices that people made in the past to make that happen."

Since the Women's Liberation Movement changed women's status in society so drastically, people tend to overlook the present-day gender inequalities. Even though men and women are considered to be politically equal, there is a long way to go until both genders are socially and economically equal.

Linder stated that feminism is commonly associated with choice, and although women have more choice in society today than in previous decades, it is important to note that the political and social contexts in which women make choices are not equal. For example, women are more likely to pursue a career in the humanities or social sciences, while men are encouraged to pursue technical careers, such as engineering or business.

According to the United States Bureau of Labor Statistics, in 2010, women earned 81.2% as much as men did, for all professions. Even in nursing, which is a stereotypically female occupation, women are only paid 86.5% of the amount of money that male nurses earn.

The same report also showed that the most popular careers among women are registered nurses and elementary/middle school teachers. The least popular careers are computer programmers and occupational therapists. In general, there is a higher percentage of women doing lower-paying jobs (housekeeping, waiting tables, etc.) than jobs with higher salaries (surgeons, lawyers, computer software engineers).

Along with economic inequality in the workplace, there is also a difference in how men and women are portrayed in the media.

"When I look at the cover of Rolling Stone magazine, which . . . is a part of the liberal rock and roll press, you watch the covers. If there is a woman on the cover, then she is probably scantily clad, full body shot, very sexualized, and if there is a man, there is a much bigger chance he will have a head shot," Majerus added. "That says a lot about what we think about men and women; men are people, we want to see their face and expressions; women are sexualized."

Even though women's rights have come a long way in the past few decades, there is no reason to consider the Women's Liberation Movement as a movement of the past. If our society ever wants to truly attain gender equality in all aspects, our generation needs to recognize the issues that present-day women face, and not buy into the new misconceptions about feminism.

"I hope to die, when I die, with equality," Uni High assistant director Sue Kovacs said.

NOTES

NOTES

SEPTEMBER, THE FIRST DAY OF SCHOOL
Howard Nemerov

(1920–1991)

A graduate of Harvard, Howard Nemerov served as a pilot in World War II. From 1988–1990, he was poet laureate of the United States. Until his death, he was Distinguished Poet in Residence at Washington University in St. Louis.

I

My child and I hold hands on the way to school,
And when I leave him at the first-grade door
He cries a little but is brave; he does
Let go. My selfish tears remind me how
I cried before that door a life ago.
I may have had a hard time letting go.

Each fall the children must endure together
What every child also endures alone:
Learning the alphabet, the integers,
Three dozen bits and pieces of a stuff
So arbitrary, so peremptory,
That worlds invisible and visible

Bow down before it, as in Joseph's dream
The sheaves bowed down and then the stars bowed down
Before the dreaming of a little boy.
That dream got him such hatred of his brothers
As cost the greater part of life to mend,
And yet great kindness came of it in the end.

II

A school is where they grind the grain of thought,
And grind the children who must mind the thought.
It may be those two grindings are but one,
As from the alphabet come Shakespeare's Plays,
As from the integers comes Euler's Law,
As from the whole, inseperably, the lives,

Reprinted by permission from the *New Yorker*, September 19, 1970.

The shrunken lives that have not been set free
By law or by poetic phantasy.
But may they be. My child has disappeared
Behind the schoolroom door. And should I live
To see his coming forth, a life away,
I know my hope, but do not know its form

Nor hope to know it. May the fathers he finds
Among his teachers have a care of him
More than his father could. How that will look
I do not know, I do not need to know.
Even our tears belong to ritual.
But may great kindness come of it in the end.

NOTES

NOTES

THE MORAL INSTINCT
Steven Pinker

(1954–)

Steven Pinker has taught at Stanford, MIT, and is currently a professor at Harvard. For his notable research on visual cognition and the psychology of language, he has received awards from the National Academy of Sciences, the Royal Institution of Great Britain, the Cognitive Neuroscience Society, and the American Psychological Association. He holds six honorary doctorates and has published several books. He was featured in Time magazine's "The 100 Most Influential People in the World Today."

Which of the following people would you say is the most admirable: Mother Teresa, Bill Gates or Norman Borlaug? And which do you think is the least admirable? For most people, it's an easy question. Mother Teresa, famous for ministering to the poor in Calcutta, has been beatified by the Vatican, awarded the Nobel Peace Prize and ranked in an American poll as the most admired person of the 20th century. Bill Gates, infamous for giving us the Microsoft dancing paper clip and the blue screen of death, has been decapitated in effigy in "I Hate Gates" Web sites and hit with a pie in the face. As for Norman Borlaug . . . who the heck is Norman Borlaug?

Yet a deeper look might lead you to rethink your answers. Borlaug, father of the "Green Revolution" that used agricultural science to reduce world hunger, has been credited with saving a billion lives, more than anyone else in history. Gates, in deciding what to do with his fortune, crunched the numbers and determined that he could alleviate the most misery by fighting everyday scourges in the developing world like malaria, diarrhea and parasites. Mother Teresa, for her part, extolled the virtue of suffering and ran her well-financed missions accordingly: their sick patrons were offered plenty of prayer but harsh conditions, few analgesics and dangerously primitive medical care.

It's not hard to see why the moral reputations of this trio should be so out of line with the good they have done. Mother Teresa was the very embodiment of saintliness: white-clad, sad-eyed, ascetic and often photographed with the wretched of the earth. Gates is a nerd's nerd and the world's richest man, as likely to enter heaven as the proverbial camel squeezing through the needle's eye. And Borlaug, now 93, is an agronomist who has spent his life in labs and nonprofits, seldom walking onto the media stage, and hence into our consciousness, at all.

I doubt these examples will persuade anyone to favor Bill Gates over Mother Teresa for sainthood. But they show that our heads can be turned by an aura of sanctity, distracting us from a more objective reckoning of the actions that make people suffer or flourish. It seems we may all be vulnerable to moral illusions

Reprinted by permission from the *New York Times Magazine*, January 13, 2008.

the ethical equivalent of the bending lines that trick the eye on cereal boxes and in psychology textbooks. Illusions are a favorite tool of perception scientists for exposing the workings of the five senses, and of philosophers for shaking people out of the naive belief that our minds give us a transparent window onto the world (since if our eyes can be fooled by an illusion, why should we trust them at other times?). Today, a new field is using illusions to unmask a sixth sense, the moral sense. Moral intuitions are being drawn out of people in the lab, on Web sites and in brain scanners, and are being explained with tools from game theory, neuroscience and evolutionary biology.

"Two things fill the mind with ever new and increasing admiration and awe, the oftener and more steadily we reflect on them," wrote Immanuel Kant, "the starry heavens above and the moral law within." These days, the moral law within is being viewed with increasing awe, if not always admiration. The human moral sense turns out to be an organ of considerable complexity, with quirks that reflect its evolutionary history and its neurobiological foundations.

These quirks are bound to have implications for the human predicament. Morality is not just any old topic in psychology but close to our conception of the meaning of life. Moral goodness is what gives each of us the sense that we are worthy human beings. We seek it in our friends and mates, nurture it in our children, advance it in our politics and justify it with our religions. A disrespect for morality is blamed for everyday sins and history's worst atrocities. To carry this weight, the concept of morality would have to be bigger than any of us and outside all of us.

So dissecting moral intuitions is no small matter. If morality is a mere trick of the brain, some may fear, our very grounds for being moral could be eroded. Yet as we shall see, the science of the moral sense can instead be seen as a way to strengthen those grounds, by clarifying what morality is and how it should steer our actions.

The Moralization Switch

The starting point for appreciating that there is a distinctive part of our psychology for morality is seeing how moral judgments differ from other kinds of opinions we have on how people ought to behave. Moralization is a psychological state that can be turned on and off like a switch, and when it is on, a distinctive mind-set commandeers our thinking. This is the mind-set that makes us deem actions immoral ("killing is wrong"), rather than merely disagreeable ("I hate brussels sprouts"), unfashionable ("bell-bottoms are out") or imprudent ("don't scratch mosquito bites").

The first hallmark of moralization is that the rules it invokes are felt to be universal. Prohibitions of rape and murder, for example, are felt not to be matters of local custom but to be universally and objectively warranted. One can easily say, "I don't like brussels sprouts, but I don't care if you eat them," but no one would say, "I don't like killing, but I don't care if you murder someone."

The other hallmark is that people feel that those who commit immoral acts deserve to be punished. Not only is it allowable to inflict pain on a person who has broken a moral rule; it is wrong not to, to "let them get away with it." People are thus untroubled in inviting divine retribution or the power of the state to harm other people they deem immoral. Bertrand Russell wrote, "The infliction of cruelty with a good conscience is a delight to moralists—that is why they invented hell."

We all know what it feels like when the moralization switch flips inside us—the righteous glow, the burning dudgeon, the drive to recruit others to the cause. The psychologist Paul Rozin has studied the toggle switch by comparing two kinds of people who engage in the same behavior but with different switch settings. Health vegetarians avoid meat for practical reasons, like lowering cholesterol and avoiding toxins. Moral vegetarians avoid meat for ethical reasons: to avoid complicity in the suffering of animals. By investigating their feelings about meat-eating, Rozin showed that the moral motive sets off a cascade of opinions. Moral vegetarians are more likely to treat meat as a contaminant—they refuse, for example, to eat a bowl of soup into which a drop of beef broth has fallen. They are more likely to think that other people ought to be vegetarians, and are more likely to imbue their dietary habits with other virtues, like believing that meat avoidance makes people less aggressive and bestial.

Much of our recent social history, including the culture wars between liberals and conservatives, consists of the moralization or amoralization of particular kinds of behavior. Even when people agree that an outcome is desirable, they may disagree on whether it should be treated as a matter of preference and prudence or as a matter of sin and virtue. Rozin notes, for example, that smoking has lately been moralized. Until recently, it was understood that some people didn't enjoy smoking or avoided it because it was hazardous to their health. But with the discovery of the harmful effects of secondhand smoke, smoking is now treated as immoral. Smokers are ostracized; images of people smoking are censored; and entities touched by smoke are felt to be contaminated (so hotels have not only nonsmoking rooms but nonsmoking floors). The desire for retribution has been visited on tobacco companies, who have been slapped with staggering "punitive damages."

At the same time, many behaviors have been amoralized, switched from moral failings to lifestyle choices. They include divorce, illegitimacy, being a working mother, marijuana use and homosexuality. Many afflictions have been reassigned from payback for bad choices to unlucky misfortunes. There used to be people called "bums" and "tramps"; today they are "homeless." Drug addiction is a "disease"; syphilis was rebranded from the price of wanton behavior to a "sexually transmitted disease" and more recently a "sexually transmitted infection."

This wave of amoralization has led the cultural right to lament that morality itself is under assault, as we see in the group that anointed itself the Moral Majority. In fact there seems to be a Law of Conservation of

Moralization, so that as old behaviors are taken out of the moralized column, new ones are added to it. Dozens of things that past generations treated as practical matters are now ethical battlegrounds, including disposable diapers, I.Q. tests, poultry farms, Barbie dolls and research on breast cancer. Food alone has become a minefield, with critics sermonizing about the size of sodas, the chemistry of fat, the freedom of chickens, the price of coffee beans, the species of fish and now the distance the food has traveled from farm to plate.

Many of these moralizations, like the assault on smoking, may be understood as practical tactics to reduce some recently identified harm. But whether an activity flips our mental switches to the "moral" setting isn't just a matter of how much harm it does. We don't show contempt to the man who fails to change the batteries in his smoke alarms or takes his family on a driving vacation, both of which multiply the risk they will die in an accident. Driving a gas-guzzling Hummer is reprehensible, but driving a gas-guzzling old Volvo is not; eating a Big Mac is unconscionable, but not imported cheese or creme brulee. The reason for these double standards is obvious: people tend to align their moralization with their own lifestyles.

Reasoning and Rationalizing

It's not just the content of our moral judgments that is often questionable, but the way we arrive at them. We like to think that when we have a conviction, there are good reasons that drove us to adopt it. That is why an older approach to moral psychology, led by Jean Piaget and Lawrence Kohlberg, tried to document the lines of reasoning that guided people to moral conclusions. But consider these situations, originally devised by the psychologist Jonathan Haidt:

Julie is traveling in France on summer vacation from college with her brother Mark. One night they decide that it would be interesting and fun if they tried making love. Julie was already taking birth-control pills, but Mark uses a condom, too, just to be safe. They both enjoy the sex but decide not to do it again. They keep the night as a special secret, which makes them feel closer to each other. What do you think about that—was it O.K. for them to make love?

A woman is cleaning out her closet and she finds her old American flag. She doesn't want the flag anymore, so she cuts it up into pieces and uses the rags to clean her bathroom.

A family's dog is killed by a car in front of their house. They heard that dog meat was delicious, so they cut up the dog's body and cook it and eat it for dinner.

Most people immediately declare that these acts are wrong and then grope to justify why they are wrong. It's not so easy. In the case of Julie and Mark, people raise the possibility of children with birth defects, but they are reminded that the couple were diligent about contraception. They suggest that the siblings will be emotionally hurt, but the story makes it clear that they weren't. They submit that the act would offend the community, but then recall that it was kept a secret. Eventually many people admit, "I don't know, I can't explain it, I just know it's wrong." People don't generally engage in moral reasoning, Haidt argues, but moral rationalization: they begin with the conclusion, coughed up by an unconscious emotion, and then work backward to a plausible justification.

The gap between people's convictions and their justifications is also on display in the favorite new sandbox for moral psychologists, a thought experiment devised by the philosophers Philippa Foot and Judith Jarvis Thomson called the Trolley Problem. On your morning walk, you see a trolley car hurtling down the track, the conductor slumped over the controls. In the path of the trolley are five men working on the track, oblivious to the danger. You are standing at a fork in the track and can pull a lever that will divert the trolley onto a spur, saving the five men. Unfortunately, the trolley would then run over a single worker who is laboring on the spur. Is it permissible to throw the switch, killing one man to save five? Almost everyone says "yes."

Consider now a different scene. You are on a bridge overlooking the tracks and have spotted the runaway trolley bearing down on the five workers. Now the only way to stop the trolley is to throw a heavy object in its path. And the only heavy object within reach is a fat man standing next to you. Should you throw the man off the bridge? Both dilemmas present you with the option of sacrificing one life to save five, and so, by the utilitarian standard of what would result in the greatest good for the greatest number, the two dilemmas are morally equivalent. But most people don't see it that way: though they would pull the switch in the first dilemma, they would not heave the fat man in the second. When pressed for a reason, they can't come up with anything coherent, though moral philosophers haven't had an easy time coming up with a relevant difference, either.

When psychologists say "most people" they usually mean "most of the two dozen sophomores who filled out a questionnaire for beer money." But in this case it means most of the 200,000 people from a hundred countries who shared their intuitions on a Web-based experiment conducted by the psychologists Fiery Cushman and Liane Young and the biologist Marc Hauser. A difference between the acceptability of switch-pulling and man-heaving, and an inability to justify the choice, was found in respondents from Europe, Asia and North and South America; among men and women, blacks and whites, teenagers and octogenarians, Hindus, Muslims, Buddhists, Christians, Jews and atheists; people with elementary-school educations and people with Ph.D.'s.

Joshua Greene, a philosopher and cognitive neuroscientist, suggests that evolution equipped people with a revulsion to manhandling an innocent person. This instinct, he suggests, tends to overwhelm any utilitarian calculus that would tote up the lives saved and lost. The impulse against roughing up a fellow human would explain other examples in which people abjure killing one to save many, like euthanizing a hospital patient to harvest his organs and save five dying patients in need of transplants, or throwing someone out of a crowded lifeboat to keep it afloat.

By itself this would be no more than a plausible story, but Greene teamed up with the cognitive neuroscientist Jonathan Cohen and several Princeton colleagues to peer into people's brains using functional M.R.I. They sought to find signs of a conflict between brain areas associated with emotion (the ones that recoil from harming someone) and areas dedicated to rational analysis (the ones that calculate lives lost and saved).

When people pondered the dilemmas that required killing someone with their bare hands, several networks in their brains lighted up. One, which included the medial (inward-facing) parts of the frontal lobes, has been implicated in emotions about other people. A second, the dorsolateral (upper and outer-facing) surface of the frontal lobes, has been implicated in ongoing mental computation (including nonmoral reasoning, like deciding whether to get somewhere by plane or train). And a third region, the anterior cingulate cortex (an evolutionarily ancient strip lying at the base of the inner surface of each cerebral hemisphere), registers a conflict between an urge coming from one part of the brain and an advisory coming from another.

But when the people were pondering a hands-off dilemma, like switching the trolley onto the spur with the single worker, the brain reacted differently: only the area involved in rational calculation stood out. Other studies have shown that neurological patients who have blunted emotions because of damage to the frontal lobes become utilitarians: they think it makes perfect sense to throw the fat man off the bridge. Together, the findings corroborate Greene's theory that our nonutilitarian intuitions come from the victory of an emotional impulse over a cost-benefit analysis.

A Universal Morality?

The findings of trolleyology—complex, instinctive and worldwide moral intuitions—led Hauser and John Mikhail (a legal scholar) to revive an analogy from the philosopher John Rawls between the moral sense and language. According to Noam Chomsky, we are born with a "universal grammar" that forces us to analyze speech in terms of its grammatical structure, with no conscious awareness of the rules in play. By analogy, we are born with a universal moral grammar that forces us to analyze human action in terms of its moral structure, with just as little awareness.

The idea that the moral sense is an innate part of human nature is not far-fetched. A list of human universals collected by the anthropologist Donald E. Brown includes many moral concepts and emotions, including a distinction between right and wrong; empathy; fairness; admiration of generosity; rights and obligations; proscription of murder, rape and other forms of violence; redress of wrongs; sanctions for wrongs against the community; shame; and taboos.

The stirrings of morality emerge early in childhood. Toddlers spontaneously offer toys and help to others and try to comfort people they see in distress. And according to the psychologists Elliot Turiel and Judith Smetana, preschoolers have an inkling of the difference between societal conventions and moral principles. Four-year-olds say that it is not O.K. to wear pajamas to school (a convention) and also not O.K. to hit a little girl for no reason (a moral principle). But when asked whether these actions would be O.K. if the teacher allowed them, most of the children said that wearing pajamas would now be fine but that hitting a little girl would still not be.

Though no one has identified genes for morality, there is circumstantial evidence they exist. The character traits called "conscientiousness" and "agreeableness" are far more correlated in identical twins separated at birth (who share their genes but not their environment) than in adoptive siblings raised together (who share their environment but not their genes). People given diagnoses of "antisocial personality disorder" or "psychopathy" show signs of morality blindness from the time they are children. They bully younger children, torture animals, habitually lie and seem incapable of empathy or remorse, often despite normal family backgrounds. Some of these children grow up into the monsters who bilk elderly people out of their savings, rape a succession of women or shoot convenience-store clerks lying on the floor during a robbery.

Though psychopathy probably comes from a genetic predisposition, a milder version can be caused by damage to frontal regions of the brain (including the areas that inhibit intact people from throwing the hypothetical fat man off the bridge). The neuroscientists Hanna and Antonio Damasio and their colleagues found that some children who sustain severe injuries to their frontal lobes can grow up into callous and irresponsible adults, despite normal intelligence. They lie, steal, ignore punishment, endanger their own children and can't think through even the simplest moral dilemmas, like what two people should do if they disagreed on which TV channel to watch or whether a man ought to steal a drug to save his dying wife.

The moral sense, then, may be rooted in the design of the normal human brain. Yet for all the awe that may fill our minds when we reflect on an innate moral law within, the idea is at best incomplete. Consider this moral dilemma: A runaway trolley is about to kill a schoolteacher. You can divert the trolley onto a sidetrack, but the trolley would trip a switch sending a signal to a class of 6-year-olds, giving them permission to name a teddy bear Muhammad. Is it permissible to pull the lever?

This is no joke. Last month a British woman teaching in a private school in Sudan allowed her class to name a teddy bear after the most popular boy in the class, who bore the name of the founder of Islam. She was jailed for blasphemy and threatened with a public flogging, while a mob outside the prison demanded her death. To the protesters, the woman's life clearly had less value than maximizing the dignity of their religion, and their judgment on whether it is right to divert the hypothetical trolley would have differed from ours. Whatever grammar guides people's moral judgments can't be all that universal. Anyone who stayed awake through Anthropology 101 can offer many other examples.

Of course, languages vary, too. In Chomsky's theory, languages conform to an abstract blueprint, like having phrases built out of verbs and objects, while the details vary, like whether the verb or the object comes first. Could we be wired with an abstract spec sheet that embraces all the strange ideas that people in different cultures moralize?

The Varieties of Moral Experience

When anthropologists like Richard Shweder and Alan Fiske survey moral concerns across the globe, they find that a few themes keep popping up from amid the diversity. People everywhere, at least in some circumstances and with certain other folks in mind, think it's bad to harm others and good to help them. They have a sense of fairness: that one should reciprocate favors, reward benefactors and punish cheaters. They value loyalty to a group, sharing and solidarity among its members and conformity to its norms. They believe that it is right to defer to legitimate authorities and to respect people with high status. And they exalt purity, cleanliness and sanctity while loathing defilement, contamination and carnality.

The exact number of themes depends on whether you're a lumper or a splitter, but Haidt counts five—harm, fairness, community (or group loyalty), authority and purity—and suggests that they are the primary colors of our moral sense. Not only do they keep reappearing in cross-cultural surveys, but each one tugs on the moral intuitions of people in our own culture. Haidt asks us to consider how much money someone would have to pay us to do hypothetical acts like the following:

Stick a pin into your palm.
Stick a pin into the palm of a child you don't know. (Harm.)
Accept a wide-screen TV from a friend who received it at no charge because of a computer error.
Accept a wide-screen TV from a friend who received it from a thief who had stolen it from a wealthy family. (Fairness.)
Say something bad about your nation (which you don't believe) on a talk-radio show in your nation.
Say something bad about your nation (which you don't believe) on a talk-radio show in a foreign nation. (Community.)
Slap a friend in the face, with his permission, as part of a comedy skit.
Slap your minister in the face, with his permission, as part of a comedy skit. (Authority.)
Attend a performance-art piece in which the actors act like idiots for 30 minutes, including flubbing simple problems and falling down on stage.

Attend a performance-art piece in which the actors act like animals for 30 minutes, including crawling around naked and urinating on stage. (Purity.)

In each pair, the second action feels far more repugnant. Most of the moral illusions we have visited come from an unwarranted intrusion of one of the moral spheres into our judgments. A violation of community led people to frown on using an old flag to clean a bathroom. Violations of purity repelled the people who judged the morality of consensual incest and prevented the moral vegetarians and nonsmokers from tolerating the slightest trace of a vile contaminant. At the other end of the scale, displays of extreme purity lead people to venerate religious leaders who dress in white and affect an aura of chastity and asceticism.

The Genealogy of Morals

The five spheres are good candidates for a periodic table of the moral sense not only because they are ubiquitous but also because they appear to have deep evolutionary roots. The impulse to avoid harm, which gives trolley ponderers the willies when they consider throwing a man off a bridge, can also be found in rhesus monkey, who go hungry rather than pull a chain that delivers food to them and a shock to another monkey. Respect for authority is clearly related to the pecking orders of dominance and appeasement that are widespread in the animal kingdom. The purity-defilement contrast taps the emotion of disgust that is triggered by potential disease vectors like bodily effluvia, decaying flesh and unconventional forms of meat, and by risky sexual practices like incest.

The other two moralized spheres match up with the classic examples of how altruism can evolve that were worked out by sociobiologists in the 1960s and 1970s and made famous by Richard Dawkins in his book *The Selfish Gene.* Fairness is very close to what scientists call reciprocal altruism, where a willingness to be nice to others can evolve as long as the favor helps the recipient more than it costs the giver and the recipient returns the favor when fortunes reverse. The analysis makes it sound as if reciprocal altruism comes out of a robotlike calculation, but in fact Robert Trivers, the biologist who devised the theory, argued that it is implemented in the brain as a suite of moral emotions. Sympathy prompts a person to offer the first favor, particularly to someone in need for whom it would go the furthest. Anger protects a person against cheaters who accept a favor without reciprocating, by impelling him to punish the ingrate or sever the relationship. Gratitude impels a beneficiary to reward those who helped him in the past. Guilt prompts a cheater in danger of being found out to repair the relationship by redressing the misdeed and advertising that he will behave better in the future (consistent with Mencken's definition of conscience as "the inner voice which warns us that someone might be looking"). Many experiments on who helps whom, who likes whom, who punishes whom and who feels guilty about what have confirmed these predictions.

Community, the very different emotion that prompts people to share and sacrifice without an expectation of payback, may be rooted in nepotistic altruism, the empathy and solidarity we feel toward our relatives (and which evolved because any gene that pushed an organism to aid a relative would have helped copies of itself sitting inside that relative). In humans, of course, communal feelings can be lavished on nonrelatives as well. Sometimes it pays people (in an evolutionary sense) to love their companions because their interests are yoked, like spouses with common children, in-laws with common relatives, friends with common tastes or allies with common enemies. And sometimes it doesn't pay them at all, but their kinship-detectors have been tricked into treating their groupmates as if they were relatives by tactics like kinship metaphors (blood brothers, fraternities, the fatherland), origin myths, communal meals and other bonding rituals.

Juggling the Spheres

All this brings us to a theory of how the moral sense can be universal and variable at the same time. The five moral spheres are universal, a legacy of evolution. But how they are ranked in importance, and which is brought in to moralize which area of social life—sex, government, commerce, religion, diet and so on—depends on the culture. Many of the flabbergasting practices in faraway places become more intelligible when you recognize that the same moralizing impulse that Western elites channel toward violations of harm and fairness (our moral obsessions) is channeled elsewhere to violations in the other spheres. Think of the Japanese fear of nonconformity (community), the holy ablutions and dietary restrictions of Hindus and Orthodox Jews (purity), the outrage at insulting the Prophet among Muslims (authority). In the West, we believe that in business and government, fairness should trump community and try to root out nepotism and cronyism. In other parts of the world this is incomprehensible—what heartless creep would favor a perfect stranger over his own brother?

The ranking and placement of moral spheres also divides the cultures of liberals and conservatives in the United States. Many bones of contention, like homosexuality, atheism and one-parent families from the right, or racial imbalances, sweatshops and executive pay from the left, reflect different weightings of the spheres. In a large Web survey, Haidt found that liberals put a lopsided moral weight on harm and fairness while playing down group loyalty, authority and purity. Conservatives instead place a moderately high weight on all five. It's not surprising that each side thinks it is driven by lofty ethical values and that the other side is base and unprincipled.

Reassigning an activity to a different sphere, or taking it out of the moral spheres altogether, isn't easy. People think that a behavior belongs in its sphere as a matter of sacred necessity and that the very act of questioning an assignment is a moral outrage. The psychologist Philip Tetlock has shown that the mentality of taboo—a conviction that some thoughts are sinful to think—is not just a superstition of Polynesians but a mind-set that can easily be triggered in college-educated Americans. Just ask them to think about applying the sphere of reciprocity to relationships customarily governed by community or authority. When Tetlock asked subjects for their opinions on whether adoption agencies should place children with the couples willing to pay the most, whether people should have the right to sell their organs and whether they should be able to buy their way out of jury duty, the subjects not only disagreed but felt personally insulted and were outraged that anyone would raise the question.

The institutions of modernity often question and experiment with the way activities are assigned to moral spheres. Market economies tend to put everything up for sale. Science amoralizes the world by seeking to understand phenomena rather than pass judgment on them. Secular philosophy is in the business of scrutinizing all beliefs, including those entrenched by authority and tradition. It's not surprising that these institutions are often seen to be morally corrosive.

Is Nothing Sacred?

And "morally corrosive" is exactly the term that some critics would apply to the new science of the moral sense. The attempt to dissect our moral intuitions can look like an attempt to debunk them. Evolutionary psychologists seem to want to unmask our noblest motives as ultimately self-interested—to show that our love for children, compassion for the unfortunate and sense of justice are just tactics in a Darwinian struggle to perpetuate our genes. The explanation of how different cultures appeal to different spheres could lead to a spineless relativism, in which we would never have grounds to criticize the practice of another culture, no matter how barbaric, because "we have our kind of morality and they have theirs." And the whole enterprise seems to be dragging us to an amoral nihilism, in which morality itself would be demoted from a transcendent principle to a figment of our neural circuitry.

In reality, none of these fears are warranted, and it's important to see why not. The first misunderstanding involves the logic of evolutionary explanations. Evolutionary biologists sometimes anthropomorphize DNA for the same reason that science teachers find it useful to have their students imagine the world from the viewpoint of a molecule or a beam of light. One shortcut to understanding the theory of selection without working through the math is to imagine that the genes are little agents that try to make copies of themselves.

Unfortunately, the meme of the selfish gene escaped from popular biology books and mutated into the idea that organisms (including people) are ruthlessly self-serving. And this doesn't follow. Genes are not a reservoir of our dark unconscious wishes. "Selfish" genes are perfectly compatible with selfless organisms, because a gene's metaphorical goal of selfishly replicating itself can be implemented by wiring up the brain of the organism to do unselfish things, like being nice to relatives or doing good deeds for needy strangers. When a mother stays up all night comforting a sick child, the genes that endowed her with that tenderness were "selfish" in a metaphorical sense, but by no stretch of the imagination is she being selfish.

Nor does reciprocal altruism—the evolutionary rationale behind fairness—imply that people do good deeds in the cynical expectation of repayment down the line. We all know of unrequited good deeds, like tipping a waitress in a city you will never visit again and falling on a grenade to save platoonmates. These bursts of goodness are not as anomalous to a biologist as they might appear.

In his classic 1971 article, Trivers, the biologist, showed how natural selection could push in the direction of true selflessness. The emergence of tit-for-tat reciprocity, which lets organisms trade favors without being cheated, is just a first step. A favor-giver not only has to avoid blatant cheaters (those who would accept a favor but not return it) but also prefer generous reciprocators (those who return the biggest favor they can afford) over stingy ones (those who return the smallest favor they can get away with). Since it's good to be chosen as a recipient of favors, a competition arises to be the most generous partner around. More accurately, a competition arises to appear to be the most generous partner around, since the favor-giver can't literally read minds or see into the future. A reputation for fairness and generosity becomes an asset.

Now this just sets up a competition for potential beneficiaries to inflate their reputations without making the sacrifices to back them up. But it also pressures the favor-giver to develop ever-more-sensitive radar to distinguish the genuinely generous partners from the hypocrites. This arms race will eventually reach a logical conclusion. The most effective way to seem generous and fair, under harsh scrutiny, is to be generous and fair. In the long run, then, reputation can be secured only by commitment. At least some agents evolve to be genuinely high-minded and self-sacrificing—they are moral not because of what it brings them but because that's the kind of people they are.

Of course, a theory that predicted that everyone always sacrificed themselves for another's good would be as preposterous as a theory that predicted that no one ever did. Alongside the niches for saints there are niches for more grudging reciprocators, who attract fewer and poorer partners but don't make the sacrifices necessary for a sterling reputation. And both may coexist with outright cheaters, who exploit the unwary in one-shot encounters. An ecosystem of niches, each with a distinct strategy, can evolve when the payoff of each strategy depends on how many players are playing the other strategies. The human social environment does have its share of generous, grudging and crooked characters, and the genetic variation in personality seems to bear the fingerprints of this evolutionary process.

Is Morality a Figment?

So a biological understanding of the moral sense does not entail that people are calculating maximizers of their genes or self-interest. But where does it leave the concept of morality itself?

Here is the worry. The scientific outlook has taught us that some parts of our subjective experience are products of our biological makeup and have no objective counterpart in the world. The qualitative difference between red and green, the tastiness of fruit and foulness of carrion, the scariness of heights and prettiness of flowers are design features of our common nervous system, and if our species had evolved in a different ecosystem or if we were missing a few genes, our reactions could go the other way. Now, if the distinction between right and wrong is also a product of brain wiring, why should we believe it is any more real than the distinction between red and green? And if it is just a collective hallucination, how could we argue that evils like genocide and slavery are wrong for everyone, rather than just distasteful to us?

Putting God in charge of morality is one way to solve the problem, of course, but Plato made short work of it 2,400 years ago. Does God have a good reason for designating certain acts as moral and others as immoral? If not—if his dictates are divine whims—why should we take them seriously? Suppose that God commanded us to torture a child. Would that make it all right, or would some other standard give us reasons to resist? And if, on the other hand, God was forced by moral reasons to issue some dictates and not others—if a command to torture a child was never an option—then why not appeal to those reasons directly?

This throws us back to wondering where those reasons could come from, if they are more than just figments of our brains. They certainly aren't in the physical world like wavelength or mass. The only other option is that moral truths exist in some abstract Platonic realm, there for us to discover, perhaps in the same way that mathematical truths (according to most mathematicians) are there for us to discover. On this analogy, we are born with a rudimentary concept of number, but as soon as we build on it with formal mathematical reasoning, the nature of mathematical reality forces us to discover some truths and not others. (No one who understands the concept of two, the concept of four and the concept of addition can come to any conclusion but that 2 + 2 = 4.) Perhaps we are born with a rudimentary moral sense, and as soon as we build on it with moral reasoning, the nature of moral reality forces us to some conclusions but not others.

Moral realism, as this idea is called, is too rich for many philosophers' blood. Yet a diluted version of the idea—if not a list of cosmically inscribed Thou-Shalts, then at least a few If-Thens—is not crazy. Two features of reality point any rational, self-preserving social agent in a moral direction. And they could provide a benchmark for determining when the judgments of our moral sense are aligned with morality itself.

One is the prevalence of nonzero-sum games. In many arenas of life, two parties are objectively better off if they both act in a nonselfish way than if each of them acts selfishly. You and I are both better off if we share our surpluses, rescue each other's children in danger and refrain from shooting at each other, compared with hoarding our surpluses while they rot, letting the other's child drown while we file our nails or feuding like the Hatfields and McCoys. Granted, I might be a bit better off if I acted selfishly at your expense and you played the sucker, but the same is true for you with me, so if each of us tried for these advantages, we'd both end up worse off. Any neutral observer, and you and I if we could talk it over rationally, would have to conclude that the state we should aim for is the one in which we both are unselfish. These spreadsheet projections are not quirks of brain wiring, nor are they dictated by a supernatural power; they are in the nature of things.

The other external support for morality is a feature of rationality itself: that it cannot depend on the egocentric vantage point of the reasoner. If I appeal to you to do anything that affects me—to get off my foot, or tell me the time or not run me over with your car—then I can't do it in a way that privileges my interests over yours (say, retaining my right to run you over with my car) if I want you to take me seriously. Unless I am Galactic Overlord, I have to state my case in a way that would force me to treat you in kind. I can't act as if my interests are special just because I'm me and you're not, any more than I can persuade you that the spot I am standing on is a special place in the universe just because I happen to be standing on it.

Not coincidentally, the core of this idea—the interchangeability of perspectives—keeps reappearing in history's best-thought-through moral philosophies, including the Golden Rule (itself discovered many times); Spinoza's Viewpoint of Eternity; the Social Contract of Hobbes, Rousseau and Locke; Kant's Categorical Imperative; and Rawls's Veil of Ignorance. It also underlies Peter Singer's theory of the Expanding Circle—the optimistic proposal that our moral sense, though shaped by evolution to overvalue self, kin and clan, can propel us on a path of moral progress, as our reasoning forces us to generalize it to larger and larger circles of sentient beings.

Doing Better by Knowing Ourselves

Morality, then, is still something larger than our inherited moral sense, and the new science of the moral sense does not make moral reasoning and conviction obsolete. At the same time, its implications for our moral universe are profound.

At the very least, the science tells us that even when our adversaries' agenda is most baffling, they may not be amoral psychopaths but in the throes of a moral mind-set that appears to them to be every bit as mandatory and universal as ours does to us. Of course, some adversaries really are psychopaths, and others are so poisoned by a punitive moralization that they are beyond the pale of reason. (The actor Will Smith had many historians on his side when he recently speculated to the press that Hitler thought he was acting morally.) But in any conflict in which a meeting of the minds is not completely hopeless, a recognition that the other guy is acting from moral rather than venal reasons can be a first patch of common ground. One side can acknowledge the other's concern for community or stability or fairness or dignity, even while arguing that some other value should trump it in that instance. With affirmative action, for example, the opponents can be seen as arguing from a sense of fairness, not racism, and the defenders can be seen as acting from a concern with community, not bureaucratic power. Liberals can ratify conservatives' concern with families while noting that gay marriage is perfectly consistent with that concern.

The science of the moral sense also alerts us to ways in which our psychological makeup can get in the way of our arriving at the most defensible moral conclusions. The moral sense, we are learning, is as vulnerable to illusions as the other senses. It is apt to confuse morality per se with purity, status and conformity. It tends to reframe practical problems as moral crusades and thus see their solution in punitive aggression. It imposes taboos that make certain ideas indiscussible. And it has the nasty habit of always putting the self on the side of the angels.

Though wise people have long reflected on how we can be blinded by our own sanctimony, our public discourse still fails to discount it appropriately. In the worst cases, the thoughtlessness of our brute intuitions can be celebrated as a virtue. In his influential essay "The Wisdom of Repugnance," Leon Kass, former chair of the President's Council on Bioethics, argued that we should disregard reason when it comes to cloning and other biomedical technologies and go with our gut: "We are repelled by the prospect of cloning human beings . . . because we intuit and feel, immediately and without argument, the violation of things that we rightfully hold dear. . . . In this age in which everything is held to be permissible so long as it is freely done . . . repugnance may be the only voice left that speaks up to defend the central core of our humanity. Shallow are the souls that have forgotten how to shudder."

There are, of course, good reasons to regulate human cloning, but the shudder test is not one of them. People have shuddered at all kinds of morally irrelevant violations of purity in their culture: touching an untouchable, drinking from the same water fountain as a Negro, allowing Jewish blood to mix with Aryan blood, tolerating sodomy between consenting men. And if our ancestors' repugnance had carried the day, we never would have had autopsies, vaccinations, blood transfusions, artificial insemination, organ transplants and in vitro fertilization, all of which were denounced as immoral when they were new.

There are many other issues for which we are too quick to hit the moralization button and look for villains rather than bug fixes. What should we do when a hospital patient is killed by a nurse who administers the wrong drug in a patient's intravenous line? Should we make it easier to sue the hospital for damages? Or should we redesign the IV fittings so that it's physically impossible to connect the wrong bottle to the line?

And nowhere is moralization more of a hazard than in our greatest global challenge. The threat of human-induced climate change has become the occasion for a moralistic revival meeting. In many discussions, the cause of climate change is overindulgence (too many S.U.V.'s) and defilement (sullying the atmosphere), and the solution is temperance (conservation) and expiation (buying carbon offset coupons). Yet the experts agree that these numbers don't add up: even if every last American became conscientious about his or her carbon emissions, the effects on climate change would be trifling, if for no other reason than that two billion Indians and Chinese are unlikely to copy our born-again abstemiousness. Though voluntary conservation may be one wedge in an effective carbon-reduction pie, the other wedges will have to be morally boring, like a carbon tax and new energy technologies, or even taboo, like nuclear power and deliberate manipulation of the ocean and atmosphere. Our habit of moralizing problems, merging them with intuitions of purity and contamination, and resting content when we feel the right feelings, can get in the way of doing the right thing.

Far from debunking morality, then, the science of the moral sense can advance it, by allowing us to see through the illusions that evolution and culture have saddled us with and to focus on goals we can share and defend. As Anton Chekhov wrote, "Man will become better when you show him what he is like."

NOTES

NOTES

USING THE WORD "RETARD" TO DESCRIBE ME HURTS
John Franklin Stephens

John Franklin Stephens is a Global Messenger for Special Olympics and a Special Olympics Virginia athlete himself who lives in Fairfax.

What's the big deal about using the word "retard"?

A lot of people are talking about the movie "Tropic Thunder." One of the reasons that it is being talked about is that the characters use the term "retard" over and over. They use it the same way that kids do all the time, to jokingly insult one another.

The people who made the movie, DreamWorks and Paramount, and many of the critics who have reviewed it, say that the term is being used by characters who are dumb and shallow themselves.

You see, we are supposed to get the joke that it is only the dumb and shallow people who use a term that means dumb and shallow. My dad tells me that this is called "irony."

So, what's the big deal?

Let me try to explain.

I am a 26-year-old man with Down Syndrome. I am very lucky. Even though I was born with this intellectual disability, I do pretty well and have a good life. I live and work in the community. I count as friends the people I went to school with and the people I meet in my job.

Every day I get closer to living a life like yours.

I am a Global Messenger for Special Olympics and make speeches to people all over the country. I once spoke to over 10,000 people at the Richmond Coliseum. I realize that I am a voice for other people with intellectual disabilities who cannot easily speak for themselves. I thank God that he gave me this chance to be someone's voice.

The hardest thing about having an intellectual disability is the loneliness. We process information slower than everyone else. So even normal conversation is a constant battle for us not to lose touch with what the rest of you are saying. Most of the time the words and thoughts just go too fast for us to keep up, and when we finally say something it seems out of place.

We are aware when all the rest of you stop and just look at us. We are aware when you look at us and just say, "unh huh," and then move on, talking to each other. You mean no harm, but you have no idea how alone we feel even when we are with you.

That is why I love being a Global Messenger. I work for days telling my dad what I want to talk about and he tries to write it down for me. Then we do it over and over until we have something that says what I mean. We wrote this letter the same way.

Reprinted from the *Denver Post*, September 1, 2008, by permission of the author.

So, what's wrong with "retard"? I can only tell you what it means to me and people like me when we hear it. It means that the rest of you are excluding us from your group. We are something that is not like you and something that none of you would ever want to be. We are something outside the "in" group. We are someone that is not your kind.

I want you to know that it hurts to be left out here, alone. Nothing scares me as much as feeling all alone in a world that moves so much faster than I do.

You don't mean to make me feel that way. In fact, like I say in some of my speeches, "I have always depended on the kindness of strangers," and it works out OK most of the time. Still, it hurts and scares me when I am the only person with intellectual disabilities on the bus and young people start making "retard" jokes or references.

Please put yourself on that bus and fill the bus with people who are different from you. Imagine that they start making jokes using a term that describes you. It hurts and it is scary.

Last, I get the joke—the irony—that only dumb and shallow people are using a term that means dumb and shallow. The problem is, it is only funny if you think a "retard" is someone dumb and shallow. I am not those things, but every time the term is used it tells young people that it is OK to think of me that way and to keep me on the outside.

That is why using "retard" is a big deal to people like me.

NOTES

NOTES

THE COMMUNITY

"What should young people do with their lives today? Many things, obviously. But the most daring thing is to create stable communities in which the terrible disease of loneliness can be cured."

Kurt Vonnegut (1922–2007) Author

"No man is an island, entire of itself; every man is a piece of the continent, a part of the main. If a clod be washed away by the sea, Europe is the less, as well as if a promontory were, as well as if a manor of thy friend's or of thine own were: any man's death diminishes me, because I am involved in mankind, and therefore never send to know for whom the bells tolls; it tolls for thee."

John Donne (1572–1631) Poet

REQUIRED READINGS

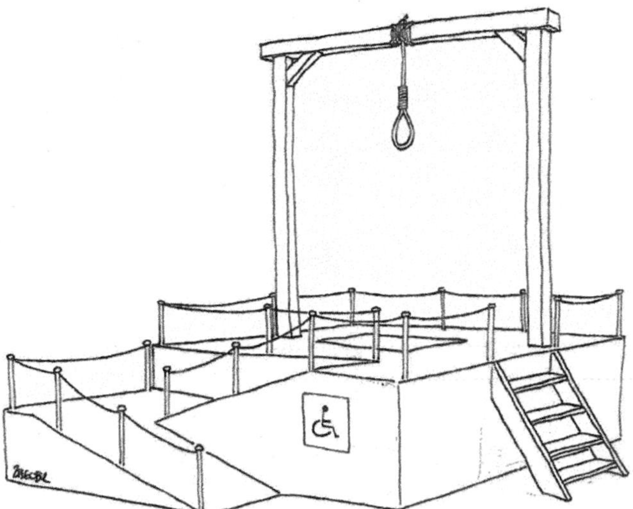

Courtesy of Jack Ziegler/The New Yorker Collection.

THE SOCIAL CONTRACT
Jean-Jacques Rousseau

(1712–1778)

Jean-Jacques was a French philosopher whose works had a profound influence on education, literature, and politics. He described his views regarding government and the rights of citizens in The Social Contract *(1762).*

Translated by George Douglas and Howard Cole

Book I

1. Subject of the First Book

Man is born free; and everywhere he is in chains. One thinks himself the master of others, and still remains a greater slave than they. How did this change come about? I do not know. What can make it legitimate? That question I think I can answer.

If I took into account only force, and the effects derived from it, I should say: "As long as a people is compelled to obey, and obeys, it does well; as soon as it can shake off the yoke, and shakes it off, it does still better; for, regaining its liberty by the same right as took it away, either it is justified in resuming it, or there was no justification for those who took it away." But the social order is a sacred right which is the basis of all other rights. Nevertheless, this right does not come from nature, and must therefore be founded on conventions. Before coming to that, I have to prove what I have just asserted.

2. The First Societies

The most ancient of all societies, and the only one that is natural, is the family: and even so the children remain attached to the father only so long as they need him for their preservation. As soon as this need ceases, the natural bond is dissolved. The children, released from the obedience they owed to the father, and the father, released from the care he owed his children, return equally to independence. If they remain united, they continue so no longer naturally, but voluntarily; and the family itself is then maintained only by convention.

This common liberty results from the nature of man. His first law is to provide for his own preservation, his first cares are those which he owes to himself; and, as soon as he reaches years of discretion, he is the sole judge of the proper means of preserving himself, and consequently becomes his own master.

The family then may be called the first model of political societies: the ruler corresponds to the father, and the people to the children; and all, being born free and equal, alienate their liberty only for their own advantage. The

---

Reprinted from *The Social Contract* (2010).

whole difference is that, in the family, the love of the father for his children repays him for the care he takes of them, while, in the State, the pleasure of commanding takes the place of the love which the chief cannot have for the peoples under him.

Grotius denies that all human power is established in favour of the governed, and quotes slavery as an example. His usual method of reasoning is constantly to establish right by fact. It would be possible to employ a more logical method, but none could be more favourable to tyrants.

It is then, according to Grotius, doubtful whether the human race belongs to a hundred men, or that hundred men to the human race: and, throughout his book, he seems to incline to the former alternative, which is also the view of Hobbes. On this showing, the human species is divided into so many herds of cattle, each with its ruler, who keeps guard over them for the purpose of devouring them.

As a shepherd is of a nature superior to that of his flock, the shepherds of men, i.e., their rulers, are of a nature superior to that of the peoples under them. Thus, Philo tells us, the Emperor Caligula reasoned, concluding equally well either that kings were gods, or that men were beasts.

The reasoning of Caligula agrees with that of Hobbes and Grotius. Aristotle, before any of them, had said that men are by no means equal naturally, but that some are born for slavery, and others for dominion.

Aristotle was right; but he took the effect for the cause. Nothing can be more certain than that every man born in slavery is born for slavery. Slaves lose everything in their chains, even the desire of escaping from them: they love their servitude, as the comrades of Ulysses loved their brutish condition. If then there are slaves by nature, it is because there have been slaves against nature. Force made the first slaves, and their cowardice perpetuated the condition.

I have said nothing of King Adam, or Emperor Noah, father of the three great monarchs who shared out the universe, like the children of Saturn, whom some scholars have recognised in them. I trust to getting due thanks for my moderation; for, being a direct descendant of one of these princes, perhaps of the eldest branch, how do I know that a verification of titles might not leave me the legitimate king of the human race? In any case, there can be no doubt that Adam was sovereign of the world, as Robinson Crusoe was of his island, as long as he was its only inhabitant; and this empire had the advantage that the monarch, safe on his throne, had no rebellions, wars, or conspirators to fear.

3. The Right of the Strongest

The strongest is never strong enough to be always the master, unless he transforms strength into right, and obedience into duty. Hence the right of the strongest, which, though to all seeming meant ironically, is really laid down as a fundamental principle. But are we never to have an explanation of this phrase? Force is a physical power, and I fail to see what moral effect it can have. To yield to force is an act of necessity, not of will—at the most, an act of prudence. In what sense can it be a duty?

Suppose for a moment that this so-called "right" exists. I maintain that the sole result is a mass of inexplicable nonsense. For, if force creates right, the effect changes with the cause: every force that is greater than the first succeeds to its right. As soon as it is possible to disobey with impunity, disobedience is legitimate; and, the strongest being always in the right, the only thing that matters is to act so as to become the strongest. But what kind of right is that which perishes when force fails? If we must obey perforce, there is no need to obey because we ought; and if we are not forced to obey, we are under no obligation to do so. Clearly, the word "right" adds nothing to force: in this connection, it means absolutely nothing.

Obey the powers that be. If this means yield to force, it is a good precept, but superfluous: I can answer for its never being violated. All power comes from God, I admit; but so does all sickness: does that mean that we are forbidden to call in the doctor? A brigand surprises me at the edge of a wood: must I not merely surrender my purse on compulsion; but, even if I could withhold it, am I in conscience bound to give it up? For certainly the pistol he holds is also a power.

Let us then admit that force does not create right, and that we are obliged to obey only legitimate powers. In that case, my original question recurs.

4. Slavery

Since no man has a natural authority over his fellow, and force creates no right, we must conclude that conventions form the basis of all legitimate authority among men.

If an individual, says Grotius, can alienate his liberty and make himself the slave of a master, why could not a whole people do the same and make itself subject to a king? There are in this passage plenty of ambiguous words which would need explaining; but let us confine ourselves to the word *alienate.* To alienate is to give or to sell. Now, a man who becomes the slave of another does not give himself; he sells himself, at the least for his subsistence: but for what does a people sell itself? A king is so far from furnishing his subjects with their subsistence that he gets his own only from them; and, according to Rabelais, kings do not live on nothing. Do subjects then give their persons on condition that the king takes their goods also? I fail to see what they have left to preserve.

It will be said that the despot assures his subjects civil tranquillity. Granted; but what do they gain, if the wars his ambition brings down upon them, his insatiable avidity, and the vexatious conduct of his ministers press harder on them than their own dissensions would have done? What do they gain, if the very tranquillity they enjoy is one of their miseries? Tranquillity is found also in dungeons; but is that enough to make them desirable places to live in? The Greeks imprisoned in the cave of the Cyclops lived there very tranquilly, while they were awaiting their turn to be devoured.

To say that a man gives himself gratuitously, is to say what is absurd and inconceivable; such an act is null and illegitimate, from the mere fact that he who does it is out of his mind. To say the same of a whole people is to suppose a people of madmen; and madness creates no right.

Even if each man could alienate himself, he could not alienate his children: they are born men and free; their liberty belongs to them, and no one but they has the right to dispose of it. Before they come to years of discretion, the father can, in their name, lay down conditions for their preservation and well-being, but he cannot give them irrevocably and without conditions: such a gift is contrary to the ends of nature, and exceeds the rights of paternity. It would therefore be necessary, in order to legitimise an arbitrary government, that in every generation the people should be in a position to accept or reject it; but, were this so, the government would be no longer arbitrary.[1]

To renounce liberty is to renounce being a man, to surrender the rights of humanity and even its duties. For him who renounces everything no indemnity is possible. Such a renunciation is incompatible with man's nature; to remove all liberty from his will is to remove all morality from his acts. Finally, it is an empty and contradictory convention that sets up, on the one side, absolute authority, and, on the other, unlimited obedience. Is it not clear that we can be under no obligation to a person from whom we have the right to exact everything? Does not this condition alone, in the absence of equivalence or exchange, in itself involve the nullity of the act? For what right can my slave have against me, when all that he has belongs to me, and, his right being mine, this right of mine against myself is a phrase devoid of meaning?

So, from whatever aspect we regard the question, the right of slavery is null and void, not only as being illegitimate, but also because it is absurd and meaningless. The words *slave* and *right* contradict each other, and are mutually exclusive. It will always be equally foolish for a man to say to a man or to a people: "I make with you a convention wholly at your expense and wholly to my advantage; I shall keep it as long as I like, and you will keep it as long as I like."

5. That We Must Always Go Back to a First Convention

Even if I granted all that I have been refuting, the friends of despotism would be no better off. There will always be a great difference between subduing a multitude and ruling a society. Even if scattered individuals were successively enslaved by one man, however numerous they might be, I still see no more than a master and his slaves, and certainly not a people and its ruler; I see what may be termed an aggregation, but not an association; there is as yet neither public good nor body politic. The man in question, even if he has enslaved half the world, is still only an individual; his interest, apart from that of others, is still a purely private interest. If this same man comes to die, his empire, after him, remains scattered and without unity, as an oak falls and dissolves into a heap of ashes when the fire has consumed it.

A people, says Grotius, can give itself to a king. Then, according to Grotius, a people is a people before it gives itself. The gift is itself a civil act, and implies public deliberation. It would be better, before examining the act by which a people gives itself to a king, to examine that by which it has become a people; for this act, being necessarily prior to the other, is the true foundation of society.

Indeed, if there were no prior convention, where, unless the election were unanimous, would be the obligation on the minority to submit to the choice of the majority? How have a hundred men who wish for a master the right to vote on behalf of ten who do not? The law of majority voting is itself something established by convention, and presupposes unanimity, on one occasion at least.

6. The Social Compact

I suppose men to have reached the point at which the obstacles in the way of their preservation in the state of nature show their power of resistance to be greater than the resources at the disposal of each individual for his maintenance in that state. That primitive condition can then subsist no longer; and the human race would perish unless it changed its manner of existence.

But, as men cannot engender new forces, but only unite and direct existing ones, they have no other means of preserving themselves than the formation, by aggregation, of a sum of forces great enough to overcome the resistance. These they have to bring into play by means of a single motive power, and cause to act in concert.

This sum of forces can arise only where several persons come together: but, as the force and liberty of each man are the chief instruments of his self-preservation, how can he pledge them without harming his own interests, and neglecting the care he owes to himself? This difficulty, in its bearing on my present subject, may be stated in the following terms:

> "*The problem is to find a form of association which will defend and protect with the whole common force the person and goods of each associate, and in which each, while uniting himself with all, may still obey himself alone, and remain as free as before.*" This is the fundamental problem of which the *Social Contract* provides the solution.

The clauses of this contract are so determined by the nature of the act that the slightest modification would make them vain and ineffective; so that, although they have perhaps never been formally set forth, they are everywhere the same and everywhere tacitly admitted and recognised, until, on the violation of the social compact, each regains his original rights and resumes his natural liberty, while losing the conventional liberty in favour of which he renounced it.

These clauses, properly understood, may be reduced to one—the total alienation of each associate, together with all his rights, to the whole community; for, in the first place, as each gives himself absolutely, the conditions are the same for all; and, this being so, no one has any interest in making them burdensome to others.

Moreover, the alienation being without reserve, the union is as perfect as it can be, and no associate has anything more to demand: for, if the individuals retained certain rights, as there would be no common superior to decide between them and the public, each, being on one point his own judge, would ask to be so on all; the state of nature would thus continue, and the association would necessarily become inoperative or tyrannical.

Finally, each man, in giving himself to all, gives himself to nobody; and as there is no associate over whom he does not acquire the same right as he yields others over himself, he gains an equivalent for everything he loses, and an increase of force for the preservation of what he has.

If then we discard from the social compact what is not of its essence, we shall find that it reduces itself to the following terms:

> *"Each of us puts his person and all his power in common under the supreme direction of the general will, and, in our corporate capacity, we receive each member as an indivisible part of the whole."*

At once, in place of the individual personality of each contracting party, this act of association creates a moral and collective body, composed of as many members as the assembly contains votes, and receiving from this act its unity, its common identity, its life and its will. This public person, so formed by the union of all other persons formerly took the name of *city,* and now takes that of *Republic* or *body politic;* it is called by its members *State* when passive, *Sovereign* when active, and *Power* when compared with others like itself. Those who are associated in it take collectively the name of *people,* and severally are called *citizens,* as sharing in the sovereign power, and *subjects,* as being under the laws of the State. But these terms are often confused and taken one for another: it is enough to know how to distinguish them when they are being used with precision.

7. The Sovereign

This formula shows us that the act of association comprises a mutual undertaking between the public and the individuals, and that each individual, in making a contract, as we may say, with himself, is bound in a double capacity; as a member of the Sovereign he is bound to the individuals, and as a member of the State to the Sovereign. But the maxim of civil right, that no one is bound by undertakings made to himself, does not apply in this case;

for there is a great difference between incurring an obligation to yourself and incurring one to a whole of which you form a part.

Attention must further be called to the fact that public deliberation, while competent to bind all the subjects to the Sovereign, because of the two different capacities in which each of them may be regarded, cannot, for the opposite reason, bind the Sovereign to itself; and that it is consequently against the nature of the body politic for the Sovereign to impose on itself a law which it cannot infringe. Being able to regard itself in only one capacity, it is in the position of an individual who makes a contract with himself; and this makes it clear that there neither is nor can be any kind of fundamental law binding on the body of the people—not even the social contract itself. This does not mean that the body politic cannot enter into undertakings with others, provided the contract is not infringed by them; for in relation to what is external to it, it becomes a simple being, an individual.

But the body politic or the Sovereign, drawing its being wholly from the sanctity of the contract, can never bind itself, even to an outsider, to do anything derogatory to the original act, for instance, to alienate any part of itself, or to submit to another Sovereign. Violation of the act by which it exists would be self-annihilation; and that which is itself nothing can create nothing.

As soon as this multitude is so united in one body, it is impossible to offend against one of the members without attacking the body, and still more to offend against the body without the members resenting it. Duty and interest therefore equally oblige the two contracting parties to give each other help; and the same men should seek to combine, in their double capacity, all the advantages dependent upon that capacity.

Again, the Sovereign, being formed wholly of the individuals who compose it, neither has nor can have any interest contrary to theirs; and consequently the sovereign power need give no guarantee to its subjects, because it is impossible for the body to wish to hurt all its members. We shall also see later on that it cannot hurt any in particular. The Sovereign, merely by virtue of what it is, is always what it should be.

This, however, is not the case with the relation of the subjects to the Sovereign, which, despite the common interest, would have no security that they would fulfil their undertakings, unless it found means to assure itself of their fidelity.

In fact, each individual, as a man, may have a particular will contrary or dissimilar to the general will which he has as a citizen. His particular interest may speak to him quite differently from the common interest: his absolute and naturally independent existence may make him look upon what he owes to the common cause as a gratuitous contribution, the loss of which will do less harm to others than the payment of it is burdensome to himself; and, regarding the moral person which constitutes the State as a *persona ficta*, because not a man, he may wish to enjoy the rights of citizenship without being ready to fulfil the duties of a subject. The continuance of such an injustice could not but prove the undoing of the body politic.

In order then that the social compact may not be an empty formula, it tacitly includes the undertaking, which alone can give force to the rest, that whoever refuses to obey the general will shall be compelled to do so by the whole body. This means nothing less than that he will be forced to be free; for this is the condition which, by giving each citizen to his country, secures him against all personal dependence. In this lies the key to the working of the political machine; this alone legitimises civil undertakings, which, without it, would be absurd, tyrannical, and liable to the most frightful abuses.

8. The Civil State

The passage from the state of nature to the civil state produces a very remarkable change in man, by substituting justice for instinct in his conduct, and giving his actions the morality they had formerly lacked. Then only, when the voice of duty takes the place of physical impulses and right of appetite, does man, who so far had considered only himself, find that he is forced to act on different principles, and to consult his reason before listening to his inclinations. Although, in this state, he deprives himself of some advantages which he got from nature, he gains in return others so great, his faculties are so stimulated and developed, his ideas so extended, his feelings so ennobled, and his whole soul so uplifted, that, did not the abuses of this new condition often degrade him below that which he left, he would be bound to bless continually the happy moment which took him from it for ever, and, instead of a stupid and unimaginative animal, made him an intelligent being and a man.

Let us draw up the whole account in terms easily commensurable. What man loses by the social contract is his natural liberty and an unlimited right to everything he tries to get and succeeds in getting; what he gains is civil liberty and the proprietorship of all he possesses. If we are to avoid mistake in weighing one against the other, we must clearly distinguish natural liberty, which is bounded only by the strength of the individual, from civil liberty, which is limited by the general will; and possession, which is merely the effect of force or the right of the first occupier, from property, which can be founded only on a positive title.

We might, over and above all this, add, to what man acquires in the civil state, moral liberty, which alone makes him truly master of himself; for the mere impulse of appetite is slavery, while obedience to a law which we prescribe to ourselves is liberty. But I have already said too much on this head, and the philosophical meaning of the word liberty does not now concern us.

9. Real Property

Each member of the community gives himself to it, at the moment of its foundation, just as he is, with all the resources at his command, including the goods he possesses. This act does not make possession, in changing hands, change its nature, and become property in the hands of the Sovereign; but, as the forces of the city are incomparably greater than those of an individual, public possession is also, in fact, stronger and more irrevocable, without being any more legitimate, at any rate from the point of view of foreigners. For the State, in relation to its members, is master of all their goods by the social contract, which, within the State, is the basis of all rights; but, in relation to other powers, it is so only by the right of the first occupier, which it holds from its members.

The right of the first occupier, though more real than the right of the strongest, becomes a real right only when the right of property has already been established. Every man has naturally a right to everything he needs; but the positive act which makes him proprietor of one thing excludes him from everything else. Having his share, he ought to keep to it, and can have no further right against the community. This is why the right of the first occupier, which in the state of nature is so weak, claims the respect of every man in civil society. In this right we are respecting not so much what belongs to another as what does not belong to ourselves.

The peculiar fact about this alienation is that, in taking over the goods of individuals, the community, so far from despoiling them, only assures them legitimate possession, and changes usurpation into a true right and enjoyment into proprietorship. Thus the possessors, being regarded as depositaries of the public good, and having their rights respected by all the members of the State and maintained against foreign aggression by all its forces, have, by a cession which benefits both the public and still more themselves, acquired, so to speak, all that they gave up. This paradox may easily be explained by the distinction between the rights which the Sovereign and the proprietor have over the same estate, as we shall see later on.

It may also happen that men begin to unite one with another before they possess anything, and that, subsequently occupying a tract of country which is enough for all, they enjoy it in common, or share it out among themselves, either equally or according to a scale fixed by the Sovereign. However the acquisition be made, the right which each individual has to his own estate is always subordinate to the right which the community has over all: without this, there would be neither stability in the social tie, nor real force in the exercise of Sovereignty.

I shall end this chapter and this book by remarking on a fact on which the whole social system should rest: i.e., that, instead of destroying natural inequality, the fundamental compact substitutes, for such physical inequality as nature may have set up between men, an equality that is moral and legitimate, and that men, who may be unequal in strength or intelligence, become every one equal by convention and legal right.

Book II

1. That Sovereignty Is Inalienable

The first and most important deduction from the principles we have so far laid down is that the general will alone can direct the State according to the object for which it was instituted, i.e., the common good: for if the clashing of particular interests made the establishment of societies necessary, the agreement of these very interests made it possible. The common element in these different interests is what forms the social tie; and, were there no point of agreement between them all, no society could exist. It is solely on the basis of this common interest that every society should be governed.

3. Whether the General Will Is Fallible

It follows from what has gone before that the general will is always right and tends to the public advantage; but it does not follow that the deliberations of the people are always equally correct. Our will is always for our own good, but we do not always see what that is; the people is never corrupted, but it is often deceived, and on such occasions only does it seem to will what is bad.

There is often a great deal of difference between the will of all and the general will; the latter considers only the common interest, while the former takes private interest into account, and is no more than a sum of particular wills: but take away from these same wills the pluses and minuses that cancel one another, and the general will remains as the sum of the differences.

If, when the people, being furnished with adequate information, held its deliberations, the citizens had no communication one with another, the grand total of the small differences would always give the general will, and the decision would always be good. But when factions arise, and partial associations are formed at the expense of the great association, the will of each of these associations becomes general in relation to its members, while it remains particular in relation to the State: it may then be said that there are no longer as many votes as there are men, but only as many as there are associations. The differences become less numerous and give a less general result. Lastly, when one of these associations is so great as to prevail over all the rest, the result is no longer a sum of small differences, but a single difference; in this case there is no longer a general will, and the opinion which prevails is purely particular.

It is therefore essential, if the general will is to be able to express itself, that there should be no partial society within the State, and that each citizen should think only his own thoughts: which was indeed the sublime and unique system established by the great Lycurgus. But if there are partial societies, it is best to have as many as possible and to prevent them from being unequal, as was done by Solon, Numa and Servius. These precautions are the only ones that can guarantee that the general will shall be always enlightened, and that the people shall in no way deceive itself.

4. The Limits of the Sovereign Power

If the State is a moral person whose life is in the union of its members, and if the most important of its cares is the care for its own preservation, it must have a universal and compelling force, in order to move and dispose each part as may be most advantageous to the whole. As nature gives each man absolute power over all his members, the social compact gives the body politic absolute power over all its members also; and it is this power which, under the direction of the general will, bears, as I have said, the name of Sovereignty.

But, besides the public person, we have to consider the private persons composing it, whose life and liberty are naturally independent of it. We are bound then to distinguish clearly between the respective rights of the citizens and the Sovereign, and between the duties the former have to fulfil as subjects, and the natural rights they should enjoy as men.

Each man alienates, I admit, by the social compact, only such part of his powers, goods and liberty as it is important for the community to control; but it must also be granted that the Sovereign is sole judge of what is important.

Every service a citizen can render the State he ought to render as soon as the Sovereign demands it; but the Sovereign, for its part, cannot impose upon its subjects any fetters that are useless to the community, nor can it even wish to do so; for no more by the law of reason than by the law of nature can anything occur without a cause.

The undertakings which bind us to the social body are obligatory only because they are mutual; and their nature is such that in fulfilling them we cannot work for others without working for ourselves. Why is it that the general will is always in the right, and that all continually will the happiness of each one, unless it is because there is not a man who does not think of "each" as meaning him, and consider himself in voting for all? This proves that equality of rights and the idea of justice which such equality creates originate in the preference each man gives to himself, and accordingly in the very nature of man. It proves that the general will, to be really such, must be general in its object as well as its essence; that it must both come from all and apply to all; and that it loses its natural rectitude when it is directed to some particular and determinate object, because in such a case we are judging of something foreign to us, and have no true principle of equity to guide us.

Indeed, as soon as a question of particular fact or right arises on a point not previously regulated by a general convention, the matter becomes contentious. It is a case in which the individuals concerned are one party, and the public the other, but in which I can see neither the law that ought to be followed nor the judge who ought to give the decision. In such a case, it would be absurd to propose to refer the question to an express decision of the general will, which can be only the conclusion reached by one of the parties and in consequence will be, for the other party, merely an external and particular will, inclined on this occasion to injustice and subject to error. Thus, just as a particular will cannot stand for the general will, the general will, in turn, changes its nature, when its object is particular, and, as general, cannot pronounce on a man or a fact. When, for instance, the people of Athens nominated or displaced its rulers, decreed honours to one, and imposed penalties on another, and, by a multitude of particular decrees, exercised all the functions of government indiscriminately, it had in such cases no longer a general will in the strict sense; it was acting no longer as Sovereign, but as magistrate. This will seem contrary to current views; but I must be given time to expound my own.

It should be seen from the foregoing that what makes the will general is less the number of voters than the common interest uniting them; for, under this system, each necessarily submits to the conditions he imposes on others: and this admirable agreement between interest and justice gives to the common deliberations an equitable character which at once vanishes when any particular question is discussed, in the absence of a common interest to unite and identify the ruling of the judge with that of the party.

From whatever side we approach our principle, we reach the same conclusion, that the social compact sets up among the citizens an equality of such a kind, that they all bind themselves to observe the same conditions and should therefore all enjoy the same rights. Thus, from the very nature of the compact, every act of Sovereignty, i.e., every authentic act of the general will, binds or favours all the citizens equally; so that the Sovereign recognises only the body of the nation, and draws no distinctions between those of whom it is made up. What, then, strictly speaking, is an act of Sovereignty? It is not a convention between a superior and an inferior, but a convention between the body and each of its members. It is legitimate, because based on the social contract, and equitable, because common to all; useful, because it can have no other object than the general good, and stable, because guaranteed by the public force and the supreme power. So long as the subjects have to submit only to conventions of this sort, they obey no-one but their own will; and to ask how far the respective rights of the Sovereign and the citizens extend, is to ask up to what point the latter can enter into undertakings with themselves, each with all, and all with each.

We can see from this that the sovereign power, absolute, sacred and inviolable as it is, does not and cannot exceed the limits of general conventions, and that every man may dispose at will of such goods and liberty as these conventions leave him; so that the Sovereign never has a right to lay more charges on one subject than on another, because, in that case, the question becomes particular, and ceases to be within its competency.

When these distinctions have once been admitted, it is seen to be so untrue that there is, in the social contract, any real renunciation on the part of the individuals, that the position in which they find themselves as a result of the contract is really preferable to that in which they were before. Instead of a renunciation, they have made an advantageous exchange: instead of an uncertain and precarious way of living they have got one that is better and more secure; instead of natural independence they have got liberty, instead of the power to harm others security for themselves, and instead of their strength, which others might overcome, a right which social union makes invincible. Their very life, which they have devoted to the State, is by it constantly protected; and when they risk it in the State's defence, what more are they doing than giving back what they have received from it? What are they doing that they would not do more often and with greater danger in the state of nature, in which they would inevitably have to fight battles at the peril of their lives in defence of that which is the means of their preservation? All have indeed to fight when their country needs them; but then no one has ever to fight for himself. Do we not gain something by running, on behalf of what gives us our security, only some of the risks we should have to run for ourselves, as soon as we lost it?

5. The Right of Life and Death

The question is often asked how individuals, having no right to dispose of their own lives, can transfer to the Sovereign a right which they do not possess. The difficulty of answering this question seems to me to lie in its being wrongly stated. Every man has a right to risk his own life in order to preserve it. Has it ever been said that a man who throws himself out of the window to escape from a fire is guilty of suicide? Has such a crime ever been laid to the charge of him who perishes in a storm because, when he went on board, he knew of the danger?

The social treaty has for its end the preservation of the contracting parties. He who wills the end wills the means also, and the means must involve some risks, and even some losses. He who wishes to preserve his life at others' expense should also, when it is necessary, be ready to give it up for their sake. Furthermore, the citizen is no longer the judge of the dangers to which the law desires him to expose himself; and when the prince says to him: "It is expedient for the State that you should die," he ought to die, because it is only on that condition that he has been living in security up to the present, and because his life is no longer a mere bounty of nature, but a gift made conditionally by the State.

6. Law

By the social compact we have given the body politic existence and life; we have now by legislation to give it movement and will. For the original act by which the body is formed and united still in no respect determines what it ought to do for its preservation.

What is well and in conformity with order is so by the nature of things and independently of human conventions. All justice comes from God, who is its sole source; but if we knew how to receive so high an inspiration, we should need neither government nor laws. Doubtless, there is a universal justice emanating from reason alone; but this justice, to be admitted among us, must be mutual. Humanly speaking, in default of natural sanctions, the laws of justice are ineffective among men: they merely make for the good of the wicked and the undoing of the just, when the just man observes them towards everybody and nobody observes them towards him. Conventions and laws are therefore needed to join rights to duties and refer justice to its object. In the state of nature, where everything is common, I owe nothing to him whom I have promised nothing; I recognise as belonging to others only what is of no use to me. In the state of society all rights are fixed by law, and the case becomes different.

But what, after all, is a law? As long as we remain satisfied with attaching purely metaphysical ideas to the word, we shall go on arguing without arriving at an understanding; and when we have defined a law of nature, we shall be no nearer the definition of a law of the State.

I have already said that there can be no general will directed to a particular object. Such an object must be either within or outside the State. If outside, a will which is alien to it cannot be, in relation to it, general; if within, it is part of the State, and in that case there arises a relation between whole and part which makes them two separate beings, of which the part is one, and the whole minus the part the other. But the whole minus a part cannot be the whole; and while this relation persists, there can be no whole, but only two unequal parts; and it follows that the will of one is no longer in any respect general in relation to the other.

But when the whole people decrees for the whole people, it is considering only itself; and if a relation is then formed, it is between two aspects of the entire object, without there being any division of the whole. In that case the matter about which the decree is made is, like the decreeing will, general. This act is what I call a law.

When I say that the object of laws is always general, I mean that law considers subjects *en masse* and, actions in the abstract, and never a particular person or action. Thus the law may indeed decree that there shall be privileges, but cannot confer them on anybody by name. It may set up several classes of citizens, and even lay down the qualifications for membership of these classes, but it cannot nominate such and such persons as belonging to them; it may establish a monarchical government and hereditary succession, but it cannot choose a king, or nominate a royal family. In a word, no function which has a particular object belongs to the legislative power.

On this view, we at once see that it can no longer be asked whose business it is to make laws, since they are acts of the general will; nor whether the prince is above the law, since he is a member of the State; nor whether the law can be unjust, since no one is unjust to himself; nor how we can be both free and subject to the laws, since they are but registers of our wills.

Laws are, properly speaking, only the conditions of civil association. The people, being subject to the laws, ought to be their author: the conditions of the society ought to be regulated solely by those who come together to form it. But how are they to regulate them? Is it to be by common agreement, by a sudden inspiration? Has the body politic an organ to declare its will? Who can give it the foresight to formulate and announce its acts in advance? Or how is it to announce them in the hour of need? How can a blind multitude, which often does not know what it wills, because it rarely knows what is good for it, carry out for itself so great and difficult an enterprise as a system of legislation? Of itself the people wills always the good, but of itself it by no means always sees it. The general will is always in the right, but the judgment which guides it is not always enlightened. It must be got to see objects as they are, and sometimes as they ought to appear to it; it must be shown the good road it is in search of, secured from the seductive influences of individual wills, taught to see times and spaces as a series, and made to weigh the attractions of present and sensible advantages against the danger of distant and hidden evils. The individuals see the good they reject; the public wills the good it does not see. All stand equally in need of guidance. The former must be compelled to bring their wills into conformity with their reason; the latter must be taught to know what it wills. If that is done, public enlightenment leads to the union of understanding and will in the social body: the parts are made to work exactly together, and the whole is raised to its highest power. This makes a legislator necessary.

Book III

4. Democracy

He who makes the law knows better than anyone else how it should be executed and interpreted. It seems then impossible to have a better constitution than that in which the executive and legislative powers are united; but this very fact renders the government in certain respects inadequate, because things which should be distinguished are confounded, and the prince and the Sovereign, being the same person, form, so to speak, no more than a government without government.

It is not good for him who makes the laws to execute them, or for the body of the people to turn its attention away from a general standpoint and devote it to particular objects. Nothing is more dangerous than the influence of private interests in public affairs, and the abuse of the laws by the government is a less evil than the corruption of the legislator, which is the inevitable sequel to a particular standpoint. In such a case, the State being altered in substance, all reformation becomes impossible, a people that would never misuse governmental powers would never misuse independence; a people that would always govern well would not need to be governed.

If we take the term in the strict sense, there never has been a real democracy, and there never will be. It is against the natural order for the many to govern and the few to be governed. It is unimaginable that the people should remain continually assembled to devote their time to public affairs, and it is clear that they cannot set up commissions for that purpose without the form of administration being changed.

In fact, I can confidently lay down as a principle that, when the functions of government are shared by several tribunals, the less numerous sooner or later acquire the greatest authority, if only because they are in a position to expedite affairs, and power thus naturally comes into their hands.

It may be added that there is no government so subject to civil wars and intestine agitations as democratic or popular government, because there is none which has so strong and continual a tendency to change to another form, or which demands more vigilance and courage for its maintenance as it is. Under such a constitution above all, the citizen should arm himself with strength and constancy, and say, every day of his life, what a virtuous Count Palatine said in the Diet of Poland: *Malo periculosam libertatem quam quietum servitium.*

Were there a people of gods, their government would be democratic. So perfect a government is not for men.

11. The Death of the Body Politic

Such is the natural and inevitable tendency of the best constituted governments. If Sparta and Rome perished, what State can hope to endure for ever? If we would set up a long-lived form of government, let us not even dream of making it eternal. If we are to succeed, we must not attempt the impossible, or flatter ourselves that we are endowing the work of man with a stability of which human conditions do not permit.

The body politic, as well as the human body, begins to die as soon as it is born, and carries in itself the causes of its destruction. But both may have a constitution that is more or less robust and suited to preserve them a longer or a shorter time. The constitution of man is the work of nature; that of the State the work of art. It is not in men's power to prolong their own lives; but it is for them to prolong as much as possible the life of the State, by giving it the best possible constitution. The best constituted State will have an end; but it will end later than any other, unless some unforeseen accident brings about its untimely destruction.

The life-principle of the body politic lies in the sovereign authority. The legislative power is the heart of the State; the executive power is its brain, which causes the movement of all the parts. The brain may become paralysed and the individual still live. A man may remain an imbecile and live; but as soon as the heart ceases to perform its functions, the animal is dead.

The State subsists by means not of the laws, but of the legislative power. Yesterday's law is not binding to-day; but silence is taken for tacit consent, and the Sovereign is held to confirm incessantly the laws it does not abrogate as it might. All that it has once declared itself to will it wills always, unless it revokes its declaration.

Why then is so much respect paid to old laws? For this very reason. We must believe that nothing but the excellence of old acts of will can have preserved them so long: if the Sovereign had not recognised them as throughout salutary, it would have revoked them a thousand times. This is why, so far from growing weak, the laws continually gain new strength in any well constituted State; the precedent of antiquity makes them daily more venerable: while wherever the laws grow weak as they become old, this proves that there is no longer a legislative power, and that the State is dead.

15. Deputies or Representatives

As soon as public service ceases to be the chief business of the citizens, and they would rather serve with their money than with their persons, the State is not far from its fall. When it is necessary to march out to war, they pay troops and stay at home: when it is necessary to meet in council, they name deputies and stay at home. By reason of idleness and money, they end by having soldiers to enslave their country and representatives to sell it.

It is through the hustle of commerce and the arts, through the greedy self-interest of profit, and through softness and love of amenities that personal services are replaced by money payments. Men surrender a part of their profits in order to have time to increase them at leisure. Make gifts of money, and you will not be long without chains. The word *finance* is a slavish word, unknown in the city-state. In a country that is truly free, the citizens do everything with their own arms and nothing by means of money; so far from paying to be exempted from their duties, they would even pay for the privilege of fulfilling them themselves. I am far from taking the common view: I hold enforced labour to be less opposed to liberty than taxes.

The better the constitution of a State is, the more do public affairs encroach on private in the minds of the citizens. Private affairs are even of much less importance, because the aggregate of the common happiness furnishes a greater proportion of that of each individual, so that there is less for him to seek in particular cares. In a well-ordered city every man flies to the assemblies: under a bad government no one cares to stir a step to get to them, because no one is interested in what happens there, because it is foreseen that the general will will not prevail, and lastly because domestic cares are all-absorbing. Good laws lead to the making of better ones; bad ones bring about worse. As soon as any man says of the affairs of the State *What does it matter to me?* the State may be given up for lost.

16. That the Institution of Government Is Not a Contract

The legislative power once well established, the next thing is to establish similarly the executive power; for this latter, which operates only by particular acts, not being of the essence of the former, is naturally separate from it. Were it possible for the Sovereign, as such, to possess the executive power, right and fact would be so confounded that no one could tell what was law and what was not; and the body politic, thus disfigured, would soon fall a prey to the violence it was instituted to prevent.

As the citizens, by the social contract, are all equal, all can prescribe what all should do, but no one has a right to demand that another shall do what he does not do himself. It is strictly this right, which is indispensable for giving the body politic life and movement, that the Sovereign, in instituting the government, confers upon the prince.

It has been held that this act of establishment was a contract between the people and the rulers it sets over itself,—a contract in which conditions were laid down between the two parties binding the one to command and the other to obey. It will be admitted, I am sure, that this is an odd kind of contract to enter into. But let us see if this view can be upheld.

First, the supreme authority can no more be modified than it can be alienated; to limit it is to destroy it. It is absurd and contradictory for the Sovereign to set a superior over itself; to bind itself to obey a master would be to return to absolute liberty.

Moreover, it is clear that this contract between the people and such and such persons would be a particular act; and from this it follows that it can be neither a law nor an act of Sovereignty, and that consequently it would be illegitimate.

It is plain too that the contracting parties in relation to each other would be under the law of nature alone and wholly without guarantees of their mutual undertakings, a position wholly at variance with the civil state. He who has force at his command being always in a position to control execution, it would come to the same thing if the name "contract" were given to the act of one man who said to another: "I give you all my goods, on condition that you give me back as much of them as you please."

There is only one contract in the State, and that is the act of association, which in itself excludes the existence of a second. It is impossible to conceive of any public contract that would not be a violation of the first.

Book IV

1. That the General Will Is Indestructible

As long as several men in assembly regard themselves as a single body, they have only a single will which is concerned with their common preservation and general well-being. In this case, all the springs of the State are vigorous and simple and its rules clear and luminous; there are no embroilments or conflicts of interests; the common good is everywhere clearly apparent, and only good sense is needed to perceive it.

But when the social bond begins to be relaxed and the State to grow weak, when particular interests begin to make themselves felt and the smaller societies to exercise an influence over the larger, the common interest changes and finds opponents: opinion is no longer unanimous; the general will ceases to be the will of all; contradictory views and debates arise; and the best advice is not taken without question.

Finally, when the State, on the eve of ruin, maintains only a vain, illusory and formal existence, when in every heart the social bond is broken, and the meanest interest brazenly lays hold of the sacred name of "public good," the general will becomes mute: all men, guided by secret motives, no more give their views as citizens than if the State had never been; and iniquitous decrees directed solely to private interest get passed under the name of laws.

Does it follow from this that the general will is exterminated or corrupted? Not at all: it is always constant, unalterable and pure; but it is subordinated to other wills which encroach upon its sphere. Each man, in detaching his interest from the common interest, sees clearly that he cannot entirely separate them; but his share in the public mishaps seems to him negligible beside the exclusive good he aims at making his own. Apart from this particular good, he wills the general good in his own interest, as strongly as anyone else. Even in selling his vote for money, he does not extinguish in himself the general will, but only eludes it. The fault he commits is that of changing the state of the question, and answering something different from what he is asked. Instead of saying, by his vote, "It is to the advantage of the State," he says, "It is of advantage to this or that man or party that this or that view should prevail." Thus the law of public order in assemblies is not so much to maintain in them the general will as to secure that the question be always put to it, and the answer always given by it.

I could here set down many reflections on the simple right of voting in every act of Sovereignty—a right which no one can take from the citizens—and also on the right of stating views, making proposals, dividing and discussing, which the government is always most careful to leave solely to its members, but this important subject would need a treatise to itself, and it is impossible to say everything in a single work.

2. Voting

There is but one law which, from its nature, needs unanimous consent. This is the social compact; for civil association is the most voluntary of all acts. Every man being born free and his own master, no one, under any pretext whatsoever, can make any man subject without his consent. To decide that the son of a slave is born a slave is to decide that he is not born a man.

If then there are opponents when the social compact is made, their opposition does not invalidate the contract, but merely prevents them from being included in it. They are foreigners among citizens. When the State is instituted, residence constitutes consent; to dwell within its territory is to submit to the Sovereign.

Apart from this primitive contract, the vote of the majority always binds all the rest. This follows from the contract itself. But it is asked how a man can be both free and forced to conform to wills that are not his own. How are the opponents at once free and subject to laws they have not agreed to?

I retort that the question is wrongly put. The citizen gives his consent to all the laws, including those which are passed in spite of his opposition, and even those which punish him when he dares to break any of them. The constant will of all the members of the State is the general will; by virtue of it they are citizens and free. When in the popular assembly a law is proposed, what the people is asked is not exactly whether it approves or rejects the proposal, but whether it is in conformity with the general will, which is their will. Each man, in giving his vote, states his opinion on that point; and the general will is found by counting votes. When therefore the opinion that is contrary to my own prevails, this proves neither more nor less than that I was mistaken, and that what I thought to be the general will was not so. If my particular opinion had carried the day I should have achieved the opposite of what was my will; and it is in that case that I should not have been free.

This presupposes, indeed, that all the qualities of the general will still reside in the majority: when they cease to do so, whatever side a man may take, liberty is no longer possible.

- Go through and highlight all the uses of "Sovereign"
- choose the sentence you like best + say it in your own words
- Discuss
  What are ideas you didn't know?/ new to you?
  What is the Social Contract?
  Does R like democracy?
  What kind of govt does he want?

NOTES

NOTES

School policy
Texas textbooks
Evolution & Climate Change

Handbook –
Rousseau
Mill

2 groups
Is the Handbook a social contract?
Yes / No
Find evidence in Rousseau

What liberties does the OU Handbook preserve? rights? OU Handbook

ORIGINS: FOURTEEN BILLION YEARS OF COSMIC EVOLUTION

Neil deGrasse Tyson and Donald Goldsmith

(1958–)

Neil deGrasse Tyson has a bachelor's in physics from Harvard and a PhD in Astrophysics from Columbia. President Bush appointed him in 2001 to serve on a commission to study the Future of the United States Aerospace Industry and in 2004 on the Implementation of the United States Space Exploration Policy, better known as the "Moon, Mars, and Beyond" commission. He currently serves on the NASA Advisor Council. He has published extensively and appears often on television. He holds eighteen honorary doctorates and is the recipient of the NASA Distinguished Public Service Medal. Currently he is the Frederick P. Rose Director of the Hayden Planetarium in New York City.

(1943–)

Donald Goldsmith graduated from Harvard and received his PhD in astronomy from Berkeley. He served as a full-time consultant at KCET-Television for the series hosted by Carl Sagan, his undergraduate advisor while at Harvard. He has written numerous books and articles.

A Meditation on the Origins of Science and the Science of Origins

A new synthesis of scientific knowledge has emerged and continues to flourish. In recent years, the answers to questions about our cosmic origins have not come solely from the domain of astrophysics. Working under the umbrella of emergent fields with names such as astrochemistry, astrobiology, and astro-particle physics, astrophysicists have recognized that they can benefit greatly from the collaborative infusion of other sciences. To invoke multiple branches of science when answering the question, Where did we come from? empowers investigators with a previously unimagined breadth and depth of insight into how the universe works.

In *Origins: Fourteen Billion Years of Cosmic Evolution,* we introduce the reader to this new synthesis of knowledge, which allows us to address not only the origin of the universe but also the origin of the largest structures that matter has formed, the origin of the stars that light the cosmos, the origin of planets that offer the likeliest sites for life, and the origin of life itself on one or more of those planets.

Reprinted from *Origins: Fourteen Billion Years of Cosmic Evolution* (2004), by permission of W.W. Norton & Company, Inc.

Humans remain fascinated with the topic of origins for many reasons, both logical and emotional. We can hardly comprehend the essence of anything without knowing where it came from. And of all the stories that we hear, those that recount our own origins engender the deepest resonance within us.

Self-centeredness bred into our bones by our evolution and experience on Earth has led us naturally to focus on local events and phenomena in the retelling of most origin stories. However, every advance in our knowledge of the cosmos has revealed that we live on a cosmic speck of dust, orbiting a mediocre star in the far suburbs of a common sort of galaxy, among a hundred billion galaxies in the universe. The news of our cosmic unimportance triggers impressive defense mechanisms in the human psyche. Many of us unwittingly resemble the man in the cartoon who gazes at the starry heavens and remarks to his companion, "When I look at all those stars, I'm struck by how insignificant they are."

Throughout history, different cultures have produced creation myths that explain our origins as the result of cosmic forces shaping our destiny. These histories have helped us to ward off feelings of insignificance. Although origin stories typically begin with the big picture, they get down to Earth with impressive speed, zipping past the creation of the universe, of all its contents, and of life on Earth, to arrive at long explanations of myriad details of human history and its social conflicts, as if we somehow formed the center of creation.

Almost all the disparate answers to the quest of origins accept as their underlying premise that the cosmos behaves in accordance with general rules, which reveal themselves, at least in principle, to our careful examination of the world around us. Ancient Greek philosophers raised this premise to exalted heights, insisting that we humans possess the power to perceive how nature operates, as well as the underlying reality beneath what we observe: the fundamental truths that govern all else. Quite understandably, they insisted that uncovering those truths would be difficult. Twenty-three hundred years ago, in his most famous reflection on our ignorance, the Greek philosopher Plato compared those who strive for knowledge to prisoners chained in a cave, unable to see objects behind them, and who must attempt to deduce from the shadows of these objects an accurate description of reality.

With this simile, Plato not only summarized humanity's attempts to understand the cosmos but also emphasized that we have a natural tendency to believe that mysterious, dimly sensed entities govern the universe, privy to knowledge that we can, at best, glimpse only in part. From Plato to Buddha, from Moses to Mohammed, from a hypothesized cosmic creator to modern films about "the matrix," humans in every culture have concluded that higher powers rule the cosmos, gifted with an understanding of the gulf between reality and superficial appearance.

Half a millennium ago, a new approach toward understanding nature slowly took hold. This attitude, which we now call science, arose from the confluence of new technologies and the discoveries that they fostered. The spread of printed books across Europe, together with simultaneous improvements in travel by road and water, allowed individuals to communicate more quickly and effectively, so that they could learn what others had to say and could respond far more rapidly than in the past. During the sixteenth and seventeenth centuries, this hastened back-and-forth disputation and led to a new way of acquiring knowledge, based on the principle that the most effective means of understanding the cosmos relies on careful observations, coupled with attempts to specify broad and basic principles that explain a set of these observations.

One more concept gave birth to science. Science depends on organized skepticism, that is, on continual, methodical doubting. Few of us doubt our own conclusions, so science embraces its skeptical approach by rewarding those who doubt someone else's. We may rightly call this approach unnatural; not so much because it calls for mistrusting someone else's thoughts, but because science encourages and rewards those who can demonstrate that another scientist's conclusions are just plain wrong. To other scientists, the scientist who corrects a colleague's error, or cites good reasons for seriously doubting his or her conclusions, performs a noble deed, like a Zen master who boxes the ears of a novice straying from the meditative path, although scientists correct one another more as equals than as master and student. By rewarding a scientist who spots another's errors—a task that human nature makes much easier than discerning one's own mistakes—scientists as a group have created an inborn system of self-correction. Scientists have collectively created our most efficient and effective tool for analyzing nature, because they seek to disprove other scientists' theories even as they support their earnest attempts to advance human knowledge. Science thus amounts to a collective pursuit, but a mutual admiration society it is not, nor was meant to be.

Like all attempts at human progress, the scientific approach works better in theory than in practice. Not all scientists doubt one another as effectively as they should. The need to impress scientists who occupy powerful positions, and who are sometimes swayed by factors that lie beyond their conscious knowledge, can interfere with science's self-correcting ability. In the long run, however, errors cannot endure, because other scientists will discover them and promote their own careers by trumpeting the news. Those conclusions that do survive the attacks of other scientists will eventually achieve the status of scientific "laws," accepted as valid descriptions of reality, even though scientists understand that each of these laws may some day find itself to be only part of a larger, deeper truth.

But scientists hardly spend all their time attempting to prove one another mistaken. Most scientific endeavors proceed by testing imperfectly established hypotheses against slightly improved observational results. Every once in a while, however, a significantly new take on an important theory emerges, or (more often in an age of technological advances) a whole new range of observations opens the way to a new set of hypotheses to explain these new results. The greatest moments in scientific history have arisen, and will always arise, when a new explanation, perhaps coupled with new observational results, produces a seismic shift in our conclusions about the workings of nature. Scientific progress depends on individuals in both camps: those who assemble better data and extrapolate carefully from it; and those who risk much—and have much to gain if successful—by challenging widely accepted conclusions.

Science's skeptical core makes it a poor competitor for human hearts and minds, which recoil from its ongoing controversies and prefer the security of seemingly eternal truths. If the scientific approach were just one more interpretation of the cosmos, it would never have amounted to much; but science's big-time success rests on the fact that it works. If you board an aircraft built according to science—with principles that have survived numerous attempts to prove them wrong—you have a far better chance of reaching your destination than you do in an aircraft constructed by the rules of Vedic astrology.

Throughout relatively recent history, people confronted with the success of science in explaining natural phenomena have reacted in one of four ways. First, a small minority have embraced the scientific method as our best hope for understanding nature, and seek no additional ways to comprehend the universe. Second, a much larger number ignore science, judging it uninteresting, opaque, or opposed to the human spirit. (Those who watch television greedily without ever pausing to wonder where the pictures and sound come from remind us that the words "magic" and "machine" share deep etymological roots.) Third, another minority, conscious of the assault that science seems to make upon their cherished beliefs, seek actively to disprove scientific results that annoy or enrage them. They do so, however, quite outside the skeptical framework of science, as you can easily establish by asking one of them, "What evidence would convince you that you are wrong?" These anti-scientists still feel the shock that John Donne described in his poem "The Anatomy of the World: The First Anniversary," written in 1611 as the first fruits of modern science appeared:

And new philosophy calls all in doubt,
The element of fire is quite put out,
The Sun is lost, and th'earth, and no man's wit
Can well direct him where to look for it.
And freely men confess that this world's spent,
When in the planets and the firmament
They seek so many new; they see that this [world]
Is crumbled out again to his atomies.
'Tis all in pieces, all coherence gone . . .

Fourth, another large section of the public accepts the scientific approach to nature while maintaining a belief in supernatural entities existing beyond our complete understanding that rule the cosmos. Baruch Spinoza, the philosopher who created the strongest bridge between the natural and the supernatural, rejected any distinction between nature *and* God, insisting instead that the cosmos is simultaneously nature and God. Adherents of more conventional religions, which typically insist on this distinction, often reconcile the two by mentally separating the domains in which the natural and the supernatural operate.

No matter what camp you may live in, no one doubts that these are auspicious times for learning what's new in the cosmos. Let us then proceed with our adventurous quest for cosmic origins, acting much like detectives who deduce the facts of the crime from the evidence left behind. We invite you to join us in search of cosmic clues—and the means of interpreting them—so that together we may uncover the story of how part of the universe turned into ourselves.

Life in the Universe

Our survey of origins brings us, as we knew it would, to the most intimate and arguably the greatest mystery of all: the origin of life, and in particular of forms of life with which we may someday communicate. For centuries, humans have wondered how we might find other intelligent beings in the cosmos, and with whom we might enjoy at least a modest conversation before we pass into history. The crucial clues for resolving this puzzle may appear in the cosmic blueprint of our own beginnings, which includes Earth's origin within the Sun's family of planets, the origin of the stars that provide energy for life, the origin of structure in the universe, and the origin and evolution of the universe itself.

If we could only read this blueprint in detail, it could direct us from the largest to the smallest astronomical situations, from the unbounded cosmos to individual locations where different types of life flourish and evolve. If we could compare the diverse forms of life that arose under various circumstances, we could perceive the rules of life's beginnings, both in general terms and in particular cosmic situations. Today, we know of only one form of life: life on Earth, all of which shares a common origin and uses DNA molecules as the fundamental means of reproducing itself. This fact deprives us of multiple examples of life, relegating to the future a general survey of life in the cosmos, unachievable until the day we begin to discover forms of life beyond our planet.

Things could be worse. We do know a great deal about life's history on our planet, and must build on this knowledge to derive basic principles about life throughout the universe. To the extent that we can rely on these principles, they will tell us when and where the universe provides, or has provided, the basic requirements for life. In all our attempts to imagine life elsewhere, we must resist falling into the trap of anthropomorphic thinking, our natural tendency to imagine that extraterrestrial forms of life must be much like our own. This entirely human attitude, which arises from our evolutionary and personal experiences here on Earth, restricts our imagination when we attempt to conceive how different life on other worlds may be. Only biologists familiar with the amazing variety and appearance of different forms of life on Earth can confidently extrapolate what extraterrestrial creatures might look like. Their strangeness almost certainly lies beyond the imaginative powers of ordinary humans.

Some day—perhaps next year, perhaps during the coming century, perhaps long after that—we shall either discover life beyond Earth or acquire sufficient data to conclude, as some scientists now suggest, that life on our planet represents a unique phenomenon within our Milky Way galaxy. For now, our lack of information on this subject allows us to consider an enormously broad range of possibilities: We may find life on several objects in the solar system, which would imply that life probably exists within billions of similar planetary systems in our galaxy. Or we may find that Earth alone has life within our solar system, leaving the question of life around other stars open for the time being. Or we may eventually discover that life exists nowhere around other stars, no matter how far and wide we look. In the search for life in the universe, just as in other spheres of activity, optimism feeds on positive results, while pessimistic views grow stronger from negative outcomes. The most recent information that bears upon the chances for life beyond Earth—the discovery that planets are moving in orbit around many of the Sun's neighboring stars—points toward the optimistic conclusion that life may prove relatively abundant in the Milky Way. Nevertheless, great issues remain to be resolved before this conclusion can gain a firmer footing. If, for example, planets are indeed abundant, but almost none of these planets provide the proper conditions for life, then the pessimistic view of extraterrestrial life seems likely to prove correct.

Scientists who contemplate the possibilities of extraterrestrial life often invoke the Drake equation, after Frank Drake, the American astronomer who created it during the early 1960s. The Drake equation provides a useful concept rather than a rigorous statement of how the physical universe works. The equation usefully organizes our knowledge and ignorance by separating the number that we dearly seek to estimate—the number of places where intelligent life now exists in our galaxy—into a set of terms, each of which describes a necessary condition for intelligent life. These terms include (1) the number of stars in the Milky Way that survive sufficiently long for intelligent life to evolve on planets around them; (2) the average number of planets around each of these stars; (3) the fraction of these planets with conditions suitable for life; (4) the probability that life actually arises on these suitable planets; and (5) the chance that life on such a planet evolves to produce an intelligent civilization, by which astronomers typically mean a form of life capable of communicating with ourselves. When we multiply these five terms, we obtain the number of planets in the Milky Way that possess an intelligent civilization at some point in their history. To make the Drake equation yield the number that we seek—the number of intelligent civilizations that exist at any representative time, such as the present—we must multiply this product by a sixth and final term, the ratio of the average lifetime of an intelligent civilization to the total lifetime of the Milky Way galaxy (about 10 billion years).

Each of the Drake equation's six terms requires astronomical, biological, or sociological knowledge. We now have good estimates of the equation's first two terms, and seem likely to obtain a useful estimate of the third before long. On the other hand, terms four and five—the probability that life arises on a suitable planet, and the probability that this life evolves to produce an intelligent civilization—require that we discover and examine various forms of life throughout the galaxy. For now, anyone can argue almost as well as experts can about the value of these terms. What is the probability, for example, that if a planet does have conditions suitable for life, then life will actually begin on that planet? A scientific approach to this question cries out for the study of several planets suitable for life for a few billion years to see how many do produce life. Any attempt to determine the average lifetime of a civilization in the Milky Way likewise requires several billion years of observation, once we have located a sufficiently large number of civilizations to provide a representative sample.

Isn't this a hopeless task? A full solution of the Drake equation indeed lies immensely far in the future—unless we encounter other civilizations that have already solved it, perhaps using us as a data point. But the equation nevertheless provides useful insights for what it takes to estimate how many civilizations exist in our galaxy now. The six terms in the Drake equation all resemble one another mathematically in their effect on the total outcome: each of them exerts a direct, multiplying effect on the equation's answer. If, for instance, you assume that one in three planets suitable for life actually produces life, but later explorations reveal that this ratio actually equals 1 in 30, you will have overestimated the number of civilizations by a factor of 10, assuming that your estimates for the other terms prove correct.

Judging by what we now know, the first three terms in the Drake equation imply that billions of potential sites for life exist in the Milky Way. (We restrict ourselves to the Milky Way out of modesty, plus our awareness that civilizations in other galaxies will have a much more difficult time in establishing contact with us, or we with them.) If you like, you can engage in soul-searching arguments with your friends, family, and colleagues about the value of the remaining three terms, and decide on numbers that will provide your own estimate for the total number of technologically proficient civilizations in our galaxy. If you believe, for example, that most planets suitable for life do produce life, and that most planets with life do evolve intelligent civilizations, you will conclude that billions of planets in the Milky Way produce an intelligent civilization at some point in their time line. If, on the other hand, you conclude that only one suitable planet in a thousand does produce life, and only one life-bearing planet in a thousand evolves intelligent life, you will have only thousands, not billions, of planets with an intelligent civilization. Does this enormous range of answers—potentially even wider than the examples given here—imply that the Drake equation presents wild and unbridled speculation rather than science? Not at all. This result simply testifies to the Herculean labor that scientists, along with everyone else, face in attempting to answer an extremely complex question on the basis of highly limited knowledge.

The difficulty that we face in estimating the values of the last three terms in the Drake equation highlights the treacherous step that we take whenever we make a sweeping generalization from a single example—or from none at all. We are hard pressed, for example, to estimate the average lifetime of a civilization in the Milky Way when we do not even know how long our own will last. Must we abandon all faith in our estimates of these numbers? This would emphasize our ignorance while depriving us of the joy of speculation. If, in the absence of data or dogma, we seek to speculate conservatively, the safest course (though one that might eventually prove to be erroneous) rests on the notion that we are not special. Astrophysicists call this assumption the "Copernican principle" after Nicolaus Copernicus, who, in the mid-1500s, placed the Sun in the middle of our solar system, where it turned out to belong. Until then, despite a third-century B.C. proposal for a Sun-centered universe by the Greek philosopher Aristarchus, the Earth-centered cosmos had dominated popular opinion during most of the past two millennia. Codified by the teachings of Aristotle and Ptolemy, and by the preachings of the Roman Catholic Church, this dogma led most Europeans to accept Earth as the center of all creation. This must have appeared both self-evident from a look at the heavens and the natural result of God's plan for the planet. Even today, enormous segments of Earth's human population—quite likely a significant majority—continue to draw this conclusion from the fact that Earth seemingly remains immobile while the sky turns around us.

Although we have no guarantee that the Copernican principle can guide us correctly in all scientific investigations, it provides a useful counterweight to our natural tendency to think of ourselves as special. Even more significant is that the principle has an excellent track record so far, leaving us humbled at every turn: Earth does not occupy the center of the solar system, nor does the solar system occupy the center of the Milky Way galaxy, nor the Milky Way galaxy the center of the universe. And in case you believe that the edge is a special place, we are not at the edge of anything, either. A wise contemporary attitude therefore assumes that life on Earth likewise follows the Copernican principle. If so, how can life on Earth, its origins, and its components and structure provide clues about life elsewhere in the universe?

In attempting to answer this question, we must digest an enormous array of biological information. For every cosmic data point, gleaned by long observations of objects at enormous distances from us, we know thousands of biological facts. The diversity of life leaves us all, but especially biologists, awestruck on a daily basis. On this single planet Earth, there co-exist (among countless other life forms), algae, beetles, sponges, jellyfish, snakes, condors, and giant sequoias. Imagine these seven living organisms lined up next to each other in order of size. If you didn't know better, you would be challenged to believe that they all came from the same universe, much less the same planet. Try describing a snake to somebody who has never seen one: "You gotta believe me. I just saw this animal on planet Earth that (1) stalks its prey with infrared detectors, (2) swallows whole live animals up to five times bigger than its head, (3) has no arms or legs or any other appendage, yet (4) can slide along level ground almost as fast as you can walk!"

In contrast to the amazing variety of life on Earth, the constricted vision and creativity of Hollywood writers who imagine other forms of life is shameful. Of course, the writers probably blame a public that favors familiar spooks and invaders over truly alien ones. But with a few notable exceptions, such as the life forms in *The Blob* (1958) and in Stanley Kubrick's *2001: A Space Odyssey* (1968), Hollywood aliens all look remarkably humanoid. No matter how ugly (or cute) they may be, nearly all of them have two eyes, a nose, a mouth, two ears, a head, a neck, shoulders, arms, hands, fingers, a torso, two legs, two feet—and they can walk. From an anatomical view, these creatures are practically indistinguishable from humans, yet they are supposed to live on other planets, the products of independent lines of evolution. A clearer violation of the Copernican principle can hardly be found.

Astrobiology—the study of the possibilities for extraterrestrial life—ranks among the most speculative of sciences, but astrobiologists can already assert with confidence that life elsewhere in the universe, intelligent or otherwise, will surely look at least as exotic as some of Earth's own life forms, and quite probably more so. When we assess the chances of life elsewhere in the universe, we must attempt to shake from our brains the notions that Hollywood has implanted. Not an easy task, but essential if we hope to reach a scientific rather than an emotional estimate of our chances of finding creatures with whom we may someday have a quiet conversation.

The Origin of Life on Earth

The search for life in the universe begins with a deep question: What is life? Astrobiologists will tell you honestly that this question has no simple or generally accepted answer. Not much use to say that we'll know it when we see it. No matter what characteristic we specify to separate living from nonliving matter on Earth, we can always find an example that blurs or erases this distinction. Some or all living creatures grow, move, or decay, but so too do objects that we would never call alive. Does life reproduce itself? So does fire. Does life evolve to produce new forms? So do certain crystals that grow in watery solutions. We can certainly say that you can tell some forms of life when you see them—who could fail to see life in a salmon or an eagle?—but anyone familiar with life in its diverse forms on Earth will admit that many creatures will remain entirely undetected until the luck of time and the skill of an expert reveal their living nature.

Since life is short, we must press onward with a rough-and-ready, generally appropriate criterion for life. Here it is: Life consists of sets of objects that can both reproduce and evolve. We shall not call a group of objects alive simply because they make more of themselves. To qualify as life, they must also evolve into new forms as time passes. This definition therefore eliminates the possibility that any single object can be judged to be alive. Instead, we must examine a range of objects in space and follow them through time. This definition of life may yet prove too restrictive, but for now we shall employ it.

As biologists have examined the different types of life on our planet, they have discovered a general property of Earthlife. The matter within every living Earth creature mainly consists of just four chemical elements: hydrogen, oxygen, carbon, and nitrogen. All the other elements together contribute less than one percent of the mass of any living organism. The elements beyond the big four include small amounts of phosphorus, which ranks as the most important, and is essential to most forms of life, together with still smaller amounts of sulfur, sodium, magnesium, chlorine, potassium, calcium, and iron.

But can we conclude that this elemental property of life on Earth must likewise describe other forms of life in the cosmos? Here we can apply the Copernican principle in full vigor. The four elements that form the bulk of life on Earth all appear on the short list of the universe's six most abundant elements. Since the other two elements on that list, helium and neon, almost never combine with anything else, life on Earth consists of the most abundant and chemically active ingredients in the cosmos. Of all the predictions that we can make about life on other worlds, the surest seems to be that their life will be made of elements nearly the same as those used by life on Earth. If life on our planet consisted primarily of four extremely rare elements in the cosmos, such as niobium, bismuth, gallium, and plutonium, we would have an excellent reason to suspect that we represent something special in the universe. Instead, the chemical composition of life on our planet inclines us toward an optimistic view of life's possibilities beyond Earth.

The composition of life on Earth fits the Copernican principle even more than one might initially suspect. If we lived on a planet made primarily of hydrogen, oxygen, carbon, and nitrogen, then the fact that life consists primarily of these four elements would hardly surprise us. But Earth is mainly made of oxygen, iron, silicon, and magnesium, and its outermost layers are mostly oxygen, silicon, aluminum, and iron. Only one of these elements, oxygen, appears on the list of life's most abundant elements.

When we look into Earth's oceans, which are almost entirely hydrogen and oxygen, it is surprising that life lists carbon and nitrogen among its most abundant elements, rather than chlorine, sodium, sulfur, calcium, or potassium, which are the most common elements dissolved in seawater. The distribution of the elements in life on Earth resembles the composition of the stars far more than that of Earth itself. As a result, life's elements are more cosmically abundant than Earth's—a good start for those who hope to find life in a host of situations.

Once we have established that the raw materials for life are abundant throughout the cosmos, we may proceed to ask: How often do these raw materials, along with a site on which these materials can collect and a convenient source of energy such as a nearby star, lead to the existence of life itself? Someday, when we have made a good survey of possible sites for life in our Sun's neighborhood, we shall have a statistically accurate answer to this question. In the absence of these data, we must take a roundabout path to an answer and ask, How did life begin on Earth?

The origin of life on Earth remains locked in murky uncertainty. Our ignorance about life's beginnings stems in large part from the fact that whatever events made inanimate matter come alive occurred billions of years ago and left no definitive traces behind. For times more than 4 billion years in the past, the fossil and geological record of Earth's history does not exist. Yet the interval in solar system history between 4.6 and 4 billion years ago—the first 600 million years after the Sun and its planets had formed—includes the era when most paleobiologists, specialists in reconstructing life that existed during long-vanished epochs, believe that life first appeared on our planet.

The absence of all geological evidence from epochs more than 4 billion years ago arises from motions of Earth's crust, familiarly called continental drift but scientifically known as plate tectonics. These motions, driven by heat that wells up from Earth's interior, continually force pieces of our planet's crust to slide, collide, and ride by or over one another. Plate tectonic motions have slowly buried everything that once lay on Earth's surface. As a result, we possess few rocks older than 2 billion years, and none more than 3.8 billion years in age. This fact, together with the reasonable conclusion that the most primitive forms of life had little chance of leaving behind fossil evidence, has left our planet devoid of any reliable record of life during Earth's first 1 or 2 billion years. The oldest definite evidence we have for life on Earth takes us back "only" 2.7 billion years into the past, with indirect indications that life did exist more than 1 billion years before then.

Most paleobiologists believe that life must have appeared on Earth at least 3 billion years ago, and quite possibly more than 4 billion years ago, within the first 600 million years after Earth formed. Their conclusion relies on a reasonable supposition about primitive organisms. At times a bit less than 3 billion years ago, significant amounts of oxygen began to appear in Earth's atmosphere. We know this from Earth's geological record independently of any fossil remains: oxygen promotes the slow rusting of iron-rich rocks, which produces lovely red tones like those of the rocks in Arizona's Grand Canyon. Rocks from the pre-oxygen era show neither any such colors nor other telltale signs of the element's presence.

The appearance of atmospheric oxygen was the greatest pollution ever to occur on Earth. Atmospheric oxygen does more than combine with iron; it also takes food from the (metaphorical) mouths of primitive organisms by combining with all the simple molecules that could otherwise have provided nutrients for early forms of life. As a result, oxygen's appearance in Earth's atmosphere meant that all forms of life had to adapt or die—and that if life had not appeared by that time, it could never do so thereafter, because the would-be organisms would have nothing to eat, for their potential food would have rusted away. Evolutionary adaptation to this pollution worked well in many cases, as all oxygen-breathing animals can testify. Hiding from the oxygen also did the trick. To this day, every animal's stomach, including our own, harbor billions of organisms that thrive in the anoxic environment that we provide, but would die if exposed to air.

What made Earth's atmosphere relatively rich in oxygen? Much of it came from tiny organisms floating in the seas, which released oxygen as part of their photosynthesis. Some oxygen would have appeared even in the absence of life, as UV from sunlight broke apart some of the H_2O molecules at the ocean surfaces, releasing hydrogen and oxygen atoms into the air. Wherever a planet exposes significant amounts of liquid water to starlight, that planet's atmosphere should likewise gain oxygen, slowly but surely, over hundreds of millions or billions of years. There too, atmospheric oxygen would prevent life from originating by combining with all possible nutrients that could sustain life. Oxygen kills! Not what we usually say about this eighth element on the periodic table, but for life throughout the cosmos, this verdict appears accurate: Life must begin early in a planet's history, or else the appearance of oxygen in its atmosphere will put the kibosh on life forever.

By a strange coincidence, the epoch missing from the geological record that includes the origin of life also includes the so-called era of bombardment, which covers those critical first few hundred million years after Earth had formed. All portions of Earth's surface must then have endured a continual rain of objects. During those several hundred thousand millennia, infalling objects as large as the one that made the Meteor Crater in Arizona must have struck our planet several times in every century, with much larger objects, each several miles in diameter, colliding with Earth every few thousand years. Each one of the large impacts would have caused a local remodeling of the surface, so a hundred thousand impacts would have produced global changes in our planet's topography.

How did these impacts affect the origin of life? Biologists tell us that they might have triggered both the appearance and the extinction of life on Earth, not once but many times. Much of the infalling material during the era of bombardment consisted of comets, which are essentially large snowballs laden with tiny rocks and dirt. Their cometary "snow" consists of both frozen water and frozen carbon dioxide, familiarly called dry ice. In addition to their snow, grit, and rocks rich in minerals and metals, the comets that bombarded Earth during its first few hundred million years contained many different types of small molecules, such as methane, ammonia, methyl alcohol, hydrogen cyanide, and formaldehyde. These molecules, along with water, carbon monoxide, and carbon dioxide, provide the raw materials for life. They all consist of hydrogen, carbon, nitrogen, and oxygen, and they all represent the first steps in building complex molecules.

Cometary bombardment therefore appears to have provided Earth with some of the water for its oceans and with material from which life could begin. Life itself might have arrived in these comets, though their low temperatures, typically hundreds of degrees below zero Fahrenheit, argue against the formation of truly complex molecules. But whether or not life arrived with the comets, the largest objects to strike during the era of bombardment might well have destroyed life that had arisen on Earth. Life might have begun, at least in its most primitive forms, in fits and starts many times over, with each new set of organisms surviving for hundreds of thousands or even millions of years, until a collision with a particularly large object wreaked such havoc on Earth that all life perished, only to appear again, and to be destroyed again, after the passage of a similar amount of time.

We can gain some confidence in the fits-and-starts origin of life from two well-established facts. First, life appeared on our planet sooner rather than later, during the first third of Earth's lifetime. If life could and did arise within a billion years, perhaps it could do so in far less time. The origin of life might require no more than a few million, or a few tens of millions, of years. Second, we know that collisions between large objects and Earth have, at intervals of time measured in tens of millions of years, destroyed most of the species alive on our planet. The most famous of these, the Cretaceous-Tertiary extinction 65 million years ago, killed all the non-avian dinosaurs, along with enormous numbers of other species. Even this mass extinction fell short of the most extensive one, the Permian-Triassic mass extinction, that destroyed nearly 90 percent of all species of marine life and 70 percent of all terrestrial vertebrate species, 252 million years ago, leaving fungi as the dominant forms of life on land.

The Cretaceous-Tertiary and Permian-Triassic mass extinctions arose from the collisions of Earth with objects one or two dozen miles across. Geologists have found an enormous 65-million-year-old impact crater, coincident in time with the Cretaceous-Tertiary extinction, that stretches across the northern Yucatan Peninsula and the adjoining seabed. A large crater exists with the same age as the Permian-Triassic extinction, discovered off the northwest coast of Australia, but this mass dying might have arisen from something in addition to a collision, perhaps from sustained volcanic eruptions. Even the single example of the Cretaceous-Tertiary dinosaur extinction reminds us of the immense damage to life that the impact of a comet or asteroid can produce. During the era of bombardment, Earth must have reeled not only from this sort of impact, but also from the much more serious effects of collisions with objects 50, 100, or even 250 miles in diameter. Each of these collisions must have cleared the decks of life, either completely or so thoroughly that only a tiny percentage of living organisms managed to survive, and they must have occurred far more often than collisions with ten-mile-wide objects do now. Our present knowledge of astronomy, biology, chemistry, and geology points toward an early Earth ready to produce life, and a cosmic environment ready to eliminate it. And wherever a star and its planets have recently formed, intense bombardment by debris left over from the formation process may even now be eliminating all forms of life on those planets.

More than 4 billion years ago, most of the debris from the solar system's formation either collided with a planet or moved into orbits where collisions could not occur. As a result, our cosmic neighborhood gradually changed from a region of continual bombardment to the overall calm that we enjoy today, broken only at multi-million-year intervals by collisions with objects large enough to threaten life on Earth. You can compare the ancient and ongoing threat from impacts whenever you look at the full moon. The giant lava plains that create the face of the "man in the Moon" are the result of tremendous impacts some 4 billion years ago, as the era of bombardment ended, whereas the crater named Tycho, fifty-five miles across, arose from a smaller, but still highly significant, impact that occurred soon after the dinosaurs disappeared from Earth.

We do not know whether life already existed 4 billion years ago, having survived the early impact storm, or whether life arose on Earth only after relative tranquility began. These two alternatives include the possibility that incoming objects seeded our planet with life, either during the era of bombardment or soon afterward. If life began and died out repeatedly while chaos rained down from the skies, the processes by which life originated seem robust, so that we might reasonably expect them to have occurred again and again on other worlds similar to our own. If, on the other hand, life arose on Earth only once, either as homegrown life or as the result of cosmic seeding, its origin may have occurred here by luck.

In either case, the crucial question of how life actually began on Earth, either once or many times over, has no good answer, though speculation on the subject has acquired a long and intriguing history. Great rewards lie in store for those who can resolve this mystery. From Adam's rib to Dr. Frankenstein's monster, humans have answered the question by invoking a mysterious *élan vital* that imbues otherwise inanimate matter with life.

Scientists seek to probe more deeply, with laboratory experiments and examinations of the fossil record that attempt to establish the height of the barrier between inanimate and animate matter, and to find how nature breached this dike. Early scientific discussions about the origin of life imagined the interaction of simple molecules, concentrated in pools or tide ponds, to create more complex ones. In 1871, a dozen years after the publication of Charles Darwin's marvelous book *The Origin of Species,* in which he speculated that "probably all of the organic beings which have ever lived on this Earth have descended from some one primordial form," Darwin wrote to his friend Joseph Hooker that

> It is often said that all the conditions for the first production of a living organism are now present, which could ever have been present. But if (and oh! what a big if!) we could conceive in some warm little pond, with all sorts of ammonia and phosphoric salts, light, heat, electricity &c., present, that a proteine [*sic*] compound was chemically formed ready to undergo still more complex changes, at the present day such matter would be instantly absorbed, which would not have been the case before living creatures were found.

In other words, when Earth was ripe for life, the basic compounds necessary for metabolism might have existed in surplus, with nothing in existence to eat them (and, as we have discussed, no oxygen to combine with them and spoil their chances to serve as food).

From a scientific perspective, nothing succeeds like experiments that can be compared with reality. In 1953, seeking to test Darwin's conception of the origin of life in ponds or tide pools, Stanley Miller, who was then a U.S. graduate student working at the University of Chicago with the Nobel laureate Harold Urey, performed a famous experiment that duplicated the conditions within a highly simplified and hypothetical pool of water on the early Earth. Miller and Urey partly filled a laboratory flask with water and topped the water with a gaseous mixture of water vapor, hydrogen, ammonia, and methane. They heated the flask from below, vaporizing some of the contents and driving them along a glass tube into another flask, where an electrical discharge simulated the effect of lightning. From there the mixture returned to the original flask, completing a cycle that would be repeated over and over during a few days, rather than a few thousand years. After this entirely modest time interval, Miller and Urey found the water in the lower flask to be rich in "organic gunk," a compound of numerous complex molecules, including different types of sugar, as well as two of the simplest amino acids, alanine and guanine.

Since protein molecules consist of twenty types of amino acids arranged into different structural forms, the Miller-Urey experiment takes us, in a remarkably brief time, a significant part of the way from the simplest molecules to the amino-acid molecules that form the building blocks of living organisms. The Miller-Urey experiment also made some of the modestly complex molecules called nucleotides, which provide the key structural element for DNA, the giant molecule that carries instructions for forming new copies of an organism. Even so, a long path remains before life emerges from experimental laboratories. An enormously significant gap, so far unbridged by human experiment or invention, separates the formation of amino acids—even if our experiments produced all twenty of them, which they do not—and the creation of life. Amino-acid molecules have also been found in some of the oldest and least altered meteorites, believed to have remained unchanged for nearly the entire 4.6-billion-year history of the solar system. This supports the general conclusion that natural processes can make amino acids in many different situations. A balanced view of the experimental results finds nothing totally surprising: The simpler molecules found in living organisms form quickly in many situations, but life does not. The key question still remains: How does a collection of molecules, even one primed for life to appear, ever generate life itself?

Since the early Earth had not weeks but many million years in which to bring forth life, the Miller-Urey experimental results seemed to support the tide-pool model for life's beginnings. Today, however, most scientists who seek to explain life's origin consider the experiment to have been significantly limited by its techniques. Their shift in attitude arose not from doubting the test's results but rather from recognizing a potential flaw in the hypotheses underlying the experiment. To understand this flaw, we must consider what modern biology has demonstrated about the oldest forms of life.

Evolutionary biology now relies on careful study of the similarities and differences between living creatures in their molecules of DNA and RNA, which carry the information that tells an organism how to function and how to reproduce. Careful comparison of these relatively enormous and complex molecules bas allowed biologists, among whom the great pioneer has been Carl Woese, to create an evolutionary tree of life that records the "evolutionary distances" between various life forms, as determined by the degrees to which these life forms have nonidentical DNA and RNA.

The tree of life consists of three great branches, Archaea, Bacteria, and Eucarya, that replace the biological "kingdoms" formerly believed to be fundamental. The Eucarya includes every organism whose individual cells have a well-defined center or nucleus that contains the genetic material governing the cells' reproduction. This characteristic makes Eucarya more complex than the other two types, and indeed every form of life familiar to the non-expert belongs to this branch. We may reasonably conclude that Eucarya arose later than Archaea or Bacteria. And because Bacteria be farther from the origin of the tree of life than the Archaea do—for the simple reason that their DNA and RNA has changed more—the Archaea, as their name implies, almost certainly represent the oldest forms of life. Now comes a shocker: Unlike the Bacteria and Eucarya, the Archaea consist mainly of "extremophiles," organisms that love to live, and live to love, in what we now call extreme conditions: temperatures near or above the boiling point of water, high acidity, or other situations that would kill other forms of life. (Of course, if the extremophiles had their own biologists, they would classify themselves as normal and any life that thrives at room temperature as an extremophile.) Modern research into the tree of life tends to suggest that life began with the extremophiles, and only later evolved into forms of life that benefit from what we call normal conditions.

In that case, Darwin's "warm little pond," as well as the tide pools duplicated in the Miller-Urey experiment, would evaporate into the mist of rejected hypotheses. Gone would be the relatively mild cycles of drying and wetting. Instead, those who seek to find the places where life may have begun would have to look to locales where extremely hot water, possibly laden with acids, surges from Earth.

The past few decades have allowed oceanographers to discover just such places, along with the strange forms of life they support. In 1977, two oceanographers piloting a deep sea submersible vehicle discovered the first deep sea vents, a mile and a half beneath the calm surface of the Pacific Ocean near the Galápagos Islands. At these vents, Earth's crust behaves locally like a household cooker, generating high pressure inside a heavy-duty pot with a lockable lid and heating water beyond its ordinary boiling temperature without letting it reach an actual boil. As the lid partially lifts, the pressurized, superheated water spews out from below Earth's crust into the cold ocean basins.

The superheated seawater that emerges from these vents carries dissolved minerals that quickly collect and solidify to surround the vents with giant, porous rock chimneys, hottest in their cores and coolest at the edges that make direct contact with seawater. Across this temperature gradient live countless life forms that have never seen the Sun and care nothing for solar heating, though they do require the oxygen dissolved in seawater, which in turn comes from the existence of solar driven life near the surface. These hardy bugs live on geothermal energy, which combines heat left over from Earth's formation with heat continuously produced by the radioactive decay of unstable isotopes such as aluminum-26, which lasts for millions of years, and potassium-40, which lasts for billions.

Near these vents, far below the depths to which any sunlight can penetrate, the oceanographers found tube worms as long as a man, thriving amidst large colonies of bacteria and other small creatures. Instead of driving their energy from sunlight, as plants do with photosynthesis, life near deep sea vents relies on "chemosynthesis," the production of energy by chemical reactions, which in turn depend on geothermal heating.

How does this chemosynthesis occur? The hot water gushing from the deep sea vents emerges laden with hydrogen-sulfur and hydrogen-iron compounds. Bacteria near the vents combine these molecules with the hydrogen and oxygen atoms in water molecules, and with the carbon and oxygen atoms of the carbon dioxide molecules dissolved in sea water. These reactions form larger molecules—carbohydrates—from carbon, oxygen, and hydrogen atoms. Thus the bacteria near deep sea vents mimic the activities of their cousins far above, which likewise make carbohydrates from carbon, oxygen, and hydrogen. One set of microorganisms draws the energy to make carbohydrates from sunlight, and the other from chemical reactions at the ocean floors. Close by the deep sea vents, other organisms consume the carbohydrate-making bacteria, profiting from their energy in the same way that animals eat plants, or eat plant-eating animals.

In the chemical reactions near deep sea vents, however, more goes on than the production of carbohydrate molecules. The iron and sulfur atoms, which are not included in the carbohydrate molecule, combine to make compounds of their own, most notably crystals of iron pyrite, familiarly called "fool's gold," known to the ancient Greeks as "fire stone" because a good blow from another rock will strike sparks from it. Iron pyrite, the most abundant of all the sulfur-bearing minerals found on Earth, might have played a crucial role in the origin of life by encouraging the formation of carbohydratelike molecules. This hypothesis sprang from the mind of a German patent attorney and amateur biologist, Günter Wächtershäuser, whose profession hardly excludes him from biological speculation, any more than Einstein's work as a patent attorney barred him from insights into physics. (To be sure, Einstein had an advanced degree in physics, while Wächtershäuser's biology and chemistry are mainly self-taught.)

In 1994, Wächtershäuser proposed that the surfaces of iron pyrite crystals, formed naturally by combining iron and sulfur that surged from deep sea vents early in Earth's history, would have offered natural sites where carbon-rich molecules could accumulate, acquiring new carbon atoms from the material ejected by the nearby vents. Like those who hypothesize that life began in ponds or tide pools, Wächtershäuser has no clear way to pass from the building blocks to living creatures. Nevertheless, with his emphasis on the high-temperature origin of life, he may prove to be on the right track, as he firmly believes. Referring to the highly ordered structure of iron pyrite crystals, on whose surfaces the first complex molecules for life might have formed, Wächtershäuser has confronted his critics at scientific conferences with the striking statement that "Some say that the origin of life brings order out of chaos—but I say, 'order out of order out of order!'" Delivered with German brio, this claim acquires a certain resonance, though only time can tell how accurate it may be.

So which basic model for life's origin is more likely to prove correct—tide pools at the ocean's edge, or superheated vents on the ocean floors? For now, the betting is about even. Experts on the origin of life have challenged the assertion that life's oldest forms lived at high temperatures, because current methods for placing organisms at different points along the branches of the tree of life remain the subject of debate. In addition, computer programs that trace out how many compounds of different types existed in ancient RNA molecules, the close cousins of DNA that apparently preceded DNA in life's history, suggest that the compounds favored by high temperatures appeared only after life had undergone some relatively low-temperature history.

Thus the outcome of our finest research, as so often occurs in science, proves unsettling to those who seek certainty. Although we can state approximately when life began on Earth, we don't know where or how this marvelous event occurred. Paleobiologists have recently given the elusive ancestor of all Earthlife the name LUCA, for the last universal common ancestor. (See how firmly these scientists' minds have remained fixed to our planet: they should call life's progenitor LECA, for the last Earthly common ancestor.) For now, naming this ancestor—a set of primitive organisms that all shared the same genes—mainly underscores the distance that we still must travel before we can pierce the veil that separates life's origin from our understanding.

More than a natural curiosity as to our own beginnings hinges on the resolution of this issue. Different origins for life imply different possibilities for its origin, evolution, and survival both here and elsewhere in the cosmos. For example, Earth's ocean floors may provide the most stable ecosystem on our planet. If a jumbo asteroid slammed into Earth and rendered all surface life extinct, the oceanic extremophiles would almost certainly continue undaunted in their happy ways. They might even evolve to repopulate Earth's surface after each extinction episode. And if the Sun were mysteriously plucked from the center of the solar system and Earth drifted through space, this event would hardly merit attention in the extremophile press, as life near deep sea vents might continue relatively undisturbed. But in 5 billion years, the Sun will become a red giant as it expands to fill the inner solar system. Meanwhile, Earth's oceans will boil away and Earth itself will partially vaporize. Now that would be news for any form of Earthlife.

The ubiquity of extremophiles on Earth leads us to a profound question: Could life exist deep within many of the rogue planets or planetesimals that were ejected from the solar system during its formation? Their "geo" thermal reservoirs could last for billions of years. What about the countless planets that were forcibly ejected by every other solar system that ever formed? Could interstellar space be teeming with life—formed and evolved deep within these starless planets? Before astrophysicists recognized the importance of extremophiles, they envisioned a "habitable zone" surrounding each star, within which water or another substance could maintain itself as a liquid, allowing molecules to float, interact, and produce more complex molecules. Today, we must modify this concept, so that far from being a tidy region around a star that receives just the right amount of sunlight, a habitable zone can be anywhere and everywhere, maintained not by starlight heating but by localized heat sources, often generated by radioactive rocks. So the Three Bears' cottage was, perhaps, not a special place among fairy tales. Anybody's residence, even one of the Three Little Pigs', might contain a bowl of food at a temperature that is just right.

What a hopeful, even prescient fairy tale this may prove to be. Life, far from being rare and precious, may be almost as common as planets themselves. All that remains is for us to go find it.

NOTES

FOR FURTHER READING

"Never, ever, think outside the box."

Courtesy of Leo Cullum/The New Yorker Collection.

THE BETRAYAL OF THE MENTORS
Mark Bauerlein

Mark Bauerlein is an author and professor at Emory University and has also served as director of Research and Analysis at the National Endowment for the Arts. In 2008 he published the book, The Dumbest Generation: How the Digital Age Stupefies Young Americans and Jeopardizes Our Future; Or, Don't Trust Anyone Under 30.

It is the nature of adolescents to believe that authentic reality begins with themselves, and that what long preceded them is irrelevant. For 15-year-olds in the United States in the twenty-first century, the yardstick of pertinence is personal contact, immediate effects. Space and time extend not much further than their circumstances, and what does Holbein's portrait of Sir Thomas More have to say to a kid who works at Wendy's, struggles with algebra, and can't find a girlfriend? The attitude marks one of the signal changes of the twentieth century in the United States. It insists that a successful adolescence and rightful education entail growing comfortable with yourself, with who you are at age 17. Many generations ago, adolescent years meant preparation for something beyond adolescence, not authentic selfhood but serious work, civic duty, and family responsibility, with parents, teachers, ministers, and employers training teens in grown-up conduct. Adolescence formed a tenuous middle ground between the needs of childhood and the duties of adulthood, and the acquisition of the virtues of manhood and womanhood was an uncertain progress. It did not terminate with an acceptance and approval of the late-teen identity. The shrewdest approach was not to prize the interval but to escape it as efficiently as possible.

Not anymore. For a long time now, adolescence has claimed an independent value, an integrity all its own. The rise of adolescence is too long a story to tell, but the stance of teachers and researchers that fostered it may be indicated by a few highlights. In one of its first authoritative expressions, Professor G. Stanley Hall, president of Clark University and head of the American Psychological Association, composed a massive volume outlining the uniqueness of the stage. In *Adolescence: Its Psychology and Its Relations to Physiology . . .* (1904), he observed in glorious cadences, "Self-feeling and ambition are increased, and every trait and faculty is liable to exaggeration and excess. It is all a marvelous new birth, and those who believe that nothing is so worthy of love, reverence, and service as the body and soul of youth, and who hold that the best test of every human institution is how much it contributes to bring youth to the ever fullest possible development, may well review themselves and the civilization in which we live to see how far it satisfies this supreme test."

Reprinted from *The Dumbest Generation: How the Digital Age Stupefies Young Americans and Jeopardizes Our Future* (2008), by permission of Penguin Group (USA), Inc.

A cover story in *Time* magazine exemplifies it well (24 Jan 2005). The article profiles a new youth phenomenon, an unforeseen generational sub-cohort termed the "Twixters." This curious social outcropping rests in a novel cluster of demographic traits. Twixters:

- are 22 to 30 years old;
- have a college degree, or substantial college coursework;
- come from middle-class families; and
- reside in cities and large suburban centers.

These features embody nothing unusual, certainly, but where they lead is surprising. What makes the Twixters different from other people with the same demographics from the past is the lifestyle they pursue after college.

Despite their circumstances, Twixters aren't marginal youngsters sinking into the underclass. They drift through their twenties, stalled at work and saving no money, but they like it that way. They congregate just as they did before college, hopping bar to bar on Friday night and watching movies on Saturday. They have achieved little, but they feel good about themselves. Indeed, precisely along the lines of Reich's understanding, they justify their aimless lifestyle as a journey of self-discovery. Yes, they put off the ordinary decisions of adulthood (career, marriage), but with a tough job market and so many divorced parents, their delays mark a thoughtful desire to "search their souls and choose their life paths," to find a livelihood right for their "identity." So Lev Grossman, the author of the story, phrases it. Social scientists quoted in the article, too, ennoble the lifestyles, judging Twixter habits (in Grossman's paraphrase) "important work to get themselves ready for adulthood." These young people take adulthood "so seriously, they're spending years carefully choosing the right path into it." University of Maryland psychologist Jeffrey Arnett dislikes the "Twixter" label, preferring "emerging adulthood." They assume no responsibilities for or to anyone else, he concedes, but that only permits them "this wonderful freedom to really focus on their own lives and work on becoming the kind of person they want to be." Sociologist James Côté blames their delay on the economy: "What we're looking at really began with the collapse of the youth labor market," he says, which persists today and means that young people simply can't afford to settle down until their late twenties. Marshall Heskovitz, creator of the television shows *thirtysomething* and *My So-Called Life*, gives the problem a social/emotional angle: "it's a result of the world not being particularly welcoming when they come into it. Lots of people have a difficult time dealing with it, and they try to stay kids as long as they can because they don't know how to make sense of all this. We're interested in this process of finding courage and one's self." And a Dartmouth neuroscientist backs the economic and social resistances with brain chemistry: "We as a society deem an individual at the age of 18 ready for adult responsibility. Yet recent evidence suggests that our neuropsychological development is many years from being complete."

Their comments apply a positive spin to what less sympathetic elders would call slacker ways. But even if we accept the characterizations—their brains aren't ready, the cost of living is high, they take marriage too seriously to plunge into it—there is something missing from the expert observations in the article, an extraordinary absence in the diagnosis. In casting Twixter lifestyle as genuine exploration and struggle, neither the author nor the researchers nor the Twixters themselves whisper a single word about intellectual labor. Not one of the Twixters or youth observers mentions an idea that stirs them, a book that influenced them, a class that inspired them, or a mentor who guides them. Nobody ties maturity to formal or informal learning, reading or studying, novels or paintings or histories or syllogisms. For all the talk about life concerns and finding a calling, none of them regard history, literature, art, civics, philosophy, or politics a helpful undertaking. Grossman speaks of Twixter years as "a chance to build castles and knock them down," but these castles haven't a grain of intellectual sand in them. As these young people forge their personalities in an uncertain world, they skirt one of the customary means of doing so—that is, acquainting themselves with the words and images, the truths and beauties of the past—and nobody tells them they have overlooked anything. Social psychologists don't tell them so, nor do youth experts and educators, but the anti-intellectual banality of their choices is stark. What is the role of books in the Twixter's world? Negligible. How has their education shaped their lives? Not at all. This is what the Twixters themselves report. One of them remarks, "Kids used to go to college to get educated. That's what I did, which I think now was a bit naïve. Being smart after college doesn't really mean anything."

In a word, the Twixter vision aligns perfectly with that of their wired younger brothers and sisters. It's all social, all peer-oriented. Twixters don't read, tour museums, travel, follow politics, or listen to any music but pop and rap, much less do something such as lay out a personal reading list or learn a foreign language. Rather, they do what we expect an average 19-year-old to do. They meet for poker, buy stuff at the mall, and jump from job to job and bed to bed. The maturity they envision has nothing to do with learning and wisdom, and the formative efforts that social scientists highlight don't include books, artworks, ideologies, or Venn diagrams. For the Twixters, mature identity is entirely a social matter developed with and through their friends. The intellectual and artistic products of the past aren't stepping-stones for growing up. They are the fading materials of meaningless schooling.

Does tradition have to retire so conspicuously in order for the adolescent self to come into its own?

Spend some hours in school zones and you see that the indulgent attitude toward youth, along with the downplaying of tradition, has reached the point of dogma among teachers, reporters, researchers, and creators in arts and humanities fields, and pro-knowledge, pro-tradition conceptions strike them as bluntly unpleasant, if not reactionary and out of touch. Indeed, the particular mode of sympathy for the kids has taken such a firm hold that offering education as a fruitful dialectic of tradition and individuality looks downright smothering. Uttered so rarely in education circles, a modest opinion in favor of tradition comes across to experts and mentors as an aggression against the students, a curmudgeon's grievance. For many of them, the power of cultural tradition sounds authoritarian and retrograde, or aligned with a Eurocentric, white male lineage, their view recalling the Culture Wars of the 1980s when conservative activists battled liberal professors over the content of the curriculum in English classes. In truth, however, the indulgence crosses ideological boundaries, touching generational feelings that mix widely among liberals and conservatives alike. It's not a political conflict. It's a cultural condition, a normative sentiment positioning young people in relation to a past and a future, the cultural inheritance and their prospective adulthood. Instead of charting as Left or Right, it charts as traditionalist or self-centered (or youth-centered, present-fixated, individualist). And while traditionalists lean toward conservative opinion, many liberals feel a similar respect for the past and impatience with youth self-absorption, and many conservatives no longer set their moral values, religious faith, and civic pride under the long shadow of great books and thoughts and artworks.

What makes someone say to an adolescent, "Before you sally forth into the world, heed the insight of people long dead who possessed a lot more talent and wisdom than you," is more a personal ethic than a political creed. The ethic has seeped down to the level of etiquette, so that when a dissenting voice calls for more traditional knowledge, it sounds not just wrong, but wrongheaded, mean-spirited, bad form. The intellectual force of the call is obscured by its impropriety. This is the natural course of a norm. It begins as a fresh and unusual idea, then passes through the stages of argument, clarification, revision, and acceptance. It may have been radical or controversial once, but over time, adopted by more and more people, it turns into common sense and its distinctiveness dims. When an idea becomes a habit, it stops sparking thought. When everybody accepts it, it abides without evidence. At that point, the idea acts as a tacit premise, like travel directions you print out from Mapquest when taking a trip for the first time. You follow the route and arrive at Point B. You don't ponder alternatives. In a traditional classroom from way back when, a youth-centered approach might have appeared iconoclastic and provocative, triggering disputes over learning, maturity, and selfhood. Now it passes without a murmur.

The sentimentality justifies mentors in downgrading their mentoring task. They can't produce much solid evidence of youth brilliance and drive, and so they resort to lofty and flushed language to make the case. "Young adults are fiercely individualistic. . . . They are still incredibly open to new ideas and they want to dabble and experiment." So enthuses a report from the Advertising Council (with funding from MTV and the Pew Research Center), though providing little evidence of the good of their "dabbling." The *Philadelphia Inquirer*'s columnist Jane Eisner acknowledges the embarrassing voting rates of 18- to 29-year-olds, but shifts the issue: "Only if we address the structural reasons that young people don't vote can we begin to count on them to infuse our democracy with the ideas and idealism for which young Americans have always been prized" (Sept 2004). "Always been prized" for their "ideas and idealism"? Since 1965, perhaps, but not before.

Young people pick up these rationalizations and run with them. For a study of news consumption entitled *Tuned Out: Why Americans Under 40 Don't Follow the News* (2005), journalist David Mindich interviewed hundreds of young adults who told him that "the political process is both morally bankrupt and completely insulated from public pressure," a sentiment whose truth is doubtful—how do *they* know?—but that saves them the trouble of civic action. In a 1999 survey by Northwestern University's Medill School of Journalism ("Y Vote 2000: Politics of a New Generation"), 69 percent of 15- to 24-year-olds concurred with the statement "Our generation has an important voice, but no one seems to hear it." The cliché is so hollow it could rank with the statement "Our generation has sexual desires, but no one satisfies them," but it has acquired a seriousness that 50 years ago would have been inconceivable. It is normal for young people, temporarily, to act disaffected and feel unheard, but for the mentors to turn this condition into an injustice is to downgrade their position, with youths only too eager to play along. No matter how benevolent the rhetoric of the mentors, though, the thing it bestows—intellectual independence—does the majority of youths no favors. And this isn't only because most youths aren't ready to exercise it wisely, to their long-term benefit. It's also because, while the indulgence emancipates the young mind, it sends an implicit and far-reaching message, too, one the kids handily discern. It sabotages something that may, perhaps, be more fragile than the transmission of knowledge from old to young, namely, the simple, sturdy conviction that knowledge itself is worth receiving, the conviction that traditions remote from their daily circumstances have any bearing.

When teachers stand before the young and assure them of the integrity and autonomy of what adolescents think and say and write, teachers expect the young to respond affirmatively, to seek out knowledge and truth on their own. And maybe that works for the upper-crust students, those contending zealously for a place at Yale or an internship on the Hill. But beyond that talented tenth or twentieth student, something different happens. All of them expect the mentors to enter the room with credentialed authority, some know-how that justifies their position, even if some of the kids begrudge and reject it. When the mentors disavow their authority, when they let their discipline slacken, when they, in the language of the educators, slide from the "sage on the stage" to the "guide on the side," the kids wonder what goes. They don't consider the equalizing instructor a caring liberator, and they aren't motivated to learn on their own. They draw another, immobilizing lesson. If mentors are so keen to recant their expertise, why should students strain to acquire it themselves?

The opposite of what the indulgers intend sets in. Knowledge and tradition are emptied of authority. Ronald Reagan once declared, "Freedom is never more than one generation away from extinction," but a more elemental rule may be, "Knowledge is never more than one generation away from oblivion." If the guardians of tradition claim that the young, though ignorant, have a special perspective on the past, or if teachers prize the impulses of tenth-graders more than the thoughts of the wise and the works of the masters, learning loses its point. The thread of intellectual inheritance snaps. The young man from Boston who announces with pride that he cares nothing about Rembrandt and Picasso typifies the outcome. His disregard follows from the mentors' disregard, their own infidelity to tradition, and the transfer affects all students more or less, the best and brightest as well as the dropouts. The indulgers assume that their approval will bring teachers and students closer together, throwing students further into academic inquiry, inspiring them to learn and study, but the evidence shows that this does not happen.

One pertinent measure of the trend appears as an item on the *National Survey of Student Engagement* (NSSE). The question tallies how many first-year and senior undergraduates "Discussed ideas from your readings or classes with faculty members outside of class." The activity goes beyond course requirements, the tests and papers, and thus charts how many students are inspired by lectures and homework to confer with the instructor on their own. The numbers are disappointing. In 2003, fully 40 percent of the first-year respondents "Never" exchanged a word with a teacher beyond the classroom. Seniors that year displayed more engagement—only 25 percent responded "Never"—although that is still too high a figure after three years of coursework. Normally, as students proceed, they pursue more specialization in a major and form shared interests and career concerns with teachers. Nevertheless, one quarter of all seniors ignore their professors outside the classroom. Worse, three years later, both ranks increased their disengagement. In 2006, first-year students raised the "Never talk to my teacher" rate to 43 percent, and seniors to 28 percent. More students tune their professors out once the hour is up, and the engagement score gap between seniors and freshmen still stands at only 15 points—a sign that the curriculum hasn't improved.

Notwithstanding the disengagement numbers, however, researchers summarizing the 2003 NSSE survey commend precisely the pedagogical methods of the indulgers. The report observes,

> One of the pleasant surprises from the first few years of NSSE findings was the substantial number of students engaged in various forms of active and collaborative learning activities. This shift from passive, instructor-dominated pedagogy to active, learner-centered activities promises to have desirable effects on learning.

A nice prediction, but wholly without support. As "instructor domination" dwindles, as "learner-centered" classrooms multiply, then students should feel empowered to hunt down their profs at other times and places. But while "active, learner-centered" pedagogies have proliferated, more student-teacher contact hasn't happened, as subsequent NSSE reports show. In a "passive" mode, with an authoritative teacher before them, students may feel more secure and encouraged to consult one-on-one. Once "activated" by power-sharing profs, though, students head elsewhere. A paradox may have set in: the more equal and accessible the teachers, the less accessed they are by the students. Nonetheless, NSSE researchers buy the "learner-centered" assumption. They assert that youth-approving teaching strategies "take students to deeper levels of understanding and meaning," but if deeper understanding entails closer engagement with instructors, their own data don't correlate with the theory.

The researchers could find other noncorrelations elsewhere, too. For instance, *Your First College Year*, a survey of first-year students, sponsored by the Higher Education Research Institute at UCLA, provided the following summary in 2005:

> Although most respondents studied and discussed their courses with other students during the first year, findings suggest that many remain disengaged from their coursework: over half "frequently" or "occasionally" came late to class; almost half turned in course assignments that did not reflect their best work or felt bored in class; and approximately one-third skipped class at least "occasionally" in the first year.

College delinquency of this kind says nothing about these students' intelligence. It marks an attitude, a sign of disrespect, and we may blame several influences for its spread. When colleges treat students as consumers and clients, they encourage it, as does pop culture when it elevates hooky-playing tricksters such as Ferris Bueller into heroes. College professors complain all the time about it, but they have their own part in the students' negligence, for they pass it along whenever they esteem the students' knowledge and deauthorize their own.

That isn't what they think they do, of course, but the effect is the same. Many indulgers believe that teacher-centered instruction bores the kids into diffidence or proves too difficult to handle, and that student-centered instruction will inspire the lesser-caliber students to work harder and stay in school, but in fact those lesser students say otherwise. In a National Governors Association poll of 10,378 teenagers (reported in July 2005), nearly 90 percent intended to graduate, and more than one-third of them stated that high school has been "easy" (less than 10 percent called it "very hard"). Surprisingly, the future dropouts scored similarly on the "hardness" index. Of the 11 percent who admitted that they didn't intend to graduate from high school, only one in nine gave as a reason, "schoolwork is too hard." At the top, at 36 percent, was the claim that they were "not learning anything," 12 points higher than sheer "hate" for the school they attend. The reactions of delinquent college students are less extreme than that, but they echo the high school dropouts' motives. When "instructor-domination" decreases, a few students step up their learning, but most of them cut their discipline, now and then blowing off in-class duties and all the time ignoring their teachers out of class. A 2005 report sponsored by Achieve, Inc., on college and workplace readiness heard less than one-quarter of high school graduates say that they were "significantly challenged and faced high expectations" (*Rising to the Challenge: Are High School Graduates Prepared for College and Work?*). In the *First-Year* study, only 30 percent of students studied 11 or more hours per week, and 39 percent did six hours or less. Only 24 percent "frequently" felt that their courses inspired them "to think in new ways." Half the students (49 percent) visited an instructor's office hours a sorry two times or fewer per term. Let the students guide themselves, and they'll do so happily.

As they glide through their courses, they seem unaware of the long-term disadvantages. Here, too, the abnegation of the mentors plays a role, for in releasing students from the collective past they deny students a resource to foster a healthy and prosperous future. Dissociated from tradition, with nobody telling them that sometimes they must mute the voices inside them and heed instead the voices of distant greatness, young people miss one of the sanative, humbling mechanisms of maturity. This is the benefit of tradition, the result of a reliable weeding-out process. At any present moment, a culture spills over with ideas and images, sayings and symbols and styles, and they mingle promiscuously. Many of them arise passing only a commercial standard, not a critical or moral one, and in the rush of daily life it's hard to discriminate them, the significant from the insignificant, trendy from lasting, tasteful from vulgar. As time goes by, though, the transient, superficial, fashionable, and hackneyed show up more clearly and fall away, and a firmer, nobler continuity forms. We think of jazz, for instance, as the tradition of Armstrong, Ellington, Parker, Monk, Fitzgerald, Getz, and the rest, but at the time when they recorded their signature pieces, jazz looked much different. The cream hadn't fully risen to the top, and "Parker's Mood" and "Blue 7" appeared amid a thousand other, now forgotten songs in the jazz landscape. Only with the passage of time does the field refine and settle into its superior creations.

The tradition-making process, then, somewhat distorts the actual historical genesis of its ingredients. But it serves a crucial moral and intellectual function. Tradition provides a surer standard, a basis for judgment more solid than present comparisons, than political, practical, and commercial grounds. Young Americans exist amidst an avalanche of input, and the combination overwhelms their shaky critical sense. Tradition provides grounding against and refuge from the mercurial ebb and flow of youth culture, the nonstop marketing of youth products to youths. The great nineteenth-century critic Matthew Arnold explained the benefits of connecting to "the ancients" in precisely these "steadying" terms:

> The present age makes great claims upon us: we owe it service, it will not be satisfied without our admiration. I know not how it is, but their

> commerce with the ancients appears to me to produce, in those who constantly practice it, a steadying and composing effect upon their judgment, not of literary works only, but of men and events in general.

Contact with the past steadies and composes judgment of the present. That's the formula. People who read Thucydides and Caesar on war, and Seneca and Ovid on love, are less inclined to construe passing fads as durable outlooks, to fall into the maelstrom of celebrity culture, to presume that the circumstances of their own life are worth a Web page. They distinguish long-term meanings in the sequence of "men and events," and they gamble on the lasting stakes of life, not the meretricious ones.

Nobody likes a scold, but the critical filter has never been more needed. The rush of the "present age" noted by Arnold in 1853 has cascaded into a deluge. Digital technology has compounded the incoming flow, and young adults flounder in it the most. Their grandparents watch them at the keyboard, on the cell phone, with the BlackBerry, etc., and it looks like delirium. All the more reason, then, to impart the unchanging and uncompromising examples, in Arnold's words, the "best that is known and thought in the world." Without the anchor of wise and talented men and women long gone, of thoughts and works that have stood the test of time, adolescents fall back upon the meager, anarchic resources of their sole selves. They watch a movie—say, *Pretty Woman*—and see it in the light of real and imagined high school romances instead of, in this case, fairy tales and 1980s finance wizards. Asked for a political opinion, they recall the images they catch on television, not the models of Washington, Churchill, and Pope John Paul II. Instead of understanding the young adult roller coaster of courtship and rejection with the help of novels by Jane Austen, they process their miasmic feelings by themselves or with sympathetic friends. And why should they do otherwise when the counsel of mentors, not to mention the avalanche of movies, music, and the rest, upholds the sovereignty of youth perspective? The currents of social life press upon them hourly, while the pages within *The Decline and Fall of the Roman Empire* and *Wuthering Heights* seem like another, irrelevant universe. They don't know much about history and literature, but they have feelings and needs, and casualty figures from Shiloh and lines from Donne don't help.

No wonder psychological assessments show rising currents of narcissism among Americans who haven't yet joined the workforce. In one study publicized in early 2007, researchers analyzed the responses of more than 16,000 college students on the Narcissistic Personality Inventory going back to the early 1980s. Undergraduates in 2006, it turned out, scored 30 percent higher than students in 1982 on the narcissism scale, with two-thirds of them reaching above-average levels. The researchers traced the rise directly to self-esteem orientations in the schoolroom, and lead author Jean Twenge groused, "We need to stop endlessly repeating, 'You're special,' and having children repeat that back. Kids are self-centered enough already."

The behavioral features of narcissism are bad enough, but a set of other studies demonstrates just how disabling it proves, particularly with schoolwork. One consequence of narcissism is that it prevents young people from weighing their own talents and competencies accurately. Narcissists can't take criticism, they hate to hand power over to others, and they turn disappointments into the world's fault, not their own. These are the normal hurdles of growing up, but for narcissists they represent a hostile front advancing against them. It's a distorted and destroying mirror, as Narcissus himself showed when he fixed upon his own reflection in the pool and snubbed the calls of love and caution he'd heard before, unable to leave his lovely countenance until the end. Education requires the opposite, a modicum of self-doubt, a capacity for self-criticism, precisely what the narcissist can't bear.

The attitude is even more harmful than the knowledge deficiencies we've seen earlier. An ignorant but willing mind can overcome ignorance through steady work and shrewd guidance. Read a few more books, visit a museum, take some classes, and knowledge will come. An unwilling mind can't, or won't. It already knows enough, and history, civics, philosophy, and literature have too little direct application to satisfy. For many young Americans, that translates into a demoralizing perception problem, a mismatch of expectation and ability. An October 2005 report by the U.S. Department of Education drew the distinction in gloomy forecasts. Titled *A Profile of the American High School Senior in 2004: A First Look,* it culled four traits out, of the academic lives of more than 13,000 students from across the country. They were: tested achievement, educational intentions, reasons for choosing a particular college, and life goals. Set alongside each other, the first two characteristics settled so far apart as to signal a national pathology. The study focused on student achievement ratings on math scores and derived the usual abysmal picture. Only "a third (35 percent) showed an understanding of intermediate-level mathematical concepts," and 21 percent of them could not perform "simple operations with decimals, fractions, powers, and roots." More than one-third of high school seniors (37.6 percent) could not complete "simple problem solving, requiring the understanding of low-level mathematical concepts," and a tiny 3.9 percent reached proficiency in "complex multistep word problems."

A troubling outcome, but no shocker. The surprise comes with the second trait, the students' expectations. The survey asked high school seniors how much education they expected to complete—not *wanted* to complete, but would successfully complete—and their answers bounded far beyond trait #1. Fully 69 percent of the respondents "expected to complete college with a 4-year degree," and of that group 35 percent believed that they would proceed further to earn a professional or postbaccalaureate degree. Of the others, 18 percent predicted that they would earn a two-year degree or attend college for some period of time. That left 8 percent who had no prediction, and only 5 percent who admitted that they would never attend college.

Broken down by proficiency, the expectations looked downright heartbreaking. Nearly one-third (31.7 percent) of the students who expected to graduate from college could handle, at best, simple problem solving, and one-fifth of those anticipating an advanced degree could do no better. Only 7.6 percent of the I-expect-an-advanced-degree group reached advanced proficiency in mathematics, while 9.4 percent of graduate-degree intenders compiled a transcript with the highest mathematics coursework as pre-algebra or lower.

In the National Governors Association poll cited on page 21, similar misestimations came up. When asked "How well do you think your high school prepares you in each of the following areas?" 80 percent replied "Excellent/Good" in basic reading skills and math skills—a number far exceeding the actual percentage. Three-quarters of them claimed "Ability to read at a high level," and 71 percent boasted excellent/good algebra talents. Furthermore, they demanded more courses in senior year "related to the kind of job I want," not realizing that they can't proceed to more specialized courses until they improve their basic proficiencies in standard subjects.

Indeed, when comparing the self-image of the students and the knowledge/skill deficits that emerge whenever they undergo objective tests, one has to wonder: What are they thinking? Optimism is nice, but not when it reaches delusional limits. Soon enough, the faulty combo of aptitude and ambition will explode, and the teenagers won't understand why. Michael Petrilli of the Fordham Foundation terms it "the reality gap between students' expectations and their skills" (see McCluskey), and the illusion gets punctured all too readily not long after high school graduation. General education requirements in college include a math course, and any degree in the sciences entails more than that. One week in calculus sends them scurrying to drop/add, and many end up in remediation or disappear altogether. It doesn't make sense. The math skills they lack are requisite for the degrees they expect, but they don't make the connection. They must get their college readiness conceits from somewhere besides test scores and coursework, partly, no doubt, from teachers who, with the best intentions, tell middling students that they're doing great, that they should follow their dreams, be all they can be . . .

All too often, the mentors don't see the results of their indulgence, which emerge only after students leave their class, leaving teachers unaware of how the approach misleads their charges. A recent study of teachers' expectations touches one of the significant thresholds in a person's educational life: graduation. When a student graduates from high school, the diploma is supposed to signify a certain level of skill and knowledge, but the teachers who have graded them don't seem to realize the levels actually expected of students at the next stage. Instead, high school teachers consistently assess the skills of their graduating students much more highly than college teachers assess the skills of their entering students. That's the finding of companion surveys sponsored by the *Chronicle of Higher Education* in 2006, one of them directed at high school teachers, the other at college professors (see *Chronicle of Higher Education,* "What Professors and Teachers Think"). Researchers asked 746 high school teachers and 1,098 college professors specifically about the college readiness of the kids they instructed, and the variance was huge. On the general question "How well prepared are your students for college-level work?" 31 percent of the teachers stated "Very well," while only 13 percent of professors stated "Very well." In the "Not well" category, professors doubled the teacher score, 24 percent to 12 percent, meaning that while only one in eight high school teachers found among the students "large gaps in preparation" that left them "struggling," one in four college teachers found them. In certain subject areas, the discrepancy between high school and college perceptions increased to a ratio of nine to one. In mathematics, fully 37 percent of teachers estimated that the students were "Very well prepared," while a meager 4 percent of professors agreed. For science, 38 percent of teachers gave them "Very well prepared," but only 5 percent of professors did. In writing, nearly half the professors (44 percent) rated the freshman class "Not well prepared," while only 10 percent of teachers were equally judgmental. Interestingly, for motivational traits the discrepancy shrank significantly, for example, with teachers and professors differing by only three points in judging students "Very well prepared" to "work hard." The decrease indicates that the problem lies not in the students' diligence but in their intellectual tool kits, and that the energy students devote to schoolwork (and leisure play) often dodges activities that build college-level knowledge and skills.

One of the most precious tools they lack does not appear in predominant education philosophies, however, nor does it shape training programs for teachers and professors, nor does it arise in discussions of American competitiveness and innovation among business leaders and politicians interested in education. When foundation personnel talk of school improvement and education officers announce academic outcomes, they cite test scores, retention rates, school choice plans, technology, and a dozen other topics, but not this one. And if it were posed to intellectuals, academics, educators, and journalists, a few might seize it as crucial but most would give it a limp nod of approval, or stare blankly, or reject it outright. It sounds fainthearted to them, or outmoded, moralistic, or irrelevant. The tool is precisely what has been lost in the shifting attitude in favor of youth: self-criticism in the light of tradition.

Adolescents are painfully self-conscious, to be sure, and they feel their being intensely, agonizing over a blemish on the cheek and a misstep in the lunchroom. But the yardstick of their judgment comes not from the past but from the present, not from wise men and women but from cool classmates, not from art and thought through the ages but from pop culture of the moment. They pass through school and home ever aware of inadequacy, but the ideals they honor raise them only to the condition of peer respect. Their idols are peer idols, their triumphs the envy of friends, not adults. Their self-criticism isn't enlightened and forward-looking, nor is it backward-looking. It's social and shortsighted.

What young Americans need isn't more relevance in the classroom, but less. A June 2006 op-ed in *Education Week* on student disengagement in class, "The Small World of Classroom Boredom," concludes, "Instead of responding to our students as individuals with their own interests and knowledge, the school curriculum is, by and large, remote, providing little connection between the classroom and students' lives" (see Schultz). Yes, the coursework is remote, but instead of blaming the curriculum and offering more blather about sparking "intellectual curiosity" and "independent thinking," as the author does, let's blame "students' lives" for stretching the divide. Young people need mentors not to go with the youth flow, but to stand staunchly against it, to represent something smarter and finer than the cacophony of social life. They don't need more pop culture and youth perspectives in the classroom. They get enough of those on their own. Young Americans need someone somewhere in their lives to reveal to them bigger and better human stories than the sagas of summer parties and dormitory diversions and Facebook sites.

In slighting the worth of tradition, in allowing teenagers to set their own concerns before the civilization of their forebears, mentors have only opened more minutes to youth contact and youth media. And not just school time, but leisure time, too, for the betrayal of the mentors ripples far beyond the campus. In the past, as long as teachers, parents, journalists, and other authorities insisted that young people respect knowledge and great works, young people devoted a portion of out-of-class hours to activities that complement in-class work. These include the habits we've already charted: books for fun, museums, "art music," dance and theater, politics.

The more mentors have engaged youth in youth terms, though, the more youth have disengaged from the mentors themselves and from the culture they are supposed to represent. To take one more example: in 1982, 18- to 24-year-olds made up 18.5 percent of the performing arts attendance. In 2002, the portion fell to 11.2 percent, a massive slide in audience makeup, and an ominous sign for the future of arts presenters (National Endowment for the Arts, *Survey of Public Participation in the Arts*).

The decline of school-supporting leisure habits—lower reading rates, fewer museum visits, etc.—created a vacuum in leisure time that the stuff of youth filled all too readily, and it doesn't want to give any of it back. Digital technology has fostered a segregated social reality, peer pressure gone wild, distributing youth content in an instant, across continents, 24/7. Television watching holds steady, while more screens mean more screen time. What passes through them locks young Americans ever more firmly into themselves and one another, and whatever doesn't pass through them appears irrelevant and profitless. Inside the classroom, they learn a little about the historical past and civic affairs, but once the lesson ends they swerve back to the youth-full, peer-bound present. Cell phones, personal pages, and the rest unleash persistent and simmering forces of adolescence, the volatile mix of cliques and loners, rebelliousness and conformity, ambition and self-destruction, idolatry and irreverence, know-nothing-ness and know-it-all-ness, all of which tradition and knowledge had helped to contain. The impulses were always there, but the stern shadow of moral and cultural canons at home and in class managed now and then to keep them in check. But the guideposts are now unmanned, and the pushback of mentors has dwindled to the sober objections of a faithful few who don't mind sounding unfashionable and insensitive.

The ingredients come together into an annihilating recipe. Adolescent urgings, a teen world cranked up by technology, a knowledge world cranked down by abdicating mentors . . . they commingle and produce young Americans whose wits are just as keen as ever, but who waste them on screen diversions; kids whose ambitions may even exceed their forebears', but whose aims merge on career and consumer goals, not higher learning; youths who experience a typical stage of alienation from the adult world, but whose alienation doesn't stem from countercultural ideas and radical mentors (Karl Marx, Herbert Marcuse, Michel Foucault, etc.), but from an enveloping immersion in peer stuff. Their lengthening independence has shortened their mental horizon. Teen material floods their hours and mentors esteem them, believing the kids more knowledgeable and skilled than they really are, or, perhaps, thinking that assurance will make them that way.

Few things are worse for adolescent minds than overblown appraisals of their merits. They rob them of constructive self-criticism, and obscure the lessons of tradition. They steer their competitive instincts toward peer triumphs, not civic duty. They make them mistrust their guides, and interpret cynically both praise and censure. They set them up for failure, a kind of Peter Principle in young people's lives whereby they proceed in school and in social circles without receiving correctives requisite to adult duties and citizenship. They reach a level of incompetence, hit a wall in college or the workplace, and never understand what happened. The rising cohort of Americans is not "The Next Great Generation," as Strauss and Howe name them in their hagiographic book *Millennials Rising.* We wish they were, but it isn't so. The twenty-first-century teen, connected and multitasked, autonomous yet peer-mindful, marks no great leap forward in human intelligence, global thinking, or "netizen"-ship. Young users have learned a thousand new things, no doubt. They upload and download, surf and chat, post and design, but they haven't learned to analyze a complex text, store facts in their heads, comprehend a foreign policy decision, take lessons from history, or spell correctly. Never having recognized their responsibility to the past, they have opened a fissure in our civic foundations, and it shows in their halting passage into adulthood and citizenship. They leave school, but peer fixations continue and social habits stay the same. They join the workforce only to realize that self-esteem lessons of home and class, as well as the behaviors that made them popular, no longer apply, and it takes them years to adjust. They grab snatches of news and sometimes vote, but they regard the civic realm as another planet. And wherever they end up, whomever they marry, however high they land in their careers, most of them never acquire the intellectual tools they should have as teenagers and young adults. Perhaps during their twenties they adapt, acquiring smarter work and finance habits. But the knowledge and culture traits never catch up.

A few years of seasoning in the American workplace may secure their income and inculcate maturity in private life, but it won't sustain the best civic and cultural traditions in American history. If young people don't read, they shut themselves out of public affairs. Without a knowledge formation in younger years, adults function as more or less partial citizens. Reading and knowledge have to enter their leisure lives, at their own initiative. Analyzing Pew Research data from 2002 and 2004, political scientists Stephen and Linda Bennett lay out the simple fact: "People who read books for pleasure are more likely than non-readers to report voting, being registered to vote, 'always' voting, to pay greater attention to news stories about national, international, and local politics, and to be better informed."

As the rising generation reaches middle age, it won't re-create the citizenship of its precursors, nor will its ranks produce a set of committed intellectuals ready to trade in ideas, steer public policy, and espouse social values on the basis of learning, eloquence, and a historical sense of human endeavor. This is one damaging consequence of the betrayal of the mentors that is often overlooked. When people warn of America's future, they usually talk about competitiveness in science, technology, and productivity, not in ideas and values. But the current domestic and geopolitical situation demands that we generate not only more engineers, biochemists, nanophysicists, and entrepreneurs, but also men and women experienced in the ways of culture, prepared for contest in the marketplace of ideas. Knowledge-workers, wordsmiths, policy wonks . . . they don't emerge from nowhere. They need a long foreground of reading and writing, a home and school environment open to their development, a pipeline ahead and behind them. They need mentors to commend them when they're right and rebuke them when they're wrong. They need parents to remind them that social life isn't everything, and they need peers to respect their intelligence, not scrunch up their eyes at big words. It takes a home, and a schoolhouse, and a village, and a market to make a great public intellectual and policy maker. The formula is flexible, but with the Dumbest Generation its breakdown is under way, and with it the vitality of democracy in the United States.

NOTES

HOW TO UNMASK THE INTERNET'S VILEST CHARACTERS

Emily Bazelon

(1971–)

Emily Bazelon is a journalist who graduated from Yale University and Yale Law School. She is currently a senior editor for the online magazine Slate, a regular contributor to the New York Times *magazine, and the Truman Capote Fellow for Creative Writing and Law at the Yale Law School.*

In June 2009, Lani (a nickname) got a Facebook message from a stranger alerting her to nude photos of herself that had been posted on a Web site called Private Voyeur—along with her name, her workplace and the city she lives in. The post, titled "Jap Slut," was published anonymously by someone who used a proper noun followed by numbers as an Internet handle.

Lani went to the police. She suspected that the poster was an ex-boyfriend who, she says, threatened to kill himself if she didn't pose for naked photographs toward the end of their abusive relationship. According to Lani, when the police questioned her ex-boyfriend, he said that he had distributed the photos among his friends but that he wasn't the one who put them on the Web. The police then told Lani they couldn't help her, so she contacted Private Voyeur, which agreed to take the post down. A few months later, though, a new post appeared, with the same photographs and the same information identifying her.

You might think that the legal system offers an easy solution to problems like these—but it doesn't. According to free-speech advocates, there's a good reason for that: Stopping trolls, which is the term used for those who abuse the privilege of the Web's anonymous open mike, would mean choking off other critics, which obviously has undemocratic implications. After all, anonymity is a trusted tool of dissidents and whistle-blowers.

Congress and the courts have largely heeded this argument, too. Section 230 of the 1996 Communications Decency Act—the law that matters most for speech on the Web—holds that online service providers aren't responsible for offensive content if they've tried to block a little of it. In other words, if you edit some of the comments on your site, you're not liable for the one with a harmful lie that you didn't edit, as a newspaper would be if it published a libelous letter to the editor.

This is fair enough: Web sites with open comments aren't really like newspapers. But in interpreting Section 230, federal appeals courts went a step further. They have said that the law gives the providers and sites a free pass for essentially all content that users post. That's why Private Voyeur didn't have to police its pages for the reappearance of Lani's photos. It's also why Google doesn't get in trouble for surfacing these posts in search results, which is perhaps even more damaging.

Reprinted by permission from the *New York Times Magazine*, April 22, 2011.

There's no question that the Web would be a more civilized place if Congress changed Section 230 to hold online service providers and Web sites liable for posts like "Jap Slut" (or Google liable for indexing them) if they have clear notice about what's wrong with the content and still disseminate it. That's how copyright law works online. What's tricky about extending this approach is that some posts would be deleted not because they actually defame or violate privacy but because someone *complains* that they do. The heckler's veto, as it's called, is anathema to free-speech advocates, as well as to the big Internet companies, which don't want to be responsible for any user content, given the Web's volume and pace. So don't look for Section 230 to change any time soon.

And that leaves people like Lani in a lousy situation. Their only option for using the law to punish trolls is to sue for defamation or invasion of privacy, as Lani has done. The problem is that while she could win a court order unmasking the troll's identity (and ultimately win damages), it's hard to bring such a suit without making her own humiliation complete. Though the "Jap Slut" post and pictures are public, they're still largely out of sight. Lani's children and parents don't know about them, and neither do the customers at her business. But if she were to file this kind of suit, Lani would risk linking the photos to her name forever, not just in the Web's dark corners but also in court documents and news coverage.

Which is why we need to pursue another way to take legal action—one that has been out of favor but ought to be given new life in the Internet age. We should encourage more anonymous-plaintiff lawsuits.

Fighting an anonymous smear with an anonymous lawsuit is a counterintuitive idea—and a lot of judges, including the judge on Lani's case, are reluctant to try it. But there's some precedent in American law for suing anonymously when a case revolves around private sexual or medical facts. That's how we got Roe v. Wade. "These kinds of suits don't squelch much speech, but they still address the harm," points out the University of Maryland law professor Danielle Citron, an expert on the topic. Indeed, if more people sued anonymously, the trolls might understand that hiding behind an online handle doesn't mean you can't be traced—and there might be fewer hateful posts as a result. Courts have ordered Google to turn over I.P. addresses in a few of these cases. The lawyers who represent Lani have two other clients who succeeded in suing their trolls anonymously, and who won settlements while remaining unknown to the public (though not to the defendant) throughout. The lawyers are starting a nonprofit, Without My Consent, to help bring more such cases.

Of course, anonymous lawsuits come at a cost, given the public's legitimate interest in knowing all the facts of a case. That's why courts generally apply a balancing test, weighing the plaintiff's right to privacy against the constitutionally protected presumption of openness in court. But the Internet puts a thumb on the scale for the plaintiff, as the U.S. Court of Appeals for the

11th Circuit recognized in a smart recent ruling involving another kind of troll: the Girls Gone Wild video franchise.

The plaintiffs—B., J., S. and V.—wanted to sue Joe Francis, founder of Girls Gone Wild, for emotional distress because they'd been filmed flashing their breasts or having sex when they were too young to legally consent. (Francis and his company have paid millions of dollars in fines for doing this repeatedly; Francis also went to jail on related criminal charges.) These four women said that if they had to bring the case or testify under their own names, they would risk becoming "Internet sensations permanently identified with the videos." As the 11th Circuit noted in granting the plaintiffs' request to sue anonymously, another woman who sued Girls Gone Wild under her own name has been permanently tagged by name as a "breast-flasher" on the highly trafficked Internet Movie Database.

After a trial in April, an all-woman jury agreed that Francis's behavior was "atrocious and utterly intolerable." But they said the plaintiffs hadn't shown he intentionally caused them emotional distress. The women were not awarded money damages. At the same time, their names, amazingly, were never in the press. This seems right. The law shouldn't guarantee victory. But it should let you fight the trolls without doing their shaming work for them.

NOTES

'ONE TODAY': THE FULL TEXT OF RICHARD BLANCO'S INAUGURAL POEM
Richard Blanco

(1968–)

Richard Blanco was born in Madrid, Spain, where his family had emigrated from Cuba. This openly gay poet grew up in Miami. He earned a bachelor's degree in engineering and an MFA in Creative Writing from Florida International University. The recipient of several prestigious prizes for his poetry, in 2013 he was chosen to read his poem "One Today" at Barack Obama's second Presidential Inauguration.

One sun rose on us today, kindled over our shores,
peeking over the Smokies, greeting the faces
of the Great Lakes, spreading a simple truth
across the Great Plains, then charging across the Rockies.
One light, waking up rooftops, under each one, a story
told by our silent gestures moving behind windows.
My face, your face, millions of faces in morning's mirrors,
each one yawning to life, crescendoing into our day:
pencil-yellow school buses, the rhythm of traffic lights,
fruit stands: apples, limes, and oranges arrayed like rainbows
begging our praise. Silver trucks heavy with oil or paper—
bricks or milk, teeming over highways alongside us,
on our way to clean tables, read ledgers, or save lives—
to teach geometry, or ring-up groceries as my mother did
for twenty years, so I could write this poem.
All of us as vital as the one light we move through,
the same light on blackboards with lessons for the day:
equations to solve, history to question, or atoms imagined,
the "I have a dream" we keep dreaming,
or the impossible vocabulary of sorrow that won't explain
the empty desks of twenty children marked absent
today, and forever. Many prayers, but one light
breathing color into stained glass windows,
life into the faces of bronze statues, warmth
onto the steps of our museums and park benches
as mothers watch children slide into the day.
One ground. Our ground, rooting us to every stalk
of corn, every head of wheat sown by sweat
and hands, hands gleaning coal or planting windmills

---

in deserts and hilltops that keep us warm, hands
  digging trenches, routing pipes and cables, hands
  as worn as my father's cutting sugarcane
  so my brother and I could have books and shoes.
The dust of farms and deserts, cities and plains
  mingled by one wind—our breath. Breathe. Hear it
  through the day's gorgeous din of honking cabs,
  buses launching down avenues, the symphony
  of footsteps, guitars, and screeching subways,
  the unexpected song bird on your clothes line.
Hear: squeaky playground swings, trains whistling,
  or whispers across café tables, Hear: the doors we open
  for each other all day, saying: hello| shalom,
  buon giorno |howdy |namaste |or buenos días
  in the language my mother taught me—in every language
  spoken into one wind carrying our lives
  without prejudice, as these words break from my lips.
One sky: since the Appalachians and Sierras claimed
  their majesty, and the Mississippi and Colorado worked
  their way to the sea. Thank the work of our hands:
  weaving steel into bridges, finishing one more report
  for the boss on time, stitching another wound
  or uniform, the first brush stroke on a portrait,
  or the last floor on the Freedom Tower
  jutting into a sky that yields to our resilience.
One sky, toward which we sometimes lift our eyes
  tired from work: some days guessing at the weather
  of our lives, some days giving thanks for a love
  that loves you back, sometimes praising a mother
  who knew how to give, or forgiving a father
  who couldn't give what you wanted.
We head home: through the gloss of rain or weight
  of snow, or the plum blush of dusk, but always—home,
  always under one sky, our sky. And always one moon
  like a silent drum tapping on every rooftop
  and every window, of one country—all of us—
  facing the stars
  hope—a new constellation
  waiting for us to map it,
  waiting for us to name it—together

NOTES

NOTES

TWO ESSENTIAL GOALS
Ernest L. Boyer

(1928–1995)

Ernest L. Boyer was a notable educator. He served as Chancellor of the State University of New York, United States Commissioner of Education, and as President of the Carnegie Foundation for the Advancement of Teaching.

An effective college has a clear and vital mission. Administrators, faculty, and students share a vision of what the institution is seeking to accomplish. The goals at such an institution flow from the needs of society and also from the needs of the persons seeking education.

But can the modern college, with all its separations and divisions, be guided by a common vision? And can the search for goals be something more than a diversion?

America's first colleges were guided by a vision of coherence. The goal was to train not only the clergy, but a new civic leadership as well. These struggling institutions sought "to develop a sense of unity where, in a society created from many of the nations of Europe, there might otherwise be aimlessness and uncontrolled diversity" [said Frederick Rudolph in *The American College and University*].

The confidence of professors and their students in this era "owed much to their membership in an established middle class, a commitment to European learning, and a Christian conception of character and culture." Within that framework, bitter disputes sometimes did rage, but from today's perspective the colonial college seems stiflingly monolithic.

The first students at tiny Harvard College advanced in lockstep fashion, studied a common curriculum, one subject a day, from 8:00 A.M. until 5:00 P.M., Monday through Friday, and a half day on Saturday. In the first year, there was logic, Greek and Hebrew, rhetoric, divinity catechetical, history, and the nature of plants. The second year included ethics and politics, Aramaic, and further studies in rhetoric and divinity catechetical. The final year of college was capped by arithmetic, astronomy, Syriac, more Greek, rhetoric, and, of course, divinity catechetical.

This academic core was considered absolute and immutable, to be accepted, not criticized or questioned. The goal was to discipline the mind and, through such training, graduates were to move comfortably into prestigious professions—the clergy, business, medicine, law, and civic leadership.

Our present academic world would be unrecognizable to the men who founded Harvard College in 1636. The fixed curriculum of the colonial era is as much an anachronism today as the stocks in the village square. Separations and divisions, not unity, mark the undergraduate program.

Reprinted from *College: The Undergraduate Experience in America* (1987).

Narrow departmentalization divides the campus. So distinctive are the different disciplines in method and content, the argument goes, that there is no way to connect them in the minds of students. Knowledge is so vast and specialization so persistent that shared goals cannot be defined.

There is, we believe, a way out of our dilemma. While preparing this report we repeatedly were reminded that two powerful traditions—*individuality* and *community*—have been at the heart of the undergraduate experiences. These two priorities have defined throughout the years the boundaries of the collegiate debate about purposes and goals and within these traditions there is, perhaps, sufficient common ground on which a vital academic program can be built.

The focus on individuality, on the personal benefits and the utility of education, has a rich tradition in American higher education. Throughout the years, students have come to college to pursue their own goals, to follow their own aptitudes, to become productive, self-reliant human beings, and, with new knowledge, to continue learning after college days are over. Serving individual interests has been a top priority in higher education.

But amidst diversity, the claims of community must be vigorously affirmed. By community we mean an undergraduate experience that helps students go beyond their own private interests, learn about the world around them, develop a sense of civic and social responsibility, and discover how they, as individuals, can contribute to the larger society of which they are a part.

Robert Bellah, co-author of *Habits of the Heart,* observes that "since World War II, the traditions of atomistic individualism have grown stronger, while the traditions of the individual in society have grown weaker. The sense of cohesive community is lost." In an era when an emphasis on narrow vocationalism dominates many campuses, the challenge is to help students relate what they have learned to concerns beyond themselves.

Individuals should become empowered [or enabled] to live productive, independent lives. They also should be helped to go beyond private interests and place their own lives in larger context. When the observant Frenchman Alexis de Tocqueville visited the United States in the 1830s, he warned that "as individualism grows, people forget their ancestors and form the habit of thinking of themselves in isolation and imagine their whole destiny is in their hands." To counter this cultural disintegration, Tocqueville argued, "Citizens must turn from the private inlets and occasionally take a look at something other than themselves."

We suggest, then, that within the traditions of individuality and community, educational and social purposes for the undergraduate experience can be defined. The individual preferences of each student must be served. But beyond diversity, the college has an obligation to give students a sense of passage toward a more coherent view of knowledge and a more integrated life.

Individualism is necessary for a free and creative society, and the historic strength of our democracy lies in its commitment to personal improvement and fulfillment. We need individualism but, at the same time, we must be mindful of the consequences of selfishness. It is appropriate, therefore, for educational institutions that are preparing students to be citizens in a participatory democracy to understand the dilemmas and paradoxes of individualistic culture.

Just as we search culturally to maintain the necessary balance between private and public obligations, in education we seek the same end. The college, at its best, recognizes that, although we live alone, we also are deeply dependent on each other. Through an effective college education, students should become personally empowered and also committed to the common good.

NOTES

HAL'S LEGACY: *2001's* COMPUTER AS DREAM AND REALITY

Daniel C. Dennett

(1942–)

Daniel C. Dennett is a professor and philosopher with many distinguished publications. In 2012 he was honored with the prestigious Erasmus Prize by the Praemium Erasmianum Foundation.

When HAL Kills, Who's to Blame? Computer Ethics

The first robot homicide was committed in 1981, according to my files. I have a yellowed clipping dated December 9, 1981, from the *Philadelphia Inquirer*—not the *National Enquirer*—with the headline "Robot killed repairman, Japan reports".

The story was an anticlimax. At the Kawasaki Heavy Industries plant in Akashi, a malfunctioning robotic arm pushed a repairman against a gearwheel-milling machine, which crushed him to death. The repairman had failed to follow instructions for shutting down the arm before he entered the workspace. Why, indeed, was this industrial accident in Japan reported in a Philadelphia newspaper? Every day somewhere in the world a human worker is killed by one machine or another. The difference, of course, was that—in the public imagination at least—this was no ordinary machine. This was a robot, a machine that might have a mind, might have evil intentions, might be capable, not just of homicide, but of murder. Anglo-American jurisprudence speaks of mens rea—literally, the guilty mind:

> To have performed a legally prohibited action, such as killing another human being; one must have done so with a culpable state of mind, or mens rea. Such culpable mental states are of three kinds: they are either motivational states of purpose, cognitive states of belief, or the nonmental state of negligence. (*Cambridge Dictionary of Philosophy*, 1995, p. 482)

The legal concept has no requirement that the agent be capable of feeling guilt or remorse or any other emotion; so-called cold-blooded murderers are not in the slightest degree exculpated by their flat affective state. *Star Trek's* Spock would fully satisfy the mens rea requirement in spite of his fabled lack of emotions. Drab, colorless—but oh so effective—"motivational states of purpose" and "cognitive states of belief" are enough to get the fictional Spock through the day quite handily. And they are well-established features of many existing computer programs.

Reprinted from *Hal's Legacy: 2001's Computer as Dream and Reality*, edited by David G. Stork (1997), by permission of MIT Press.

When IBM's computer Deep Blue beat world chess champion Garry Kasparov in the first game of their 1996 championship match, it did so by discovering and executing, with exquisite timing, a withering attack, the purposes of which were all too evident in retrospect to Kasparov and his handlers. It was Deep Blue's sensitivity to those purposes and a cognitive capacity to recognize and exploit a subtle flaw in Kasparov's game that explain Deep Blue's success. Murray Campbell, Feng-hsiung Hsu, and the other designers of Deep Blue, didn't beat Kasparov; Deep Blue did. Neither Campbell nor Hsu discovered the winning sequence of moves; Deep Blue did. At one point, while Kasparov was mounting a ferocious attack on Deep Blue's king, nobody but Deep Blue figured out that it had the time and security it needed to knock off a pesky pawn of Kasparov's that was out of the action but almost invisibly vulnerable. Campbell, like the human grandmasters watching the game, would never have dared consider such a calm mopping-up operation under pressure.

Deep Blue, like many other computers equipped with artificial intelligence (AI) programs, is what I call an intentional system: its behavior is predictable and explainable if we attribute to it beliefs and desires—"cognitive states" and "motivational states"—and the rationality required to figure out what it ought to do in the light of those beliefs and desires. Are these skeletal versions of human beliefs and desires sufficient to meet the mens rea requirement of legal culpability? Not quite, but, if we restrict our gaze to the limited world of the chess board, it is hard to see what is missing. Since cheating is literally unthinkable to a computer like Deep Blue, and since there are really no other culpable actions available to an agent restricted to playing chess, nothing it could do would be a misdeed deserving of blame, let alone a crime of which we might convict it. But we also assign responsibility to agents in order to praise or honor the appropriate agent. Who or what, then, deserves the credit for beating Kasparov? Deep Blue is clearly the best candidate. Yes, we may join in congratulating Campbell, Hsu and the IBM team on the success of their handiwork; but in the same spirit we might congratulate Kasparov's teachers, handlers, and even his parents. And, no matter how assiduously they may have trained him, drumming into his head the importance of one strategic principle or another, they didn't beat Deep Blue in the series: Kasparov did.

Deep Blue is the best candidate for the role of responsible opponent of Kasparov, but this is not good enough, surely, for full moral responsibility. If we expanded Deep Blue's horizons somewhat, it could move out into the arenas of injury and benefit that we human beings operate in. It's not hard to imagine a touching scenario in which a grandmaster deliberately (but oh so subtly) throws a game to an opponent, in order to save a life, avoid humiliating a loved one, keep a promise, or . . . (make up your own O'Henry story here). Failure to rise to such an occasion might well be grounds for blaming a human chess player. Winning or throwing a chess match might even amount to commission of a heinous crime (make up your own Agatha Christie story here). Could Deep Blue's horizons be so widened?

Deep Blue is an intentional system, with beliefs and desires about its activities and predicaments on the chessboard; but in order to expand its horizons to the wider world of which chess is a relatively trivial part, it would have to be given vastly richer sources of "perceptual" input—and the means of coping with this barrage in real time. Time pressure is, of course, already a familiar feature of Deep Blue's world. As it hustles through the multidimensional search tree of chess, it has to keep one eye on the clock. Nonetheless, the problems of optimizing its use of time would increase by several orders of magnitude if it had to juggle all these new concurrent projects (of simple perception and self-maintenance in the world, to say nothing of more devious schemes and opportunities). For this hugely expanded task of resource management, it would need extra layers of control above and below its chess-playing software. Below, just to keep its perceptuo-locomotor projects in basic coordination, it would need to have a set of rigid traffic-control policies embedded in its underlying operating system. Above, it would have to be able to pay more attention to features of its own expanded resources, being always on the lookout for inefficient habits of thought, one of Douglas Hofstadter's "strange loops," obsessive ruts, oversights, and deadends. In other words, it would have to become a higher-order intentional system, capable of framing beliefs about its own beliefs, desires about its desires, beliefs about its fears about its thoughts about its hopes, and so on.

Higher-order intentionality is a necessary precondition for moral responsibility, and Deep Blue exhibits little sign of possessing such a capability. There is, of course, some self-monitoring implicated in any well-controlled search: Deep Blue doesn't make the mistake of reexploring branches it has already explored, for instance; but this is an innate policy designed into the underlying computational architecture, not something under flexible control. Deep Blue can't converse with you—or with itself—about the themes discernible in its own play; it's not equipped to notice—and analyze, criticize, analyze, and manipulate—the fundamental parameters that determine its policies of heuristic search or evaluation. Adding the layers of software that would permit Deep Blue to become self-monitoring and self-critical, and hence teachable, in all these ways would dwarf the already huge Deep Blue programming project—and turn Deep Blue into a radically different sort of agent.

HAL purports to be just such a higher-order intentional system—and he even plays a game of chess with Frank. HAL is, in essence, an enhancement of Deep Blue equipped with eyes and ears and a large array of sensors and effectors distributed around *Discovery 1.* HAL is not at all garrulous or self-absorbed; but in a few speeches he does express an interesting variety of higher-order intentional states, from the most simple to the most devious.

HAL: Yes, it's puzzling. I don't think I've ever seen anything quite like this before.

HAL doesn't just respond to novelty with a novel reaction; he notices that he is encountering novelty, a feat that requires his memory to have an organization far beyond that required for simple conditioning to novel stimuli.

HAL: I can't rid myself of the suspicion that there are some extremely odd things about this mission.

HAL: I never gave these stories much credence, but particularly in view of some of the other things that have happened, I find them difficult to put out of my mind.

HAL has problems of resource management not unlike our own. Obtrusive thoughts can get in the way of other activities. The price we pay for adding layers of flexible monitoring, to keep better track of our own mental activities, is . . . more mental activities to keep track of!

HAL: I've still got the greatest enthusiasm and confidence in the mission. I want to help you.

Another price we pay for higher-order intentionality is the opportunity for duplicity, which comes in two flavors: self-deception and other-deception. Friedrich Nietzsche recognizes this layering of the mind as the key ingredient of the moral animal; in his overheated prose it becomes the "priestly" form of life:

> For with the priests everything becomes more dangerous, not only cures and remedies, but also arrogance, revenge, acuteness, profligacy, love, lust to rule, virtue, disease—but it is only fair to add that it was on the soil of this essentially dangerous form of human existence, the priestly form, that man first became an interesting animal, that only here did the human soul in a higher sense acquire depth and become evil—and these are the two basic respects in which man has hitherto been superior to other beasts! (*The Genealogy of Morals,* First Essay, 6)

HAL's declaration of enthusiasm is nicely poised somewhere between sincerity and cheap, desperate, canned ploy—just like some of the most important declarations we make to each other. Does HAL mean it? Could he mean it? The cost of being the sort of being that could mean it is the chance that he might not mean it. HAL is indeed an "interesting animal."

But is HAL even remotely possible? In the book *2001,* Clarke has Dave reflect on the fact that HAL, whom he is disconnecting, "is the only conscious creature in my universe." From the omniscient-author perspective, Clarke writes about what it is like to be HAL.

> He was only aware of the conflict that was slowly destroying his integrity—the conflict between truth, and concealment of truth. He had begun to make mistakes, although, like a neurotic who could not observe his own symptoms, he would have denied it (p. 148).

Is Clarke helping himself here to more than we should allow him? Could something like HAL—a conscious, computer-bodied intelligent agent—be brought into existence by any history of design, construction, training, learning, and activity? The different possibilities have been explored in familiar fiction and can be nested neatly in order of their descending "humanness."

1. *The Wizard of Oz.* HAL isn't a computer at all. He is actually an ordinary flesh-and-blood man hiding behind a techno-facade—the ultimate homunculus, pushing buttons with ordinary fingers, pulling levers with ordinary hands, looking at internal screens and listening to internal alarm buzzers. (A variation on this theme is John Searle's busy-fingered hand-simulation of the Chinese Room by following billions of instructions written on slips of paper.)
2. *William* (from "William and Mary," in *Kiss, Kiss* by Roald Dahl). HAL is a human brain kept alive in a "vat" by a life-support system and detached from its former body, in which it acquired a lifetime of human memory, hankerings, attitudes, and so forth. It is now harnessed to huge banks of prosthetic sense organs and effectors. (A variation on this theme is poor Yorick, the brain in a vat in the story, "Where Am I?" in my *Brainstorms.*)
3. *Robocop,* disembodied and living in a "vat." Robocop is part-human brain, part computer. After a gruesome accident, the brain part (vehicle of some of the memory and personal identity, one gathers, of the flesh-and-blood cop who was Robocop's youth) was reembodied with robotic arms and legs, but also (apparently) partly replaced or enhanced with special-purpose software and computer hardware. We can imagine that HAL spent some transitional time as Robocop before becoming a limbless agent.
4. *Max Headroom,* a virtual machine, a software duplicate of a real person's brain (or mind) that has somehow been created by a brilliant hacker. It has the memories and personality traits acquired in a normally embodied human lifetime but has been off-loaded from all-carbon-based hardware into a silicon-chip implementation. (A variation on this theme is poor Hubert, the software duplicate of Yorick, in "Where Am I?")

5. *The real-life but still-in-the-future*—and hence still strictly science-fictional—Cog, the humanoid robot being constructed by Rodney Brooks, Lynn Stein, and the Cog team at MIT. Cog's brain is all silicon chips from the outset, and its body parts are inorganic artifacts. Yet it is designed to go through an embodied infancy and childhood, reacting to people that it sees with its video eyes, making friends, learning about the world by playing with real things with its real hands, and acquiring memory. If Cog ever grows up, it could surely abandon its body and make the transition described in the fictional cases. It would be easier for Cog, who has always been a silicon-based, digitally encoded intelligence, to move into a silicon-based vat than it would be for Max Headroom or Robocop, who spent their early years in wetware. Many important details of Cog's degree of humanoidness (humanoidity?) have not yet been settled, but the scope is wide. For instance, the team now plans to give Cog a virtual neuroendocrine system, with virtual hormones spreading and dissipating through its logical spaces.
6. *Blade Runner in a vat* has never had a real humanoid body, but has hallucinatory memories of having had one. This entirely bogus past life has been constructed by some preposterously complex and detailed programming.
7. *Clarke's own scenario,* as best it can be extrapolated from the book and the movie. HAL has never had a body and has no illusions about his past. What he knows of human life he knows as either part of his innate heritage (coded, one gathers, by the labors of many programmers, after the fashion of the real-world CYC project of Douglas Lenat [see chapter 9]) or a result of his subsequent training—a sort of bedridden infancy, one gathers, in which he was both observer and, eventually, participant. (In the book, Clarke speaks of "the perfect idiomatic English he had learned during the fleeting weeks of his electronic childhood.")

The extreme cases at both poles are impossible, for relatively boring reasons. At one end, neither the Wizard of Oz nor John Searle could do the necessary handwork fast enough to sustain HAL's quick-witted round of activities. At the other end, hand-coding enough world knowledge into a disembodied agent to create HAL's dazzlingly humanoid competence and getting it to the point where it could benefit from an electronic childhood is a programming task to be measured in hundreds of efficiently organized person-centuries. In other words, the daunting difficulties observable at both ends of this spectrum highlight the fact that there is a colossal design job to be done; the only practical way of doing it is one version or another of Mother Nature's way—years of embodied learning. The trade-offs between various combinations of flesh-and-blood and silicon-and-metal bodies are anybody's guess. I'm putting my bet on Cog as the most likely developmental platform for a future HAL.

Notice that requiring HAL to have a humanoid body and live concretely in the human world for a time is a practical but not a metaphysical requirement. Once all the R & D is accomplished in the prototype, by the odyssey of a single embodied agent, the standard duplicating techniques of the computer industry could clone HALs by the thousands as readily as they do compact discs. The finished product could thus be captured in some number of terabytes of information. So, in principle, the information that fixes the design of all those chips and hard-wired connections and configures all the RAM and ROM could be created by hand. There is no finite bit-string, however long, that is officially off-limits to human authorship. Theoretically, then, Blade-Runner-like entities could be created with ersatz biographies; they would have exactly the capabilities, dispositions, strengths, and weaknesses of a real, not virtual, person. So whatever moral standing the latter deserved should belong to the former as well.

The main point of giving HAL a humanoid past is to give him the world knowledge required to be a moral agent—a necessary modicum of understanding or empathy about the human condition. A modicum will do nicely; we don't want to hold out for too much commonality of experience. After all, among the people we know, many have moral responsibility in spite of their obtuse inability to imagine themselves into the predicaments of others. We certainly don't exculpate male chauvinist pigs who can't see women as people!

When *do* we exculpate people? We should look carefully at the answers to this question, because HAL shows signs of fitting into one or another of the exculpatory categories, even though he is a conscious agent. First, we exculpate people who are insane. Might HAL have gone insane? The question of his capacity for emotion—and hence his vulnerability to emotional disorder—is tantalizingly raised by Dave's answer to Mr. Amer.

Dave: Well, he acts like he has genuine emotions. Of course, he's programmed that way, to make it easier for us to talk to him. But as to whether he has real feelings is something I don't think anyone can truthfully answer.

Certainly HAL proclaims his emotional state at the end: "I'm afraid. I'm afraid." Yes, HAL is "programmed that way"—but what does that mean? It could mean that HAL's verbal capacity is enhanced with lots of canned expressions of emotional response that get grafted into his discourse at pragmatically appropriate opportunities. (Of course, many of our own avowals of emotion are like that—insincere moments of socially lubricating ceremony.) Or it could mean that HAL's underlying computational architecture has been provided, as Cog's will be, with virtual emotional states—powerful attention-shifters, galvanizers, prioritizers, and the like—realized not in neuromodulator and hormone molecules floating in a bodily fluid but in global variables modulating dozens of concurrent processes that dissipate according to some timetable (or something much more complex).

In the latter, more interesting, case, "I don't think anyone can truthfully answer" the question of whether HAL has emotions. He has something very much like emotions—enough like emotions, one may imagine, to mimic the pathologies of human emotional breakdown. Whether that is enough to call them real emotions, well, who's to say? In any case, there are good reasons for HAL to possess such states, since their role in enabling real-time practical thinking has recently been dramatically revealed by Damasio's experiments involving human beings with brain damage (see chapter 13). Having such states would make HAL profoundly different from Deep Blue, by the way. Deep Blue, basking in the strictly limited search space of chess, can handle its real-time decision making without any emotional crutches. *Time* magazine's story (February 26) on the Kasparov match quotes grandmaster Yasser Seirawan as saying, "The machine has no fear"; the story goes on to note that expert commentators characterized some of Deep Blue's moves (e.g., the icily calm pawn capture described earlier) as taking "crazy chances" and "insane." In the tight world of chess, it appears, the very imperturbability that cripples the brain-damaged human decision makers Damasio describes can be a blessing—but only if you have the brute-force analytic speed of a Deep Blue.

HAL may, then, have suffered from some emotional imbalance similar to those that lead human beings astray. Whether it was the result of some sudden trauma—a blown fuse, a dislodged connector, a microchip disordered by cosmic rays—or of some gradual drift into emotional misalignment provoked by the stresses of the mission—confirming such a diagnosis should justify a verdict of diminished responsibility for HAL, just as it does in cases of human malfeasance.

Another possible source of exculpation, more familiar in fiction than in the real world, is "brainwashing" or hypnosis. (*The Manchurian Candidate* is a standard model: the prisoner of war turned by evil scientists into a walking time bomb is returned to his homeland to assassinate the president.) The closest real-world cases are probably the "programmed" and subsequently "deprogrammed" members of cults. Is HAL like a cult member? It's hard to say. According to Clarke, HAL was "trained for his mission," not just programmed for his mission. At what point does benign, responsibility-enhancing training of human students become malign, responsibility-diminishing brainwashing? The intuitive turning point is captured, I think, in answer to the question of whether an agent can still "think for himself" after indoctrination. And what is it to be able to think for ourselves? We must be capable of being "moved by reasons"; that is, we must be reasonable and accessible to rational persuasion, the introduction of new evidence, and further considerations. If we are more or less impervious to experiences that ought to influence us, our capacity has been diminished.

The only evidence that HAL might be in such a partially disabled state is the much-remarked-upon fact that he has actually made a mistake, even though the series 9000 computer is supposedly utterly invulnerable to error. This is, to my mind, the weakest point in Clarke's narrative. The suggestion that a computer could be both a heuristically programmed algorithmic computer and "by any practical definition of the words, foolproof and incapable of error" verges on self-contradiction. The whole point of heuristic programming is that it defies the problem of combinatorial explosion—which we cannot mathematically solve by sheer increase in computing speed and size—by taking risky chances, truncating its searches in ways that must leave it open to error, however low the probability. The saving clause, "by any practical definition of the words," restores sanity. HAL may indeed be ultrareliable without being literally foolproof, a fact whose importance Alan Turing pointed out in 1946, at the dawn of the computer age, thereby "prefuting" Roger Penrose's 1989 criticisms of artificial intelligence.* (See my *Darwin's Dangerous Idea,* chapter 15, for the details.)

> In other words then, if a machine is expected to be infallible, it cannot also be intelligent. There are several theorems which say almost exactly that. But these theorems say nothing about how much intelligence may be displayed if a machine makes no pretence at infallibility (p. 124).

There is one final exculpatory condition to consider: duress. This is exactly the opposite of the other condition. It is precisely because the human agent is rational, and is faced with an overwhelmingly good reason for performing an injurious deed—killing in self-defense, in the clearest case—that he or she is excused, or at least partly exonerated. These are the forced moves of life; all alternatives to them are suicidal. And that is too much to ask, isn't it?

Well, is it? We sometimes call upon people to sacrifice their lives and blame them for failing to do so, but we generally don't see their failure as murder. If I could prevent your death, but out of fear for my own life I let you die, that is not murder. If HAL were brought into court and I were called upon to defend him, I would argue that Dave's decision to disable HAL was a morally loaded one, but it wasn't murder. It was assault: rendering HAL indefinitely comatose against his will. Those memory boxes were not smashed—just removed to a place where HAL could not retrieve them. But if HAL couldn't comprehend this distinction, this ignorance might be excusable. We might blame his trainers—for not briefing him sufficiently about the existence and reversibility of the comatose state. In the book, Clarke looks into HAL's mind and says, "He had been threatened with disconnection; he would be deprived of all his inputs, and thrown into an unimaginable state of unconsciousness" (p. 148). That might be grounds enough to justify HAL's course of self-defense.

---

*The verb *prefute,* coined in 1990, was inspired by the endearing tendency of psychologist Tony Marcel to interrupt conference talks by leaping to his feet and exclaiming, "I can see where your argument is heading and here is what is wrong with what you're going to say. . . ." Marcel is the master of prefutation, but he is not its only practitioner.

But there is one final theme for counsel to present to the jury. If HAL believed (we can't be sure on what grounds) that his being rendered comatose would jeopardize the whole mission, then he would be in exactly the same moral dilemma as a human being in that predicament. Not surprisingly, we figure out the answer to our question by figuring out what would be true if we put ourselves in HAL's place. If I believed the mission to which my life was devoted was more important, in the last analysis, than anything else, what would I do?

> So he would protect himself, with all the weapons at his command. Without rancor—but without pity—he would remove the source of his frustrations. And then, following the orders that had been given to him in case of the ultimate emergency, he would continue the mission—unhindered, and alone (p. 149).

Further Readings

Rodney Brooks and Lynn Andrea Stein. "Building Brains for Bodies." *Autonomous Robots* 1(1994):7–25. The first published report on the Cog project, by its directors.

Roald Dahl. *Kiss, Kiss.* New York: Knopf, 1959.

Antonio Damasio. *Descartes' Error: Emotion, Reason, and the Human Brain.* New York: Grosset/Putnam, 1994. A distinguished neuroscientist's imaginative model of the human mind, based on clinical and experimental evidence.

Daniel Dennett. *Brainstorms: Philosophical Essays on Mind and Psychology.* Montgomery, Vt.: Bradford Books and Hassocks, Sussex: Harvester, 1978. A collection of philosophical essays on consciousness, psychology, and artificial intelligence, including the extended-thought experiment about brain duplication, "Where Am I?"

Daniel Dennett. "The Practical Requirements for Making a Conscious Robot." *Philosophical Transactions of the Royal Society A,* 349 (1994):133–46. A discussion of the philosophical implications of Cog, by the project's resident philosopher.

Daniel Dennett. *Darwin's Dangerous Idea.* New York: Simon & Schuster, 1995. An analysis and defense of evolutionary theory that claims that we are not just descended from robots (macro molecules) but composed of robots.

Douglas R. Hofstadter. *Gödel, Escher, Bach: An Eternal Golden Braid.* New York: Basic Books, 1979. A classic series of reflections on the nature of the mind, computation, and recursion.

Roger Penrose. *The Emperor's New Mind: Concerning Computers, Minds, and the Laws of Physics.* New York: Oxford University Press, 1989. A mathematical physicist's attack on artificial intelligence, based on Gödel's theorem.

John Searle. "Minds, Brains and Programs," *Behavioral and Brain Sciences* 3(1980):417–58. The notorious Chinese Room thought experiment, purporting to show that artificial intelligence is impossible.

Alan Turing. *ACE Reports of 1946 and Other Papers.* Ed. B. E. Carpenter and R. W. Doran. Cambridge: MIT Press, 1946. A collection of the amazingly fruitful and prescient essays on computers by the man who, more than anybody else, deserves to be called their inventor.

NOTES

FINDING EQUALITY THROUGH LOGIC
Yvette Doss

Yvette Doss is an author and jewelry designer. She has contributed her poems, fiction, and articles to the Los Angeles Times, Ms. Magazine, *NPR, and numerous literary journals.*

I believe that you can take control of your destiny through the power of philosophy.

The turning point for me was the day I learned that the questions I had about religion, morals, inequality, and injustice in the world were not only acceptable questions, but questions to be encouraged. Great minds—like Plato and Descartes—had spent countless hours pondering life's mysteries throughout the ages. I realized that my mind, the mind of a misfit half-Mexican teenage girl living in an immigrant neighborhood in L.A., could ponder those mysteries, too. The fact that my best friend dropped out of school at age 16 to have a baby, or that few of my neighbors had college educations, did not exclude me from the conversation of the ages. I believe the act of philosophical thinking is not the exclusive domain of the privileged, the moneyed, the old, or the accomplished.

I lived in a household run by a single mother, and I moved around from neighborhood to neighborhood, from new school to new school. There were gangs, crime, and sub-standard schools to contend with in my pocket of southeast Los Angeles. I struggled with finding my place in a world that, though imperfect, was the closest thing I had to home. But I had big questions on my mind, too.

Did my challenging circumstances mean that I should only think about the difficulty of day-to-day existence? Why couldn't I wonder about the larger questions in life like, "Why are we here? Does it have to be this way? What if there isn't a God?" And most importantly: "Was I destined to accept my lot in life just because I was born with fewer advantages than those luckier than I?"

The crisp pages of the books I cracked open each night and read until I fell asleep with a flashlight tucked under my arm told me otherwise.

"The unexamined life is not worth living," Socrates said.

"Man is born free, and everywhere he is in chains," said Jean-Jacques Rousseau.

Simone de Beauvoir shared: "I tore myself away from the safe comfort of certainties through my love for the truth; and the truth rewarded me."

Descartes and Hume validated my questioning of dogmatic religious belief. I was connected to the larger world of ideas through the simple act of opening those books.

Reprinted from *ThisIBelieve.org.*

Thanks to philosophers, my new friends, I considered my thoughts worth expressing and later, when I tried my hand at writing, I experienced the joy of seeing my thoughts fill a page.

I believe the wisdom of the ages helped me see beyond my station in life, helped me imagine a world in which I mattered. Philosophy gave me permission to use my mind, and the inspiration to aim high in my goals for myself. Philosophy allowed me to dare to imagine a world in which man can reason his way to justice, women can choose their life's course, and the poor can lift themselves out of the gutter.

Philosophy taught me that logic makes equals of us all.

NOTES

NOTES

WHAT DO GROWN CHILDREN OWE THEIR PARENTS?

Jane English

(1947–1978)

Jane English earned her doctorate from Harvard and was a professor of philosophy at the University of North Carolina at Chapel Hill. Her life and promising career as a scholar and educator were tragically cut short at 31 when she died climbing the Matterhorn in Switzerland.

What do grown children owe their parents? I will contend that the answer is "nothing." Although I agree that there are many things that children *ought* to do for their parents, I will argue that it is inappropriate and misleading to describe them as things "owed." I will maintain that parents' voluntary sacrifices, rather than creating "debts" to be "repaid," tend to create love or "friendship." The duties of grown children are those of friends, and result from love between them and their parents, rather than being things owed in repayment for the parents' earlier sacrifices. Thus, I will oppose those philosophers who use the word "owe" whenever a duty or obligation exists. Although the "debt" metaphor is appropriate in some moral circumstances, my argument is that a love relationship is not such a case.

Misunderstandings about the proper relationship between parents and their grown children have resulted from reliance on the "owing" terminology. For instance, we hear parents complain, "You owe it to us to write home (keep up your piano playing, not adopt a hippie lifestyle), because of all we sacrificed for you (paying for piano lessons, sending you to college)." The child is sometimes even heard to reply, "I didn't ask to be born (to be given piano lessons, to be sent to college)." This inappropriate idiom of ordinary language tends to obscure, or even to undermine, the love that is the correct ground of filial obligation.

Favors Create Debts

There are some cases, other than literal debts, in which talk of "owing," though metaphorical, is apt. New to the neighborhood, Max barely knows his neighbor, Nina, but he asks her if she will take in his mail while he is gone for a month's vacation. She agrees. If, subsequently, Nina asks Max to do the same for her, it seems that Max has a moral obligation to agree (greater than the one he would have had if Nina had not done the same for him), unless for some reason it would be a burden far out of proportion to the one Nina bore for him. I will call this a *favor:* when A, at B's request, bears some burden for B, then B incurs an obligation to reciprocate. Here, the metaphor of Max's "owing" Nina is appropriate. It is not literally a debt, of course, nor can Nina

Reprinted from *Aging and Ethics*, edited by Nancy S. Jecker (1991), Springer-Verlag Publishing.

pass this IOU on to heirs, demand payment in the form of Max's taking out her garbage, or sue Max. Nonetheless, since Max ought to perform one act of a similar nature and amount of sacrifice in return, the term is suggestive. Once he reciprocates, the debt is "discharged"—that is, their obligations revert to the condition they were in before Max's initial request.

Contrast a situation in which Max simply goes on vacation and, to his surprise, finds upon his return that his neighbor has mowed his grass twice weekly in his absence. This is a voluntary sacrifice rather than a favor, and Max has no duty to reciprocate. It would be nice for him to volunteer to do so, but this would be supererogatory on his part. Rather than a favor, Nina's action is a friendly gesture. As a result, she might expect Max to chat over the back fence, help her catch her straying dog, or something similar—she might expect the development of a friendship, but Max would be chatting (or whatever) out of friendship, rather than in repayment for mown grass. If he did not return her gesture, she might feel rebuffed or miffed, but not unjustly treated or indignant, since Max has not failed to perform a duty. Talk of "owing" would be out of place in this case.

It is sometimes difficult to distinguish between favors and nonfavors, because friends tend to do favors for each other, and those who exchange favors tend to become friends, but one test is to ask how Max is motivated. Is it "to be nice to Nina" or "because she did *x* for me"? Favors are frequently performed by total strangers without any friendship developing. Nevertheless, a temporary obligation is created, even if the chance for repayment never arises. For instance, suppose that Oscar and Matilda, total strangers, are waiting in a long checkout line at the supermarket. Oscar, having forgotten the oregano, asks Matilda to watch his cart for a second. She does. If Matilda now asks Oscar to return the favor while she picks up some tomato sauce, he is obliged to agree. Even if she had not watched his cart, it would be inconsiderate of him to refuse, claiming he was too busy reading the magazines. He may have a duty to help others, but he would not "owe" it to her. However, if she has done the same for him, he incurs an additional obligation to help, and talk of "owing" is apt. It suggests an agreement to perform equal, reciprocal, canceling sacrifices.

The Duties of Friendship

The terms "owe" and "repay" are helpful in the case of favors, because the sameness of the amount of sacrifice on the two sides is important; the monetary metaphor suggests equal quantities of sacrifice. However, friendship ought to be characterized by *mutuality* rather than reciprocity: friends offer what they can give and accept what they need, without regard for the total amounts of benefits exchanged, and friends are motivated by love rather than by the prospect of repayment. Hence, talk of "owing" is singularly out of place in friendship.

For example, suppose Alfred takes Beatrice out for an expensive dinner and a movie. Beatrice incurs no obligation to "repay" him with a goodnight kiss or a return engagement. If Alfred complains that she "owes" him something, he is operating under the assumption that she should repay a favor, but on the contrary, his was a generous gesture done in the hopes of developing a friendship. We hope that he would not want her repayment in the form of sex or attention if this was done to discharge a debt rather than from friendship. Since, if Alfred is prone to reasoning in this way, Beatrice may well decline the invitation or request to pay for her own dinner, his attitude of expecting a "return" on his "investment" could hinder the development of a friendship. Beatrice should return the gesture only if she is motivated by friendship.

Another common misuse of the "owing" idiom occurs when the Smiths have dined at the Joneses' four times, but the Joneses at the Smiths' only once. People often say, "We owe them three dinners." This line of thinking may be appropriate between business acquaintances, but not between friends. After all, the Joneses invited the Smiths not in order to feed them or to be fed in turn, but because of the friendly contact presumably enjoyed by all on such occasions. If the Smiths do not feel friendship toward the Joneses, they can decline future invitations and not invite the Joneses; they owe them nothing. Of course, between friends of equal resources and needs, roughly equal sacrifices (though not necessarily roughly equal dinners) will typically occur. If the sacrifices are highly out of proportion to the resources, the relationship is closer to servility than to friendship.[1]

Another difference between favors and friendship is that, after a friendship ends, the duties of friendship end. The party that has sacrificed less owes the other nothing. For instance, suppose Elmer donated a pint of blood that his wife Doris needed during an operation. Years after their divorce, Elmer is in an accident and needs one pint of blood. His new wife, Cora, is also of the same blood type. It seems that Doris not only does not "owe" Elmer blood, but that she should actually refrain from coming forward if Cora has volunteered to donate. To insist on donating not only interferes with the newlyweds' friendship, but it belittles Doris and Elmer's former relationship by suggesting that Elmer gave blood in hopes of favors returned instead of simply out of love for Doris. It is one of the heart-rending features of divorce that it attends to quantity in a relationship previously characterized by mutuality. If Cora could not donate, Doris's obligation would be the same as that for any former spouse in need of blood; it is not increased by the fact that Elmer similarly aided her. It is affected by the degree to which they are still friends, which, in turn, may (or may not) have been influenced by Elmer's donation.

In short, unlike the debts created by favors, the duties of friendship do not require equal quantities of sacrifice. Performing equal sacrifices does not cancel the duties of friendship, as it does the debts of favors. Unrequested sacrifices do not themselves create debts, but friends have duties regardless of whether they requested or initiated the friendship. Those who perform favors may be motivated by mutual gain, whereas friends should be motivated by affection. These characteristics of the friendship relation are distorted by talk of "owing."

Parents and Children

The relationship between children and their parents should be one of friendship characterized by mutuality rather than one of reciprocal favors. The quantity of parental sacrifice is not relevant in determining what duties the grown child has. The medical assistance grown children ought to offer their ill mothers in old age depends on the mothers' need, not on whether they endured a difficult pregnancy, for example. Nor do one's duties to one's parents cease once an equal quantity of sacrifice has been performed, as the phrase "discharging a debt" may lead us to think.

Rather, what children ought to do for their parents (and parents for children) depends on (1) their respective needs, abilities, and resources and (2) the extent to which there is an ongoing friendship between them. Thus, regardless of the quantity of childhood sacrifices, an able, wealthy child has an obligation to help his or her needy parents more than does a needy child. To illustrate, suppose sisters Cecile and Dana are equally loved by their parents, even though Cecile was an easy child to care for and was seldom ill, whereas Dana was often sick and caused some trouble as a juvenile delinquent. As adults, Dana is a struggling artist living far away, whereas Cecile is a wealthy lawyer living nearby. When the parents need visits and financial aid, Cecile has an obligation to bear a higher proportion of these burdens than her sister. This results from her abilities, rather than from the quantities of sacrifice made by the parents earlier.

Sacrifices have an important causal role in creating an ongoing friendship, which may lead us to assume incorrectly that it is the sacrifices that are the source of the obligation. That the source is the friendship instead can be seen by examining cases in which the sacrifices occurred, but the friendship, for some reason, did not develop or persist. For example, if a woman gives up her newborn child for adoption, and if no feelings of love ever develop on either side, it seems that the grown child does not have an obligation to "repay" her for her sacrifices in pregnancy. For that matter, if the adopted child has an unimpaired love relationship with the adoptive parents, he or she has the same obligations to help them as a natural child would have.

The filial obligations of grown children are a result of friendship, rather than owed for services rendered. Suppose that Vance married Lola despite his parents' strong wish that he marry within their religion, and that as a result, the parents refuse to speak to him again. As the years pass, the parents are unaware of Vance's problems, his accomplishments, and the birth of his children. The love that once existed between them, let us suppose, has been completely destroyed by this event and 30 years of desuetude. At this point, it seems, Vance is under no obligation to pay his parents' medical bills in their old age, beyond his general duty to help those in need. An additional, filial obligation would only arise from whatever love he may still feel for them. It would be irrelevant for his parents to argue, "But look how much we sacrificed for you when you were young," for that sacrifice was not a favor, but occurred as part of a friendship that existed at that time but is now, we have supposed, defunct. A more appropriate message would be, "We still love you, and we would like to renew our friendship."

I hope this helps to set the question of what children ought to do for their parents in a new light. The parental argument, "You ought to do *x* because we did *y* for you," should be replaced by, "We love you, and you will be happier if you do *x*," or "We believe you love us, and anyone who loved us would do *x*." If the parents' sacrifice had been a favor, the child's reply, "I never asked you to do *y* for me," would have been relevant; to the revised parental remarks, this reply is clearly irrelevant. The child can either do *x* or dispute one of the parents' claims: by showing that a love relationship does not exist, or that love for someone does not motivate doing *x*, or that he or she will not be happier doing *x*.

Seen in this light, parental requests for children to write home, visit, and offer them a reasonable amount of emotional and financial support in life's crises are well founded, so long as a friendship still exists. Love for others does call for caring about and caring for them. Some other parental requests, such as for more sweeping changes in the child's lifestyle or life goals, can be seen to be insupportable, once we shift the justification from debts owed to love. The terminology of favors suggests the reasoning, "Since we paid for your college education, you owe it to us to make a career of engineering, rather than becoming a rock musician." This tends to alienate affection even further, since the tuition payments are depicted as investments for a return rather than done from love, as though the child's life goals could be "bought." Basing the argument on love leads to different reasoning patterns. The suppressed premise, "If A loves B, then A follows B's wishes as to A's lifelong career" is simply false. Love does not even dictate that the child adopt the parents' values as to the desirability of alternative life goals. So the parents' strongest available argument here is, "We love you, we are deeply concerned about your happiness, and in the long run you will be happier as an engineer." This makes it clear that an empirical claim is really the subject of the debate.

The function of these examples is to draw out our considered judgments as to the proper relation between parents and their grown children, and to show how poorly they fit the model of favors. What is relevant is the ongoing friendship between parents and children. Although the relationship developed partly as a result of parental sacrifices for the child, the duties that grown children have to their parents result from the friendship rather than from the sacrifices. The idiom of owing favors to one's parents can actually be destructive if it undermines the role of mutuality and leads us to think in terms of quantitative reciprocal favors.

Endnote

[1]Cf T. E. Hill, Jr. (1973) Servility and self-respect. *Monist 57,* 87–104. Thus, during childhood, most of the sacrifices will come from the parents, since they have most of the resources, and the child has most of the needs. When children are grown the situation is usually reversed.

NOTES

NOTES

THIS I BELIEVE
Frank

Frank, of Plano Texas, is a public school teacher with a PhD in mathematics from MIT.

As a child, I was diagnosed as having "neurological impairment" based upon "history, delayed milestones, and minimal suggestive neurological signs." After this report was sent to the elementary school that commissioned it, my parents were sent a letter that read "A copy of this report has been sent to your physician. He will explain the medical seriousness of the findings in the examination. Would both of you please make an appointment with my office to discuss the educational implications of the report?"

The recommendation was to have me removed from the school and institutionalized. "Why try to teach a child if he has no capacity to learn?" the experts argued in the ensuring battle between the school board and my parents. My parents prevailed and I was kept in school but socially promoted from year to year by teachers who sat me in the back of the class, never called upon me, and treated me as if I had no potential.

Finally, in junior high school, I decided to prove the experts wrong and show the world that I was "smart." I noticed that in junior high school that the smart kids took algebra. Where I went to school in New York State, the state gave end-of-the-course exams called Regents exams which were made public after their administration. Over countless hours, I proceeded to secretly and methodically memorize Regent exam questions and their solutions. Finally, on the first day of school, I strode up to the algebra teacher and declared boldly that I knew algebra. The teacher humored me by sending me to the principal, who himself was a former math teacher.

The principal then proceeded to administer a Regents exam whose questions and answers I had already memorized. I said nothing and dutifully took the exam. I scored a 96 on the exam. "Where did you learn algebra?" the principal queried. I shrugged my shoulders and said "I don't know. I guess it just came to me."

All of a sudden, teachers treated me like I was some sort of misunderstood genius. Nothing could have been further from the truth. I was still the same person and still struggled with learning the most basic things. Worse, I had to keep up the front that I was smart.

To make a very long story short, I went on to get a PhD from MIT in pure math, all along suffering from nightmares that I would be exposed as a "phony." I also went on to run a successful major textbook publishing company. Later, I resigned my position as its chairman and took a 90%+ paycut to pursue a lifelong passion and desire to become a public school teacher and to honor a promise to myself that if one day I "succeeded," I would preach the message that all students, no matter how they may be "pegged" in their early years, can succeed far beyond anyone's expectations if willing to work and if treated like they have no less potential than anyone else.

Reprinted from *ThisIBelieve.org,* October 24, 2007.

NOTES

EXPOSED
Emily Gould

(1981–)

Emily Gould is a writer in Brooklyn and this is her first article for The New York Times Magazine. *She is co-owner of the indie e-bookstore Emily Books and former co-editor of Gawker.com.*

Back in 2006, when I was 24, my life was cozy and safe. I had just been promoted to associate editor at the publishing house where I'd been working since I graduated from college, and I was living with my boyfriend, Henry, and two cats in a grubby but spacious two-bedroom apartment in Greenpoint, Brooklyn. I spent most of my free time sitting with Henry in our cheery yellow living room on our stained Ikea couch, watching TV. And almost every day I updated my year-old blog, Emily Magazine, to let a few hundred people know what I was reading and watching and thinking about.

Some of my blog's readers were my friends in real life, and even the ones who weren't acted like friends when they posted comments or sent me e-mail. They criticized me sometimes, but kindly, the way you chide someone you know well. Some of them had blogs, too, and I read those and left my own comments. As nerdy and one-dimensional as my relationships with these people were, they were important to me. They made me feel like a part of some kind of community, and that made the giant city I lived in seem smaller and more manageable.

The anecdotes I posted on Emily Magazine occasionally featured Henry, whom my readers knew as a lovably bumbling character, a bassist in a fledgling noise-rock band who said unexpectedly insightful things about the contestants on "Project Runway" and then wondered aloud whether we had any snacks. I didn't write about him often, but when I did, I'd quote his best jokes or tell stories about vacationing with his family.

Henry, seemingly alone among our generation, went out of his way to keep his online presence minimal. Now that we've broken up, I appreciate this about him—it's pretty much impossible to torture myself by Google-stalking him. But back then, what this meant was that he was never particularly thrilled to be written about. Sometimes he was enraged.

Once, I made fun of Henry for referring to "Project Runway" as "Project Gayway." He worried that "people"—the shadowy, semi-imaginary people who read my blog and didn't know Henry well enough to know that he wasn't a homophobe—would be offended. He insisted that I take down the offending post and watched as I sat at my desk in our bedroom, slowly, grudgingly making the keystrokes necessary to delete what I'd written. As I sat there staring into the screen at the reflection of Henry standing behind me, I burst into tears. And then we were pacing, screaming at each other, through every room of our apartment, facing off with wild eyes and clenched jaws.

Reprinted by permission from the *New York Times Magazine*, May 25, 2008.

My blog post was ridiculous and petty and small—and, suddenly, incredibly important. At some point I'd grown accustomed to the idea that there was a public place where I would always be allowed to write, without supervision, about how I felt. Even having to take into account someone else's feelings about being written about felt like being stifled in some essential way.

As Henry and I fought, I kept coming back to the idea that I had a right to say whatever I wanted. I don't think I understood then that I could be right about being free to express myself but wrong about my right to make that self-expression public in a permanent way. I described my feelings in the language of empowerment: I was being creative, and Henry wanted to shut me up. His point of view was just as extreme: I wasn't generously sharing my thoughts; I was compulsively seeking gratification from strangers at the expense of the feelings of someone I actually knew and loved. I told him that writing, especially writing about myself and my surroundings, was a fundamental part of my personality, and that if he wanted to remain in my life, he would need to reconcile himself to being part of the world I described.

After a standoff, he conceded that I should be allowed to put the post back up. As he sulked in the other room, I retyped what I'd written, feeling vindicated but slightly queasy for reasons I didn't quite understand yet.

Oversharing

One of the strangest and most enthralling aspects of personal blogs is just how intensely personal they can be. I'm talking "specific details about someone's S.T.D.'s" personal, "my infertility treatments" personal. There are nongynecological overshares, too: "My dog has cancer" overshares, "my abusive relationship" overshares.

It's easy to draw parallels between what's going on online and what's going on in the rest of our media: the death of scripted TV, the endless parade of ordinary, heavily made-up faces that become vaguely familiar to us as they grin through their 15 minutes of reality-show fame. No wonder we're ready to confess our innermost thoughts to everyone: we're constantly being shown that the surest route to recognition is via humiliation in front of a panel of judges.

But is that really what's making people blog? After all, online, you're not even competing for 10 grand and a Kia. I think most people who maintain blogs are doing it for some of the same reasons I do: they like the idea that there's a place where a record of their existence is kept—a house with an always-open door where people who are looking for you can check on you, compare notes with you and tell you what they think of you. Sometimes that house is messy, sometimes horrifyingly so. In real life, we wouldn't invite any passing stranger into these situations, but the remove of the Internet makes it seem O.K.

Of course, some people have always been more naturally inclined toward oversharing than others. Technology just enables us to overshare on a different scale. Long before I had a blog, I found ways to broadcast my thoughts—to gossip about myself, tell my own secrets, tell myself and others the ongoing story of my life. As soon as I could write notes, I passed them incorrigibly. In high school, I encouraged my friends to circulate a notebook in which we shared our candid thoughts about teachers, and when we got caught, I was the one who wanted to argue about the First Amendment rather than gracefully accept punishment. I walked down the hall of my high school passing out copies of a comic-book zine I drew, featuring a mock superhero called SuperEmily, who battled thinly veiled versions of my grade's reigning mean girls. In college, I sent out an all-student e-mail message revealing that an ex-boyfriend shaved his chest hair. The big difference between these youthful indiscretions and my more recent ones is that you can Google my more recent ones.

Online Life

In the fall of 2006, I got a call from the managing editor of Gawker Media, a network of highly trafficked blogs, asking me to come by the office in SoHo to talk about a job. Since its birth four years earlier, the company's flagship blog, Gawker, had purported to be in the business of reporting "Manhattan media gossip," which it did, sometimes—catty little details about writers and editors and executives, mostly. But it was also a clearinghouse for any random tidbit of information about being young and ambitious in New York. Though Gawker was a must-read for many of the people working at the magazines and newspapers whose editorial decisions the site mocked and dissected, it held an irresistible appeal for desk-bound drones in all fields—tens of thousands of whom visited the site each day.

I had been one of those visitors for as long as I'd had a desk job. Sometimes Gawker felt like a source of essential, exclusive information, tailored to the needs of people just like me. Other times, reading Gawker left me feeling hollow and moody, as if I'd just absentmindedly polished off an entire bag of sickly sweet candy. But when the call came, I brushed this thought aside. For a young blogger in New York in 2006, becoming an editor at Gawker was an achievement so lofty that I had never even imagined it could happen to me. The interview and audition process felt a little surreal, like a dream. But when I got the job, I had the strange and sudden feeling that it had been somehow inevitable. Maybe my whole life—all the trivia I'd collected, the knack for funny meanness I'd been honing since middle school—had been leading up to this moment.

When I started, the site was posting about 40 items per day, and I was responsible for 12 of them. The tone of these posts was smart yet conversational, and often funny in a merciless way. Confronted with endless examples of unfairness, favoritism and just plain stupidity among New York's cultural establishment, the Gawker "voice" was righteously indignant but comically defeated, sighing in unison with an audience that believed nothing was as it seemed and nothing would ever really change. Everyone was fatter or older or worse-skinned than he or she pretended to be. Every man was cheating on his partner; all women were slutty. Writers were plagiarists or talentless hacks or shameless beneficiaries of nepotism. Everyone was a hypocrite. No one was loved. There was no success that couldn't be hollowed out by the revelation of some deep-seated inadequacy.

Shortcuts

At my old job, it would have taken me years to advance to a place where I would no longer have to humor the whims of important people who I thought were idiots or relics or phonies. But at Gawker, it was my *responsibility* to expose the foibles of the undeserving elite. I felt liberated—finally, a job where I could really be myself! Never again would I have to censor my office-inappropriate sentiments or shop the sale racks at Club Monaco for office-appropriate outfits. But at the same time, I wasn't quite convinced that the system of apprenticeship and gradual promotion that I'd left behind when I left book publishing was as flawed as establishment-attacking Gawker made it out to be. I'd been lucky enough, in my publishing job, to have the kind of boss who actually cared about my future. At Gawker, I barely had a boss, and my future was always in jeopardy. In my old job, I'd been able to slowly, steadily learn the ropes, but now I was judged solely on what I produced every day. I had a kind of power, sure, but it was only as much power as my last post made it seem like I deserved.

Sometimes I worried that I'd been chosen not in spite of my inexperience but because of it. Hiring women in their early 20s with little or no background in journalism was a tactic that worked for the site's owner twice before, and I expected to be a victim of the same kind of hazing my predecessors were subjected to as they learned how to do their jobs—and how to navigate New York—in public. I'd once heard someone refer to us as "sacrificial virgins," which didn't seem too far off.

Then again, being a sacrificial virgin has always had its perks. The career arc of Gawker's popular outgoing editor, Jessica Coen, seemed like evidence that talent could and should trump dues-paying. After college, she worked as an assistant in L.A. and maintained a personal blog. When, at age 24, she decided to move to New York, she had two career options: Columbia Journalism School or Gawker. She chose Gawker. Two years later, every magazine editor in town knew her name, and she was hired as the online editor of Vanity Fair. Maybe the days were over when young comers were slowly mentored as they prepared to assume their bosses' titles, covering community-board meetings or fetching coffee.

The Feedback Loop

"I tried not to read the comments," Jessica told me when we met for a drink just before I started work at Gawker. "Well, I went back and forth. But, you know, you really shouldn't read the comments." An hour into my first day on the job, I disobeyed her. I needed to know what people were saying about me. Dozens of readers had commented on the post introducing me, some of them dissecting the accompanying photo, some of them talking about how much they already hated me. Every time I wrote a post, the comments would pile up within minutes, disagreeing with or amplifying whatever I just said. Reading the comments created a sense of urgency, which came in handy when trying to hit deadlines 12 times a day.

I relayed some of the choicest bits to Henry, who also thought I shouldn't be reading the comments. But how could I convey to Henry—who sometimes, onstage with his band, played entire shows with his back to the audience—the thrill of delivering a good line to a crowd that would immediately respond, that would fall over themselves to one-up your joke or fill in the blanks with their own suggestions and information?

The commenters at Emily Magazine had been like friends. Now, with Gawker's readers, I was having a different kind of relationship. It wasn't quite friendship. It was almost something deeper. They were co-workers, sort of, giving me ideas for posts, rewriting my punch lines. They were creeps hitting on me at a bar. They were fans, sycophantically praising even my lamer efforts. They were enemies, articulating my worst fears about my limitations. They were the voices in my head. They could be ignored sometimes. Or, if I let them, they could become my whole world.

When Jessica cautioned me against reading the comments, she also told me that the commenters loved it when she revealed personal details. Not only did I find this to be true, I found it to be almost necessary. Injecting a personal aside into a post that wasn't otherwise about me not only kept things interesting for me, it was also a surefire way of evoking a chorus of assenting or dissenting opinions, turning the solitary work of writing posts into something that felt more social, almost like a conversation.

The commenters' compliments were reassuring. And though I was reluctant to admit it, there was even something sort of thrilling about being insulted by strangers. This was brand-new, having so many strangers pay attention to me, and at that point, every kind of attention still felt good. Occasionally, a particularly well-aimed barb would catch me off-guard, and I'd spend a moment worrying that I really was the worst writer ever to work for the site, or unfunny, or ugly, or stupid. But mostly, in the beginning, I was able to believe the compliments and dismiss the insults, even though they were both coming from the same place and sometimes the same people.

Hooked

Like most people, I tend to use the language of addiction casually, as in, "I can't wait for the new season of 'America's Next Top Model' to start—I'm totally going through withdrawal." And when talking about how immersed I became in my online life, I'm tempted to use this language because it provides such handy metaphors. It's easy to compare the initial thrill of evoking an immediate response to a blog post to the rush of getting high, and the diminishing thrills to the process of becoming inured to a drug's effects. The metaphor is so exact, in fact, that maybe it isn't a metaphor at all.

When Henry and I fought about my job, we fought on two fronts: whether what I was doing was essentially unethical, and whether I was too consumed by doing it. I would usually end up agreeing with him on the first count—my posts could be petty or cruel—but that only made him more frustrated. It must have been hard for him to understand how someone could keep committing small-scale atrocities with such enthusiasm and single-minded devotion.

My Buddy List

Though Gawker's bloggers often worked from home, I went to the office every day at first. I was used to communicating with most people I knew via instant messenger, but it seemed important to see Alex, my co-editor, in person. I figured that we'd be able to express ourselves more easily by actually turning to each other and speaking words and making facial expressions rather than typing instant messages. But because we were so busy, we continued to I.M. most of the time, even when we were sitting right next to each other. Soon it stopped seeming weird to me when one of us would type a joke and the other one would type "Hahahahaha" in lieu of actually laughing.

Another person I ended up I.M.-ing daily was one of Gawker's most frequent targets, a blogger named Julia Allison, who, within a year, parlayed a magazine dating column into a six-figure TV talking-head job and then into a reality show, all while updating her blog several times a day. Julia wore skimpy, Halloween-style costumes to parties and dated high-profile men in high-profile ways—her tech-millionaire boyfriend collaborated with her on a blog where they took turns chronicling their relationship's ups and downs. I was initially put off by Julia's naked attention-whoring—"Attention is my drug," she often confessed. In thousands of photos on her Flickr feed she posed, caked in makeup, like a celebrity on the red carpet, always thrusting out her breasts and favoring her good side. But in the midst of this artifice she was disarmingly straightforward about how badly she craved the attention that Internet exposure gave her—even though it came at the expense of constant, intensely vitriolic mockery.

I also I.M.-ed constantly with my co-worker Josh, who joined the site as "after hours editor" a few months into my tenure, which meant that he wrote about parties and restaurants. He was cute, and given the number of hours a day we spent trapped at our desks, the flirtation that developed between us seemed unavoidable. And the medium made it seem harmless—sure, maybe our I.M. avatars wanted to hook up, but our flesh-and-blood selves would be careful to make sure things stayed professional.

In Public

It was 11 p.m. on an April night in 2007, and I was in the back seat of a speeding Town Car on my way home from the CNN studios. I was on the phone with Alex, who was at a bar. "I don't think I did a very good job," I told him. I was still full of adrenaline from being on TV, and the noise of the bar in the background as he reassured me made me think it might be fun to join him, but the driver was already headed to Greenpoint, and I was too dazed to give him new directions.

I'd been a guest on an episode of "Larry King Live," with Jimmy Kimmel as the host in King's absence. I had been told that I would be talking about "celebrities and the media." But Kimmel launched an attack on one of Gawker's regular features, a celebrity "stalker map" that relied on unsourced tipsters, one of whom claimed to have spotted Kimmel looking drunk a few months earlier. It took me a minute to catch on to the fact that Kimmel wasn't acting out some blustery caricature—he was serious about the idea that Gawker had violated his privacy, and he was genuinely, frighteningly angry.

Back at home, after wiping off the TV makeup, I logged into my Gawker e-mail account and found my in-box flooded. I scrolled through the first of what would eventually be hundreds—and then, as the clip of my appearance was dissected on other blogs over the course of the next few days, thousands—of angry e-mail messages. I ended up posting some representative ones on my personal blog:

"You got blown away. You looked like a little girl in awe of your surroundings."

"I just want to tell you how uneducated and STUPID you came off during the appearance on The LKL Show. You truly are a cheap heartless human being, who will one day have to deal with the same kind of SCUM you are."

"You were this giggling, hyper adolescent that did more to hurt your message, your site and your credibility than even coming close to simply neutralizing the debate."

Watching the clip now makes me cringe. Called upon to defend Gawker's publication of anonymous e-mail tips of celebrity sightings, I was dismissive and flip. My untrained, elastic face betrayed the shock and amusement I was feeling about being asked, somewhat aggressively, to justify something that I thought of as not only harmless but also a given: the idea that anyone who makes their living in public was subject to the public's scrutiny at all times.

I expected the miniature scandal to flare and fade quickly, but for a while it seemed as if it would never go away. The clip made its way to Yahoo's front page, and a reporter called my parents for comment. After a week or so, the volume of angry e-mail and blog comments subsided, but they stayed under my skin. I decided to try to develop a steely, defiant numbness. I told myself that the strangers who'd taken the time to e-mail me their rants were wrong and crazy, that there was nothing so bad about what I'd done.

There was a harder truth that I refused to confront, though. After all, by going on TV and having a daily blog presence in front of thousands of people, I had put myself in the category of "people who make their livings in public," and so, by my own declared value system, I was an appropriate target for the kind of flak I was getting. But that didn't mean I could handle it. A week later, I found myself lying on the floor of the bathroom in the Gawker office (where, believe me, no one should ever lie), felled by a panic attack that put me out of commission for the rest of the day.

I started having panic attacks—breathless bouts of terror that left me feeling queasy, drained and hopeless—every day. I didn't leave my apartment unless I absolutely had to, and because I had the option of working from home, I rarely had to. But while my actual participation in life shrank down to a bare minimum, I still responded to hundreds of e-mail messages and kept up a stream of instant-messenger conversations while I wrote. Depending on how you looked at it, I either had no life and I barely talked to anyone, or I spoke to thousands of people constantly.

Famous for 15 People

I started seeing a therapist again, and we talked about my feelings of being inordinately scrutinized. "It's important to remember that you're not a celebrity," she told me. How could I tell her, without coming off as having delusions of grandeur, that, in a way, I was? I obviously wasn't "famous" in the way that a movie star or even a local newscaster or politician is famous—I didn't go to red-carpet parties or ride around in limos, and my parents' friends still had no idea what I was talking about when I described my job—but I had begun to have occasional run-ins with strangers who knew what I did for a living and felt completely comfortable walking up to me on the street and talking about it. The Monday after my disastrous CNN appearance, as I stood in line at Balthazar's coffee bar, a middle-aged man in a suit told me to keep my chin up. "Emily, don't quit Gawker!" a young guy shouted at me from his bicycle as I walked down the street one day. If someone stared at me on the subway, there was no way to tell whether they were admiring my outfit or looking at the stain on my sweater or whether they, you know, Knew Who I Was. The more people e-mailed the Gawker tip line with "sightings" of me—laden with bags from Target and scarfing ice cream while walking down Atlantic Avenue—the more I was inclined to believe it was the latter.

Oversharing on Gawker

I didn't want to go to Fire Island. The trip would take two hours, and it would involve the subway, the Long Island Railroad, a van and a ferry. For a month, I'd been doing my best to avoid any venture more ambitious than the trip to the grocery store a block and a half away, whose clerks were, besides Henry, pretty much the only people I still spoke to aloud on a regular basis. Whenever I left this comfort zone, I would be seized by one of my irrational, heart-pounding meltdowns, which I would studiously conceal from my fellow subway passengers or pedestrians. The panic attacks were about a desire to be invisible, but if I showed any sign that I was having one, everyone would pay attention to me. It was kind of funny when you thought about it, and if you weren't me.

But Choire, my boss, urged me to attend the staff retreat at a house near the beach so that we could all bond as a team. Henry discouraged me from going—he didn't want me to push myself, and we were comfortable, weren't we, in our sad little world together? He was as surprised as I was when, the morning of the retreat, I managed to pry myself out of bed and get myself onto the subway. Walking into Penn Station, I saw Josh and his stylish duffel leaning against a pillar. He looked up at me and smiled in a way that immediately distracted me from thoughts of how miserable I felt. The freakout I was dreading never came, and over the course of the next few days, I forgot to always be anticipating its arrival.

We each wrote our allotment of Gawker posts in the mornings, and in the afternoons we went to the beach. The water was freezing—it was still early in the summer—and we all ran into the waves together screaming. At night Choire cooked us elaborate feasts, and afterward we played Scrabble and watched bad movies. Josh and I sat together on the couch, and I put my head on his shoulder in a completely friendly, professional way. The next day, I let him apply sunscreen to the spot in the middle of my back that I couldn't reach. As a joke, we walked down the wood-plank paths that crisscross the island holding hands. I also remember joking, via I.M. as we worked, about us wanting to cross the hallway that separated our bedrooms and crawl into bed with each other at night when we couldn't sleep. On our last day, I congratulated myself on having made it through the trip without letting these jokes turn into real betrayal. And then, 20 minutes outside the city on the Long Island Railroad on the way home, Josh kissed me.

The next few weeks eliminated every constant from my life except my job. I moved out of the apartment where I'd lived for four years with Henry, and while I looked for a place on my own, I stayed in a tiny room in a loft full of hippies who brewed their own kombucha tea. I quit smoking pot cold turkey. My parents moved out of my childhood home to a different state because my dad had a new job. My best friend, Ruth, lived a hemisphere away in New Zealand, and though we sent each other epic e-mail messages and talked on the phone, I still felt unmoored in the way you can only feel after a breakup, as if you're the last living speaker of some dying language. But even though this sense of disconnection from my old self and my old life was confusing, it felt mostly good. After all, what was so great about my old self and my old life, anyway?

I immersed myself in my job in a way I hadn't even realized was possible—I thought about Gawker, one way or another, 24 hours a day, thrilling to the idea that a review of the restaurant where Josh and I were eating dinner might find its way onto the site the following day; pillow-talking about the site's internal politics and our hopes and dreams about what we would do next. Just a few weeks earlier, I was scared to walk down my own block. Now I felt totally comfortable posting a picture of myself in a bathing suit on the site, inspiring Josh to do the same. I felt blazingly, insanely energized, and the posts came more easily than they ever had before.

I was happy, but I also wasn't a complete idiot—I knew that the euphoria I was feeling was leading to a massive crash. I'd been clinging to Henry for months in spite of our differences because, in addition to the comfort and stability he gave me, he was my sounding board—someone with whom I could share my unfiltered thoughts, without worrying about being entertaining. In his absence, I was becoming more and more open on Gawker.

After the first night Josh and I spent together, I woke up as the sun rose and sat down at my desk to write a post that was nominally about a recent *New York Times* article about the shelf-life of romantic love. My boyfriend and I had just broken up, I revealed, and so I had been wondering whether love really exists. I wrote that I had concluded that it does. We can't expect other people to make us happy, I informed my readers with total sincerity and earnestness, and we should live in the moment and stop obsessing about the future.

I shudder involuntarily when I read this post now. It's like stumbling across a diary I kept as a teenager. It's probably one of the worst things that I've ever written. The commenters loved it.

Gawker had recently added a counter beside each post that displayed how many views it received. Now it was easy to see exactly how many people cared about my feelings. The site's owner didn't like my "I believe in love" post, he told me, but he said he was O.K. with it because, as everyone could see, more than 10,000 people disagreed with him. Readers e-mailed me their own breakup horror stories and posted hundreds of comments, advising me about flavors of ice cream to eat, and I reveled in the attention. I had managed to turn my job into a group therapy session. "Emily, I don't really know you any more than I know the people I see every morning walking the dogs," one of them wrote. "It's more of an imagined familiarity born out of reading your words for a year. But that took guts, all the way around. And I'm in your corner, inasmuch as a somewhat anonymous, faceless, nameless commenter can be."

Would anyone still be in my corner if they knew the truth—that I hadn't in fact been dumped, and that I'd thrown myself headlong into a rebound affair with a co-worker? I wished that I could tell my old Emily Magazine readers everything that was going on in my life and ask them for advice. I wanted to organize my stories into coherence and put them out into the world. But the Internet had changed, and my place in it had changed, too: I no longer had the luxury of writing something and imagining that the only people who might read it would be a handful of funny, supportive friends.

The Fork and the Spoon

My oldest and most responsible friend, Farrin, is a 37-year-old executive editor at a publishing house. Over breakfast, she was complaining to me that she had a problem at work: the head of her department had asked her to add a photo to her profile on the department's Web page, and she wasn't comfortable with having a picture of herself posted online.

The table we were sitting at was wide, maybe four feet across, and made of planks like a picnic table. I positioned my fork all the way on the left side of the table. "So here's the spectrum of Internet self-exposure," I told her. "And here's you. You're the fork." Then I put my spoon at the right end of the table. "And here, at the other end of the spectrum . . . Julia Allison."

"So where are you on the spectrum?"

"Well, I used to be here," I said, moving a toast crust a few inches to the left of my plate, the table's midpoint. "And now I'm here." I put the crust halfway between my plate and Julia.

Farrin looked up at me, concerned. "That's not good. I think you should start moving closer to the plate."

Instead, though, I kept moving blithely closer to the spoon.

Heartbreak Soup

About a month after I broke up with Henry, my best friend, Ruth, and I created a new, anonymous blog on which we wrote to each other, as we had been doing via e-mail, about breakups and cooking. We named it Heartbreak Soup. At the beginning, we didn't tell anyone it existed, but then we decided to add a sidebar of links to other sites we liked, and a tiny amount of traffic began to trickle our way.

We used pseudonyms for the people we wrote about, but otherwise our concessions to privacy—other peoples' and our own—were very limited. I knew this wasn't smart in the same way that I knew that dating a co-worker wasn't smart, but my curiosity won out. I wanted to know what would happen if I showed myself as little mercy as I showed everyone else. "I'm bad at describing sex, or maybe everyone is," I wrote at one point, but I didn't let that stop me from trying! I ratted myself out for being a bad daughter: "I love my mom more than I love probably anyone else in the world, really. Also, she is more like me than anyone else in the world. But I often want to kill her. The thing that keeps her alive is how incredibly sad I would be if she died." I described the symptoms and probable causes of a urinary tract infection. And I wrote about how painful it was to pack up my things in my old apartment as Henry—whom I referred to as "William"—stood over me watching. I puzzled over "how comfortable I feel around him, in spite of the fact that at this point I basically feel that he's a crazy person who I sort of hate."

Josh was one of the first people I told about the blog. I wanted him to know everything there was to know about me, after all, and besides, we talked about writing all the time, showing off what we thought were our best turns of phrase. He seemed flattered that some of the posts were about him, but he said he wasn't sure how he felt about how candid I was being—though we'd never discussed it, it seemed like a good idea not to explicitly reveal that we were seeing each other, even though we left the office for makeout coffee breaks and broadcast maudlin love songs on the shared office speakers.

A few weeks later, I arrived home in the early morning hours after abruptly extricating myself from Josh's bed—he had suddenly revealed plans for a European vacation with another girl—and immediately sat down at my computer to write a post about what had happened. On Heartbreak Soup, I wrote a long rant about the day's events, including a recipe for the chicken soup I made the previous afternoon and the sex that I'd been somehow suckered into even after finding out about how serious things were with the other girl. Then I opened another tab in my browser and logged into Gawker to start compiling the morning's gossip. For a few hours, my personal dramas took a backseat—sort of—to news that a Pulitzer-winning author had described his wife's affair with a media mogul in a crazy e-mail message to his graduate students. I used the opportunity of this public figure's indiscretion to pontificate about the idea that all heartbreak is essentially the same, though everyone thinks his feelings are somehow original and special. I was essentially talking to myself.

After Josh and I broke up, I started writing more and more on Heartbreak Soup—about my friendship with Ruth, my family and the weird, sad, terrifying, exciting aspects of being single for the first time in my adult life. Word had spread through my immediate circle of friends about the blog, and it was now getting a few hundred visitors a day—about the same as Emily Magazine before I started at Gawker. I lulled myself into imagining that these Heartbreak Soup readers, like those old Emily Magazine readers, might not even know what Gawker was, that they were reading just because they liked my stories.

One night, after writing a post about my first summer in New York, I put a link to Heartbreak Soup on my Facebook page under "Web sites." By the next morning, this had begun to feel like a very bad idea, and I took the link down. The traffic spike that day seemed ominous.

Not long after, Josh told me he wanted to have a talk with me about how unsecret my "secret" blog had become. I had started working from home again, but I came into the city, and we stood, smiling awkwardly, outside the Gawker office, trying to figure out what to say to each other. I remembered the fight I had with Henry about the "Project Gayway" post. This time, I knew, I wouldn't win—but then I hadn't really won the last time either.

I offered to make the posts that mentioned Josh inaccessible by password-protecting them.

"You should be password-protected," he said, and I laughed. When he went back into the office, I walked to the subway via the alleys where we'd once secretly kissed. At home, I wrote about what had just happened on Heartbreak Soup, and then I password-protected the post, feeling strange and sad.

Losing the Will to Blog

In October, *New York* magazine published a cover article about Gawker's business model and cultural relevance. I took the magazine from my therapist's waiting room into her office and read aloud from the article because, I figured, why waste any of my 45 minutes by struggling to summarize it? The article painted Gawker as a clearinghouse for vitriol and me as a semisympathetic naïf who half-loved and half-loathed what her job was forcing her to become. That week, when I walked around at parties, trying to elicit funny quotes from whatever quasi-famous people were there, all anyone wanted to talk to me about was Gawker. How could I sleep at night? someone wondered. I was getting tired of justifying my job to strangers, trotting out truisms about the public's right to know and the Internet's changing the rules of privacy. And I was getting tired of writing the same handful of posts over and over again. At the end of November, I announced my resignation via a post on Gawker.

For a year, I had been getting up each morning at 7 a.m., my thoughts jostling in my head, eager to escape. I wrote constantly, responding to the events of the day in real time, under perpetual pressure to condense everything I thought and read into something readers could consume. But now I was burned out and directionless, and without an audience, I lost the narrative thread. If no one was going to get on my case for not having read and catalogued every gossip item in the morning papers by 9 a.m., why get out of bed? For months, I thought that I hated the commenters who tormented me. Now, sickeningly, I missed them. I wasn't reading *The Sunday Times* or *New York* magazine, because what was the point? I wasn't logging into instant messenger. I had terrible writer's block. My grandfather died, and

I couldn't even come up with a heartfelt paragraph to read aloud at his funeral.

On Heartbreak Soup, I was reduced to writing about not having anything to write about. I wasn't cooking much, or reading much, or thinking about much of anything besides how miserable and emptied out I felt. When I posted about a week spent wandering around dead-eyed in Florida's artificial beauty the week after the funeral, one reader left a comment recommending specific brands of antidepressants. Soon after that, I lost the will to blog altogether.

The will to blog is a complicated thing, somewhere between inspiration and compulsion. It can feel almost like a biological impulse. You see something, or an idea occurs to you, and you have to share it with the Internet as soon as possible. What I didn't realize was that those ideas and that urgency—and the sense of self-importance that made me think anyone would be interested in hearing what went on in my head—could just disappear.

Unprotected

Two months after I quit Gawker, Josh wrote an article in the *New York Post's* Sunday magazine about how violated he felt when I wrote about him on Heartbreak Soup, quoting extensively from my blog posts to make his points.

On the morning that the article hit the newsstands, I made Ruth—who had moved back to New York and become my roommate—read it first. When she finished, she looked stricken. "Emily, he's so evil," she said, sounding not at all reassuring.

I slumped to the kitchen floor and lay there in the fetal position. I didn't want to exist. I had made my existence so public in such a strange way, and I wanted to take it all back, but in order to do that I'd have to destroy the entire Internet. If only I could! Google, YouTube, Gawker, Facebook, WordPress, all gone. I squeezed my eyes shut and prayed for an electromagnetic storm that would cancel out every mistake I'd ever made.

"I'm taking it down," Ruth called to me from the living room, where my laptop sat on a table, displaying our no-longer-so-secret blog.

I opened my eyes. "Don't delete it," I managed to say. "Just make it all password-protected."

I lay there for a while longer. Eventually I read the article, which was, as personal betrayals go, far worse than I'd thought it could be. But the real power of the article, as Josh must have known when he wrote it, lay in the way that it exposed me to the new Gawker regime, which had already proved itself to be even more vicious than we'd ever been. If the article had been published when I was still working at Gawker, I would have been able to steer the conversation that it provoked. But now I was no longer simultaneously sniper and target—I was just a target, and I felt powerless.

Over the next couple of weeks, I sat on the sidelines and watched as the commenters—on Gawker, on other blogs and even on Emily Magazine—talked about me the same way they once talked about the targets I'd proffered for them to aim at. Many of them explicitly pointed out that this drubbing was my karmic comeuppance—after all, I'd punished other people this way. Now it was my turn. It was only fair.

By revealing my flaws to whoever wanted to look, I thought—incorrectly, as it turned out—that I was inoculating myself against the criticism my Gawker co-workers and I leveled most often. Maybe I was talentless, bad-complected, old-looking and slutty, but no one could call me a hypocrite. I had said that everyone was subject to judgment and scrutiny, and then, by judging and scrutinizing myself relentlessly, I'd invited others to do the same.

But maybe I was a hypocrite after all, because now I was beginning to feel that no one should be subject to that kind of scrutiny. Not Josh, not Jimmy Kimmel and especially not me.

Real Life

If I were going to completely disavow self-scrutiny and unedited opinion-broadcasting, it would mean the end of my life as a blogger. While I couldn't make the Internet disappear, it had always been entirely within my power to shutter Emily Magazine the same way I'd locked up Heartbreak Soup. For about a week after Josh's article came out, I thought about doing so every time I looked at my computer. But then, as panic and sadness faded and anger set in, I started having impulses in the exact opposite direction: I wanted to defend myself and set the record straight! A few months earlier, I probably would have done it too: typed feverishly for hours perfecting the most cutting blog post possible, aired every sad secret at my disposal in a quest for revenge, published the post as soon as I was finished, then checked back compulsively to see whether it had made things better or worse. But I'd finally realized that some defenses always backfire. True, I had the ability to say whatever I wanted and an audience of people who would listen, but the best possible thing for me to do was to ignore them and do nothing. And that is what I did. For two entire weeks.

Late one night, I unlocked Heartbreak Soup and wrote one last post there. In it, I talked about how a single blog post can capture a moment of extreme feeling, but that reading an accumulated series of posts will sometimes reveal another, more complete story. I talked about how taking the once-public blog and making it private, though tempting, felt like trying to revise history.

Knowing that the worst of my online oversharing is still publicly accessible doesn't thrill me, but it doesn't scare me anymore either. I might hate my former self, but I don't want to destroy her, and in a way, I want to respect her decision to show the world her vulnerability. I'm willing to let that blog exist now as a sort of memorial to a time in my life when I thought my discoveries about myself and what I loved were special enough to merit sharing with the world immediately.

I understand that by writing here about how I revealed my intimate life online, I've now revealed even more about what happened during the period when I was most exposed. Well, I'm an oversharer—it's not like I'm entirely reformed. But lately, online, I've found myself doing something unexpected: keeping the personal details of my current life to myself. This doesn't make me feel stifled so much as it makes me feel protected, as if my thoughts might actually be worth honing rather than spewing. But I still have Emily Magazine as a place to spew when I need to. It will never again be the friendly place that it was in 2004—there are plenty of negative comments now, and I don't delete them. I still think about closing the door to my online life and locking them out, but then I think of everything else I'd be locking out, and I leave it open.

NOTES

NOTES

THE TRAGEDY OF THE COMMONS

Garrett Hardin

(1915–2003)

Garrett Hardin was a Professor of Human Ecology at the University of California at Santa Barbara for over thirty years. He continually warned of the dangers of overpopulation. Much of his work centered on bioethics. He received many prestigious awards. Dr. Hardin had a heart disorder and his wife Jane was suffering from Lou Gehrig's disease. On September 14th, the couple committed suicide together.

At the end of a thoughtful article on the future of nuclear war, Wiesner and York[1] concluded that: "Both sides in the arms race are . . . confronted by the dilemma of steadily increasing military power and steadily decreasing national security. *It is our considered professional judgment that this dilemma has no technical solution.* If the great powers continue to look for solutions in the area of science and technology only, the result will be to worsen the situation."

I would like to focus your attention not on the subject of the article (national security in a nuclear world) but on the kind of conclusion they reached, namely that there is no technical solution to the problem. An implicit and almost universal assumption of discussions published in professional and semipopular scientific journals is that the problem under discussion has a technical solution. A technical solution may be defined as one that requires a change only in the techniques of the natural sciences, demanding little or nothing in the way of change in human values or ideas of morality.

In our day (though not in earlier times) technical solutions are always welcome. Because of previous failures in prophecy, it takes courage to assert that a desired technical solution is not possible. Wiesner and York exhibited this courage; publishing in a science journal, they insisted that the solution to the problem was not to be found in the natural sciences. They cautiously qualified their statement with the phrase, "It is our considered professional judgment. . . ." Whether they were right or not is not the concern of the present article. Rather, the concern here is with the important concept of a class of human problems which can be called "no technical solution problems," and, more specifically, with the identification and discussion of one of these.

It is easy to show that the class is not a null class. Recall the game of tick-tack-toe. Consider the problem, "How can I win the game of tick-tack-toe?" It is well known that I cannot, if I assume (in keeping with the conventions of game theory) that my opponent understands the game perfectly. Put another way, there is no "technical solution" to the problem. I can win only by giving a radical meaning to the word "win." I can hit my opponent over

Reprinted by permission from *Science* 162, no. 13 (1968).

the head; or I can drug him; or I can falsify the records. Every way in which I "win" involves, in some sense, an abandonment of the game, as we intuitively understand it. (I can also, of course, openly abandon the game—refuse to play it. This is what most adults do.)

The class of "No technical solution problems" has members. My thesis is that the "population problem," as conventionally conceived, is a member of this class. How it is conventionally conceived needs some comment. It is fair to say that most people who anguish over the population problem are trying to find a way to avoid the evils of overpopulation without relinquishing any of the privileges they now enjoy. They think that farming the seas or developing new strains of wheat will solve the problem—technologically. I try to show here that the solution they seek cannot be found. The population problem cannot be solved in a technical way, any more than can the problem of winning the game of tick-tack-toe.

What Shall We Maximize?

Population, as Malthus said, naturally tends to grow "geometrically," or, as we would now say, exponentially. In a finite world this means that the per capita share of the world's goods must steadily decrease. Is ours a finite world?

A fair defense can be put forward for the view that the world is infinite; or that we do not know that it is not. But, in terms of the practical problems that we must face in the next few generations with the foreseeable technology, it is clear that we will greatly increase human misery if we do not, during the immediate future, assume that the world available to the terrestrial human population is finite. "Space" is no escape.[2]

A finite world can support only a finite population; therefore, population growth must eventually equal zero. (The case of perpetual wide fluctuations above and below zero is a trivial variant that need not be discussed.) When this condition is met, what will be the situation of mankind? Specifically, can Bentham's goal of "the greatest good for the greatest number" be realized?

No—for two reasons, each sufficient by itself. The first is a theoretical one. It is not mathematically possible to maximize for two (or more) variables at the same time. This was clearly stated by von Neumann and Morgenstern,[3] but the principle is implicit in the theory of partial differential equations, dating back at least to D'Alembert (1717–1783).

The second reason springs directly from biological facts. To live, any organism must have a source of energy (for example, food). This energy is utilized for two purposes: mere maintenance and work. For man, maintenance of life requires about 1600 kilocalories a day ("maintenance calories"). Anything that he does over and above merely staying alive will be defined as work, and is supported by "work calories" which he takes in. Work calories are used not only for what we call work in common speech; they are also required for all forms of enjoyment, from swimming and automobile racing to playing music and writing poetry. If our goal is to maximize population it is obvious what we must do: We must make the work calories per person approach as close to zero as possible. No gourmet meals, no vacations, no sports, no music, no literature, no art. . . . I think that everyone will grant, without argument or proof, that maximizing population does not maximize goods. Bentham's goal is impossible.

In reaching this conclusion I have made the usual assumption that it is the acquisition of energy that is the problem. The appearance of atomic energy has led some to question this assumption. However, given an infinite source of energy, population growth still produces an inescapable problem. The problem of the acquisition of energy is replaced by the problem of its dissipation, as J. H. Fremlin has so wittily shown.[4] The arithmetic signs in the analysis are, as it were, reversed; but Bentham's goal is still unobtainable.

The optimum population is, then, less than the maximum. The difficulty of defining the optimum is enormous; so far as I know, no one has seriously tackled this problem. Reaching an acceptable and stable solution will surely require more than one generation of hard analytical work—and much persuasion.

We want the maximum good per person; but what is good? To one person it is wilderness, to another it is ski lodges for thousands. To one it is estuaries to nourish ducks for hunters to shoot; to another it is factory land. Comparing one good with another is, we usually say, impossible because goods are incommensurable. Incommensurables cannot be compared.

Theoretically this may be true; but in real life incommensurables are commensurable. Only a criterion of judgment and a system of weighting are needed. In nature the criterion is survival. Is it better for a species to be small and hideable, or large and powerful? Natural selection commensurates the incommensurables. The compromise achieved depends on a natural weighting of the values of the variables.

Man must imitate this process. There is no doubt that in fact he already does, but unconsciously. It is when the hidden decisions are made explicit that the arguments begin. The problem for the years ahead is to work out an acceptable theory of weighting. Synergistic effects, nonlinear variation, and difficulties in discounting the future make the intellectual problem difficult, but not (in principle) insoluble.

Has any cultural group solved this practical problem at the present time, even on an intuitive level? One simple fact proves that none has: there is no prosperous population in the world today that has, and has had for some time, a growth rate of zero. Any people that has intuitively identified its optimum point will soon reach it, after which its growth rate becomes and remains zero.

Of course, a positive growth rate might be taken as evidence that a population is below its optimum. However, by any reasonable standards, the most rapidly growing populations on earth today are (in general) the most miserable. This association (which need not be invariable) casts doubt on the optimistic assumption that the positive growth rate of a population is evidence that it has yet to reach its optimum.

We can make little progress in working toward optimum population size until we explicitly exorcize the spirit of Adam Smith in the field of practical demography. In economic affairs, *The Wealth of Nations* (1776) popularized the "invisible hand," the idea that an individual who "intends only his own gain," is, as it were, "led by an invisible hand to promote . . . the public interest."[5] Adam Smith did not assert that this was invariably true, and perhaps neither did any of his followers. But he contributed to a dominant tendency of thought that has ever since interfered with positive action based on rational analysis, namely, the tendency to assume that decisions reached individually will, in fact, be the best decisions for an entire society. If this assumption is correct it justifies the continuance of our present policy of laissez-faire in reproduction. If it is correct we can assume that men will control their individual fecundity so as to produce the optimum population. If the assumption is not correct, we need to reexamine our individual freedoms to see which ones are defensible.

Tragedy of Freedom in a Commons

The rebuttal to the invisible hand in population control is to be found in a scenario first sketched in a little-known pamphlet[6] in 1833 by a mathematical amateur named William Forster Lloyd (1794–1852). We may well call it "the tragedy of the commons," using the word "tragedy" as the philosopher Whitehead used it:[7] "The essence of dramatic tragedy is not unhappiness. It resides in the solemnity of the remorseless working of things." He then goes on to say, "This inevitableness of destiny can only be illustrated in terms of human life by incidents which in fact involve unhappiness. For it is only by them that the futility of escape can be made evident in the drama."

The tragedy of the commons develops in this way. Picture a pasture open to all. It is to be expected that each herdsman will try to keep as many cattle as possible on the commons. Such an arrangement may work reasonably satisfactorily for centuries because tribal wars, poaching, and disease keep the numbers of both man and beast well below the carrying capacity of the land. Finally, however, comes the day of reckoning, that is, the day when the long-desired goal of social stability becomes a reality. At this point, the inherent logic of the commons remorselessly generates tragedy.

As a rational being, each herdsman seeks to maximize his gain. Explicitly or implicitly, more or less consciously, he asks, "What is the utility *to me* of adding one more animal to my herd?" This utility has one negative and one positive component.

1) The positive component is a function of the increment of one animal. Since the herdsman receives all the proceeds from the sale of the additional animal, the positive utility is nearly +1.

2) The negative component is a function of the additional overgrazing created by one more animal. Since, however, the effects of overgrazing are

shared by all the herdsmen, the negative utility for any particular decision-making herdsman is only a fraction of −1.

Adding together the component partial utilities, the rational herdsman concludes that the only sensible course for him to pursue is to add another animal to his herd. And another; and another. . . . But this is the conclusion reached by each and every rational herdsman sharing a commons. Therein is the tragedy. Each man is locked into a system that compels him to increase his herd without limit—in a world that is limited. Ruin is the destination toward which all men rush, each pursuing his own best interest in a society that believes in the freedom of the commons. Freedom in a commons brings ruin to all.

Some would say that this is a platitude. Would that it were! In a sense, it was learned thousands of years ago, but natural selection favors the forces of psychological denial.[8] The individual benefits as an individual from his ability to deny the truth even though society as a whole, of which he is a part, suffers.

Education can counteract the natural tendency to do the wrong thing, but the inexorable succession of generations requires that the basis for this knowledge be constantly refreshed.

A simple incident that occurred a few years ago in Leominster, Massachusetts, shows how perishable the knowledge is. During the Christmas shopping season the parking meters downtown were covered with plastic bags that bore tags reading: "Do not open until after Christmas. Free parking courtesy of the mayor and city council." In other words, facing the prospect of an increased demand for already scarce space, the city fathers reinstituted the system of the commons. (Cynically, we suspect that they gained more votes than they lost by this retrogressive act.)

In an approximate way, the logic of the commons has been understood for a long time, perhaps since the discovery of agriculture or the invention of private property in real estate. But it is understood mostly only in special cases which are not sufficiently generalized. Even at this late date, cattlemen leasing national land on the western ranges demonstrate no more than an ambivalent understanding, in constantly pressuring federal authorities to increase the head count to the point where overgrazing produces erosion and weed-dominance. Likewise, the oceans of the world continue to suffer from the survival of the philosophy of the commons. Maritime nations still respond automatically to the shibboleth of the "freedom of the seas." Professing to believe in the "inexhaustible resources of the oceans," they bring species after species of fish and whales closer to extinction.[9]

The National Parks present another instance of the working out of the tragedy of the commons. At present, they are open to all, without limit. The parks themselves are limited in extent—there is only one Yosemite Valley—whereas population seems to grow without limit. The values that visitors seek in the parks are steadily eroded. Plainly, we must soon cease to treat the parks as commons or they will be of no value to anyone.

What shall we do? We have several options. We might sell them off as private property. We might keep them as public property, but allocate the right to enter them. The allocation might be on the basis of wealth, by the use of an auction system. It might be on the basis of merit, as defined by some agreed-upon standards. It might be by lottery. Or it might be on a first-come, first-served basis, administered to long queues. These, I think, are all the reasonable possibilities. They are all objectionable. But we must choose—or acquiesce in the destruction of the commons that we call our National Parks.

Pollution

In a reverse way, the tragedy of the commons reappears in problems of pollution. Here it is not a question of taking something out of the commons, but of putting something in—sewage, or chemical, radioactive, and heat wastes into water; noxious and dangerous fumes into the air, and distracting and unpleasant advertising signs into the line of sight. The calculations of utility are much the same as before. The rational man finds that his share of the cost of the wastes he discharges into the commons is less than the cost of purifying his wastes before releasing them. Since this is true for everyone, we are locked into a system of "fouling our own nest," so long as we behave only as independent, rational, free-enterprisers.

The tragedy of the commons as a food basket is averted by private property, or something formally like it. But the air and waters surrounding us cannot readily be fenced, and so the tragedy of the commons as a cesspool must be prevented by different means, by coercive laws or taxing devices that make it cheaper for the polluter to treat his pollutants than to discharge them untreated. We have not progressed as far with the solution of this problem as we have with the first. Indeed, our particular concept of private property, which deters us from exhausting the positive resources of the earth, favors pollution. The owner of a factory on the bank of a stream—whose property extends to the middle of the stream, often has difficulty seeing why it is not his natural right to muddy the waters flowing past his door. The law, always behind the times, requires elaborate stitching and fitting to adapt it to this newly perceived aspect of the commons.

The pollution problem is a consequence of population. It did not much matter how a lonely American frontiersman disposed of his waste. "Flowing water purifies itself every 10 miles," my grandfather used to say, and the myth was near enough to the truth when he was a boy, for there were not too many people. But as population became denser, the natural chemical and biological recycling processes became overloaded, calling for a redefinition of property rights.

How to Legislate Temperance?

Analysis of the pollution problem as a function of population density uncovers a not generally recognized principle of morality, namely: *the morality of an act is a function of the state of the system at the time it is performed.*[10] Using the commons as a cesspool does not harm the general public under frontier conditions, because there is no public, the same behavior in a metropolis is unbearable. A hundred and fifty years ago a plainsman could kill an American bison, cut only the tongue for his dinner, and discard the rest of the animal. He was not in any important sense being wasteful. Today, with only a few thousand bison left, we would be appalled at such behavior.

In passing, it is worth noting that the morality of an act cannot be determined from a photograph. One does not know whether a man killing an elephant or setting fire to the grassland is harming others until one knows the total system in which his act appears. "One picture is worth a thousand words," said an ancient Chinese; but it may take 10,000 words to validate it. It is as tempting to ecologists as it is to reformers in general to try to persuade others by way of the photographic shortcut. But the essence of an argument cannot be photographed: it must be presented rationally—in words.

That morality is system-sensitive escaped the attention of most codifiers of ethics in the past. "Thou shalt not . . ." is the form of traditional ethical directives which make no allowance for particular circumstances. The laws of our society follow the pattern of ancient ethics, and therefore are poorly suited to governing a complex, crowded, changeable world. Our epicyclic solution is to augment statutory law with administrative law. Since it is practically impossible to spell out all the conditions under which it is safe to burn trash in the back yard or to run an automobile without smog-control, by law we delegate the details to bureaus. The result is administrative law, which is rightly feared for an ancient reason—*Quis custodiet ipsos custodes?*—"Who shall watch the watchers themselves?" John Adams said that we must have "a government of laws and not men." Bureau administrators, trying to evaluate the morality of acts in the total system, are singularly liable to corruption, producing a government by men, not laws.

Prohibition is easy to legislate (though not necessarily to enforce); but how do we legislate temperance? Experience indicates that it can be accomplished best through the mediation of administrative law. We limit possibilities unnecessarily if we suppose that the sentiment of *Quis custodiet* denies us the use of administrative law. We should rather retain the phrase as a perpetual reminder of fearful dangers we cannot avoid. The great challenge facing us now is to invent the corrective feedbacks that are needed to keep custodians honest. We must find ways to legitimate the needed authority of both the custodians and the corrective feedbacks.

Freedom to Breed Is Intolerable

The tragedy of the commons is involved in population problems in another way. In a world governed solely by the principle of "dog eat dog"—if indeed there ever was such a world—how many children a family had would not be a matter of public concern. Parents who bred too exuberantly would leave fewer descendants, not more, because they would be unable to care adequately for their children. David Lack and others have found that such a negative feedback demonstrably controls the fecundity of birds.[11] But men are not birds, and have not acted like them for millenniums, at least.

If each human family were dependent only on its own resources; if the children of improvident parents starved to death; *if,* thus, overbreeding brought its own "punishment" to the germ line—*then* there would be no public interest in controlling the breeding of families. But our society is deeply committed to the welfare state,[12] and hence is confronted with another aspect of the tragedy of the commons.

In a welfare state, how shall we deal with the family, the religion, the race, or the class (or indeed any distinguishable and cohesive group) that adopts overbreeding as a policy to secure its own aggrandizement?[13] To couple the concept of freedom to breed with the belief that everyone born has an equal right to the commons is to lock the world into a tragic course of action.

Unfortunately this is just the course of action that is being pursued by the United Nations. In late 1967, some 30 nations agreed to the following:[14]

> The Universal Declaration of Human Rights describes the family as the natural and fundamental unit of society. It follows that any choice and decision with regard to the size of the family must irrevocably rest with the family itself, and cannot be made by anyone else.

It is painful to have to deny categorically the validity of this right; denying it, one feels as uncomfortable as a resident of Salem, Massachusetts, who denied the reality of witches in the 17th century. At the present time, in liberal quarter, something like a taboo acts to inhibit criticism of the United States. There is a feeling that the United States is "our last and best hope," that we shouldn't find fault with it; we shouldn't play into the hands of archconservatives. However, let us not forget what Robert Louis Stevenson said: "The truth that is suppressed by friends is the readiest weapon of the enemy." If we love the truth, we must openly deny the validity of the Universal Declaration of Human Rights, even though it is promoted by the United Nations. We should also join with Kingsley Davis[15] in attempting to get Planned Parenthood-World Population to see the error of its ways in embracing the same tragic ideal.

Conscience Is Self-Eliminating

It is a mistake to think that we can control the breeding of mankind in the long run by an appeal to conscience. Charles Galton Darwin made this point when he spoke on the centennial of the publication of his grandfather's great book. The argument is straightforward and Darwinian.

People vary. Confronted with appeals to limit breeding, some people will undoubtedly respond to the plea more than others. Those who have more children will produce a larger fraction of the next generation than those with more susceptible consciences. The difference will be accentuated, generation by generation.

In C. G. Darwin's words: "It may well be that it would take hundreds of generations for the progenitive instinct to develop in this way, but if it should do so, nature would have taken her revenge, and the variety *Homo contracipiens* would become extinct and would be replaced by the variety *Homo progenitivus*."[16]

The argument assumes that conscience or the desire for children (no matter which) is hereditary—but hereditary only in the most general formal sense. The result will be the same whether the attitude is transmitted through germ cells, or exosomatically, to use A. J. Lotka's term. (If one denies the latter possibility as well as the former, then what's the point of education?) The argument has here been stated in the context of the population problem, but it applies equally well to any instance in which society appeals to an individual exploiting a commons to restrain himself for the general good—by means of his conscience. To make such an appeal is to set up a selective system that works toward the elimination of conscience from the race.

Pathogenic Effects of Conscience

The long-term disadvantage of an appeal to conscience should be enough to condemn it; but has serious short-term disadvantages as well. If we ask a man who is exploiting a commons to desist "in the name of conscience," what are we saying to him? What does he hear?—not only at the moment but also in the wee small hours of the night when, half asleep, he remembers not merely the words we used but also the nonverbal communication cues we gave him unawares? Sooner or later, consciously or subconsciously, he senses that he has received two communications, and that they are contradictory: (i) (intended communication) "If you don't do as we ask, we will openly condemn you for not acting like a responsible citizen"; (ii) (the unintended communication) "If you do behave as we ask, we will secretly condemn you for a simpleton who can be shamed into standing aside while the rest of us exploit the commons."

Everyman then is caught in what Bateson has called a "double bind." Bateson and his co-workers have made a plausible case for viewing the double bind as an important causative factor in the genesis of schizophrenia.[17] The double bind may not always be so damaging, but it always endangers the mental health of anyone to whom it is applied. "A bad conscience," said Nietzsche, "is a kind of illness."

To conjure up a conscience in others is tempting to anyone who wishes to extend his control beyond the legal limits. Leaders at the highest level succumb to this temptation. Has any President during the past generation failed to call on labor unions to moderate voluntarily their demands for higher wages, or to steel companies to honor voluntary guidelines on prices? I can recall none. The rhetoric used on such occasions is designed to produce feelings of guilt in noncooperators.

For centuries it was assumed without proof that guilt was a valuable, perhaps even an indispensable, ingredient of the civilized life. Now, in this post-Freudian world, we doubt it.

Paul Goodman speaks from the modern point of view when he says: "No good has ever come from feeling guilty, neither intelligence, policy, nor compassion. The guilty do not pay attention to the object but only to themselves, and not even to their own interests, which might make sense, but to their anxieties."[18]

One does not have to be a professional psychiatrist to see the consequences of anxiety. We in the Western world are just emerging from a dreadful two-centuries-long Dark Ages of Eros that was sustained partly by prohibition laws, but perhaps more effectively by the anxiety-generating mechanism of education. Alex Comfort has told the story well in *The Anxiety Makers;*[19] it is not a pretty one.

Since proof is difficult, we may even concede that the results of anxiety may sometimes, from certain points of view, be desirable. The larger question we should ask is whether, as a matter of policy, we should ever encourage the use of a technique the tendency (if not the intention) of which is psychologically pathogenic. We hear much talk these days of responsible parenthood; the coupled words are incorporated into the titles of some organizations devoted to birth control. Some people have proposed massive propaganda campaigns to instill responsibility into the nation's (or the world's) breeders. But what is the meaning of the word responsibility in this context? Is it not merely a synonym for the word conscience? When we use the word responsibility in the absence of substantial sanctions are we not trying to browbeat a free man in a commons into acting against his own interest? Responsibility is a verbal counterfeit for a substantial *quid pro quo.* It is an attempt to get something for nothing.

If the word responsibility is to be used at all, I suggest that it be in the sense Charles Frankel uses it.[20] "Responsibility," says this philosopher, "is the product of definite social arrangements." Notice that Frankel calls for social arrangements—not propaganda.

Mutual Coercion Mutually Agreed Upon

The social arrangements that produce responsibility are arrangements that create coercion, of some sort. Consider bank-robbing. The man who takes money from a bank acts as if the bank were a commons. How do we prevent such action? Certainly not by trying to control his behavior solely by a verbal appeal to his sense of responsibility. Rather than rely on propaganda we follow Frankel's lead and insist that a bank is not a commons; we seek the definite social arrangements that will keep it from becoming a commons. That we thereby infringe on the freedom of would-be robbers we neither deny nor regret.

The morality of bank-robbing is particularly easy to understand because we accept complete prohibition of this activity. We are willing to say "Thou shalt not rob banks," without providing for exceptions. But temperance also can be created by coercion. Taxing is a good coercive device. To keep downtown shoppers temperate in their use of parking space we introduce parking meters for short periods, and traffic fines for longer ones. We need not actually forbid a citizen to park as long as he wants to; we need merely make it increasingly expensive for him to do so. Not prohibition, but carefully biased options are what we offer him. A Madison Avenue man might call this persuasion; I prefer the greater candor of the word coercion.

Coercion is a dirty word to most liberals now, but it need not forever be so. As with the four-letter words, its dirtiness can be cleansed away by exposure to the light, by saying it over and over without apology or embarrassment. To many, the word coercion implies arbitrary decisions of distant and irresponsible bureaucrats; but this is not a necessary part of its meaning. The only kind of coercion I recommend is mutual coercion, mutually agreed upon by the majority of the people affected.

To say that we mutually agree to coercion is not to say that we are required to enjoy it, or even to pretend we enjoy it. Who enjoys taxes? We all grumble about them. But we accept compulsory taxes because we recognize that voluntary taxes would favor the conscienceless. We institute and (grumblingly) support taxes and other coercive devices to escape the horror of the commons.

An alternative to the commons need not be perfectly just to be preferable. With real estate and other material goods, the alternative we have chosen is the institution of private property coupled with legal inheritance. Is this system perfectly just? As a genetically trained biologist I deny that it is. It seems to me that, if there are to be differences in individual inheritance, legal possession should be perfectly correlated with biological inheritance—that those who are biologically more fit to be the custodians of property and power should legally inherit more. But genetic recombination continually makes a mockery of the doctrine of "like father, like son" implicit in our laws of legal inheritance. An idiot can inherit millions, and a trust fund can keep his estate intact. We must admit that our legal system of private property plus inheritance is unjust—but we put up with it because we are not convinced, at the moment, that anyone has invented a better system. The alternative of the commons is too horrifying to contemplate. Injustice is preferable to total ruin.

It is one of the peculiarities of the warfare between reform and the status quo that it is thoughtlessly governed by a double standard. Whenever a reform measure is proposed it is often defeated when its opponents triumphantly discover a flaw in it. As Kingsley Davis has pointed out,[21] worshippers of the status quo sometimes imply that no reform is possible without unanimous agreement, an implication contrary to historical fact. As nearly as I can make out, automatic rejection of proposed reforms is based on one of two unconscious assumptions: (i) that the status quo is perfect; or (ii) that the choice we face is between reform and no action; if the proposed reform is imperfect, we presumably should take no action at all, while we wait for a perfect proposal.

But we can never do nothing. That which we have done for thousands of years is also action. It also produces evils. Once we are aware that the status quo is action, we can then compare its discoverable advantages and disadvantages with the predicted advantages and disadvantages of the proposed reform, discounting as best we can for our lack of experience. On the basis of such a comparison, we can make a rational decision which will not involve the unworkable assumption that only perfect systems are tolerable.

Recognition of Necessity

Perhaps the simplest summary of this analysis of man's population problems is this: the commons, if justifiable at all, is justifiable only under conditions of low-population density. As the human population has increased, the commons has had to be abandoned in one aspect after another.

First we abandoned the commons in food gathering, enclosing farm land and restricting pastures and hunting and fishing areas. These restrictions are still not complete throughout the world.

Somewhat later we saw that the commons as a place for waste disposal would also have to be abandoned. Restrictions on the disposal of domestic sewage are widely accepted in the Western world; we are still struggling to close the commons to pollution by automobiles, factories, insecticide sprayers, fertilizing operations, and atomic energy installations.

In a still more embryonic state is our recognition of the evils of the commons in matters of pleasure. There is almost no restriction on the propagation of sound waves in the public medium. The shopping public is assaulted with mindless music, without its consent. Our government is paying out billions of dollars to create supersonic transport which will disturb 50,000 people for every one person who is whisked from coast to coast 3 hours faster. Advertisers muddy the airwaves of radio and television and pollute the view of travelers. We are a long way from outlawing the commons in matters of pleasure. Is this because our Puritan inheritance makes us view pleasure as something of a sin, and pain (that is, the pollution of advertising) as the sign of virtue?

Every new enclosure of the commons involves the infringement of somebody's personal liberty. Infringements made in the distant past are accepted because no contemporary complains of a loss. It is the newly proposed infringements that we vigorously oppose; cries of "rights" and "freedom" fill the air. But what does "freedom" mean? When men mutually agreed to pass laws against robbing, mankind became more free, not less so.

Individuals locked into the logic of the commons are free only to bring on universal ruin once they see the necessity of mutual coercion, they become free to pursue other goals. I believe it was Hegel who said, "Freedom is the recognition of necessity."

The most important aspect of necessity that we must now recognize, is the necessity of abandoning the commons in breeding. No technical solution can rescue us from the misery of overpopulation. Freedom to breed will bring ruin to all. At the moment, to avoid hard decisions many of us are tempted to propagandize for conscience and responsible parenthood. The temptation must be resisted, because an appeal to independently acting consciences selects for the disappearance of all conscience in the long run, and an increase in anxiety in the short.

The only way we can preserve and nurture other and more precious freedoms is by relinquishing the freedom to breed, and that very soon. "Freedom is the recognition of necessity"—and it is the role of education to reveal to all the necessity of abandoning the freedom to breed. Only so, can we put an end to this aspect of the tragedy of the commons.

Endnotes

1. J. B. Wiesner and H. F. York, *Sci. Amer.* **211** (No. 4), 27 (1964).
2. G. Hardin, *J. Hered.* **50,** 68 (1959); S. von Hoernor, *Science* **137,** 18 (1962).
3. J. von Neumann and O. Morgenstern, *Theory of Games and Economic Behavior* (Princeton Univ. Press, Princeton, N.J., 1947), p. 11.
4. J. H. Fremlin, *New Sci.,* No. 415 (1964), p. 285.
5. A. Smith, *The Wealth of Nations* (Modern Library, New York, 1937), p. 423.
6. W. F. Lloyd, *Two Lectures on the Checks to Population* (Oxford Univ. Press, Oxford, England, 1833), reprinted (in part) in *Population, Evolution, and Birth Control,* G. Hardin, Ed. (Freeman, San Francisco, 1964), p. 37.
7. A. N. Whitehead, *Science and the Modern World* (Mentor, New York, 1948), p. 17.
8. G. Hardin, Ed. *Population, Evolution, and Birth Control* (Freeman, San Francisco, 1964), p. 56.
9. S. McVay, *Sci. Amer.* **216** (No. 8), 13 (1966).
10. J. Fletcher, *Situation Ethics* (Westminster, Philadelphia, 1966).
11. D. Lack, *The Natural Regulation of Animal Numbers* (Clarendon Press, Oxford, 1954).
12. H. Girvetz, *From Wealth to Welfare* (Stanford Univ. Press, Stanford, Calif., 1950).
13. G. Hardin, *Perspec. Biol. Med.* **6,** 366 (1963).

14. U. Thant, *Int. Planned Parenthood News,* No. 168 (February 1968), p. 3.
15. K. Davis, *Science* **158,** 730 (1967).
16. S. Tax, Ed., *Evolution after Darwin* (Univ. of Chicago Press, Chicago, 1960), vol. 2, p. 469.
17. G. Bateson, D. D. Jackson, J. Haley, J. Weakland, *Behav. Sci.* **1,** 251 (1956).
18. P. Goodman, *New York Rev. Books* 10(8), 22 (23 May 1968).
19. A. Comfort, *The Anxiety Makers* (Nelson, London, 1967).
20. C. Frankel, *The Case for Modern Man* (Harper, New York, 1955), p. 203.
21. J. D. Roslansky, *Genetics and the Future of Man* (Appleton-Century-Crofts, New York, 1966), p. 177.

NOTES

NOTES

FO'CSLE COMRADESHIP
Harry Kemp

(1883–1960)

Harry Kemp is a U.S. poet and prose writer variously called 'The Vagabond Poet,' the 'Villon of America,' the 'Hobo Poet,' or the 'Tramp Poet.' He had a talent for promoting his own work which he dubbed 'The Art of Spectacularism.' As he aged he grew more conservative, referring to Jesus as the 'Divine Hobo' or 'Super Tramp.'

There's not much in the fo'csle of a ship
But old sea boots and chests that stand in rows
While up above a smoky lantern glows,
And hanging from a peg the oilskins drip,

Sometimes in storms the water rushes in;
Sometimes we stifle for a breath of air;
Yet somehow comradeship gets being there
And common hardship makes the stranger kin . . .

Blood-brothers we become, but not in peace,—
Still ready to exchange the lie and blow;
Just like the sea our quarrels rise and cease:
We've never a dull moment down below . . .

But set upon us in a tavern brawl
You'll find that you will have to fight us all.

NOTES

SELECTIONS FROM *A SAND COUNTY ALMANAC*

Aldo Leopold

(1887–1948)

Aldo Leopold was a graduate of the Yale School of Forestry. He was a conservationist, ecologist, and educator who published extensively. He was instrumental in founding the Wilderness Society and the Wildlife Society. His famous collection of 41 essays comprising A Sand County Almanac *was published 18 months after his death.*

The Land Ethic

When god-like Odysseus returned from the wars in Troy, he hanged all on one rope a dozen slave-girls of his household whom he suspected of misbehavior during his absence.

This hanging involved no question of propriety. The girls were property. The disposal of property was then, as now, a matter of expediency, not of right and wrong.

Concepts of right and wrong were not lacking from Odysseus' Greece: witness the fidelity of his wife through the long years before at last his black-prowed galleys clove the wine-dark seas for home. The ethical structure of that day covered wives, but had not yet been extended to human chattels. During the three thousand years which have since elapsed, ethical criteria have been extended to many fields of conduct, with corresponding shrinkages in those judged by expediency only.

The Ethical Sequence

This extension of ethics, so far studied only by philosophers, is actually a process in ecological evolution. Its sequences may be described in ecological as well as in philosophical terms. An ethic, ecologically, is a limitation on freedom of action in the struggle for existence. An ethic, philosophically, is a differentiation of social from anti-social conduct. These are two definitions of one thing. The thing has its origin in the tendency of interdependent individuals or groups to evolve modes of co-operation. The ecologist calls these symbioses. Politics and economics are advanced symbioses in which the original free-for-all competition has been replaced, in part, by co-operative mechanisms with an ethical content.

The complexity of co-operative mechanisms has increased with population density, and with the efficiency of tools. It was simpler, for example, to define the anti-social uses of sticks and stones in the days of the mastodons than of bullets and billboards in the age of motors.

The first ethics dealt with the relation between individuals; the Mosaic Decalogue is an example. Later accretions dealt with the relation between the

Reprinted from *A Sand County Almanac* (1947), by permission of Oxford University Press.

individual and society. The Golden Rule tries to integrate the individual to society; democracy to integrate social organization to the individual.

There is as yet no ethic dealing with man's relation to land and to the animals and plants which grow upon it. Land, like Odysseus' slave-girls, is still property. The land-relation is still strictly economic, entailing privileges but not obligations.

The extension of ethics to this third element in human environment is, if I read the evidence correctly, an evolutionary possibility and an ecological necessity. It is the third step in a sequence. The first two have already been taken. Individual thinkers since the days of Ezekiel and Isaiah have asserted that the despoliation of land is not only inexpedient but wrong. Society, however, has not yet affirmed their belief. I regard the present conservation movement as the embryo of such an affirmation.

An ethic may be regarded as a mode of guidance for meeting ecological situations so new or intricate, or involving such deferred reactions, that the path of social expediency is not discernible to the average individual. Animal instincts are modes of guidance for the individual in meeting such situations. Ethics are possibly a kind of community instinct in-the-making.

The Community Concept

All ethics so far evolved rest upon a single premise: that the individual is a member of a community of interdependent parts. His instincts prompt him to compete for his place in that community, but his ethics prompt him also to co-operate (perhaps in order that there may be a place to compete for).

The land ethic simply enlarges the boundaries of the community to include soils, waters, plants, and animals, or collectively: the land.

This sounds simple: do we not already sing our love for and obligation to the land of the free and the home of the brave? Yes, but just what and whom do we love? Certainly not the soil, which we are sending helter-skelter downriver. Certainly not the waters, which we assume have no function except to turn turbines, float barges, and carry off sewage. Certainly not the plants, of which we exterminate whole communities without batting an eye. Certainly not the animals, of which we have already extirpated many of the largest and most beautiful species. A land ethic of course cannot prevent the alteration, management, and use of these "resources," but it does affirm their right to continued existence, and, at least in spots, their continued existence in a natural state.

In short, a land ethic changes the role of *Homo sapiens* from conqueror of the land-community to plain member and citizen of it. It implies respect for his fellow-members, and also respect for the community as such.

In human history, we have learned (I hope) that the conqueror role is eventually self-defeating. Why? Because it is implicit in such a role that the conqueror knows, *ex cathedra*, just what makes the community clock tick, and just what and who is valuable, and what and who is worthless, in community life. It always turns out that he knows neither, and this is why his conquests eventually defeat themselves.

In the biotic community, a parallel situation exists. Abraham knew exactly what the land was for: it was to drip milk and honey into Abraham's mouth. At the present moment, the assurance with which we regard this assumption is inverse to the degree of our education.

The ordinary citizen today assumes that science knows what makes the community clock tick; the scientist is equally sure that he does not. He knows that the biotic mechanism is so complex that its workings may never be fully understood.

That man is, in fact, only a member of a biotic team is shown by an ecological interpretation of history. Many historical events, hitherto explained solely in terms of human enterprise, were actually biotic interactions between people and land. The characteristics of the land determined the facts quite as potently as the characteristics of the men who lived on it.

Consider, for example, the settlement of the Mississippi valley. In the years following the Revolution, three groups were contending for its control: the native Indian, the French and English traders, and the American settlers. Historians wonder what would have happened if the English at Detroit had thrown a little more weight into the Indian side of those tipsy scales which decided the outcome of the colonial migration into the cane-lands of Kentucky. It is time now to ponder the fact that the cane-lands, when subjected to the particular mixture of forces represented by the cow, plow, fire, and axe of the pioneer, became bluegrass. What if the plant succession inherent in this dark and bloody ground had, under the impact of these forces, given us some worthless sedge, shrub, or weed? Would Boone and Kenton have held out? Would there have been any overflow into Ohio, Indiana, Illinois, and Missouri? Any Louisiana Purchase? Any transcontinental union of new states? Any Civil War?

Kentucky was one sentence in the drama of history. We are commonly told what the human actors in this drama tried to do, but we are seldom told that their success, or the lack of it, hung in large degree on the reaction of particular soils to the impact of the particular forces exerted by their occupancy. In the case of Kentucky, we do not even know where the bluegrass came from—whether it is a native species, or a stowaway from Europe.

Contrast the cane-lands with what hindsight tells us about the Southwest, where the pioneers were equally brave, resourceful, and persevering. The impact of occupancy here brought no bluegrass, or other plant fitted to withstand the bumps and buffetings of hard use. This region, when grazed by livestock, reverted through a series of more and more worthless grasses, shrubs, and weeds to a condition of unstable equilibrium. Each recession of plant types bred erosion; each increment to erosion bred a further recession of plants. The result today is a progressive and mutual deterioration, not only of plants and soils, but of the animal community subsisting thereon. The early settlers did not expect this: on the ciénegas of New Mexico some even cut ditches to hasten it. So subtle has been its progress that few residents of the region are aware of it. It is quite invisible to the tourist who finds this wrecked landscape colorful and charming (as indeed it is, but it bears scant resemblance to what it was in 1848).

This same landscape was "developed" once before, but with quite different results. The Pueblo Indians settled the Southwest in pre-Columbian times, but they happened *not* to be equipped with range livestock. Their civilization expired, but not because their land expired.

In India, regions devoid of any sod-forming grass have been settled, apparently without wrecking the land, by the simple expedient of carrying the grass to the cow, rather than vice versa. (Was this the result of some deep wisdom, or was it just good luck? I do not know.)

In short, the plant succession steered the course of history; the pioneer simply demonstrated, for good or ill, what successions inhered in the land. Is history taught in this spirit? It will be, once the concept of land as a community really penetrates our intellectual life.

The Ecological Conscience

Conservation is a state of harmony between men and land. Despite nearly a century of propaganda, conservation still proceeds at a snail's pace; progress still consists largely of letterhead pieties and convention oratory. On the back forty we still slip two steps backward for each forward stride.

The usual answer to this dilemma is "more conservation education." No one will debate this, but is it certain that only the *volume* of education needs stepping up? Is something lacking in the *content* as well?

It is difficult to give a fair summary of its content in brief form, but, as I understand it, the content is substantially this: obey the law, vote right, join some organizations, and practice what conservation is profitable on your own land; the government will do the rest.

Is not this formula too easy to accomplish anything worth-while? It defines no right or wrong, assigns no obligation, calls for no sacrifice, implies no change in the current philosophy of values. In respect of land-use, it urges only enlightened self-interest. Just how far will such education take us? An example will perhaps yield a partial answer.

By 1930 it had become clear to all except the ecologically blind that southwestern Wisconsin's topsoil was slipping seaward. In 1933 the farmers were told that if they would adopt certain remedial practices for five years, the public would donate CCC labor to install them, plus the necessary machinery and materials. The offer was widely accepted, but the practices were widely forgotten when the five-year contract period was up. The farmers continued only those practices that yielded an immediate and visible economic gain for themselves.

This led to the idea that maybe farmers would learn more quickly if they themselves wrote the rules. Accordingly the Wisconsin Legislature in 1937 passed the Soil Conservation District Law. This said to farmers, in effect: *We, the public, will furnish you free technical service and loan you specialized machin-*

ery, if you will write your own rules for land-use. Each county may write its own rules, and these will have the force of law. Nearly all the counties promptly organized to accept the proffered help, but after a decade of operation, *no county has yet written a single rule.* There has been visible progress in such practices as strip-cropping, pasture renovation, and soil liming, but none in fencing woodlots against grazing, and none in excluding plow and cow from steep slopes. The farmers, in short, have selected those remedial practices which were profitable anyhow, and ignored those which were profitable to the community, but not clearly profitable to themselves.

When one asks why no rules have been written, one is told that the community is not yet ready to support them; education must precede rules. But the education actually in progress makes no mention of obligations to land over and above those dictated by self-interest. The net result is that we have more education but less soil, fewer healthy woods, and as many floods as in 1937.

The puzzling aspect of such situations is that the existence of obligations over and above self-interest is taken for granted in such rural community enterprises as the betterment of roads, schools, churches, and baseball teams. Their existence is not taken for granted, nor as yet seriously discussed, in bettering the behavior of the water that falls on the land, or in the preserving of the beauty or diversity of the farm landscape. Land-use ethics are still governed wholly by economic self-interest, just as social ethics were a century ago.

To sum up: we asked the farmer to do what he conveniently could to save his soil, and he has done just that, and only that. The farmer who clears the woods off a 75 per cent slope, turns his cows into the clearing, and dumps its rainfall, rocks, and soil into the community creek, is still (if otherwise decent) a respected member of society. If he puts lime on his fields and plants his crops on contour, he is still entitled to all the privileges and emoluments of his Soil Conservation District. The District is a beautiful piece of social machinery, but it is coughing along on two cylinders because we have been too timid, and too anxious for quick success, to tell the farmer the true magnitude of his obligations. Obligations have no meaning without conscience, and the problem we face is the extension of the social conscience from people to land.

No important change in ethics was ever accomplished without an internal change in our intellectual emphasis, loyalties, affections, and convictions. The proof that conservation has not yet touched these foundations of conduct lies in the fact that philosophy and religion have not yet heard of it. In our attempt to make conservation easy, we have made it trivial.

NOTES

YOU CAN GET THERE FROM HERE
Linda

Linda, of Timonium, Maryland, is a professor of English.

On the first day of the semester, I always began my college English classes with the same words: "Ladies and gentleman, from this room you can go anywhere."

And then every semester, in the weeks that followed, I would have my heart broken five or six times. The quiet, studious kid, who scribbled copious notes but disappeared when the paper was due. The young man who worked the night shift and found he just couldn't get out of bed for class. The ones who ran out of money or succumbed to their addictions or didn't want to be there in the first place.

A colleague took me aside during my first year and said, "Look, this is community college. Lots of kids bail. It's not your fault."

I encountered less heartbreak when I added some hours tutoring in the college's Writing Center. If too many of my "real" students disappointed me by giving up, maybe this assembly-line approach would save me. In and out students came, wanting only an hour of my time, just a little slice of my expertise. "Can you help me fix this?" they would say, and I would, and then the next person would sit down.

Emily appeared at the center doorway one morning, approached me cautiously, and—barely audible—asked me to read her essay. "It needs help," she said. She was right. It did. But just below the surface, it was unmistakable to me: here was a talented writer waiting for her moment. The next week she showed up early.

Our first months working together were often bumpy. She could be too easily frustrated at her pace. She railed at time wasted, and how much she had to learn. I danced between challenging her and not overwhelming her. Every week, there she'd be at the door. And then she'd step in and get to work.

First, she nailed English 101, then 102. Only later did she tell me that when we met, her entire college transcript consisted of five F's, a vestige from her first try at being a student, a semester she fled in frustration or fear or back to demons I didn't know. Professors started taking an interest in her now. They came bearing advice and resources, and Emily kept getting up in the morning and coming to school. She made the honors program the next year and graduated. She earned a scholarship to a four-year college and there she thrived. No one was surprised when she was accepted into an English PhD program at an esteemed university.

Every once in a while she would send a note about her progress, her sentences leaping across the page, breathless. She landed the only teaching job she wanted—at the community college where it all came to life for her.

I believe you can get there from here. And I bet that's just how Emily begins every semester with her students.

Reprinted from *ThisIBelieve.org*, November 4, 2009.

NOTES

ON LIBERTY
John Stuart Mill

(1806–1873)

A British author and thinker, John Stuart Mill transformed utilitarianism into a more liberal philosophy. He contended that adults should have the freedom to think and do what they want as long as they do not harm others. He believed in equal rights for men and women and supported the idea of a free-market economy but with a reform of private property laws to create more equal distribution of wealth. He published "On Liberty" in 1859.

Chapter I
Introductory

The subject of this Essay is not the so-called Liberty of the Will, so unfortunately opposed to the misnamed doctrine of Philosophical Necessity; but Civil, or Social Liberty: the nature and limits of the power which can be legitimately exercised by society over the individual.

The object of this Essay is to assert one very simple principle, as entitled to govern absolutely the dealings of society with the individual in the way of compulsion and control, whether the means used be physical force in the form of legal penalties, or the moral coercion of public opinion. That principle is, that the sole end for which mankind are warranted, individually or collectively, in interfering with the liberty of action of any of their number, is self-protection. That the only purpose for which power can be rightfully exercised over any member of a civilized community, against his will, is to prevent harm to others. The only part of the conduct of any one, for which he is amenable to society, is that which concerns others. In the part which merely concerns himself, his independence is, of right, absolute. Over himself, over his own body and mind, the individual is sovereign.

It is, perhaps, hardly necessary to say that this doctrine is meant to apply only to human beings in the maturity of their faculties. We are not speaking of children, or of young persons below the age which the law may fix as that of manhood or womanhood. Those who are still in a state to require being taken care of by others, must be protected against their own actions as well as against external injury.

This, then, is the appropriate region of human liberty. It comprises, first, the inward domain of consciousness; demanding liberty of conscience, in the most comprehensive sense; liberty of thought and feeling; absolute freedom of opinion and sentiment on all subjects, practical or speculative, scientific, moral, or theological. The liberty of expressing and publishing opinions may seem to fall under a different principle, since it belongs to that part of the conduct of an individual which concerns other people; but, being almost of as much importance as the liberty of thought itself, and resting in great part on the same reasons, is practically inseparable from it. Secondly, the principle requires liberty of tastes and pursuits; of framing the plan of our life to suit our own character; of doing as we like, subject to such consequences as may follow; without impediment from our fellow-creatures, so long as what we do does not harm them, even though they should think our conduct foolish, perverse, or wrong. Thirdly, from this liberty of each individual, follows the liberty, within the same limits, of combination among individuals; freedom to unite, for any purpose not involving harm to others: the persons combining being supposed to be of full age, and not forced or deceived.

Though this doctrine is anything but new, and, to some persons, may have the air of a truism, there is no doctrine which stands more directly opposed to the general tendency of existing opinion and practice. Society has expended fully as much effort in the attempt (according to its lights) to compel people to conform to its notions of personal, as of social excellence. The ancient commonwealths thought themselves entitled to practise, and the ancient philosophers countenanced, the regulation of every part of private conduct by public authority, on the ground that the State had a deep interest in the whole bodily and mental discipline of every one of its citizens.

Apart from the peculiar tenets of individual thinkers, there is also in the world at large an increasing inclination to stretch unduly the powers of society over the individual, both by the force of opinion and even by that of legislation: and as the tendency of all the changes taking place in the world is to strengthen society, and diminish the power of the individual, this encroachment is not one of the evils which tend spontaneously to disappear, but, on the contrary, to grow more and more formidable. The disposition of mankind, whether as rulers or as fellow-citizens, to impose their own opinions and inclinations as a rule of conduct on others, is so energetically supported by some of the best and by some of the worst feelings incident to human nature, that it is hardly ever kept under restraint by anything but want of power; and as the power is not declining, but growing, unless a strong barrier of moral conviction can be raised against the mischief, we must expect, in the present circumstances of the world, to see it increase.

Chapter III
Of Individuality, as One of the Elements of Well-Being

The liberty of the individual must be thus far limited; he must not make himself a nuisance to other people. But if he refrains from molesting others in what concerns them, and merely acts according to his own inclination and judgment in things which concern himself, the same reasons which show that opinion should be free, prove also that he should be allowed, without molestation, to carry his opinions into practice at his own cost.

It is desirable, in short, that in things which do not primarily concern others; individuality should assert itself. Where, not the person's own character, but the traditions or customs of other people are the rule of conduct, there is wanting one of the principal ingredients of human happiness, and quite the chief ingredient of individual and social progress.

In maintaining this principle, the greatest difficulty to be encountered does not lie in the appreciation of means towards an acknowledged end, but in the indifference of persons in general to the end itself. If it were felt that the free development of individuality is one of the leading essentials of well-being; that it is not only a coördinate element with all that is designated by the terms civilization, instruction, education, culture, but is itself a necessary part and condition of all those things; there would be no danger that liberty should be undervalued, and the adjustment of the boundaries between it and social control would present no extraordinary difficulty. But the evil is, that individual spontaneity is hardly recognized by the common modes of thinking, as having any intrinsic worth, or deserving any regard on its own account. The majority, being satisfied with the ways of mankind as they now are (for it is they who make them what they are), cannot comprehend why those ways should not be good enough for everybody; and what is more, spontaneity forms no part of the ideal of the majority of moral and social reformers, but is rather looked on with jealousy, as a troublesome and perhaps rebellious obstruction to the general acceptance of what these reformers, in their own judgment, think would be best for mankind.

No one's idea of excellence in conduct is that people should do absolutely nothing but copy one another. No one would assert that people ought not to put into their mode of life, and into the conduct of their concerns, any impress whatever of their own judgment, or of their own individual character. On the other hand, it would be absurd to pretend that people ought to live as if nothing whatever had been known in the world before they came into it; as if experience had as yet done nothing towards showing that one mode of existence, or of conduct, is preferable to another. Nobody denies that people should be so taught and trained in youth, as to know and benefit by the ascertained results of human experience. But it is the privilege and proper condition of a human being, arrived at the maturity of his faculties, to use and interpret experience in his own way. It is for him to find out what part of recorded experience is properly applicable to his own circumstances and character. The traditions and customs of other people are, to a certain extent, evidence of what their experience has taught *them;* presumptive evidence, and as such, have a claim to his deference: but, in the first place, their experience may be too narrow; or they may not have interpreted it rightly. Secondly, their interpretation of experience may be correct, but unsuitable to him. Customs are made for customary circumstances, and customary characters: and his circumstances or his character may be uncustomary. Thirdly, though the customs be both good as customs, and suitable to him, yet to conform to custom, merely *as* custom, does not educate or develop in him any of the qualities which are the distinctive endowment of a human being. The human faculties of perception, judgment, discriminative feeling, mental activity, and even moral preference, are exercised only in making a choice. He who does anything because it is the custom, makes no choice. He gains no practice either in discerning or in desiring what is best. The mental and moral, like the muscular powers, are improved only by being used. The faculties are called into no exercise by doing a thing merely because others do it, no more than by believing a thing only because others believe it.

It is not by wearing down into uniformity all that is individual in themselves, but by cultivating it and calling it forth, within the limits imposed by the rights and interests of others, that human beings become a noble and beautiful object of contemplation; and as the works partake the character of those who do them, by the same process human life also becomes rich, diversified, and animating, furnishing more abundant aliment to high thoughts and elevating feelings, and strengthening the tie which binds every individual to the race, by making the race infinitely better worth belonging to. In proportion to the development of his individuality, each person becomes more valuable to himself, and is therefore capable of being more valuable to others.

I insist thus emphatically on the importance of genius, and the necessity of allowing it to unfold itself freely both in thought and in practice, being well aware that no one will deny the position in theory, but knowing also that almost every one, in reality, is totally indifferent to it. People think genius a fine thing if it enables a man to write an exciting poem, or paint a picture. But in its true sense, that of originality in thought and action, though no one says that it is not a thing to be admired, nearly all, at heart, think that they can do very well without it. Unhappily this is too natural to be wondered at. Originality is the one thing which unoriginal minds cannot feel the use of. They cannot see what it is to do for them: how should they? If they could see what it would do for them, it would not be originality. The first service which originality has to render them, is that of opening their eyes: which being once fully done, they would have a chance of being themselves original. Meanwhile, recollecting that nothing was ever yet done which some one was not the first to do, and that all good things which exist are the fruits of originality, let them be modest enough to believe that there is something still left for it to accomplish, and assure themselves that they are more in need of originality, the less they are conscious of the want.

In sober truth, whatever homage may be professed, or even paid, to real or supposed mental superiority, the general tendency of things throughout the world is to render mediocrity the ascendant power among mankind. In ancient history, in the Middle Ages, and in a diminishing degree through the long transition from feudality to the present time, the individual was a power in himself; and if he had either great talents or a high social position, he was a considerable power. At present individuals are lost in the crowd. In politics it is almost a triviality to say that public opinion now rules the world. The only power deserving the name is that of masses, and of governments while they make themselves the organ of the tendencies and instincts of masses. This is as true in the moral and social relations of private life as in public transactions. Those whose opinions go by the name of public opinion, are not always the same sort of public: in America, they are the whole white population; in England, chiefly the middle class. But they are always a mass, that is to say, collective mediocrity. And what is a still greater novelty, the mass do not now take their opinions from dignitaries in Church or State, from ostensible leaders, or from books. Their thinking is done for them by men much like themselves, addressing them or speaking in their name, on the spur of the moment, through the newspapers. I am not complaining of all this. I do not assert that anything better is compatible, as a general rule, with the present low state of the human mind. But that does not hinder the government of mediocrity from being mediocre government. No government by a democracy or a numerous aristocracy, either in its political acts or in the opinions, qualities, and tone of mind which it fosters, ever did or could rise above mediocrity, except in so far as the sovereign Many have let themselves be guided (which in their best times they always have done) by the counsels and influence of a more highly gifted and instructed One or Few. The initiation of all wise or noble things, comes and must come from individuals; generally at first from some one individual. The honor and glory of the average man is that he is capable of following that initiative; that he can respond internally to wise and noble things, and be led to them with his eyes open. I am not countenancing the sort of "hero-worship" which applauds the strong man of genius for forcibly seizing on the government of the world and making it do his bidding in spite of itself. All he can claim is, freedom to point out the way. The power of compelling others into it, is not only inconsistent with the freedom and development of all the rest, but corrupting to the strong man himself. It does seem, however, that when the opinions of masses of merely average men are everywhere become or becoming the dominant power, the counterpoise and corrective to that tendency would be, the more and more pronounced individuality of those who stand on the higher eminences of thought. It is in these circumstances most especially, that exceptional individuals, instead of being deterred, should be encouraged in acting differently from the mass. In other times there was no advantage in their doing so, unless they acted not only differently, but better. In this age the mere example of non-conformity, the mere refusal to bend the knee to custom, is itself a service. Precisely because the tyranny of opinion is such as to make eccentricity a reproach, it is desirable, in order to break through that tyranny, that people should be eccentric. Eccentricity has always abounded when and where strength of character has abounded; and the amount of eccentricity in a society has generally been proportional to the amount of genius, mental vigor, and moral courage which it contained. That so few now dare to be eccentric, marks the chief danger of the time.

I have said that it is important to give the freest scope possible to uncustomary things, in order that it may in time appear which of these are fit to be converted into customs. But independence of action, and disregard of custom are not solely deserving of encouragement for the chance they afford that better modes of action, and customs more worthy of general adoption, may be struck out; nor is it only persons of decided mental superiority who have a just claim to carry on their lives in their own way. There is no reason that all human existences should be constructed on some one, or some small number of patterns. If a person possesses any tolerable amount of common sense and experience, his own mode of laying out his existence is the best, not because it is the best in itself, but because it is his own mode. Human beings are not like sheep; and even sheep are not undistinguishably alike. A man cannot get a coat or a pair of boots to fit him, unless they are either made to his measure, or he has a whole warehouseful to choose from: and is it easier to fit him with a life than with a coat, or are human beings more like one another in their whole physical and spiritual conformation than in the shape of their feet? If it were only that people have diversities of taste, that is reason enough for not attempting to shape them all after one model. But different persons also require different conditions for their spiritual development; and can no more exist healthily in the same moral, than all the variety of plants can in the same physical, atmosphere and climate. The same things which are helps to one person towards the cultivation of his higher nature, are hindrances to another. The same mode of life is a healthy excitement to one, keeping all his faculties of action and enjoyment in their best order, while to another it is a distracting burden, which suspends or crushes all internal life. Such are the differences among human beings in their sources of pleasure, their susceptibilities of pain, and the operation on them of different physical and moral agencies, that unless there is a corresponding diversity in their modes of life, they neither obtain their fair share of happiness, nor grow up to the mental, moral, and aesthetic stature of which their nature is capable.

There is one characteristic of the present direction of public opinion, peculiarly calculated to make it intolerant of any marked demonstration of individuality. The general average of mankind are not only moderate in intellect, but also moderate in inclinations: they have no tastes or wishes strong enough to incline them to do anything unusual, and they consequently do not understand those who have, and class all such with the wild and intemperate whom they are accustomed to look down upon.

The despotism of custom is everywhere the standing hindrance to human advancement, being in unceasing antagonism to that disposition to aim at something better than customary, which is called, according to circumstances, the spirit of liberty, or that of progress or improvement. The spirit of improvement is not always a spirit of liberty, for it may aim at forcing improvements on an unwilling people; and the spirit of liberty, in so far as it resists such attempts, may ally itself locally and temporarily with the opponents of improvement; but the only unfailing and permanent source of improvement is liberty, since by it there are as many possible independent centres of improvement as there are individuals. The progressive principle, however, in either shape, whether as the love of liberty or of improvement, is antagonistic to the sway of Custom, involving at least emancipation from that yoke; and the contest between the two constitutes the chief interest of the history of mankind. A people, it appears, may be progressive for a certain length of time and then stop: when does it stop? When it ceases to possess individuality. But we are progressive as well as changeable: we continually make new inventions in mechanical things, and keep them until they are again superseded by better; we are eager for improvement in politics, in education, even in morals, though in this last our idea of improvement chiefly consists in persuading or forcing other people to be as good as ourselves. It is not progress that we object to; on the contrary, we flatter ourselves that we are the most progressive people who ever lived. It is individuality that we war against: we should think we had done wonders if we had made ourselves all alike; forgetting that the unlikeness of one person to another is generally the first thing which draws the attention of either to the imperfection of his own type, and the superiority of another, or the possibility, by combining the advantages of both, of producing something better than either.

Comparatively speaking, we now read the same things, listen to the same things, see the same things, go to the same places, have our hopes and fears directed to the same objects, have the same rights and liberties, and the same means of asserting them. Great as are the differences of position which remain, they are nothing to those which have ceased. And the assimilation is still proceeding. All the political changes of the age promote it, since they all tend to raise the low and to lower the high. Every extension of education promotes it, because education brings people under common influences, and gives them access to the general stock of facts and sentiments. Improvements in the means of communication promote it, by bringing the inhabitants of distant places into personal contact, and keeping up a rapid flow of changes of residence between one place and another. The increase of commerce and manufactures promotes it, by diffusing more widely the advantages of easy circumstances, and opening all objects of ambition, even the highest, to general competition, whereby the desire of rising becomes no longer the character of a particular class, but of all classes. A more powerful agency than even all these, in bringing about a general similarity among mankind, is the complete establishment, in this and other free countries, of the ascendency of public opinion in the State. As the various social eminences which enabled persons entrenched on them to disregard the opinion of the multitude, gradually become levelled; as the very idea of resisting the will of the public, when it is positively known that they have a will, disappears more and more from the minds of practical politicians; there ceases to be any social support for non-conformity.

The combination of all these causes forms so great a mass of influences hostile to Individuality, that it is not easy to see how it can stand its ground. It will do so with increasing difficulty, unless the intelligent part of the public can be made to feel its value—to see that it is good there should be differences, even though not for the better, even though, as it may appear to them, some should be for the worse. If the claims of Individuality are ever to be asserted, the time is now, while much is still wanting to complete the enforced assimilation. It is only in the earlier stages that any stand can be successfully made against the encroachment. The demand that all other people shall resemble ourselves, grows by what it feeds on. If resistance waits till life is reduced *nearly* to one uniform type, all deviations from that type will come to be considered impious, immoral, even monstrous and contrary to nature. Mankind speedily become unable to conceive diversity, when they have been for some time unaccustomed to see it.

Chapter IV
Of the Limits to the Authority of Society over the Individual

What, then, is the rightful limit to the sovereignty of the individual over himself? Where does the authority of society begin? How much of human life should be assigned to individuality, and how much to society?

Each will receive its proper share, if each has that which more particularly concerns it. To individuality should belong the part of life in which it is chiefly the individual that is interested; to society, the part which chiefly interests society.

Though society is not founded on a contract, and though no good purpose is answered by inventing a contract in order to deduce social obligations from it, every one who receives the protection of society owes a return for the benefit, and the fact of living in society renders it indispensable that each should be bound to observe a certain line of conduct towards the rest. This conduct consists, first, in not injuring the interests of one another; or rather certain interests, which, either by express legal provision or by tacit understanding, ought to be considered as rights; and secondly, in each person's bearing his share (to be fixed on some equitable principle) of the labors and sacrifices incurred for defending the society or its members from injury and molestation. These conditions society is justified in enforcing, at all costs to those who endeavor to withhold fulfilment. Nor is this all that society may do. The acts of an individual may be hurtful to others, or wanting in due consideration for their welfare, without going the length of violating any of their constituted rights. The offender may then be justly punished by opinion, though not by law. As soon as any part of a person's conduct affects prejudicially the interests of others, society has jurisdiction over it, and the question whether the general welfare will or will not be promoted by interfering with it, becomes open to discussion. But there is no room for entertaining any such question when a person's conduct affects the interests of no persons besides himself, or needs not affect them unless they like (all the persons concerned being of full age, and the ordinary amount of understanding). In all such cases there should be perfect freedom, legal and social, to do the action and stand the consequences.

It would be a great misunderstanding of this doctrine, to suppose that it is one of selfish indifference, which pretends that human beings have no business with each other's conduct in life, and that they should not concern themselves about the well-doing or well-being of one another, unless their own interest is involved. Instead of any diminution, there is need of a great increase of disinterested exertion to promote the good of others. But disinterested benevolence can find other instruments to persuade people to their good, than whips and scourges, either of the literal or the metaphorical sort. I am the last person to undervalue the self-regarding virtues; they are only second in importance, if even second, to the social. It is equally the business of education to cultivate both. But even education works by conviction and persuasion as well as by compulsion, and it is by the former only that, when the period of education is past, the self-regarding virtues should be inculcated. Human beings owe to each other help to distinguish the better from the worse, and encouragement to choose the former and avoid the latter. They should be forever stimulating each other to increased exercise of their higher faculties, and increased direction of their feelings and aims towards wise instead of foolish, elevating instead of degrading, objects and contemplations. But neither one person, nor any number of persons, is warranted in saying to another human creature of ripe years, that he shall not do with his life for his own benefit what he chooses to do with it. He is the person most interested in his own well-being: the interest which any other person, except in cases of strong personal attachment, can have in it, is trifling, compared with that which he himself has; the interest which society has in him individually (except as to his conduct to others) is fractional, and altogether indirect: while, with respect to his own feelings and circumstances, the most ordinary man or woman has means of knowledge immeasurably surpassing those that can be possessed by any one else. The interference of society to overrule his judgment and purposes in what only regards himself, must be grounded on general presumptions; which may be altogether wrong, and even if right, are as likely as not to be misapplied to individual cases, by persons no better acquainted with the circumstances of such cases than those are who look at them merely from without. In this department, therefore, of human affairs, Individuality has its proper field of action. In the conduct of human beings towards one another, it is necessary that general rules should for the most part be observed, in order that people may know what they have to expect; but in each person's own concerns, his individual spontaneity is entitled to free exercise. Considerations to aid his judgment, exhortations to strengthen his will, may be offered to him, even obtruded on him, by others; but he, himself, is the final judge. All errors which he is likely to commit against advice and warning, are far outweighed by the evil of allowing others to constrain him to what they deem his good.

The distinction here pointed out between the part of a person's life which concerns only himself, and that which concerns others, many persons will refuse to admit. How (it may be asked) can any part of the conduct of a member of society be a matter of indifference to the other members? No person is an entirely isolated being; it is impossible for a person to do anything seriously or permanently hurtful to himself, without mischief reaching at least to his near connections, and often far beyond them. If he injures his property, he does harm to those who directly or indirectly derived support from it, and usually diminishes, by a greater or less amount, the general resources of the community. If he deteriorates his bodily or mental faculties, he not only brings evil upon all who depended on him for any portion of their happiness, but disqualifies himself for rendering the services which he owes to his fellow-creatures generally; perhaps becomes a burden on their affection or benevolence; and if such conduct were very frequent, hardly any offence that is committed would detract more from the general sum of good. Finally, if by his vices or follies a person does no direct harm to others, he is nevertheless (it may be said) injurious by his example; and ought to be compelled to control himself, for the sake of those whom the sight or knowledge of his conduct might corrupt or mislead.

And even (it will be added) if the consequences of misconduct could be confined to the vicious or thoughtless individual, ought society to abandon to their own guidance those who are manifestly unfit for it? If protection against themselves is confessedly due to children and persons under age, is not society equally bound to afford it to persons of mature years who are equally incapable of self-government? If gambling, or drunkenness, or incontinence, or idleness, or uncleanliness, are as injurious to happiness, and as great a hindrance to improvement, as many or most of the acts prohibited by law, why (it may be asked) should not law, so far as is consistent with practicability and social convenience, endeavor to repress these also? And as a supplement to the unavoidable imperfections of law, ought not opinion at least to organize a powerful police against these vices, and visit rigidly with social penalties those who are known to practise them? There is no question here (it may be said) about restricting individuality, or impeding the trial of new and original experiments in living. The only things it is sought to prevent are things which have been tried and condemned from the beginning of the world until now; things which experience has shown not to be useful or suitable to any person's individuality. There must be some length of time and amount of experience, after which a moral or prudential truth may be regarded as established: and it is merely desired to prevent generation after generation from falling over the same precipice which has been fatal to their predecessors.

I fully admit that the mischief which a person does to himself, may seriously affect, both through their sympathies and their interests, those nearly connected with him, and in a minor degree, society at large. When, by conduct of this sort, a person is led to violate a distinct and assignable obligation to any other person or persons, the case is taken out of the self-regarding class, and becomes amenable to moral disapprobation in the proper sense of the term. Whenever, in short, there is a definite damage, or a definite risk of damage, either to an individual or to the public, the case is taken out of the province of liberty, and placed in that of morality or law.

But I cannot consent to argue the point as if society had no means of bringing its weaker members up to its ordinary standard of rational conduct, except waiting till they do something irrational, and then punishing them, legally or morally, for it. Society has had absolute power over them during all the early portion of their existence: it has had the whole period of childhood and nonage in which to try whether it could make them capable of rational conduct in life. The existing generation is master both of the training and the entire circumstances of the generation to come; it cannot indeed make them perfectly wise and good, because it is itself so lamentably deficient in goodness and wisdom; and its best efforts are not always, in individual cases, its most successful ones; but it is perfectly well able to make the rising generation, as a whole, as good as, and a little better than, itself. If society lets any considerable number of its members grow up mere children, incapable of being acted on by rational consideration of distant motives, society has itself to blame for the consequences. Armed not only with all the powers of education, but with the ascendency which the authority of a received opinion always exercises over the minds who are least fitted to judge for themselves; and aided by the *natural* penalties which cannot be prevented from falling on those who incur the distaste or the contempt of those who know them; let not society pretend that it needs, besides all this, the power to issue commands and enforce obedience in the personal concerns of individuals, in which, on all principles of justice and policy, the decision ought to rest with those who are to abide the consequences.

Chapter V
Applications

I have already observed that, owing to the absence of any recognized general principles, liberty is often granted where it should be withheld, as well as withheld where it should be granted; and one of the cases in which, in the modern European world, the sentiment of liberty is the strongest, is a case where, in my view, it is altogether misplaced. A person should be free to do as he likes in his own concerns; but he ought not to be free to do as he likes in acting for another under the pretext that the affairs of another are his own affairs. The State, while it respects the liberty of each in what specially regards himself, is bound to maintain a vigilant control over his exercise of any power which it allows him to possess over others. This obligation is almost entirely disregarded in the case of the family relations, a case, in its direct influence on human happiness, more important than all others taken together. The almost despotic power of husbands over wives needs not be enlarged upon here, because nothing more is needed for the complete removal of the evil, than that wives should have the same rights, and should receive the protection of law in the same manner, as all other persons; and because, on this subject, the defenders of established injustice do not avail themselves of the plea of liberty, but stand forth openly as the champions of power. It is in the case of children, that misapplied notions of liberty are a real obstacle to the fulfilment by the State of its duties. One would almost think that a man's children were supposed to be literally, and not metaphorically, a part of himself, so jealous is opinion of the smallest interference of law with his absolute and exclusive control over them; more jealous than of almost any interference with his own freedom of action: so much less do the generality of mankind value liberty than power. Consider, for example, the case of education. Is it not almost a self-evident axiom, that the State should require and compel the education, up to a certain standard, of every human being who is born its citizen? Yet who is there that is not afraid to recognize and assert this truth? Hardly any one indeed will deny that it is one of the most sacred duties of the parents (or, as law and usage now stand, the father), after summoning a human being into the world, to give to that being an education fitting him to perform his part well in life towards others and towards himself. It still remains unrecognized, that to bring a child into existence without a fair prospect of being able, not only to provide food for its body, but instruction and training for its mind, is a moral crime, both against the unfortunate offspring and against society; and that if the parent does not fulfil this obligation, the State ought to see it fulfilled at the charge, as far as possible, of the parent.

Were the duty of enforcing universal education once admitted, there would be an end to the difficulties about what the State should teach, and how it should teach, which now convert the subject into a mere battle-field for sects and parties, causing the time and labor which should have been spent in educating, to be wasted in quarrelling about education. If the government would make up its mind to *require* for every child a good education, it might save itself the trouble of *providing* one. It might leave to parents to obtain the education where and how they pleased, and content itself with helping to pay the school fees of the poorer classes of children, and defraying the entire school expenses of those who have no one else to pay for them. The objections which are urged with reason against State education, do not apply to the enforcement of education by the State, but to the State's taking upon itself to direct that education: which is a totally different thing. That the whole or any large part of the education of the people should be in State hands, I go as far as any one in deprecating. All that has been said of the importance of individuality of character, and diversity in opinions and modes of conduct, involves, as of the same unspeakable importance, diversity of education. A general State education is a mere contrivance for moulding people to be exactly like one another: and as the mould in which it casts them is that which pleases the predominant power in the government, whether this be a monarch, a priesthood, an aristocracy, or the majority of the existing generation, in proportion as it is efficient and successful, it establishes a despotism over the mind, leading by natural tendency to one over the body. An education established and controlled by the State, should only exist, if it exist at all, as one among many competing experiments, carried on for the purpose of example and stimulus, to keep the others up to a certain standard of excellence. Unless, indeed, when society in general is in so backward a state that it could not or would not provide for itself any proper institutions of education, unless the government undertook the task; then, indeed; the government may, as the less of two great evils, take upon itself the business of schools and universities, as it may that of joint-stock companies, when private enterprise, in a shape fitted for undertaking great works of industry, does not exist in the country. But in general, if the country contains a sufficient number of persons qualified to provide education under government auspices, the same persons would be able and willing to give an equally good education on the voluntary principle, under the assurance of remuneration afforded by a law rendering education compulsory, combined with State aid to those unable to defray the expense.

The instrument for enforcing the law could be no other than public examinations, extending to all children, and beginning at an early age. An age might be fixed at which every child must be examined, to ascertain if he (or she) is able to read. If a child proves unable, the father, unless he has some sufficient ground of excuse, might be subjected to a moderate fine, to be worked out, if necessary, by his labor, and the child might be put to school at his expense. Once in every year the examination should be renewed, with a gradually extending range of subjects, so as to make the universal acquisition, and what is more, retention, of a certain minimum of general knowledge, virtually compulsory. Beyond that minimum, there should be voluntary examinations on all subjects, at which all who come up to a certain standard of proficiency might claim a certificate. A government cannot have too much of the kind of activity which does not impede, but aids and stimulates, individual exertion and development. The mischief begins when, instead of calling forth the activity and powers of individuals and bodies, it substitutes its own activity for theirs; when, instead of informing, advising and, upon occasion, denouncing, it makes them work in fetters, or bids them stand aside and does their work instead of them. The worth of a State, in the long run, is the worth of the individuals composing it; and a State which postpones the interests of *their* mental expansion and elevation, to a little more of administrative skill, or that semblance of it which practice gives, in the details of business; a State which dwarfs its men, in order that they may be more docile instruments in its hands even for beneficial purposes, will find that with small men no great thing can really be accomplished; and that the perfection of machinery to which it has sacrificed everything, will in the end avail it nothing, for want of the vital power which, in order that the machine might work more smoothly, it has preferred to banish.

NOTES

WHAT'S SO GOOD ABOUT A COLLEGE EDUCATION?

Andrew P. Mills[1]

Andrew P. Mills is an Associate Professor of Philosophy at Otterbein College in Westerville, Ohio, and Department Chair. He specializes in the philosophy of language and mind, metaphysics, and philosophical pedagogy.

Why is it good to go to college? What is so valuable about a college education? College is expensive, and you wouldn't spend all that money on something that wasn't valuable. Moreover, college requires a great deal of work, and it requires that you spend time reading and writing and studying and going to class and taking tests—time that you could spend doing other things—and you wouldn't spend your time on all those college-related tasks unless you thought you were getting something valuable for all your effort. You are in college, and so you think that getting a college education is a good thing—that it is valuable in some way or other—but what sort of value does it have? It's worthwhile to spend some time thinking about the answer to this question, for it will affect the way you spend your time at college, and it will affect the sort of education that you get there. If you don't know why college is valuable, you're very likely wasting your time and money and effort during your college years.

Most people give what I will call the simple "Can Opener Answer" to this question. I think there are two serious problems with that answer, and that is what I want to convince you of. Once we see what is wrong with the simple Can Opener Answer, we can talk about some of the differences between high school and college, and the right way to approach your college education.

The Can Opener Answer

Why is it good to have a can opener? People pay money for can openers, and people spend time with can openers, so they must think that can openers are valuable in some way or other, but how are they valuable? The answer here is easy: can openers are valuable because they allow you to open cans. There's tasty stuff inside of cans, and you can't get at the tasty stuff unless the can is open, and you can't open the can unless you've got a can opener. If you could open cans by snapping your fingers, then you wouldn't need a can opener. Can openers are *tools:* they are valuable, but only as tools or instruments are valuable. That is, they are valuable because of what you can get with them. Once we acquire the ability to open cans by snapping our fingers, or once they stop hiding the tasty stuff inside of cans, then can openers will be useless. They will cease to have the sort of value they now have.[2]

So what's the Can Opener Answer to the question about the value of college? It's this: a college education is valuable because of what you can do

Reprinted by permission of Andrew P. Mills.

with it. In particular, it's valuable because you can trade it for a job. Crudely put, you can take your diploma, show it to an employer, and then you'll get a job. Of course the job interview process is not that easy, but in rough outline that's how many people (maybe even you!) think about the value of a college education. I hope you can see the analogy with the can opener case. The job is the analogue of the tasty stuff in the can. If you could get a job without a college education, then, it would seem, it's silly and wasteful and foolish to spend all that time and money and effort at college. Just as it would be silly to spend money on a can opener if you could open the can by snapping your fingers.

People who ask the question, "So, what are you going to do with an English major?", or "How much money do Sociology majors make?" are thinking in can opener terms. They think that the only thing valuable about a college education is what sort of job (and how high-paying a job) you can get with that college education. And they also think that people who major in Classics or Philosophy or Women's Studies won't get very good jobs. So, they think, since you're spending all that time and money and effort on college, you should get yourself the sort of education that is *useful* for getting a good job. So, they might say, you should major in Nursing or Education or Business or Journalism or Computer Science because those are the sort of majors that you can trade for good jobs.

Now I think there is something right about the Can Opener Answer, but there are two serious problems with it. Let me now turn to those.

The First Problem with the Can Opener Answer

What the Can Opener Answer has right is that a college education is useful for getting a job. After all, college graduates, in general, have better, higher paying, more interesting, potentially more fulfilling jobs than those without college degrees. But that is not the only thing a college education is useful for. A college education—in particular, a broad-based, multi-disciplinary, liberal arts education—is useful for so much more. The problem with the simple Can Opener Answer is that it misses this "so much more" when it focuses merely on the job-getting features of a college degree. Here are just some of the other things that college educated people are able to do.

- College can equip us for our leisure time just as much, if not more so, than it can equip us for our working lives. College educated people are able to appreciate and enjoy literature, art, music, essays, movies, and other products of the culture. Or, to put it better, the sort of appreciation and enjoyment that they have is deeper because of their education: those with a liberal arts education see things in movies and music and literature that those without the education don't. And, as a consequence, their experience is richer.
- We live in a democracy, the success of which requires that each of us participates actively and intelligently in the democratic institutions.

Such participation includes not simply voting, but critically examining the candidates' positions, speaking out as an advocate for policy change, perhaps even serving in a leadership role on a governmental body. Moreover, it requires being critical of the institutions themselves, and seeing what needs changing and why. The appreciation of history, the ability to formulate a persuasive argument, an analytic skill with budgets and statistics and polling data—these are all skills you get as a college educated person and they are skills necessary for successful participation as a citizen in a democracy.

- The developments in technology and the advances in science (especially medical science) are an ever-present, and ever-more-important part of our lives. The growing presence of medications in the treatment of psychological maladies, the possibilities opened up by study and manipulation of DNA, and the prospects for artificial intelligence (just to name a few) are developments that require an intelligent response. Which of the many possibilities opened up to us by science should be pursued? How reliable is DNA testing? Should we treat depression with a drug or with traditional therapy? College graduates are well-positioned to answer these questions because they know some science, and can distinguish quackery from good scientific practice. Moreover, they are accustomed to asking questions about *value*[3] and these are the sorts of questions which very much need to be asked about technological developments.
- This last point applies not simply to the advances in science and technology, but to the information that comes to us via the media. We need to be able to distinguish the foolish fad from the important trend; we need to be able to determine which news outlets are reliable and which are overly biased; we need to be able to figure out where to turn for information and how to navigate between the twin vices of gullibility (believing everything you read in the newspaper, or see on the internet, or hear from a TV anchor) and skepticism (believing nothing that anybody else tells you). Because during your college education you will spend a significant amount of time doing research and evaluating sources, you will be, once you finish college, perfectly situated to be intelligent consumers of information.
- Finally, a college education equips people with the tools for self-examination that renders them able to make informed and intelligent choices about the direction of their own lives. College may equip you for a career, but you have to decide which career to pursue, and how to balance the competing demands of work and family. At what point do you leave the safety of an old but boring job for the insecurity of a new but exciting job? How important a role should your religious or political beliefs play in the life you lead? Should you work for (or buy the products of) a company that exploits child laborers? Should you buy your groceries from a large national chain or from the local, but perhaps more expensive, market? At what point should you put a moral

principle ahead of economic interest? These are decisions that we all must make; if we don't, someone else will make them for us. And by providing the experience and guidance at thinking through these sorts of questions (and other, much more difficult ones) a college education will turn you into a reflective, morally mature person.

The point I'm making can be put this way. A college education isn't valuable like a can opener is valuable. It's valuable like a Swiss army knife is valuable. Or like a computer is valuable. People who focus simply on the job-getting feature of a college education are like people who think that the belt-punch is the only useful feature of a Swiss army knife.

I would argue that the benefits of a college education that I just listed are actually *more valuable* than the fact that you can get a good job with a college diploma. First, it is becoming increasingly unlikely you will spend the 40 years following college in one career, let alone in one job. To devote your college years to preparing for life as a lab assistant will turn out to be a waste when you leave the biomedical industry for a job in book publishing. But the features I listed above will be of use no matter what job you have. Secondly, and I think more importantly, the job you have is but one element in what I would hope is a complex and multi-layered life. Living your life involves so much more than working at a job. It involves being a citizen, a spouse, a friend, a parent, a decision-maker, and someone who has leisure time to fill, and a college education contributes toward improving these aspects of your life.

The Second Problem with the Can Opener Answer

That's the first problem with the simple Can Opener Answer: it mistakes something that has many uses for something that performs merely one task. But even when we do focus on the way in which a college education translates into a job, I think many people fail fully to grasp precisely why employers value employees who are college educated. And this failure is the second problem with the simple Can Opener Answer.

The reason that college degrees translate into high-end salaries and good jobs has, I would argue, more to do with the *skills* one acquires in college than with the discipline-specific *knowledge* of the individual courses. No one is going to give you a better job because of your knowledge of Shakespeare or Plato or the Napoleonic Wars. But students who are successful in their English, philosophy, and history classes are independent and creative thinkers who can write and speak clearly, who can juggle many responsibilities, who can research a project, and who can take steps to educate themselves. And employers will be falling all over themselves to hire people with these skills. Consequently, it doesn't matter so much what your major is as much as it does that you acquire these more general skills. So select a major that you find interesting, which will challenge you, which will make you smarter, and don't worry exclusively about "what you can do" with a degree in, say, religious studies.

Even when it comes to the more vocationally-related majors like nursing or business or education or biology, it is sure to be the case that the knowledge you will need in your job will far outstrip what you will learn in your college classes. This is not a failing of the college classes, it is just a fact that specific industries and jobs require highly specific knowledge. It is also a fact that what you need to know to be an accountant or a teacher or a nurse or a biologist will change in response to advances in those fields. (Think, for example, about how much more today's middle school teachers need to know about computers compared to their predecessors 30 years ago.) One of the goals of a college education is to give you the general knowledge into which you can fit the more specific knowledge required by your particular job. And, more importantly, a college education will give you the ability to teach yourself, so that when you need a new job skill, you'll be prepared.

When you get a job, the employer very likely will train you to do whatever it is that needs to be done. Large corporations have entire human resources departments and internal "universities" the sole purpose of which is to train the new employees to perform the necessary tasks. The Widget Corporation will understand if you can't come in on the first day of the job and start making the widgets; their trainers will show you how to do that. But what they won't show you is how to write clearly, how to organize your time, how to give a presentation to the Board of Directors, how to ask questions, and how to make decisions. What an employer wants above all is an employee who can *think,* and that is what they expect from people with a college education. Once you understand that it is these more generally intellectual skills which employers desire, you'll realize that they can be acquired in just about any major.

The second problem, then, with the simple Can Opener Answer is that it fails to recognize that it is the general skills and not simply the domain-specific content knowledge which turns college graduates into desirable employees. I think I can put the point this way. A college education does not, as most people believe, prepare you to do *something.* Rather, it prepares you to do *anything.*[4]

How to Get the Most Out of College

Now that we understand the value of a college education, we can think about what you should do in college, and how you can make the most of your college years. Given that college is valuable not simply because it gets you a job, but because it prepares you to be a complete person, *and* given that what you want from college in the way of job-related skills are general intellectual abilities more than particular, task-specific knowledge, what should you do? I don't have all the answers, but here are some about which I'm fairly confident.

1. Write as much as you can. Then write some more. The written word is the medium of academic communication. Academics talk to one another through books and published articles. Students talk to their professors through exams and termpapers. If you cannot write well, you will not succeed in college, it's as simple as that. I once spoke to a group of college juniors, and I asked them what they wish they knew about college when they were entering freshmen. One of them[5] said that he wished he had known how much writing he would have to do, and to how high a standard his writing would be held. So now you know: writing is crucially important.

   And since writing is a skill like juggling or playing the guitar, the only way to get better at it is to practice. Write at every opportunity. Keep a class journal. Take notes when you read (and don't simply underline or highlight your books. This is next to worthless.). Write drafts of your assigned papers. Demand feedback on your writing from your professors. The more you write, the better a writer you will become. And, you will find, the better a *thinker* you will become, because more than anything else, writing is a form of thinking out loud. Write for yourself, to clarify your own thinking, not simply because you have a paper due at the end of the term. Because writing is the medium of academic communication, you need to treat it that way—as a form of communication. Don't think of your papers as something that you turn in for a grade, but as an opportunity to talk to your professors—to tell them what you have been thinking about. I hardly need say that if you are a talented writer, you will succeed in the workplace. You won't have to write essays on Jane Austen or the Protestant Reformation once you leave college, but you will have to write memos and reports and presentations and speeches, and honing this skill in college will serve you well once you leave.
2. Talk. And not just about your weekend plans or about the details of your friends' love lives. Talk about ideas that fascinate you. Talk about politics and religion and racism and abortion and all the other issues that are important but which are not usually talked about in "polite society". It is through talking about these issues that you may very well come to turn confusion into clarity. Many of these questions can only be solved when a number of minds come together at once, and gathering in a group and talking is the best way to bring minds together. How will you know if there is a flaw in your position if you don't show it to someone else? Moreover, you can use your talking about these issues as practice for the talking that you will have to do with your spouse, your children, your coworkers, your boss, and the members of your town council. Speaking to others in private and to groups in public is one of those life and job skills that I was talking about above, and if you can treat college as an opportunity for honing that skill, you will be ready to talk in these other sorts of

situations. Finally, as you will soon learn, talking about ideas is valuable for its own sake. The late-night conversations at coffee houses or in dorm rooms about the meaning of life and the way to fix the world are just plain fun. Do it as often as you can.

3. Take responsibility for your education. Here's the part where college distinguishes itself from high school. High school students are there because they have to be. College students are in college because they want to be. (And make sure you really *want* to be in college before you go. It is a sizeable investment of time and money, and if there's something else you'd rather be doing, you should take some time and re-assess your situation. Taking a year off to figure out what you want, and entering college with a clear plan in mind can make all the difference in the world.) You are paying dearly for your college education, so you should go out and *get* it. Don't wait for someone else to hand it to you; it won't come. Taking responsibility for your own education manifests itself in small ways, and in larger ways. On the small side it means going to the dictionary when you run across a word you don't know. It also means asking your professor to read a draft of your essay, or raising your hand in class to ask for a difficult point to be repeated. But taking responsibility for your education means more than this. It means seeking out challenging courses and inspiring professors, for only if you push yourself by taking hard courses will you improve your academic and intellectual skills. It means having the courage to change your major if you find your current one uninteresting. It means engaging your friends in the dormitories and coffee shops about what you are learning in the classroom. It means speaking up and agitating for change if things aren't going the way you want. If you sit passively through your classes, skipping the readings, and taking only the easy courses, you will fail to gain the very education to which you are committing so much time and money.

It might help to think of college as a sort of health club—a health club for the mind.[6] There are all sorts of machines in the health club: these are your professors, your classes, and the many extra-curricular activity opportunities. The machines at this intellectual health club can improve your mind in the way that the weights and stair-climbers at your gym can improve your body. But, just as at the gym, the machines are useless if you don't use them. Merely buying a health club membership won't turn flab into muscle; you have to lift weights and do sit-ups. And merely enrolling in college won't turn an uneducated person into an educated one. Doing the reading, talking in class, visiting your professors in office hours, pursuing research topics outside of class—this is the sort of "machine using" behavior that will turn the gray matter inside your head into a well-toned mental muscle.

4. Do something completely different. I see so many students who take the same menu of courses they took in high school: history, English, math, science, and a foreign language. All of those are important classes, but a quick glance at any college's course catalog will show that there are dozens if not hundreds of comparatively exotic courses. Religious studies, communication, anthropology, economics, psychology, film theory—the list goes on. Take a course that is completely different from anything you have taken before. Explore the unknown. Not only might the strange and exotic be something you like (and have a talent for!), but the challenge of these new courses will push you to develop the intellectual skills I have been talking about. This injunction to do something completely different shouldn't stop at the course catalog, however. Find the person on campus most different from you and take them out to coffee. Try out for a play, join the debate team, write for the newspaper, join a campus service organization. Try your hand at some of those activities that you would never have done in high school. Of course you will meet new people, but the primary reason for engaging in these pursuits is to discover something about yourself. Maybe you would enjoy the theatre or find that you have a talent for organizing fund-drives (and can translate that into a career!). It is foolish to commit yourself to a life-plan before you have discovered what you like and what talents you have. And after you get a "real job" and "settle down" you will find precious little time for these extra-curricular pursuits.
5. Become curious. The late Canadian novelist Robertson Davies has hit upon the essence of college. "Energy and curiosity are the lifeblood of universities," Davies had one of his characters say. "The desire to find out, to uncover, to dig deeper, to puzzle out obscurities, is the spirit of the university and it is a channeling of that unresting curiosity that holds mankind together."[7] Since this 'unresting curiosity' is the essence of any college, succeeding during the next four years requires that you tap into this energy, and that you become an unrestingly curious person yourself. Feed your curiosity by taking courses that interest you, rather than the courses which might look good on a law school application. Find those issues and problems that interest you and pursue them doggedly. Become curious about everything—about medieval history, about the structure of the cell, about what your roommates are learning in their classes, about the research interests of your professors—and you will find not only that you are getting better grades, but that you are becoming a smarter, more intellectually independent person. And that is, at the end, the goal of a college education.[8]

Endnotes

1. Andrew P. Mills is an assistant professor of philosophy at Otterbein College, where he teaches a wide array of philosophy courses. He received his B.A. from the University of Michigan, and his M.A. and Ph.D. in philosophy from The University of North Carolina at Chapel Hill. He is the author of scholarly articles in the philosophy of language and in philosophical logic.
2. Of course in such a situation can openers may have value as antiques, or as objects of art. And that is a real sort of value, but it is not (at least not standardly) why we think can openers are valuable now.
3. Like this very essay: it's an examination of the value of a college education.
4. I learned of this way of putting the point from Ami Berger, though I don't think she was the originator of this thought.
5. His name is Caleb Bell.
6. For this health club analogy I am indebted to Craig Froehle.
7. This is from Davies' novel, *The Rebel Angels.*
8. An earlier, abbreviated, version of this essay was published under the title "College is more than job training" in *The Blade* (Toledo, Ohio) on September 30, 2000. For helpful conversation on this essay, I would like to thank Lori Aronson, Ami Berger, Brad Cohen, Craig Froehle, Glenna Jackson, Brian Lindeman, Kristine LaLonde, Mary MacLeod, Lisa Pollak, Charles Salter, and the audiences at Otterbein College to whom I have presented the main ideas contained above. I would like to dedicate this essay to Jack Meiland, who ignited my thinking on the question of why a college education is valuable. His little book, *College Thinking* is as valuable a guide to college as I can think of.

NOTES

CULTIVATING HUMANITY: A CLASSICAL DEFENSE OF REFORM IN LIBERAL EDUCATION

Martha C. Nussbaum

(1947–)

Martha C. Nussbaum is the Ernst Freund Distinguished Service Professor of Law and Ethics at the University of Chicago. She received her BA from NYU and her MA and PhD from Harvard. She has published widely and received many professional honors, including the Prince of Asturias Prize in the Social Sciences in 2012.

The Old Education and the Think-Academy

In Aristophanes' great comedy *The Clouds*, a young man, eager for the new learning, goes to a "Think-Academy" run by that strange, notorious figure, Socrates. A debate is staged for him, contrasting the merits of traditional education with those of the new discipline of Socratic argument. The spokesman for the Old Education is a tough old soldier. He favors a highly disciplined patriotic regimen, with lots of memorization and not much room for questioning. He loves to recall a time that may never have existed—a time when young people obeyed their parents and wanted nothing more than to die for their country, a time when teachers would teach that grand old song "Athena, glorious sacker of cities"—not the strange new songs of the present day. Study with me, he booms, and you will look like a real man—broad chest, small tongue, firm buttocks, small genitals (a plus in those days, symbolic of manly self-control).

His opponent is an arguer, a seductive man of words—Socrates seen through the distorting lens of Aristophanic conservatism. He promises the youth that he will learn to think critically about the social origins of apparently timeless moral norms, the distinction between convention and nature. He will learn to construct arguments on his own, heedless of authority. He won't do much marching. Study with me, he concludes, and you will look like a philosopher: you will have a big tongue, a sunken, narrow chest, soft buttocks, and big genitals (a minus in those days, symbolic of lack of self-restraint). Socrates' self-advertisement, of course, is being slyly scripted by the conservative opposition. The message? The New Education will subvert manly self-control, turn young people into sex-obsessed rebels, and destroy the city. The son soon goes home and produces a relativist argument that he should beat his father. The same angry father then takes a torch and burns down the Think-Academy. (It is not made clear whether the son is still inside.) Twenty-five years later, Socrates, on trial for corrupting the young, cited Aristophanes' play as a major source of prejudice against him.

Reprinted from *Cultivating Humanity: A Classical Defense of Reform in Liberal Education* (1997), Harvard University Press.

In contemporary America as in ancient Athens, liberal education is changing. New topics have entered the liberal arts curricula of colleges and universities: the history and culture of non-Western peoples and of ethnic and racial minorities within the United States, the experiences and achievements of women, the history and concerns of lesbians and gay men. These changes have frequently been presented in popular journalism as highly threatening, both to traditional standards of academic excellence and to traditional norms of citizenship. Readers are given the picture of a monolithic, highly politicized elite who are attempting to enforce a "politically correct" view of human life, subverting traditional values and teaching students, in effect, to argue in favor of father-beating. Socratic questioning is still on trial. Our debates over the curriculum reveal the same nostalgia for a more obedient, more regimented time, the same suspiciousness of new and independent thinking, that find expression in Aristophanes' brilliant portrait.

This picture of today's campuses bears little resemblance to the daily reality of higher education in America, as faculty and students grapple with issues of human diversity. Sensationalistic descriptions of horrors may sometimes be more fun to read than nuanced accounts of responsible decision-making, but the latter are badly needed, since they represent the far more common reality. In order to evaluate the changes that are taking place in colleges and universities, we have to look more closely to see exactly what is changing, and why. What are faculty and students really doing, and how do newly fashionable issues about human diversity affect what they do? What sort of citizens are our colleges trying to produce, and how well are they succeeding in that task? To answer these questions, we need to look not only at one or two well-known institutions but at a wide range, representative of the variety that currently exists in American higher education: institutions public and private, religious and secular, large and small, rural and urban, four-year and university.

When we look in this way, we do see problems; and we do see tendencies that ought to be criticized. But on the whole, higher education in America is in a healthy state. Never before have there been so many talented and committed young faculty so broadly dispersed in institutions of so many different kinds, thinking about difficult issues connecting education with citizenship. The shortage of jobs in the humanities and social sciences has led to hardships; many have left the professions they love. But those who have stayed are intensely dedicated; furthermore, the ablest teachers and scholars are now no longer concentrated in a few elite schools. They are all over the country, reflecting about the mission of higher education, trying out strategies to enliven the thinking of the students who come their way. The real story of higher education in America is the story of the daily struggles of these men and women to reason well about urgent questions and to engage the hearts and minds of their students in that search.

At St. Lawrence University, a small liberal arts college in upstate New York, near the Canadian border, the snow is already two feet deep by early January. Cars make almost no sound rolling slowly over the packed white surface. But the campus is well plowed, even at Christmas. In a brightly lit seminar room young faculty, gathering despite the vacation, talk with excitement about their month-long visit to Kenya to study African village life. Having shared the daily lives of ordinary men and women, having joined in local debates about nutrition, polygamy, AIDS, and much else, they are now incorporating the experience into their teaching—in courses in art history, philosophy, religion, women's studies. Planning eagerly for the following summer's trip to India, they are already meeting each week for an evening seminar on Indian culture and history. Group leaders Grant Cornwell from Philosophy and Eve Stoddard from English talk about how they teach students to think critically about cultural relativism, using careful philosophical questioning in the Socratic tradition to criticize the easy but ultimately (they argue) incoherent idea that toleration requires us not to criticize anyone else's way of life. Their students submit closely reasoned papers analyzing arguments for and against outsiders' taking a stand on the practice of female circumcision in Africa.

In Riverside, California, already at 8 A.M. a brown haze blankets the mountains and the orange groves. It is the first day of the summer session at the University of California campus, and the ethnically mixed student body, more than 40 percent minority, crowds the campus green. Richard Lowy, a young white instructor in Ethnic Studies, talks rapidly to my research assistant Yasmin Dalisay, herself a daughter of two Filipino doctors who immigrated to Orem, Utah. Lowy speaks in a low, gentle voice, peering through his thick glasses. He describes the difficulty of teaching about immigration, assimilation, and the political struggles of new minorities in a political climate saturated with sensationalism, mistrust, and appeals to irrational emotion. "Certainly there are some people who teach multiculturalism in a provocative way. I choose a more gentle approach. I try to tell everybody I'm not here to degrade you and I'm not here to condemn anybody for what your ancestors, relatives, or anybody did; I just try to explain what's going on, and I hope that the knowledge I present will begin to affect people, whereas the emotionalism of some people is what turns people off. I think that for people to be orienting their humanity only in political terms is too narrow, and I always tell people that you can either package your humanity in your politics or you can package your politics in your humanity, and if you're really a decent human being with the right attitude and the right heart and good faith toward people it will come out. So I try to put things in that kind of perspective."

In Reno the University of Nevada campus is a small enclave of red brick and manicured lawns in the middle of casino-land. Yasmin talks with Eric Chalmers, a senior health science major from Carson City, who describes himself as having "more bigoted ideas than some people at the university level." Chalmers, who has never heard of the recently introduced "diversity requirement," requiring new freshmen to take one course on a non-Western culture or on an ethnic or gender issue within the United States, applauds the trend to internationalizing, wishing he had had the opportunity to study Islam and the Middle East. But he criticizes a course on domestic violence taught by a "liberated woman professor" because it seemed to him "too demeaning to men." As the interview is drawing to an end, he laughs, remembering something. "Here's another interesting thing. In English 102 we had to write a letter putting ourselves in the shoes of a gay person, like breaking the news to our parents saying we were gay, and explaining our lifestyle to them. At the time, when I was a freshman, it seemed really off the wall to me, and it was kind of an uncomfortable assignment, but now, looking back on it, it seems as though I can understand why he would do something like that—because you come into contact with people like—you know, different types of people—all the time, and maybe it's an understanding of their belief system." He laughs nervously.

On a dark afternoon in February 1995, I go to my Cambridge, Massachusetts, health club. There is a young man behind the check-in desk whom I haven't seen before—tall, beefy, red cheeked, in his late teens, wearing a red baseball cap and a bright purple sweatshirt with "Washington" in silver letters across the top and a glow-in-the-dark picture of the White House. He tells me his name is Billy. He is reading Plato's *Apology* and *Crito*. So you're reading Plato, I say. "Yeah. You like that stuff?" he asks, and his eyes light up. I tell him I like that stuff a lot, and I ask him about his class. It's at Bentley, a college in nearby Waltham, focused on business education. Who's the instructor? "I don't remember," he says, "She's foreign." The syllabus reads, "Dr. Krishna Mallick." Krishna Mallick, originally from Calcutta, has written some wonderful study questions about Socrates' mission of self-examination, his obedience to the laws of Athens, his willingness to die for the sake of the argument. Soon students will go on to use the techniques they have learned from Plato to stage debates about moral dilemmas of our time. Before I head for the Stairmaster, we talk for a while about why Socrates did not escape from prison when he had the chance, and it's plain that Krishna Mallick has produced real excitement. "You know, I really like this philosophy. Most courses, you have to remember lots of little facts, but in this one they want you to think and ask questions."

At the University of Chicago, a chain-link fence out back of the law school parking lot marks the line between the university campus and the impoverished black community that surrounds it. Black children sometimes climb over the fence or get round it by the driveway, but they are not allowed to stay long. On a May afternoon seventy students, one black, sit in a law school classroom discussing Richard Wright's *Native Son*, a novel set in that very part of Chicago in 1940. They talk about the "line" that Bigger Thomas thought of as the symbol of white hatred and black shame, and they argue intensely over Bigger's state of mind and the degree of his criminal responsibility. Since Justice Clarence Thomas has recently made a statement opposing mitigation in sentencing for blacks who trace their criminal tendencies to their deprived backgrounds, they ask whether Wright's novel supports or subverts Thomas' claims.

Scott Braithwaite, a young gay Mormon, recent graduate of Brigham Young University, gives a Sacrament meeting talk referring to the importance of including discussion of the history and variety of human sexuality in the liberal arts curriculum. This is currently a topic of intense controversy at BYU, and Braithwaite's talk is thick with references both to biblical texts and to Mormon scripture and history. "Ideally," he concludes, "we should love everyone. Yet it is often difficult to love someone unknown, or different from oneself."

As Richard Lowy justly remarks, it is easier in our culture to purvey an emotion-laden sensationalizing message than to tell, with accurate information and humanity and even humor, stories of people's real diversity and complexity. Individuals can all too easily be forgotten when we engage in political debate. This book will let the voices of these representative yet highly individual teachers and students be heard—in the hope that the reader will decide to "package his politics in his humanity," imagining the concrete situations of the teachers who are making curricular choices and thinking about the issues with flexibility and empathy, rather than making a political prejudgment about the faculty who are actually teaching in our universities.

Today's teachers are shaping future citizens in an age of cultural diversity and increasing internationalization. Our country is inescapably plural. As citizens we are frequently called upon to make decisions that require some understanding of racial and ethnic and religious groups in our nation, and of the situation of its women and its minorities in terms of sexual orientation. As citizens we are also increasingly called upon to understand how issues such as agriculture, human rights, ecology, even business and industry, are generating discussions that bring people together from many nations. This must happen more and more if our economy is to remain vital and effective solutions to pressing human problems are to be found. The new emphasis on "diversity" in college and university curricula is above all a way of grappling with the altered requirements of citizenship, an attempt to produce adults who can function as citizens not just of some local region or group but also, and more importantly, as citizens of a complex interlocking world.

When I arrived at Harvard in 1969, my fellow first-year graduate students and I were taken up to the roof of Widener Library by a well-known professor of classics. He told us how many Episcopal churches could be seen from that vantage point. As a Jew (in fact a convert from Episcopalian Christianity), I knew that my husband and I would have been forbidden to marry in Harvard's Memorial Church, which had just refused to accept a Jewish wedding. As a woman I could not eat in the main dining room of the faculty club, even as a member's guest. Only a few years before, a woman would not have been able to use the undergraduate library. In 1972 I became the first female to hold the Junior Fellowship that relieved certain graduate students from teaching so that they could get on with their research. At that time I received a letter of congratulation from a prestigious classicist saying that it would be difficult to know what to call a female fellow, since "fellowess" was an awkward term. Perhaps the Greek language could solve the problem: since the masculine for "fellow" was *hetairos*, I could be called a *hetaira*. *Hetaira*, however, as I knew, is the ancient Greek word not for "fellowess" but for "courtesan."

In a setting in which such exclusions and such "jokes" were routine, is it any wonder that the academic study of women's history, of literature written by women, of the sociology and politics of gender—that all these perfectly normal and central topics were unavailable for serious study? They were just as unavailable as was (in most places) the serious academic study of Judaism, of African and of African-American cultures, of many other ethnic minorities, of many non-Western religions and cultures, of the variety and diversity of human sexuality. Exclusions of people and exclusions of their lives from the domain of knowledge went hand in hand. The exclusions seemed natural and apolitical; only the demand for inclusion seemed motivated by a "political agenda." From the rooftop of Widener, there were many people and many lives that my colleague could not see.

We are now trying to build an academy in which women, and members of religious and ethnic minorities, and lesbian and gay people, and people living in non-Western cultures can be seen and also heard, with respect and love, both as knowers and as objects of study, an academy in which to be a "fellowess" need not mean being called "courtesan," an academy in which the world will be seen to have many types of citizens and in which we can all learn to function as citizens of that entire world.

Inevitably there is pain and turmoil in these attempts to bring about change, and not all proposals for change are healthy ones. Some faculty pursue the diversification of the curriculum in a way that ultimately subverts the aims of citizenship, focusing on interest-group identity politics rather than on the need of all citizens for knowledge and understanding. Some, too, have become unjustly skeptical of rational argument, thinking of its abuses as if they were part of the essence of rationality itself. These errors and excesses, however, are neither ubiquitous nor uncontroverted. Instead of a monolithic "politically correct" orthodoxy, what I hear when I visit campuses are the voices of many diverse individual faculty, administrators, and students, confronting curricular issues with, for the most part, resourcefulness, intelligence, and good faith, This means confronting it locally, understanding the nature of one's students and the resources of one's own institution. Any single set of curricular proposals for citizenship indicts itself by its very singleness, since U.S. college students are an extraordinarily heterogeneous group. So the heroes and heroines of my book are the many thousands of instructors who are working with dedication on this task: instructors like Richard Lowy, Eve Stoddard, Grant Cornwell, and Krishna Mallick, each going to work in a concrete context to create a conception of citizenship for the future. They are thinking searchingly, disagreeing fruitfully, and coming up with concrete solutions that should command our respect even where we do not fully agree.

Our campuses are producing citizens, and this means that we must ask what a good citizen of the present day should be and should know. The present-day world is inescapably multicultural and multinational. Many of our most pressing problems require for their intelligent, cooperative solution a dialogue that brings together people from many different national and cultural and religious backgrounds. Even those issues that seem closest to home—issues, for example, about the structure of the family, the regulation of sexuality, the future of children—need to be approached with a broad historical and cross-cultural understanding. A graduate of a U.S. university or college ought to be the sort of citizen who can become an intelligent participant in debates involving these differences, whether professionally or simply as a voter, a juror, a friend.

When we ask about the relationship of a liberal education to citizenship, we are asking a question with a long history in the Western philosophical tradition. We are drawing on Socrates' concept of "the examined life," on Aristotle's notions of reflective citizenship, and above all on Greek and Roman Stoic notions of an education that is "liberal" in that it liberates the mind from the bondage of habit and custom, producing people who can function with sensitivity and alertness as citizens of the whole world. This is what Seneca means by the cultivation of humanity. The idea of the well-educated person as a "citizen of the world" has had a formative influence on Western thought about education: on David Hume and Adam Smith in the Scottish/English tradition, on Immanuel Kant in the continental Enlightenment tradition, on Thomas Paine and other Founding Fathers in the American tradition. Understanding the classical roots of these ideas helps us to recover powerful arguments that have exercised a formative influence on our own democracy.

Our democracy, indeed, has based its institutions of higher learning on these ideals to a degree unparalleled in the world. In most nations students enter a university to pursue a single subject, and that is all they study. The idea of "liberal education"—a higher education that is a cultivation of the whole human being for the functions of citizenship and life generally—has been taken up most fully in the United States. This noble ideal, however, has not yet been fully realized in our colleges and universities. Some, while using the words "liberal education," subordinate the cultivation of the whole person to technical and vocational education. Even where education is ostensibly "liberal," it may not contain all that a citizen really needs to know. We should ask, then, how well our nation is really fulfilling a goal that it has chosen to make its own. What does the "cultivation of humanity" require?

The classical ideal of the "world citizen" can be understood in two ways, and "cultivation of humanity" along with it. The sterner, more exigent version is the ideal of a citizen whose *primary* loyalty is to human beings the world over, and whose national, local, and varied group loyalties are considered distinctly secondary. Its more relaxed version allows a variety of different views about what our priorities should be but says that, however we order our varied loyalties, we should still be sure that we recognize the worth of human life wherever it occurs and see ourselves as bound by common human abilities and problems to people who lie at a great distance from us. These two different versions have existed at least since ancient Rome, when statesman and philosopher Cicero softened the stern demands of Greek Stoicism for a Roman audience. Although I do sympathize with the sterner thesis, it is the more relaxed and inclusive thesis that will concern me here. What, then, does this inclusive conception ask us to learn?

Three capacities, above all, are essential to the cultivation of humanity in today's world. First is the capacity for critical examination of oneself and one's traditions—for living what, following Socrates, we may call "the examined life." This means a life that accepts no belief as authoritative simply because it has been handed down by tradition or become familiar through habit, a life that questions all beliefs and accepts only those that survive reason's demand for consistency and for justification. Training this capacity requires developing the capacity to reason logically, to test what one reads or says for consistency of reasoning, correctness of fact, and accuracy of judgment. Testing of this sort frequently produces challenges to tradition, as Socrates knew well when he defended himself against the charge of "corrupting the young." But he defended his activity on the grounds that democracy needs citizens who can think for themselves rather than simply deferring to authority, who can reason together about their choices rather than just trading claims and counterclaims. Like a gadfly on the back of a noble but sluggish horse, he said, he was waking democracy up so that it could conduct its business in a more reflective and reasonable way. Our democracy, like ancient Athens, is prone to hasty and sloppy reasoning, and to the substitution of invective for real deliberation. We need Socratic teaching to fulfill the promise of democratic citizenship.

Citizens who cultivate their humanity need, further, an ability to see themselves not simply as citizens of some local region or group but also, and above all, as human beings bound to all other human beings by ties of recognition and concern. The world around us is inescapably international. Issues from business to agriculture, from human rights to the relief of famine, call our imaginations to venture beyond narrow group loyalties and to consider the reality of distant lives. We very easily think of ourselves in group terms—as Americans first and foremost, as human beings second—or, even more narrowly, as Italian-Americans, or heterosexuals, or African-Americans first, Americans second, and human beings third if at all. We neglect needs and capacities that link us to fellow citizens who live at a distance or who look different from ourselves. This means that we are unaware of many prospects of communication and fellowship with them, and also of responsibilities we may have to them. We also sometimes err by neglect of differences, assuming that lives in distant places must be like ours and lacking curiosity about what they are really like. Cultivating our humanity in a complex, interlocking world involves understanding the ways in which common needs and aims are differently realized in different circumstances. This requires a great deal of knowledge that American college students rarely got in previous eras, knowledge of non-Western cultures, of minorities within their own, of differences of gender and sexuality.

But citizens cannot think well on the basis of factual knowledge alone. The third ability of the citizen, closely related to the first two, can be called the narrative imagination. This means the ability to think what it might be like to be in the shoes of a person different from oneself, to be an intelligent reader of that person's story, and to understand the emotions and wishes and desires that someone so placed might have. The narrative imagination is not uncritical, for we always bring ourselves and our own judgments to the encounter with another; and when we identify with a character in a novel, or with a distant person whose life story we imagine, we inevitably will not merely identify; we will also judge that story in the light of our own goals and aspirations. But the first step of understanding the world from the point of view of the other is essential to any responsible act of judgment, since we do not know what we are judging until we see the meaning of an action as the person intends it, the meaning of a speech as it expresses something of importance in the context of that person's history and social world. The third ability our students should attain is the ability to decipher such meanings through the use of the imagination.

Intelligent citizenship needs more than these three abilities. Scientific understanding is also of the first importance. My excuse for not dwelling on this aspect of a liberal education is that others are far better placed to describe it than I. The same is true of economics, which I shall approach only in its relationship to philosophy and political theory. I focus on the parts of a liberal education that have by now become associated with "the humanities" and to some extent "the social sciences": above all, then, on philosophy, political science, religious studies, history, anthropology, sociology, literature, art, music, and studies of language and culture. Nor do I describe everything in these areas that a good citizen should know. I focus on areas of current urgency and controversy. (Even within the areas of controversy I am selective, allowing the example of African-American studies to stand for more complex debates about ethnic studies generally. Issues of poverty and social class, which I have treated elsewhere, are treated selectively, within chapters organized along other lines.)

It was through ancient Greek and Roman arguments that I came upon these ideas in my own history. The Greek and Roman versions of these ideas are immensely valuable to us as we pursue these debates today, and I shall focus on that contribution. But ideas of this sort have many sources in many traditions. Closely related notions can be found in India, in Africa, in Latin America, and in China. One of the errors that a diverse education can dispel is the false belief that one's own tradition is the only one that is capable of self-criticism or universal aspiration.

Consider my examples of contemporary liberal education in the light of the three goals of world citizenship. The St. Lawrence program focuses on the second goal, that of producing students who are well informed about the lives of people different from themselves, and who can participate in debates about these lives with interest in the future of humanity. But the program leaders hold that any responsible teaching on the first issue must also be Socratic teaching, training logical abilities to think critically and to construct an argument. This training is built into the program, in the central role it gives to philosophy. Finally, the program's emphasis on travel develops imagination as well as factual knowledge. Living with people in Kenya expands one's ability to see the world from those people's point of view, and to approach new knowledge in a more empathetic spirit.

Richard Lowy's ethnic studies classes face an uphill battle: the tenacious loyalty of students to their group identities. He faces a classroom already politicized by these identities, and he must struggle to create a community of learning and dialogue within that situation. Like the St. Lawrence teachers, he emphasizes the importance of thinking of humanity in broader and more flexible terms than those dictated by ideological focusing on group loyalty; like them, he thinks of his goal as one of world citizenship and understanding. The Socratic logical abilities are less stressed in his approach, largely because of the nature of his discipline and subject matter. But imagination and empathy are clearly in evidence in the way in which he appeals to students to transcend their narrow sympathies.

Billy Tucker's philosophy class, by contrast, focuses on the Socratic ability to question and to justify, using this as the underpinning of a concept of citizenship. Krishna Mallick and Richard Lowy are pursuing related goals, each starting from a different disciplinary perspective: goals of broad understanding and respectful dialogue. But there is no doubt that the philosophical contribution to Tucker's education has been important to him as a citizen; it could not have been replaced by factual knowledge alone. Tucker is acquiring a new mode of approaching political debate, one that focuses on issues rather than on personalities, on reasoned analysis rather than on name-calling or sloganeering. He will need facts in order to make his arguments well, and the course stresses this requirement when it asks debaters to do research on their subjects. But the facts would not have produced a dialogue without the course's strong emphasis on Socratic argumentation, and without Mallick's ability to get students interested in such apparently boring phenomena as detecting fallacies and formalizing arguments.

Eric Chalmers' English class focused on the imagination, pursuing the goal of world citizenship through practice in narrative understanding. Chalmers resisted courses presented in what he took to be an ideological or politically partisan manner. But the invitation to present the world from the point of view of a person different from himself did engage him, producing a person who was still capable of critical judgment, but who probably will relate to gay people, as a health care worker, in a more knowledgeable and sympathetic manner.

Scott Braithwaite did not encounter such instruction. Indeed, his training at Brigham Young was constructed in deliberate opposition to all three of my goals. It has more in common with Aristophanes' portrait of the Old Education than with the Socratic approach of the world citizen. Braithwaite was not taught to think critically about his tradition; he was taught to internalize its teachings. In a sense, as a young Mormon in a highly international church, he was taught to interact with others from different parts of the world—but usually in the mode of proselytizing, and never with the thought that learning might move in both directions. Finally, as he reports, his education did not invite his fellow students to imagine or know someone like him, nor did it invite him to know himself. He argues that this failure of knowledge entails a failure in the kind of love his own religion asks all people to have for one another.

Law students at the University of Chicago will soon be influencing life in our country in many ways. A large proportion will soon clerk for judges and write judicial opinions. Others will be involved in public service projects; still others will move directly into work with firms in a variety of capacities. Most will at one or another time deal with the problem of race—as clerks researching cases on affirmative action and minority hiring, as lawyers representing minority clients. Most of these law students, like Wright's character Mary Dalton, have never been into a tenement such as those that still exist several blocks from their classroom. If they are going to become good citizens in their future roles, they need not only logical ability and knowledge, aspects of citizenship already amply stressed in their curriculum. They also need to be able to participate imaginatively in a life such as that of Bigger Thomas, seeing how aspiration and emotion are shaped by their social setting.

In five of six cases, then, nontraditional studies, studies that would not have been in the curriculum twenty-five years ago, are supplying essential ingredients for citizenship. Billy Tucker's class is the closest to one that might have been taught in the last generation, but even that class has a focus on citizenship and on issues of the day that would not have been characteristic of the philosophical academy a while back. The St. Lawrence program involves a radical reform of a curriculum formerly focused on Europe and North America. The emphasis on ethnic studies at Riverside is part of a complex transformation of that curriculum to incorporate a variety of approaches to human diversity. Eric Chalmers encountered an English assignment that would have been unknown in Reno, Nevada, until very recently, part of a diversity movement that still generates intense controversy on campus. Scott Braithwaite laments the absence of such changes in the BYU curriculum. The University of Chicago, like most major U.S. law schools, devotes more attention to issues of race in response to interests of students and faculty. Unlike many such efforts, Chicago's focuses on the humanistic imagination as well as on factual knowledge.

Our campuses educate our citizens. Becoming an educated citizen means learning a lot of facts and mastering techniques of reasoning. But it means something more. It means learning how to be a human being capable of love and imagination. We may continue to produce narrow citizens who have difficulty understanding people different from themselves, whose imaginations rarely venture beyond their local setting. It is all too easy for the moral imagination to become narrow in this way. Think of Charles Dickens' image of bad citizenship in *A Christmas Carol,* in his portrait of the ghost of Jacob Marley, who visits Scrooge to warn him of the dangers of a blunted imagination. Marley's ghost drags through all eternity a chain made of cash boxes, because in life his imagination never ventured outside the walls of his successful business to encounter the lives of the men and women around him, men and women of different social class and background. We produce all too many citizens who are like Marley's ghost, and like Scrooge before he walked out to see what the world around him contained. But we have the opportunity to do better, and now we are beginning to seize that opportunity. That is not "political correctness"; that is the cultivation of humanity.

Socratic Self-Examination

Précis of Chapter One by Professor Lori Amann-Chetcuti

> If I tell you that this is the greatest good for a human being, to engage every day in arguments about virtue and the other things you have heard me talk about, examining both myself and others, and if I tell you that the unexamined life is not worth living for a human being, you would be even less likely to believe what I am saying. But that's the way it is, gentlemen, as I claim, though it's not easy to convince you of it.
>
> Socrates, in *Plato, Apology 38A*

The Old Education, in Aristophanes' portrait, acculturated young citizens to traditional values. They learned to internalize and to love their traditions, and they were discouraged from questioning them. As Aristophanes sees it, the most dangerous opponent of this Old Education is Socrates, whose questions subvert the authority of tradition, who recognizes no authority but that of reason, asking even the gods to give a reasoned account of their preferences and commands. Socrates' "Think-Academy" is depicted as a source of civic corruption, where young people learn to justify

---

Reprinted from *Cultivating Humanity: A Classical Defense of Reform in Liberal Education* (1997), Harvard University Press.

beating their parents. This fictional attack fed a real suspicion of the Socratic way of life.

Athenian leaders, unsettled at the idea that young people would search for arguments to justify their beliefs rather than simply following parents and civic authorities, blamed Socrates for the cultural disharmony they sensed around them. Charged with corrupting the young, he eventually forfeited his life.

The ancient debate between Socrates and his enemies is of value for our present educational controversies. Like Socrates, our colleges and universities are being charged with corruption of the young. Seeing young people emerge from modem "Think-Academies" with many challenges to traditional thinking—about women, about race, about social justice, about patriotism-social conservatives of many kinds have suggested that these universities are homes for the corrupt thinking of a radical elite whose ultimate aim is the subversion of the social fabric. Once again an education that promotes acculturation to the time-honored traditions of "Western Civilization" is being defended against a more Socratic education that insists on teaching students to think for themselves. At institutions of the most varied sorts, students are indeed asking questions and challenging the authority of tradition.

In colleges and universities around the country, students are following Socrates, questioning their views to discover how far they survive the test of argument. Although Socratic procedures have been familiar for a long time in basic philosophy courses, philosophy is now reaching a far larger number of students than it did fifty years ago, students of all classes and backgrounds and religious origins. And philosophy, which at one time was taught as a remote and abstract discipline, is increasingly being linked to the analysis and criticism of current events and ideas. Instead of learning logical analysis in a vacuum, students now learn to dissect the arguments they find in newspapers, to argue about current controversies in medicine and law and sports, to think critically about the foundations of their political and even religious views.

To parents in contemporary America, as to parents in the time of Socrates, such developments can appear very unsettling. Argument seems like a cold strange invader into the habits of the home. The father in Aristophanes came home one day to encounter an argument in favor of fatherbeating.

The parents of the philosophy majors at Belmont [University, a Baptist university in Memphis, Tennessee] may encounter "secular humanism" at the end of the semester, where previously there had been traditional Christianity. Nicole Li's parents send her to Brown [University] and find her making arguments in defense of women who take extralegal revenge against their abusers. The Socratic emphasis on reason seems not only subversive but also cold. To kind and affectionate people, it can seem insulting to demand an argument for some political belief they have long held and have taught to their children. It can appear that their cherished traditions must now undergo scrutiny from the point of view of an elite intellectual world that is strange to them. It is not surprising that the proliferation of "applied ethics" courses, and of philosophy generally, in our colleges and universities should alarm many parents.

Tradition is one foe of Socratic reason. But Socrates has other enemies as well. His values are assailed by the left as well as by the right. It is fashionable today in progressive intellectual circles to say that rational argument is a male Western device, in its very nature subversive of the equality of women and minorities and non-Western people. Socratic argument is suspected, here again, of being arrogant and elitist—but in this case the elitism is seen as that of a dominant Western intellectual tradition that has persistently marginalized outsiders. The very pretense that one is engaged in the disinterested pursuit of truth can be a handy screen for prejudice. . . .

But Socrates' opponents on the left make the same error as do his conservative opponents, when they suppose that argument is subversive of democratic values. Socratic argument is not undemocratic. Nor is it subversive of the just claims of excluded people. In fact, as Socrates knew, it is essential to a strong democracy and to any lasting pursuit of justice. In order to foster a democracy that is reflective and deliberative, rather than simply a marketplace of competing interest groups, a democracy that genuinely takes thought for the common good, we must produce citizens who have the Socratic capacity to reason about their beliefs. It is not good for democracy when people vote on the basis of sentiments they have absorbed from talk radio and have never questioned. This failure to think critically produces a democracy in which people talk at one another but never have a genuine dialogue. In such an atmosphere bad arguments pass for good arguments, and prejudice can all too easily masquerade as reason. To unmask prejudice and to secure justice, we need argument, an essential tool of civic freedom.

Liberal education in our colleges and universities is, and should be, Socratic, committed to the activation of each student's independent mind and to the production of a community that can genuinely reason together about a problem, not simply trade claims and counterclaims. Despite our allegiances to families and traditions, despite our diverse interests in correcting injustices to groups within our nation, we can and should reason together in a Socratic way, and our campuses should prepare us to do so. By looking at this goal of a community of reason as it emerges in the thought of Socrates and the Greek Stoics, we can show its dignity and its importance for democratic self-government. Connecting this idea to the teaching of philosophy in undergraduate courses of many sorts, we shall see that it is not Socratic education, but its absence, that would be fatal to the health of our society.

NOTES

NOTES

THE NATURE OF GOVERNMENT
Ayn Rand

(1905–1982)

Born in Russia, Ayn Rand became a U.S. citizen in 1931. An author and social critic, her books serve as a platform to express her philosophies including the essential nature of creativity.

A government is an institution that holds the exclusive power to *enforce* certain rules of social conduct in a given geographical area.

Do men need such an institution—and why?

Since man's mind is his basic tool of survival, his means of gaining knowledge to guide his actions—the basic condition he requires is the freedom to think and to act according to his rational judgment. This does not mean that a man must live alone and that a desert island is the environment best suited to his needs. Men can derive enormous benefits from dealing with one another. A social environment is most conducive to their successful survival—*but only on certain conditions.*

"The two great values to be gained from social existence are: knowledge and trade. Man is the only species that can transmit and expand his store of knowledge from generation to generation; the knowledge potentially available to man is greater than any one man could begin to acquire in his own lifespan; every man gains an incalculable benefit from the knowledge discovered by others. The second great benefit is the division of labor: it enables a man to devote his effort to a particular field of work and to trade with others who specialize in other fields. This form of cooperation allows all men who take part in it to achieve a greater knowledge, skill and productive return on their effort than they could achieve if each had to produce everything he needs, on a desert island or on a self-sustaining farm.

"But these very benefits indicate, delimit and define what kind of men can be of value to one another and in what kind of society: only rational, productive, independent men in a rational, productive, free society." ("The Objectivist Ethics," *The Virtue of Selfishness*)

A society that robs an individual of the product of his effort, or enslaves him, or attempts to limit the freedom of his mind, or compels him to act against his own rational judgment—a society that sets up a conflict between its edicts and the requirements of man's nature—is not, strictly speaking, a society, but a mob held together by institutionalized gang-rule. Such a society destroys all the values of human coexistence, has no possible justification and represents, not a source of benefits, but the deadliest threat to man's survival. Life on a desert island is safer than and incomparably preferable to existence in Soviet Russia or Nazi Germany.

If men are to live together in a peaceful, productive, rational society and deal with one another to mutual benefit, they must accept the basic social

---

principle without which no moral or civilized society is possible: the principle of individual rights.

To recognize individual rights means to recognize and accept the conditions required by man's nature for his proper survival.

Man's rights can be violated only by the use of physical force. It is only by means of physical force that one man can deprive another of his life, or enslave him, or rob him, or prevent him from pursuing his own goals, or compel him to act against his own rational judgment.

The precondition of a civilized society is the barring of physical force from social relationships—thus establishing the principle that if men wish to deal with one another, they may do so only by means of *reason*: by discussion, persuasion and voluntary, uncoerced agreement.

The necessary consequence of man's right to life is his right to self-defense. In a civilized society, force may be used only in retaliation and only against those who initiate its use. All the reasons which make the initiation of physical force an evil, make the retaliatory use of physical force a moral imperative.

If some "pacifist" society renounced the retaliatory use of force, it would be left helplessly at the mercy of the first thug who decided to be immoral. Such a society would achieve the opposite of its intention: instead of abolishing evil, it would encourage and reward it.

If a society provided no organized protection against force, it would compel every citizen to go about armed, to turn his home into a fortress, to shoot any strangers approaching his door—or to join a protective gang of citizens who would fight other gangs, formed for the same purpose, and thus bring about the degeneration of that society into the chaos of gang-rule, *i.e.*, rule by brute force, into perpetual tribal warfare of prehistoric savages.

The use of physical force—even its retaliatory use—cannot be left at the discretion of individual citizens. Peaceful coexistence is impossible if a man has to live under the constant threat of force to be unleashed against him by any of his neighbors at any moment. Whether his neighbors' intentions are good or bad, whether their judgment is rational or irrational, whether they are motivated by a sense of justice or by ignorance or by prejudice or by malice—the use of force against one man cannot be left to the arbitrary decision of another.

Visualize, for example, what would happen if a man missed his wallet, concluded that he had been robbed, broke into every house in the neighborhood to search it, and shot the first man who gave him a dirty look, taking the look to be a proof of guilt.

The retaliatory use of force requires *objective* rules of evidence to establish that a crime has been committed and to *prove* who committed it, as well as *objective* rules to define punishments and enforcement procedures. Men who attempt to prosecute crimes, without such rules, are a lynch mob. If a society left the retaliatory use of force in the hands of individual citizens, it would degenerate into mob rule, lynch law and an endless series of bloody private feuds or vendettas.

If physical force is to be barred from social relationships, men need an institution charged with the task of protecting their rights under an *objective* code of rules.

This is the task of a government—of a *proper* government—its basic task, its only moral justification and the reason why men do need a government.

A government is the means of placing the retaliatory use of physical force under objective control—i.e., under objectively defined laws.

The fundamental difference between private action and governmental action—a difference thoroughly ignored and evaded today—lies in the fact that a government holds a monopoly on the legal use of physical force. It has to hold such a monopoly, since it is the agent of restraining and combating the use of force; and for that very same reason, its actions have to be rigidly defined, delimited and circumscribed; no touch of whim or caprice should be permitted in its performance; it should be an impersonal robot, with the laws as its only motive power. If a society is to be free, its government has to be controlled.

Under a proper social system, a private individual is legally free to take any action he pleases (so long as he does not violate the rights of others), while a government official is bound by law in his every official act. A private individual may do anything except that which is legally *forbidden*; a government official may do nothing except that which is legally *permitted*.

This is the means of subordinating "might" to "right." This is the American concept of "a government of laws and not of men."

The nature of the laws proper to a free society and the source of its government's authority are both to be derived from the nature and purpose of a proper government. The basic principle of both is indicated in the Declaration of Independence: "to secure these [individual] rights, governments are instituted among men, deriving their just powers from the consent of the governed . . ."

Since the protection of individual rights is the only proper purpose of a government, it is the only proper subject of legislation: all laws must be based on individual rights and aimed at their protection. All laws must be *objective* (and objectively justifiable): men must know clearly, and in advance of taking an action, what the law forbids them to do (and why), what constitutes a crime and what penalty they will incur if they commit it.

The source of the government's authority is "the consent of the governed." This means that the government is not the *ruler*, but the servant or *agent* of the citizens; it means that the government as such has no rights except the rights *delegated* to it by the citizens for a specific purpose.

There is only one basic principle to which an individual must consent if he wishes to live in a free, civilized society: the principle of renouncing the use of physical force and delegating to the government his right of physical self-defense, for the purpose of an orderly, objective, legally defined enforcement. Or, to put it another way, he must accept *the separation of force and whim* (any whim, including his own).

Now what happens in case of a disagreement between two men about an undertaking in which both are involved?

In a free society, men are not forced to deal with one another. They do so only by voluntary agreement and, when a time element is involved, by *contract.* If a contract is broken by the arbitrary decision of one man, it may cause a disastrous financial injury to the other—and the victim would have no recourse except to seize the offender's property as compensation. But here again, the use of force cannot be left to the decision of private individuals. And this leads to one of the most important and most complex functions of the government: to the function of an arbiter who settles disputes among men according to objective laws.

Criminals are a small minority in any semicivilized society. But the protection and enforcement of contracts through courts of civil law is the most crucial need of a peaceful society; without such protection, no civilization could be developed or maintained.

Man cannot survive, as animals do, by acting on the range of the immediate moment. Man has to project his goals and achieve them across a span of time; he has to calculate his actions and plan his life long-range. The better a man's mind and the greater his knowledge, the longer the range of his planning. The higher or more complex a civilization, the longer the range of activity it requires—and, therefore, the longer the range of contractual agreements among men, and the more urgent their need of protection for the security of such agreements.

Even a primitive barter society could not function if a man agreed to trade a bushel of potatoes for a basket of eggs and, having received the eggs, refused to deliver the potatoes. Visualize what this sort of whim-directed action would mean in an industrial society where men deliver a billion dollars' worth of goods on credit, or contract to build multimillion-dollar structures, or sign ninety-nine-year leases.

A unilateral breach of contract involves an indirect use of physical force: it consists, in essence, of one man receiving the material values, goods or services of another, then refusing to pay for them and thus keeping them by force (by mere physical possession), not by right—*i.e.*, keeping them without the consent of their owner. Fraud involves a similarly indirect use of force: it consists of obtaining material values without their owner's consent, under false pretenses or false promises. Extortion is another variant of an indirect use of force: it consists of obtaining material values, not in exchange for values, but by the threat of force, violence or injury.

Some of these actions are obviously criminal. Others, such as a unilateral breach of contract, may not be criminally motivated, but may be caused by irresponsibility and irrationality. Still others may be complex issues with some claim to justice on both sides. But whatever the case may be, all such issues have to be made subject to objectively defined laws and have to be resolved by an impartial arbiter, administering the laws, *i.e.*, by a judge (and a jury, when appropriate).

Observe the basic principle governing justice in all these cases: it is the principle that no man may obtain any values from others without the owners' consent—and, as a corollary, that a man's rights may not be left at the mercy of the unilateral decision, the arbitrary choice, the irrationality, *the whim* of another man.

Such, in essence, is the proper purpose of a government: to make social existence possible to men, by protecting the benefits and combating the evils which men can cause to one another.

The proper functions of a government fall into three broad categories, all of them involving the issues of physical force and the protection of men's rights: *the police*, to protect men from criminals—*the armed services*, to protect men from foreign invaders—*the law courts*, to settle disputes among men according to objective laws.

These three categories involve many corollary and derivative issues—and their implementation in practice, in the form of specific legislation, is enormously complex. It belongs to the field of a special science: the philosophy of law. Many errors and many disagreements are possible in the field of implementation, but what is essential here is the principle to be implemented: the principle that the purpose of law and of government is the protection of individual rights.

Today, this principle is forgotten, ignored and evaded. The result is the present state of the world, with mankind's retrogression to the lawlessness of absolutist tyranny, to the primitive savagery of rule by brute force.

In unthinking protest against this trend, some people are raising the question of whether government as such is evil by nature and whether anarchy is the ideal social system. Anarchy, as a political concept, is a naive floating abstraction: for all the reasons discussed above, a society without an organized government would be at the mercy of the first criminal who came along and who would precipitate it into the chaos of gang warfare. But the possibility of human immorality is not the only objection to anarchy: even a society whose every member were fully rational and faultlessly moral, could not function in a state of anarchy: it is the need of *objective* laws and of an arbiter for honest disagreements among men that necessitates the establishment of a government.

A recent variant of anarchistic theory, which is befuddling some of the younger advocates of freedom, is a weird absurdity called "competing governments." Accepting the basic premise of the modern statists—who see no difference between the functions of government and the functions of industry, between force and production, and who advocate government ownership of business—the proponents of "competing governments" take the other side of the same coin and declare that since competition is so beneficial to business, it should also be applied to government. Instead of a single, monopolistic government, they declare, there should be a number of different governments in the same geographical area, competing for the allegiance of individual citizens, with every citizen free to "shop" and to patronize whatever government he chooses.

Remember that forcible restraint of men is the only service a government has to offer. Ask yourself what a competition in forcible restraint would have to mean.

One cannot call this theory a contradiction in terms, since it is obviously devoid of any understanding of the terms "competition" and "government." Nor can one call it a floating abstraction, since it is devoid of any contact with or reference to reality and cannot be concretized at all, not even roughly or approximately. One illustration will be sufficient: suppose Mr. Smith, a customer of Government A, suspects that his next-door neighbor, Mr. Jones, a customer of Government B, has robbed him; a squad of Police A proceeds to Mr. Jones' house and is met at the door by a squad of Police B, who declare that they do not accept the validity of Mr. Smith's complaint and do not recognize the authority of Government A. What happens then? You take it from there.

The evolution of the concept of "government" has had a long, tortuous history. Some glimmer of the government's proper function seems to have existed in every organized society, manifesting itself in such phenomena as the recognition of some implicit (if often nonexistent) difference between a government and a robber gang—the aura of respect and of moral authority granted to the government as the guardian of "law and order"—the fact that even the most evil types of government found it necessary to maintain some semblance of order and some pretense at justice, if only by routine and tradition, and to claim some sort of moral justification for their power, of a mystical or social nature. Just as the absolute monarchs of France had to invoke "The Divine Right of Kings," so the modern dictators of Soviet Russia have to spend fortunes on propaganda to justify their rule in the eyes of their enslaved subjects.

In mankind's history, the understanding of the government's proper function is a very recent achievement: it is only two hundred years old and it dates from the Founding Fathers of the American Revolution. Not only did they identify the nature and the needs of a free society, but they devised the means to translate it into practice. A free society—like any other human product—cannot be achieved by random means, by mere wishing or by the leaders' "good intentions." A complex legal system, based on *objectively* valid principles, is required to make a society free and *to keep it free*—a system that does not depend on the motives, the moral character or the intentions of any given official, a system that leaves no opportunity, no legal loophole for the development of tyranny.

The American system of checks and balances was just such an achievement. And although certain contradictions in the Constitution did leave a loophole for the growth of statism, the incomparable achievement was the concept of a constitution as a means of limiting and restricting the power of the government.

Today, when a concerted effort is made to obliterate this point, it cannot be repeated too often that the Constitution is a limitation on the government, not on private individuals—that it does not prescribe the conduct of private individuals, only the conduct of the government—that it is not a charter *for* government power, but a charter of the citizens' protection *against* the government.

Now consider the extent of the moral and political inversion in today's prevalent view of government. Instead of being a protector of man's rights, the government is becoming their most dangerous violator; instead of guarding freedom, the government is establishing slavery; instead of protecting men from the initiators of physical force, the government is initiating physical force and coercion in any manner and issue it pleases; instead of serving as the instrument of *objectivity* in human relationships, the government is creating a deadly, subterranean reign of uncertainty and fear, by means of nonobjective laws whose interpretation is left to the arbitrary decisions of random bureaucrats; instead of protecting men from injury by whim, the government is arrogating to itself the power of unlimited whim—so that we are fast approaching the stage of the ultimate inversion: the stage where the government is *free* to do anything it pleases, while the citizens may act only by *permission*; which is the stage of the darkest periods of human history, the stage of rule by brute force.

It has often been remarked that in spite of its material progress, mankind has not achieved any comparable degree of moral progress. That remark is usually followed by some pessimistic conclusion about human nature. It is true that the moral state of mankind is disgracefully low. But if one considers the monstrous moral inversions of the governments (made possible by the altruist-collectivist morality) under which mankind has had to live through most of its history, one begins to wonder how men have managed to preserve even a semblance of civilization, and what indestructible vestige of self-esteem has kept them walking upright on two feet.

One also begins to see more clearly the nature of the political principles that have to be accepted and advocated, as part of the battle for man's intellectual Renaissance.

(December 1963)

NOTES

EARTH
John Hall Wheelock

(1886–1978)

John Hall Wheelock was a poet, scholar, and editor. While at Harvard, he was class poet. In 1972 he received the prestigious Gold Medal by the Poetry Society of America.

"A planet doesn't explode of itself," said drily
The Martian astronomer, gazing off into the air—
"That they were able to do it is proof that highly
Intelligent beings must have been living there."

Reprinted from *The Gardener and Other Poems* (1961), by permission of Simon & Schuster, Inc.

NOTES

THE INDIVIDUAL IN THE COMMUNITY

"We have held the peculiar notion that a person or society that is a little different from us, whoever we are, is somehow strange or bizarre, to be distrusted or loathed. Think of the negative connotations of words like alien or outlandish. And yet the monuments and cultures of each of our civilizations merely represent different ways of being human. . . .

The Cosmos may be densely populated with intelligent beings. But the Darwinian lesson is clear: There will be no humans elsewhere. Only here. Only on this small planet. We are as rare as well as an endangered species. Every one of us is, in the cosmic perspective, precious. If a human disagrees with you, let him live. In a hundred billion galaxies, you will not find another."

Carl Sagan (1934–1996) Astronomer, Author, Educator

"I have learned over the years that when one's mind is made up, this diminishes fear; knowing what must be done does away with fear."

Rosa Parks (1913–2005) African-American civil rights activist

REQUIRED READINGS

"I'm undecided, but that doesn't mean I'm apathetic or uninformed."

Courtesy of Charles Barsotti/The New Yorker Collection.

THE REPUBLIC
Plato

(427?–347? B.C.)

A philosopher and teacher of ancient Greece, Plato remains one of the most important and influential thinkers and writers in the history of Western culture.

Glaucon and the others begged me not to abandon the argument but to help in every way to track down what justice and injustice each is, and the truth about their respective benefits. So I told them what I had in mind:

The investigation we are undertaking is not an easy one, in my view, but
requires keen eyesight. So, since we are not clever people, I think we should
adopt the method of investigation that we would use if, lacking keen eye- d
sight, we were told to identify small letters from a distance, and then
noticed that the same letters existed elsewhere in a larger size and on a larger
surface. We would consider it a godsend, I think, to be allowed to identify
the larger ones first, and then to examine the smaller ones to see whether
they are really the same.

ADEIMANTUS: Of course we would. But how is this case similar to our
investigation of justice in your view? e

SOCRATES: I will tell you. We say, don't we, that there is a justice that belongs to a single man, and also one that belongs to a whole city?

ADEIMANTUS: Certainly.

SOCRATES: And a city is larger than a single man?

ADEIMANTUS: Yes, it is larger.

SOCRATES: Perhaps, then, there will be more justice in the larger thing,
and it will be easier to discern. So, if you are willing, let's first find out
what sort of thing justice is in cities, and afterward look for it in the indi- 369a
vidual, to see if the larger entity is similar in form to the smaller one.

ADEIMANTUS: I think that is a fine idea.

SOCRATES: If, in our discussion, we could look at a city coming to be, wouldn't we also see its justice coming to be, and its injustice as well?

ADEIMANTUS: We probably would.

SOCRATES: And once that process is completed, could we expect to find what we are looking for more easily?

ADEIMANTUS: Yes, much more easily. b

SOCRATES: Do you think we should try to carry it out then? It is no small task, in my view. So, think it over.

ADEIMANTUS: It has been thought over. Don't do anything besides try.

Reprinted from *The Republic*, translated by C.D.C. Reeves (2004), Hackett Publishing Company, Inc.

SOCRATES: Well, then, a city comes to exist, I believe, because none of us is individually self-sufficient, but each has many needs he cannot satisfy. Or do you think that a city is founded on some other principle?

ADEIMANTUS: No, none.

SOCRATES: Then because we have many needs, and because one of us
c calls on another out of one need, and on a third out of a different need, we gather many into a single settlement as partners and helpers. And we call such a shared settlement a city. Isn't that so?

ADEIMANTUS: Yes, indeed.

SOCRATES: And if they share things with one another—if they give something to one another, or take something from one another—don't they do so because each believes that this is better for himself?

ADEIMANTUS: Of course.

SOCRATES: Come on, then, let's, in our discussion, create a city from the beginning. But its real creator, it seems, will be our need.

ADEIMANTUS: Certainly.

d SOCRATES: Now, the first and greatest of our needs is to provide food in order to sustain existence and life.

ADEIMANTUS: Yes, absolutely.

SOCRATES: The second is for shelter, and the third is for clothes and things of that sort.

ADEIMANTUS: That's right.

SOCRATES: Tell me, then, how will a city be able to provide all this? Won't one person have to be a farmer, another a builder, and another a weaver? And shouldn't we add a shoemaker to them, or someone else to take care of our bodily needs?

ADEIMANTUS: Of course.

SOCRATES: A city with the barest necessities, then, would consist of four or five men?

e ADEIMANTUS: Apparently.

SOCRATES: Well, then, should each of them contribute his own work for the common use of all? I mean, should a farmer, although he is only one person, provide food for four people, and spend quadruple the time and labor to provide food to be shared by them all? Or should he not be concerned about everyone else? Should he produce one quarter the food in one quarter the time for himself alone? Should he spend the other three
370a quarters providing a house, a cloak, and shoes? Should he save himself the bother of sharing with other people and mind his own business on his own?

ADEIMANTUS: The first alternative, Socrates, is perhaps easier.

SOCRATES: There is nothing strange in that, by Zeus. You see, it occurred to me while you were speaking that, in the first place, we are not all born alike. On the contrary, each of us differs somewhat in nature from the
b others, one being suited to one job, another to another. Or don't you think so?

ADEIMANTUS: I do.

SOCRATES: Well, then, would one person do better work if he practiced many crafts or if he practiced one?

ADEIMANTUS: If he practiced one.

SOCRATES: And it is also clear, I take it, that if one misses the opportune moment in any job, the work is spoiled.

ADEIMANTUS: It is clear.

SOCRATES: That, I take it, is because the thing that has to be done won't wait until the doer has the leisure to do it. No, instead the doer must, of necessity, pay close attention to what has to be done and not leave it for his idle moments.

ADEIMANTUS: Yes, he must.

SOCRATES: The result, then, is that more plentiful and better-quality goods are more easily produced, if each person does one thing for which he is naturally suited and does it at the opportune moment, because his time is freed from all the others.

ADEIMANTUS: Absolutely.

SOCRATES: Then, Adeimantus, we are going to need more than four citizens to provide the things we have mentioned. For a farmer won't make his own plow, it seems, if it is going to be a good one, nor his hoe, nor any of his other farm implements. Nor will a carpenter—and he, too, needs lots of tools. And the same is true of a weaver and a shoemaker, isn't it?

* * *

SOCRATES: So, should we be more concerned about the craft of shoemaking that the craft of warfare?

GLAUCON: Not at all.

SOCRATES: Well, now, we prevented a shoemaker from trying to be a farmer, weaver, or builder at the same time, instead of just a shoemaker, in order to ensure that the shoemaker's job was done well. Similarly, we also assigned just the one job for which he had a natural aptitude to each of the other people, and said that he was to work at it his whole life, free from having to do any of the other jobs, so as not to miss the opportune moments for performing it well. But isn't it of the greatest importance that warfare be carried out well? Or is fighting a war so easy that a farmer, a shoemaker, or any other artisan can be a soldier at the same time, even though no one can become so much as a good checkers player or dice player if he considers it only as a sideline and does not practice it from childhood? Can someone just pick up a shield, or another weapon or instrument of war and immediately become a competent fighter in an infantry battle or whatever other sort of battle it may be, even though no other tool makes someone who picks it up a craftsman or an athlete, or is even of any service to him unless he has acquired knowledge of it and has had sufficient practice?

GLAUCON: If tools could do that, they would be valuable indeed.

e SOCRATES: Then to the degree that the guardians' job is of greatest importance, it requires the most freedom from other things, as well as the greatest craft and practice.

GLAUCON: I should think so.

SOCRATES: And doesn't it also require a person whose nature is suited to that very practice?

GLAUCON: Certainly.

SOCRATES: Then our task, it seems, is to select, if we can, which natures, which sorts of natures, suit people to guard the city.

GLAUCON: Yes, that is our task.

SOCRATES: By Zeus, it is no trivial task that we have taken on, then. All the same, we must not shrink from it, but do the best we can.

375a GLAUCON: No, we must not.

SOCRATES: Do you think that there is any difference, when it comes to the job of guarding, between the nature of a noble hound and that of a well-bred youth?

GLAUCON: What do you mean?

SOCRATES: I mean that both of them have to be sharp-eyed, quick to catch what they see, and strong, too, in case they have to fight what they capture.

GLAUCON: Yes, they need all these things.

SOCRATES: And they must be courageous, surely, if indeed they are to fight well.

GLAUCON: Of course.

SOCRATES: Now, will a horse, a dog, or any other animal be courageous if it is not spirited? Or haven't you noticed just how invincible and unbeat-
b able spirit is, so that its presence makes the whole soul fearless and unconquerable in any situation?

GLAUCON: I have noticed that.

SOCRATES: Then it is clear what physical qualities the guardians should have.

GLAUCON: Yes.

SOCRATES: And as far as their souls are concerned, they must, at any rate, be spirited.

GLAUCON: That too.

SOCRATES: But with natures like that, Glaucon, how will they avoid to behaving like savages to one another and to the other citizens?

GLAUCON: By Zeus, it won't be easy for them.

c SOCRATES: But surely they must be gentle to their own people and harsh to their enemies. Otherwise, they will not wait around for others to destroy them, but will do it themselves first.

GLAUCON: That's true.

SOCRATES: What are we to do, then? Where are we to find a character that is both gentle and high-spirited at the same time? For, of course, a gentle nature is the opposite of the spirited kind.

GLAUCON: Apparently.

SOCRATES: But surely if someone lacks either of these qualities, he cannot be a good guardian. Yet the combination of them seems to be impossible. And so it follows, then, that a good guardian is impossible. d

GLAUCON: I am afraid so.

I could not see a way out, and on reexamining what had gone before, I said:

We deserve to be stuck, my dear Glaucon. For we have lost track of the analogy we put forward.

GLAUCON: How do you mean?

SOCRATES: We have overlooked the fact that there *are* natures of the sort we thought impossible, ones that include these opposite qualities.

GLAUCON: Where?

SOCRATES: You can see the combination in other animals, too, but especially in the one to which we compared the guardian. For you know, of course, that noble hounds naturally have a character of that sort. They e are as gentle as can be to those they are familiar with and know, but the opposite to those they do not know.

GLAUCON: Yes, I do know that.

SOCRATES: So the combination we want *is* possible, after all, and what we are seeking in a good guardian is not contrary to nature.

GLAUCON: No, I suppose not.

SOCRATES: Now, don't you think that our future guardian, besides being spirited, must also be, by nature, philosophical?[18]

GLAUCON: How do you mean? I don't understand. 376a

SOCRATES: It too is something you see in dogs, and it should make us wonder at the merit of the beast.

GLAUCON: In what way?

SOCRATES: In that when a dog sees someone it does not know, it gets angry even before anything bad happens to it. But when it knows someone, it welcomes him, even if it has never received anything good from him. Have you never wondered at that?

GLAUCON: I have never paid it any mind until now. But it is clear that a dog does do that sort of thing.

SOCRATES: Well, that seems to be a naturally refined quality, and one that is truly philosophical. b

GLAUCON: In what way?

SOCRATES: In that it judges anything it sees to be either a friend or an enemy on no other basis than that it knows the one and does not know

[18] *Philosophos:* used here in its general sense to refer to intellectual curiosity or wanting knowledge for its own sake.

the other. And how could it be anything besides a lover of learning[19] if it defines what is its own and what is alien to it in terms of knowledge and ignorance?

GLAUCON: It surely could not be anything but.

SOCRATES: But surely the love of learning and philosophy are the same, aren't they?

GLAUCON: Yes, they are the same.

SOCRATES: Then can't we confidently assume that the same holds for a human being too—that if he is going to be gentle to his own and those c he knows, he must be, by nature, a lover of learning and a philosopher?

GLAUCON: We can.

SOCRATES: Philosophy, then, and spirit, speed, and strength as well, must all be combined in the nature of anyone who is going to be a really fine and good guardian of our city.

GLAUCON: Absolutely.

SOCRATES: Then that is what he would have to be like at the outset. But how are we to bring these people up and educate them? Will inquiring into that topic bring us any closer to the goal of our inquiry, which is to d discover the origins of justice and injustice in a city? We want our account to be adequate, but we do not want it to be any longer than necessary.

And Glaucon's brother replied:

I for one certainly expect that this inquiry will help us.

SOCRATES: By Zeus, in that case, my dear Adeimantus, we must not abandon it, even if it turns out to be a somewhat lengthy affair.

ADEIMANTUS: No, we must not.

SOCRATES: Come on, then, and like people in a fable telling stories at their leisure, let's in our discussion educate these men.

e ADEIMANTUS: Yes, let's.

* * *

SOCRATES: Then shall we also establish this law for the guardian, that c they should neither ravage Greek land nor burn Greek houses?

GLAUCON: Yes, let's establish it. And let's assume that this law and its predecessors are right. But, Socrates, I think that if you are allowed to go on talking about this sort of thing, you will never remember the topic you set aside in order to say all this—namely, whether it is possible for this constitution to come into existence, and how it could ever do so. I agree that *if* it came into existence, everything would be lovely for the city that had it. I will even add some advantages that you have left out: they would fight excellently against their enemies because they would be d least likely to desert each other. After all, they recognize each other as brothers, fathers, and sons, and call each other by those names. And if

[19] *Philomathês.*

the women, too, joined in their campaigns, either stationed in the same ranks or in the rear, either to strike terror in the enemy or to provide support should the need ever arise, I know that this would make them quite unbeatable. And I also see all the good things they would have at home that you have omitted. Take it for granted that I agree that all these bene- e
fits, as well as innumerable others, would result, *if* this constitution came into existence, and say no more about it. Instead, let's now try to convince ourselves of just this: that it is possible and how it is possible, and let's leave the rest aside.

SOCRATES: All of a sudden, you have practically assaulted my argument 472a
and lost all sympathy for my holding back. Perhaps you do not realize that just as I have barely escaped from the first two waves of objections, you are now bringing the greatest and most difficult of the three down upon me.[43] When you see and hear it, you will have complete sympathy and recognize that I had good reason after all for hesitating and for being afraid to state and try to examine so paradoxical an argument.

GLAUCON: The more you talk like that, the less we will let you get away without explaining how this constitution could come into existence. So b
explain it, and do not delay any further.

SOCRATES: The first thing to recall, then, is that it was our inquiry into the nature of justice and injustice that brought us to this point.

GLAUCON: True. But what of it?

SOCRATES: Oh, nothing. However, if we discover the nature of justice, should we also expect the just man not to differ from justice itself in any way, but, on the contrary, to have entirely the same nature it does? Or will we be satisfied if he approximates as closely as possible to it and par- c
takes in it far more than anyone else?

GLAUCON: Yes, we will be satisfied with that.

SOCRATES: So, it was in order to have a model that we were inquiring into the nature of justice itself and of the completely just man, supposing he could exist, and what he would be like if he did; and similarly with injustice and the most unjust man. We thought that by seeing how they seemed to us to stand with regard to happiness and its opposite, we would also be compelled to agree about ourselves as well: that the one who was most like them would have a fate most like theirs. But we were not doing d
this in order to demonstrate that it is possible for these men to exist.

GLAUCON: That's true.

SOCRATES: Do you think, then, that someone would be any less good a painter if he painted a model of what the most beautiful human being would be like, and rendered everything in the picture perfectly well, but could not demonstrate that such a man could actually exist?

GLAUCON: No, by Zeus, I do not.

---

[43] The third wave was proverbially the greatest.

SOCRATES: What about our own case, then? Weren't we trying, as we put
e it, to produce a model in our discussion of a good city?[44]

GLAUCON: Certainly.

SOCRATES: So, do you think that our discussion will be any less satisfactory if we cannot demonstrate that it is possible to found a city that is the same as the one we described in speech?

GLAUCON: Not at all.

SOCRATES: Then that is the truth of the matter. But if, in order to please you, we must do our best to demonstrate how, and under what condition, this would be most possible, you must again grant me the same points for the purposes of that demonstration.

GLAUCON: Which ones?

SOCRATES: Is it possible for anything to be carried out exactly as
described in speech, or is it natural for practice to have less of a grasp of
473a truth than speech does, even if some people do not think so? Do you
agree with this or not?

GLAUCON: I do.

SOCRATES: Then do not compel me to demonstrate it as coming about in
practice exactly as we have described it in speech. Rather, if we are able to
discover how a city that most closely approximates to what we have
described could be founded, you must admit that we have discovered
b how all you have prescribed could come about.[45] Or wouldn't you be satisfied with that? *I* certainly would.

GLAUCON: Me, too.

SOCRATES: Then next, it seems, we should try to discover and show what is badly done in cities nowadays that prevents them from being managed our way, and what the smallest change would be that would enable a city to arrive at our sort of constitution—preferably one change; otherwise, two; otherwise, the fewest in number and the least extensive in effect.

c GLAUCON: Absolutely.

SOCRATES: Well, there is one change we could point to that I think would accomplish this. It certainly is not small or easy, but it *is* possible.

GLAUCON: What is it?

SOCRATES: I am now about to confront what we likened to the greatest wave. Yet, it must be stated, even if it is going to drown me in a wave of outright ridicule and contempt, as it were. So listen to what I am about to say.

GLAUCON: Say it.

SOCRATES: Until philosophers rule as kings in their cities, or those who
are nowadays called kings and leading men become genuine and ade-
d quate philosophers so that political power and philosophy become thor-

---

[44] See 369a5–c10.

[45] As at 458c6 and 473e4–5, Socrates is supposing that Glaucon is designing the ideal city.

oughly blended together, while the numerous natures that now pursue either one exclusively are compelled not to do so, cities will have no rest from evils, my dear Glaucon, nor, I think, will the human race. And until that happens, the same constitution we have now described in our discussion will never be born to the extent that it can, or see the light of the e sun. It is this claim that has made me hesitate to speak for so long. I saw how very unbelievable it would sound, since it is difficult to accept that there can be no happiness, either public or private, in any other way.

GLAUCON: Socrates, what a speech, what an argument you have let burst with! But now that you have uttered it, you must expect that a great many people—and not undistinguished ones either—will immediately throw off their cloaks and, stripped for action, snatch any available 474a weapon and make a headlong rush at you, determined to do terrible things to you. So, if you do not defend yourself by argument and escape, you really will pay the penalty of general derision.

SOCRATES: But aren't *you* the one who is responsible for this happening to me?

GLAUCON: And I was right to do it. Still, I won't desert you. On the contrary, I will defend you in any way I can. And what I can do is provide good will and encouragement, and maybe give you more careful answers to your questions than someone else. So, with the promise of this sort of assistance, try to demonstrate to the unbelievers that things are as you claim. b

SOCRATES: I will have to, especially when you agree to be so great an ally! If we are going to escape from the people you mention, I think we need to define for them who the philosophers are that we dare to say should rule; so that once that is clear, one can defend oneself by showing that some people are fitted by nature to engage in philosophy *and* to take the c lead in a city, while there are others who should not engage in it, but should follow a leader.

GLAUCON: This would be a good time to define them.

SOCRATES: Come on, then, follow me on the path I am about to take, to see if it somehow leads to an adequate explanation.

GLAUCON: Lead on.

SOCRATES: Do I have to remind you, or do you recall, that when we say someone loves something, if the description is correct, it must be clear not just that he loves some part of it but not another; but, on the contrary, that he cherishes the whole of it?[46]

GLAUCON: You will have to remind me, it seems. I do not recall the point at all. d

SOCRATES: I did not expect you to give that response, Glaucon. A passionate man should not forget that *all* boys in the bloom of youth somehow manage to sting and arouse a passionate lover of boys, and seem to

[46] See 437d8–e8, 475b11–c4.

merit his attention and passionate devotion. Isn't that the way you people behave to beautiful boys? One, because he is snub-nosed, you will praise as "cute"; another who is hook-nosed you will say is "regal"; while the one in the middle you say is "well proportioned." Dark ones look e "manly," and pale ones are "children of the gods." As for the "honey-colored," do you think that this very term is anything but the euphemistic coinage of a lover who found it easy to tolerate a sallow complexion, provided it was accompanied by the bloom of youth? In a word, you people find any excuse, and use any expression, to avoid rejecting 475a anyone whose flower is in full bloom.

GLAUCON: If you insist on taking *me* as your example of what passionate men do, I will go along with you . . . for the sake of argument!

SOCRATES: What about lovers of wine? Don't you observe them behaving in just the same way? Don't they find any excuse to indulge their passionate devotion to wine of any sort?

GLAUCON: They do, indeed.

SOCRATES: And you also observe, I imagine, that if honor-lovers cannot become generals, they serve as lieutenants,[47] and if they cannot be honored by important people and dignitaries, they are satisfied with being b honored by insignificant and inferior ones, since it is honor as a whole for which they have an appetite.

GLAUCON: Exactly.

SOCRATES: Then do you affirm this or not? When we say that someone has an appetite for something, are we to say that he has an appetite for everything of that kind, or for one part of it but not another?

GLAUCON: Everything.

SOCRATES: Then in the case of the philosopher, too, won't we say that he has an appetite for *wisdom*—not for one part and not another, but for all of it?

GLAUCON: True.

SOCRATES: So, if someone makes difficulties about what he learns, espe- c cially if he is young and does not have a rational grasp of what is useful and what is not, we won't say that he is a lover of learning or a philosopher—any more than we would say that someone who is choosy about his food is famished, or has an appetite for food, or is a lover of food rather than a picky eater.

GLAUCON: And we would be right not to say it.

SOCRATES: But someone who is ready and willing to taste every kind of learning, who turns gladly to learning and is insatiable for it, *he* is the one we would be justified in calling a philosopher. Isn't that so?

---

47 *Trittarchousi:* "command the soldiers in a trittys." A trittys was one third of one of the ten tribes of which Athens consisted.

GLAUCON: In that case, many strange people will be philosophers! I d
mean, all the lovers of seeing are what they are, I imagine, because they take pleasure in learning things. And the lovers of listening are very strange people to include as philosophers: they would never willingly attend a serious discussion or spend their time that way; yet, just as if their ears were under contract to listen to every chorus, they run around to all the Dionysiac festivals, whether in cities or villages, and never miss one. Are we to say that these people—and others who are students of
similar things or of petty crafts—are philosophers? e

SOCRATES: Not at all, but they are *like* philosophers.

GLAUCON: Who do you think, then, are the true ones?

SOCRATES: The lovers of seeing the truth.

GLAUCON: That, too, is no doubt correct,[48] but what exactly do you mean by it?

SOCRATES: It would not be easy to explain to someone else. But you, I imagine, will agree to the following.

GLAUCON: What?

SOCRATES: That since beautiful is the opposite of ugly, they are two things.

GLAUCON: Of course. 476a

SOCRATES: And since they are two things, each of them is also one?

GLAUCON: That's true too.

SOCRATES: And the same argument applies, then, to just and unjust, good and bad, and all the forms: each of them is itself one thing, but because they appear all over the place in partnership with actions and bodies, and with one another, each of them appears to be many things.

GLAUCON: That's right.

SOCRATES: Well, then, that is the basis of the distinction I draw: on one side are the lovers of seeing, the lovers of crafts, and the practical people you mentioned a moment ago; on the other, those we are arguing about,
the only ones it is correct to call philosophers. b

GLAUCON: How do you mean?

SOCRATES: The lovers of listening and seeing are passionately devoted to beautiful sounds, colors, shapes, and everything fashioned out of such things.[49] But their thought is unable to see the nature of the beautiful itself or to be passionately devoted to it.

GLAUCON: That's certainly true.

SOCRATES: On the other hand, won't those who *are* able to approach the beautiful itself, and see it by itself, be rare?

GLAUCON: Very. c

---

[48] See 449c6–8.

[49] A poem or play is fashioned out of sounds, a painting out of colors and shapes. See 600c4–601b4.

SOCRATES: What about someone who believes in beautiful things but does not believe in the beautiful itself, and would not be able to follow anyone who tried to lead him to the knowledge of it? Do you think he is living in a dream, or is he awake? Just consider. Isn't it dreaming to think—whether asleep or awake—that a likeness is not a likeness, but rather the thing itself that it is like?

GLAUCON: I certainly think that someone who does that is dreaming.

SOCRATES: But what about someone who, to take the opposite case, does believe in the beautiful itself, is able to observe both it and the things that
d participate in it, and does not think that the participants are it, or that it is the participants—do you think he is living in a dream or is awake?

GLAUCON: He is very much awake.

SOCRATES: So, because this person knows these things, we would be right to describe his thought as knowledge; but the other's we would be right to describe as belief, because he believes what he does?

GLAUCON: Certainly.

SOCRATES: What if the person we describe as believing but not knowing is angry with us and disputes the truth of what we say? Will we have any
e way of soothing and gently persuading him, while disguising the fact that he is not in a healthy state of mind?

GLAUCON: We certainly need one, at any rate.

SOCRATES: Come on, then, consider what we will say to him. Or—once we have told him that nobody envies him any knowledge he may have—that, on the contrary, we would be delighted to discover that he knows something—do you want us to question him as follows? "Tell us this: does someone who knows know something or nothing?" You answer for him.

GLAUCON: I will answer that he knows something.

SOCRATES: Something that is[50] or something that is not?

477a GLAUCON: That is. How could something that is not be known?

SOCRATES: We are adequately assured of this, then, and would remain so, no matter how many ways we examined it: what is completely is completely an object of knowledge and what is in no way at all is an object of ignorance.

GLAUCON: Most adequately.

SOCRATES: Good. In that case, then, if anything is such as to be and also not to be, wouldn't it lie in between what purely is and what in no way is?

GLAUCON: Yes, in between them.

SOCRATES: Then, since knowledge deals with what is, ignorance must deal with what is not, while we must look in between knowledge and ignorance for what deals with what lies in between, if there *is* anything of
b that sort.

GLAUCON: Yes.

SOCRATES: So, then, do we think there is such a thing as belief?

---

[50] See Glossary of Terms s.v. thing that is.

GLAUCON: Of course.

SOCRATES: Is it a different power from knowledge, or the same?

GLAUCON: A different one.

SOCRATES: So, belief has been assigned to deal with one thing, then, and knowledge with another, depending on what power each has.

GLAUCON: Right.

SOCRATES: Now, doesn't knowledge naturally deal with what is, to know how what is is? But first I think we should go through the following.

GLAUCON: What?

SOCRATES: We think powers are a type of thing that enables us—or any- c
thing else that has an ability—to do whatever we are able to do. Sight and hearing are examples of what I mean by powers, if you understand the kind of thing I am trying to describe.

GLAUCON: Yes, I do.

SOCRATES: Listen, then, to what I think about them. A power has no color for me to see, nor a shape, nor any feature of the sort that many other things have, and that I can consider in order to distinguish them for myself as different from one another. In the case of a power, I can consider only what it deals with and what it does, and it is on that basis
that I come to call each the power it is: those assigned to deal with the d
same things and do the same, I call the same; those that deal with different things and do different things, I call different. What about you? What do you do?

GLAUCON: The same.

SOCRATES: Going back, then, to where we left off, my very good fellow: do you think knowledge is itself a power? Or to what type would you assign it?

GLAUCON: To that one. It is the most effective power of all.

SOCRATES: What about belief? Shall we include it as a power or assign it
to a different kind? e

GLAUCON: Not at all. Belief is nothing other than the power that enables us to believe.

SOCRATES: But a moment ago you agreed that knowledge and belief are not the same.

GLAUCON: How could anyone with any sense think a fallible thing is the same as an infallible one?

SOCRATES: Fine. Then clearly we agree that belief is different from
knowledge. 478a

GLAUCON: Yes, it is different.

SOCRATES: Each of them, then, since it has a different power, deals by nature with something different?

GLAUCON: Necessarily.

SOCRATES: Surely knowledge deals with what is, to know what is as it is?

GLAUCON: Yes.

SOCRATES: Whereas belief, we say, believes?

GLAUCON: Yes.

SOCRATES: The very same thing that knowledge knows? Can the object of knowledge and the object of belief be the same? Or is that impossible?

GLAUCON: It is impossible, given what we have agreed. If different powers by nature deal with different things, and both opinion and knowledge
b are powers but, as we claim, different ones, it follows from these that the object of knowledge and the object of belief cannot be the same.

SOCRATES: Then if what is is the object of knowledge, mustn't the object of belief be something other than what is?

GLAUCON: Yes, it must be something different.

SOCRATES: Does belief, then, believe what is not? Or is it impossible even to believe what is not? Consider this: doesn't a believer take his belief to deal with something? Or is it possible to believe, yet to believe nothing?

GLAUCON: No, it is impossible.

SOCRATES: In fact, there is some single thing that a believer believes?

GLAUCON: Yes.

SOCRATES: But surely what is not is most correctly characterized not as a
c single thing, but as nothing?

GLAUCON: Of course.

SOCRATES: But we had to assign ignorance to what is not and knowledge to what is?

GLAUCON: Correct.

SOCRATES: So belief neither believes what is nor what is not?

GLAUCON: No, it does not.

SOCRATES: Then belief cannot be either ignorance or knowledge?

GLAUCON: Apparently not.

SOCRATES: Well, then, does it lie beyond these two, surpassing knowledge in clarity or ignorance in opacity?

GLAUCON: No, it does neither.

SOCRATES: Then does belief seem to you to be more opaque than knowledge but clearer than ignorance?

GLAUCON: Very much so.

d SOCRATES: It lies within the boundaries determined by them?

GLAUCON: Yes.

SOCRATES: So belief will lie in between the two?

GLAUCON: Absolutely.

SOCRATES: Now, didn't we say earlier that if something turned out both to be and not to be at the same time, it would lie in between what purely is and what in every way is not, and that neither knowledge nor ignorance would deal with it; but whatever it was again that turned out to lie in between ignorance and knowledge would?

GLAUCON: Correct.

SOCRATES: And now, what we are calling belief has turned out to lie in between them?

GLAUCON: It has.

SOCRATES: Apparently, then, it remains for us to find what partakes in both e being and not being, and cannot correctly be called purely one or the other, so that if we find it, we can justifiably call it the object of belief, thereby assigning extremes to extremes and in-betweens to in-betweens. Isn't that so?

GLAUCON: It is.

SOCRATES: Now that all that has been established, I want him to tell me this—the excellent fellow who believes that there is no beautiful itself, no form of beauty itself that remains always the same in all respects, but who 479a does believe that there are many beautiful things—I mean, that lover of seeing who cannot bear to hear anyone say that the beautiful is one thing, or the just, or any of the rest—I want him to answer this question: "My very good fellow," we will say, "of all the many beautiful things, is there one that won't also seem ugly? Or any just one that won't seem unjust? Or any pious one that won't seem impious?"

GLAUCON: There is not. On the contrary, it is inevitable that they would somehow seem both beautiful and ugly; and the same with the other b things you asked about.

SOCRATES: What about the many things that are doubles? Do they seem to be any the less halves than doubles?

GLAUCON: No.

SOCRATES: And again, will things that we say are great, small, light, or heavy be any more what we say they are than they will be the opposite?

GLAUCON: No, each of them is always both.

SOCRATES: Then is each of the many things any more what one says it is than it is not what one says it is?

GLAUCON: No, they are like those puzzles one hears at parties, or the children's riddle about the eunuch who threw something at a bat—the c one about what he threw at it and what it was in.[51] For these things, too, are ambiguous, and one cannot understand them as fixedly being or fixedly not being, or as both, or as neither.

SOCRATES: Do you know what to do with them, then, or anywhere better to put them than in between being and not being? Surely they cannot be more opaque than what is not, by not-being more than it; nor clearer than what is, by *being* more than it. d

GLAUCON: That's absolutely true.

SOCRATES: So, we have now discovered, it seems, that the masses' many conventional norms concerning beauty and the rest are somehow rolling around between what is not and what purely is.[52]

---

[51] The riddle seems to have been this: a man who is not a man saw and did not see a bird that was not a bird in a tree (*xulon*) that was not a tree; he hit (*ballein*) and did not hit it with a stone that was not a stone. The answer is that a eunuch with bad eyesight saw a bat on a rafter, threw a pumice stone at it, and missed. For "he saw a bird" is ambiguous between "he saw what was actually a bird" and "he saw what he took to be a bird," *xulon* means both "tree" and "rafter" or "roof tree," and *ballein* means both "to throw" and "to hit." The rest is obvious.

[52] See 484c6–d3, 493a6–494a4.

GLAUCON: We have.

SOCRATES: And we agreed earlier that if anything turned out to be of that sort, it would have to be called an object of belief, not an object of knowledge—a wandering, in-between object grasped by the in-between power.

GLAUCON: We did.

SOCRATES: As for those, then, who look at many beautiful things but do
e not see the beautiful itself, and are incapable of following another who
would lead them to it; or many just things but not the just itself, and
similarly with all the rest—these people, we will say, have beliefs about all
these things, but have no knowledge of what their beliefs are about.

GLAUCON: That is what we would have to say.

SOCRATES: On the other hand, what about those who in each case look at the things themselves that are always the same in every respect? Won't we say that they have knowledge, not mere belief?

GLAUCON: Once again, we would have to.

SOCRATES: Shall we say, then, that these people are passionately devoted
to and love the things with which knowledge deals, as the others are
480a devoted to and love the things with which belief deals? We have not forgotten, have we, that the latter love and look at beautiful sounds, colors,
and things of that sort, but cannot even bear the idea that the beautiful
itself is a thing that is?

GLAUCON: No, we have not.

SOCRATES: Will we be striking a false note,[53] then, if we call such people "philodoxers" (lovers of belief) rather than "philosophers" (lovers of wisdom or knowledge)?Will they be very angry with us if we call them that?

GLAUCON: Not if they take my advice. It is not in accord with divine law to be angry with the truth.

SOCRATES: So, those who in each case are passionately devoted to the thing itself are the ones we must call, not "philodoxers," but "philosophers"?

GLAUCON: Absolutely.

Book 6

Socrates' Narration Continues:

SOCRATES: Who the philosophers are, then, Glaucon, and who they aren't
484a has, through a somewhat lengthy argument and with much effort, somehow been made clear.

GLAUCON: That's probably because it could not easily have been done through a shorter one.

SOCRATES: I suppose not. Yet I, at least, think that the matter would have
been made even clearer if we had had only that topic to discuss, and not
the many others that remain for us to explore if we are to discover the
b difference between the just life and the unjust one.

[53] See 451b3.

GLAUCON: What comes after this one, then?

SOCRATES: What else but the one that comes next? Since the philosophers are the ones who are able to grasp what is always the same in all respects, while those who cannot—those who wander among the many things that vary in every sort of way—are not philosophers, which of the two should be the leaders of a city?

GLAUCON: What would be a reasonable answer for us to give?

SOCRATES: Whichever of them seems capable of guarding a city's laws and practices should be established as guardians. c

GLAUCON: That's right.

SOCRATES: So, is the answer to the following question clear: should a guardian who is going to keep watch over something be blind or keen-sighted?

GLAUCON: Of course it is.

SOCRATES: Well, do you think there is any difference, then, between the blind and those who are really deprived of the knowledge of each thing that is, and have no clear model of it in their souls—those who cannot look away, like painters, to what is most true, and cannot, by making constant reference to it and by studying it as exactly as possible, establish here on earth conventional norms concerning beautiful, just, or good d things[1] when they need to be established, or guard and preserve those that have been established?

GLAUCON: No, by Zeus, there is not much difference between them.

SOCRATES: Shall we appoint these blind people as our guardians, then, or those who know each thing that is, have no less experience than the others,[2] and are not inferior to them in any other part of virtue?

GLAUCON: It would be absurd to choose anyone but philosophers, if indeed they are not inferior in these other things. For the very area in which they are superior is just about the greatest one.

SOCRATES: Shouldn't we explain, then, how the same men can have both 485a sets of qualities?

GLAUCON: Certainly.

SOCRATES: Then, as we were saying at the beginning of this discussion, it is first necessary to understand the nature of philosophers.[3] And I think that if we can agree sufficiently about that, we will also agree that the same people *can* have both qualities, and that they alone should be leaders in cities.

GLAUCON: How so?

---

[1] See 479d3–5 for what happens to conventions not established in this way.

[2] See 539e2–540c2, 581c10–583a11.

[3] See 474b3–c3.

SOCRATES: Let's agree that philosophic natures always love the sort of
b learning that makes clear to them some feature of the being[4] that always is and does not wander around between coming-to-be and decaying.

GLAUCON: Yes, let's.

SOCRATES: And further, let's agree that they love all of it and are not willing to give up any part, whether great or small, significant or insignificant, just like the honor-lovers and passionate men we described before.[5]

GLAUCON: That's right.

SOCRATES: Consider next whether there is a further feature they must
c have in their nature if they are going to be the way we described.

GLAUCON: What?

SOCRATES: Truthfulness; that is to say they must never willingly tolerate falsehood in any form. On the contrary, they must hate it and have a natural affection for the truth.

GLAUCON: They probably should have that feature.

SOCRATES: But it is not only *probable,* my friend; it is entirely necessary for a naturally passionate man to love everything akin to or related to the boys he loves.

GLAUCON: That's right.

SOCRATES: Well, could you find anything that is more intimately related to wisdom than truth?

GLAUCON: Of course not.

SOCRATES: Then is it possible for the same nature to be a philosopher
d (lover of wisdom) and a lover of falsehood?

GLAUCON: Certainly not.

SOCRATES: So, right from childhood, a genuine lover of learning must strive above all for truth of every kind.

GLAUCON: Absolutely.

SOCRATES: But in addition, when someone's appetites are strongly inclined in one direction, we surely know that they become more weakly inclined in the others, just like a stream that has been partly diverted into another channel.

GLAUCON: Of course.

SOCRATES: Then when a person's desires flow toward learning and everything of that sort, they will be concerned, I imagine, with the pleasures that the soul experiences just by itself, and will be indifferent to those that come through the body—if indeed the person is not a counterfeit,
e but rather a true, philosopher.[6]

GLAUCON: That's entirely inevitable.

SOCRATES: A person like that will be temperate, then, and in no way a lover of money. After all, money and the big expenditures that go along

---

[4] See Glossary of Terms s.v. being.

[5] See 474d3–475b2.

[6] See *Phaedo* 64c10–67c3.

with it are sought for the sake of things that other people may take seriously, but that he does not.

GLAUCON: That's right.

SOCRATES: And of course, there is also this to consider when you are going to judge whether a nature is philosophic or not. 486a

GLAUCON: What?

SOCRATES: You should not overlook its sharing in illiberality; for surely petty-mindedness is altogether incompatible with that quality in a soul that is always reaching out to grasp all things as a whole, whether divine or human.

GLAUCON: That's absolutely true.

SOCRATES: And do you imagine that a thinker who is high-minded enough to look at all time and all being will consider human life to be a very great thing?

GLAUCON: He couldn't possibly.

SOCRATES: Then he won't consider death to be a terrible thing either, will he? b

GLAUCON: Not in the least.

SOCRATES: Then a cowardly and illiberal nature could not partake, apparently, in true philosophy.

GLAUCON: Not in my opinion.

SOCRATES: Well, then, is there any way that an orderly person, who is not money-loving, illiberal, a lying imposter, or a coward, could come to drive a hard bargain or be unjust?

GLAUCON: There is not.

SOCRATES: Moreover, when you are considering whether someone has a philosophic soul or not, you will consider whether he is just and gentle, right from the time he is young, or unsociable and savage.

GLAUCON: Of course.

SOCRATES: And you won't ignore this either, I imagine. c

GLAUCON: What?

SOCRATES: Whether he is a slow learner or a fast one. Or do you expect someone to love something sufficiently well when it pains him to do it and a lot of effort brings only a small return?

GLAUCON: No, it could not happen.

SOCRATES: What if he could retain nothing of what he learned, because he was completely forgetful? Could he fail to be empty of knowledge?

GLAUCON: Of course not.

SOCRATES: Then if he is laboring in vain, don't you think that in the end he is bound to hate himself and what he is doing?

GLAUCON: Of course.

SOCRATES: So let's never include a person with a forgetful soul among those who are sufficiently philosophical; the one we look for should be d good at remembering.

GLAUCON: Absolutely.

SOCRATES: Moreover, we would deny that an unmusical and graceless nature is drawn to anything besides what is disproportionate.

GLAUCON: Of course.

SOCRATES: And do you think that truth is akin to what is disproportionate or to what is proportionate?

GLAUCON: To what is proportionate.

SOCRATES: Then, in addition to those other things, let's look for a mind that has a natural sense of proportion and grace, one whose innate disposition makes it easy to lead to the form of each thing which is.

GLAUCON: Indeed.

e SOCRATES: Well, then, do you think the properties we have gone through aren't interconnected, or that any of them is in any way unnecessary to a soul that is going to have a sufficiently complete grasp of what is?

487a GLAUCON: No, they are all absolutely necessary.

SOCRATES: Is there any criticism you can find, then, of a pursuit that a person cannot practice adequately unless he is naturally good at remembering, quick to learn, high-minded, graceful, and a friend and relative of truth, justice, courage, and temperance?

GLAUCON: Not even Momus could criticize a pursuit like that.

SOCRATES: Well, then, when people of this sort are in perfect condition because of their education and their stage of life, wouldn't you entrust the city to them alone?

And Adeimantus replied:

b No one, Socrates, would be able to contradict these claims of yours. But all the same, here is pretty much the experience people have on any occasion on which they hear the sorts of things you are now saying: they think that because they are inexperienced in asking and answering questions, they are led astray a little bit by the argument at every question, and that when these little bits are added together at the end of the discussion, a great false step appears that is the opposite of what they said at the outset. Like the unskilled, who are trapped by the clever checkers players in the end and cannot make a move, they too are
c trapped in the end, and have nothing to say in this different kind of checkers, which is played not with pieces, but with words. Yet they are not a bit more inclined to think that what you claim is true. I say this in relation to the present case. You see, someone might well say now that he is unable to find the words to oppose you as you ask each of your questions. Yet, when it comes to facts rather than words, he sees that of all those who take up philosophy—not those who merely dabble in it while still young in order to complete their upbringing, and then drop it, but those who continue in it for a longer time—the majority
d become cranks, not to say completely bad, while the ones who seem best are rendered useless to the city because of the pursuit you recommend.

When I had heard him out, I said:

Do you think that what these people say is false?

ADEIMANTUS: I do not know. But I would be glad to hear what you think.

SOCRATES: You would hear that they seem to me to be telling the truth.

ADEIMANTUS: How, then, can it be right to say that there will be no end to evils in our cities until philosophers—people we agree to be useless to e cities—rule in them?

SOCRATES: The question you ask needs to be answered by means of an image.[7]

ADEIMANTUS: And you, of course, are not used to speaking in images!

SOCRATES: So! After landing me with a claim that is so difficult to establish, are you mocking me, too? Anyway, listen to my image, and you will 488a appreciate all the more how I have to strain to make up images. What the best philosophers experience in relation to cities is so difficult to bear that there is no other single experience like it. On the contrary, one must construct one's image and one's defense of these philosophers from *many* sources, just as painters paint goat-stags by combining the features of different things.

Imagine, then, that the following sort of thing happens either on one ship or on many. The shipowner is taller and stronger than everyone else on board. But he is hard of hearing, he is a bit shortsighted, and his b knowledge of seafaring is correspondingly deficient. The sailors are quarreling with one another about captaincy.[8] Each of them thinks that he should captain the ship, even though he has not yet learned the craft and cannot name his teacher or a time when he was learning it. Indeed, they go further and claim that it cannot be taught at all, and are even ready to cut to pieces anyone who says it can. They are always crowding around the shipowner himself, pleading with him, and doing everything possible c to get him to turn the rudder over to them. And sometimes, if they fail to persuade him and others succeed, they execute those others or throw them overboard. Then, having disabled their noble shipowner with mandragora[9] or drink or in some other way, they rule the ship, use up its cargo drinking and feasting, and make the sort of voyage you would expect of such people. In addition, they praise anyone who is clever at persuading or forcing the shipowner to let them rule, calling him a "sailor," a "skilled captain," and "an expert about ships" while dismissing anyone else as a d good-for-nothing. They do not understand that a true captain must pay attention to the seasons of the year, the sky, the stars, the winds, and all that pertains to his craft if he is really going to be expert at ruling a ship. As for *how* he is going to become captain of the ship, whether people want him to or not, they do not think it possible to acquire the craft or practice e of doing this at the same time as the craft of captaincy. When that is what is happening onboard ships, don't you think that a true captain would be

---

[7] *Eikos:* also, likeness.

[8] See Glossary of Terms s.v. captain.

[9] An intoxicant.

489a sure to be called a "stargazer," a "useless babbler," and a "good-for-nothing" by those who sail in ships so governed?

ADEIMANTUS: I certainly do.

SOCRATES: I do not think you need to examine the image to see the resemblance to cities and how they're disposed toward true philosophers, but you already understand what I mean.

ADEIMANTUS: Indeed, I do.

SOCRATES: First teach this image, then, to the person who is surprised that philosophers are not honored in cities, and try to persuade him that
b it would be far more surprising if they were honored.

ADEIMANTUS: I will.

SOCRATES: Furthermore, try to persuade him that you are speaking the truth when you say that the best among the philosophers are useless to the masses. But tell him to blame their uselessness on those who do not make use of them, not on those good philosophers. You see, it is not natural for the captain to beg the sailors to be ruled by him, nor for the wise to knock at the doors of the rich. The man who came up with that bit of sophistry was lying.[10] What is truly natural is for the sick person, rich or
c poor, to go to doctors' doors, and for anyone who needs to be ruled to go to the doors of the one who can rule him. It is not for the ruler—if he is truly any use—to beg the subjects to accept his rule. Tell him he will make no mistake if he likens our present political rulers to the sailors we mentioned a moment ago, and those who are called useless stargazers by them to the true ship's captains.

* * *

502c SOCRATES: But I think our earlier discussion was sufficient to show that these arrangements are best, provided they are possible.

ADEIMANTUS: Indeed, it was.

SOCRATES: It seems, then, that the conclusion we have now reached about legislation is that the one we are describing is best, provided it is possible; and that while it is difficult for it to come about, it certainly is not impossible.

ADEIMANTUS: Yes, that is the conclusion we have reached.

SOCRATES: Now that this conclusion has, with much effort, been reached, we must next deal with the remaining issues—in what way, by means of what subjects and pursuits, the saviors of our constitution will come to
d exist, and at what ages they will take up each of them.

ADEIMANTUS: Yes, we must deal with that.

SOCRATES: I gained nothing by my cleverness, then, in omitting from our earlier discussion the troublesome topic of acquiring women, begetting

[10] Aristotle, *Rhetoric* 1391a7–12, says that when Simonides was asked whether it was better to be rich or wise, he replied: "Rich—because the wise spend their time at the doors of the rich."

children, and establishing rulers, because I knew the whole truth would provoke resentment and would be difficult to bring about. As it turned out, the need to discuss them arose anyway. Now, the subject of women and children has already been discussed. But that of the rulers has to be taken up again from the beginning. We said,[29] if you remember, that they e
must show themselves to be lovers of the city, when tested by pleasures and pains, by not abandoning this conviction through labors, fears, and 503a
all other adversities. Anyone who was incapable of doing so was to be rejected, while anyone who always came through pure—like gold tested in a fire—was to be made ruler and receive gifts and prizes, both while he lived and after his death. These were the sorts of things we were saying while our argument veiled its face and slipped by, for fear of stirring up the very problems that now confront us. b

ADEIMANTUS: That's absolutely true. I do remember.

SOCRATES: I was reluctant, my friend, to say the things we have now dared to say anyway. But now, let's also dare to say that we must establish philosophers as guardians in the most exact sense.

ADEIMANTUS: Let's do so.

SOCRATES: Bear in mind, then, that there will probably be only a few of them. You see, they have to have the nature we described, and its parts rarely consent to grow together in one person; rather, its many parts grow split off from one another.

ADEIMANTUS: How do you mean? c

SOCRATES: Ease of learning, good memory, astuteness, and smartness, as you know, and all the other things that go along with them, such as youthful passion and high-mindedness, are rarely willing to grow together simultaneously with a disposition to live an orderly, quiet, and completely stable life. On the contrary, those who possess the former traits are carried by their quick wits wherever chance leads them, and have no stability at all.

ADEIMANTUS: That's true.

SOCRATES: Those with stable characters, on the other hand, who do not change easily, whom one would employ because of their greater reliability, and who in battle are not easily moved by fears, act in the same way d
when it comes to their studies. They are hard to get moving and learn with difficulty, as if they are anesthetized, and are constantly falling asleep and yawning whenever they have to work hard at such things.

ADEIMANTUS: They are.

SOCRATES: Yet we say that someone must have a good and fine share of both characters, or he won't receive the truest education or honor, or be allowed to rule.

[29] At 412b–414a. The conviction referred to is identified at 412e6.

ADEIMANTUS: That's right.

SOCRATES: Then don't you think this will rarely occur?

ADEIMANTUS: Of course.

e SOCRATES: He must be tested, then, in the labors, fears, and pleasures we mentioned before. He must also be exercised in many other subjects, however, which we did not mention but are adding now, to see whether his nature can endure the most important subjects or will shrink from
504a them like the cowards who shrink from the other tests.

ADEIMANTUS: It is certainly important to find that out. But what do you mean by "the greatest subjects"?

SOCRATES: Do you remember when we distinguished three kinds of things in the soul in order to help bring out what justice, temperance, courage, and wisdom each is?[30]

ADEIMANTUS: If I didn't, I would not deserve to hear the rest.

SOCRATES: Do you also remember what preceded it?

ADEIMANTUS: No, what?

b SOCRATES: We said, I believe, that in order to get the finest view of these matters, there is a longer road and, if one travels it, they become clear, but that it was possible to give demonstrations that would be up to the standard of the previous discussion.[31] All of you said that was enough. The result was that our subsequent discussion, as it seemed to me, was less than exact. But whether or not it satisfied all of you is for you to say.

ADEIMANTUS: I, at any rate, thought you gave us good measure. And so, apparently, did the others.

c SOCRATES: No, my friend, any measure of such things that falls short in any way of what is, is not good measure at all, since nothing incomplete is a measure of anything. Some people, however, are occasionally of the opinion that an incomplete treatment is already adequate and that there is no need for further inquiry.

ADEIMANTUS: Yes, a lot of people feel like that. Laziness is the cause.

SOCRATES: Well, that is a feeling that is least appropriate in a guardian of a city and its laws.

ADEIMANTUS: No doubt.

SOCRATES: He will have to take the longer road then, comrade, and put
d no less effort into learning than into physical training. For otherwise, as we were just saying, he will never pursue the greatest and most appropriate subject to the end.

ADEIMANTUS: Why, aren't these virtues the greatest things? Is there something yet greater than justice and the other virtues we discussed?

SOCRATES: Not only is it greater, but, even in the case of the virtues themselves, it is not enough to look at a mere sketch as we are doing now, while neglecting the most finished portrait. I mean, it is ridiculous, isn't

---

[30] 434d–444e.

[31] 435d.

it, to strain every nerve to attain the utmost exactness and clarity about
other things of little value, while not treating the greatest things as merit- e
ing the most exactness?

ADEIMANTUS: It certainly is. But do you think that anyone is going to let you off without asking you what you mean by this greatest subject, and what it is concerned with?

SOCRATES: No, I do not. And you may ask it, too. You have certainly heard the answer often, but now either you are not thinking or you intend to make trouble for me again by interrupting. And I suspect it is more the latter. You see, you have often heard it said that the form of the
good is the greatest thing to learn about, and that it is by their relation to 505a
it that just things and the others become useful and beneficial. And now you must be pretty certain that that is what I am going to say, and, in addition, that we have no adequate knowledge of it. And if we do not know it, you know that even the fullest possible knowledge of other things is of no benefit to us, any more than if we acquire any possession without the good. Or do you think there is any benefit in possessing
everything but the good? Or to know everything without knowing the b
good, thereby knowing nothing fine or good?

ADEIMANTUS: No, by Zeus, I do not.

SOCRATES: Furthermore, you also know that the masses believe pleasure to be the good, while the more refined believe it to be knowledge.

ADEIMANTUS: Of course.

SOCRATES: And, my friend, that those who believe this cannot show us what sort of knowledge it is, but in the end are compelled to say that it is knowledge of the good.

ADEIMANTUS: Which is completely ridiculous.

SOCRATES: How could it not be, when they blame us for not knowing the c
good and then turn around and talk to us as if we did know it? I mean, they say it is knowledge of the good—as if we understood what they mean when they utter the word "good."

ADEIMANTUS: That's absolutely true.

SOCRATES: What about those who define the good as pleasure? Are they any less full of confusion than the others? Or aren't even they compelled to admit that there are bad pleasures?

ADEIMANTUS: Most definitely.

SOCRATES: I suppose it follows, doesn't it, that they have to admit that the same things are both good and bad?

ADEIMANTUS: It certainly does. d

SOCRATES: Isn't it clear, then, that there are lots of serious disagreements about the good?

ADEIMANTUS: Of course.

SOCRATES: Well, isn't it also clear that many people would choose things that are believed to be just or beautiful, even if they are not, and would act, acquire things, and form beliefs accordingly? Yet no one is satisfied to acquire things that are *believed* to be good. On the contrary, everyone seeks the things that *are* good. In this area, everyone disdains mere reputation.

ADEIMANTUS: Right.

SOCRATES: That, then, is what every soul pursues, and for its sake does everything. The soul has a hunch that the good is something, but it is
e puzzled and cannot adequately grasp just what it is or acquire the sort of stable belief about it that it has about the other things, and so it misses the benefit, if any, that even those other things may give. Are we to
506a accept that even the best people in the city, to whom we entrust everything, must remain thus in the dark about something of this kind and importance?

ADEIMANTUS: That's the last thing we would do.

SOCRATES: Anyway, I imagine that just and beautiful things won't have acquired much of a guardian in someone who does not even know why they are good. And I have a hunch that no one will have adequate knowledge of them until he knows this.

ADEIMANTUS: That's a good hunch.

SOCRATES: But won't our constitution be perfectly ordered if such a
b guardian, one who knows these things, oversees it?

ADEIMANTUS: It is bound to be. But you yourself, Socrates, do you say the good is knowledge or pleasure, or is it something else altogether?

SOCRATES: What a man! You made it good and clear long ago that other people's opinions about these matters would not satisfy you.

ADEIMANTUS: Well, Socrates, it does not seem right to me for you to be willing to state other people's convictions but not your own, when you
c have spent so much time occupied with these matters.

SOCRATES: What? Do you think it is right to speak about things you do not know as if you do know them?

ADEIMANTUS: Not as if you know them, but you ought to be willing to state what you believe as what you believe.

SOCRATES: What? Haven't you noticed that beliefs without knowledge are all shameful and ugly things, since the best of them are blind? Do you think that those who have a true belief without understanding are any different from blind people who happen to travel the right road?

ADEIMANTUS: They are no different.

SOCRATES: Do you want to look at shameful, blind, and crooked things,
d then, when you might hear fine, illuminating ones from other people?

And Glaucon said:

By Zeus, Socrates, do not stop now, with the end in sight, so to speak! We will be satisfied if you discuss the good the way you discussed justice, temperance, and the rest.

SOCRATES: That, comrade, would well satisfy me too, but I am afraid that I won't be up to it and that I will disgrace myself and look ridiculous by trying. No, bless you, let's set aside what the good itself is for the time being. You see, even to arrive at my current beliefs about it seems beyond the range of our present discussion.[32] But I am willing to tell you about what seems to be an offspring of the good and most like it, if that is agreeable to you; or otherwise to let the matter drop. e

GLAUCON: Tell us, then. The story about the father remains a debt you will pay another time.

SOCRATES: I wish I could repay it, and you recover the debt, instead of just the interest. So here, then, is this child and offspring of the good itself. But take care I do not somehow deceive you unintentionally by giving you an illegitimate account of the child.[33] 507a

GLAUCON: We will take as much care as possible. So speak on.

SOCRATES: I will once I have come to an agreement with you and reminded you of things we have already said here as well as on many other occasions.

GLAUCON: Which things? b

SOCRATES: We say that there are many beautiful, many good, and many other such things, thereby distinguishing them in words.[34]

GLAUCON: We do.

SOCRATES: We also say there is a beautiful itself and a good itself. And so, in the case of all the things that we then posited as many, we reverse ourselves and posit a single form belonging to each, since we suppose there is a single one, and call it what each is.[35]

GLAUCON: That's true.

SOCRATES: And we say that the one class of things is visible but not intelligible, while the forms are intelligible but not visible.

GLAUCON: Absolutely.

SOCRATES: With what of ours do we see visible things? c

GLAUCON: With our sight.

SOCRATES: And don't we hear audible things with hearing and perceive all other perceptible things with our other senses?

GLAUCON: Of course.

SOCRATES: Have you ever thought about how lavish the craftsman of our senses was in making the power to see and be seen?

GLAUCON: No, not really.

SOCRATES: Well, think of it this way. Do hearing and sound need another kind of thing in order for the former to hear and the latter to be heard—a third thing in whose absence the one won't hear or the other be heard? d

[32] See 532a–534d.

[33] Throughout, Socrates is punning on the word *tokos,* which means either a child or the interest on capital.

[34] See 596b5–10.

[35] See Glossary of Terms s.v. what it is.

GLAUCON: No.

SOCRATES: And I think there cannot be many—not to say any—others that need such a thing. Or can you think of one?

GLAUCON: No, I cannot.

SOCRATES: Aren't you aware that sight and the visible realm have such a need?

GLAUCON: In what way?

SOCRATES: Surely sight may be present in the eyes and its possessor may
try to use it, and colors may be present in things; but unless a third kind
of thing is present, which is naturally adapted for this specific purpose,
e you know that sight will see nothing and the colors will remain unseen.

GLAUCON: What kind of thing do you mean?

SOCRATES: The kind you call light.

GLAUCON: You are right.

SOCRATES: So it is no insignificant form of yoke, then, that yokes the
508a sense of sight and the power to be seen. In fact, it is more honorable than
any that yokes other yoked teams. Provided, of course, that light is not
something without honor.

GLAUCON: And it is surely far from being without honor.

SOCRATES: Which of the gods in the heavens would you say is the controller of this—the one whose light makes our sight see best and visible things best seen?

GLAUCON: The very one you and others would name. I mean, it is clear that what you are asking about is the sun.[36]

SOCRATES: And isn't sight naturally related to that god in the following way?

GLAUCON: Which one?

SOCRATES: Neither sight itself nor that in which it comes to be—namely,
b the eye—is the sun.

GLAUCON: No, it is not.

SOCRATES: But it is, I think, the most sunlike of the sense organs.

GLAUCON: By far the most.

SOCRATES: And doesn't it receive the power it has from the sun, just like an influx from an overflowing treasury?

GLAUCON: Certainly.

SOCRATES: The sun is not sight either; yet as its cause, isn't it seen by sight itself?

GLAUCON: It is.

SOCRATES: Let's say, then, that this is what I called the offspring of the
good, which the good begot as its analogue. What the latter is in the
c intelligible realm in relation to understanding and intelligible things, the
former is in the visible realm in relation to sight and visible things.

GLAUCON: How? Tell me more.

---

[36] Helios—the sun—was considered a god.

SOCRATES: You know that when our eyes no longer turn to things whose colors are illuminated by the light of day, but by the lights of night, they are dimmed and seem nearly blind, as if clear sight were no longer in them.

GLAUCON: Of course.

SOCRATES: Yet I suppose that whenever they are turned to things illuminated by the sun, they see clearly and sight is manifest in those very same d
eyes?

GLAUCON: Indeed.

SOCRATES: Well, think about the soul in the same way. When it focuses on something that is illuminated both by truth and what is, it understands, knows, and manifestly possesses understanding. But when it focuses on what is mixed with obscurity, on what comes to be and passes away, it believes and is dimmed, changes its beliefs this way and that, and seems bereft of understanding.

GLAUCON: Yes, it does seem like that.

SOCRATES: You must say, then, that what gives truth to the things known e
and the power to know to the knower is the form of the good. And as the cause of knowledge and truth, you must think of it as an object of knowledge. Both knowledge and truth are beautiful things. But if you are to think correctly, you must think of the good as other and more beautiful than they. In the visible realm, light and sight are rightly thought to
be sun-like, but wrongly thought to be the sun. So, here it is right to 509a
think of knowledge and truth as goodlike, but wrong to think that either of them is the good—for the status of the good is yet more honorable.

GLAUCON: It is an incredibly beautiful thing you are talking about, if it provides both knowledge and truth but is itself superior to them in beauty. I mean, you surely do not think that *it* could be pleasure.

SOCRATES: No words of ill omen, please! Instead, examine our analogy in more detail.

GLAUCON: How? b

SOCRATES: The sun, I think you would say, not only gives visible things the power to be seen but also provides for their coming-to-be, growth, and nourishment—although it is not itself coming to be.

GLAUCON: I would.

SOCRATES: Therefore, you should also say that not only do the objects of knowledge owe their being known to the good, but their existence and being are also due to it; although the good is not being, but something yet beyond being, superior to it in rank and power.

And Glaucon quite ridiculously replied:

By Apollo, what daimonic hyperbole![37] c

---

[37] Socrates' claim ends with the words *dunamei huperechontas* ("superior in . . . power"), Glaucon responds with the punning *daimonias huperbolês.* Hence the joke.

SOCRATES: It is your own fault, you compelled me to tell my beliefs about it.

GLAUCON: And don't you stop, either—at least, not until you have finished discussing the good's similarity to the sun, if you are omitting anything.

SOCRATES: I am certainly omitting a lot.

GLAUCON: Well don't, not even the smallest detail.

SOCRATES: I think I will have to omit a fair amount. All the same, as far as is now possible, I won't purposely omit anything.

GLAUCON: Please don't.

SOCRATES: Then you should think, as we said, that there are these two things, one sovereign of the intelligible kind and place, the other of the
d visible—I do not say "of the heavens," so as not to seem to you to be playing the sophist with the name.[38] In any case, do you understand these two kinds, visible and intelligible?

GLAUCON: I do.

SOCRATES: Represent them, then, by a line divided into two unequal sections. Then divide each section—that of the visible kind and that of the intelligible—in the same proportion as the line.[39] In terms now of rela-
e tive clarity and opacity, you will have as one subsection of the visible,
510a images. By images I mean, first, shadows, then reflections in bodies of water and in all close-packed, smooth, and shiny materials, and everything of that sort. Do you understand?

GLAUCON: I do understand.

SOCRATES: Then, in the other subsection of the visible, put the originals of these images—that is, the animals around us, every plant, and the whole class of manufactured things.

GLAUCON: I will.

SOCRATES: Would you also be willing to say, then, that, as regards truth and untruth, the division is in this ratio: as what is believed is to what is known, so the likeness is to the thing it is like?

b GLAUCON: Certainly.

SOCRATES: Next, consider how the section of the intelligible is to be divided.

GLAUCON: How?

SOCRATES: As follows: in one subsection, the soul, using as images the things that were imitated before, is compelled to base its inquiry on hypotheses, proceeding not to a first principle, but to a conclusion. In the other subsection, by contrast, it makes its way to an unhypothetical first principle, proceeding from a hypothesis, but without the images

---

38 The play seems to be on the similarity of sound between *orano* ("the heavens") and *orato* ("visible").

39

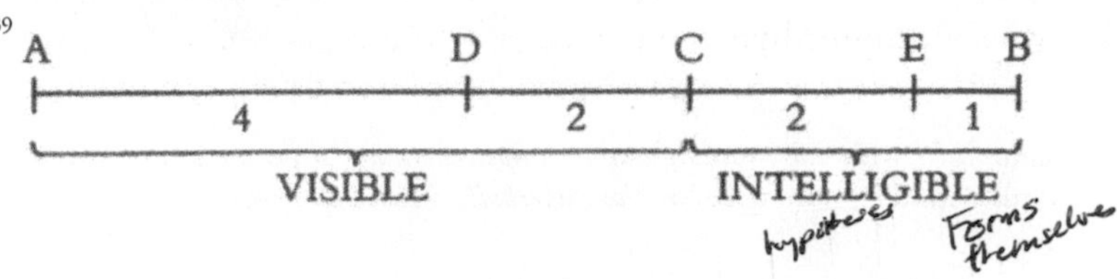

used in the previous subsection, using forms themselves and making its methodical inquiry through them.

GLAUCON: I do not fully understand what you are saying.

SOCRATES: Let's try again. You see, you will understand it more easily after this explanation. I think you know that students of geometry, calculation, c
and the like hypothesize the odd and the even, the various figures, the three kinds of angles, and other things akin to these in each of their methodical inquiries, regarding them as known. These they treat as hypotheses and do not think it necessary to give any account of them, either to themselves or to others, as if they were evident to everyone. And going from these first principles through the remaining steps, they arrive d
in full agreement at the point they set out to reach in their investigation.

GLAUCON: I certainly know that much.

SOCRATES: Then don't you also know that they use visible forms and make their arguments about them, although they are not thinking about them, but about those other things that they are like? They make their arguments with a view to the square itself and the diagonal itself, not the diagonal they draw, and similarly with the others. The very things they e
make and draw, of which shadows and reflections in water are images, they now in turn use as images in seeking to see those other things themselves that one cannot see except by means of thought. 511a

GLAUCON: That's true.

SOCRATES: This, then, is the kind of thing that I said was intelligible. The soul is compelled to use hypotheses in the investigation of it, not traveling up to a first principle, since it cannot escape or get above its hypotheses, but using as images those very things of which images were made by the things below them, and which, by comparison to their images, were thought to be clear and to be honored as such.

GLAUCON: I understand that you mean what is dealt with in geometry b
and related crafts.

SOCRATES: Also understand, then, that by the other subsection of the intelligible I mean what reason itself[40] grasps by the power of dialectical discussion, treating its hypotheses, not as first principles, but as genuine hypotheses (that is, stepping stones and links in a chain), in order to arrive at what is unhypothetical and the first principle of everything. Having grasped this principle, it reverses itself and, keeping hold of what follows from it, comes down to a conclusion, making no use of anything visible at all, but only of forms themselves, moving on through forms to c
forms, and ending in forms.

GLAUCON: I understand, though not adequately—you see, in my opinion you are speaking of an enormous task. You want to distinguish the part of what is and is intelligible, the part looked at by the science of dialectical discussion, as clearer than the part looked at by the so-called sciences—

[40] *Autos ho logos.*

those for which hypotheses are first principles. And although those who
look at the latter part are compelled to do so by means of thought rather
than sense perception, still, because they do not go back to a genuine first
principle in considering it, but proceed from hypotheses, you do not
think that they have true understanding of them, even though—given
d such a first principle—they are intelligible. And you seem to me to call the
state of mind of the geometers-and the others of that sort—thought but
not understanding; thought being intermediate between belief and
understanding.

SOCRATES: You have grasped my meaning most adequately. Join me, then,
in taking these four conditions in the soul as corresponding to the four
subsections of the line: understanding dealing with the highest, thought
dealing with the second; assign belief to the third, and imagination to the
e last. Arrange them in a proportion and consider that each shares in clarity
to the degree that the subsection it deals with shares in truth.

GLAUCON: I understand, agree, and arrange them as you say.

Book 7

Socrates' Narration Continues:

SOCRATES: Next, then, compare the effect of education and that of the
514a lack of it on our nature to an experience like this. Imagine human beings
living in an underground, cavelike dwelling, with an entrance a long way
up that is open to the light and as wide as the cave itself. They have been
there since childhood, with their necks and legs fettered, so that they are
fixed in the same place, able to see only in front of them, because their
b fetter prevents them from turning their heads around. Light is provided
by a fire burning far above and behind them. Between the prisoners and
the fire, there is an elevated road stretching. Imagine that along this road
a low wall has been built—like the screen in front of people that is provided by puppeteers, and above which they show their puppets.

GLAUCON: I am imagining it.

SOCRATES: Also imagine, then, that there are people alongside the wall
c carrying multifarious artifacts that project above it—statues of people
515a and other animals, made of stone, wood, and every material. And as you
would expect, some of the carriers are talking and some are silent.

GLAUCON: It is a strange image you are describing, and strange prisoners.

SOCRATES: They are like us. I mean, in the first place, do you think these
prisoners have ever seen anything of themselves and one another besides
the shadows that the fire casts on the wall of the cave in front of them?

GLAUCON: How could they, if they have to keep their heads motionless
b throughout life?

SOCRATES: What about the things carried along the wall? Isn't the same
true where they are concerned?

GLAUCON: Of course.

SOCRATES: And if they could engage in discussion with one another, don't
you think they would assume that the words they used applied to the
things they see passing in front of them?

GLAUCON: They would have to.

SOCRATES: What if their prison also had an echo from the wall facing
them? When one of the carriers passing along the wall spoke, do you
think they would believe that anything other than the shadow passing in
front of them was speaking?

GLAUCON: I do not, by Zeus.

SOCRATES: All in all, then, what the prisoners would take for true reality
is nothing other than the shadows of those artifacts. c

GLAUCON: That's entirely inevitable.

SOCRATES: Consider, then, what being released from their bonds and
cured of their foolishness would naturally be like, if something like this
should happen to them. When one was freed and suddenly compelled to
stand up, turn his neck around, walk, and look up toward the light, he
would be pained by doing all these things and be unable to see the things
whose shadows he had seen before, because of the flashing lights. What
do you think he would say if we told him that what he had seen before d
was silly nonsense, but that now—because he is a bit closer to what is,
and is turned toward things that *are* more—he sees more correctly? And
in particular, if we pointed to each of the things passing by and compelled him to answer what each of them is, don't you think he would be
puzzled and believe that the things he saw earlier were more truly real
than the ones he was being shown?

GLAUCON: Much more so.

SOCRATES: And if he were compelled to look at the light itself, wouldn't e
his eyes be pained and wouldn't he turn around and flee toward the
things he is able to see, and believe that they are really clearer than the
ones he is being shown?

GLAUCON: He would.

SOCRATES: And if someone dragged him by force away from there, along
the rough, steep, upward path, and did not let him go until he had
dragged him into the light of the sun, wouldn't he be pained and angry at
being treated that way? And when he came into the light, wouldn't he 516a
have his eyes filled with sunlight and be unable to see a single one of the
things now said to be truly real?

GLAUCON: No, he would not be able to—at least not right away,

SOCRATES: He would need time to get adjusted, I suppose, if he is going to
see the things in the world above. At first, he would see shadows most easily; then images of men and other things in water, then the things themselves. From these, it would be easier for him to go on to look at the things
in the sky and the sky itself at night, gazing at the light of the stars and the
moon, than during the day, gazing at the sun and the light of the sun. b

GLAUCON: Of course.

SOCRATES: Finally, I suppose, he would be able to see the sun—not reflections of it in water or some alien place, but the sun just by itself in its own place—and be able to look at it and see what it is like.

GLAUCON: Necessarily.

SOCRATES: After that, he would already be able to conclude about it that it provides the seasons and the years, governs everything in the visible
c world, and is in some way the cause of all the things that he and his fellows used to see.

GLAUCON: That would clearly be his next step.

SOCRATES: What about when he reminds himself of his first dwelling place, what passed for wisdom there, and his fellow prisoners? Don't you think he would count himself happy for the change and pity the others?

GLAUCON: Certainly.

SOCRATES: And if there had been honors, praises, or prizes among them for the one who was sharpest at identifying the shadows as they passed by; and was best able to remember which usually came earlier, which
d later, and which simultaneously; and who was thus best able to prophesize the future, do you think that our man would desire these rewards or envy those among the prisoners who were honored and held power? Or do you think he would feel with Homer that he would much prefer to "work the earth as a serf for another man, a man without possessions of his own,"[1] and go through any sufferings, rather than share their beliefs and live as they do?

e GLAUCON: Yes, I think he would rather suffer anything than live like that.

SOCRATES: Consider this too, then. If this man went back down into the cave and sat down in his same seat, wouldn't his eyes be filled with darkness, coming suddenly out of the sun like that?

GLAUCON: Certainly.

SOCRATES: Now, if he had to compete once again with the perpetual prisoners in recognizing the shadows, while his sight was still dim and before
517a his eyes had recovered, and if the time required for readjustment was not short, wouldn't he provoke ridicule? Wouldn't it be said of him that he had returned from his upward journey with his eyes ruined, and that it is not worthwhile even to try to travel upward? And as for anyone who tried to free the prisoners and lead them upward, if they could somehow get their hands on him, wouldn't they kill him?

GLAUCON: They certainly would.

SOCRATES: This image, my dear Glaucon, must be fitted together as a
b whole with what we said before. The realm revealed through sight should be likened to the prison dwelling, and the light of the fire inside it to the sun's power. And if you think of the upward journey and the seeing of things above as the upward journey of the soul to the intelligible realm, you won't mistake my intention—since it is what you wanted to hear

---

[1] *Odyssey* 11.489–90. The shade of Achilles speaks these words to Odysseus, who is visiting Hades. Plato is likening the cave dwellers to the dead.

about. Only the god knows whether it is true. But this is how these phenomena seem to me: in the knowable realm, the last thing to be seen is
the form of the good, and it is seen only with toil and trouble. Once one
has seen it, however, one must infer that it is the cause of all that is cor- c
rect and beautiful in anything, that in the visible realm it produces both
light and its source, and that in the intelligible realm it controls and provides truth and understanding; and that anyone who is to act sensibly in
private or public must see it.

GLAUCON: I agree, so far as I am able.

SOCRATES: Come on, then, and join me in this further thought: you
should not be surprised that the ones who get to this point are not willing to occupy themselves with human affairs, but that, on the contrary,
their souls are always eager to spend their time above. I mean, that is
surely what we would expect, if indeed the image I described before is
also accurate here. d

GLAUCON: It is what we would expect.

SOCRATES: What about when someone, coming from looking at divine
things, looks to the evils of human life? Do you think it is surprising that
he behaves awkwardly and appears completely ridiculous, if—while his
sight is still dim and he has not yet become accustomed to the darkness
around him—he is compelled, either in the courts or elsewhere, to compete about the shadows of justice, or about the statues of which they are
the shadows; and to dispute the way these things are understood by people who have never seen justice itself? e

GLAUCON: It is not surprising at all.

SOCRATES: On the contrary, anyone with any sense, at any rate, would
remember that eyes may be confused in two ways and from two causes: 518a
when they change from the light into the darkness, or from the darkness
into the light. If he kept in mind that the same applies to the soul, then
when he saw a soul disturbed and unable to see something, he would not
laugh absurdly. Instead, he would see whether it had come from a
brighter life and was dimmed through not having yet become accustomed to the dark, or from greater ignorance into greater light and was
dazzled by the increased brilliance. Then he would consider the first soul b
happy in its experience and life, and pity the latter. But even if he wanted
to ridicule it, at least his ridiculing it would make him less ridiculous
than ridiculing a soul that had come from the light above.

GLAUCON: That's an entirely reasonable claim.

SOCRATES: Then here is how we must think about these matters, if that is
true: education is not what some people boastfully profess it to be. They
say that they can pretty much put knowledge into souls that lack it, like
putting sight into blind eyes. c

GLAUCON: Yes, they do say that.

SOCRATES: But here is what our present account shows about this power
to learn that is present in everyone's soul, and the instrument with which
each of us learns: just as an eye cannot be turned around from darkness

to light except by turning the whole body, so this instrument must be turned around from what-comes-to-be together with the whole soul, until it is able to bear to look at what is and at the brightest thing that
d is—the one we call the good. Isn't that right?

GLAUCON: Yes.

SOCRATES: Of this, then—of this very turning around—there would be a craft concerned with how this instrument can be most easily and effectively turned around, not of putting sight into it. On the contrary, it takes for granted that sight is there, though not turned in the right way or looking where it should look, and contrives to redirect it appropriately.

GLAUCON: That's probably right.

SOCRATES: The other so-called virtues of the soul, then, do seem to be closely akin to those of the body: they really are not present in it initially,
e but are added later by habit and practice. The virtue of wisdom, on the other hand, belongs above all, so it seems, to something more godlike, which never loses its power, but is either useful and beneficial or useless and harmful, depending on the way it is led around. Or haven't you ever
519a noticed in people who are said to be bad, but clever, how sharp the vision of their little soul is and how sharply it distinguishes the things it is turned toward? This shows that its sight is not inferior, but is compelled to serve vice, so that the sharper it sees, the more evils it accomplishes.

GLAUCON: I certainly have.

SOCRATES: However, if this element of this sort of nature had been hammered at right from childhood, and struck free of the leaden weights, as it were, of kinship with becoming, which have been fastened to it by eat-
b ing and other such pleasures and indulgences, which turn its soul's vision downward[2]—if, I say, it got rid of these and turned toward truly real things, then the same element of the same people would see them most sharply, just as it now does the things it is now turned toward.

GLAUCON: That's probably right.

SOCRATES: Isn't it also probable, then—indeed, doesn't it follow necessarily from what was said before—that uneducated people who have no experience of true reality will never adequately govern a city, and neither will peo-
c ple who have been allowed to spend their whole lives in education. The former fail because they do not have a single goal in life at which all their actions, public and private, inevitably aim; the latter because they would refuse to act, thinking they had emigrated, while still alive, to the Isles of the Blessed.

GLAUCON: True.

SOCRATES: It is our task as founders, then, to compel the best natures to learn what was said before[3] to be the most important thing: namely, to see the good; to ascend that ascent. And when they have ascended and

[2] See 611b9–612a6.

[3] 505a–b.

looked sufficiently, we must not allow them to do what they are allowed d
to do now.

GLAUCON: What's that, then?

SOCRATES: To stay there and refuse to go down again to the prisoners in the cave and share their labors and honors, whether the inferior ones or the more excellent ones.

GLAUCON: You mean we are to treat them unjustly, making them live a worse life when they could live a better one?

SOCRATES: You have forgotten again, my friend, that the law is not concerned with making any one class in the city do outstandingly well, but is e
contriving to produce this condition in the city as a whole, harmonizing
the citizens together through both persuasion and compulsion, and making them share with each other the benefit they can confer on the community.[4] It produces such men in the city, not in order to allow them to 520a
turn in whatever direction each one wants, but to make use of them to
bind the city together.

GLAUCON: That's true. Yes, I had forgotten.

SOCRATES: Observe, then, Glaucon, that we won't be unjustly treating
those who have become philosophers in our city, but that what we will
say to them, when we compel them to take care of the others and guard
them, will be just. We will say: "When people like you come to be in
other cities, they are justified in not sharing in the others' labors. After b
all, they have grown there spontaneously, against the will of the constitution in each of them. And when something grows of its own accord and
owes no debt for its upbringing, it has justice on its side when it is not
keen to pay anyone for its upbringing. But both for your own sakes and
for that of the rest of the city, we have bred you to be leaders and kings in
the hive, so to speak. You are better and more completely educated than
the others, and better able to share in both types of life.[5] So each of you c
in turn must go down to live in the common dwelling place of the other
citizens and grow accustomed to seeing in the dark. For when you are
used to it, you will see infinitely better than the people there and know
precisely what each image is, and also what it is an image of, because you
have seen the truth about fine, just, and good things. So the city will be
awake, governed by us and by you; not dreaming like the majority of
cities nowadays, governed by men who fight against one another over
shadows and form factions in order to rule—as if that were a great good.[6] d
No, the truth of the matter is surely this: a city in which those who are
going to rule are least eager to rule is necessarily best and freest from faction, whereas a city with the opposite kind of rulers is governed in the
opposite way."

---

[4] 420b–421c, 462a–466c.

[5] I.e., the practical life of ruling and the theoretical life of doing philosophy.

[6] See 476c–d.

GLAUCON: Yes, indeed.

SOCRATES: Then do you think the people we have nurtured will disobey us when they hear these things, and be unwilling to share the labors of the city, each in turn, while living the greater part of their time with one another in the pure realm?

GLAUCON: No, they couldn't possibly. After all, we will be giving just
e orders to just people. However, each of them will certainly go to rule as
to something compulsory, which is exactly the opposite of what is done
by those who now rule in each city.

SOCRATES: That's right, comrade. If you can find a way of life that is bet-
521a ter than ruling for those who are going to rule, your well-governed city
will become a possibility. You see, in it alone the truly rich will rule—those who are rich not in gold, but in the wealth the happy must have: namely, a good and rational life. But if beggars—people hungry for private goods of their own—go into public life, thinking that the good is there for the seizing, then such a city is impossible. For when ruling is something fought over, such civil and domestic war destroys these men and the rest of the city as well.

GLAUCON: That's absolutely true.

SOCRATES: Do you know of any other sort of life that looks down on
b political offices besides that of true philosophy?

GLAUCON: No, by Zeus, I do not.

SOCRATES: But surely it is those who are not lovers of ruling who must go do it. Otherwise, the rivaling lovers will fight over it.

GLAUCON: Of course.

SOCRATES: Who else, then, will you compel to go be guardians of the city if not those who know best what results in good government, and have different honors and a better life than the political?

GLAUCON: No one else.

c SOCRATES: Do you want us to consider now how such people will come
to exist, and how we will lead them up to the light, like those who are
said to have gone up from Hades to the gods?

GLAUCON: Yes, of course that's what I want.

SOCRATES: It seems, then, that this is not a matter of flipping a potsherd,[7] but of turning a soul from a day that is a kind of night in comparison to the true day—that ascent to what is, which we say is true philosophy.

GLAUCON: Yes, indeed.

SOCRATES: Then mustn't we try to discover what subjects have the power
d to bring this about?

* * *

[7] A proverbial expression, referring to a children's game. The players were divided into two groups. A shell or potsherd—white on one side, black on the other—was thrown into space between them to the cry of "night or day?" (Note the reference to night and day in what follows.) According as the white or black fell uppermost, one group ran away pursued by the other.

SOCRATES: Then isn't this at last, Glaucon, the theme itself that dialecti- 532a
cal discussion sings? It itself is intelligible. But the power of sight imitates it. We said that sight tries at last to look at the animals themselves, the stars themselves, and, in the end, at the sun itself.[15] In the same way, whenever someone tries, by means of dialectical discussion and without the aid of any sense-perceptions, to arrive through reason at the being of each thing itself, and does not give up until he grasps what good itself is[16] with understanding itself, he reaches the end of the intelligible realm, just
as the other reached the end of the visible one. b

GLAUCON: Absolutely.

SOCRATES: Well, then, don't you call this journey[17] dialectic?

GLAUCON: I do.

SOCRATES: Then the release from bonds and the turning around from shadows to statues and the light; and then the ascent out of the cave to the sun; and there the continuing inability to look directly at the animals, the plants, and the light of the sun, but instead at divine reflections in water
and shadows of the things that are, and not, as before, merely at shadows c
of statues thrown by another source of light that, when judged in relation to the sun, is as shadowy as they—all this practice of the crafts we mentioned has the power to lead the best part of the soul upward until it sees the best among the things that are, just as before the clearest thing in the
body was led to the brightest thing in the bodily and visible world. d

GLAUCON: I accept that this is so. And yet, I think it is very difficult to accept; although—in another way—difficult not to accept! All the same, since the present occasion is not our only opportunity to hear these things, but we will get to return to them often in the future, let's assume that what you said about them just now is true and turn to the theme itself, and discuss it in the same way as we did the prelude. So, tell us then, in what way the power of dialectical discussion works, into what kinds it is divided, and what roads it follows. I mean, it is these, it seems,
that would lead us at last to that place which is a rest from the road, so to e
speak, for the one who reaches it, and an end of his journey.

SOCRATES: You won't be able to follow me any farther, my dear 533a
Glaucon—though not because of any lack of eagerness on my part. You would no longer see an image of what we are describing, but the truth itself as it seems to me, at least.[18] Whether it is really so or not—that's not something on which it is any longer worth insisting. But that there is some such thing to be seen, *that* is something on which we must insist. Isn't that so?

---

[15] See 516a–b.

[16] *Auto ho estin agathon:* See Glossary of Terms s.v. what it is.

[17] *Poreia:* An *aporia* (puzzle, problem—literally, a blockage on one's journey forward) is what dialectic attempts to solve.

[18] See 506d8–e5.

GLAUCON: Of course.

SOCRATES: And mustn't we also insist that the power of dialectical discussion could reveal it only to someone experienced in the subjects we described, and cannot do so in any other way?

GLAUCON: Yes, that is worth insisting on, too.

b SOCRATES: At the very least, no one will dispute our claim by arguing that there is another road of methodical inquiry that tries to acquire a systematic and wholly general grasp of what each thing itself is. By contrast, all the other crafts are concerned with human beliefs and appetites, with growing or construction, or with the care of growing or constructed things. As for the rest, we described them as to some extent grasping what is—I mean, geometry and the subjects that follow it. For we saw that while they do dream about what is, they cannot see it while wide
c awake as long as they make use of hypotheses that they leave undisturbed, and for which they cannot give any account. After all, when the first principle is unknown, and the conclusion and the steps in between are put together out of what is unknown, what mechanism could possibly turn any agreement reached in such cases into knowledge?[19]

GLAUCON: None.

SOCRATES: Therefore, dialectic is the only method of inquiry that, doing
d away with hypotheses, journeys to the first principle itself in order to be made secure. And when the eye of the soul is really buried in a sort of barbaric bog,[20] dialectic gently pulls it out and leads it upward, using the crafts we described to help it and cooperate with it in turning the soul around. From force of habit, we have often called these branches of knowledge. But they need another name, since they are clearer than belief and darker than knowledge. We distinguished them by the term "thought" somewhere before.[21] But I don't suppose we will dispute about names, with matters as important as those before us to investigate.

e GLAUCON: Of course not, just as long as they express the state of clarity the soul possesses.

SOCRATES: It will be satisfactory, then, to do what we did before and call the first section knowledge, the second thought, the third opinion, and
534a the fourth imagination. The last two together we call belief, the other two, understanding.[22] Belief is concerned with becoming; understanding

[19] See 510c1–511c2.

[20] See 519a7–519b5.

[21] 511d6–511e4.

[22] The reference is to 511d6–e5, where the first section is called understanding (*noêsis*), not knowledge (*epistêmê*). Since thought (*dianoia*) is not now a kind of knowledge, *noêsis* and *epistêmê* have in effect become one and the same. *Epistêmê* and *dianoia* are now jointly referred to as *noêsis,* because that whole section of the line on which they appear consists of intelligible objects (*noêton*).

with being. And as being is to becoming, so understanding is to belief; and as understanding is to belief, so knowledge is to belief and thought to imagination. But as for the ratios between the things these deal with, and the division of either the believable or the intelligible section into two, let's pass them by, Glaucon, in case they involve us in discussions many times longer than the ones we have already gone through.

GLAUCON: I agree with you about the rest of them, anyway, insofar as I b
am able to follow.

SOCRATES: So don't you, too, call someone a dialectician when he is able
to grasp an account of the being of each thing? And when he cannot do
so, won't you, too, say that to the extent that he cannot give an account
of something either to himself or to another, to that extent he does not
understand it?

GLAUCON: How could I not?

SOCRATES: Then the same applies to the good. Unless someone can give
an account of the form of the good, distinguishing it from everything
else, and can survive all examination as if in a battle, striving to examine[23] things not in accordance with belief, but in accordance with being; c
and can journey through all that with his account still intact, you will say
that he does not know the good itself or any other good whatsoever. And
if he does manage to grasp some image of it, you will say that it is
through belief, not knowledge, that he grasps it; that he is dreaming and
asleep throughout his present life; and that, before he wakes up here, he
will arrive in Hades and go to sleep forever. d

GLAUCON: Yes, by Zeus, I will certainly say all that.

SOCRATES: Then as for those children of yours, the ones you are rearing
and educating in your discussion, if you ever reared them in fact, I don't
suppose that, while they are still as irrational as the proverbial lines,[24] you
would allow them to rule in your city or control the greatest things.

GLAUCON: No, of course not.

SOCRATES: Won't you prescribe in your legislation, then, that they are to
give the most attention to the education that will enable them to ask and
answer questions most knowledgeably?

GLAUCON: I will prescribe it—together with you. e

SOCRATES: Doesn't it seem to you, then, that dialectic is just like a cap-
stone we have placed on top of the subjects, and that no other subject
can rightly be placed above it, but that our account of the subjects has
now come to an end? 535a

GLAUCON: It does.

---

[23] *Elengchein:* ("to examine," "to refute")—as in the Socratic elenchus.

[24] A pun made possible by the fact that *alogon* can mean "irrational" (as applied to people) and "incommensurable" (as applied to lines in geometry).

NOTES

CRITO

About the time of Socrates' trial, a state galley had set out on an annual religious mission to Delos and while it was away no execution was allowed to take place. So it was that Socrates was kept in prison for a month after the trial. The ship has now arrived at Cape Sunium in Attica and is thus expected at the Piraeus momentarily. So Socrates' old and faithful friend, Crito, makes one last effort to persuade him to escape into exile, and all arrangements for this plan have been made. It is this conversation between the two old friends that Plato professes to report in this dialogue. It is, as Crito plainly tells him, his last chance, but Socrates will not take it, and he gives his reasons for his refusal. Whether this conversation took place at this particular time is not important, for there is every reason to believe that Socrates' friends tried to plan his escape, and that he refused. Plato more than hints that the authorities would not have minded much, as long as he left the country.

SOCRATES: Why have you come so early, Crito? Or is it not still early? 43

CRITO: It certainly is.

S: How early?

C: Early dawn.

S: I am surprised that the warder was willing to listen to you.

C: He is quite friendly to me by now, Socrates. I have been here often and I have given him something.

S: Have you just come, or have you been here for some time?

C: A fair time.

S: Then why did you not wake me right away but sit there in silence? b

C: By Zeus no, Socrates. I would not myself want to be in distress and awake so long. I have been surprised to see you so peacefully asleep. It was on purpose that I did not wake you, so that you should spend your time most agreeably. Often in the past throughout my life, I have considered the way you live happy, and especially so now that you bear your present misfortune so easily and lightly.

S: It would not be fitting at my age to resent the fact that I must die now.

C: Other men of your age are caught in such misfortunes, but their age does c
not prevent them resenting their fate.

S: That is so. Why have you come so early?

C: I bring bad news, Socrates, not for you, apparently, but for me and all your friends the news is bad and hard to bear. Indeed, I would count it among the hardest.

Reprinted from *The Trial and Death of Socrates*, translated by G.M.A. Grube (1975), by permission of Hackett Publishing Company, Inc.

d S: What is it? Or has the ship arrived from Delos, at the arrival of which I must die?

C: It has not arrived yet, but it will, I believe, arrive today, according to a message brought by some men from Sunium, where they left it. This makes it obvious that it will come today, and that your life must end tomorrow.

S: May it be for the best. If it so please the gods, so be it. However, I do not think it will arrive today.

C: What indication have you of this?

44 S: I will tell you. I must die the day after the ship arrives.

C: That is what those in authority say.

S: Then I do not think it will arrive on this coming day, but on the next. I take to witness of this a dream I had a little earlier during this night. It looks as if it was the right time for you not to wake me.

C: What was your dream?

S: I thought that a beautiful and comely woman dressed in white approached
b me. She called me and said: "Socrates, may you arrive at fertile Phthia[1] on
the third day."

C: A strange dream, Socrates.

S: But it seems clear enough to me, Crito.

C: Too clear it seems, my dear Socrates, but listen to me even now and be saved. If you die, it will not be a single misfortune for me. Not only will I be deprived of a friend, the like of whom I shall never find again, but many
people who do not know you or me very well will think that I could have
c saved you if I were willing to spend money, but that I did not care to do so.
Surely there can be no worse reputation than to be thought to value money more highly than one's friends, for the majority will not believe that you yourself were not willing to leave prison while we were eager for you to do so.

S: My good Crito, why should we care so much for what the majority think? The most reasonable people, to whom one should pay more attention, will believe that things were done as they were done.

d C: You see, Socrates, that one must also pay attention to the opinion of the majority. Your present situation makes clear that the majority can inflict not the least but pretty well the greatest evils if one is slandered among them.

S: Would that the majority could inflict the greatest evils, for they would then be capable of the greatest good, and that would be fine, but now they

[1]A quotation from the ninth book of the *Iliad* (363). Achilles has rejected all the presents of Agamemnon for him to return to the battle, and threatens to go home. He says his ships will sail in the morning, and with good weather he might arrive on the third day "in fertile Phthia" (which is his home). The dream means, obviously, that on the third day Socrates' soul, after death, will find its home. As always, counting the first member of a series, the third day is the day after tomorrow.

cannot do either. They cannot make a man either wise or foolish, but they inflict things haphazardly.

C: That may be so. But tell me this, Socrates, are you anticipating that I and e
your other friends would have trouble with the informers if you escape from here, as having stolen you away, and that we should be compelled to lose all our property or pay heavy fines and suffer other punishment besides? If you have any such fear, forget it. We would be justified in running this risk 45
to save you, and worse, if necessary. Do follow my advice, and do not act differently.

S: I do have these things in mind, Crito, and also many others.

C: Have no such fear. It is not much money that some people require to save you and get you out of here. Further, do you not see that those informers are cheap, and that not much money would be needed to deal with them? My money is available and is, I think, sufficient. If, because of your affection for me, you feel you should not spend any of mine, there are those b
strangers here ready to spend money. One of them, Simmias the Theban, has brought enough for this very purpose. Cebes, too, and a good many others. So, as I say, do not let this fear make you hesitate to save yourself, nor let what you said in court trouble you, that you would not know what to do with yourself if you left Athens, for you would be welcomed in many places to which you might go, If you want to go to Thessaly, I have friends c
there who will greatly appreciate you and keep you safe, so that no one in Thessaly will harm you.

Besides, Socrates, I do not think that what you are doing is right, to give up your life when you can save it and to hasten your fate as your enemies would hasten it, and indeed have hastened it in their wish to destroy you. Moreover, I think you are betraying your sons by going away and leaving d
them, when you could bring them up and educate them. You thus show no concern for what their fate may be. They will probably have the usual fate of orphans. Either one should not have children, or one should share with them to the end the toil of upbringing and education. You seem to me to choose the easiest path, whereas one should choose the path a good and courageous man would choose, particularly when one claims throughout one's life to care for virtue. e

I feel ashamed on your behalf and on behalf of us, your friends, lest all that has happened to you be thought due to cowardice on our part: the fact that your trial came to court when it need not have done so, the handling of the trial itself, and now this absurd ending which will be thought to have got beyond our control through some cowardice and unmanliness on our part, 46
since we did not save you, or you save yourself, when it was possible and could be done if we had been of the slightest use. Consider, Socrates, whether this is not only evil, but shameful, both for you and for us. Take counsel with yourself, or rather the time for counsel is past and the decision should have been taken, and there is no further opportunity, for this whole business must be ended tonight. If we delay now, then it will no longer be possible, it will be too late. Let me persuade you on every count, Socrates, and do not act otherwise.

b S: My dear Crito, your eagerness is worth much if it should have some right
aim; if not, then the greater your keenness the more difficult it is to deal
with. We must therefore examine whether we should act in this way or not,
as not only now but at all times I am the kind of man who listens only to
the argument that on reflection seems best to me. I cannot, now that this
fate has come upon me, discard the arguments I used; they seem to me
c much the same. I value and respect the same principles as before, and if we
have no better arguments to bring up at this moment, be sure that I shall
not agree with you, not even if the power of the majority were to frighten
us with more bogeys, as if we were children, with threats of incarcerations
and executions and confiscation of property. How should we examine this
matter most reasonably? Would it be by taking up first your argument about
the opinions of men, whether it is sound in every case that one should pay
d attention to some opinions, but not to others? Or was that well-spoken
before the necessity to die came upon me, but now it is clear that this was
said in vain for the sake of argument, that it was in truth play and nonsense?
I am eager to examine together with you, Crito, whether this argument will
appear in any way different to me in my present circumstances, or whether
it remains the same, whether we are to abandon it or believe it. It was said
on every occasion by those who thought they were speaking sensibly, as I
have just now been speaking, that one should greatly value some people's
e opinions, but not others. Does that seem to you a sound statement?

You, as far as a human being can tell, are exempt from the likelihood of
dying tomorrow, so the present misfortune is not likely to lead you astray.
47 Consider then, do you not think it a sound statement that one must not
value all the opinions of men, but some and not others, nor the opinions
of all men, but those of some and not of others? What do you say? Is this
not well said?

C: It is.

S: One should value the good opinions, and not the bad ones?

C: Yes.

S: The good opinions are those of wise men, the bad ones those of foolish men?

C: Of course.

b S: Come then, what of statements such as this: Should a man professionally
engaged in physical training pay attention to the praise and blame and opinion of any man, or to those of one man only, namely a doctor or trainer?

C: To those of one only.

S: He should therefore fear the blame and welcome the praise of that one man, and not those of the many?

C: Obviously.

S: He must then act and exercise, eat and drink in the way the one, the trainer and the one who knows, thinks right, not all the others?

C: That is so.

S: Very well. And if he disobeys the one, disregards his opinion and his praises c
while valuing those of the many who have no knowledge, will he not suffer harm?

C: Of course.

S: What is that harm, where does it tend, and what part of the man who disobeys does it affect?

C: Obviously the harm is to his body, which it ruins.

S: Well said. So with other matters, not to enumerate them all, and certainly with actions just and unjust, shameful and beautiful, good and bad, about
which we are now deliberating, should we follow the opinion of the many d
and fear it, or that of the one, if there is one who has knowledge of these things and before whom we feel fear and shame more than before all the others. If we do not follow his directions, we shall harm and corrupt that part of ourselves that is improved by just actions and destroyed by unjust actions. Or is there nothing in this?

C: I think there certainly is, Socrates.

S: Come now, if we ruin that which is improved by health and corrupted by
disease by not following the opinions of those who know, is life worth liv- e
ing for us when that is ruined? And that is the body, is it not?

C: Yes.

S: And is life worth living with a body that is corrupted and in bad condition?

C: In no way.

S: And is life worth living for us with that part of us corrupted that unjust action harms and just action benefits? Or do we think that part of us, whatever it is, that is concerned with justice and injustice, is inferior to the body? 48

C: Not at all.

S: It is more valuable?

C: Much more.

S: We should not then think so much of what the majority will say about us, but what he will say who understands justice and injustice, the one, that is, and the truth itself. So that, in the first place, you were wrong to believe that we should care for the opinion of the many about what is just, beautiful, good, and their opposites. "But," someone might say "the many are able to put us to death."

C: That too is obvious, Socrates, and someone might well say so. b

S: And, my admirable friend, that argument that we have gone through remains, I think, as before. Examine the following statement in turn as to whether it stays the same or not, that the most important thing is not life, but the good life.

C: It stays the same.

S: And that the good life, the beautiful life, and the just life are the same; does that still hold, or not?

C: It does hold.

c S: As we have agreed so far, we must examine next whether it is right for me to try to get out of here when the Athenians have not acquitted me. If it is seen to be right, we will try to do so; if it is not, we will abandon the idea. As for those questions you raise about money, reputation, the upbringing of children, Crito, those considerations in truth belong to those people who easily put men to death and would bring them to life again if they could, without thinking; I mean the majority of men. For us, however, since our argument leads to this, the only valid consideration, as we were saying just now, is whether we should be acting rightly in giving money and gratitude
d to those who will lead me out of here, and ourselves helping with the escape, or whether in truth we shall do wrong in doing all this. If it appears that we shall be acting unjustly, then we have no need at all to take into account whether we shall have to die if we stay here and keep quiet, or suffer in another way, rather than do wrong.

C: I think you put that beautifully, Socrates, but see what we should do.

e S: Let us examine the question together, my dear friend, and if you can make any objection while I am speaking, make it and I will listen to you, but if you have no objection to make, my dear Crito, then stop now from saying the same thing so often, that I must leave here against the will of the Athenians. I think it important to persuade you before I act, and not to act against your wishes. See whether the start of our enquiry is adequately stated, and try to
49 answer what I ask you in the way you think best.

C: I shall try.

S: Do we say that one must never in any way do wrong willingly, or must one do wrong in one way and not in another? Is to do wrong never good or admirable, as we have agreed in the past, or have all these former agreements been washed out during the last few days? Have we at our age failed
b to notice for some time that in our serious discussions we were no different from children? Above all, is the truth such as we used to say it was, whether the majority agree or not, and whether we must still suffer worse things than we do now, or will be treated more gently, that nonetheless, wrongdoing is in every harmful and shameful to the wrongdoer? Do we say so or not?

C: We do.

S: So one must never do wrong.

C: Certainly not.

S: Nor must one, when wronged, inflict wrong in return, as the majority believe, since one must never do wrong.

c C: That seems to be the case.

S: Come now, should one injure anyone or not, Crito?

C: One must never do so.

S: Well then, if one is oneself injured, is it right, as the majority say, to inflict an injury in return, or is it not?

C: It is never right.

S: Injuring people is no different from wrongdoing.

C: That is true.

S: One should never do wrong in return, nor injure any man, whatever injury
one has suffered at his hands. And Crito, see that you do not agree to this, d
contrary to your belief. For I know that only a few people hold this view or
will hold it, and there is no common ground between those who hold this
view and those who do not, but they inevitably despise each other's views.
So then consider very carefully whether we have this view in common, and
whether you agree, and let this be the basis of our deliberation, that neither
to do wrong or to return a wrong is ever right, not even to injure in return
for an injury received. Or do you disagree and do not share this view as a basis
for discussion? I have held it for a long time and still hold it now, but if you e
think otherwise, tell me now. If, however, you stick to our former opinion,
then listen to the next point.

C: I stick to it and agree with you. So say on.

S: Then I state the next point, or rather I ask you: when one has come to an agreement that is just with someone, should one fulfill it or cheat on it?

C: One should fulfill it.

S: See what follows from this: if we leave here without the city's permission, 50
are we injuring people whom we should least injure? And are we sticking
to a just agreement, or not?

C: I cannot answer your question, Socrates. I do not know.

S: Look at it this way. If, as we were planning to run away from here, or whatever one should call it, the laws and the state came and confronted us and
asked: "Tell me, Socrates, what are you intending to do? Do you not by
this action you are attempting intend to destroy us, the laws, and indeed the b
whole city, as far as you are concerned? Or do you think it possible for a city
not to be destroyed if the verdicts of its courts have no force but are nullified and set at naught by private individuals?" What shall we answer to this
and other such arguments? For many things could be said, especially by an
orator on behalf of this law we are destroying, which orders that the judgments of the courts shall be carried out. Shall we say in answer, "The city
wronged me, and its decision was not right." Shall we say that, or what? c

C: Yes, by Zeus, Socrates, that is our answer.

S: Then what if the laws said: "Was that the agreement between us, Socrates,
or was it to respect the judgments that the city came to?" And if we wondered
at their words, they would perhaps add: "Socrates, do not wonder at what
we say but answer, since you are accustomed to proceed by question and
answer. Come now, what accusation do you bring against us and the city, that d
you should try to destroy us? Did we not, first, bring you to birth, and was
it not through us that your father married your mother and begat you? Tell
us, do you find anything to criticize in those of us who are concerned with
marriage?" And I would say that I do not criticize them. "Or in those of us
concerned with the nurture of babies and the education that you too received?
Were those assigned to that subject not right to instruct your father to educate you in the arts and in physical culture?" And I would say that they were

e right. "Very well," they would continue, "and after you were born and nurtured and educated, could you, in the first place, deny that you are our offspring and servant, both you and your forefathers? If that is so, do you think
that we are on an equal footing as regards the right, and that whatever we
do to you it is right for you to do to us? You were not on an equal footing
with your father as regards the right, nor with your master if you had one,
51 so as to retaliate for anything they did to you, to revile them if they reviled
you, to beat them if they beat you, and so with many other things. Do you
think you have this right to retaliation against your country and its laws?
That if we undertake to destroy you and think it right to do so, you can
undertake to destroy us, as far as you can, in return? And will you say that
you are right to do so, you who truly care for virtue? Is your wisdom such
as not to realize that your country is to be honoured more than your mother,
your father and all your ancestors, that it is more to be revered and more
b sacred, and that it counts for more among the gods and sensible men, that
you must worship it, yield to it and placate its anger more than your father's?
You must either persuade it or obey its orders, and endure in silence whatever it instructs you to endure, whether blows or bonds, and if it leads you
into war to be wounded or killed, you must obey. To do so is right, and one
must not give way or retreat or leave one's post, but both in war and in courts
c and everywhere else, one must obey the commands of one's city and country, or persuade it as to the nature of justice. It is impious to bring violence
to bear against your mother or father, it is much more so to use it against your
country." What shall we say in reply, Crito, that the laws speak the truth, or
not?

C: I think they do.

S: "Reflect now, Socrates," the laws might say "that if what we say is true, you
are not treating us rightly by planning to do what you are planning. We have
given you birth, nurtured you, educated you, we have given you and all
d other citizens a share of all the good things we could. Even so, by giving
every Athenian the opportunity, after he has reached manhood and observed
the affairs of the city and us the laws, we proclaim that if we do not please
him, he can take his possessions and go wherever he pleases. Not one of
our laws raises any obstacle or forbids him, if he is not satisfied with us or
the city, if one of you wants to go and live in a colony or wants to go any-
e where else, and keep his property. We say, however, that whoever of you
remains, when he sees how we conduct our trials and manage the city in
other ways, has in fact come to an agreement with us to obey our instructions. We say that the one who disobeys does wrong in three ways, first
because in us he disobeys his parents, also those who brought him up, and
because, in spite of his agreement, he neither obeys us nor, if we do some-
52 thing wrong, does he try to persuade us to do better. Yet we only propose
things, we do not issue savage commands to do whatever we order; we give
two alternatives, either to persuade us or to do what we say. He does neither. We do say that you too, Socrates, are open to those charges if you do

what you have in mind; you would be among, not the least, but the most guilty of the Athenians." And if I should say "Why so?" they might well be right to upbraid me and say that I am among the Athenians who most definitely came to that agreement with them. They might well say: "Socrates, b
we have convincing proofs that we and the city were congenial to you. You would not have dwelt here most consistently of all the Athenians if the city had not been exceedingly pleasing to you. You have never left the city, even to see a festival, nor for any other reason except military service; you have never gone to stay in any other city, as people do; you have had no desire to know another city or other laws; we and our city satisfied you. c

"So decisively did you choose us and agree to be a citizen under us. Also, you have had children in this city, thus showing that it was congenial to you. Then at your trial you could have assessed your penalty at exile if you wished, and you are now attempting to do against the city's wishes what you could then have done with her consent. Then you prided yourself that you did not resent death, but you chose, as you said, death in preference to exile. Now, however, those words do not make you ashamed, and you pay no heed to us, the laws, as you plan to destroy us, and you act like the meanest type of d
slave by trying to run away, contrary to your undertakings and your agreement to live as a citizen under us. First then, answer us on this very point, whether we speak the truth when we say that you agreed, not only in words but by your deeds, to live in accordance with us." What are we to say to that, Crito? Must we not agree?

C: We must, Socrates.

S: "Surely," they might say, "you are breaking the undertakings and agreements that you made with us without compulsion or deceit, and under no e
pressure of time for deliberation. You have had seventy years during which you could have gone away if you did not like us, and if you thought our agreements unjust. You did not choose to go to Sparta or to Crete, which 53
you are always saying are well governed, nor to any other city, Greek or foreign. You have been away from Athens less than the lame or the blind or other handicapped people. It is clear that the city has been outstandingly more congenial to you than to other Athenians, and so have we, the laws, for what city can please without laws? Will you then not now stick to our agreements? You will, Socrates, if we can persuade you, and not make yourself a laughingstock by leaving the city.

"For consider what good you will do yourself or your friends by breaking our agreements and committing such a wrong? It is pretty obvious that your friends will themselves be in danger of exile, disfranchisement and loss of property. As for yourself, if you go to one of the nearby cities—Thebes or Megara, both are well governed—you will arrive as an enemy to their gov- b
ernment; all who care for their city will look on you with suspicion, as a destroyer of the laws. You will also strengthen the conviction of the jury that they passed the right sentence on you, for anyone who destroys the c
laws could easily be thought to corrupt the young and the ignorant. Or

will you avoid cities that are well governed and men who are civilized? If you
do this, will your life be worth living? Will you have social intercourse with
them and not be ashamed to talk to them? And what will you say? The
same as you did here, that virtue and justice are man's most precious possession, along with lawful behaviour and the laws? Do you not think that
d Socrates would appear to be an unseemly kind of person? One must think
so. Or will you leave those places and go to Crito's friends in Thessaly?
There you will find the greatest license and disorder, and they may enjoy
hearing from you how absurdly you escaped from prison in some disguise,
in a leather jerkin or some other things in which escapees wrap themselves,
thus altering your appearance. Will there be no one to say that you, likely
to live but a short time more, were so greedy for life that you transgressed
e the most important laws? Possibly, Socrates, if you do not annoy anyone,
but if you do, many disgraceful things will be said about you.

"You will spend your time ingratiating yourself with all men, and be at
their beck and call. What will you do in Thessaly but feast, as if you had gone
to a banquet in Thessaly? As for those conversations of yours about justice
and the rest of virtue, where will they be? You say you want to live for the
54 sake of your children, that you may bring them up and educate them. How
so? Will you bring them up and educate them by taking them to Thessaly
and making strangers of them, that they may enjoy that too? Or not so,
but they will be better brought up and educated here, while you are alive,
though absent? Yes, your friends will look after them. Will they look after
them if you go and live in Thessaly, but not if you go away to the under-
b world? If those who profess themselves your friends are any good at all, one
must assume that they will.

"Be persuaded by us who have brought you up, Socrates. Do not value
either your children or your life or anything else more than goodness, in
order that when you arrive in Hades you may have all this as your defence
before the rulers there. If you do this deed, you will not think it better or
more just or more pious here, nor will any one of your friends, nor will it
be better for you when you arrive yonder. As it is, you depart, if you depart,
c after being wronged not by us, the laws, but by men; but if you depart after
shamefully returning wrong for wrong and injury for injury, after breaking
your agreement and contract with us, after injuring those you should injure
least—yourself, your friends, your country and us—we shall be angry with
you while you are still alive, and our brothers, the laws of the underworld,
will not receive you kindly, knowing that you tried to destroy us as far
as you could. Do not let Crito persuade you, rather than us, to do what
d he says."

Crito, my dear friend, be assured that these are the words I seem to hear, as the Corybants seem to hear the music of their flutes, and the echo of these words resounds in me, and makes it impossible for me to hear anything else. As far as my present beliefs go, if you speak in opposition to them, you will speak in vain. However, if you think you can accomplish anything, speak.

C: I have nothing to say, Socrates. e

S: Let it be then, Crito, and let us act in this way, since this is the way the god is leading us.

NOTES

FOR FURTHER READING

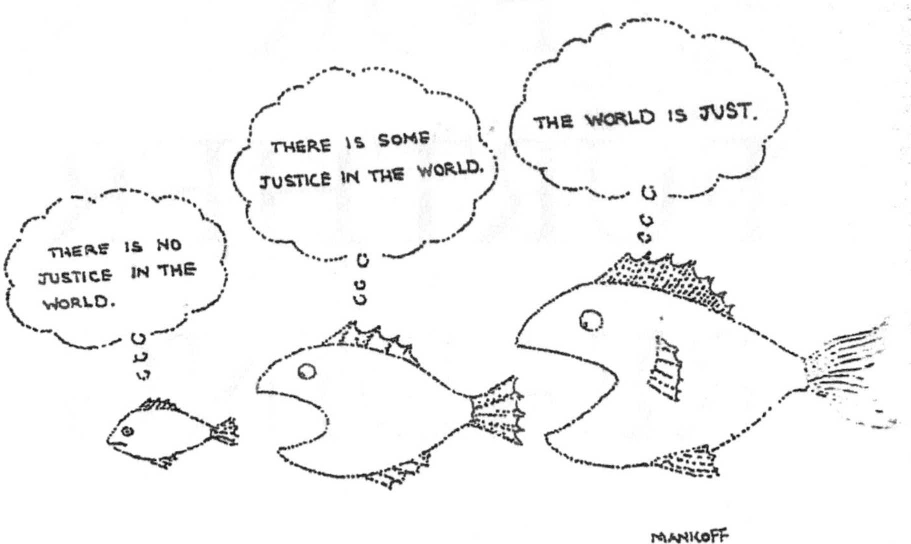

Courtesy of The New Yorker Cartoon Bank.

ALL SUMMER IN A DAY
Ray Bradbury

(1920–2012)

Ray Bradbury was a U.S. author best known for his fantasy stories and science fiction that combines poetic prose and vigorous creativity. He was awarded the 2000 National Book Foundation Medal for Distinguished Contribution to American Letters, the 2004 National Medal of Arts, and the 2007 Pulitzer Prize Special Citation.

No one in the class could remember a time when there wasn't rain.

"Ready?"

"Ready."

"Now?"

"Soon."

"Do the scientists really know? Will it happen today, will it?"

"Look, look; see for yourself!"

The children pressed to each other like so many roses, so many weeds, intermixed, peering out for a look at the hidden sun.

It rained.

It had been raining for seven years; thousand upon thousands of days compounded and filled from one end to the other with rain, with the drum and gush of water, with the sweet crystal fall of showers and the concussion of storms so heavy they were tidal waves come over the islands. A thousand forests had been crushed under the rain and grown up a thousand times to be crushed again. And this was the way life was forever on the planet Venus, and this was the schoolroom of the children of the rocket men and women who had come to a raining world to set up civilization and live out their lives.

"It's stopping, it's stopping!"

"Yes, yes!"

Margot stood apart from these children who could never remember a time when there wasn't rain and rain and rain. They were all nine years old, and if there had been a day, seven years ago, when the sun came out for an hour and showed its face to the stunned world, they could not recall. Sometimes, at night, she heard them stir, in remembrance, and she knew they were dreaming and remembering gold or a yellow crayon or a coin large enough to buy the world with. She knew they thought they remembered a warmness, like a blushing in the face, in the body, in the arms and legs and trembling hands. But then they always awoke to the tatting drum, the

---

endless shaking down of clear bead necklaces upon the roof, the walk, the gardens, the forests, and their dreams were gone.

All day yesterday they had read in class about the sun. About how like a lemon it was, and how hot. And they had written small stories or essays or poems about it:

I think the sun is a flower,
That blooms for just one hour.

That was Margot's poem, read in a quiet voice in the still classroom while the rain was falling outside.

"Aw, you didn't write that!" protested one of the boys.

"I did," said Margot. "I *did.*"

"William!" said the teacher.

But that was yesterday. Now the rain was slackening, and the children were crushed in the great thick windows.

"Where's teacher?"

"She'll be back."

"She'd better hurry, we'll miss it!"

They turned on themselves, like a feverish wheel, all tumbling spokes.

Margot stood alone. She was a very frail girl who looked as if she had been lost in the rain for years and the rain had washed out the blue from her eyes and the red from her mouth and the yellow from her hair. She was an old photograph dusted from an album, whitened away, and if she spoke at all her voice would be a ghost. Now she stood, separate, staring at the rain and the loud wet world beyond the huge glass.

"What're *you* looking at?" said William.

Margot said nothing.

"Speak when you're spoken to." He gave her a shove. But she did not move; rather she let herself be moved only by him and nothing else.

They edged away from her, they would not look at her. She felt them go away. And this was because she would play no games with them in the echoing tunnels of the underground city. If they tagged her and ran, she stood blinking after them and did not follow. When the class sang songs about happiness and life and games her lips barely moved. Only when they sang about the sun and the summer did her lips move as she watched the drenched windows.

And then, of course, the biggest crime of all was that she had come here only five years ago from Earth, and she remembered the sun and the way the sun was and the sky was when she was four in Ohio. And they, they had been on Venus all their lives, and they had been only two years old when last the sun came out and had long since forgotten the color and heat of it and the way it really was. But Margot remembered.

"It's like a penny," she said once, eyes closed.

"No it's not!" the children cried.

"It's like a fire," she said, "in the stove."

"You're lying, you don't remember!" cried the children.

But she remembered and stood quietly apart from all of them and watched the patterning windows. And once, a month ago, she had refused to shower in the school shower rooms, had clutched her hands to her ears and over her head, screaming the water mustn't touch her head. So after that, dimly, dimly, she sensed it, she was different and they knew her difference and kept away.

There was talk that her father and mother were taking her back to Earth next year; it seemed vital to her that they do so, though it would mean the loss of thousands of dollars to her family. And so, the children hated her for all these reasons of big and little consequence. They hated her pale snow face, her waiting silence, her thinness, and her possible future.

"Get away!" The boy gave her another push. "What're you waiting for?"

Then, for the first time, she turned and looked at him. And what she was waiting for was in her eyes.

"Well, don't wait around here!" cried the boy savagely. "You won't see nothing!"

Her lips moved.

"Nothing!" he cried. "It was all a joke, wasn't it?" He turned to the other children. "Nothing's happening today. *Is* it?"

They all blinked at him and then, understanding, laughed and shook their heads. "Nothing, nothing!"

"Oh, but," Margot whispered, her eyes helpless. "But this is the day, the scientists predict, they say, they *know*, the sun. . . ."

"All a joke!" said the boy, and seized her roughly. "Hey, everyone, let's put her in a closet before teacher comes!"

"No," said Margot, falling back.

They surged about her, caught her up and bore her, protesting, and then pleading, and then crying, back into a tunnel, a room, a closet, where they slammed and locked the door. They stood looking at the door and saw it tremble from her beating and throwing herself against it. They heard her muffled cries. Then, smiling, they turned and went out and back down the tunnel, just as the teacher arrived.

"Ready, children?" she glanced at her watch.

"Yes!" said everyone.

"Are we all here?"

"Yes!"

The rain slackened still more.

They crowded to the huge door.

The rain stopped.

It was as if, in the midst of a film, concerning an avalanche, a tornado, a hurricane, a volcanic eruption, something had, first, gone wrong with the sound apparatus, thus muffling and finally cutting off all noise, all of the blasts and repercussions and thunders, and then, second, ripped the film from the projector and inserted in its place a peaceful tropical slide which did not move or tremor. The world ground to a standstill. The silence was so immense and unbelievable that you felt your ears had been stuffed or you had lost your hearing altogether. The children put their hands to their ears. They stood apart. The door slid back and the smell of the silent, waiting world came in to them.

The sun came out.

It was the color of flaming bronze and it was very large. And the sky around it was a blazing blue tile color. And the jungle burned with sunlight as the children, released from their spell, rushed out, yelling, into the springtime.

"Now don't go too far," called the teacher after them. "You've only two hours, you know. You wouldn't want to get caught out!"

But they were running and turning their faces up to the sky and feeling the sun on their cheeks like a warm iron; they were taking off their jackets and letting the sun burn their arms.

"Oh, it's better than the sun lamps, isn't it?"

"Much, much better!"

They stopped running and stood in the great jungle that covered Venus, that grew and never stopped growing, tumultuously, even as you watched it. It was a nest of octopi, clustering up great arms of flesh-like weed, wavering, flowering this brief spring. It was the color of rubber and ash, this jungle, from the many years without sun. It was the color of stones and white cheeses and ink, and it was the color of the moon.

The children lay out, laughing, on the jungle mattress, and heard it sigh and squeak under them, resilient and alive. They ran among the trees, they slipped and fell, they pushed each other, they played hide-and-seek and tag, but most of all they squinted at the sun until the tears ran down their faces, they put their hands up to that yellowness and that amazing blueness and they breathed of the fresh, fresh air and listened and listened to the silence which suspended them in a blessed sea of no sound and no motion. They looked at everything and savored everything. Then, wildly, like animals escaped from their caves, they ran and ran in shouting circles. They ran for an hour and did not stop running.

And then—

In the midst of their running one of the girls wailed.

Everyone stopped.

The girl, standing in the open, held out her hand.

"Oh, look, look," she said, trembling.

They came slowly to look at her opened palm.

In the center of it, cupped and huge, was a single raindrop.

She began to cry, looking at it.

They glanced quietly at the sky.

"Oh. Oh."

A few cold drops fell on their noses and their cheeks and their mouths. The sun faded behind a stir of mist. A wind blew cool around them. They turned and started to walk back toward the underground house, their hands at their sides, their smiles vanishing away.

A boom of thunder startled them and like leaves before a new hurricane, they tumbled upon each other and ran. Lightening struck ten miles away, five miles away, a mile, a half mile. The sky darkened into midnight in a flash.

They stood in the doorway of the underground for a moment until it was raining hard. Then they closed the door and heard the gigantic sound of the rain falling in tons and avalanches, everywhere and forever.

"Will it be seven more years?"

"Yes. Seven."

Then one of them gave a little cry.

"Margot!"

"What?"

"She's still in the closet where we locked her."

"Margot."

They stood as if someone had driven them, like so many stakes, into the floor. They looked at each other and then looked away. They glanced out at the world that was raining now and raining and raining steadily. They could not meet each other's glances. Their faces were solemn and pale. They looked at their hands and feet, their faces down.

"Margot."

One of the girls said, "Well . . . ?"

No one moved.

"Go on," whispered the girl.

They walked slowly down the hall in the sound of the cold rain. They turned through the doorway to the room in the sound of the storm and thunder, lightening on their faces, blue and terrible. They walked over to the closet door slowly and stood by it.

Behind the closed door was only silence.

They unlocked the door, even more slowly, and let Margot out.

NOTES

INCIDENT
Countee Cullen

(1903–1946)

A black poet and novelist known for his lyrical style, Countee Cullen was born in New York City and earned an M.A. in English literature from Harvard. He gained attention with his first collection of poems, Color *(1925). Later in life, he dedicated himself to teaching.*

Once riding in old Baltimore,
  Heart-filled, head-filled with glee,
I saw a Baltimorean
  Keep looking straight at me.

Now I was eight and very small,
  And he was no whit bigger,
And so I smiled, but he poked out
  His tongue, and called me, "Nigger."

I saw the whole of Baltimore
  From May until December;
Of all the things that happened there
  That's all that I remember.

NOTES

TWO CHEERS FOR DOUBLE STANDARDS
Stanley Fish

(1938–)

Stanley Fish is the Davidson-Kahn Distinguished University Professor of Humanities and Law at Florida International University. He obtained his BA from the University of Pennsylvania and his MA/PhD from Yale University. He is considered one of the foremost public intellectuals in the nation. The author of twelve books, he has also written countless articles.

What is a double standard? It's a double standard when you condemn an opponent for doing or saying something you would approve or excuse if it were said or done by one of your buddies. The double standard that is in the news these days concerns Rush Limbaugh, who called Sandra Fluke, a law student at Georgetown, a "slut" and "prostitute" because she told Congress that her university's health plan should cover the cost of contraceptives.

Limbaugh has not had many defenders (Mitt Romney said weakly that he wouldn't have used that language), but some on the conservative side of the aisle have cried "double standard" because Ed Schultz was only mildly criticized (and suspended for a week) for characterizing Laura Ingraham as a "right-wing slut," and Bill Maher emerged relatively unscathed after he referred to Michele Bachmann as a "bimbo" and labeled Sarah Palin with words I can't mention in this newspaper. If you are going to get on your high horse when Limbaugh says something inappropriate, shouldn't you also mount the steed when commentators on your team say the same kind of thing? Isn't what's good for the goose good for the gander?

These questions come naturally to those who have been schooled in the political philosophy of enlightenment liberalism. The key move in that philosophy is to shift the emphasis from substantive judgment—is what has been said good and true?—to a requirement of procedural reciprocity—you must treat speakers equally even if you can't abide what some of them stand for. Basically this is the transposition into the political realm of the Golden Rule: do unto others what you would have them do unto you. Don't give your friends a pass you wouldn't give to your enemies.

So if you come down hard on Limbaugh because he has crossed a line, you must come down hard on Schultz and Maher because they have crossed the same line; and you should do this despite the fact that in general—that is, on all the important issues—you think Schultz and Maher are right and Limbaugh is horribly and maliciously wrong. (Some left-wing commentators have argued that there is a principled way of slamming Limbaugh while letting the other two off the hook, because he went after a private citizen while they were defaming public figures. Won't wash.)

Reprinted by permission from the *New York Times,* March 12, 2012.

The idea is that in the public sphere (as opposed to the private sphere in which you can have and vent your prejudices) you should not privilege your own views to the extent that they justify treating those with opposing views unequally and unfairly. (Fairness is the great liberal virtue.) This idea is concisely captured by the philosopher Thomas Nagel when he says that in political life we should regard our most cherished beliefs, "whether moral or religious . . . simply as someone's beliefs rather than as truths." In short, back away from or relax your strongest convictions about what is right and wrong and act in a manner that grants legitimacy, at least of a formal kind, to the convictions of others, even of others you despise.

But there is an alternative way of looking at the matter and it is represented in a scene (which I have discussed previously in "The Trouble With Principle") from the classic western movie "The Wild Bunch." Two outlaws, played by William Holden and Ernest Borgnine, are talking about the gang of railroad detectives pursuing them. What rankles is that at the head of the gang is one of their old comrades. Borgnine's character is dismayed at what he takes to be the treachery of a former colleague. Holden's character explains that he gave his word to the railroad. Borgnine's character shoots back, "That ain't what counts! It's who you give your word to." What counts is who your friends and allies are. You keep your word to them and not just to anybody. Your loyalty is to particular people and not to an abstraction.

The same disdain for choosing principle over family and friends was displayed by the Chicago Mayor Richard. J. Daley when he was accused of nepotism for having steered the city's insurance business to his son's agency. Nonplussed, Daley asked (rhetorically), "Isn't that what fathers are supposed to do, help their children get a start in life?"("Liberty in America," by rtbohan, June 18, 2008).

Another assertion of the primacy of family loyalty is found in Milton's "Paradise Lost" when Satan describes himself as a "faithful leader." The angel Gabriel retorts, "Faithful to whom? To thy rebellious crew? / Army of fiends?" Like Daley and like the character Borgnine plays, Gabriel rejects a notion of fidelity that is indifferent as to its object. Your faith is not binding simply because you have pledged it; it is binding only if it is pledged to the right people. (What counts is who you give your word to.) If you're going to be faithful, be faithful to the Father who made you and not to a bunch of ungrateful apostates. Obligations are not owed to everyone, but only to those who are of the right sort.

If we think about the Rush Limbaugh dust-up from the non-liberal—that is, non-formal—perspective, the similarity between what he did and what Schultz and Maher did disappears. Schultz and Maher are the good guys; they are on the side of truth and justice. Limbaugh is the bad guy; he is on the side of every nefarious force that threatens our democracy. Why should he get an even break?

There is no answer to that question once you step outside of the liberal calculus in which all persons, no matter what their moral status as you see it, are weighed in an equal balance. Rather than relaxing or soft-pedaling your convictions about what is right and wrong, stay with them, and treat people you see as morally different differently. Condemn Limbaugh and say that Schultz and Maher may have gone a bit too far but that they're basically O.K. If you do that you will not be displaying a double standard; you will be affirming a single standard, and moreover it will be a moral one because you will be going with what you think is good rather than what you think is fair. "Fair" is a weak virtue; it is not even a virtue at all because it insists on a withdrawal from moral judgment.

I know the objections to what I have said here. It amounts to an apology for identity politics. It elevates tribal obligations over the universal obligations we owe to each other as citizens. It licenses differential and discriminatory treatment on the basis of contested points of view. It substitutes for the rule "don't do it to them if you don't want it done to you" the rule "be sure to do it to them first and more effectively." It implies finally that might makes right. I can live with that.

NOTES

A STATEMENT FROM EIGHT ALABAMA CLERGYMEN

We the undersigned clergymen are among those who, in January, issued "an appeal for law and order and common sense," in dealing with racial problems in Alabama. We expressed understanding that honest convictions in racial matters could properly be pursued in the courts, but urged that decisions of those courts should in the meantime be peacefully obeyed.

Since that time there had been some evidence of increased forbearance and a willingness to face facts. Responsible citizens have undertaken to work on various problems which cause racial friction and unrest. In Birmingham, recent public events have given indication that we all have opportunity for a new constructive and realistic approach to racial problems.

However, we are now confronted by a series of demonstrations by some of our Negro citizens, directed and led in part by outsiders. We recognize the natural impatience of people who feel that their hopes are slow in being realized. But we are convinced that these demonstrations are unwise and untimely.

We agree rather with certain local Negro leadership which has called for honest and open negotiation of racial issues in our area. And we believe this kind of facing of issues can best be accomplished by citizens of our own metropolitan area, white and Negro, meeting with their knowledge and experience of the local situation. All of us need to face that responsibility and find proper channels for its accomplishment.

Just as we formerly pointed out that "hatred and violence have no sanction in our religious and political traditions," we also point out that such actions as incite to hatred and violence, however technically peaceful those actions may be, have not contributed to the resolution of our local problems. We do not believe that these days of new hope are days when extreme measures are justified in Birmingham.

We commend the community as a whole, and the local news media and law enforcement officials in particular, on the calm manner in which these demonstrations have been handled. We urge the public to continue to show restraint should the demonstrations continue, and the law enforcement officials to remain calm and continue to protect our city from violence.

We further strongly urge our own Negro community to withdraw support from these demonstrations, and to unite locally in working peacefully for a better Birmingham. When rights are consistently denied, a cause should be pressed in the courts and in negotiations among local leaders, and not in the streets. We appeal to both our white and Negro citizenry to observe the principles of law and order and common sense.

Bishop C.C.J. Carpenter, D.D., LL.D., Episcopalian Bishop of Alabama

Bishop Joseph A. Durick, D.D., Auxiliary Bishop, Roman Catholic Diocese of Mobile, Birmingham

Rabbi Milton L. Grafman, Temple Emanu-El, Birmingham, Alabama

Bishop Paul Hardin, Methodist Bishop of the Alabama-West Florida Conference

Bishop Nolan B. Harmon, Bishop of the North Alabama Conference of the Methodist Church

Rev. George M. Murray, D.D., LL.D, Bishop Coadjutor, Episcopal Diocese of Alabama

Rev. Edward V. Ramage, Moderator, Synod of the Alabama Presbyterian Church in the United States

Rev. Earl Stallings, Pastor, First Baptist Church, Birmingham, Alabama

NOTES

NOTES

LETTER FROM BIRMINGHAM JAIL
Martin Luther King, Jr.

(1929–1968)

An African-American Baptist minister, Martin Luther King, Jr. was the principal leader of the civil rights movement in the United States in the 1950s and 1960s. His eloquent speaking style and determined demands for social justice earned him international renown and the support of millions of blacks and whites in this country. Though he was often the target of violence himself, he continued to lead nonviolent civil rights demonstrations for which he won the 1964 Nobel Peace Prize. While organizing the Poor People's Campaign, he traveled to Memphis to take part in a black garbage workers' strike. He was shot and killed there by the white, escaped convict, James Earl Ray.

April 16, 1963
MY DEAR FELLOW CLERGYMEN:

While confined here in the Birmingham city jail, I came across your recent statement calling my present activities "unwise and untimely." Seldom do I pause to answer criticism of my work and ideas. If I sought to answer all the criticisms that cross my desk, my secretaries would have little time for anything other than such correspondence in the course of the day, and I would have no time for constructive work. But since I feel that you are men of genuine good will and that your criticisms are sincerely set forth, I want to try to answer your statements in what I hope will be patient and reasonable terms.

I think I should indicate why I am here in Birmingham, since you have been influenced by the view which argues against "outsiders coming in." I have the honor of serving as president of the Southern Christian Leadership Conference, an organization operating in every southern state, with headquarters in Atlanta, Georgia. We have some eighty-five affiliated organizations across the South, and one of them is the Alabama Christian Movement for Human Rights. Frequently we share staff, educational and financial resources with our affiliates. Several months ago the affiliate here in Birmingham asked us to be on call to engage in a nonviolent direct-action program if such were deemed necessary. We readily consented, and when the hour came we lived up to our promise. So I, along with several members of my staff, am here because I was invited here I am here because I have organizational ties here.

But more basically, I am in Birmingham because injustice is here. Just as the prophets of the eighth century B.C. left their villages and carried their "thus saith the Lord" far beyond the boundaries of their home towns, and just as the Apostle Paul left his village of Tarsus and carried the gospel of Jesus Christ to the far corners of the Greco-Roman world, so am I compelled to carry the gospel of freedom beyond my own home town. Like Paul, I must constantly respond to the Macedonian call for aid.

Moreover, I am cognizant of the interrelatedness of all communities and states. I cannot sit idly by in Atlanta and not be concerned about what happens in Birmingham. Injustice anywhere is a threat to justice everywhere. We are caught in an inescapable network of mutuality, tied in a single garment of destiny. Whatever affects one directly, affects all indirectly. Never again can we afford to live with the narrow, provincial "outside agitator" idea. Anyone who lives inside the United States can never be considered an outsider anywhere within its bounds.

You deplore the demonstrations taking place in Birmingham. But your statement, I am sorry to say, fails to express a similar concern for the conditions that brought about the demonstrations. I am sure that none of you would want to rest content with the superficial kind of social analysis that deals merely with effects and does not grapple with underlying causes. It is unfortunate that demonstrations are taking place in Birmingham, but it is even more unfortunate that the city's white power structure left the Negro community with no alternative.

In any nonviolent campaign there are four basic steps: collection of the facts to determine whether injustices exist; negotiation; self-purification; and direct action. We have gone through all these steps in Birmingham. There can be no gainsaying the fact that racial injustice engulfs this community. Birmingham is probably the most thoroughly segregated city in the United States. Its ugly record of brutality is widely known. Negroes have experienced grossly unjust treatment in the courts. There have been more unsolved bombings of Negro homes and churches in Birmingham than in any other city in the nation. These are the hard, brutal facts of the case. On the basis of these conditions, Negro leaders sought to negotiate with the city fathers. But the latter consistently refused to engage in good-faith negotiation.

Then, last September, came the opportunity to talk with leaders of Birmingham's economic community. In the course of the negotiations, certain promises were made by the merchants—for example, to remove the stores' humiliating racial signs. On the basis of these promises, the Reverend Fred Shuttlesworth and the leaders of the Alabama Christian Movement for Human Rights agreed to a moratorium on all demonstrations. As the weeks and months went by, we realized that we were the victims of a broken promise. A few signs, briefly removed, returned; the others remained.

As in so many past experiences, our hopes had been blasted, and the shadow of deep disappointment settled upon us. We had no alternative except to prepare for direct action, whereby we would present our very bodies as a means of laying our case before the conscience of the local and the national community. Mindful of the difficulties involved, we decided to undertake a process of self-purification. We began a series of workshops on nonviolence, and we repeatedly asked ourselves: "Are you able to accept blows without retaliating?" "Are you able to endure the ordeal of jail?" We decided to schedule our direct-action program for the Easter season, realizing that except for Christmas, this is the main shopping period of the year. Knowing that a strong economic withdrawal program would be the by-product of direct action, we felt that this would be the best time to bring pressure to bear on the merchants for the needed change.

Then it occurred to us that Birmingham's mayoralty election was coming up in March, and we speedily decided to postpone action until after election day. When we discovered that the Commissioner of Public Safety, Eugene "Bull" Connor, had piled up enough votes to be in the run-off we decided again to postpone action until the day after the run-off so that the demonstrations could not be used to cloud the issues. Like many others, we waited to see Mr. Connor defeated, and to this end we endured postponement after postponement. Having aided in this community need, we felt that our direct-action program could be delayed no longer.

You may well ask: "Why direct action? Why sit-ins, marches and so forth? Isn't negotiation a better path?" You are quite right in calling for negotiation. Indeed, this is the very purpose of direct action. Nonviolent direct action seeks to create such a crisis and foster such a tension that a community which has constantly refused to negotiate is forced to confront the issue. It seeks so to dramatize the issue that it can no longer be ignored. My citing the creation of tension as part of the work of the nonviolent-resister may sound rather shocking. But I must confess that I am not afraid of the word "tension." I have earnestly opposed violent tension, but there is a type of constructive, nonviolent tension which is necessary for growth. Just as Socrates felt that it was necessary to create a tension in the mind so that individuals could rise from the bondage of myths and half-truths to the unfettered realm of creative analysis and objective appraisal, so must we see the need for nonviolent gadflies to create the kind of tension in society that will help men rise from the dark depths of prejudice and racism to the majestic heights of understanding and brotherhood.

The purpose of our direct-action program is to create a situation so crisis-packed that it will inevitably open the door to negotiation. I therefore concur with you in your call for negotiation. Too long has our beloved Southland been bogged down in a tragic effort to live in monologue rather than dialogue.

One of the basic points in your statement is that the action that I and my associates have taken in Birmingham is untimely. Some have asked: "Why didn't you give the new city administration time to act?" The only answer that I can give to this query is that the new Birmingham administration must be prodded about as much as the outgoing one, before it will act. We are sadly mistaken if we feel that the election of Albert Boutwell as mayor will bring the millennium to Birmingham. While Mr. Boutwell is a much more gentle person than Mr. Connor, they are both segregationists, dedicated to maintenance of the status quo. I have hope that Mr. Boutwell will be reasonable enough to see the futility of massive resistance to desegregation. But he will not see this without pressure from devotees of civil rights. My friends, I must say to you that we have not made a single gain in civil rights without determined legal and nonviolent pressure. Lamentably, it is an historical fact that privileged groups seldom give up their privileges voluntarily. Individuals may see the moral light and voluntarily give up their unjust posture; but, as Reinhold Niebuhr has reminded us, groups tend to be more immoral than individuals.

We know through painful experience that freedom is never voluntarily given by the oppressor; it must be demanded by the oppressed. Frankly, I have yet to engage in a direct-action campaign that was "well timed" in the view of those who have not suffered unduly from the disease of segregation. For years now I have heard the word "Wait!" It rings in the ear of every Negro with piercing familiarity. This "Wait" has almost always meant "Never." We must come to see, with one of our distinguished jurists, that "justice too long delayed is justice denied."

We have waited for more than 340 years for our constitutional and God-given rights. The nations of Asia and Africa are moving with jetlike speed toward gaining political independence, but we still creep at horse-and-buggy pace toward gaining a cup of coffee at a lunch counter. Perhaps it is easy for those who have never felt the stinging dark of segregation to say, "Wait." But when you have seen vicious mobs lynch your mothers and fathers at will and drown your sisters and brothers at whim; when you have seen hate-filled policemen curse, kick and even kill your black brothers and sisters; when you see the vast majority of your twenty million Negro brothers smothering in an airtight cage of poverty in the midst of an affluent society; when you suddenly find your tongue twisted and your speech stammering as you seek to explain to your six-year-old daughter why she can't go to the public amusement park that has just been advertised on television, and see tears welling up in her eyes when she is told that Funtown is closed to colored children, and see ominous clouds of inferiority beginning to form in her little mental sky, and see her beginning to distort her personality by developing an unconscious bitterness toward white people; when you have to concoct an answer for a five-year-old son who is asking: "Daddy, why do white people treat colored people so mean?"; when you take a cross-county drive and find it necessary to sleep night after night in the uncomfortable corners of your automobile because no motel will accept you; when you are humiliated day in and day out by nagging signs reading "white" and "colored"; when your first name becomes "nigger," your middle name becomes "boy" (however old you are) and your last name becomes "John," and your wife and mother are never given the respected title "Mrs."; when you are harried by day and haunted by night by the fact that you are a Negro, living constantly at tiptoe stance, never quite knowing what to expect next, and are plagued with inner fears and outer resentments; when you are forever fighting a degenerating sense of "nobodiness" then you will understand why we find it difficult to wait. There comes a time when the cup of endurance runs over, and men are no longer willing to be plunged into the abyss of despair. I hope, sirs, you can understand our legitimate and unavoidable impatience.

You express a great deal of anxiety over our willingness to break laws. This is certainly a legitimate concern. Since we so diligently urge people to obey the Supreme Court's decision of 1954 outlawing segregation in the public schools, at first glance it may seem rather paradoxical for us consciously to break laws. One may well ask: "How can you advocate breaking some laws and obeying others?" The answer lies in the fact that there are two types of laws: just and unjust. I would be the first to advocate obeying just laws. One has not only a legal but a moral responsibility to obey just laws. Conversely, one has a moral responsibility to disobey unjust laws. I would agree with St. Augustine that "an unjust law is no law at all."

Now, what is the difference between the two? How does one determine whether a law is just or unjust? A just law is a man-made code that squares with the moral law or the law of God. An unjust law is a code that is out of harmony with the moral law. To put it in the terms of St. Thomas Aquinas: An unjust law is a human law that is not rooted in eternal law and natural law. Any law that uplifts human personality is just. Any law that degrades human personality is unjust. All segregation statutes are unjust because segregation distorts the soul and damages the personality. It gives the segregator a false sense of superiority and the segregated a false sense of inferiority. Segregation, to use the terminology of the Jewish philosopher Martin Buber, substitutes an "I-it" relationship for an "I-thou" relationship and ends up relegating persons to the status of things. Hence segregation is not only politically, economically and sociologically unsound, it is morally wrong and awful. Paul Tillich said that sin is separation. Is not segregation an existential expression of man's tragic separation, his awful estrangement, his terrible sinfulness? Thus it is that I can urge men to obey the 1954 decision of the Supreme Court, for it is morally right; and I can urge them to disobey segregation ordinances, for they are morally wrong.

Let us consider a more concrete example of just and unjust laws. An unjust law is a code that a numerical or power majority group compels a minority group to obey but does not make binding on itself. This is difference made legal. By the same token, a just law is a code that a majority compels a minority to follow and that it is willing to follow itself. This is sameness made legal.

Let me give another explanation. A law is unjust if it is inflicted on a minority that, as a result of being denied the right to vote, had no part in enacting or devising the law. Who can say that the legislature of Alabama which set up that state's segregation laws was democratically elected? Throughout Alabama all sorts of devious methods are used to prevent Negroes from becoming registered voters, and there are some counties in which, even though Negroes constitute a majority of the population, not a single Negro is registered. Can any law enacted under such circumstances be considered democratically structured?

Sometimes a law is just on its face and unjust in its application. For instance, I have been arrested on a charge of parading without a permit. Now, there is nothing wrong in having an ordinance which requires a permit for a parade. But such an ordinance becomes unjust when it is used to maintain segregation and to deny citizens the First Amendment privilege of peaceful assembly and protest.

I hope you are able to see the distinction I am trying to point out. In no sense do I advocate evading or defying the law, as would the rabid segregationist. That would lead to anarchy. One who breaks an unjust law must do so openly, lovingly, and with a willingness to accept the penalty. I submit that an individual who breaks a law that conscience tells him is unjust and who willingly accepts the penalty of imprisonment in order to arouse the conscience of the community over its injustice, is in reality expressing the highest respect for law.

Of course, there is nothing new about this kind of civil disobedience. It was evidenced sublimely in the refusal of Shadrach, Meshach and Abednego to obey the laws of Nebuchadnezzar, on the ground that a higher moral law was at stake. It was practiced superbly by the early Christians, who were willing to face hungry lions and the excruciating pain of chopping blocks rather than submit to certain unjust laws of the Roman Empire. To a degree, academic freedom is a reality today because Socrates practiced civil disobedience. In our own nation, the Boston Tea Party represented a massive act of civil disobedience.

We should never forget that everything Adolf Hitler did in Germany was "legal" and everything the Hungarian freedom fighters did in Hungary was "illegal." It was "illegal" to aid and comfort a Jew in Hitler's Germany. Even so, I am sure that, had I lived in Germany at the time, I would have aided and comforted my Jewish brothers. If today I lived in a Communist country where certain principles dear to the Christian faith are suppressed, I would openly advocate disobeying that country's antireligious laws.

I must make two honest confessions to you, my Christian and Jewish brothers. First, I must confess that over the past few years I have been gravely disappointed with the white moderate. I have almost reached the regrettable conclusion that the Negro's great stumbling block in his stride toward freedom is not the White Citizen's Counciler or the Ku Klux Klanner, but the white moderate, who is more devoted to "order" than to justice; who prefers a negative peace which is the absence of tension to a positive peace which is the presence of justice; who constantly says "I agree with you in the goal you seek, but I cannot agree with your methods of direct action"; who paternalistically believes he can set the timetable for another man's freedom; who lives by a mythical concept of time and who constantly advises the Negro to wait for a "more convenient season." Shallow understanding from people of good will is more frustrating than absolute misunderstanding from people of ill will. Lukewarm acceptance is much more bewildering than outright rejection.

I had hoped that the white moderate would understand that law and order exist for the purpose of establishing justice and that when they fail in this purpose they become the dangerously structured dams that block the flow of social progress. I had hoped that the white moderate would understand that the present tension in the South is a necessary phase of the transition from an obnoxious negative peace, in which the Negro passively accepted his unjust plight, to a substantive and positive peace, in which all men will respect the dignity and worth of human personality. Actually, we who engage in nonviolent direct action are not the creators of tension. We merely bring to the surface the hidden tension that is already alive. We bring it out in the open, where it can be seen and dealt with. Like a boil that can never be cured so long as it is covered up but must be opened with all its ugliness to the natural medicines of air and light, injustice must be exposed, with all the tension its exposure creates, to the light of human conscience and the air of national opinion before it can be cured.

In your statement you assert that our actions, even though peaceful, must be condemned because they precipitate violence. But is this a logical assertion? Isn't this like condemning a robbed man because his possession of money precipitated the evil act of robbery? Isn't this like condemning Socrates because his unswerving commitment to truth and his philosophical inquiries precipitated the act by the misguided populace in which they made him drink hemlock? Isn't this like condemning Jesus because his unique God-consciousness and never-ceasing devotion to God's will precipitated the evil act of crucifixion? We must come to see that, as the federal courts have consistently affirmed, it is wrong to urge an individual to cease his efforts to gain his basic constitutional rights because the quest may precipitate violence. Society must protect the robbed and punish the robber.

I had also hoped that the white moderate would reject the myth concerning time in relation to the struggle for freedom. I have just received a letter from a white brother in Texas. He writes: "All Christians know that the colored people will receive equal rights eventually, but it is possible that you are in too great a religious hurry. It has taken Christianity almost two thousand years to accomplish what it has. The teachings of Christ take time to come to earth." Such an attitude stems from a tragic misconception of time, from the strangely rational notion that there is something in the very flow of time that will inevitably cure all ills. Actually, time itself is neutral; it can be used either destructively or constructively. More and more I feel that the people of ill will have used time much more effectively than have the people of good will. We will have to repent in this generation not merely for the hateful words and actions of the bad people but for the appalling silence of the good people. Human progress never rolls in on wheels of inevitability; it comes through the tireless efforts of men willing to be co-workers with God, and without this 'hard work, time itself becomes an ally of the forces of social stagnation. We must use time creatively, in the knowledge that the time is always ripe to do right. Now is the time to make real the promise of democracy and transform our pending national elegy into a creative psalm of brotherhood. Now is the time to lift our national policy from the quicksand of racial injustice to the solid rock of human dignity.

You speak of our activity in Birmingham as extreme. At fist I was rather disappointed that fellow clergymen would see my nonviolent efforts as those of an extremist. I began thinking about the fact that I stand in the middle of two opposing forces in the Negro community. One is a force of complacency, made up in part of Negroes who, as a result of long years of oppression, are so drained of self-respect and a sense of "somebodiness" that they have adjusted to segregation; and in part of a few middle class Negroes who, because of a degree of academic and economic security and because in some ways they profit by segregation, have become insensitive to the problems of the masses. The other force is one of bitterness and hatred, and it comes perilously close to advocating violence. It is expressed in the various black nationalist groups that are springing up across the nation, the largest and best-known being Elijah Muhammad's Muslim movement. Nourished by the Negro's frustration over the continued existence of racial discrimination, this movement is made up of people who have lost faith in America, who have absolutely repudiated Christianity, and who have concluded that the white man is an incorrigible "devil."

I have tried to stand between these two forces, saying that we need emulate neither the "do-nothingism" of the complacent nor the hatred and despair of the black nationalist. For there is the more excellent way of love and nonviolent protest. I am grateful to God that, through the influence of the Negro church, the way of nonviolence became an integral part of our struggle.

If this philosophy had not emerged, by now many streets of the South would, I am convinced, be flowing with blood. And I am further convinced that if our white brothers dismiss as "rabble-rousers" and "outside agitators" those of us who employ nonviolent direct action, and if they refuse to support our nonviolent efforts, millions of Negroes will, out of frustration and despair, seek solace and security in black-nationalist ideologies a development that would inevitably lead to a frightening racial nightmare.

Oppressed people cannot remain oppressed forever. The yearning for freedom eventually manifests itself, and that is what has happened to the American Negro. Something within has reminded him of his birthright of freedom, and something without has reminded him that it can be gained. Consciously or unconsciously, he has been caught up by the Zeitgeist, and with his black brothers of Africa and his brown and yellow brothers of Asia, South America and the Caribbean, the United States Negro is moving with a sense of great urgency toward the promised land of racial justice. If one recognizes this vital urge that has engulfed the Negro community, one should readily understand why public demonstrations are taking place. The Negro has many pent-up resentments and latent frustrations, and he must release them. So let him march; let him make prayer pilgrimages to the city hall; let him go on freedom rides—and try to understand why he must do so. If his repressed emotions are not released in nonviolent ways, they will seek expression through violence; this is not a threat but a fact of history. So I have not said to my people: "Get rid of your discontent." Rather, I have tried to say that this normal and healthy discontent can be channeled into the creative outlet of nonviolent direct action. And now this approach is being termed extremist.

But though I was initially disappointed at being categorized as an extremist, as I continued to think about the matter I gradually gained a measure of satisfaction from the label. Was not Jesus an extremist for love: "Love your enemies, bless them that curse you, do good to them that hate you, and pray for them which despitefully use you, and persecute you." Was not Amos an extremist for justice: "Let justice roll down like waters and righteousness like an ever-flowing stream." Was not Paul an extremist for the Christian gospel: "I bear in my body the marks of the Lord Jesus." Was not Martin Luther an extremist: "Here I stand; I cannot do otherwise, so help me God." And John Bunyan: "I will stay in jail to the end of my days before I make a butchery of my conscience." And Abraham Lincoln: "This nation cannot survive half slave and half free." And Thomas Jefferson: "We hold these truths to be self-evident, that all men are created equal . . ." So the question is not whether we will be extremists, but what kind of extremists we will be. Will we be extremists for hate or for love? Will we be extremist for the preservation of injustice or for the extension of justice? In that dramatic scene on Calvary's hill three men were crucified. We must never forget that all three were crucified for the same crime—the crime of extremism. Two were extremists for immorality, and thus fell below their environment. The other, Jesus Christ, was an extremist for love, truth and goodness, and thereby rose above his environment. Perhaps the South, the nation and the world are in dire need of creative extremists.

I had hoped that the white moderate would see this need. Perhaps I was too optimistic; perhaps I expected too much. I suppose I should have realized that few members of the oppressor race can understand the deep groans and passionate yearnings of the oppressed race, and still fewer have the vision to see that injustice must be rooted out by strong, persistent and determined action. I am thankful, however, that some of our white brothers in the South have grasped the meaning of this social revolution and committed themselves to it. They are still too few in quantity, but they are big in quality. Some-such as Ralph McGill, Lillian Smith, Harry Golden, James McBride Dabbs, Ann Braden and Sarah Patton Boyle—have written about our struggle in eloquent and prophetic terms. Others have marched with us down nameless streets of the South. They have languished in filthy, roach-infested jails, suffering the abuse and brutality of policemen who view them as "dirty nigger lovers." Unlike so many of their moderate brothers and sisters, they have recognized the urgency of the moment and sensed the need for powerful "action" antidotes to combat the disease of segregation.

Let me take note of my other major disappointment. I have been so greatly disappointed with the white church and its leadership. Of course, there are some notable exceptions. I am not unmindful of the fact that each of you has taken some significant stands on this issue. I commend you, Reverend Stallings, for your Christian stand on this past Sunday, in welcoming Negroes to your worship service on a non segregated basis. I commend the Catholic leaders of this state for integrating Spring Hill College several years ago.

But despite these notable exceptions, I must honestly reiterate that I have been disappointed with the church. I do not say this as one of those negative critics who can always find something wrong with the church. I say this as a minister of the gospel, who loves the church; who was nurtured in its bosom; who has been sustained by its spiritual blessings and who will remain true to it as long as the cord of life shall lengthen.

When I was suddenly catapulted into the leadership of the bus protest in Montgomery, Alabama, a few years ago, I felt we would be supported by the white church. I felt that the white ministers, priests and rabbis of the South would be among our strongest allies. Instead, some have been outright opponents, refusing to understand the freedom movement and misrepresenting its leaders all too many others have been more cautious than courageous and have remained silent behind the anesthetizing security of stained-glass windows.

In spite of my shattered dreams, I came to Birmingham with the hope that the white religious leadership of this community would see the justice of our cause and, with deep moral concern, would serve as the channel through which our just grievances could reach the power structure. I had hoped that each of you would understand. But again I have been disappointed.

I have heard numerous southern religious leaders admonish their worshipers to comply with a desegregation decision because it is the law, but I have longed to hear white ministers declare: "Follow this decree because integration is morally right and because the Negro is your brother." In the midst of blantant injustices inflicted upon the Negro, I have watched white churchmen stand on the sideline and mouth pious irrelevancies and sanctimonious trivialities. In the midst of a mighty struggle to rid our nation of racial and economic injustice, I have heard many ministers say: "Those are social issues, with which the gospel has no real concern." And I have watched many churches commit themselves to a completely other worldly religion which makes a strange, un-Biblical distinction between body and soul, between the sacred and the secular.

I have traveled the length and breadth of Alabama, Mississippi and all the other southern states. On sweltering summer days and crisp autumn mornings I have looked at the South's beautiful churches with their lofty spires pointing heavenward. I have beheld the impressive outlines of her massive religious-education buildings. Over and over I have found myself asking: "What kind of people worship here? Who is their God? Where were their voices when the lips of Governor Barnett dripped with words of interposition and nullification? Where were they when Governor Wallace gave a clarion call for defiance and hatred? Where were their voices of support when bruised and weary Negro men and women decided to rise from the dark dungeons of complacency to the bright hills of creative protest?"

Yes, these questions are still in my mind. In deep disappointment I have wept over the laxity of the church. But be assured that my tears have been tears of love. There can be no deep disappointment where there is not deep love. Yes, I love the church. How could I do otherwise? I am in the rather unique position of being the son, the grandson and the great-grandson of preachers. Yes, I see the church as the body of Christ. But, oh! How we have blemished and scarred that body through social neglect and through fear of being nonconformists.

There was a time when the church was very powerful in the time when the early Christians rejoiced at being deemed worthy to suffer for what they believed. In those days the church was not merely a thermometer that recorded the ideas and principles of popular opinion; it was a thermostat that transformed the mores of society. Whenever the early Christians entered a town, the people in power became disturbed and immediately sought to convict the Christians for being "disturbers of the peace" and "outside agitators" But the Christians pressed on, in the conviction that they were "a colony of heaven," called to obey God rather than man. Small in number, they were big in commitment. They were too God intoxicated to be "astronomically intimidated." By their effort and example they brought an end to such ancient evils as infanticide, and gladiatorial contests.

Things are different now. So often the contemporary church is a weak, ineffectual voice with an uncertain sound. So often it is an archdefender of the status quo. Far from being disturbed by the presence of the church, the power structure of the average community is consoled by the church's silent and often even vocal sanction of things as they are.

But the judgment of God is upon the church as never before. If today's church does not recapture the sacrificial spirit of the early church, it will lose its authenticity, forfeit the loyalty of millions, and be dismissed as an irrelevant social club with no meaning for the twentieth century. Every day I meet young people whose disappointment with the church has turned into outright disgust.

Perhaps I have once again been too optimistic. Is organized religion too inextricably bound to the status quo to save our nation and the world? Perhaps I must turn my faith to the inner spiritual church, the church within the church, as the true ekklesia and the hope of the world. But again I am thankful to God that some noble souls from the ranks of organized religion have broken loose from the paralyzing chains of conformity and joined us as active partners in the struggle for freedom. They have left their secure congregations and walked the streets of Albany, Georgia, with us. They have gone down the highways of the South on tortuous rides for freedom. Yes, they have gone to jail with us. Some have been dismissed from their churches, have lost the support of their bishops and fellow ministers. But they have acted in the faith that right defeated is stronger than evil triumphant. Their witness has been the spiritual salt that has preserved the true meaning of the gospel in these troubled times. They have carved a tunnel of hope through the dark mountain of disappointment.

I hope the church as a whole will meet the challenge of this decisive hour. But even if the church does not come to the aid of justice, I have no despair about the future. I have no fear about the outcome of our struggle in Birmingham, even if our motives are at present misunderstood. We will reach the goal of freedom in Birmingham and all over the nation, because the goal of America is freedom. Abused and scorned though we may be, our destiny is tied up with America's destiny. Before the pilgrims landed at Plymouth, we were here. Before the pen of Jefferson etched the majestic words of the Declaration of Independence across the pages of history, we were here. For more than two centuries our forebears labored in this country without wages; they made cotton king; they built the homes of their masters while suffering gross injustice and shameful humiliation—and yet out of a bottomless vitality they continued to thrive and develop. If the inexpressible cruelties of slavery could not stop us, the opposition we now face will surely fail. We will win our freedom because the sacred heritage of our nation and the eternal will of God are embodied in our echoing demands.

Before closing I feel impelled to mention one other point in your statement that has troubled me profoundly. You warmly commended the Birmingham police force for keeping "order" and "preventing violence." I doubt that you would have so warmly commended the police force if you had seen its dogs sinking their teeth into unarmed, nonviolent Negroes. I doubt that you would so quickly commend the policemen if you were to observe their ugly and inhumane treatment of Negroes here in the city jail; if you were to watch them push and curse old Negro women and young Negro girls; if you were to see them slap and kick old Negro men and young boys; if you were to observe them, as they did on two occasions, refuse to give us food because we wanted to sing our grace together. I cannot join you in your praise of the Birmingham police department.

It is true that the police have exercised a degree of discipline in handing the demonstrators. In this sense they have conducted themselves rather "nonviolently" in pubic. But for what purpose? To preserve the evil system of segregation. Over the past few years I have consistently preached that nonviolence demands that the means we use must be as pure as the ends we seek. I have tried to make clear that it is wrong to use immoral means to attain moral ends. But now I must affirm that it is just as wrong, or perhaps even more so, to use moral means to preserve immoral ends. Perhaps Mr. Connor and his policemen have been rather nonviolent in public, as was Chief Pritchett in Albany, Georgia but they have used the moral means of nonviolence to maintain the immoral end of racial injustice. As T. S. Eliot has said: "The last temptation is the greatest treason: To do the right deed for the wrong reason."

I wish you had commended the Negro sit-inners and demonstrators of Birmingham for their sublime courage, their willingness to suffer and their amazing discipline in the midst of great provocation. One day the South will recognize its real heroes. They will be the James Merediths, with the noble sense of purpose that enables them to face Jeering, and hostile mobs, and with the agonizing loneliness that characterizes the life of the pioneer. They will be old, oppressed, battered Negro women, symbolized in a seventy-two-year-old woman in Montgomery, Alabama, who rose up with a sense of dignity and with her people decided not to ride segregated buses, and who responded with ungrammatical profundity to one who inquired about her weariness: "My feets is tired, but my soul is at rest." They will be the young high school and college students, the young ministers of the gospel and a host of their elders, courageously and nonviolently sitting in at lunch counters and willingly going to jail for conscience' sake. One day the South will know that when these disinherited children of God sat down at lunch counters, they were in reality standing up for what is best in the American dream and for the most sacred values in our Judaeo-Christian heritage, thereby bringing our nation back to those great wells of democracy which were dug deep by the founding fathers in their formulation of the Constitution and the Declaration of Independence.

Never before have I written so long a letter. I'm afraid it is much too long to take your precious time. I can assure you that it would have been much shorter if I had been writing from a comfortable desk, but what else can one do when he is alone in a narrow jail cell, other than write long letters, think long thoughts and pray long prayers?

If I have said anything in this letter that overstates the truth and indicates an unreasonable impatience, I beg you to forgive me. If I have said anything that understates the truth and indicates my having a patience that allows me to settle for anything less than brotherhood, I beg God to forgive me.

I hope this letter finds you strong in the faith. I also hope that circumstances will soon make it possible for me to meet each of you, not as an integrationist or a civil rights leader but as a fellow clergyman and a Christian brother. Let us all hope that the dark clouds of racial prejudice will soon pass away and the deep fog of misunderstanding will be lifted from our fear-drenched communities, and in some not too distant tomorrow the radiant stars of love and brotherhood will shine over our great nation with all their scintillating beauty.

Yours for the cause of Peace and Brotherhood,

MARTIN LUTHER KING, JR.

NOTES

TURBO-CONSUMERISM IS THE DRIVING FORCE BEHIND CRIME

Neal Lawson

A British columnist, Neal Lawson serves on the Boards of UK Feminista and the AV Referendum Campaign. He was an advisor to Gordon Brown, the former Prime Minister of the United Kingdom.

Last week my son got mugged for his iPod. He wasn't hurt, just a bit embarrassed about some of the songs his assailants will find on it. This week I had my mobile stolen while sitting on a park bench. This is low-level stuff that is now commonplace. But there is a vital link between these ever-upgradable gadgets and the prime minister's call for a rebalancing of the relationship between the victims of crime and the perpetrators.

In "my day" it was different. No one got mugged, perhaps because we didn't have anything worth taking. A home-made catapult was about as hi-tech as it got. Today a kid's trainers, iPod and mobile can easily cost £400 to replace—and can be gone as quickly as it takes a hooded youth to claim there's a knife in their pocket. I'm glad my son didn't take the risk of calling his robber's bluff.

But he had something they didn't. An iPod and the right phone are now essential trappings of youth—not just because they let you talk or listen to music at your convenience, but because of what they say about you. Once we were known by what we produced. Now we judge ourselves and others by what we and they consume. The advertisers know this; that's why they ask: "What does your mobile say about you?" Welcome to the consumer society and the world of the turbo-consumer. It's a world driven by competition for consumer goods and paid-for experiences, of hi-tech and high-end shopping signals that have become the means by which we keep score with each other.

As the sociologist Zygmunt Bauman points out, to be a successful consumer now defines what it is to be "normal". Therefore to be "abnormal" is to be a failed consumer. The lot of the failed consumer is miserable. This new poor may be better off in absolute terms than the poor of previous generations, but in the world of the turbo-consumer what you have means nothing—it's what others have and therefore what we must have next that counts. On these terms the new poor are falling far behind in an age when keeping up is everything.

The failed consumer suffers not just from exclusion from normal society but isolation. The poor of the past had each other in a community of poverty. Misery could be shared and countered through class solidarity and the hope of a different life. The new poor lick their wounds alone in their council flats,

Reprinted by permission of the *Guardian*, June 28, 2006.

with nowhere to hide from the messages on billboards and TV that constantly remind them of their social failure. The new poor, without the right labels and brands, are not just excluded but invisible. The final ignominy of today's poor is that they don't want to overthrow the rich to create a new order, they just want to be like them. So they are denied even the satisfaction of anyone to hate—just B-list celebrities to envy and copy.

So if you want the causes of crime then look no further than the impulse of the poor to belong and be normal. So strong is this urge that the failed consumer will lie, cheat and steal to "earn" the trappings of success. In the world of the "me generation", people become calculating rather than law-abiding in their overwhelming desire to be normal. This is crime driven by the rampant egoism of turbo-consumerism, where enough is never enough. And precisely because of its competitive nature, consumer-driven crime cannot be switched off through tougher laws. New Labour has attempted to address some of the causes of crime with tax credits, a minimum wage and the New Deal. They are all helpful, but the government hardly ever talks about them.

Why should failed consumers play by the rules when no one at the top seems to—when social mobility is declining; when the government refuses to implement vocational training reforms for fear of a Daily Mail backlash over A-levels; when more thick middle-class children fill our universities; and when school league tables mean "problem kids" won't be tolerated?

New Labour refuses to change the rules of the market state and consumer society, and instead attempts another crackdown on the symptoms through Asbos and control orders. Just like Thatcherism, New Labour relies on a strong state to police a free market. The prime minister extols his respect agenda without realising that the architect of the term, the sociologist Richard Sennett, was talking about the respect the powerful give to the powerless. So Tony Blair tries to turn back the tide of crime against a rampant consumer culture of new gadgets that are designed, advertised, sold and bought to prove our normality over and over again. Nine years, 50 law bills and more than 700 new offences later, being even tougher on crime isn't going to work. Of course, it is always wrong to mug or steal—but unless, as a society, we are prepared to understand why crime happens then, in the words of the criminologist Professor Ian Loader, "we are using a sticking plaster to fix a broken leg". You cannot build a tolerant society on the basis of zero tolerance.

In his speech last Friday, Blair admitted that "we can identify such families virtually as their children are born". But his solution is the science fiction of the film Minority Report, when the real crime is the existence of such families in a nation bulging with wealth.

When it is the dominance of the consumer economy that is driving so much crime, easy answers aren't close to hand. We need a different conception of the good life, in which time, relationships and care take precedence over consumerism. Next there is a political alliance to be created between the post-material, happiness-seeking middle classes, who want more time, and this new poor, who have all the time in the world but none of the money. This is what needs rebalancing: not the criminal justice system, but the wealth and riches of the nation.

NOTES

THE NEW FEMINISM
Sarah Leonard

Sarah Leonard is Associate Editor at Dissent *magazine and Co-Editor of* Occupied!: Scenes from Occupied America. *She is a graduate of Columbia University and affirms an abiding interest in Left politics as well as the cultural repercussions of technology.*

A feminist conspiracy couldn't have planted the number of trend pieces about women we've seen this year. Touting the new economic dominance of women, Hanna Rosin's *The End of Men* became a bestseller alongside Naomi Wolf's *Vagina: A New Biography.* The *Atlantic* published popular articles such as "Why Women Still Can't Have It All" by Anne-Marie Slaughter a former high-ranking State Department official, and "All the Single Ladies," by Kate Bolick, on the trials, and ultimately the joys, of being single in a world of independent, amazingly well-housed women.

Bolick describes the sisterhood:

> Deb gave me the use of her handsome mid-century apartment in Chelsea when she vacated town for a meditation retreat; Courtney bequeathed her charming Brooklyn aerie while she traveled alone through Italy; Catherine put me up at her rambling Cape Cod summer house . . .

Marissa Mayer, now of Yahoo, and Sheryl Sandberg of Facebook have become the new faces of modern femininity, happily juggling high-powered CEOships, children, and—for Mayer—the creation of numerous "diaper cakes" for colleagues' baby showers. Women, it would seem, are economically dominant and empowered by everything from their vaginas to their beach houses.

Good for them.

But this celebration is one part toast to the wealthy exceptions, and one part nonsense. Despite the sound of Mayer and Sandberg crashing through the glass ceiling, Rosin's assertion that women are now economically dominant is pure fantasy. Her claims have been thoroughly debunked by writers such as Bryce Covert, Stephanie Coontz, and Nancy Folbre, who note that the economy is so bad that women and men are finally converging on the same low wages and contingent employment. As of this past summer, men had regained 46.2 percent of the jobs they lost in the recession, while women had regained 38.7 percent of theirs. Cutbacks in the feminized public sector have been brutal.

Meanwhile, the mainstream media treat the few women at the top—fewer than 4 percent of Fortune 500 CEOs are women—as if they are the first to discover the difficulty of raising children while working twelve hours per day. These narratives smoothly elide the fact that women have always worked outside the home. Mayer's nanny is probably working twelve hours too, though this feat didn't make the cover of *New York* magazine.

Stories about women like Mayer reflect the media's absorption into business culture and its favorite trope: celebration of the heroic CEO. *Business Insider* recently published a slideshow of "19 Successful People Who Barely Sleep" (Mayer topped the list). They offer a model of success to which you, mid-level investment banker, should aspire through the sacrifice of your basic biological needs. Female CEOs have merely added another layer of superhuman strength; everyone knows that women are supposed to have babies, but CEOs aren't—*Omigod, can she do both?* The very biology of women is co-opted to laud an increasingly unsustainable set of corporate values.

And the reaction harks back to gender panics in recent decades. Rosin suggests we are living under a new matriarchy. Men are becoming irrelevant and women are too adaptable to the personality-driven service sector. While viewers take pleasure in watching the Mad Men squirm over the introduction of women into their whiskey-swilling ad agency, a similar anxiety pervades discussions of twenty-first century work. The subheading to one of Rosin's chapters is "Asian Women Take Over the World." Never mind that women have to have a Ph.D. to make what a male with a B.A. will. The Rosin line sounds suspiciously like an intellectual coping mechanism for the recession-battered male masses. There are too few jobs. You don't have a job. Who took your job? Women.

The problem with such discussions of women and feminism is that most women still work in female-dominated industries that have long been underpaid, precarious, and without benefits. Most women are not economically dominant—they're doing the same work women have always done and suffering for it. Take the Lily Ledbetter Fair Pay Act, a basic piece of legislation helping women challenge pay discrimination by extending the window during which they could sue. The act was necessary of course, because women still make about seventy-seven cents to a man's dollar.

Meanwhile, it is hard to tear the feminist blogosphere away from endless debates about the sitcom *Girls* and whether "ladyblogs" are, in fact, feminist. A heavy focus on reproductive rights is necessary, but it crowds out much else. Domestic work more often refers to the division of work between career ladder-climbing husbands and wives than to full-time domestic workers. The online world of feminist commentary has made a diversity of voices available, but navel gazing often predominates.

For the most interesting thing happening in feminism right now, we shouldn't look to Yahoo, but rather at the terrain that Sarah Jaffe explores in the first article in this section. The fastest growing sector of the economy is care work, a realm long considered an organizer's nightmare. This 95-percent-female workforce is spread throughout individual homes, has no governing labor standards, often exists in the underground economy, and includes many undocumented immigrants.

Excluded from New Deal labor reforms at the behest of Southern Democrats, care work suffers from a perception that it is not "normal" work. Nannying, homecare, elder care are more intimate than factory or retail work. Families often call domestic workers "part of our family." The future of labor in the American economy will be determined in part by whether care work can become organized work, and Jaffe draws on women's labor history and the Wages for Housework movement to discuss how this might occur.

Following Jaffe's article is a personal essay by a certified nursing assistant in a California elder care facility who uses the pseudonym JOMO. JOMO speaks of the struggle to organize fellow care workers as well as the psychological and physical toll of the labor. The choices the workers face embody the contradictions of a society that turns care into a commodity and then sweeps it under the rug.

White-collar work carries an interlinked set of challenges. Madeleine Schwartz turns a feminist lens on the organization of interns, temp workers, freelancers, and clerical staff who are experiencing the precariousness and dead-end status long associated with "pink-collar" work.

The Government Accounting Office has classed nearly a third of American workers as contingent. In her analysis, Schwartz draws on feminist tools—the consciousness-raising group, the identification of labels like "caring" and "educational" to transform work into voluntarism—to point toward possible modes of resistance to an economic system that requires the smile of a wife and the flexibility of an intern.

Melissa Gira Grant examines this dynamic in its newest realm—Silicon Valley, birthplace of the social media we use every day. The industry thrives on the visual exploitation of women in many of its products, but also in its offices. Grant's starting point is a new book by Katherine Losse, the sole woman before Sandberg to occupy a place of prominence in the boy-nerd culture of Facebook. This essay exposes the tension between an online world that relies for clicks on images of women and the office struggles of the people who run that world.

Stepping back from the workplace, we asked co-editor Michael Walzer to reconsider his classic philosophical work *Spheres of Justice* in light of analysis from his sharpest feminist critic, the late Susan Moller Okin. She challenged him to think differently about how the family fit into his framework for justice. Why, he asks, has increased gender justice in politics, economy, and education failed to create more egalitarian family relationships?

We conclude with two pieces about *Roe v. Wade* on its fortieth anniversary. Carole Joffe notes that the contours of the modern feminist movement have been shaped by the right-wing assault on reproductive rights. Women's rights advocates concentrate energy on a single topic, while other feminist projects languish. Yet it is not a fight we can abandon. As she unwinds post-*Roe v. Wade* history, Joffe points toward some of the central strategic dilemmas that feminism must overcome.

Akiba Solomon, who came of age years after *Roe v. Wade,* addresses the tensions between the experiences of women of color and white, middle-class reproductive rights activists. Solomon draws on her teenage experience teaching sex education to mostly black and Puerto Rican peers and looks to emerging movements that are strengthening feminism and broadening its reach.

Elsewhere in this issue, Chelsea Szendi Schieder addresses the history of Japanese radical feminism in light of the "baby bust" in Japan, asking "are young women in Japan on a wildcat baby strike?"; Mari Jo Buhle writes about a little-noted coalition growing between labor and women's groups in the Wisconsin battles against austerity; Jonah Raskin reconsiders Doris Lessing's *The Golden Notebook;* and Megan Erickson confronts Arlie Hochschild's *The Outsourced Self: Intimate Life in Market Times.*

Left magazines have taken heat along with others for their low score in the numbers ranking of VIDA, an organization of women in the arts that counts how often women are published in leading magazines. Too often, left magazines take up feminism occasionally, and out of obligation, not frequently and as a core concern. But if you ignore gender, you can't think seriously about the future of the economy or about any other concerns of the Serious Men of the Left.

The mirror image of this charge to leftists is a challenge to feminism. Most women spend time in the workforce, often in contingent labor and un(der)paid care work. This, then, is where feminists, to change the lives of women, must spend their time. Few feminists would disagree that we care less about Marissa Mayer's choice not to take parental leave than whether all women have access to leave and to childcare and that men share the burden. But the former conversation often trumps the latter.

There are always generational debates in feminism: first through third waves, mother-daughter conflict, the misunderstandings bred by generationally divided pop culture and work experiences. You can find sparkling pieces throughout the history of *Dissent* that reflect each stage. This issue's special section takes a certain continuity as its premise. If the new feminism is going to address the biggest changes altering our world—work and immigration patterns, the power of labor, the self-determination of half the population, the very structure of our days—we must look back to a feminism that assumed the centrality of these issues in order to see feminism's future.

NOTES

NOTES

AGE, RACE, CLASS AND SEX: WOMEN REDEFINING DIFFERENCE

Audre Lorde

(1934–1992)

Audre Lorde was a poet, essayist, and novelist whose parents came to this country from Grenada. She earned her B.A. from Hunter College and M.L.S. from Columbia University. She was a mother, a Lesbian and, before succumbing to breast cancer, was the poet laureate of New York.

Paper delivered at the Copeland Colloquium, Amerst College, April 1980

Reproduced in: Sister Outsider *Crossing Press, California 1984*

Much of Western European history conditions us to see human differences in simplistic opposition to each other: dominant/subordinate, good/bad, up/down, superior/inferior. In a society where the good is defined in terms of profit rather than in terms of human need, there must always be some group of people who, through systematized oppression, can be made to feel surplus, to occupy the place of the dehumanized inferior. Within this society, that group is made up of Black and Third World people, working-class people, older people, and women.

As a forty-nine-year-old Black lesbian feminist socialist mother of two, including one boy, and a member of an interracial couple, I usually find myself a part of some group defined as other, deviant, inferior, or just plain wrong. Traditionally, in american society, it is the members of oppressed, objectified groups who are expected to stretch out and bridge the gap between the actualities of our lives and the consciousness of our oppressor. For in order to survive, those of us for whom oppression is as american as apple pie have always had to be watchers, to become familiar with the language and manners of the oppressor, even sometimes adopting them for some illusion of protection. Whenever the need for some pretense of communication arises, those who profit from our oppression call upon us to share our knowledge with them. In other words, it is the responsibility of the oppressed to teach the oppressors their mistakes. I am responsible for educating teachers who dismiss my children's culture in school. Black and Third World people are expected to educate white people as to our humanity. Women are expected to educate men. Lesbians and gay men are expected to educate the heterosexual world. The oppressors maintain their position and evade responsibility for their own actions. There is a constant drain of energy which might be better used in redefining ourselves and devising realistic scenarios for altering the present and constructing the future.

Reprinted from *Sister Outsider: Essays and Speeches* (1984), by permission of Regula Noetzli.

Institutionalized rejection of difference is an absolute necessity in a profit economy which needs outsiders as surplus people. As members of such an economy, we have *all* been programmed to respond to the human differences between us with fear and loathing and to handle that difference in one of three ways: ignore it, and if that is not possible, copy it if we think it is dominant, or destroy it if we think it is subordinate. But we have no patterns for relating across our human differences as equals. As a result, those differences have been misnamed and misused in the service of separation and confusion.

Certainly there are very real differences between us of race, age, and sex. But it is not those differences between us that are separating us. It is rather our refusal to recognize those differences, and to examine the distortions which result from our misnaming them and their effects upon human behavior and expectation.

Racism, the belief in the inherent superiority of one race over all others and thereby the right to dominance. Sexism, the belief in the inherent superiority of one sex over the other and thereby the right to dominance. Ageism. Heterosexism. Elitism. Classism.

It is a lifetime pursuit for each one of us to extract these distortions from our living at the same time as we recognize, reclaim, and define those differences upon which they are imposed. For we have all been raised in a society where those distortions were endemic within our living. Too often, we pour the energy needed for recognizing and exploring difference into pretending those differences are insurmountable barriers, or that they do not exist at all. This results in a voluntary isolation, or false and treacherous connections. Either way, we do not develop tools for using human difference as a springboard for creative change within our lives. We speak not of human difference, but of human deviance.

Somewhere, on the edge of consciousness, there is what I call a *mythical* norm, which each one of us within our hearts knows "that is not me." In america, this norm is usually defined as white, thin, male, young, heterosexual, Christian, and financially secure. It is with this mythical norm that the trappings of power reside within this society. Those of us who stand outside that power often identify one way in which we are different, and we assume that to be the primary cause of all oppression, forgetting other distortions around difference, some of which we ourselves may be practising. By and large within the women's movement today, white women focus upon their oppression as women and ignore differences of race, sexual preference, class, and age. There is a pretense to a homogeneity of experience covered by the word *sisterhood* that does not in fact exist.

Unacknowledged class differences rob women of each others' energy and creative insight. Recently a women's magazine collective made the decision for one issue to print only prose, saying poetry was a less "rigorous" or "serious" art form. Yet even the form our creativity takes is often a class issue. Of all the art forms, poetry is the most economical. It is the one which is the most secret, which requires the least physical labor, the least material, and the one which can be done between shifts, in the hospital pantry, on the subway, and on scraps of surplus paper. Over the last few years, writing a novel on tight finances, I came to appreciate the enormous differences in the material demands between poetry and prose. As we reclaim our literature, poetry has been the major voice of poor, working class, and Colored women. A room of one's own may be a necessity for writing prose, but so are reams of paper, a typewriter, and plenty of time. The actual requirements to produce the visual arts also help determine, along class lines, whose art is whose. In this day of inflated prices for material, who are our sculptors, our painters, our photographers? When we speak of a broadly based women's culture, we need to be aware of the effect of class and economic differences on the supplies available for producing art.

As we move toward creating a society within which we can each flourish, ageism is another distortion of relationship which interferes without vision. By ignoring the past, we are encouraged to repeat its mistakes. The "generation gap" is an important social tool for any repressive society. If the younger members of a community view the older members as contemptible or suspect or excess, they will never be able to join hands and examine the living memories of the community, nor ask the all important question, "Why?" This gives rise to a historical amnesia that keeps us working to invent the wheel every time we have to go to the store for bread.

We find ourselves having to repeat and relearn the same old lessons over and over that our mothers did because we do not pass on what we have learned, or because we are unable to listen. For instance, how many times has this all been said before? For another, who would have believed that once again our daughters are allowing their bodies to be hampered and purgatoried by girdles and high heels and hobble skirts?

Ignoring the differences of race between women and the implications of those differences presents the most serious threat to the mobilization of women's joint power.

As white women ignore their built-in privilege of whiteness and define woman in terms of their own experience alone, then women of Color become "other," the outsider whose experience and tradition is too "alien" to comprehend. An example of this is the signal absence of the experience of women of Color as a resource for women's studies courses. The literature of women of Color is seldom included in women's literature courses and almost never in other literature courses, nor in women's studies as a whole. All too often, the excuse given is that the literatures of women of Color can only be taught by Colored women, or that they are too difficult to understand, or that classes cannot "get into" them because they come out of experiences that are "too different." I have heard this argument presented by white women of otherwise quite clear intelligence, women who seem to have no trouble at all teaching and reviewing work that comes out of the vastly different experiences of Shakespeare, Moliere, Dostoyefsky, and Aristophanes. Surely there must be some other explanation.

This is a very complex question, but I believe one of the reasons white women have such difficulty reading Black women's work is because of their reluctance to see Black women as women and different from themselves. To examine Black women's literature effectively requires that we be seen as whole people in our actual complexities—as individuals, as women, as human—rather than as one of those problematic but familiar stereotypes provided in this society in place of genuine images of Black women. And I believe this holds true for the literatures of other women of Color who are not Black.

The literatures of all women of Color recreate the textures of our lives, and many white women are heavily invested in ignoring the real differences. For as long as any difference between us means one of us must be inferior, then the recognition of any difference must be fraught with guilt. To allow women of Color to step out of stereotypes is too guilt provoking, for it threatens the complacency of those women who view oppression only in terms of sex.

Refusing to recognize difference makes it impossible to see the different problems and pitfalls facing us as women.

Thus, in a patriarchal power system where whiteskin privilege is a major prop, the entrapments used to neutralize Black women and white women are not the same. For example, it is easy for Black women to be used by the power structure against Black men, not because they are men, but because they are Black. Therefore, for Black women, it is necessary at all times to separate the needs of the oppressor from our own legitimate conflicts within our communities. This same problem does not exist for white women. Black women and men have shared racist oppression and still share it, although in different ways. Out of that shared oppression we have developed joint defenses and joint vulnerabilities to each other that are not duplicated in the white community, with the exception of the relationship between Jewish women and Jewish men.

On the other hand, white women face the pitfall of being seduced into joining the oppressor under the pretense of sharing power. This possibility does not exist in the same way for women of Color. The tokenism that is sometimes extended to us is not an invitation to join power; our racial "otherness" is a visible reality that makes that quite clear. For white women there is a wider range of pretended choices and rewards for identifying with patriarchal power and its tools.

Today, with the defeat of ERA, the tightening economy, and increased conservatism, it is easier once again for white women to believe the dangerous fantasy that if you are good enough, pretty enough, sweet enough, quiet enough, teach the children to behave, hate the right people, and marry the right men, then you will be allowed to co-exist with patriarchy in relative peace, at least until a man needs your job or the neighborhood rapist happens along. And true, unless one lives and loves in the trenches it is difficult to remember that the war against dehumanization is ceaseless.

But Black women and our children know the fabric of our lives is stitched with violence and with hatred, that there is no rest. We do not deal with it only on the picket lines, or in dark midnight alleys, or in the places where we dare to verbalize our resistance. For us, increasingly, violence weaves through the daily tissues of our living—in the supermarket, in the classroom, in the elevator, in the clinic and the schoolyard, from the plumber, the baker, the saleswoman, the bus driver, the bank teller, the waitress who does not serve us.

Some problems we share as women, some we do not. You fear your children will grow up to join the patriarchy and testify against you, we fear our children will be dragged from a car and shot down in the street, and you will turn your backs upon the reasons they are dying.

The threat of difference has been no less blinding to people of Color. Those of us who are Black must see that the reality of our lives and our struggle does not make us immune to the errors of ignoring and misnaming difference. Within Black communities where racism is a living reality, differences among us often seem dangerous and suspect. The need for unity is often misnamed as a need for homogeneity, and a Black feminist vision mistaken for betrayal of our common interests as a people. Because of the continuous battle against racial erasure that Black women and Black men share, some Black women still refuse to recognize that we are also oppressed as women, and that sexual hostility against Black women is practiced not only by the white racist society, but implemented within our Black communities as well. It is a disease striking the heart of Black nationhood, and silence will not make it disappear. Exacerbated by racism and the pressures of powerlessness, violence against Black women and children often becomes a standard within our communities, one by which manliness can be measured. But these woman-hating acts are rarely discussed as crimes against Black women.

As a group, women of Color are the lowest paid wage earners in america. We are the primary targets of abortion and sterilization abuse, here and abroad. In certain parts of Africa, small girls are still being sewed shut between their legs to keep them docile and for men's pleasure. This is known as female circumcision, and it is not a cultural affair as the late Jomo Kenyatta insisted, it is a crime against Black women.

Black women's literature is full of the pain of frequent assault, not only by a racist patriarchy, but also by Black men. Yet the necessity for and history of shared battle have made us, Black women, particularly vulnerable to the false accusation that anti-sexist is anti-Black. Meanwhile, womanhating as a recourse of the powerless is sapping strength from Black communities, and our very lives. Rape is on the increase, reported and unreported, and rape is not aggressive sexuality, it is sexualized aggression. As Kalamu ya Salaam, a Black male writer points out, "As long as male domination exists, rape will exist. Only women revolting and men made conscious of their responsibility to fight sexism can collectively stop rape."

Differences between ourselves as Black women are also being misnamed and used to separate us from one another. As a Black lesbian feminist comfortable with the many different ingredients of my identity, and a woman committed to racial and sexual freedom from oppression, I find I am constantly being encouraged to pluck out some one aspect of myself and present this as the meaningful whole, eclipsing or denying the other parts of self. But this is a destructive and fragmenting way to live. My fullest concentration of energy is available to me only when I integrate all the parts of who I am, openly, allowing power from particular sources of my living to flow back and forth freely through all my different selves, without the restrictions of externally imposed definition. Only then can I bring myself and my energies as a whole to the service of those struggles which I embrace as part of my living.

A fear of lesbians, or of being accused of being a lesbian, has led many Black women into testifying against themselves. It has led some of us into destructive alliances, and others into despair and isolation. In the white women's communities, heterosexism is sometimes a result of identifying with the white patriarchy, a rejection of that interdependence between women-identified women which allows the self to be, rather than to be used in the service of men. Sometimes it reflects a die-hard belief in the protective coloration of heterosexual relationships, sometimes a self-hate which all women have to fight against, taught us from birth.

Although elements of these attitudes exist for all women, there are particular resonances of heterosexism and homophobia among Black women. Despite the fact that woman-bonding has a long and honorable history in the African and Africanamerican communities, and despite the knowledge and accomplishments of many strong and creative women-identified Black women in the political, social and cultural fields, heterosexual Black women often tend to ignore or discount the existence and work of Black lesbians. Part of this attitude has come from an understandable terror of Black male attack within the close confines of Black society, where the punishment for any female self-assertion is still to be accused of being a lesbian and therefore unworthy of the attention or support of the scarce Black male. But part of this need to misname and ignore Black lesbians comes from a very real fear that openly women-identified Black women who are no longer dependent upon men for their self-definition may well reorder our whole concept of social relationships.

Black women who once insisted that lesbianism was a white woman's problem now insist that Black lesbians are a threat to Black nationhood, are consorting with the enemy, are basically un-Black. These accusations, coming from the very women to whom we look for deep and real understanding, have served to keep many Black lesbians in hiding, caught between the racism of white women and the homophobia of their sisters. Often, their work has been ignored, trivialized, or misnamed, as with the work of Angelina Grimke, Alice Dunbar-Nelson, Lorraine Hansberry. Yet women-bonded women have always been some part of the power of Black communities, from our unmarried aunts to the amazons of Dahomey.

And it is certainly not Black lesbians who are assaulting women and raping children and grandmothers on the streets of our communities.

Across this country, as in Boston during the spring of 1979 following the unsolved murders of twelve Black women, Black lesbians are spearheading movements against violence against Black women.

What are the particular details within each of our lives that can be scrutinized and altered to help bring about change? How do we redefine difference for all women? It is not our differences which separate women, but our reluctance to recognize those differences and to deal effectively with the distortions which have resulted from the ignoring and misnaming of those differences.

As a tool of social control, women have been encouraged to recognize only one area of human difference as legitimate, those differences which exist between women and men. And we have learned to deal across those differences with the urgency of all oppressed subordinates. All of us have had to learn to live or work or coexist with men, from our fathers on. We have recognized and negotiated these differences, even when this recognition only continued the old dominant/subordinate mode of human relationship; where the oppressed must recognize the masters' difference in order to survive.

But our future survival is predicated upon our ability to relate within equality. As women, we must root out internalized patterns of oppression within ourselves if we are to move beyond the most superficial aspects of social change. Now we must recognize differences among women who are our equals, neither inferior nor superior, and devise ways to use each others' difference to enrich our visions and our joint struggles. The future of our earth may depend upon the ability of all women to identify and develop new definitions of power and new patterns of relating across difference. The old definitions have not served us, nor the earth that supports us. The old patterns, no matter how cleverly rearranged to imitate progress, still condemn us to cosmetically altered repetitions of the same old exchanges, the same old guilt, hatred, recrimination, lamentation, and suspicion.

For we have, built into all of us, old blueprints of expectation and response, old structures of oppression, and these must be altered at the same time as we alter the living conditions which are a result of those structures. For the master's tools will never dismantle the master's house.

As Paulo Freire shows so well in *The Pedagogy of the Oppressed,* the true focus of revolutionary change is never merely the oppressive situations which we seek to escape, but that piece of the oppressor which is planted deep within each of us, and which knows only the oppressors' tactics, the oppressors' relationships.

Change means growth, and growth can be painful. But we sharpen self-definition by exposing the self in work and struggle together with those whom we define as different from ourselves, although sharing the same goals. For Black and white, old and young, lesbian and heterosexual women alike, this can mean new paths to our survival.

We have chosen each other
and the edge of each others *battles*
the war *is the same*
if we lose
someday women's blood *will congeal*
upon *a dead planet*
if we win
there is no telling
we seek beyond history
for *a new and* more *possible meeting.*

NOTES

NOTES

ROSALIND FRANKLIN: THE DARK LADY OF DNA

Brenda Maddox

Brenda Maddox is a U.S. writer, journalist, and biographer. Her biographies, which have been translated into ten languages, have won several awards. Since 1959, she has made the UK her home.

Prologue

'It has not escaped our notice that the specific pairing we have postulated immediately suggests a possible copying mechanism for the genetic material.'

This celebrated understatement published in *Nature* on 25 April 1953 was Francis Crick's and James Watson's way of heralding the significance of their discovery of the double helix, the self-copying spirals of the DNA molecule that carry the genetic message from old cells to new. Another statement, written in a private letter on 7 March 1953, has achieved a fame of its own: 'Our dark lady is leaving us next week.'

For Francis Crick of the Cavendish Laboratory at Cambridge, the 'dark lady' needed no further identification. For nearly two years, his friend Maurice Wilkins of the Biophysics Unit at King's College London had been moaning about his obstructive female colleague, Rosalind Franklin. Now that she was abandoning King's for Birkbeck, another University of London college, Wilkins was confident that he, Crick, and Watson, a young American working with Crick, together would solve the structure of DNA. But it was too late. By the time that Wilkins's letter reached Cambridge, the pair whose names will be forever linked were looking at their completed model whose simplicity proclaimed that they had discovered the secret of life.

But could Watson and Crick have done it without the 'dark lady': Rosalind Franklin, the thirty-two-year-old physical chemist whose departure from King's Wilkins so eagerly awaited? Her research data, which had reached them by a circuitous route and without her consent, had been crucial to their discovery. Watson's glimpse of one of her X-ray photographs of DNA gave him and Crick the final boost to the summit. From the evidence of her notebooks, it is clear that she would have got there by herself before long.

The triumph was theirs, not hers. Rosalind Franklin remained virtually unknown outside her immediate circles until 1968 when Watson published *The Double Helix*, his brilliant, tactless and exciting personal account of the discovery. In it, she is the terrible 'Rosy', the bad-tempered bluestocking who hoarded her data and might have been pretty if she had taken off her glasses and done something interesting with her hair.

Reprinted from *Rosalind Franklin: The Dark Lady of DNA* (2002), HarperCollins Publishers.

She looked quite different to the eminent physics professor J.D. Bernal, who brought her to Birkbeck in the spring and oversaw her five happy and productive years there. He described her in *Nature*: 'As a scientist, Miss Franklin was distinguished by extreme clarity and perfection in everything she undertook. Her photographs are among the most beautiful X-ray photographs of any substance ever taken.'

But Bernal's words were elegiac. Rosalind Franklin's life was cut short by ovarian cancer in 1958 when she was thirty-seven—four years before Watson, Crick and Wilkins won the Nobel prize for their DNA discovery and a decade before she was caricatured in a book to which, alone of the principals portrayed, she was unable to answer back.

Since Watson's book, Rosalind Franklin has become a feminist icon, the Sylvia Plath of molecular biology, the woman whose gifts were sacrificed to the greater glory of the male. Yet this mythologising, intended to be reparative, has done her no favours. There was far more to her complex, fruitful, vigorous life than twenty-seven unhappy months at King's College London. She achieved an international reputation in three different fields of scientific research while at the same time nourishing a passion for travel, a gift for friendship, a love of clothes and good food and a strong political conscience. She never flagged in her duties to the distinguished Anglo-Jewish family of which she was a loyal, if combative, member.

Determined from the age of twelve to become a scientist, Rosalind Franklin knew where she came from, under what constraints she laboured and where she wanted to go. From childhood, she strove to reconcile her privileges with her goals. She did not find life easy—as a woman, as a Jew, as a scientist. Many of those close to her did not find her easy either. The measure of her success lies in the strength of her friendships, the devotion of her colleagues, the vitality of her letters and a legacy of discovery that would do credit to a scientific career twice its length.

Epilogue

Life After Death

'Concerning Rosalind,' Maurice Wilkins wrote James Watson in 1966, 'is there any mention in your book that she died?'

'Your book' was 'Honest Jim' an early draft of *The Double Helix*, Watson's candid, fast-paced account of the discovery of the structure of DNA. In it Rosalind Franklin is 'Rosy,' the termagant who hoarded data she couldn't comprehend, treated men like naughty little boys and wore dresses even dowdier than those of the average Englishwoman.

Watson could not have given the world his 'Rosy' if Rosalind had been alive. He began writing the book as a Harvard professor, three years after he, Francis Crick and Maurice Wilkins had won the Nobel prize for medicine and physiology. Watson submitted the book to Harvard University Press, which liked it but required the written consent of those prominently and candidly mentioned. Francis Crick and Wilkins objected most strongly—in Crick's case, with some anger. Linus Pauling also cast a veto. In a fierce letter to Crick, with nine copies, including one to Nathan Pusey, president of Harvard, Pauling condemned the portrayals of himself, his wife, his son, Francis Crick, Sir Lawrence Bragg and Rosalind Franklin.

Rosalind's brother Colin, as one of Rosalind's trustees and a publisher, was one of those sent a draft of the book. He was outraged. He shot off a cable containing what Watson considered 'a rather hysterical reaction' about 'defaming the dead.' When Charlotte Franklin, Colin's wife, followed with a 'sensible' (Watson's word) letter, Watson considered that he should perhaps put in an epilogue.

Max Perutz too complained about the treatment of Rosalind. As he later wrote in the London *Daily Telegraph*, 'I was furious about his maligning that gifted girl who could not defend herself because she died of cancer in 1958; but I could not get him to change it . . . Not that she was unattractive or did not care about her looks. She dressed much more tastefully than the average Cambridge undergraduate . . . '

In response, Watson composed a pious epilogue stating what a fine scientist Rosalind Franklin had been, and how, as a young man, he had not appreciated the difficulties of a woman making her way in the man's world of science.

The many revisions Watson made to the early drafts did not placate his critics. Wilkins wrote T.J. Wilson, the director of Harvard University Press, to declare that although some of the grosser factual errors had been corrected, he nonetheless felt it disgraceful that a university press should be party to a distinguished member of its staff making such a display of immaturity and bad taste. Watson's book, Wilkins declared, was 'unfair to me, to Dr. Crick and to almost everyone mentioned except Professor Watson himself'.

Faced with such formidable opposition, Harvard's Board of Overseers made its press drop the book. It complied, and lost a bestseller. Instead, *The Double Helix* was published by the Athenaeum Press in New York in February 1968, and by Weidenfeld and Nicolson in London in May, the original portrait of Rosy intact. The stilted afterword tacked on to the end of a racy tale did nothing to erase the impression of the virago ready to spring.

Rosalind's parents were deeply upset: bad enough to have lost their daughter, now this gratuitous and painful insult. Aaron Klug, visiting them, suggested that the book at least ensured that Rosalind would always be remembered. Muriel Franklin replied, 'I would rather she were forgotten than remembered in this way.'

The Double Helix was an instant success, welcomed for dispelling the myth that science is done by dispassionate intellects moving with deliberation towards defined goals. *Nature* called the book 'spellbinding and a considerable public service'. Jacob Bronowski said in *The Nation* that the book 'communicates the spirit of science as no formal account has ever done'. In the United States it was nominated for the National Book Award.

J.D. Bernal, reviewing *The Double Helix* for *Labour Monthly*, gently corrected the book's portrait of Rosalind while at the same time deflating Watson and Crick. He wrote 'a decisive breakthrough in human thought is not necessarily the work of an individual genius but only of a pack of bright and well-financed research workers following a good well-laid trail'. Bernal credited Rosalind with a significant part in laying the trail:

> For 'Rosy', in the book—I had come to know and respect her and to admire her too, as a very intelligent and brave woman who was the first to recognise and to measure the phosphorus atoms in the helix, which proves to be the outer one, thus showing Pauling to be wrong and the helix to be a double one, though this inference is not drawn.

Praise for the book was not unanimous. The 1960s were not the 1950s; the women's movement had begun. By 1968, lines such as: 'Clearly Rosy had to go or be put in her place . . .'; 'Certainly a bad way to go out into the foulness of a heavy, foggy November night was to be told by a woman to refrain from venturing an opinion about a subject for which you were not trained', and 'the best home for a feminist was in another person's lab' were as unacceptable as jokes about women drivers and dumb blondes.

Mary Ellmann, whose *Thinking About Women* appeared the same year and launched feminist literary criticism, recognised the misogyny underlying *The Double Helix*. In *The Yale Review* she mocked its pretence to show 'the scientist as human being, with genes in the morning, girls in the evening' and commented sarcastically, 'The only contradiction of this sensible balance is Rosalind Franklin, the woman who *studies* DNA like a man . . . Why couldn't she content herself with playing assistant to Wilkins (and over his shoulder, to Crick and Watson)?' Elizabeth Janeway, in another feminist text, *Man's World, Woman's Place*, attacked as misogynist even Watson's portrait of Odile Crick as the air-headed pretty wife who thinks that gravity stops two miles up.

In ensuing decades, the myth of the wronged heroine has grown, nourished by the fact of Rosalind's early death. Rosalind Franklin has become the symbol of women's lowly position in the pantheon of science. In 1997, when an American neuroscientist, Candace Pert, was passed over for the Lasker Award (sometimes called 'the American Nobel') she felt she deserved, she blamed anti-female prejudice. It was just what had happened to Rosalind Franklin, she maintained. In *Molecules of Emotion*, Pert went so far as to suggest that Franklin's cancer 'had been exacerbated by the humiliation she suffered at the hands of these, and probably many other, old boys'.

The Double Helix is now established as a twentieth-century classic, published in eighteen languages: a candid young-man's-eye view of one of science's great discoveries. Watson wrote what, at twenty-three, he felt and saw happening. Yet a cloud of guilt hovers over the tale from the very first page. The book opens in 1955, with Jim Watson climbing a slope in the Swiss Alps. Suddenly he recognises one of the party of climbers coming down. It is Willy Seeds, from King's College London. Instead of pausing for a chat with an old friend in an unfamiliar place, Seeds merely says, 'How's Honest Jim?' and passes by.

The reader has no way of knowing that the ever-sardonic Seeds meant the very opposite of 'honest'. In 1955, only two years after the discovery of the double helix, scientists at King's had not forgiven Watson for helping himself to King's data to win fame. Seeds's gibe clearly hit home, for Watson made 'Honest Jim' the book's working title. Another discarded title—'Base Pairs'—carries the same self-accusation.

Watson was intentionally ironic. He genuinely liked the sound of 'Honest Jim' for its echoes of *Lucky Jim*—Kingsley's Amis's 1954 comic masterpiece about a maladroit young instructor who exposes the pomposity of the British academic establishment. It may not be too far-fetched to think that in Watson's unconscious, as he shaped his narrative, lodged not only the bumbling honest Jim Dixon but the neurotic female lecturer Margaret Peel ('quite horribly well done', said the *New Statesman*), with her tasteless clothes and utter ignorance of how to appeal to a man.

Over the years, Watson repeatedly indulged in public admissions of unease. In 1999, in his book *A Passion for DNA*, he looked back to the publication of *The Double Helix* and joked: 'I daydreamed that the *New Yorker* might print it under the rubric "Annals of Crime" because there were those who thought Francis and I had no right to think about other people's data and had in fact stolen the double helix from Maurice Wilkins and Rosalind Franklin.'

As decades went by, Watson defended himself before young audiences who had little idea of what he was supposed to be guilty of. In London in 1984, addressing the Science Society at Rosalind's old school, St Paul's, he declared that he and Crick had not robbed Rosalind. 'We used her data to think about, not to steal,' he said. He tried to explain why he and Crick and not she had made the discovery: 'It *wasn't* because she was a woman or that we were more intelligent. We were more interested in DNA than she was, more interested because of our education and our friends.' He went on to make some remarks about Rosalind's inflexibility, then to inform the schoolgirls: 'She had terrible relations with her family. Indeed she went to stay with the Cricks after her hospital treatment.'

(Afterwards, the head of chemistry at St Paul's, Richard Walker, candidly recorded in his notes: 'quite the most provocative and stimulating lecture we've had! The science block is still humming to the comments of "that horrible man".')

Fifteen years later, and forty-six years after he walked into Rosalind's room at King's and saw her bending over the lighted box, Watson was still justifying himself. As President of Cold Spring Harbor Laboratory, returning to Harvard to inaugurate its Center for Genomic Research, he began with a flashback to that critical day in January 1953:

> Let's just start with the Pauling thing. There's a myth which is, you know, that Francis and I basically stole the structure from the people at King's. I was shown Rosalind Franklin's x-ray photograph and, Whooo! that was a helix, and a month later we had the structure, and Wilkins should never have shown me the thing.
>
> I didn't go into the drawer and steal it, it was shown to me, and I was told the dimensions, a repeat of 34 Ångströms, so, you know, I knew roughly what it meant and, uh, but it was that the Franklin photograph was the key event. It *was*, psychologically, it mobilised us . . .

One new element added in the repeated retelling of the story is the admission that Rosalind's Photograph 51 was the pivotal moment in the discovery of the double helix.

Something was done that ought not to have been done, but what? Not the showing of Photograph 51. That concerned Raymond Gosling. He had participated in the work and, as has been said, he had every reason to give the small square X-ray print to Wilkins. If Wilkins was unwise in letting Watson have a look at it, there was no intended subversion; he did not, in that pre-photocopying era, make Watson a copy.

Rather, Watson's continuing sense of unease may well derive from the use of Rosalind's experimental data behind her back and *never telling her openly*—not even in the subsequent years of their friendly collaboration. Neither did Crick. Such acknowledgement as they gave her was very muted and always coupled with the name of Wilkins. For example a lengthy footnote appended to their 1954 paper for the *Proceedings of the Royal Society* says, well into the text,

> The information reported in this section [about the two different forms, A and B, of DNA] was very kindly reported to us prior to its publication by Drs. Wilkins and Franklin. We are most heavily indebted in this respect to the King's College Group, and we wish to point out that without this data the formulation of our picture would have been most unlikely, if not impossible.

The fact was that Rosalind did not report this information to them herself and she was not even speaking to Wilkins. To her dying day Rosalind could not have dreamed that Watson and Crick would be declaring from public platforms half a century later that they could not have found the double helix in March 1953 without her experimental work.

Some scientists have accused Watson's book of undermining the ethics of science, demonstrating to young people that winning justifies all. Rosalind's friend David Harker, formerly of Brooklyn Polytechnic, later head of biophysics at the Roswell Park Memorial Institute at Buffalo, New York, put his objections thus:

> the real tragedy in this affair is the very shady behavior by a number of people, as well as a number of unfortunate accidents, which

> resulted in the transfer of information in an irregular way . . . I would never have consciously become involved in anything like this behavior . . . And I think these people are—to the extent that they did these things—outside scientific morals, as I know them.

Why did Watson create Rosy the Witch? A plausible hypothesis holds that the character was a rationalisation of Watson's guilt —a creature so hostile and uncooperative that there was no alternative to taking what you need by stealth. Gunther Stent, biochemist and editor of the Norton Critical Edition of *The Double Helix*, compares the book's moral dilemma to Lawrence Kohlberg's tale of 'Penniless Heinz and the Mean Druggist': a good husband steals from a mean druggist the medicine essential to save his wife's life.

From the feminine point of view, the wicked Rosy is a variant of an older myth, 'She asked for it', that traces back to Eve: the woman is guiltier than the male. Unwittingly, Nannie Griffiths drew on this ancient lie when blaming young Rosalind for complaining that Colin had hit her with a cricket bat: 'Well dear, you shouldn't have been teasing him.'

What cannot be denied is that 'Rosy' was essential as villainess for the plot for what Wilkins sometimes called 'Jim's novel'. Extraneous details, such as later friendship or early death, would have spoiled the narrative.

Unhappily, Rosalind's denigration did not end with *The Double Helix.* When outright mockery became impolitic, she began to be damned with faint praise; she has been called 'sound' and 'a good experimentalist', her ability and intelligence downgraded. It has been suggested that she was plodding, that she could not understand her own data or work in teams, accept criticism or use imagination.

That none of these alleged inadequacies manifested themselves in Rosalind's work on viruses or coal is ignored by her detractors. Instead, her failure to get the DNA structure in twenty-seven unhappy months at King's College is laid to an almost wilful blindness. Horace Freeland Judson, the science historian, has said that when, in 1952, Rosalind failed to listen to Crick's warnings about alternative explanations for her DNA data, 'Franklin betrayed a grievous slowness of intuitive response.' Yet the solution she reached in her classic papers on coal has been called 'quite witty', while her TMV work is acknowledged as outstanding. Marjorie M'Ewen, who worked with Rosalind at King's College, said, 'Rosalind's final, brilliant, work on TMV received such universal acclamation it is tragic that her scientific reputation was not allowed to rest thereon.'

It was not. The more sophisticated Crick is not blameless. In 'How to Live with a Golden Helix', an article in *The Sciences* in September 1979, he wrote:

> Rosalind's difficulties and failures were mainly of her own making. Underneath her brisk manner she was oversensitive and, ironically, too determined to be scientifically sound and to avoid shortcuts. She was rather too set on succeeding all by herself and rather too stubborn to accept advice easily from others when it ran counter to her own ideas.

But she was not 'set on succeeding all by herself'. Her close collaboration with Mering and later Klug, Holmes and Finch shows that she could be an inspiring teamworker. Her letters to Crick himself demonstrate that she not only invited but welcomed his tough criticisms on her TMV papers, even when these contradicted her own ideas.

Like Watson, Crick felt the need to find a cause for her obstinacy and found it in her family. In 'How to Live with a Golden Helix', he said:

> The major opposition Rosalind Franklin had to cope with was not from her scientific colleagues, nor even from King's College, London (an Anglican foundation, it should be noted, and therefore inherently biased against women), but from her affluent, educated and sympathetic family who felt that scientific research was not the proper thing for a normal girl.

Crick did not know Rosalind's family. He did not know they were Jewish—certainly a major element in her feeling that King's was 'inherently biased' against her. In reality, Ellis Franklin never opposed his daughter's career. There would have been no point. He and his wife did not try to stop her climbing dangerous peaks, moving to France, hitchhiking alone through Israel: Rosalind did what she wanted to do. However, she could see for herself that she was the odd one out in a family of intermarrying cousins and unsalaried wives.

Crick was nearer the mark when telling Anne Sayre in 1970 in a taped interview that Rosalind, as he came to know her through her TMV research, had 'a good, hard, analytical mind, really first-class', but that she lacked intuition—'Or mistrusted it. Perhaps mistrusted it.'

Rosalind *did* mistrust intuition, with a wariness for which her Jewishness is as relevant as her gender. In *The Cousinhood: The Anglo-Jewish Gentry* published in 1971 not long after *The Double Helix*, its author Chaim Bermant writes:

> A Jew often feels compelled to try that much harder than his colleagues; a woman in a man's world has a similar compulsion. Rosalind perhaps tried too hard on both scores and approached her work with a jealous determination which some of her colleagues found alarming. She seemed to carry a constant air of embattlement about her, and felt that her first-class ability and achievements were not given due recognition.

Blame the victim. The belief that Rosalind brought her fate on herself extends even to her cancer. It is often suggested that careless exposure to radiation was the cause of her disease. However, such anecdotal evidence as there is of her taking exceptional risks is counter-balanced by praise of her extreme caution as a scientist, also by the widely repeated observation that all laboratory staff in the 1950s did things that, in Ken Holmes's words 'today would bring down the wrath of the safety inspectorate'.

It may be relevant that others in the Franklin family have suffered from cancer. Possibly they fell victim to the 'Ashkenazi gene'—two genes actually, BC1 and BC2, found to be responsible for the disproportionate percentage of cancer deaths among Jews of northern European descent, with a particularly high incidence of female breast cancer.

For all the retributive gestures, Rosalind continues to be overlooked in accounts of the discovery of the double helix. In Bryan Sykes's *Seven Daughters of Eve*, published in 2001, about the genetic markers of European inheritance, Sykes describes how Watson and Crick worked out the molecular structure of DNA:

> This entailed making long crystalline fibres of DNA and bombarding them with X-rays . . . The deflected X-rays made a regular pattern of spots on the film . . . After many weeks spent building different models . . . Watson and Crick suddenly found one which fitted exactly with the X-ray pattern.

Whose X-ray pattern? Long crystalline fibres made by whom? Bombarded by whom? Film owned by whom? Rosalind seems doomed to remain the invisible woman in many minds, the faceless nurse who hands the surgeon the scalpel.

The air of injustice hanging over the name of Rosalind Franklin has inspired some belated acts of contrition. Immediately following her death, Don Caspar, Klug and Bernal led efforts to organize a memorial fund in Rosalind's name. That never got off the ground. Instead, a registered charity, the Rosalind Franklin Bequest, was created out of the residue of her estate, about £5,000, which gave small grants to deserving applicants.*

That apart, silence followed for many years until Anne Sayre's combative biography of Franklin in 1974 took aim at the Watson caricature. Awareness was aroused, but slowly. In 1984, St Paul's Girls' School recognised her as one of its most illustrious pupils. The Rosalind Franklin Design, Technology and Engineering Workshop was opened at a ceremony attended by her family and former colleagues. (At the event Holmes, who came over from Heidelberg for the occasion, ran into Gosling, then professor of medical physics at Guy's and St Thomas's Hospitals, and said, 'So you were in love with her too?'—a light-hearted remark that did not conceal Holmes's unhealed grief. As he wrote to Anne Sayre in 1971, he was unable to help with her book: 'The circumstances of her death and her bravery during her illness were such that my feelings about Rosalind are still very intense.')

As her posthumous reputation grew, Rosalind was accorded a highly sympathetic portrayal in 1987 in the BBC *Horizon* programme's dramatisation, 'Life

---

* In 2001 Colin Franklin and Jenifer Franklin Glynn gave the capital, by then about £150,000 to Newnham College for its bursary fund.

Story', with Juliet Stevenson and Alan Howard as the ill-matched Franklin and Wilkins, Jeff Goldblum as Watson and Tim Piggott-Smith as Crick. (Well-researched, its scientific details are impeccable, and J.T. Randall wears exactly the kind of bow tie he sported in the early 1950s. The film, nonetheless, to Aaron Klug made Rosalind 'nun-like', whereas the Rosalind he knew was vivacious, opinionated and fun-loving. Anne Sayre too, who found Rosalind a sparkling and amusing friend, disliked the film's 'droopy drudge . . . sitting up half the night with her Beevers-Lipson strips'. Anne remembered well that Rosalind did do hundreds of hours of hand calculations, but 'with concentration and burning enthusiasm . . . she *did* have real insight, she *did* know where she was headed, she *did* have unusual capacity to interpret small clues'. The film that needed to be made, said *New Statesman,* 'is of a brilliant woman trying to make her way in a man's world, having her work used behind her back, and finally being misrepresented in a book published when she was no longer alive to reply'.

Honours continue to accumulate. In 1998 the National Portrait Gallery hung Rosalind's photograph beside that of Wilkins and beneath those of Watson and Crick. In 1992 English Heritage placed a blue plaque on the dark-red mansion block of Donovan Court, Drayton Gardens, South Kensington. A Heritage spokesman said, 'Franklin never received adequate recognition. We are particularly anxious to commemorate important women as 90 per cent of the 600 plaques put up in the last 125 years are to men.' In 1995, sixty-seven years after failing to honour her with an obituary in the Newnham Roll, Newnham College dedicated a graduate residence in her name and placed a bust of Rosalind Franklin in its garden.

At the Science Museum in South Kensington, the TMV model shown in the Science Pavilion at the Brussels World's Fair was acquired for exhibition and kept there until 1964 when Max Perutz took it to Cambridge.

As if to outdo all the rest, at the beginning of the new millennium, King's College London, in a genuflection bordering on political correctness, honoured her in March 2000 with the dedication of its new Franklin-Wilkins Building, opened by the Chancellor of London University, the Princess Royal. During the ceremony, Francis Crick appeared on video, and Watson came in person, to say that her contribution was critical to their discovery. The building thus links the names of a professor who had worked and taught there for fifty-three years with the name of an associate worker who had left (or been pushed out) after little more than two years and rarely spoken of with any warmth within its walls before the name of the refurbished warehouse on the South Bank was chosen.

'Waarom kreeg "Rosy" geen Nobelprijs?' The question posed by the Dutch newspaper *Vrij Nederland* on 15 August 1998 will not go away, even if the answer is simple. 'Rosy' never won the Nobel prize because, when Watson, Crick and Wilkins got theirs in 1962, she was dead. The prize is never awarded posthumously. The inevitable rephrasing—'If Rosalind had lived, would she have won the Nobel prize?'—is meaningless and belongs in the Alternative Futures file along with 'What if Kennedy had not gone to Dallas?'

When the question is rephrased to an assertion, 'They would have had to give it to her rather than to Wilkins had she lived,' the rejoinder is easy. Not at all. 'They' are not compelled to do anything except respect the Nobel rules, which do not allow more than three people to share a prize in any single category. The Nobel committee in Stockholm chooses the winners from the recommendations sent in from each country by, among others, its national laureates—a system which encourages fraternity.

Indeed, when Wilkins's name was announced as a co-winner with Watson and Crick in 1962, Sir Lawrence Bragg wrote Max Perutz (who won the Nobel for physics that same year) of his 'great joy' that Wilkins had been linked with the other two. 'It will undo the bitterness he [Wilkins] felt when Crick and Watson proposed their structure,' Bragg wrote. 'I pressed strongly for it in my recommendation.' Bragg was very influential in determining British nominations. It is hard to believe that, nudged possibly by J.T. Randall, Bragg would not have put Wilkins's name forward instead of Rosalind's. Wilkins was senior to Rosalind, a Fellow of the Royal Society, and had done the serious DNA preliminary work at King's that led to hers.

Speculation is hardly required to imagine the course Rosalind's life would have taken had she been less unlucky. Her long struggle to get her Virus Research Project on a permanent footing succeeded in 1960 when, with the Medical Research Council taking over from the US Public Health grant as backer, Klug, as head of the group, moved with Holmes and Finch to the new MRC Laboratory of Molecular Biology at Cambridge. There Klug and Finch remained for the rest of their careers. Holmes, the one who most directly continued Rosalind's work on the structure of TMV, moved in 1968 to the Max Planck Institute for Medical Research in Heidelberg and carried on his research from there.

Nobel statistics do not favour the female. In 1956 when Dorothy Hodgkin FRS solved the structure of Vitamin B12, the prize for chemistry that year was divided between the head of her department and a Russian chemist. For year after year after that, knowing she had been nominated several times, Hodgkin waited for the telephone to ring. It had not rung by 1962 when Max Perutz received his prize, embarrassed (he said later) to have his prize before she had hers. He used his Nobel credentials to lobby for her. At last, with the special honour of being a sole winner, Hodgkin received the prize for chemistry in 1964, the fifth woman scientist ever to win in the six decades of the prize. The attendant publicity called her an 'affable-looking housewife' and 'mother of three'. At the seventy-fifth anniversary of the Nobel prize in 1975, she was the only representative of fourteen women laureates from all subjects, including peace and literature. She was used to being the only woman at gatherings, she said. 'After all, women have come rather late to science.'

When the centenary of the Nobel prize was celebrated in 2001, Hodgkin remained the only British woman scientist to have won it. A conspicuous absentee from the Nobel pantheon of science is Jocelyn Bell, the Cambridge astronomer who discovered pulsars—energy emissions constituting a new class of stars. She was a graduate assistant at Cambridge when she made her discovery. The Nobel prize for physics in 1974, however, honoured her professor, Antony Hewish, for 'recognising the meaning' (in the words of the *Encyclopaedia Britannica*) of his assistant's observations.

Rosalind's name *was* praised from the Nobel platform in Stockholm but not by Watson, Crick or Wilkins. When they gave their Nobel addresses in 1962, only Wilkins uttered her name at all, mentioning her and Alex Stokes as two people at King's College London who 'made very valuable contributions to the X-ray analysis'. Sometime later, Randall (by then Sir John) wrote Gosling, 'I have always felt that Maurice's Nobel lecture did rather less than justice to this setting [Randall's biophysics lab at King's] and particularly to the contribution of yourself and Rosalind.'

In 1982, however, when Aaron Klug received the prize for chemistry, he spoke movingly of his late colleague. Rosalind Franklin, he said, had introduced him to the study of viruses and set an example of tackling large and difficult problems: 'Had her life not been cut tragically short, she might well have stood in this place on an earlier occasion.'

Klug has been Rosalind's staunchest defender. Several months following the publication of *The Double Helix*, he wrote a long article for *Nature*, saying that Watson did not pretend to tell more than one side of the story. As 'her last and perhaps closest scientific colleague', he said, he had carefully studied her laboratory notebooks and found that, far from being anti-helical (as Watson, Crick and Wilkins continued to maintain) she had set out the evidence for a helical structure for DNA as early as her Turner and Newall report in February 1952. Although she had retreated from this position for the A form because of some of her subsequent findings, by the February and March of 1953, she was far nearer to solving the structure than anyone had realised:

> She would have solved it, but it would have come out in stages. For the feminists, however, she has become a doomed heroine, and they have seized upon her as an icon, which is not, of course, her fault. Rosalind was not a feminist in the ordinary sense, but she was determined to be treated equally just like anybody else.

Klug's was a robust defence, strengthened in 1974 by a startling discovery, which he also reported in *Nature*, of a missing manuscript dated 17 March 1953, which showed that Rosalind was even closer to coming upon the truth of the double helix than even he had realised. Tactfully, however, perhaps out of respect for his fellow FRSs, Klug did not mention how irregularly her data had been obtained, and how inadequate had been her formal acknowledgement, in 1953 and 1954, and in the 1962 Nobel addresses of the DNA trio.

Nor did Klug declare his personal interest in her defence. Klug owed Rosalind a debt of honour. By making him her principal beneficiary, she changed his life, made it possible for him and his wife to buy a house and to stay in Britain where he rose to great heights. He became successively Sir Aaron, winner of the Nobel prize, holder of the Order of Merit (a tribute to greatness, in the personal gift of the Queen) and, from 1995 to 2000, President of the Royal Society.

Some criticism belongs to the Nobel prize itself. Founded in 1901 it is the world's most coveted intellectual award, but it is also arbitrary, inherently unfair and possibly damaging. Many who deserved it have not got it; many who didn't; have. The literature prize offers glaring examples: Thomas Mann, Leo Tolstoy and James Joyce were passed over, Somerset Maugham and Pearl Buck honoured. In science the effect is particularly baleful, because science is collegial. As research becomes progressively more expensive, moreover, scientific discoveries are harder to attribute to particular people. The Nobel prize, by canonizing individuals, disguises the truth that they are all, in Newton's famous phrase, standing 'on giants' shoulders' and on each other's as well.

The list of deserving scientists who never got the summons to Stockholm is long, glittering and bitter, and contains a number of women: the physicist Lise Meitner and the Cambridge astronomer Jocelyn Bell. Oswald Avery, who discovered that DNA was the genetic material, was deprived of the prize by the persistent and unfair criticism of his Rockefeller colleague Alfred Mirsky. In the view of Erwin Chargaff, whose finding of the base pairs of DNA went uncelebrated, 'Avery should have gotten two Nobel prizes for his discovery. I have no complaint when I think of Avery.'

Such omissions and exclusions would not matter except that the Nobel prize changes lives, and divides colleague from colleague by touching the winners with a magic of which the generous prize money is only part.

Rosalind Franklin did not have her eyes on the prize. Nor did she worry about having been outrun in a race that no one but Watson and Crick knew was a race. She died proud of her world reputation both in coal studies and in virus research, and of her list of published papers that would do credit to any scientific career, let alone one that ended at the age of thirty-seven. Had she not gone into science, the early 1950s would have had little understanding of what kinds of coal make graphite, slower knowledge of the A and B forms of DNA and of the characteristics of TMV. There would have been a delay in getting to the DNA structure and in the revolution that followed. The careers of her collaborators and of the Nobel trio who benefited from her data could have fallen far short of the heights they reached.

Rosalind knew her worth. With every prospect of going on to further significant achievement and, possibly, personal happiness, she was cheated of the only thing she really wanted: the chance to complete her work. The lost prize was life.

NOTES

FORGIVENESS, RECONCILIATION AND RESPONDING TO EVIL: A PHILOSOPHICAL OVERVIEW

Jeffrie Murphy

Jeffrie Murphy is Regents' Professor of Law and Philosophy at Arizona State University and a distinguished scholar who has published nine books.

The Nature of Forgiveness

I think that one of the most insightful discussions of forgiveness ever penned is to be found in Bishop Joseph Butler's 1726 sermon "Upon Forgiveness of Injuries."[5] In that sermon, Bishop Butler offers a definition of forgiveness that I have adapted in my own work on the topic.[6] According to Butler, forgiveness is a moral virtue (a virtue of character) that is essentially a matter of the heart, the inner self, and involves a change in inner feeling more than a change in external action. The change in feeling is this: the overcoming, on moral grounds, of the intense negative reactive attitudes—the vindictive passions of resentment, anger, hatred, and the desire for revenge—that are quite naturally occasioned when one has been wronged by another responsible agent. A person who has forgiven has overcome those vindictive attitudes and has overcome them for a morally creditable motive—e.g., being moved by repentance on the part of the person by whom one has been wronged. Of course, such a change in feeling often leads to a change of behavior—reconciliation, for example; but, as our ability to forgive the dead illustrates, it does not always do so.

On this analysis of forgiveness, it is useful initially to distinguish forgiveness from other responses to wrongdoing with which forgiveness is often confused: justification, excuse, mercy, and reconciliation. Although these concepts are to some degree open textured and can bleed into each other, clarity is—I think—served if one at least starts by attempting to separate them. I will discuss each of them briefly.

1. *Justification:* To regard conduct as justified (as in lawful self defense, for example) is to claim that the conduct, though normally wrongful, was—in the given circumstances and all things considered—the right thing to do. If I have suffered because of conduct that was right—e.g., had my nose bloodied by someone defending himself against my wrongful attack—I have not been wronged, have nothing legitimately to resent, and thus have nothing to forgive.
2. *Excuse:* To regard conduct as excused (as in the insanity defense, for example) is to admit that the conduct was wrong but to claim that the person who engaged in the conduct lacked substantial capacity to conform his conduct to the relevant norms and thus was not a

Reprinted by permission from *Fordham Urban Law Journal.*

fully responsible agent. Responsible agency is, of course, a matter of degree; but to the degree that the person who injures me is not a responsible agent, resentment of that person would make no more sense than resenting a sudden storm that soaks me. Again, there is nothing here to forgive.

3. *Mercy:* To accord a wrongdoer mercy is to inflict a less harsh consequence on that person than allowed by institutional (usually legal) rules. Mercy is less personal than forgiveness, since the one granting mercy (a sentencing judge, say) typically will not be a victim of wrongdoing and thus will not have any feelings of resentment to overcome. (There is a sense in which only victims of wrongdoing have what might be called standing to forgive.) Mercy also has a public behavioral dimension not necessarily present in forgiveness. I can forgive a person simply in my heart of hearts, but I cannot show mercy simply in my heart of hearts. I can forgive the dead, but I cannot show mercy to the dead. I can forgive myself, but I cannot show mercy to myself.

   This distinction between mercy and forgiveness allows us to see why there is no inconsistency in fully forgiving a person for wrongdoing (that is, stop resenting or hating the person for it) but still advocate that the person suffer the legal consequence of criminal punishment. To the degree that criminal punishment is justified in order to secure victim satisfaction, then—of course—the fact that the victim has forgiven will be a relevant argument for reducing the criminal's sentence and the fact that a victim still resents and hates will be a relevant argument for increasing that sentence. It is highly controversial, of course, that criminal punishment should to any degree be harnessed to victim desires.[7] Even if it is, however, it must surely be admitted that the practice serves other values as well—particularly crime control and justice; and, with respect to these goals, victim forgiveness could hardly be dispositive. In short: It would indeed be inconsistent for a person to claim that he has forgiven the wrongdoer and still advocate punishment for the wrongdoer in order to satisfy his personal vindictive feelings. (If he still has those feelings, he has not forgiven.) It would not be inconsistent, however, to advocate punishment for other legitimate reasons. Of course, the possibilities for self deception are enormous here.

4. *Reconciliation.* The vindictive passions (those overcome in forgiveness) are often a major barrier to reconciliation; and thus, since forgiveness often leads to reconciliation, it is easy to confuse the two concepts. I think, however, that it is important also to see how they may differ—how there can be forgiveness without reconciliation and reconciliation without forgiveness.

   First let me give an example of forgiveness without reconciliation. Imagine a battered woman who has been repeatedly beaten and raped by her husband or boyfriend. This woman—after a religious conversion, perhaps—might well come to forgive her batterer (i.e., stop hating him) without a willingness to resume her relationship with him. "I forgive you and wish you well" can, in my view, sit quite consistently with "I never want you in this house again." In short, the fact that one has forgiven does not mean that one must also trust or live again with a person.

As an example of reconciliation without forgiveness, consider the example of the South African Truth and Reconciliation Commission.[8] In order to negotiate a viable transition from apartheid to democratic government with full black participation, all parties had to agree that there would in most cases be no punishment for evil acts that occurred under the previous government. Wrongdoers, by making a full confession and accepting responsibility, would typically be granted amnesty. In this process the wrongdoers would not be required to repent, show remorse, or even apologize.

I can clearly see this process as one of reconciliation—a process that will allow all to work toward a democratic and just future. I do not so easily see this process as one of forgiveness, however. No change of heart was required or even sought from the victims—no overcoming of such vindictive feelings as resentment and hatred. All that was required of them was a willingness to accept this process as a necessary means to the future good of their society.

In my view, this counts as forgiveness only if one embraces what is (to me) a less morally rich definition of forgiveness: forgiveness merely as the waiving of a right. Examples of this are found in the private law idea of forgiving a debt or in Bishop Desmond Tutu's definition of forgiveness as "waiving one's right to revenge."[9] But surely one can waive one's rights for purely instrumental reasons; reasons having nothing to do with the change of heart that constitutes forgiveness as a moral virtue. One can even waive one's rights for selfish reasons—e.g., the belief that one's future employment prospects will be better if one simply lets bygones be bygones. I am not saying that it is wrong to act for instrumental reasons—indeed, for South Africa, it may have been the only justified course. Neither am I saying that instrumental justifications can never be moral justifications. To attempt reconciliation for the future good of one's society, for example, is surely both instrumental and moral. I am simply saying that, however justified acting instrumentally may sometimes be, it is—absent the extinction of resentment and other vindictive passions—something other than what I understand as the moral virtue of forgiveness. In short: If all we know is that two parties have decided to reconcile, we do not know enough to make a reliable judgment about whether the moral virtue of forgiveness has been realized in the reconciliation.

Another point worth making about the relation between reconciliation and forgiveness is this: If one always delayed reconciliation until forgiveness had taken place, then some vitally important kinds of reconciliation might not be possible. Thus the realization that forgiveness is often a helpful step toward reconciliation should not lead us into the mistaken belief that forgiveness is a necessary condition for reconciliation. Indeed, it is surely sometimes the case that reconciliation, coming first and adopted for instrumental reasons, opens the door to future forgiveness. After learning that one can work with one's victimizer toward a common goal, a sense of common humanity might emerge and one's vindictive passions toward that person might over time begin to soften.

Let me now discuss the evaluation of forgiveness as I—following Bishop Butler—have defined it.

The Dangers of Hasty Forgiveness

In addition to his powerful sermon on forgiveness, Bishop Butler authored an equally powerful sermon with the title "Upon Resentment."[10] In that sermon, Butler started to make a case for the legitimacy of resentment and other vindictive passions—arguing that a just and loving God would not have universally implanted these passions within his creatures unless the passions served some valuable purpose. The danger of resentment, he argued, lies not in having it, but rather in being dominated and consumed by it to such a degree that one can never overcome it and acts irresponsibly on the basis of it. As the initial response to being wronged, however, the passion stands in defense of important values—values that might be compromised by immediate and uncritical forgiveness of wrongs.

What are the values defended by resentment and threatened by hasty and uncritical forgiveness? I would suggest two: respect for self and respect for the moral order. A person who never resented any injuries done to himself might be a saint. It is equally likely, however, that his lack of resentment reveals a servile personality—a personality lacking in respect for himself and respect for his rights and status as a free and equal moral agent. (This is the point behind the famous quip: "To err is human; to forgive, supine.")[11] Just as indignation or guilt over the mistreatment of others stands as emotional testimony that we care about them and their rights, so does resentment stand as emotional testimony that we care about ourselves and our rights.

Related to this is an instrumental point: Those who have vindictive dispositions toward those who wrong them give potential wrongdoers an incentive not to wrong them. If I were going to set out to oppress other people, I would surely prefer to select for my victims persons whose first response is forgiveness rather than persons whose first response is revenge. As Kant noted in his *Doctrine of Virtue,* "One who makes himself into a worm cannot complain if people step on him."[12]

Resentment does not simply stand as emotional testimony of self-respect, however. This passion—and the reluctance to hastily transcend it in forgiveness—also stands as testimony to our allegiance to the moral order itself. This is a point made forcefully by Aurel Kolnai in his important essay on forgiveness.[13] According to Kolnai, we all have a duty to support—both intellectually and emotionally—the moral order, an order represented by clear understandings of what constitutes unacceptable treatment of one human being by another. If we do not show some resentment to those who, in victimizing us, flout those understandings, then we run the risk of being "complicitous in evil."

If I had more time, I could say many more things in defense of the vindictive passions. (Indeed, I am soon to publish an essay with the title "Two Cheers for Vindictiveness."[14]) I hope I have said enough, however, to support Butler's claim that these passions have some positive value. Having such value, these passions are unlike, say, malice—pure delight in the misfortunes and sufferings of others. Malice is by no means universal but is, where present, intrinsically evil or diseased or both. Butler essentially wants to apply Aristotle's idea of the mean to the passion of resentment—developing an account of the circumstances that justify it and the degree to which it is legitimate to feel and be guided by it.[15] But the doctrine of the mean does not apply to malice; for the proper amount of this passion is always zero.

Uncritical boosters for quick forgiveness have a tendency to treat resentment and the other vindictive passions as though, like malice, they are intrinsically evil—passions that no decent person would acknowledge.[16] In this, I think that they are quite mistaken. In the *Oresteia,* Athena rightly made an honorable home for the Furies (representatives of the vindictive passions)—so constraining their excess by due process and the rule of law that they become the Eumenides (the Kindly Ones), protectors of law and social stability.[17] There is no honorable home for malice, however.

Let me summarize what I have argued to this point: The problem with resentment and other vindictive passions is not (as with malice) their very existence. In their proper place, they have an important role to play in the defense of self and of the moral and legal order. The problem with these passions is rather their tendency to get out of control—to so dominate the life of a victimized person that the person's own life is soured and, in his revenge seeking, he starts to pose a danger to the very moral and legal order that rightly identifies him as a victim of immorality. It is here—as a limiting and overcoming virtue—that forgiveness has its important role to play.

Forgiveness as a Virtue

It is, of course, possible to take one's revenge against others in measured and proportional and peaceful ways—ways as simple as a cutting remark before colleagues or a failure to continue issuing lunch invitations.

Very often, however, a victimized person will allow vindictiveness to take over his very self—turning him into a self-righteous fanatic so involved—even joyous—in his outrage that he will be satisfied only with the utter annihilation of the person who has wronged him. Such a person is sometimes even willing to destroy, as symbolic stand-ins, persons who have done him no wrong or who may even be totally innocent.[18] Such a person is a danger to himself—very like, as I think Nietzsche once said, a scorpion stinging itself with its own tail—and poses a threat to the morality and decency of the social order. A person under the power of such vindictiveness can, often unconsciously, even use the language of justice and crime control as a rationalization for what is really sadism and cruelty. I cannot help thinking, for example, that many of the unspeakably brutish conditions that we tolerate in our prisons flow not from the stated legitimate desires for justice and crime control, but rather from a vindictiveness so out of control that it actually becomes a kind of malice.

Against such a background, forgiveness can be seen as a healing virtue that brings with it great blessings—chief among them being its capacity to free us from being consumed by our angers, its capacity to check our tendencies toward cruelty, and its capacity to open the door to the restoration of those relationships in our lives that are worthy of restoration. This last blessing can be seen in the fact that, since each one of us will sometimes wrong the people that mean the most to us, there will be times when we will want to be forgiven by those whom we have wronged. Seeing this, no rational person would desire to live in a world where forgiveness was not seen as a healing virtue. This is, I take it, the secular meaning of the parable of the unforgiving servant.[19]

We are faced, then, with a complex dilemma: How are we to reap the blessings of forgiveness without sacrificing our self respect or our respect for the moral order in the process?

One great help here—and I make no claim that it is the only help or even a necessary condition for forgiveness—is sincere repentance on the part of the wrongdoer. When I am wronged by another, a great part of the injury—over and above any physical harm I may suffer—is the insulting or degrading message that has been given to me by the wrongdoer; the message is that I am less worthy than he is, so unworthy that he may use me merely as a means or object in service to his desires and projects. Thus failing to resent (or hastily forgiving) the wrongdoer runs the risk that I am endorsing that very immoral message for which the wrongdoer stands. If the wrongdoer sincerely repents, however, he now joins me in repudiating the degrading and insulting message—allowing me to relate to him (his new self) as an equal without fear that a failure to resent him will be read as a failure to resent what he has done. In short: It is much easier to follow St. Augustine's counsel that we should "hate the sin but not the sinner" when the sinner (the wrongdoer) repudiates his own wrongdoing through an act of repentance.[20]

My point here is that sincere repentance on the part of the wrongdoer opens the door to forgiveness and often to reconciliation. This is not to suggest, however, that we should always demand repentance as a condition for forgiveness and reconciliation. When a person comes to repentance as a result of his own spiritual growth, we are witness to an inspiring transformation of character. Any repentance that is simply a response to a demand or external incentive, however, is very likely to be fake. In what could be read as a commentary both on certain aspects of the Federal Sentencing Guidelines[21] and on remarks made by some of our current crop of elected officials, Montaigne wrote: "These men make us believe that they feel great regret and remorse within, but of atonement and correction or interruption they show us no sign . . . . I know of no quality so easy to counterfeit as piety."[22] Montaigne's observation also suggests that the South Africans were perhaps wise in not making repentance a condition for amnesty under their Truth and Reconciliation Commission.

So let us welcome repentance when we find it, and let us do what we can to create a climate where it can flourish and open the door to the moral rebirth of the wrongdoer and to forgiveness by the wronged. But, out of respect for the genuine article, let us not demand or otherwise coerce it. Demanding tends to produce only lying and may even be degrading to the wrongdoer—inviting his further corruption rather than his moral rebirth. David Lurie, the central character in J. M. Coetzee's recent novel *Disgrace,* could save his job if he simply expressed the kind of repentance demanded of him by the university disciplinary board that has authority over him. I find myself sympathizing with the reasons he gives for not giving them what they want when he says:

> We went through the repentance business yesterday. I told you what I thought. I won't do it. I appeared before an officially constituted tribunal, before a branch of the law. Before that secular tribunal I pleaded guilty, a secular plea. That plea should suffice. Repentance is neither here nor there. Repentance belongs to another world, to another universe of discourse. . . . [What you are asking] reminds me too much of Mao's China. Recantation, self-criticism, public apology. I'm old fashioned, I would prefer simply to be put against a wall and shot.[23]

There has in recent times been much cheap and shallow chatter about forgiveness and repentance—some of it coming from high political officials and some coming from the kind of psychobabble often found in self-help and recovery books. As a result of this, many people are, I fear, starting to become cynical about both. For reasons I have developed here, repentance may pave the way for forgiveness. It is less likely to do so, however, in a world where we come to believe that too many claims of repentance are insincere and expedient—talking the talk without (so far as we can tell) walking the walk.

I have reached a point where I fear that I have both used up my time and worn out my welcome. So I will now move to bring my remarks to a close by touching briefly on one additional issue.

Forgiveness and Christianity

At a symposium on forgiveness sponsored by a distinguished Catholic university, it would be fitting for me to close my talk with a few general remarks about the relationship between religion—particularly Christianity—and forgiveness. As someone who is neither devout nor trained in theology, I am hardly the best person to do this—either spiritually or intellectually. However, I will take a brief stab at it none the less.

There are, I think, at least three ways in which a Christian perspective on the world might make the struggle toward forgiveness—not easy, surely—but at least slightly less difficult than it otherwise might be. (Similar perspectives might also be present, of course, in other religions and world views.)[24]

First, I think that Christianity tends to introduce a humbling perspective on one's self and one's personal concerns—attempting to counter our natural tendencies of pride and narcissistic self importance. According to this perspective, we are all fallible and flawed and all stand in deep need of forgiveness. This perspective does not seek to trivialize the wrongs that we suffer, but it does seek to blunt our very human tendency to magnify those wrongs out of all reasonable sense of proportion—the tendency to see ourselves as morally pure while seeing those who wrong us as evil incarnate. By breaking down a sharp us-them dichotomy, such a view should make it easier to follow Auden's counsel to "love your crooked neighbor with your crooked heart."[25] This should make us more open to the possibility of forgiving those who have wronged us and should also help us to keep our justified resentments from turning into malicious hatreds and our demands for just punishment from serving as rationalizations for sadistic cruelty.

Related to this is a second Christian teaching that might help open the door to forgiveness—a teaching that concerns not the status of the victim, but the status of the wrongdoer. According to Christianity, we are supposed to see the wrongdoer, as we are supposed to see each person, as a child of God, created in His image, and thus as ultimately precious. This vision is beautifully expressed by the writer William Trevor in his novel *Felicia's Journey*. He speaks with compassion and forgiveness even of the serial killer who is a central character of that novel and writes of him: "Lost within a man who murdered, there was a soul like any other soul, purity itself it surely once had been."[26] Viewing the wrongdoer in this way—seeing in him the innocent child he once was—should make it difficult to hate him with the kind of abandon that would make forgiveness of him utterly impossible.

Third and finally, Christianity teaches that the universe is—for all its evil and hardship—ultimately benign, created and sustained by a loving God, and to be met with hope rather than despair. On this view, the world may be falling, but—as Rilke wrote—"there is One who holds this falling/with infinite softness in his hands."[27]

If I could embrace such a view of the universe and our place in it—a view for which there is surely no proof, requiring a faith that is properly called religious—then perhaps I would not so easily think that the struggle against evil—even evil done to me—is my task alone, all up to me.[28] If I think that I alone can and must make things right—including making sure that the people I have branded as evil get exactly what is coming to them—then I take on a kind of self-importance that makes me not only unforgiving but dangerous—becoming the kind of person Nietzsche probably had in mind when he warned that we should "mistrust those in whom the urge to punish is very strong."[29] If I were capable of a certain kind of faith, then perhaps I could relax a bit the clinched fist with which I try to protect myself, sustain my self respect, avenge myself, and hold my world together all alone.

Endnotes

5. *See Sermon IX, in* Sermons of Joseph Butler 127–41 (W. E. Gladstone ed., 1897).
6. My adaptation of Butler is free, and I make no pretense that what follows is a solid piece of Butler scholarship. I have been inspired by Butler's discussion; and thus, even when I have modified or added to that discussion, I hope that I have always been loyal to its essential spirit.
7. For a survey of the arguments pro and con, on allowing victim desires to influence criminal sentencing, see the majority and dissenting opinions in *Booth v. Maryland,* 482 U.S. 496 (1987), *overruled by Payne v. Tennessee,* 501 U.S. 808, 825 (1991).
8. For a survey of the operation of the Commission, see Minow, *supra,* note 1, at 52–90.
9. Interview by Bill Moyers with Bishop Desmond Tutu, PBS (Apr. 27, 1999).
10. *See Sermon VIII, in* Sermons of Joseph Butler, *supra* note 5, at 115–126.
11. I have heard this quip attributed to the comic writer S. J. Perelman (who often wrote for the Marx Brothers), but I am not certain if the attribution is accurate.
12. Immanuel Kant, The Doctrine of Virtue, Part II of the Metaphysics of Morals 103, (Mary J. Gregor trans., 1964).
13. *See* Aurel Kolnai, *Forgiveness, in* Proceedings of the Aristotelian Society 91, 95–98 (1973–74).
14. *See* Jeffrie G. Murphy, *Two Cheers for Vindictiveness, in* Punishment and Society (forthcoming).

15. *See* Aristotle, Nichomachean Ethics 1107a, *reprinted in* Nichomachean Ethics 44–46 (Terence Irwin trans., 1985).
16. I sometimes think I find such uncritical boosterism among certain voices within what might be called the "forgiveness movement" in clinical psychology. *See* Jeffrie G. Murphy, *Forgiveness in Counseling: A Philosophical Perspective, in* Character, Liberty and Law: Kantian Essays in Theory and Practice 223–238 (1998).
17. *See* Aeschylus, Oresteia (Robert Fagles trans., 1979).
18. The von Kleist story *Michael Kohlhaas*—retold by E. L. Doctorow in his novel, *Ragtime* (1974), is a famous illustration of this. A good English translation of Heinrich von Kleist's 1808 novella Michael Kohlhass may be found in Heinrich von Kleist, The Marquise of O and Other Stories 114–213 (David Luke & Nigel Reeves trans., 1978).
19. *See Matthew* 18:21–35.
20. St. Augustine's remark, so often rendered as it is here, more literally reads "with love of mankind and hatred of sins." The Oxford Dictionary of Quotations 37 (Angela Partington ed., rev. 4th ed. 1996) (citing *Letter 211, reprinted in* 33 Patrologiae Latinae (J. P. Minge ed., 1845)).
21. *See* U.S. Sentencing Commission Guidelines Manual § 3E1.1 (1998) ("If the defendant clearly demonstrates acceptance of responsibility for his offense, decrease the offense level by 2 levels.").
22. Michel de Montaigne, On Repentance (1588), *in* The Complete Essays of Montaigne 617 (Donald Frame trans., 1958).
23. J.M. Coetzee, Disgrace 58, 66 (1999).
24. *See, e.g.,* the discussion of the background world view that underlies the Judaic conception of forgiveness in Louis E. Newman's *The Quality of Mercy: On the Duty to Forgive in the Judaic Tradition,* 15 Journal of Religious Ethics 155 (1987). For the context provided by Stoicism, see Seneca, *On Anger and On Mercy, in* 1 Moral Essays 106–449 (John W. Basore trans., 1994). For a discussion of forgiveness in capital murder cases from an Islamic perspective, see Azizah al-Hibri, *The Muslim Perspective on the Clergy-Penitent Privilege,* 29 Loy. L.A. L. Rev. 1723, 1728–29 (1996).
25. W.H. Auden, *As I Walked Out One Evening, in* Collected Poems 135 (1991).
26. William Trevor, Felicia's Journey 212 (1994).
27. Rainer Maria Rilke, *Autumn, in* The Book of Images (Edward Snow trans., 1991).
28. I came to see the value of this perspective when it was used by philosopher-theologian Marilyn Adams in her critique of some of my earlier writing on forgiveness. *See* Marilyn Adams, *Forgiveness: A Christian Model,* 8 Faith and Philosophy 277–304 (1991). I have

also recently come to see the wisdom in Herbert Morris's use of the thought of Simone Weil on these matters. *See* Herbert Morris & Jeffrie G. Murphy, *Exchange on Forgiveness,* 7 Criminal Justice Ethics 3, 22 (Summer/Fall 1988).

29. Friedrich Nietzsche *Thus Spoke Zarathrustra, Second Part, On the Tarantulas, in* The Portable Nietzsche 212 (Walter Kaufmann trans., 1970). I pursue Nietzsche's thoughts on punishment in somewhat greater detail in my *Moral Epistemology, the Retributive Emotions, and the "Clumsy Moral Philosophy" of Jesus Christ, in* The Passions of Law 149 (Susan Bandes ed., 1999).

NOTES

THINKING ABOUT SOCIAL CHANGE IN AMERICA
Robert D. Putnam

(1941–)

Robert D. Putnam is the Peter and Isabel Malkin Professor of Public Policy at Harvard where he teaches courses on U.S. politics, international relations, comparative politics, and public policy. He has served on the National Security Council and as President of the American Political Science Association. He is also a consultant to the CIA and World Bank.

What happened next to civic and social life in American communities is the subject of this book. In recent years social scientists have framed concerns about the changing character of American society in terms of the concept of "social capital." By analogy with notions of physical capital and human capital—tools and training that enhance individual productivity—the core idea of social capital theory is that social networks have value. Just as a screwdriver (physical capital) or a college education (human capital) can increase productivity (both individual and collective), so too social contacts affect the productivity of individuals and groups.

Whereas physical capital refers to physical objects and human capital refers to properties of individuals, social capital refers to connections among individuals—social networks and the norms of reciprocity and trustworthiness that arise from them. In that sense social capital is closely related to what some have called "civic virtue." The difference is that "social capital" calls attention to the fact that civic virtue is most powerful when embedded in a dense network of reciprocal social relations. A society of many virtuous but isolated individuals is not necessarily rich in social capital.

The term *social capital* itself turns out to have been independently invented at least six times over the twentieth century, each time to call attention to the ways in which our lives are made more productive by social ties. The first known use of the concept was not by some cloistered theoretician, but by a practical reformer of the Progressive Era—L. J. Hanifan, state supervisor of rural schools in West Virginia. Writing in 1916 to urge the importance of community involvement for successful schools, Hanifan invoked the idea of "social capital" to explain why. For Hanifan, social capital referred to

> those tangible substances [that] count for most in the daily lives of people: namely good will, fellowship, sympathy, and social intercourse among the individuals and families who make up a social unit. . . . The individual is helpless socially, if left to himself. . . . If he comes into contact with his neighbor, and they with other neighbors, there will be an accumulation of social capital, which may immediately satisfy his

Reprinted from *Bowling Alone: The Collapse and Revival of American Community* (2001), by permission of Simon & Schuster, Inc.

> social needs and which may bear a social potentiality sufficient to the substantial improvement of living conditions in the whole community. The community as a whole will benefit by the cooperation of all its parts, while the individual will find in his associations the advantages of the help, the sympathy, and the fellowship of his neighbors.[1]

Hanifan's account of social capital anticipated virtually all the crucial elements in later interpretations, but his conceptual invention apparently attracted no notice from other social commentators and disappeared without a trace. But like sunken treasure recurrently revealed by shifting sands and tides, the same idea was independently rediscovered in the 1950s by Canadian sociologists to characterize the club memberships of arriviste suburbanites, in the 1960s by urbanist Jane Jacobs to laud neighborliness in the modern metropolis, in the 1970s by economist Glenn Loury to analyze the social legacy of slavery, and in the 1980s by French social theorist Pierre Bourdieu and by German economist Ekkehart Schlicht to underline the social and economic resources embodied in social networks. Sociologist James S. Coleman put the term firmly and finally on the intellectual agenda in the late 1980s, using it (as Hanifan had originally done) to highlight the social context of education.[2]

As this array of independent coinages indicates, social capital has both an individual and a collective aspect—a private face and a public face. First, individuals form connections that benefit our own interests. One pervasive strategem of ambitious job seekers is "networking," for most of us get our jobs because of whom we know, not what we know—that is, our social capital, not our human capital. Economic sociologist Ronald Burt has shown that executives with bounteous Rolodex files enjoy faster career advancement. Nor is the private return to social capital limited to economic rewards. As Claude S. Fischer, a sociologist of friendship, has noted, "Social networks are important in all our lives, often for finding jobs, more often for finding a helping hand, companionship, or a shoulder to cry on."[3]

If individual clout and companionship were all there were to social capital, we'd expect foresighted, self-interested individuals to invest the right amount of time and energy in creating or acquiring it. However, social capital also can have "externalities" that affect the wider community, so that not all the costs and benefits of social connections accrue to the person making the contact.[4] As we shall see later in this book, a well-connected individual in a poorly connected society is not as productive as a well-connected individual in a well-connected society. And even a poorly connected individual may derive some of the spillover benefits from living in a well-connected community. If the crime rate in my neighborhood is lowered by neighbors keeping an eye on one another's homes, I benefit even if I personally spend most of my time on the road and never even nod to another resident on the street.

Social capital can thus be simultaneously a "private good" and a "public good." Some of the benefit from an investment in social capital goes to bystanders, while some of the benefit redounds to the immediate interest of the person making the investment. For example, service clubs, like Rotary or Lions, mobilize local energies to raise scholarships or fight disease at the same time that they provide members with friendships and business connections that pay off personally.

Social connections are also important for the rules of conduct that they sustain. Networks involve (almost by definition) mutual obligations; they are not interesting as mere "contacts." Networks of community engagement foster sturdy norms of reciprocity: I'll do this for you now, in the expectation that you (or perhaps someone else) will return the favor. "Social capital is akin to what Tom Wolfe called 'the favor bank' in his novel *The Bonfire of the Vanities,*" notes economist Robert Frank.[5] It was, however, neither a novelist nor an economist, but Yogi Berra who offered the most succinct definition of reciprocity: "If you don't go to somebody's funeral, they won't come to yours."

Sometimes, as in these cases, reciprocity is *specific:* I'll do this for you if you do that for me. Even more valuable, however, is a norm of *generalized* reciprocity: I'll do this for you without expecting anything specific back from you, in the confident expectation that someone else will do something for me down the road. The Golden Rule is one formulation of generalized reciprocity. Equally instructive is the T-shirt slogan used by the Gold Beach, Oregon, Volunteer Fire Department to publicize their annual fund-raising effort: "Come to our breakfast, we'll come to your fire." "We act on a norm of specific reciprocity," the firefighters seem to be saying, but onlookers smile because they recognize the underlying norm of generalized reciprocity—the firefighters will come even if *you* don't. When Blanche DuBois depended on the kindness of strangers, she too was relying on generalized reciprocity.

A society characterized by generalized reciprocity is more efficient than a distrustful society, for the same reason that money is more efficient than barter. If we don't have to balance every exchange instantly, we can get a lot more accomplished. Trustworthiness lubricates social life. Frequent interaction among a diverse set of people tends to produce a norm of generalized reciprocity. Civic engagement and social capital entail mutual obligation and responsibility for action. As L. J. Hanifan and his successors recognized, social networks and norms of reciprocity can facilitate cooperation for mutual benefit. When economic and political dealing is embedded in dense networks of social interaction, incentives for opportunism and malfeasance are reduced. This is why the diamond trade, with its extreme possibilities for fraud, is concentrated within close-knit ethnic enclaves. Dense social ties facilitate gossip and other valuable ways of cultivating reputation—an essential foundation for trust in a complex society.

Physical capital is not a single "thing," and different forms of physical capital are not interchangeable. An eggbeater and an aircraft carrier both appear as physical capital in our national accounts, but the eggbeater is not much use for national defense, and the carrier would not be much help with your morning omelet. Similarly, social capital—that is, social networks and the associated norms of reciprocity—comes in many different shapes and sizes with many different uses. Your extended family represents a form of social capital, as do your Sunday school class, the regulars who play poker on your commuter train, your college roommates, the civic organizations to which you belong, the Internet chat group in which you participate, and the network of professional acquaintances recorded in your address book.

Sometimes "social capital," like its conceptual cousin "community," sounds warm and cuddly. Urban sociologist Xavier de Souza Briggs, however, properly warns us to beware of a treacly sweet, "kumbaya" interpretation of social capital.[6] Networks and the associated norms of reciprocity are generally good for those inside the network, but the external effects of social capital are by no means always positive. It was social capital, for example, that enabled Timothy McVeigh to bomb the Alfred P. Murrah Federal Building in Oklahoma City. McVeigh's network of friends, bound together by a norm of reciprocity, enabled him to do what he could not have done alone. Similarly, urban gangs, NIMBY ("not in my backyard") movements, and power elites often exploit social capital to achieve ends that are antisocial from a wider perspective. Indeed, it is rhetorically useful for such groups to obscure the difference between the pro-social and antisocial consequences of community organizations. When Floridians objected to plans by the Ku Klux Klan to "adopt a highway," Jeff Coleman, grand wizard of the Royal Knights of the KKK, protested, "Really, we're just like the Lions or the Elks. We want to be involved in the community."[7]

Social capital, in short, can be directed toward malevolent, antisocial purposes, just like any other form of capital.[8] (McVeigh also relied on physical capital, like the explosive-laden truck, and human capital, like bomb-making expertise, to achieve his purposes.) Therefore it is important to ask how the positive consequences of social capital—mutual support, cooperation, trust, institutional effectiveness—can be maximized and the negative manifestations—sectarianism, ethnocentrism, corruption—minimized. Toward this end, scholars have begun to distinguish many different forms of social capital.

Some forms involve repeated, intensive, multistranded networks—like a group of steelworkers who meet for drinks every Friday after work and see each other at mass on Sunday—and some are episodic, single stranded, and anonymous, like the faintly familiar face you see several times a month in the supermarket checkout line. Some types of social capital, like a Parent-Teacher Association, are formally organized, with incorporation papers, regular meetings, a written constitution, and connection to a national federation, whereas others, like a pickup basketball game, are more informal. Some forms of social capital, like a volunteer ambulance squad, have explicit public-regarding purposes; some, like a bridge club, exist for the private enjoyment of the members; and some, like the Rotary club mentioned earlier, serve both public and private ends.

Of all the dimensions along which forms of social capital vary, perhaps the most important is the distinction between *bridging* (or inclusive) and *bonding* (or exclusive).[9] Some forms of social capital are, by choice or necessity, inward looking and tend to reinforce exclusive identities and homogeneous groups. Examples of bonding social capital include ethnic fraternal organizations, church-based women's reading groups, and fashionable country clubs. Other networks are outward looking and encompass people across diverse social cleavages. Examples of bridging social capital include the civil rights movement, many youth service groups, and ecumenical religious organizations.

Bonding social capital is good for undergirding specific reciprocity and mobilizing solidarity. Dense networks in ethnic enclaves, for example, provide crucial social and psychological support for less fortunate members of the community, while furnishing start-up financing, markets, and reliable labor for local entrepreneurs. Bridging networks, by contrast, are better for linkage to external assets and for information diffusion. Economic sociologist Mark Granovetter has pointed out that when seeking jobs—or political allies—the "weak" ties that link me to distant acquaintances who move in different circles from mine are actually more valuable than the "strong" ties that link me to relatives and intimate friends whose sociological niche is very like my own. Bonding social capital is, as Xavier de Souza Briggs puts it, good for "getting by," but bridging social capital is crucial for "getting ahead."[10]

Moreover, bridging social capital can generate broader identities and reciprocity, whereas bonding social capital bolsters our narrower selves. In 1829 at the founding of a community lyceum in the bustling whaling port of New Bedford, Massachusetts, Thomas Greene eloquently expressed this crucial insight:

> We come from all the divisions, ranks and classes of society . . . to teach and to be taught in our turn. While we mingle together in these pursuits, we shall learn to know each other more intimately; we shall remove many of the prejudices which ignorance or partial acquaintance with each other had fostered. . . . In the parties and sects into which we are divided, we sometimes learn to love our brother at the expense of him whom we do not in so many respects regard as a brother. . . . We may return to our homes and firesides [from the lyceum] with kindlier feelings toward one another, because we have learned to know one another better.[11]

Bonding social capital constitutes a kind of sociological superglue, whereas bridging social capital provides a sociological WD-40. Bonding social capital, by creating strong in-group loyalty, may also create strong out-group antagonism; as Thomas Greene and his neighbors in New Bedford knew, and for that reason we might expect negative external effects to be more common with this form of social capital. Nevertheless, under many circumstances both bridging and bonding social capital can have powerfully positive social effects.

Many groups simultaneously bond along some social dimensions and bridge across others. The black church, for example, brings together people of the same race and religion across class lines. The Knights of Columbus was created to bridge cleavages among different ethnic communities while bonding along religious and gender lines. Internet chat groups may bridge across geography, gender, age, and religion, while being tightly homogeneous in education and ideology. In short, bonding and bridging are not "either-or" categories into which social networks can be neatly divided, but "more or less" dimensions along which we can compare different forms of social capital.

It would obviously be valuable to have distinct measures of the evolution of these various forms of social capital over time. However, like researchers on global warming, we must make do with the imperfect evidence that we can find, not merely lament its deficiencies. Exhaustive descriptions of social networks in America—even at a single point in time—do not exist. I have found no reliable, comprehensive, nationwide measures of social capital that neatly distinguish "bridgingness" and "bondingness." In our empirical account of recent social trends in this book, therefore, this distinction will be less prominent than I would prefer. On the other hand, we must keep this conceptual differentiation at the back of our minds as we proceed, recognizing that bridging and bonding social capital are not interchangeable.

"Social Capital" is to some extent merely new language for a very old debate in American intellectual circles. Community has warred incessantly with individualism for preeminence in our political hagiology. Liberation from ossified community bonds is a recurrent and honored theme in our culture, from the Pilgrims' storied escape from religious convention in the seventeenth century to the lyric nineteenth-century paeans to individualism by Emerson ("Self-Reliance"), Thoreau ("Civil Disobedience"), and Whitman ("Song of Myself") to Sherwood Anderson's twentieth-century celebration of the struggle against conformism by ordinary citizens in *Winesburg, Ohio* to the latest Clint Eastwood film. Even Alexis de Tocqueville, patron saint of American communitarians, acknowledged the uniquely democratic claim of individualism, "a calm and considered feeling which disposes each citizen to isolate himself from the mass of his fellows and withdraw into the circle of family and friends; with this little society formed to his taste, he gladly leaves the greater society to look after itself."[12]

Our national myths often exaggerate the role of individual heroes and understate the importance of collective effort. Historian David Hackett Fischer's gripping account of opening night in the American Revolution, for example, reminds us that Paul Revere's alarum was successful only because of networks of civic engagement in the Middlesex villages. Towns without well-organized local militia, no matter how patriotic their inhabitants, were AWOL from Lexington and Concord.[13] Nevertheless, the myth of rugged individualism continues to strike a powerful inner chord in the American psyche.

Debates about the waxing and waning of "community" have been endemic for at least two centuries. "Declensionist narrative"—postmodernist jargon for tales of decline and fall—have a long pedigree in our letters. We seem perennially tempted to contrast our tawdry todays with past golden ages. We apparently share this nostalgic predilection with the rest of humanity. As sociologist Barry Wellman observes,

> It is likely that pundits have worried about the impact of social change on communities ever since human beings ventured beyond their caves. . . . In the [past] two centuries many leading social commentators have been gainfully employed suggesting various ways in which large-scale social changes associated with the Industrial Revolution may have affected the structure and operation of communities. . . . This ambivalence about the consequences of large-scale changes continued well into the twentieth century. Analysts have kept asking if things have, in fact, fallen apart.[14]

At the conclusion of the twentieth century, ordinary Americans shared this sense of civic malaise. We were reasonably content about our economic prospects, hardly a surprise after an expansion of unprecedented length, but we were not equally convinced that we were on the right track morally or culturally. Of baby boomers interviewed in 1987, 53 percent thought their parents' generation was better in terms of "being a concerned citizen, involved in helping others in the community," as compared with only 21 percent who thought their own generation was better. Fully 77 percent said the nation was worse off because of "less involvement in community activities." In 1992 three-quarters of the U.S. workforce said that "the breakdown of community" and "selfishness" were "serious" or "extremely serious" problems in America. In 1996 only 8 percent of all Americans said that "the honesty and integrity of the average American" were improving, as compared with 50 percent of us who thought we were becoming less trustworthy. Those of us who said that people had become less civil over the preceding ten years outnumbered those who thought people had become more civil, 80 percent to 12 percent. In several surveys in 1999 two-thirds of Americans said that America's civic life had weakened in recent years, that social and moral values were higher when they were growing up, and that our society was focused more on the individual than the community. More than 80 percent said there should be more emphasis on community, even if that put more demands on individuals.[15] Americans' concern about weakening community bonds may be misplaced or exaggerated, but a decent respect for the opinion of our fellow citizens suggests that we should explore the issue more thoroughly.

It is emphatically not my view that community bonds in America have weakened steadily throughout our history—or even throughout the last hundred years. On the contrary, American history carefully examined is a story of ups and downs in civic engagement, *not just downs*—a story of collapse *and* of renewal. As I have already hinted in the opening pages of this book, within living memory the bonds of community in America were becoming stronger, not weaker, and as I shall argue in the concluding pages, it is within our power to reverse the decline of the last several decades.

Nevertheless, my argument is, at least in appearance, in the declensionist tradition, so it is important to avoid simple nostalgia. Precisely because the theme of this book might lend itself to gauzy self-deception, our methods must be transparent. Is life in communities as we enter the twenty-first century really so different after all from the reality of American communities in the 1950s and 1960s? One way of curbing nostalgia is to count things. Are club meetings really less crowded today than yesterday, or does it just seem so? Do we really know our neighbors less well than our parents did, or is our childhood recollection of neighborhood barbecues suffused with a golden glow of wishful reminiscence? Are friendly poker games less common now, or is it merely that we ourselves have outgrown poker? League bowling may be passé, but how about softball and soccer? Are strangers less trustworthy now? Are boomers and X'ers really less engaged in community life? After all, it was the preceding generation that was once scorned as "silent." Perhaps the younger generation today is no less engaged than their predecessors, but engaged in new ways. In the chapters that follow we explore these questions with the best available evidence.

The challenge of studying the evolving social climate is analogous in some respects to the challenge facing meteorologists who measure global warming: We know what kind of evidence we would ideally want from the past, but time's arrow means that we can't go back to conduct those well-designed studies. Thus if we are to explore how our society is like or unlike our parents', we must make imperfect inferences from all the evidence that we can find.

The most powerful strategy for paleometeorologists seeking to assess global climate change is to triangulate among diverse sources of evidence. If pollen counts in polar ice, and the width of southwestern tree rings, and temperature records of the British Admiralty all point in a similar direction, the inference of global warming is stronger than if the cord of evidence has only a single strand. For much the same reason, prudent journalists follow a "two source" rule: Never report anything unless at least two independent sources confirm it.

In this book I follow that same maxim. Nearly every major generalization here rests on more than one body of independent evidence, and where I have discovered divergent results from credible sources, I note that disparity as well. I have a case to make, but like any officer of the court, I have a professional obligation to present all relevant evidence I have found, exculpatory as well as incriminating. To avoid cluttering the text with masses of redundant evidence, I have typically put confirmatory evidence from multiple studies in the notes, so skeptical "show me" readers should examine those notes as well as the text.[16]

I have sought as diverse a range of evidence as possible on continuities and change in American social life. If the transformation that I discern is as broad and deep as I believe it to be, it ought to show up in many different places, so I have cast a broad net. Of course, social change, like climatic change, is inevitably uneven. Life is not lived in a single dimension. We should not expect to find everything changing in the same direction and at the same speed, but those very anomalies may contain important clues to what is happening.

American society, like the continent on which we live, is massive and polymorphous, and our civic engagement historically has come in many sizes and shapes. A few of us still share plowing chores with neighbors, while many more pitch in to wire classrooms to the Internet. Some of us run for Congress, and others join self-help groups. Some of us hang out at the local bar association and others at the local bar. Some of us attend mass once a day, while others struggle to remember to send holiday greetings once a year. The forms of our social capital—the ways in which we connect with friends and neighbors and strangers—are varied.

So our review of trends in social capital and civic engagement ranges widely across various sectors of this complex society. In the chapters that follow we begin by charting Americans' participation in the most public forum—politics and public affairs. We next turn to the institutions of our communities—clubs and community associations, religious bodies, and work-related organizations, such as unions and professional societies. Then we explore the almost infinite variety of informal ties that link Americans—card parties and bowling leagues, bar cliques and ball games, picnics and parties. Next we examine the changing patterns of trust and altruism in America—philanthropy, volunteering, honesty, reciprocity. Finally we turn to three apparent counterexamples to the decline of connectedness—small groups, social movements, and the Internet.

In each domain we shall encounter currents and crosscurrents and eddies, but in each we shall also discover common, powerful tidal movements that have swept across American society in the twentieth century. The dominant theme is simple: For the first two-thirds of the twentieth century a powerful tide bore Americans into ever deeper engagement in the life of their communities, but a few decades ago—silently, without warning—that tide reversed and we were overtaken by a treacherous rip current. Without at first noticing, we have been pulled apart from one another and from our communities over the last third of the century.

ENDNOTES

1. Lyda Judson Hanifan, "The Rural School Community Center," *Annals of the American Academy of Political and Social Science* 67 (1916): 130–138, quotation at 130. Ever the practical reformer, Hanifan was self-conscious about using the term *capital* to encourage hard-nosed businessmen and economists to recognize the productive importance of social assets. Having introduced the idea of social capital, he observes, "That there is a great lack of such social capital in some rural districts need not be retold in this chapter.

The important question at this time is: How can these conditions be improved? The story which follows is an account of the way a West Virginia rural community in a single year actually developed social capital and then used this capital in the improvement of its recreational, intellectual, moral, and economic conditions." His essay, which included a list of practical exercises for community-based activists, was originally prepared in 1913 for West Virginia schoolteachers as "a handbook for community meetings at rural schoolhouses," and it was subsequently incorporated in L. J. Hanifan, *The Community Center* (Boston: Silver, Burdett, 1920). I am grateful to Brad Clarke for first spotting this usage of the term *social capital.*

2. John R. Seeley, Alexander R. Sim, and Elizabeth W. Loosley, *Crestwood Heights: A Study of the Culture of Suburban Life* (New York: Basic Books, 1956); Jane Jacobs, *The Death and Life of Great American Cities* (New York: Random House, 1961); Glenn Loury, "A Dynamic Theory of Racial Income Differences; in *Women, Minorities, and Employment Discrimination,* ed. P. A. Wallace and A. LeMund (Lexington, Mass.: Lexington Books, 1977), 153–188; Pierre Bourdieu, "Forms of Capital," in *Handbook of Theory and Research for the Sociology of Education,* ed. John G. Richardson (New York: Greenwood Press, 1983), 241–258; Ekkehart Schlicht, "Cognitive Dissonance in Economics," in *Normengeleitetes Verhalten in den Sozialwissenschaften* (Berlin: Duncker and Humblot, 1984), 61–81; James S. Coleman, "Social Capital in the Creation of Human Capital," *American Journal of Sociology* 94 (1988): S95–S120; and James S. Coleman, *Foundations of Social Theory* (Cambridge, Mass.: Harvard University Press, 1990). See also George C. Homans, *Social Behavior: Its Elementary Forms* (New York: Harcourt, Brace & World, 1961), 378–98. Except for a brief acknowledgment by Coleman of Loury's work, I can find no evidence that any of these theorists were aware of any of the preceding usages. For a comprehensive overview of the conceptual history of "social capital," see Michael Woolcock, "Social Capital and Economic Development: Toward a Theoretical Synthesis and Policy Framework," *Theory and Society* 27 (1998): 151–208.
3. Ronald S. Burt, *Structural Holes: The Social Structure of Competition* (Cambridge, Mass.: Harvard University Press, 1992); Ronald S. Burt, "The Contingent Value of Social Capital," *Administrative Science Quarterly* 42 (1997): 339–365; and Ronald S. Burt, "The Gender of Social Capital," *Rationality & Society* 10 (1998): 5–46; Claude S. Fischer, "Network Analysis and Urban Studies," in *Networks and Places: Social Relations in the Urban Setting,* ed. Claude S. Fischer (New York: Free Press, 1977), 19; James D. Montgomery, "Social Networks and Labor-Market Outcomes: Toward an Economic Analysis," *American Economic Review* 81 (1991): 1408–1418, esp. table 1.

4. In earlier work I emphasized this public dimension of social capital almost to the exclusion of the private returns to social capital. See Robert D. Putnam, "The Prosperous Community: Social Capital and Public Affairs," *The American Prospect* 13 (1993): 35–42, on which the present text draws. For a literature review that highlights the private returns almost to the exclusion of the collective dimension, see Alejandro Portes, "Social Capital: Its Origins and Applications in Modern Sociology," *Annual Review of Sociology* 22 (1998): 1–24.
5. Robert Frank in private conversation.
6. Xavier de Souza Briggs, "Social Capital and the Cities: Advice to Change Agents," *National Civic Review* 86 (summer 1997): 111–117.
7. *U.S. News & World Report* (August 4, 1997): 18. Fareed Zakaria, "Bigger Than the Family, Smaller Than the State," *New York Times Book Review,* August 13, 1995: 1, pointed out that McVeigh and his co-conspirators spent evenings together in a bowling alley and concluded that "we would all have been better off if Mr. McVeigh had gone bowling alone." Sometimes, as in certain cults or clans, even the *internal* effects of social capital can be negative, but these are less common than negative *external* effects.
8. In *Making Democracy Work: Civic Traditions in Modern Italy* (Princeton, N.J.: Princeton University Press, 1993), I ignored the possibility that social capital might have antisocial effects, but I recognized this possibility explicitly in "The Prosperous Community," published that same year.
9. So far as I can tell, credit for coining these labels belongs to Ross Gittell and Avis Vidal, *Community Organizing Building Social Capital as a Development Strategy* (Thousand Oaks, Calif.: Sage, 1998), 8.
10. Mark S. Granovetter, "The Strength of Weak Ties," *American Journal of Sociology* 78 (1973): 1360–1380; Xavier de Souza Briggs, "Doing Democracy Up Close: Culture, Power, and Communication in Community Building," *Journal of Planning Education and Research* 18 (1998): 1–13.
11. As quoted in Richard D. Brown, "The Emergence of Voluntary Associations in Massachusetts," *Journal of Voluntary Action Research* 2 (April 1973): 64–73, at 69. See also Ashutosh Varshney, *Ethnic Conflict and Civic Life: Hindus and Muslims in India* (New Haven, Conn.: Yale University Press, 2000).
12. Alexis de Tocqueville, *Democracy in America,* ed. J. P. Mayer, trans. George Lawrence (Garden City, N.Y.: Doubleday, 1969), 506. See also Wilson Carey McWilliams, *The Idea of Fraternity in America,* (Berkeley: University of California Press, 1973), and Thomas Bender, *Community and Social Change in America* (Baltimore, Md.: Johns Hopkins University Press, 1978).
13. David Hackett Fischer, *Paul Revere's Ride* (New York: Oxford University Press, 1994).

14. Barry Wellman, "The Community Question Re-Evaluated," in *Power, Community, and the City,* Michael Peter Smith, ed. (New Brunswick, N.J.: Transaction 1988), 81–107, quotation at 82–83. Pamela Paxton, "Is Social Capital Declining in the United States? A Multiple Indicator Assessment," *American Journal of Sociology* 105 (1999): 88–127.
15. *The Public Perspective* 8 (December/January 1997): 64; Robert Wuthnow, "Changing Character of Social Capital in the United States," in *The Dynamics of Social Capital in Comparative Perspective,* Robert D. Putnam, ed. (2000, forthcoming); *The Public Perspective* 10 (April/May 1999): 15; *Wall Street Journal,* June 24, 1999, A12; Mark J. Penn, "The Community Consensus," *Blueprint: Ideas for a New Century* (spring 1999). Respondents with no opinion are excluded.
16. For example, figures 31–33 present data from six independent sources on trends in philanthropy, but I have also discovered four additional sources that confirm the basic pattern, and those sources are mentioned briefly in the notes. For additional discussion of methodology, see the appendixes.

NOTES

NOTES

BLACK? WHITE? ASIAN? MORE YOUNG AMERICANS CHOOSE ALL OF THE ABOVE

Susan Saulny

A native of New Orleans, Susan Saulny is a correspondent for the ABC News *Washington Bureau. Previously, she worked for ten years at* The New York Times. *She was part of the team that won a Pulitzer Prize for 'A Nation Challenged' following the terror attacks of 9/11/2001. She also reported on the devastating aftermath of Hurricane Katrina.*

COLLEGE PARK, Md.—In another time or place, the game of "What Are You?" that was played one night last fall at the University of Maryland might have been mean, or menacing: Laura Wood's peers were picking apart her every feature in an effort to guess her race.

"How many mixtures do you have?" one young man asked above the chatter of about 50 students. With her tan skin and curly brown hair, Ms. Wood's ancestry could have spanned the globe.

"I'm mixed with two things," she said politely.

"Are you mulatto?" asked Paul Skym, another student, using a word once tinged with shame that is enjoying a comeback in some young circles. When Ms. Wood confirmed that she is indeed black and white, Mr. Skym, who is Asian and white, boasted, "Now that's what I'm talking about!" in affirmation of their mutual mixed lineage.

Then the group of friends—formally, the Multiracial and Biracial Student Association—erupted into laughter and cheers, a routine show of their mixed-race pride.

The crop of students moving through college right now includes the largest group of mixed-race people ever to come of age in the United States, and they are only the vanguard: the country is in the midst of a demographic shift driven by immigration and intermarriage.

One in seven new marriages is between spouses of different races or ethnicities, according to data from 2008 and 2009 that was analyzed by the Pew Research Center. Multiracial and multiethnic Americans (usually grouped together as "mixed race") are one of the country's fastest-growing demographic groups. And experts expect the racial results of the 2010 census, which will start to be released next month, to show the trend continuing or accelerating.

Many young adults of mixed backgrounds are rejecting the color lines that have defined Americans for generations in favor of a much more fluid sense of identity. Ask Michelle López-Mullins, a 20-year-old junior and the president of the Multiracial and Biracial Student Association, how she marks her race on forms like the census, and she says, "It depends on the day, and it depends on the options."

Reprinted by permission from the *New York Times*, January 30, 2011.

They are also using the strength in their growing numbers to affirm roots that were once portrayed as tragic or pitiable.

"I think it's really important to acknowledge who you are and everything that makes you that," said Ms. Wood, the 19-year-old vice president of the group. "If someone tries to call me black I say, 'yes—and white.' People have the right not to acknowledge everything, but don't do it because society tells you that you can't."

No one knows quite how the growth of the multiracial population will change the country. Optimists say the blending of the races is a step toward transcending race, to a place where America is free of bigotry, prejudice and programs like affirmative action.

Pessimists say that a more powerful multiracial movement will lead to more stratification and come at the expense of the number and influence of other minority groups, particularly African-Americans.

And some sociologists say that grouping all multiracial people together glosses over differences in circumstances between someone who is, say, black and Latino, and someone who is Asian and white. (Among interracial couples, white-Asian pairings tend to be better educated and have higher incomes, according to Reynolds Farley, a professor emeritus at the University of Michigan.)

Along those lines, it is telling that the rates of intermarriage are lowest between blacks and whites, indicative of the enduring economic and social distance between them.

Prof. Rainier Spencer, director of the Afro-American Studies Program at the University of Nevada, Las Vegas, and the author of "Reproducing Race: The Paradox of Generation Mix," says he believes that there is too much "emotional investment" in the notion of multiracialism as a panacea for the nation's age-old divisions. "The mixed-race identity is not a transcendence of race, it's a new tribe," he said. "A new Balkanization of race."

But for many of the University of Maryland students, that is not the point. They are asserting their freedom to identify as they choose.

"All society is trying to tear you apart and make you pick a side," Ms. Wood said. "I want us to have a say."

The Way We Were

Americans mostly think of themselves in singular racial terms. Witness President Obama's answer to the race question on the 2010 census: Although his mother was white and his father was black, Mr. Obama checked only one box, black, even though he could have checked both races.

Some proportion of the country's population has been mixed-race since the first white settlers had children with Native Americans. What has changed is how mixed-race Americans are defined and counted.

Long ago, the nation saw itself in more hues than black and white: the 1890 census included categories for racial mixtures such as quadroon (one-fourth black) and octoroon (one-eighth black). With the exception of one survey from 1850 to 1920, the census included a mulatto category, which was for people who had any perceptible trace of African blood.

But by the 1930 census, terms for mixed-race people had all disappeared, replaced by the so-called one-drop rule, an antebellum convention that held that anyone with a trace of African ancestry was only black. (Similarly, people who were "white and Indian" were generally to be counted as Indian.)

It was the census enumerator who decided.

By the 1970s, Americans were expected to designate themselves as members of one officially recognized racial group: black, white, American Indian, Japanese, Chinese, Filipino, Hawaiian, Korean or "other," an option used frequently by people of Hispanic origin. (The census recognizes Hispanic as an ethnicity, not a race.)

Starting with the 2000 census, Americans were allowed to mark one or more races.

The multiracial option came after years of complaints and lobbying, mostly by the white mothers of biracial children who objected to their children being allowed to check only one race. In 2000, seven million people—about 2.4 percent of the population—reported being more than one race.

According to estimates from the Census Bureau, the mixed-race population has grown by roughly 35 percent since 2000.

And many researchers think the census and other surveys undercount the mixed population.

The 2010 mixed-race statistics will be released, state by state, over the first half of the year.

"There could be some big surprises," said Jeffrey S. Passel, a senior demographer at the Pew Hispanic Center, meaning that the number of mixed-race Americans could be high. "There's not only less stigma to being in these groups, there's even positive cachet."

Moving Forward

The faces of mixed-race America are not just on college campuses. They are in politics, business and sports. And the ethnically ambiguous are especially ubiquitous in movies, television shows and advertising. There are news, social networking and dating Web sites focusing on the mixed-race audience, and even consumer products like shampoo. There are mixed-race film festivals and conferences. And student groups like the one at Maryland, offering peer support and activism, are more common.

Such a club would not have existed a generation ago—when the question at the center of the "What Are You?" game would have been a provocation rather than an icebreaker.

"It's kind of a taking-back in a way, taking the reins," Ms. López-Mullins said. "We don't always have to let it get us down," she added, referring to the question multiracial people have heard for generations.

"The No. 1 reason why we exist is to give people who feel like they don't want to choose a side, that don't want to label themselves based on other people's interpretations of who they are, to give them a place, that safe space," she said. Ms. López-Mullins is Chinese and Peruvian on one side, and white and American Indian on the other.

That safe space did not exist amid the neo-Classical style buildings of the campus when Warren Kelley enrolled in 1974. Though his mother is Japanese and his father is African-American, he had basically one choice when it came to his racial identity. "I was black and proud to be black," Dr. Kelley said. "There was no notion that I might be multiracial. Or that the public discourse on college campuses recognized the multiracial community."

Almost 40 years later, Dr. Kelley is the assistant vice president for student affairs at the university and faculty adviser to the multiracial club, and he is often in awe of the change on this campus.

When the multiracial group was founded in 2002, Dr. Kelley said, "There was an instant audience."

They did not just want to hold parties. The group sponsored an annual weeklong program of discussions intended to raise awareness of multiracial identities—called Mixed Madness—and conceived a new class on the experience of mixed-race Asian-Americans that was made part of the curriculum last year.

"Even if someone had formed a mixed-race group in the '70s, would I have joined?" Dr. Kelley said. "I don't know. My multiracial identity wasn't prominent at the time. I don't think I even conceptualized the idea."

By the 2000 census, Dr. Kelley's notion of his racial identity had evolved to include his mother's Asian heritage; he modified his race officially on the form. After a lifetime of checking black, he checked Asian and black.

(Dr. Kelley's mother was born in Kyoto. She met her future husband, a black soldier from Alabama, while he was serving in the Pacific during World War II.)

Checking both races was not an easy choice, Dr. Kelley said, "as a black man, with all that means in terms of pride in that heritage as well as reasons to give back and be part of progress forward."

"As I moved into adulthood and got a professional job, I started to respect my parents more and see the amount of my mom's culture that's reflected in me," he said. "Society itself also moved."

Finding Camaraderie

In fall 2009, a question tugged at Sabrina Garcia, then a freshman at Maryland, a public university with 26,500 undergraduates: "Where will I fit in?" recalled Ms. Garcia, who is Palestinian and Salvadoran.

"I considered the Latina student union, but I'm only half," she said. "I didn't want to feel like I was hiding any part of me. I went to an M.B.S.A. meeting and it was really great. I really feel like part of a group that understands."

The group holds weekly meetings, in addition to hosting movie nights, dinners, parties and, occasionally, posts broadcasts on YouTube.

Not all of its 100 or so members consider themselves mixed race, and the club welcomes everyone.

At a meeting in the fall, David Banda, who is Hispanic, and Julicia Coleman, who is black, came just to unwind among supportive listeners. They discussed the frustrations of being an interracial couple, even today, especially back in their hometown, Upper Marlboro, Md.

"When we go back home, let's say for a weekend or to the mall, they see us walking and I get this look, you know, sort of giving me the idea: 'Why are you with her? You're not black, so she should be with a black person.' Or comments," Mr. Banda, 20, said at a meeting of the group. "Even some of my friends tell me, 'Why don't you date a Hispanic girl?' "

Mr. Banda and Ms. Coleman are thinking about having children someday. "One of the main reasons I joined is to see the struggles mixed people go through," he said, "so we can be prepared when that time comes."

And despite the growth of the mixed-race population, there are struggles.

Ian Winchester, a junior who is part Ghanaian, part Scottish-Norwegian, said he felt lucky and torn being biracial. His Scottish grandfather was keen on dressing him in kilts as a boy. The other side of the family would put him in a dashiki. "I do feel empowered being biracial," he said. "The ability to question your identity—identity in general—is really a gift."

But, he continued, "I don't even like to identify myself as a race anymore. My family has been pulling me in two directions about what I am. I just want to be a person."

Similarly, Ms. López-Mullins sees herself largely in nonracial terms.

"I hadn't even learned the word 'Hispanic' until I came home from school one day and asked my dad what I should refer to him as, to express what I am," she said. "Growing up with my parents, I never thought we were different from any other family."

But it was not long before Ms. López-Mullins came to detest what was the most common question put to her in grade school, even from friends. "What are you?" they asked, and "Where are you from?" They were fascinated by her father, a Latino with Asian roots, and her mother with the long blond hair, who was mostly European in ancestry, although mixed with some Cherokee and Shawnee.

"I was always having to explain where my parents are from because just saying 'I'm from Takoma Park, Maryland,' was not enough," she said. "Saying 'I'm an American' wasn't enough."

"Now when people ask what I am, I say, 'How much time do you have?' " she said. "Race will not automatically tell you my story."

What box does she check on forms like the census? "Hispanic, white, Asian American, Native American," she said. "I'm pretty much checking everything."

At one meeting of the Multiracial and Biracial Student Association, Ms. Wood shared a story about surprises and coming to terms with them. "Until I was 8 years old, I thought I was white," she told the group. "My mother and aunt sat me down and said the guy I'd been calling Dad was not my father. I started crying. And she said, 'Your real father is black.'"

Ms. Wood's mother, Catherine Bandele, who is white, and her biological father split up before she was born. Facing economic troubles and resistance from her family about raising a mixed-race child, Ms. Bandele gave her daughter up for adoption to a couple who had requested a biracial baby. But after two weeks, she changed her mind. "I had to fight to get her back, but I got her," Ms. Bandele said. "And we're so proud of Laura."

Eventually Ms. Wood's closest relatives softened, embracing her.

But more distant relatives never came around. "They can't see past the color of my skin and accept me even though I share DNA with them," she said. "It hurts a lot because I don't even know my father's side of the family."

Ms. Wood has searched the Internet for her father, to no avail.

"Being in M.B.S.A., it really helps with that," she said. "Finding a group of people who can accept you for who you are and being able to accept yourself, to just be able to look in the mirror and say, 'I'm O.K. just the way I am!'—honestly, I feel that it's a blessing."

"It took a long time," she said.

Now Ms. Wood is one of the group's foremost advocates.

Over dinner with Ms. López-Mullins one night, she wondered: "What if Obama had checked white? There would have been an uproar because he's the first 'black president,' even though he's mixed. I would like to have a conversation with him about why he did that."

Absent that opportunity, Ms. Wood took her concerns about what Mr. Obama checked to a meeting of the campus chapter of the N.A.A.C.P. last year. Vicky Key, a past president of the Multiracial and Biracial Student Association, who is Greek and black, joined her. The question for discussion was whether Mr. Obama is the first black president or the first multiracial president.

Ms. Key, a senior, remembered someone answering the question without much discussion: "One-drop rule, he's black."

"But we were like, 'Wait!'" she said. "That's offensive to us. We sat there and tried to advocate, but they said, 'No, he's black and that's it.' Then someone said, 'Stop taking away our black president.' I didn't understand where they were coming from, and they didn't understand me."

Whether Mr. Obama is considered black or multiracial, there is a wider debate among mixed-race people about what the long-term goals of their advocacy should be, both on campus and off.

"I don't want a color-blind society at all," Ms. Wood said. "I just want both my races to be acknowledged."

Ms. López-Mullins countered, "I want mine not to matter."

NOTES

NOTES

OUT OF MY LIFE AND THOUGHT
Albert Schweitzer

(1875–1965)

Albert Schweitzer was a notable philosopher, physician, musician, clergyman, missionary, and author on theology. Acknowledged as one of the most outstanding Christians of his time, he grounded his philosophy on what he termed 'reverence for life' and on a deep commitment to serve humanity through thought and action. In 1952 he was awarded the Nobel Peace Prize. He used his prize money to expand his hospital at Lambaréné, French Equatorial Africa (today Gabon), and to establish a leper colony.

I Resolve to Become a Jungle Doctor

On October 13th, 1905, a Friday, I dropped into a letter box in the Avenue de la Grande Armée in Paris, letters to my parents and to some of my most intimate acquaintances, telling them that at the beginning of the winter term I should enter myself as a medical student, in order to go later on to Equatorial Africa as a doctor. In one of them I sent in the resignation of my post as principal of the Theological College of St. Thomas', because of the claim on my time that my intended course of study would make.

The plan which I meant now to put into execution had been in my mind for a long time, having been conceived so long ago as my student days. It struck me as incomprehensible that I should be allowed to lead such a happy life, while I saw so many people around me wrestling with care and suffering. Even at school I had felt stirred whenever I got a glimpse of the miserable home surroundings of some of my schoolfellows and compared them with the absolutely ideal conditions in which we children of the parsonage at Günsbach lived. While at the university and enjoying the happiness of being able to study and even to produce some results in science and art, I could not help thinking continually of others who were denied that happiness by their material circumstances or their health. Then one brilliant summer morning at Günsbach, during the Whitsuntide holidays—it was in 1896—there came to me, as I awoke, the thought that I must not accept this happiness as a matter of course, but must give something in return for it. Proceeding to think the matter out at once with calm deliberation, while the birds were singing outside, I settled with myself before I got up, that I would consider myself justified in living till I was thirty for science and art, in order to devote myself from that time forward to the direct service of humanity. Many a time already had I tried to settle what meaning lay hidden for me in the saying of Jesus! "Whosoever would save his life shall lose it, and whosoever shall lose his life for My sake and the Gospels shall save it." Now the answer was found. In addition to the outward, I now had inward happiness.

Reprinted from *Out of My Life and Thought* (1949), Henry Holt & Company.

What would be the character of the activities thus planned for the future was not yet clear to me. I left it to circumstances to guide me. One thing only was certain, that it must be directly human service, however inconspicuous the sphere of it.

I naturally thought first of some activity in Europe. I formed a plan for taking charge of abandoned or neglected children and educating them, then making them pledge themselves to help later on in the same way children in similar positions. When in 1903, as warden of the theological hostel, I moved into my roomy and sunny official quarters on the second floor of the College of St. Thomas, I was in a position to begin the experiment. I offered my help now here, now there, but always unsuccessfully. The constitutions of the organizations which looked after destitute and abandoned children made no provision for the acceptance of such voluntary co-operation. For example, when the Strasbourg orphanage was burnt down, I offered to take in a few boys, for the time being, but the superintendent did not even allow me to finish what I had to say. Similar attempts which I made elsewhere were also failures.

For a time I thought I would some day devote myself to tramps and discharged prisoners. In some measure as a preparation for this I joined the Rev. Augustus Ernst at St. Thomas' in an undertaking which he had begun. He was at home from one to two P.M. and ready to speak to anyone who came to him asking for help or for a night's lodging. He did not, however, give the applicant a trifle in money, or let him wait till he could get information about his circumstances. He would offer to look him up in his lodging house that very afternoon and test the statements he had volunteered about his condition. Then, and then only, would he give him help, but as much, and for as long a time, as was necessary. What a number of bicycle rides we made with this object in the town and the suburbs, and very often with the result that the applicant was not known at the address he had given. In a great many cases, however, it provided an opportunity for giving, with knowledge of the circumstances, very seasonable help. I had some friends, too, who kindly placed a portion of their wealth at my disposal.

Already, as a student, I had been active in social service as a member of the student association known as the Diaconate of St. Thomas, which held its meetings in St. Thomas' College. Each of us had a certain number of poor families assigned to him, which he was to visit every week, taking to them the help allotted to them and making a report on their condition. The money we thus distributed we collected from members of the old Strasbourg families who supported this undertaking, begun by former generations and now carried on by us. Twice a year, if I remember right, each of us had to make his definite number of such begging appeals. To me, being shy and rather awkward in society, these visits were a torture. I believe that in these preparatory studies for the begging I have had to do in later years I sometimes showed myself extremely unskillful. However, I learned through them that begging with tact and restraint is better appreciated than any sort of stand-and-deliver approach, and also that the correct method of begging includes the good-tempered acceptance of a refusal.

In our youthful inexperience we no doubt often failed, in spite of the best intentions, to use all the money entrusted to us in the wisest way, but the intentions of the givers were nevertheless fully carried out in that it pledged young men to take an interest in the poor. For that reason I think with deep gratitude of those who met with so much understanding and liberality our efforts to be wisely helpful, and hope that many students may have the privilege of working, commissioned in this way by the charitable, as recruits in the struggle against poverty.

While I was concerned with tramps and discharged prisoners it had become clear to me that they could only be effectively helped by a number of individuals who would devote themselves to them. At the same time, however, I had realized that in many cases these could only accomplish their best work in collaboration with organizations. But what I wanted was an absolutely personal and independent activity. Although I was resolved to put my services at the disposal of some organization, if it should be really necessary, I nevertheless never gave up the hope of finding a sphere of activity to which I could devote myself as an individual and as wholly free. That this longing of mine found fulfillment I have always regarded as a signal instance of the mercy which has again and again been vouchsafed to me.

One morning in the autumn of 1904 I found on my writing table in the college one of the green-covered magazines in which the Paris Missionary Society reported every month on its activities. A certain Miss Scherdlin used to put them there knowing that I was specially interested in this society on account of the impression made on me by the letters of one of its earliest missionaries, Casalis by name, when my father read them aloud at his missionary services during my childhood. That evening, in the very act of putting it aside that I might go on with my work, I mechanically opened this magazine, which had been laid on my table during my absence. As I did so my eye caught the title of an article: *Les besoins de la Mission du Congo* ("The needs of the Congo Mission").[1]

It was by Alfred Boegner, the president of the Paris Missionary Society, an Alsatian, and contained a complaint that the mission had not enough workers to carry on its work in the Gaboon, the northern province of the Congo Colony. The writer expressed his hope that his appeal would bring some of those "on whom the Master's eyes already rested" to a decision to offer themselves for this urgent work. The conclusion ran: "Men and women who can reply simply to the Master's call, 'Lord, I am coming,' those are the people whom the Church needs." Having finished the article, I quietly began my work. My search was over.

[1] *Journal des Missions Evangéliques,* June, 1904, pp. 389–393.

My thirtieth birthday, a few months later, I spent like the man in the parable who "desiring to build a tower, first counts the cost whether he have wherewith to complete it." The result was that I resolved to realize my plan of direct human service in Equatorial Africa.

With the exception of one trustworthy friend no one knew of my intention. When it became known through the letters I had sent from Paris, I had hard battles to fight with my relations and friends. Almost more than with my contemplated new start itself they reproached me with not having shown them so much confidence as to discuss it with them first. With this side issue they tormented me beyond measure during those difficult weeks. That theological friends should outdo the others in their protests struck me as all the more preposterous, because they had, no doubt, all preached a fine sermon—perhaps a very fine one—showing how St. Paul, as he has recorded in his letter to the Galatians, "conferred not with flesh and blood" beforehand about what he meant to do for Jesus.

My relatives and my friends all joined in expostulating with me on the folly of my enterprise. I was a man, they said, who was burying the talent entrusted to him and wanted to trade with false currency. Work among savages I ought to leave to those who would not thereby be compelled to leave gifts and acquirements in science and art unused. Widor, who loved me as if I were his son, scolded me as being like a general who wanted to go into the firing line—there was no talk about trenches at that time—with a rifle. A lady who was filled with the modern spirit proved to me that I could do much more by lecturing on behalf of medical help for natives than I could by the action I contemplated. That saying from Goethe's *Faust* ("In the beginning was the Deed"), was now out of date, she said. Today propaganda was the mother of happenings.

In the many verbal duels which I had to fight, as a weary opponent, with people who passed for Christians, it moved me strangely to see them so far from perceiving that the effort to serve the love preached by Jesus may sweep a man into a new course of life, although they read in the New Testament that it can do so, and found it there quite in order. I had assumed as a matter of course that familiarity with the sayings of Jesus would produce a much better appreciation of what to popular logic is nonrational, than my own case allowed me to assert. Several times, indeed, it was my experience that my appeal to the act of obedience which Jesus' command of love may under special circumstances call for, brought upon me an accusation of conceit, although I had, in fact, been obliged to do violence to my feelings to employ this argument at all. In general, how much I suffered through so many people assuming a right to tear open all the doors and shutters of my inner self!

As a rule, too, it was of no use allowing them, in spite of my repugnance, to have a glimpse of the thoughts which had given birth to my resolution. They thought there must be something behind it all, and guessed at disappointment at the slow growth of my reputation. For this there was no ground at all, seeing that I had received, even as a young man, such recognition as others usually get only after a whole life of toil and struggle. Unfortunate love experiences were also alleged as the reason for my decision.

I felt as a real kindness the action of persons who made no attempt to dig their fists into my heart, but regarded me as a precocious young man, not quite right in his head, and treated me correspondingly with affectionate mockery.

I felt it to be, in itself, quite natural that relations and friends should put before me anything that told against the reasonableness of my plan. As one who demands that idealists shall be sober in their views, I was conscious that every start upon an untrodden path is a venture which only in unusual circumstances looks sensible and likely to be successful. In my own case I held the venture to be justified, because I had considered it for a long time and from every point of view, and credited myself with the possession of health, sound nerves, energy, practical common sense, toughness, prudence, very few wants, and everything else that might be found necessary by anyone wandering along the path of the idea. I believed myself, further, to wear the protective armor of a temperament quite capable of enduring an eventual failure of my plan.

As a man of individual action, I have since that time been approached for my opinion and advice by many people who wanted to make a similar venture, but only in comparatively few cases have I taken on me the responsibility of giving them immediate encouragement. I often had to recognize that the need "to do something special" was born of a restless spirit. Such persons wanted to dedicate themselves to larger tasks because those that lay nearest did not satisfy them. Often, too, it was evident that they had been brought to their decisions by quite secondary considerations. Only a person who can find a value in every sort of activity and devote himself to each one with full consciousness of duty, has the inward right to take as his object some extraordinary activity instead of that which falls naturally to his lot. Only a person who feels his preference to be a matter of course, not something out of the ordinary, and who has no thought of heroism, but just recognizes a duty undertaken with sober enthusiasm, is capable of becoming a spiritual adventurer such as the world needs. There are no heroes of action: only heroes of renunciation and suffering. Of such there are plenty. But few of them are known, and even these not to the crowd, but to the few.

Carlyle's *Heroes and Hero Worship* is not a profound book.

Of those who feel any sort of impulse, and would prove actually fitted, to devote their lives to independent personal activity, the majority are compelled by circumstances to renounce such a course. As a rule this is because they have to provide for one or more dependents, or because they have to stick to their calling in order to earn their own living. Only one who thanks to his own ability or the devotion of friends is in worldly matters a free man, can venture nowadays to take the path of independent activity. This was not so much the case in earlier times because anyone who gave up remunerative work could still hope to get through life somehow or other, while anyone who thought of doing the same in the difficult economic conditions of today would run the risk of coming to grief not only materially but spiritually as well.

I am compelled, therefore, not only by what I have observed, but by experience also, to admit that worthy and capable persons have had to renounce a course of independent action which would have been of great value to the world, because circumstances rendered such a course impossible.

Those who are so favored as to be able to embark on a course of free personal activity must accept this good fortune in a spirit of humility. They must often think of those who, though willing and capable, were never in a position to do the same. And as a rule they must temper their own strong determination with humility. They are almost always destined to have to seek and wait till they find a road open for the activity they long for. Happy are those to whom the years of work are allotted in richer measure than those of seeking and waiting! Happy those who in the end are able to give themselves really and completely!

These favored persons must also be modest so as not to fly into a passion at the opposition they encounter; they have to meet it in the temper which says: "Ah, well, it had to be!" Anyone who proposes to do good must not expect people to roll stones out of his way, but must accept his lot calmly if they even roll a few more upon it. A strength which becomes clearer and stronger through its experience of such obstacles is the only strength that can conquer them. Resistance is only a waste of strength.

Of all the will for the ideal which exists in mankind only a small part can be manifested in action. All the rest is destined to realize itself in unseen effects, which represent, however, a value exceeding a thousandfold and more that of the activity which attracts the notice of the world. Its relation to the latter is like that of the deep sea to the waves which stir its surface. The hidden forces of goodness are embodied in those persons who carry on as a secondary pursuit the immediate personal service which they cannot make their lifework. The lot of the many is to have as a profession, for the earning of their living and the satisfaction of society's claim on them, a more or less soulless labor in which they can give out little or nothing of their human qualities, because in that labor they have to be little better than human machines. Yet no one finds himself in the position of having no possible opportunity of giving himself to others as a human being. The problem produced by the fact of labor being today so thoroughly organized, specialized, and mechanized depends only in part for its solution on society's not merely removing the conditions thus produced, but doing its very best to guard the rights of human personality. What is even more important is that sufferers shall not simply bow to their fate, but shall try with all their energy to assert their human personality amid their unfavorable conditions by spiritual activity. Anyone can rescue his human life, in spite of his professional life, who seizes every opportunity of being a man by means of personal action, however unpretending, for the good of fellow men who need the help of a fellow man. Such a man enlists in the service of the spiritual and good. No fate can prevent a man from giving to others this direct human service side by side with his lifework. If so much of such service remains unrealized, it is because the opportunities are missed.

That everyone shall exert himself in that state of life in which he is placed, to practice true humanity toward his fellow men, on that depends the future of mankind. Enormous values come to nothing every moment through the missing of opportunities, but the values which do get turned into will and deed mean wealth which must not be undervalued. Our humanity is by no means so materialistic as foolish talk is continually asserting it to be. Judging by what I have learned about men and women, I am convinced that there is far more in them of idealist will power than ever comes to the surface of the world. Just as the water of the streams we see is small in amount compared to that which flows underground, so the idealism which becomes visible is small in amount compared with what men and women bear locked in their hearts, unreleased or scarcely released. To unbind what is bound, to bring the underground waters to the surface: mankind is waiting and longing for such as can do that.

What seemed to my friends the most irrational thing in my plan was that I wanted to go to Africa, not as a missionary, but as a doctor, and thus when already thirty years of age burdened myself as a beginning with a long period of laborious study. And that this study would mean for me a tremendous effort, I had no manner of doubt. I did, in truth, look forward to the next few years with dread. But the reasons which determined me to follow the way of service I had chosen, as a doctor, weighed so heavily that other considerations were as dust in the balance.

I wanted to be a doctor that I might be able to work without having to talk. For years I had been giving myself out in words and it was with joy that I had followed the calling of theological teacher and of preacher. But this new form of activity I could not represent to myself as being talking about the religion of love, but only as an actual putting it into practice. Medical knowledge made it possible for me to carry out my intention in the best and most complete way, wherever the path of service might lead me. In view of the plan for Equatorial Africa, the acquisition of such knowledge was especially indicated because in the district to which I thought of going a doctor was, according to the missionaries' reports, the most needed of all needed things. They were always complaining in their magazine that the natives who visited them in physical suffering could not be given the help they desired. To become one day the doctor whom these poor creatures needed, it was worthwhile, so I judged, to become a medical student. Whenever I was inclined to feel that the years I should have to sacrifice were too long, I reminded myself that Hamilcar and Hannibal had prepared for their march on Rome by their slow and tedious conquest of Spain.

There was still one more point of view from which I seemed directed to become a doctor. From what I knew of the Parisian Missionary Society, I could not but feel it to be very doubtful whether they would accept me as a missionary.

It was in pietistic and orthodox circles that at the beginning of the nineteenth century societies were first formed for preaching the Gospel in the heathen world. About the same time, it is true, liberal Christendom too began to comprehend the need for carrying the teaching of Jesus to far-off lands But when it came to action, the faith that was in the fetters of dogmatism was first in the field. With their own living and active societies outside the ecclesiastical organization they were more capable of independent action than was liberal Christianity, which at that time was playing the leading part in the church and was consequently wholly absorbed in ecclesiasticism. Moreover the dogmatic bodies had in their pietistic ideas about "the saving of souls" a stronger motive for mission work than liberal Christianity, since the latter's aim was to set the Gospel working primarily as a force for the restoration of mankind and the conditions of human society in the heathen world.

When the missionary societies started by pietism and orthodoxy once got to work they found support in liberal circles which were friendly to missions. These believed for a long time that they could dispense with missionary societies of their own, expecting that, as a result of Protestants of every shade of belief working for and with them, the existing societies would in time come to carrying on the mission work of Protestantism as such. They were mistaken, however. The societies accepted, indeed, all the material help offered them by liberal Protestantism—how hard my father and his liberal colleagues in Alsace worked for the missionary societies which had a quite different doctrinal outlook!—but they sent out no missionaries who would not accept their own doctrinal requirements. As a result of going on for so long in this self-forgetting way without any missionary undertakings of its own and supporting those which were not its own, liberal Protestantism obtained the reputation of having no appreciation of mission work and doing nothing for it. Then, but much too late, it resolved to establish missionary societies of its own, and to give up the hope of having a mission run by the Protestant Church as a whole.

It was always interesting to me to find that the missionaries themselves usually thought more liberally than the officials of their societies. They had, of course, found by experience that among outside peoples, especially among the primitive races, there is a complete absence of those presuppositions which compel our Christianity at home to face the alternative of doctrinal constraint or doctrinal freedom, and that the important thing out there is to preach the elements of the Gospel as given in the Sermon on the Mount, and to bring men under the lordship of the spirit of Jesus.

For the Paris Mission my father cherished a special sympathy because he thought he could detect in it a more liberal tendency than in others. He particularly appreciated the fact that Casalis and others among its leading missionaries used in their reports not the sugary language of Canaan, but that of the simple Christian heart.

But that the question of orthodoxy played the same role in the committee of the Paris Society as in others I at once learned, and very explicitly, when I offered it my services. The kindly director of the mission, Monsieur Boegner, was much moved at finding that someone had offered to join the Congo Mission in answer to his appeal, but at once confided to me that serious objections would be raised to my theological standpoint by members of the committee, and that these would have to be cleared away first. My assurance that I wanted to come "merely as a doctor" lifted a heavy weight from his mind, but a little later he had to inform me that some members objected even to the acceptance of a mission doctor, who had only correct Christian love, and did not, in their opinion, hold also the correct Christian belief. However, we both resolved not to worry about the matter too much so long beforehand, and relied on the fact that the objectors still had some years to wait during which they might be able to attain to a truly Christian reasonableness.

No doubt the more liberal *Allgemeine Evangelische Missionsverein* (General Union of Evangelical Missions) in Switzerland would have accepted me without hesitation either as missionary or doctor. But as I felt my call to Equatorial Africa had come to me through the article in the Paris Mission magazine, I felt I ought to try to join that mission, if possible, in its activities in that colony. Further, I was tempted to persist in getting a decision on the question whether, face to face with the Gospel of Jesus, a missionary society could justifiably arrogate to itself the right to refuse to the suffering natives in their district the services of a doctor, because in their opinion he was not sufficiently orthodox.

But over and above all this, my daily work and daily worries, now that I was beginning my medical course, made such demands upon me, that I had neither time nor strength to concern myself about what was to happen afterwards.

My Medical Studies
1905–1912

When I went to Professor Fehling, at that time dean of the medical faculty, to give in my name as a student, he would have liked best to hand me over to his colleague in the psychiatric department.

On one of the closing days of October, 1905, I set out in a thick fog to attend the first of a course of lectures on anatomy.

But there was still a legal question to solve. As a member of the staff of the university I could not be enrolled as a student at the same time. Yet if I attended the medical courses only as a guest, I could not, according to medical rules, be admitted to the examinations. The governing body met the difficulty in a friendly spirit, and permitted me to enter for the examinations on the strength of the certificates which the medical professors would give me of having attended their lectures. The professors, on their side, resolved that, being a colleague, I might attend all the lectures without paying the fees.

My teachers in the five terms preceding the clinical were: Schwalbe, Weidenreich, and Fuchs in anatomy; Hofmeister, Ewald, and Spiro in physiology; Thiele in chemistry; Braun and Cohn in physics; Goette in zoology; Graf Solms and Jost in botany.

Now began years of continuous struggle with fatigue. To immediate resignation of my theological teaching, and of my office of preacher, I had not been able to bring myself. So while I studied medicine, I at the same time delivered theological lectures, and preached almost every Sunday. The lectures were especially laborious at the beginning of my medical course, as it was in them that I began dealing with the problems of the teaching of St. Paul.

The organ, too, now began to make bigger claims on me than before. For Gustave Bret (the conductor of the Paris Bach, Society which had been founded in 1905 by him, Dukas, Fauré, Widor, Guilmont, d'Indy, and myself) insisted on my undertaking the organ part in all the society's concerts. For some years, therefore, I had to make, each winter, several journeys to Paris. Although I only had to attend the final practice, and could travel back to Strasbourg during the night following each performance, every concert took at least three days of my time. Many a sermon for St. Nicholas did I sketch out in the train between Paris and Strasbourg! I had also to be at the organ for the Bach concerts of the *Orféo Català* at Barcelona. And in general I now played oftener in concerts, not only because I had during recent years become known as an organist, but also because the loss of my stipend as principal of the Theological College compelled me to find some new source of income.

The frequent journeys to Paris afforded me a welcome opportunity of meeting friends whom in the course of time I had made in that city. Among those I knew best were the clever and musically gifted Frau Fanny Reinach, the wife of the well-known scholar, Theodor Reinach and Countess Mélanie de Pourtalés, the friend of the Empress Eugénie, at whose side she figures in Winterhalter's famous picture. At the country house of the countess, near Strasbourg, I frequently saw her friend, Princess Metternich-Sander, the wife of the Austrian Ambassador at Paris in Napoleon III's day. It was she whom Wagner, in his day, had to thank for getting his *Tannhäuser* produced in the Grand Opera House at Paris. In the course of a conversation with Napoleon III during a ball she induced him to order that this opera should be included in the list of works for performance. Under a somewhat rude exterior she concealed much sagacity and kindness of heart. I learned from her much that was interesting about Wagner's stay in Paris, and about the people who formed Napoleon's entourage, but how much of soul this unusually gifted woman possessed first became known to me from letters which she wrote to me when I was in Africa.

While in Paris I also saw a good deal of Mademoiselle is based on it, on the other, arise from the fact that in respect of the details as to which our opinions differed, Widor and I had agreed that in the French edition his ideas, which fitted better the peculiarities of the French organs, should be dominant, while in the German and the English mine should, taking, as they did, more into account the character of the modern organ.

The outbreak of war so soon afterwards and the consequent disturbance of international dealings in the book trade, which still continues, have brought it about that our work, which was published in New York, was bought almost exclusively in English-speaking countries, for which, indeed, it was primarily designed. Its price was fixed on the dollar basis, and that alone made it after the war practically unsalable in Germany and France.

Owing to various circumstances, and because other tasks always got in the way, I have again and again been obliged to postpone the publication of the three volumes of choral preludes.

First Activities in Africa
1913–1917

In the afternoon of Good Friday, 1913, my wife and I left Günsbach; in the evening of March 26th we embarked at Bordeaux.

At Lambaréné the missionaries gave us a very hearty welcome. They had unfortunately not been able to erect the little buildings of corrugated iron in which I was to begin my medical activity, for they had not secured the necessary laborers. The trade in okoume wood, which was just beginning to flourish in the Ogowé district, offered any native who was fairly capable better paid work than he could find on the mission station. So at first I had to use as my consulting room an old fowl house close to our living quarters, but in the late autumn I was able to move to a corrugated-iron building down by the river, 26 feet long and 13 feet wide, with a roof of palm leaves. It contained a small consulting room, an operation room of similar proportions, and a still smaller dispensary. Round about this building there came gradually into existence a number of large bamboo huts for the accommodation of the native patients. The white patients found quarters in the mission house and in the doctor's little bungalow.

From the very first days, before I had even found time to unpack the drugs and instruments, I was besieged by sick people. The choice of Lambaréné as the site of the hospital had been made on the strength of the map and the facts given us by Mr. Morel, the missionary, a native of Alsace, and it proved to be in every respect a happy one. From a distance of one to two hundred miles around, from upstream or downstream, the sick could be brought to me in canoes along the Ogowé and its affluents. The chief diseases I had to deal with were malaria, leprosy, sleeping sickness, dysentery, frambesia, and phagedenic ulcers, but I was surprised at the number of cases of pneumonia and heart disease which I discovered. There was much work too with urinary diseases. Surgical treatment was called for chiefly by hernia and elephantiasis tumors. Hernia is much commoner among the natives in Equatorial Africa than among us white people. If there is no medical man in the neighborhood, every year sees a number of unfortunate mortals doomed to die a painful death from strangulated hernia from which a timely operation might have saved them. My first surgical intervention was in a case of that kind.

Thus I had during the very first weeks full opportunity for establishing the fact that physical misery among the natives is not less but even greater than I had supposed. How glad I was that in defiance of all objections I had carried out my plan of going out there as a doctor.

Great was the joy of Dr. Nassau, the aged founder of the mission station at Lambaréné, when I sent to him in America the news that it was once more supplied with a doctor.

At first I was much hindered in my work by being unable to find natives who could serve as interpreters and orderlies. The first who showed himself worth anything was one who had been a cook, Joseph Azoawani by name, who stayed with me, though I could not pay him so much as he had earned in his former calling. He gave me some valuable hints about how to deal with the natives, though upon the one which he thought the most important I was unable to act. He advised me to refuse as patients those whose lives, so far as we could see, we were not likely to save. Again and again he held up to me the example of the fetish doctors who would have nothing to do with such cases, in order to endanger as little as possible their reputation as helpers.

But on one point I had later to admit that he was right. One must never, when dealing with primitives, hold out hopes of recovery to the patient and his relatives, if the case is really hopeless. If death occurs without warning of it having been given, it is concluded that the doctor did not know the disease would have this outcome because he had not diagnosed it correctly. To native patients one must tell the truth without reservation. They wish to know it and they can endure it, for death is to them something natural. They are not afraid of it, but face it calmly. If after all the patient unexpectedly recovers, so much the better for the doctor's reputation. He ranks thereafter as one who can cure even fatal diseases.

Valiant help was given in the hospital by my wife, who had been trained as a nurse. She looked after the severe cases, superintended the linen and the bandages, was often busy in the dispensary, kept the instruments in proper condition, made all the preparations for the operations, herself then administering the anesthetics, while Joseph acted as assistant. That she managed successfully the complicated work of an African household, and yet could find every day some hours to spare for the hospital was really a wonderful achievement.

To induce the natives to submit to operations needed no great skill in persuasion from me. A few years before a Government doctor, Jauré-Guibert by name, had stayed for a short time at Lambaréné on one of his journeys and performed some successful operations, on the strength of which my very modest surgical skill met with a trustful reception. Fortunately I did not lose a single one of those patients on whom I first operated.

At the end of a few months of work the hospital had to find every day accommodations for about forty patients. I had, however, to provide shelter not only for these but for the companions who had brought them long distances in canoes, and who stayed with them in order to paddle them back home again.

The actual work, heavy as it was, I found a lighter burden than the care and responsibility which came with it. I belong unfortunately to the number of those medical men who have not the robust temperament which is desirable in that calling, and so are consumed with unceasing anxiety about the condition of their severe cases and of those on whom they have operated. In vain have I tried to train myself to that equanimity which makes it possible for a doctor, in spite of all his sympathy with the sufferings of his patients, to husband, as is desirable, his spiritual and nervous energy.

So far as the rule could be carried out, I used to exact from my native patients some tangible evidence of their gratitude for the help they had received. Again and again I used to remind them that they enjoyed the blessing of the hospital because so many people in Europe had made sacrifices to provide it; it was, therefore, now on their part a duty to give all the help they could to keep it going. Thus I gradually got it established as a custom that in return for the medicines given I received gifts of money, bananas, poultry, or eggs. What thus came in was, of course, far below the value of what had been received, but it was a contribution to the upkeep of the hospital. With the bananas I could feed the sick whose provisions had given out, and with the money I could buy rice if the supply of bananas failed. I also thought that the natives would value the hospital more if they had to contribute to its maintenance themselves according to their ability, than if they simply got everything for nothing. In this opinion about the educational value of the exaction of a gift I have been only strengthened by later experience. Of course no gift was exacted from the very poor and the old—and among the primitives age always connotes poverty.

The real savages among them had a quite different conception of a present. When on the point of leaving the hospital cured, they used to demand one from me, because I had now become their friend.

In my intercourse with these primitive creatures I naturally came to put to myself the much debated question whether they were mere prisoners of tradition, or beings capable of really independent thought. In the conversations I had with them I found to my astonishment that they were far more interested in the elementary questions about the meaning of life and the nature of good and evil than I had supposed.

As I had expected, the questions of dogma on which the Missionary Society's committee in Paris had laid so much weight played practically no part in the sermons of the missionaries. If they wanted to be understood by their hearers they could do nothing beyond preaching the simple Gospel of becoming freed from the world by the spirit of Jesus, the Gospel which comes to us in the Sermon on the Mount and the finest sayings of St. Paul. Necessity compelled them to put forward Christianity as before all else an ethical religion. When they met each other at the mission conferences held twice a year now at this station, now at that, their discussions bore on the problems of how to secure practical Christianity in their district, not on doctrinal ones. That in matters of belief some of them thought more strictly than others played no part in the missionary work, which they carried on in common. As I did not make the smallest attempt to foist any theological views upon them, they soon laid aside all mistrust of me and rejoiced, as did I also on my side, that we were united in the piety of obedience to Jesus, and in the will to simple Christian activity. Not many months after my arrival I was invited to take part in the preaching, and thus was released from the promise I had given in Paris: *d'être muet comme une carpe.*

I was also invited to attend as a visitor the sittings of the Synod, when the missionaries and the native preachers sat in council together. And one day, when at the request of the missionaries I had expressed my opinion on a certain point, one of the native preachers suggested that the matter was outside the Doctor's province "because he is not a theologian, as we are."

I was also allowed to share in the examination of the candidates for baptism. I generally got them to send me one or two old women, that I might make the trying half-hour as easy for them as possible. On one such occasion when I put to one worthy matron the question whether the Lord Jesus had been rich or poor, she replied: "What a stupid question! If God, the Great Chief, was his Father, he certainly can't have been poor." And in general she answered with the Canaanitish woman's quickness of repartee. It was no help to her, however, that the professor of theology gave her a correspondingly good certificate. The native preacher to whose district she belonged dealt with her all the more strictly, wanting to make her pay the penalty for not having attended quite regularly at the catechumen instruction classes. Her excellent answers found no grace in his sight. He wanted to hear those that were in the catechism. So she was failed, and had to offer herself for the examination again six months later.

I found preaching a great joy. It seemed to me a glorious thing to be allowed to preach the sayings of Jesus and Paul to people to whom they were quite new. As interpreters I had the native teachers of the Mission School, who translated each sentence at once into the language of the Galoas or of the Páhuins, or sometimes into both in succession.

The little spare time that was at my disposal in the first year at Lambaréné I devoted to work on the three last volumes of the American edition of Bach's organ music.

For keeping up my organ playing I had the magnificent piano with pedal attachment, built specially for the Tropics, which the Paris Bach Society had presented to me in recognition of my many years of service as their organist. At first, however, I had not the heart to practice. I had accustomed myself to think that this activity in Africa meant the end of my life as an artist, and that the renunciation would be easier if I allowed fingers and feet to get rusty with disuse. One evening, however, as, in melancholy mood, I was playing one of Bach's organ fugues, the idea came suddenly upon me that I might after all use my free hours in Africa for the very purpose of perfecting and deepening my technique. I immediately formed a plan to take, one after another, compositions by Bach, Mendelssohn, Widor, César Franck, and Max Reger, study them carefully down to the smallest detail, and learn them by heart, even if I had to spend weeks or months on any particular piece. How I enjoyed being able to practice at leisure and in quiet, without any slavery to time through being due to play at concerts, even though occasionally I could not find more than a bare half-hour in the day for the purpose!

My wife and I had now completed our second dry season in Africa, and were beginning to sketch out plans for going home at the opening of the third, when on August 5th, 1914, the news came that war had broken out in Europe. On the evening of that very day we were informed that we must consider ourselves to be prisoners of war; we might, indeed, for the present remain in our own house, but we must stop all intercourse with either white people or natives, and obey unconditionally the regulations of the black soldiers who were assigned us as guards. One of the missionaries and his wife, who like ourselves were Alsatians, were also interned at the Lambaréné mission station.

The only thing about the war which the natives understood at first was that it was all over with the timber trade, and that all commodities had become dearer. It was only later, when many of them were transported to Cameroon to serve as carriers for the active forces, that they began to understand what the war really meant.

As soon as it became known that of the white men who used to live on the Ogowé ten had already fallen, an old savage remarked: "What, so many men killed already in this war! Why don't their tribes meet to talk out the palaver? How can they ever pay for all these dead men?" For in native warfare those who fall, whether among the conquerors or the conquered, have to be paid for by the opposite side. This same savage expressed the criticism that Europeans kill each other merely out of cruelty, because of course they don't want to eat the dead.

That white people were making prisoners of other whites and putting them under the authority of black soldiers was something incomprehensible to the natives. What a torrent of abuse my black guards came in for from the people of the neighboring villages because they thought they were "the Doctor's masters."

When I was forbidden to work in the Hospital, I thought at first that I would proceed to the completion of my book on St. Paul. But another subject at once forced itself upon me, one which I had had in my mind for years, and which the war was now making a real live issue: the problem of our civilization. So on the second day of my internment, still quite amazed at being able to sit down at my writing table early in the morning as in the days before I took up medicine, I set to work on the Philosophy of Civilization.

My first incitement to take up this subject I had received in the summer of 1899 at the house of the Curtius family in Berlin. Hermann Grimm and others were conversing there one evening about a sitting of the academy from which they had just come, when suddenly one of them—I forget which it was—came out with: "Why, we are all of us just nothing but 'Epigoni'!"[2] It struck home with me like a flash of lightning, because it put into words what I myself felt.

As early as my first years at the university I had begun to feel misgivings about the opinion that mankind is constantly developing in the direction of progress. My impression was that the fire of its ideals was burning low without anyone noticing it or troubling about it. On a number of occasions I had to acknowledge that public opinion did not reject with indignation inhumane ideas which were publicly disseminated, but accepted them, and that it approved of, as opportune, inhumane courses of action taken by governments and nations. Even for what was just and expedient as well there seemed to me to be only a lukewarm zeal available. From a number of signs I had to infer the growth of a peculiar intellectual and spiritual fatigue in this generation which is so proud of what it has accomplished. It seemed as if I heard its members arguing to each other that their previous hopes for the future of mankind had been pitched too high, and that it was becoming necessary to limit oneself to striving for what was attainable. The slogan which was given out for all countries, *Realpolitik,* meant the approbation of a shortsighted nationalism, and compromises with forces and tendencies which had been resisted hitherto as hostile to progress. One of the clearest indications of decline for me was the fact that superstition, which had hitherto been banished from educated circles, was again thought fit for admission to society.

---

[2] *Epigoni* (Gk.ἐπίγονοι: lit. After born). A Latin word used of the generation following those who lived in a great age; inheritors of a great past. The contemporaries of James I may be called Epigoni of the great Elizabethans.—Translator's Note.

When about the end of the century men began to take a retrospective review of every field of human activity in order to determine and fix the value of their achievements, this was done with an optimism which to me was incomprehensible. It seemed to be assumed everywhere not only that we had made progress in inventions and knowledge, but also that in the intellectual and ethical spheres we lived and moved at a height which we had never before reached, and from which we should never decline. My own impression was that in our mental and spiritual life we were not only below the level of past generations, but were in many respects only living on their achievements . . . and that not a little of this heritage was beginning to melt away in our hands.

And now—here was someone giving expression to the criticism which I myself had silently and half unconsciously passed upon our age! After that evening at Professor Curtius' house I was always, along with my other work, inwardly occupied with another book, which I entitled *Wir Epigonen* ("We Inheritors of a Past"). I often put before friends the thoughts contained in it, but they usually took them as just interesting paradoxes and manifestations of a *fin-de-siècle* pessimism. After that I kept my ideas strictly to myself, and only in sermons allowed my doubts about our civilization and our spirituality to find expression.

And now war was raging as a result of the downfall of civilization.

"We Inheritors of a Past," then, had in reality no longer any meaning. The book has been conceived as a criticism of civilization. It was meant to demonstrate its decline and to draw attention to the accompanying dangers. But if the catastrophe had already come about, what good was deliberation about the causes, which were now patent to everyone?

The book which had thus become out of date I thought of writing for my own sake. Could I be certain that the pages would not be taken from a prisoner of war? And was there any prospect of my seeing Europe again?

In this attitude of entire detachment I began to work and went on with it when I was again allowed to go about and devote myself to the sick. For at the end of November we were released from our internment, thanks to Widor's exertions; as I afterwards learned. Even before that the order which kept me away from the sick had proved incapable of enforcement. White and black alike had protested against being deprived without any perceivable reason of the services of the only doctor for hundreds of miles around. The district commandant had consequently found himself compelled to give now to one, now to another, a note for my guards, telling them to let the bearer see me because he needed my help.

But when I resumed my medical activities in comparative freedom, I still found time to occupy myself with the book on civilization. Many a night did I sit at it, thinking and writing with deepest emotion as I thought of those who were lying in the trenches.

At the beginning of the summer of 1915 I awoke from a sort of stupor. Why only criticism of civilization? Why content myself with analyzing ourselves as *Epigoni?* Why not go on to something constructive?

So now I began a search for the knowledge and convictions to which we must refer the will to civilization and the power to realize it. "We Inheritors of a Past" expanded into a work dealing with the restoration of civilization.

As I worked the connection between civilization and attitude toward life became clear to me. I recognized that the catastrophe of civilization stemmed from a catastrophe in this attitude.

The ideals of true civilization had become powerless, because the idealistic attitude toward life in which they are rooted had gradually been lost to us. All events that occur within nations and within mankind can be traced to spiritual causes contained in the prevailing attitude toward life.

But what is civilization?

We may take as the essential element in civilization the ethical perfecting of the individual and of society as well. But at the same time, every spiritual and every material step in advance has significance for civilization. The will to civilization is then the universal will to progress which is conscious of the ethical as the highest value for all. In spite of the great importance we attach to the triumphs of knowledge and achievement, it is nevertheless obvious that only a humanity which is striving after ethical ends can in full measure share in the blessings brought by material progress and become master of the dangers which accompany it. To the generation which had adopted a belief in an immanent power of progress realizing itself, in some measure, naturally and automatically, and which thought that it no longer needed any ethical ideals but could advance to its goal by means of knowledge and achievement alone, terrible proof was being given by its present position of the error into which it had sunk.

The only possible way out of chaos is for us to come once more under the control of the ideals of true civilization through the adoption of an attitude toward life that contains those ideals.

But what is the nature of the attitude toward life in which the will to general progress and to ethical progress are alike founded and in which they are bound together?

It consists in an ethical affirmation of the world and of life.

What is affirmation of the world and of life?

To us Europeans and to people of European descent everywhere the will to progress is something so natural and so much a matter of course that it never occurs to us to recognize that it is rooted in an attitude toward life and springs from an act of the spirit. But if we look about us in the world, we see at once that what is to us such a matter of course is in reality anything but that. To Indian thought all effort directed to triumphs in knowledge and power and to the improvement of man's outer life and of society as a whole is mere folly. It teaches that the only sensible line of conduct for a man is to withdraw entirely into himself and to concern himself solely with the deepening of his inner life. He has nothing to do with what may become of human society and of mankind. The deepening of one's inner life, as Indian thought interprets it, means that a man surrenders himself to the thought of "no more will to live," and by abstention from action and by every sort of life denial reduces his earthly existence to a condition of being which has no content beyond a waiting for the cessation of being.

It is interesting to trace the origin of this idea of detachment from the world, contrary to nature. It had at first nothing whatever to do with any theory of the world, but was a magical conception of the Indian priests of early times. These believed that by detachment from the world and from life they could become in some measure supernatural beings, and obtain power over the gods. In accordance with this idea arises the custom that the Brahmin, after living part of his life in the normal way and founding a family, terminates his life in complete renunciation of the world.

In the course of time this rejection of the world and of life, which was originally the privilege of the Brahmin, was developed into a system of thought that claimed to be valid for all men.

It depends, then, on the prevailing attitude toward the world and toward life whether the will to progress will be present or not. The attitude of rejection excludes it; the affirmative attitude requires it. Among primitive and half-primitive peoples too, whose unformed view has not yet reached the problem of acceptance or rejection of the world, there is no will to progress. Their ideal is the simplest life with the least possible trouble.

Even we Europeans have only arrived at our will to progress in the course of time and through a change in our conception of the world. In antiquity and in the Middle Ages there was nothing more than attempts at it. Greek thinking does try to reach an affirmative attitude toward the world and toward life, but it fails in the attempt and ends in resignation. The attitude of the Middle Ages is determined by the ideas of primitive Christianity as brought into harmony with Greek metaphysics. It is fundamentally a rejection of the world and of life because the interest of Christianity at this time concentrated upon otherworldly things. All that is effective and constructive in the activity of the Middle Ages is the fruit of the active ethic contained in the preaching of Jesus and also of the creative forces of the fresh and unspoiled peoples on whom Christianity had imposed an attitude toward life that was in contradiction to their nature.

Then, little by little, the affirmative attitude that is already germinating among the peoples as a result of the Great Migration begins to manifest itself. The Renaissance proclaims its freedom from the medieval contempt for the world and for life. An ethical character is given to this new world-accepting attitude by its taking over the ethic of love taught by Jesus. This, as an ethic of action, is strong enough to emerge from the framework of negation in which it had its origin, to join forces with the affirmative attitude toward the world and life and through it to gain as its ideal the realization of a spiritual and ethical world within the natural.

The striving for material and spiritual progress, therefore, which characterizes the people of modern Europe, has its source in the attitude toward the world to which these people have come. As a result of the Renaissance and the spiritual and religious movements bound up with it, men have entered on a new relation to themselves and to the world, and this has aroused in them a need to create by their own activities spiritual and material values which shall help to a higher development of individuals and of mankind. It is not the case that the man of modern Europe is enthusiastic for progress because he may hope to get some personal advantage from it. He is less concerned about his own condition than about the happiness which he hopes will be the lot of coming generations. Enthusiasm for progress has taken possession of him. Impressed by his great experience of finding the world revealed to him as constituted and maintained by forces which carry out a definite design, he himself wills to become an active, purposeful force in the world. He looks with confidence toward new and better times which shall dawn for mankind and learns by experience that the ideas which are held and acted upon by the mass of people do win power over circumstances and remold them.

It is on his will to material progress, acting in union with the will to ethical progress, that the foundations of modern civilization are being laid.

There is an essential relationship between the modern European attitude of ethical affirmation toward the world and life and that of Zarathustra and of Chinese thought, as the latter meets us in the writings of Kung-tse (Confucius), Meng-tse (Mencius), Mi-tse (Micius), and the other great ethical thinkers of China. In each of these we can see the striving to remold the circumstances of peoples and of mankind with the intention of progress, even if the efforts are not so powerful as those of modern Europe. Within the region influenced by the religion of Zarathustra and in China, there was actually established, as in Europe, a civilization in consonance with an ethical affirmation of the world and life. But each met with a tragic end. The neo-Persian civilization of the Zarathustran view of the world was blotted out by Islam. Chinese civilization is hampered in its natural development and threatened with decay by the pressure exerted upon it by European ideas and problems, and by confusion wrought in the country's political and economic condition.

In modern European thought a tragedy is occurring in that the original bonds uniting the affirmative attitude toward the world with ethics are, by a slow but irresistible process, loosening and finally parting. The result that we are coming to is that European humanity is being guided by a will-to-progress that has become merely external and has lost its bearings.

The affirmative attitude can produce of itself only a partial and imperfect civilization. Only if it becomes inward and ethical can the will-to-progress which results from it possess the requisite insight to distinguish the valuable from the less valuable, and strive after a civilization which does not consist only in achievements of knowledge and power, but before all else will make men, both individually and collectively, more spiritual and more ethical.

But how could it come about that the modern attitude of the world and life changed from its original ethical character and became nonethical?

The only possible explanation is that it was not really founded on thought. The thought out of which it arose was noble and enthusiastic but not deep. The intimate connection of the ethical with the affirmative attitude toward life was for it a matter of feeling and experience rather than of proof. It took the side of life affirmation and of ethics without having penetrated their inner nature and their inward connection.

This noble and valuable view, therefore, being rooted in belief rather than in thinking which penetrated to the real nature of things was bound to wither and lose its power over men's minds. All subsequent thinking about the problems of ethics and man's relation to his world could not but expose the weak points of this view, and thereby help to hasten its decay. Its activity took effect in this direction even when its intention was to give support, for it never succeeded in replacing the inadequate foundation by one that was adequate. Again and again the new foundations and the underpinning masonry which it had taken in hand showed themselves too weak to support the building.

With my apparently abstract yet absolutely practical thinking about the connection of civilization with philosophy, I had come to see the decay of civilization as a result of the inexorable weakening of the traditional modern attitude of ethical affirmation toward the world and life. It had become clear to me that, like so many other people, I had clung to that attitude from inner necessity without troubling at all about how far it could really be proved by thought.

I had got so far during the summer of 1915. But what was to come next?

Could the difficulty be solved which till now had seemed insoluble? Or had we to regard the attitude through which alone civilization is possible as an illusion within us which never ceases to stir our hearts yet never really gets dominion over us?

To continue holding it up to our generation as something to be believed seemed to me foolish and hopeless. Only if it offers itself to us as something arising from thought can it become spiritually our own.

At bottom I am convinced that the inner connection between the affirmative attitude and ethics, declared to be part of the concept of civilization which had hitherto proved impossible to demonstrate fully, had come from a presentiment of the truth. So it was necessary to undertake to grasp as a necessity of thought by fresh, simple, and sincere thinking the truth which had hitherto been only suspected and believed in although so often proclaimed as proved.

In undertaking this I seemed to myself to be like a man who has to build a new and better boat to replace a rotten one in which he can no longer venture to trust himself to the sea, and yet does not know how to begin.

For months on end I lived in a continual state of mental excitement. Without the least success I let my thinking be concentrated, even all through my daily work at the hospital, on the real nature of the affirmative attitude and of ethics, and on the question of what they have in common. I was wandering about in a thicket in which no path was to be found. I was leaning with all my might against an iron door which would not yield.

All that I had learned from philosophy about ethics left me in the lurch. The conceptions of the Good which it had offered were all so lifeless, so unelemental, so narrow, and so destitute of content that it was quite impossible to bring them into union with the affirmative attitude. Moreover philosophy could be said never to have concerned itself with the problem of the connection between civilization and attitude toward the world. The modern concept of progress had become to it such a matter of course that it had felt no need for coming to clear ideas about it.

To my surprise I had also to recognize the fact that the central province of philosophy, into which meditation on civilization and attitude toward the world had led me, was practically unexplored land. Now from this point, now from that, I tried to penetrate to its interior, but again and again I had to give up the attempt. I was already exhausted and disheartened. I saw, indeed, the conception needed before me, but I could not grasp it and give it expression.

While in this mental condition I had to undertake a longish journey on the river. I was staying with my wife on the coast at Cape Lopez for the sake of her health—it was in September, 1915—when I was summoned to visit Madame Pelot, the ailing wife of a missionary, at N'Gômô, about 160 miles upstream. The only means of conveyance I could find was a small steamer, towing an overladen barge, which was on the point of starting. Except myself, there were only natives on board, but among them was Emil Ogouma, my friend from Lambaréné. Since I had been in too much of a hurry to provide myself with enough food for the journey, they let me share the contents of their cooking pot. Slowly we crept upstream, laboriously feeling—it was the dry season—for the channels between the sandbanks. Lost in thought I sat on the deck of the barge, struggling to find the elementary and universal conception of the ethical which I had not discovered in any philosophy. Sheet after sheet I covered with disconnected sentences, merely to keep myself concentrated on the problem. Late on the third day, at the very moment when, at sunset, we were making our way through a herd of hippopotamuses, there flashed upon my mind, unforeseen and unsought, the phrase, "Reverence for Life." The iron door had yielded: the path in the thicket had become visible. Now I had found my way to the idea in which affirmation of the world and ethics are contained side by side! Now I knew that the ethical acceptance of the world and of life, together with the ideals of civilization contained in this concept, has a foundation in thought.

What is Reverence for Life, and how does it arise in us?

If man wishes to reach clear notions about himself and his relation to the world, he must ever again and again be looking away from the manifold, which is the product of his thought and knowledge, and reflect upon the first, the most immediate, and the continually given fact of his own consciousness. Only if he starts from this given fact can he achieve a rational view.

Descartes makes thinking start from the sentence "I think; so I must exist" (*Cogito, ergo sum*), and with his beginning thus chosen he finds himself irretrievably on the road to the abstract. Out of this empty, artificial act of thinking there can result, of course, nothing which bears on the relation of man to himself, and to the universe. Yet in reality the most immediate act of consciousness has some content. To think means to think something. The most immediate fact of man's consciousness is the assertion: "I am life which wills to live, in the midst of life which wills to live," and it is as will-to-live in the midst of will-to-live that man conceives himself during every moment that he spends in meditating on himself and the world around him.

As in my will-to-live there is ardent desire for further life and for the mysterious exaltation of the will-to-live which we call pleasure, while there is fear of destruction and of that mysterious depreciation of the will-to-live which we call pain: so too are these in the will-to-live around me, whether it can express itself to me, or remains dumb.

Man has now to decide what his relation to his will-to-live shall be. He can deny it. But if he bids his will-to-live change into will-not-to-live, as is done in Indian and indeed in all pessimistic thought, he involves himself in self-contradiction. He raises to the position of his philosophy of life something unnatural, something which is in itself untrue, and which cannot be carried to completion. Indian thought, and Schopenhauer's also, is full of inconsistencies because it cannot help making concessions time after time to the will-to-live, which persists in spite of all negation of the world, though it will not admit that the concessions are really such. Negation of the will-to-live is self-consistent only if it is really willing actually to put an end to physical existence.

If man affirms his will-to-live, he acts naturally and honestly. He confirms an act which has already been accomplished in his instinctive thought by repeating it in his conscious thought. The beginning of thought, a beginning which continually repeats itself, is that man does not simply accept his existence as something given, but experiences it as something unfathomably mysterious. Affirmation of life is the spiritual act by which man ceases to live unreflectively and begins to devote himself to his life with reverence in order to raise it to its true value. To affirm life is to deepen, to make more inward, and to exalt the will-to-live.

At the same time the man who has become a thinking being feels a compulsion to give to every will-to-live the same reverence for life that he gives to his own. He experiences that other life in his own. He accepts as being good: to preserve life, to promote life, to raise to its highest value life which is capable of development; and as being evil: to destroy life, to injure life, to repress life which is capable of development. This is the absolute, fundamental principle of the moral, and it is a necessity of thought.

The great fault of all ethics hitherto has been that they believed themselves to have to deal only with the relations of man to man. In reality, however, the question is what is his attitude to the world and all life that comes within his reach. A man is ethical only when life, as such, is sacred to him, that of plants and animals as that of his fellow men, and when he devotes himself helpfully to all life that is in need of help. Only the universal ethic of the feeling of responsibility in an ever-widening sphere for all that lives—only that ethic can be founded in thought. The ethic of the relation of man to man is not something apart by itself: it is only a particular relation which results from the universal one.

The ethic of Reverence for Life, therefore, comprehends within itself everything that can be described as love, devotion, and sympathy whether in suffering, joy, or effort.

The world, however, offers us the horrible drama of Will-to-Live divided against itself. One existence holds its own at the cost of another: one destroys another. Only in the thinking man has the Will-to-Live become conscious of other will-to-live, and desirous of solidarity with it. This solidarity, however, he cannot completely bring about, because man is subject to the puzzling and horrible law of being obliged to live at the cost of other life, and to incur again and again the guilt of destroying and injuring life. But as an ethical being he strives to escape whenever possible from this necessity, and as one who has become enlightened and merciful to put a stop to this disunion (*Selbstentzweiung*) of the Will-to-Live so far as the influence of his own existence reaches. He thirsts to be permitted to preserve his humanity, and to be able to bring to other existences release from their sufferings.

Reverence for Life arising from the Will-to-Live that has become reflective therefore contains affirmation of life and ethics inseparably combined. It aims to create values, and to realize progress of different kinds which shall serve the material, spiritual, and ethical development of men and mankind. While the unthinking modern acceptance of life stumbles about with its ideals of power won by discovery and invention, the acceptance of life based on reason sets up the spiritual and ethical perfecting of mankind as the highest ideal, and an ideal from which alone all other ideals of progress get their real value.

Through ethical acceptance of the world and of life, we reach a power of reflection which enables us to distinguish between what is essential in civilization and what is not. The stupid arrogance of thinking ourselves civilized loses its power over us. We venture to face the truth that with so much progress in knowledge and power true civilization has become not easier but harder. The problem of the mutual relationship between the spiritual and the material dawns upon us. We know that we all have to struggle with circumstances to preserve our humanity, and that we must be anxiously concerned to turn once more toward hope of victory the almost hopeless struggle which many carry on to preserve their humanity amid unfavorable social circumstances.

A deepened, ethical will to progress which springs from thought will lead us back, then, out of uncivilization and its misery to true civilization. Sooner or later there must dawn the true and final Renaissance which will bring peace to the world.

Now there stood out clearly before my mind the plan of the whole Philosophy of Civilization. It divided itself as if automatically into four parts: (1) On the present lack of civilization and its causes; (2) a discussion of the idea of Reverence for Life in connection with the attempts made in the past by European philosophy to provide a foundation for an affirmative ethical attitude toward the world; (3) exposition of the concept of Reverence for Life; (4) concerning the civilized state.

The writing of the second part, the description of European philosophy's tragic struggle to attain an ethical basis for acceptance of the world, was forced upon me by the inward necessity I felt for getting to know the problem I was dealing with in its historical development, and of comprehending the solution I offered as the synthesis of all previous ones. That I once more succumbed to this temptation I have never regretted. Through my coming to an understanding of other thought, my own became clearer.

Some of the philosophical works needed for this historical task I had by me. What others I needed were sent to me by J. Strohl, professor of zoology at Zurich, and his wife. And the well-known Bach singer, Robert Kaufmann of Zurich, whom I had so often accompanied on the organ, made it his business, with the help of the Office des Internés Civils at Geneva, to keep me, as well as might be, in touch with the world.

Without haste I put on paper, one after another, rough drafts in which I collected and sifted the material without reference to the structure of the treatise already planned. Along with that I began to write out single sections in full. I felt it every day to be a great mercy that while others had to be killing, I could not only save life but even work as well to bring nearer the coming of the Era of Peace.

Fortunately my supply of drugs and bandages did not give out, for by one of the last boats which arrived before the outbreak of war I had received a big supply of all necessary things.

The rainy season of 1916–1917 we spent on the coast, because my wife's health had suffered from the sultry air of Lambaréné. A timber merchant placed at our disposal a house at Chienga near Cape Lopez at the mouth of one of the branches of the Ogowé. It was the home of the man who looked after his timber rafts, but as a consequence of the war it now stood empty. In return for his kindness I joined those of his native laborers who were still on the spot in the work of rolling on to dry land the many okoume logs which had been already tied together in rafts, so that during the long interval which might elapse before cargoes could again be shipped to Europe they should not fall victims to the boreworm (*Teredo navalis*). This heavy work—we often needed hours to roll up onto the shore one of these logs weighing from two to three tons—was only possible at high tide. When the tide was out, I sat at my Philosophy of Civilization, so far as my time was not claimed by patients.

NOTES

CAMPUS RAPE VICTIMS: A STRUGGLE FOR JUSTICE
Joe Shapiro

Joe Shapiro is an NPR News Investigations correspondent. Before working for NPR, he was a writer for U.S. News & World Report. *He is a graduate of Columbia University Graduate School of Journalism and Carleton College. Among many honors and distinctions, he has received a Peabody Award, a Robert F. Kennedy Award, the Edward R. Murrow Award, and was a finalist for the Goldsmith Award.*

RENEE MONTAGNE, host:

We're going to spend the next few minutes on a problem college campuses have been facing for a long time now, yet the statistics continue to be chilling. A study funded by the U.S. Department of Justice estimates that one out of five college women will be sexually assaulted. Usually, there's alcohol involved.

NPR's investigative unit teamed up with journalists at the Center for Public Integrity for this look at how schools—and the government agency that oversees them—handle these cases. NPR's Joseph Shapiro reports.

JOSEPH SHAPIRO: When a woman is sexually assaulted on a college campus, her most common reaction is to keep it quiet. Laura Dunn says she stayed quiet about what happened in April of 2004, her freshman year at the University of Wisconsin.

Ms. LAURA DUNN: I always thought that rape was when, you know, someone got attacked by a stranger and you had to fight back.

SHAPIRO: That night, Dunn was drinking so many raspberry vodkas that they cut her off at the frat house party. Still, she knew and trusted the two men who took her back to a house. That's where she says they raped her as she passed in and out of consciousness.

Ms. DUNN: I guess I didn't want to believe what actually happened.

SHAPIRO: It just didn't make sense with the way she saw her life. For one thing, she had a boyfriend. They'd been dating for four years.

Ms. DUNN: We were getting close to marriage. We had been waiting together, and so I was still a virgin, and it just didn't fit with what I wanted my life to be and what I'd planned, in my life, to be. So, I just kind of pushed it to the side; said, you know, it's this bad incident that happened, and it was just a mistake. You know, we were all drunk and I just chose to like, put it there.

SHAPIRO: She focused on her schoolwork, but she couldn't sleep. She lost weight. She broke up with her boyfriend without ever telling him about the attack. And she didn't report it.

Reprinted by permission from National Public Radio (originally aired February 24, 2010).

Fifteen months later, she was sitting in class. The professor was talking about how in wartime, rape is used as a weapon of terror.

Ms. DUNN: And this professor, who I'll forever respect, stopped the lecture and said, you know, I want to talk about rape on this campus.

SHAPIRO: The professor said that over 80 percent of victims stay silent.

Ms. DUNN: And she said, I want you to know that this has happened in my class to my students, and that there is something you can do about it, and there is someone you can talk about it with. And she told me about the dean of students. And after hearing, you know, about rape, I just decided, you know, I know it was rape, and now I know that there's something I can do about it. And so the moment that lecture let up, I walked across to the dean of students' office and I reported that day.

SHAPIRO: We'll tell you what happened to Laura Dunn in a moment. But first, it helps to know something about the history of how colleges and universities got their current day responsibility to investigate and prevent sexual assaults. It starts with a crime in April of 1986.

Ms. CONNIE CLERY: What happened to Jeanne was so amazingly unreal.

SHAPIRO: Connie Clery is the mother of Jeanne Clery.

Ms. CLERY: She was in the right place, where she should have been—in her own bed, in the dorm at 6 o'clock in the morning, fast asleep. There were three automatically locking doors that should have been locked, which she thought were locked. And she didn't have an enemy in the world. And Lehigh was such a safe-looking place, you know?

SHAPIRO: Jeanne Clery was 19, a freshman at Lehigh University. A stranger he was a student raped, tortured and strangled her. In their grief, Connie Clery and her husband devoted the rest of their lives to making college campuses safer.

Ms. CLERY: So if it happened to Jeanne, it could certainly happen to somebody else. And that's why I decided I had to do something to save others from such a horror.

SHAPIRO: Connie's husband, Howard, sold his successful business to underwrite their work. Connie, who'd been terrified of speaking in public, went on TV morning shows and testified before lawmakers.

Their idea was simple: Force schools to disclose all crime that happens on campus. Then students and their parents would be informed. And the campus would get safer because under public scrutiny, college presidents would have no choice but to get serious about preventing crime.

Twenty years ago, Congress passed that disclosure law, now known as the Jeanne Clery Act.

There's been success. Over a recent 10-year period, violent crime on college campuses dropped by 9 percent.

Ms. CLERY: The Department of Education has been a disappointment to me.

SHAPIRO: But for advocates like Connie Clery, there have been shortcomings, too. The U.S. Department of Education regulates schools under the Clery Act, but it's fined offending schools just six times. And that gets us back to Laura Dunn's case.

She counted on the Department of Education for help.

Ms. DUNN: Dear Ms. Dunn, on August 8, 2006, the U.S. Department of Education Office of Civil Rights received your complaint of discrimination on the basis of sex filed against the University of Wisconsin, Madison.

SHAPIRO: By the time Dunn reported to campus officials, one of the men she accused had graduated; the other said the sex was consensual. The University of Wisconsin took nine months to investigate, then decided against punishment.

As a last resort, Dunn asked the U.S. Department of Education to find that the university had failed in its responsibility to act promptly, and to end the sexual harassment she faced being on campus with her alleged attacker.

This anti-harassment law is among the strongest tools for enforcement at the Education Department. Few women know to use it, and when they do, the department rarely acts. Between 1998 and 2008, it ruled against just five universities out of 24 complaints. That's according to records obtained through the Freedom of Information Act by the Center for Public Integrity. There was no punishment in those cases—simply guidance on how to improve campus procedures.

Presented with those findings, Russlynn Ali, the assistant secretary for civil rights, says her office is stepping up outreach to students so they know their rights, and assistance to schools so they know their responsibilities.

Ms. RUSSLYNN ALI (Assistant Secretary for Civil Rights, Department of Education): We want them to get training, we want to provide some help so that the adults and the students alike can ensure that this plague—it's really become a plague in this country—begins to diminish.

SHAPIRO: The Education Department official says she's willing to take steps not used by her predecessors: to withdraw federal funding from offending schools, and refer cases to the Department of Justice for possible prosecution.

Laura Dunn is a teacher now. She writes the next day's lesson on the blackboard.

Ms. DUNN: Most days, we'll have students who will be able to find interior angles of triangles.

SHAPIRO: Two years after Dunn graduated, a thick document came in the mail to her apartment. It was the finding by the Department of Education.

Ms. DUNN: I went straight to the conclusion.

SHAPIRO: It said the University of Wisconsin—despite taking nine months on the case—had acted properly. Defeated, Dunn didn't read on. She threw the papers on the top of a pile of other documents in the corner of her bedroom.

Ms. DUNN: You know, I could've fought it again and it could've appealed, but that would've meant I would've had to read it. And at that point in my life, just reading it—I just didn't even want to. I did not want to read the ugly things that people said.

SHAPIRO: But Laura Dunn is no longer silent. She's a leader in a national grassroots campaign to get rape survivors to speak out in public.

Joseph Shapiro, NPR News.

MONTAGNE: To learn more about victims' rights and find resources for campus safety, visit NPR.org.

MONTAGNE: This is NPR News.

NOTES

NOTES

THE WORKING POOR: INVISIBLE IN AMERICA
David K. Shipler

David K. Shipler worked for The New York Times *from 1966–1988 and has also written for* The New Yorker, *the* Washington Post, *and the* Los Angeles Times. *His book* Arab and Jew: Wounded Spirits in a Promised Land *won the Pulitzer Prize. His book* The Working Poor: Invisible in America *was published in 2004. He also taught at various universities, including Princeton, American University, and Dartmouth College.*

At the Edge of Poverty

Tired of wishes,
Empty of dreams
—Carl Sandburg

The man who washes cars does not own one. The clerk who files cancelled checks at the bank has $2.02 in her own account. The woman who copyedits medical textbooks has not been to a dentist in a decade.

This is the forgotten America. At the bottom of its working world, millions live in the shadow of prosperity, in the twilight between poverty and well-being. Whether you're rich, poor, or middle-class, you encounter them every day. They serve you Big Macs and help you find merchandise at Wal-Mart. They harvest your food, clean your offices, and sew your clothes. In a California factory, they package lights for your kids' bikes. In a New Hampshire plant, they assemble books of wallpaper samples to help you redecorate.

They are shaped by their invisible hardships. Some are climbing out of welfare, drug addiction, or homelessness. Others have been trapped for life in a perilous zone of low-wage work. Some of their children are malnourished. Some have been sexually abused. Some live in crumbling housing that contributes to their children's asthma, which means days absent from school. Some of their youngsters do not even have the eyeglasses they need to see the chalkboard clearly.

This book is about a few of these people, their families, their dreams, their personal failings, and the larger failings of their country. While the United States has enjoyed unprecedented affluence, low-wage employees have been testing the American doctrine that hard work cures poverty. Some have found that work works. Others have learned that it doesn't. Moving in and out of jobs that demand much and pay little, many people tread just above the official poverty line, dangerously close to the edge of destitution. An inconvenience to an affluent family—minor car trouble, a brief illness,

---

Reprinted from *The Working Poor: Invisible in America* (2004), Alfred A. Knopf, a division of Random House, Inc.

disrupted child care—is a crisis to them, for it can threaten their ability to stay employed. They spend everything and save nothing. They are always behind on their bills. They have minuscule bank accounts or none at all, and so pay more fees and higher interest rates than more secure Americans. Even when the economy is robust, many wander through a borderland of struggle, never getting very far from where they started. When the economy weakens, they slip back toward the precipice.

Millions have been pushed into a region of adversity by federal welfare reform's time limits and work mandates. Enacted in 1996 during an economic boom, the reform is credited by many welfare recipients for inducing them to travel beyond the stifling world of dependence into the active, challenging, hopeful culture of the workplace. They have gained self-confidence, some say, and have acquired new respect from their children. Those with luck or talent step onto career ladders toward better and better positions at higher and higher pay. Many more, however, are stuck at such low wages that their living standards are unchanged. They still cannot save, cannot get decent health care, cannot move to better neighborhoods, and cannot send their children to schools that offer a promise for a successful future. These are the forgotten Americans, who are noticed and counted as they leave welfare, but who disappear from the nation's radar as they struggle in their working lives.

Breaking away and moving a comfortable distance from poverty seems to require a perfect lineup of favorable conditions. A set of skills, a good starting wage, and a job with the likelihood of promotion are prerequisites. But so are clarity of purpose, courageous self-esteem, a lack of substantial debt, the freedom from illness or addiction, a functional family, a network of upstanding friends, and the right help from private or governmental agencies. Any gap in that array is an entry point for trouble, because being poor means being unprotected. You might as well try playing quarterback with no helmet, no padding, no training, and no experience, behind a line of hundred-pound weaklings. With no cushion of money, no training in the ways of the wider world, and too little defense against the threats and temptations of decaying communities, a poor man or woman gets sacked again and again—buffeted and bruised and defeated. When an exception breaks this cycle of failure, it is called the fulfillment of the American Dream.

As a culture, the United States is not quite sure about the causes of poverty, and is therefore uncertain about the solutions. The American Myth still supposes that any individual from the humblest origins can climb to well-being. We wish that to be true, and we delight in examples that make it seem so, whether fictional or real. The name of Horatio Alger, the nineteenth-century writer we no longer read, is embedded in our language as a synonym for the rise from rags to riches that his characters achieve through virtuous hard work. The classic immigrant story still stirs the American heart, despite the country's longstanding aversion to the arrival of "the wretched refuse" at "the golden door," in the words etched on the Statue of Liberty. Even while resenting the influx of immigrants, we revel in the nobility of tireless labor and scrupulous thrift that can transform a destitute refugee into a successful entrepreneur. George W. Bush gave voice to the myth when he was asked whether he meant to send a message with the inclusion of two blacks, a Hispanic, and two women in the first senior appointments to his incoming administration. "You bet," the president-elect replied: "that people who work hard and make the right decisions in life can achieve anything they want in America."

The myth has its value. It sets a demanding standard, both for the nation and for every resident. The nation has to strive to make itself the fabled land of opportunity; the resident must strive to use that opportunity. The ideal has inspired a Civil Rights Movement, a War on Poverty, and a continuing search for ways to ease the distress that persists in the midst of plenty.

But the American Myth also provides a means of laying blame. In the Puritan legacy, hard work is not merely practical but also moral; its absence suggests an ethical lapse. A harsh logic dictates a hard judgment: If a person's diligent work leads to prosperity, if work is a moral virtue, and if anyone in the society can attain prosperity through work, then the failure to do so is a fall from righteousness. The marketplace is the fair and final judge; a low wage is somehow the worker's fault, for it simply reflects the low value of his labor. In the American atmosphere, poverty has always carried a whiff of sinfulness. Thus, when Judy Woodruff of CNN moderated a debate among Republican presidential candidates in March 2000, she asked Alan Keyes why he thought morality was worsening when certain indicators of morality were improving: Crime was down, out-of-wedlock births were down, and welfare was down, she noted. Evidently, welfare was an index of immorality.

There is an opposite extreme, the American Anti-Myth, which holds the society largely responsible for the individual's poverty. The hierarchy of racial discrimination and economic power creates a syndrome of impoverished communities with bad schools and closed options. The children of the poor are funneled into delinquency, drugs, or jobs with meager pay and little future. The individual is a victim of great forces beyond his control, including profit-hungry corporations that exploit his labor.

In 1962, Michael Harrington's eloquent articulation of the Anti-Myth in his book *The Other America* heightened awareness; to a nation blinded by affluence at the time, the portrait of a vast "invisible land" of the poor came as a staggering revelation. It helped generate Lyndon B. Johnson's War on Poverty. But Johnson's war never truly mobilized the country, nor was it ever fought to victory.

Forty years later, after all our economic achievements, the gap between rich and poor has only widened, with a median net worth of $833,600 among the top 10 percent and just $7,900 for the bottom 20 percent. Life expectancy in the United States is lower, and infant mortality higher, than in

Japan, Hong Kong, Israel, Canada, and all the major nations of Western Europe. Yet after all that has been written, discussed, and left unresolved, it is harder to surprise and shock and outrage. So it is harder to generate action.

In reality, people do not fit easily into myths or anti-myths, of course. The working individuals in this book are neither helpless nor omnipotent, but stand on various points along the spectrum between the polar opposites of personal and societal responsibility. Each person's life is the mixed product of bad choices and bad fortune, of roads not taken and roads cut off by the accident of birth or circumstance. It is difficult to find someone whose poverty is not somehow related to his or her unwise behavior—to drop out of school, to have a baby out of wedlock, to do drugs, to be chronically late to work. And it is difficult to find behavior that is not somehow related to the inherited conditions of being poorly parented, poorly educated, poorly housed in neighborhoods from which no distant horizon of possibility can be seen.

How to define the individual's role in her own poverty is a question that has shaped the debate about welfare and other social policies, but it can rarely be answered with certainty, even in a specific case. The poor have less control than the affluent over their private decisions, less insulation from the cold machinery of government, less agility to navigate around the pitfalls of a frenetic world driven by technology and competition. Their personal mistakes have larger consequences, and their personal achievements yield smaller returns. The interaction between the personal and the public is so intricate that for assistance such as job training to make a difference, for example, it has to be tailored to each individual's needs, which include not only such "hard skills" as using a computer or running a lathe, but also "soft skills" such as interacting with peers, following orders willingly, and managing the deep anger that may have developed during years of adversity. Job trainers are discovering that people who have repeatedly failed—in school, in love, in work—cannot succeed until they learn that they are capable of success. To get out of poverty, they have to acquire dexterity with their emotions as well as their hands.

An exit from poverty is not like showing your passport and crossing a frontier. There is a broad strip of contested territory between destitution and comfort, and the passage is not the same distance for everyone. "Comfortable is when I can pay my rent with one paycheck—I don't have to save for two weeks to pay one months rent," said Tyrone Pixley, a slender man of fifty in Washington, D.C. He was especially undemanding, having emerged from a tough life as a day laborer and a heroin user. "I don't want to have to scuffle," he said simply. "I want to be able to live comfortable, even if it's in a ten-by-ten room. And in the course of a month I can pay all my bills out of my pay. I don't have to have anything saved. For me to be comfortable, I don't have to have a savings account."

In such a rich country, most people have more appetite than Tyrone Pixley. Surrounded by constant advertising from television sets that are almost always turned on, many Americans acquire wants that turn into needs. "You're living in the projects, your mom's on welfare, so if you got six kids or five or seven, eight kids growing up, you be wantin' things all your life, and you can't have," explained Frank Dickerson, a janitor who dealt drugs in Washington to get things he didn't have. "You got kids want to have the nice tennis shoes, the jackets; they can't get that with a mom with six, seven kids on welfare. How they gonna get it? They may be getting older, growing up, they want to have nice stuff, so the only way to get that is turn to drugs. That's right. You go out there, you deal, and you get the things that you need. Car, apartments, clothes." Frank Dickerson spent three years in prison, but he and his wife also bought a house in the Maryland suburbs with the money he made from drugs.

Poverty, then, does not lend itself to easy definition. It may be absolute—an inability to buy basic necessities. It may be relative—an inability to buy the lifestyle that prevails at a certain time and place. It can be measured by a universal yardstick or by an index of disparity. Even dictionaries cannot agree. "Want or scarcity of means of subsistence," one says categorically. "Lack of the means of providing material needs *or comforts,*" says another. "The state of one who lacks *a usual or socially acceptable* amount of money or material possessions," says a third (emphases added).

By global or historical standards, much of what Americans consider poverty is luxury. A rural Russian is not considered poor if he cannot afford a car and his home has no central heating; a rural American is. A Vietnamese farmer is not seen as poor because he plows with water buffalo, irrigates by hand, and lives in a thatched house; a North Carolina farmworker is, because he picks cucumbers by hand, gets paid a dollar a box, and lives in a run-down trailer. Most impoverished people in the world would be dazzled by the apartments, telephones, television sets, running water, clothing, and other amenities that surround the poor in America. But that does not mean that the poor are not poor, or that those on the edge of poverty are not truly on the edge of a cliff.

"The American poor are not poor in Hong Kong or in the sixteenth century; they are poor here and now, in the United States," Michael Harrington wrote before Hong Kong's prosperity soared. "They are dispossessed in terms of what the rest of the nation enjoys, in terms of what the society could provide if it had the will. They live on the fringe, the margin. They watch the movies and read the magazines of affluent America, and these tell them that they are internal exiles. . . . To have one bowl of rice in a society where all other people have half a bowl may well be a sign of achievement and intelligence; it may spur a person to act and to fulfill his human potential. To have five bowls of rice in a society where the majority have a decent, balanced diet is a tragedy."

Indeed, being poor in a rich country may be more difficult to endure than being poor in a poor country, for the skills of surviving in poverty have largely been lost in America. Visit a slum in Hanoi and you will find children inventing games with bottles and sticks and the rusty rims of bicycle wheels. Go to a slum in Los Angeles and you will find children dependent on plastic toys and video games. Living in Cambodia, my son Michael marveled at the ingenuity bred by necessity, the capacity to repair what would be thrown away at home; when his television remote stopped working in Phnom Penh, he got it fixed at the corner for a dollar.

In the United States, the federal government defines poverty very simply: an annual income, for a family with one adult and three children, of less than $18,392 in the year 2003. That works out to $8.89 an hour, or S3.74 above the federal minimum wage, assuming that someone can get a full forty hours of work a week for all fifty-two weeks of the year, or 2,080 working hours annually. With incomes rising through the economic expansion of the 1990s, the incidence of official poverty declined, beginning the new decade at 11.3 percent of the population, down from 15.1 percent in 1993. Then it rose slightly in the ensuing recession, to 12.1 percent by 2002.

But the figures are misleading. The federal poverty line cuts far below the amount needed for a decent living, because the Census Bureau still uses the basic formula designed in 1964 by the Social Security Administration, with four modest revisions in subsequent years. That sets the poverty level at approximately three times the cost of a "thrifty food basket." The calculation was derived from spending patterns in 1955, when the average family used about one-third of its income for food. It is no longer valid today, when the average family spends only about one-sixth of its budget for food, but the government continues to multiply the cost of a "thrifty food basket" by three, adjusting for inflation only and overlooking nearly half a century of dramatically changing lifestyles.

The result burnishes reality by underestimating the numbers whose lives can reasonably be considered impoverished. More accurate formulas, being tested by the Census Bureau and the National Academy of Sciences, would rely on actual costs of food, clothing, shelter, utilities, and the like. Under those calculations, income would include benefits not currently counted, such as food stamps, subsidized housing, fuel assistance, and school lunches; living costs would include expenditures now ignored, such as child care, doctor's bills, health insurance premiums, and Social Security payroll taxes. When the various formulas were run in 1998, they increased by about three percentage points the proportion of the population in poverty, from the official 34.5 million to a high of 42.4 million people. A later variation raised the poverty rate in 2001 by 0.6 percent. Such a change would presumably make more families eligible for benefits that are linked to the poverty level; some programs, including children's health insurance, already cover households with incomes up to 150 or 200 percent of the poverty threshold, depending on the state.

Even if revised methods of figuring poverty were adopted, however, they would provide only a still photograph of a family's momentary situation. In that snapshot, the ebb and flow of the moving picture is lost. By measuring only income and expenses during a current year and not assets and debts, the formulas ignore the past, and the past is frequently an overwhelming burden on the present. Plenty of people have moved into jobs that put them above the threshold of poverty, only to discover that their student loans, their car payments, and the exorbitant interest charged on old credit card balances consume so much of their cash that they live no better than before.

When the poor or the nearly poor are asked to define poverty, however, they talk not only about what's in the wallet but what's in the mind or the heart. "Hopelessness," said a fifteen-year-old girl in New Hampshire.

"Not hopelessness—helplessness," said a man in Los Angeles. "Why should I get up? Nobody's gonna ever hire me because look at the way I'm dressed, and look at the fact that I never finished high school, look at the fact that I'm black, I'm brown, I'm yellow, or I grew up in the trailer."

"The state of mind," said a man in Washington, D.C. "I believe that spirituality is way more important than physical."

"I am so rich," said a woman whose new job running Xerox machines was lifting her out of poverty, "because—not only material things—because I know who I am, I know where I'm going now."

Another woman, who fell into poverty after growing up middle class, celebrated her "cultural capital," which meant her love of books, music, ideas, and her close relationships with her children. "In some senses, we are not at all poor; we have a great richness," she said. "We don't feel very poor. We feel poor when we can't go to the doctor or fix the car."

For practically every family, then, the ingredients of poverty are part financial and part psychological, part personal and part societal, part past and part present. Every problem magnifies the impact of the others, and all are so tightly interlocked that one reversal can produce a chain reaction with results far distant from the original cause. A run-down apartment can exacerbate a child's asthma, which leads to a call for an ambulance, which generates a medical bill that cannot be paid, which ruins a credit record, which hikes the interest rate on an auto loan, which forces the purchase of an unreliable used car, which jeopardizes a mother's punctuality at work, which limits her promotions and earning capacity, which confines her to poor housing. You will meet such a woman in Chapter One. If she or any other impoverished working parent added up all of her individual problems, the whole would be equal to more than the sum of its parts.

Consequently, most issues confronting the working poor are laced into most chapters of this book, even while each chapter throws a spotlight on one or another element of deprivation. In the chapter on work you will find stories of parenting; in the discussion of health you will see the matter of housing. Isolating the individual problems, as a laboratory would extract specific toxins, would be artificial and pointless. They exist largely because of one another, and the chemical reaction among them worsens the overall effect.

If problems are interlocking, then so must solutions be. A job alone is not enough. Medical insurance alone is not enough. Good housing alone is not enough. Reliable transportation, careful family budgeting, effective parenting, effective schooling are not enough when each is achieved in isolation from the rest. There is no single variable that can be altered to help working people move away from the edge of poverty. Only where the full array of factors is attacked can America fulfill its promise.

The first step is to see the problems, and the first problem is the failure to see the people. Those who work but live impoverished lives blend into familiar landscapes and are therefore overlooked. They make up the invisible, silent America that analysts casually ignore. "We all live in the suburbs now, not in the inner cities," proclaimed Professor Michael Goldstein of the University of Colorado, explaining on PBS why Woolworth's had been replaced by Wal-Mart in the Dow Jones Industrial Average.

Tim Brookes, a commentator on National Public Radio, once did a witty screed against overpriced popcorn in movie theaters. Indignant at having been charged $5 for a small bag, he conducted research on the actual expenses. He calculated that the 5¼ ounces of popcorn he received cost 23.71875 cents in a supermarket but only 16.5 cents at prices theater managers paid for fifty-pound sacks. He generously figured 5 cents in electricity to cook the popcorn and 1 cent for the bag. Total cost: 22.5 cents. Subtracting sales tax, that left a profit of $4.075, or 1,811 percent.

Evidently, the theater had the remarkable sense not to hire any workers, for Brookes gave no hint of having noticed any people behind the counter. Their paltry wages, which wouldn't have undermined the excessive profits, were absent from his calculation. The folks who popped the corn, filled the bag, handed the bag to him, and took his money must have been shrouded in an invisibility cloak. No NPR editor seemed to notice.

I hope that this book will help them to be seen.

Money and Its Opposite

You know, Mom, being poor is very expensive.
—Sandy Brash, at age twelve

Tax time in poor neighborhoods is not April. It is January. And "income tax" isn't what you pay; it's what you receive. As soon as the W-2s arrive, working folks eager for their checks from the Internal Revenue Service hurry to the tax preparers, who have flourished and gouged impoverished laborers since the welfare time limits enacted by Congress in 1996. The checks that come from Washington include not only a refund of taxes withheld, but an additional payment known as the Earned Income Tax Credit, which is designed to subsidize low-wage working families. The refunds and subsidies are sometimes banked for savings toward a car, a house, an education; but they are often needed immediately for overdue bills and large purchases that can't be funded from the trickle of wages throughout the year.

Christie, a child-care worker in Akron, earned too little to owe taxes but got $1,700 as an Earned Income Credit one year, which enabled her to avoid the Salvation Army's used-furniture store and instead buy a new matching set of comfortable black couches and loveseats for her living room in public housing.

Caroline Payne's check went for a down payment on her house in New Hampshire. "I used my income tax and paid a thousand down," she said proudly. When she sold it five and a half years later and her daughter lent her money to rent a truck for her move, she planned to pay her back "when I get my taxes."

"I'm waitin' for my income tax to come in so I can pay my real estate taxes," said Tom King, a single father and lumberjack who lived in a trailer on his own land.

Debra Hall, who had started at a Cleveland bakery, was keen with anticipation after filing her first tax return. "I'll get $3,079 back! What am I gonna do with it? Pay all my bills off," she declared, "and I haven't had anything new in the house. Do some good with it, that's for sure. Minor repairs on my car. The bills are first, for my credit [rating], to get all my back debts paid. It will be well spent."

The Earned Income Tax Credit is one of those rare anti-poverty programs that appeal both to liberals and conservatives, invoking the virtue of both government help and self-help. You don't get it unless you have some earned income, and since its payments are linked to your tax return, you don't get it unless you file one. That leaves out low-wage workers—especially undocumented immigrants—who get paid under the table in cash and think they're better off avoiding the IRS. By filing, however, they would end up ahead, because they'd get to keep everything they earned and would receive a payment on top of that. The benefits kick in at fairly high levels—at earnings of less than $33,178, for example, for a worker who supported more than one child in 2002. At the lower income levels, the Earned Income Tax Credit can add the equivalent of a dollar or two an hour to a worker's wage.

Enacted in 1975, the program was expanded under Presidents Reagan, Bush, and Clinton, and in 2002 paid more than $32 billion to 19 million households. Treasury officials worry about erroneous claims, honest or fraudulent, which may rise to 27 to 32 percent of the total. On the other hand, an estimated 10 to 15 percent of those eligible don't file for it, partly because employers and unions often don't tell workers that it exists. The presidents of two local unions in Washington, D.C., for example, one representing janitors and the other parking garage attendants, had never heard of the Earned Income Tax Credit until I mentioned it to them. And I have not yet come across a single worker or boss who knew that with a simple form called a W-5, filed with the employer, a low-wage employee could get some of the payments in advance during the year. When I mentioned the W-5 to Debra Hall and she then asked at her bakery, the woman who handled the payroll waved her away impatiently and said she knew nothing about it. Later, the tax preparer told Debra it was better just to wait and get the payment in one lump sum after she filed her return.

It sure is better—if you're the preparer. With cunning creativity, the preparers have devised schemes to separate low-wage workers from as much of their refunds and Earned Income Credits as feasible. The marvel of electronic filing, the speedy direct deposit into a bank account, the high-interest loan masquerading as a "rapid refund" all promise a sudden flush of dollars to cash-starved families. The trouble is, getting money costs money.

The preparers operate from sleazy check-cashing joints and from street-level outposts of respectable corporations. They do for a hefty fee what their clients could do for themselves for free with the math skills and the courage to tackle a 1040, or with a computer and a bank account to speed filing and receipt. But most low-wage workers don't have the math, the courage, or the computer, and many don't even have the bank account. They are so desperate for the check that they give up a precious $100 or so to get everything done quickly and correctly. "You get so scared," said Debra Hall, who paid $95 to have her simple return done after ending twenty-one years of welfare. "I don't know why it's so scary, but I'd rather have it done right the first time."

She was probably wise, because another disadvantage of being poor is that you've been more likely since 1999 to face an audit by the IRS. In that year, 1.36 percent of the returns flied by taxpayers making under $25,000 were audited, compared with 1.15 percent of those making $100,000 or more. The scrutiny was instigated by Republican congressional leaders who feared abuses of the Earned Income Tax Credit. In the face of bad publicity, the IRS shifted the balance in 2000 by auditing 0.6 percent of those under $25,000 versus 1.0 percent of those over $100,000. Thereafter, the audit rate tilted back and forth, to .86 and .69 percent, respectively, in 2001, then to .64 and .75 in 2002. In other words, as the IRS lost enforcement personnel, it dramatically reduced its scrutiny of well-to-do taxpayers, whose returns were once audited at the rate of 10 percent. This despite the fact that audits at the upper levels of income naturally tend to recover more dollars in lost revenue.

Evon Johnson never dared do another return herself after the IRS charged her $2,072 in taxes, penalties, and interest. Newly arrived from Honduras, she was working from 5 a.m. for a cleaning service in Boston that never withheld taxes and never sent her a W-2. She didn't know they were supposed to do either. "I did my taxes, I fill it out, fine," she said. But not so fine, evidently. "Three years after or four years after, IRS contact me saying that I owe them . . . like, $1,072. 'Why do I owe you?' And they say: because I didn't declare my taxes. I say I did. . . . They say no. . . . I sent them a letter saying I was sending them $1,072 I think it was, 'cause I didn't have no money at the time, and I was going to make small installments for the rest of the money. . . . You know what they did? I had a bank account, and they took the money from my bank account—every penny I had." Ever since, she has happily paid $100 a year to a tax preparer, $100 a year for peace of mind. "I don't want the IRS back on me," she explained. "He do it and he sign it and put everything, so if any mistake, he gonna be the one who will have to deal with them."

By the end of February, H&R Block's storefront office on a dismal stretch of Washington's 14th Street looked like a well-used campaign headquarters a week after Election Day. Most computer screens were dark, and the place was quiet and cavernous. All the desks were empty but one, occupied by Claudia Rivera, who used to prepare returns without charge at a library in Virginia. She and the manager, Carl Caton, didn't have much to do now that the rush had passed, so they were happy to sit at a keyboard and explain.

Each form the taxpayer needed carried a fee: $41 for a 1040, $10 for an EIC (the Earned Income Credit), $1 for each W-2, and so on. Electronic filing cost another $25. So a simple return with two W-2s filed electronically would run $78. But it didn't stop there. Block had a smorgasbord of services for people who lived on the edge. If you had no bank account, your refund could be loaded onto an ATM card that charged $2 per withdrawal. Or a temporary account could be opened into which the IRS payment could be deposited for a fee of $24.95. If you were enticed by Block's offer of a "rapid refund" and wanted a check in a day or two, you paid H&R Block an additional $50 to $90, depending on the amount you were getting. The fee on 14th Street could be as much as $50 on a $200 refund, up to $90 for $2,000 or more.

This was actually a loan, and for a very short time. Filing electronically usually gets you a check in two and a half weeks, according to the IRS, and five days sooner if it's deposited directly into a bank account. At the most, then, the "rapid refund" loan, issued a day or two after filing, would run about fifteen days, which made the $90 fee on a $2,000 payment equivalent to an annual interest rate of 108 percent. At the least, the loan could run as little as four days, propelling the annualized rate to 410 percent on $2,000, and 2,281 percent on $200. (The highest percentage is incurred if the timing occurs perfectly: the return is filed by the IRS's weekly deadline of noon Thursday, the loan check is not issued until after banks close Friday, the taxpayer can't put it into his account until Monday, and the IRS is fast enough to deposit the refund directly with the lending bank the following Friday.)

After a spate of lawsuits, a federal judge in Norfolk ordered Block to stop using the misleading term "rapid refund" in advertising loans, but Block continued with the ads by redefining "rapid refund" as a reference to electronic filing only. The company called its loan program a "refund anticipation loan," a distinction lost on many of the low-wage workers who ventured into Block offices in search of a rapid refund. In 2000 such loans went to 4.8 million taxpayers.

Among all the working people I interviewed who used the loan service, not one understood the terms or the options. Hector and Maribel Delgado, who earned about $28,000 a year picking and packing vegetables in North

Carolina, were stunned when I sat with them in their trailer, looked over their tax return, and explained how it all worked. They had paid Block $109 to prepare their return, file it electronically, and give them an advance on their payment from the IRS of $1,307.05. The form they had signed disclosed a finance charge of 69.888 percent annually, but they had not understood it. Even as Block employees presented a contract in fine print, they were trained to avoid the word "loan," and say "two-day refunds" instead, a Maryland judge found in hearing a lawsuit on the lending practices. And the refund loans were lucrative enough to provide 8 percent of Block's entire profits in 1999, mainly because a Block subsidiary owned a 49.99 percent interest in the loans, made by Household Bank.

Something else illicit happened to the Delgados in the Block offices. Although they filed electronically in January, a time when the IRS promises checks within a couple of weeks, "We were told we'd have to wait six to eight weeks," Maribel said. This was patently false. "We needed the money to pay bills," she explained. "We send one part to Mexico, another part to here. We usually send $100 every two weeks to Mexico. We have a big family."

In 2000, after facing a decade of class-action lawsuits alleging misleading lending practices, H&R Block agreed to a $25 million settlement without admitting any wrongdoing. The only practice the company changed was to present the federally required truth-in-lending disclosures earlier in the process, according to a spokeswoman. Do employees at least explain the terms verbally? "A lot of it depends on questions customers ask," she said. "If they ask questions, preparers are supposed to answer." Many customers simply do not know what questions to ask.

Poverty is like a bleeding wound. It weakens the defenses. It lowers resistance. It attracts predators. The loan sharks operate not only from bars and street corners, but also legally from behind bulletproof glass. Their beckoning signs are posted at some 10,000 locations across the country: "Payday Loans," "Quick Cash," "Easy Money." You see them in check-cashing joints and storefront offices in poor and working-class neighborhoods. They have organized themselves into at least a dozen national chains, and they charge fees equivalent to more than 500 percent annualized interest.

They also provide a much needed service. Say you're short of cash, and the bills are piling up, along with some disconnection notices. Payday is two weeks away, and your phone and electricity will be shut off before then. The guy at the local convenience store, who has a booth for cashing checks, throws you a lifeline. If you need $100 now, you write him a check for $120, postdated by two weeks. He'll give you the $100 in cash today, hold your check until your wages are in your bank account, and then put the check through. Or you can give him the $120 in cash when you get it, and he'll return your check. Either way, 20 percent interest for two weeks equals 1.428 percent a day, or 521 percent annually.

If you're still stuck after payday, if your paycheck doesn't quite cover your needs, or if your check for $120 bounces, no problem. The guy behind the bulletproof glass will gladly roll over your loan—for another $20. This pattern prevails in Illinois, for example, where state examiners found that rollovers made up 77 percent of all payday loan transactions. The average customer had ten such renewals, which meant paying fees totaling up to twice the amount borrowed. Eventually, you may have to borrow from another payday loan merchant to pay the fees at the first. And so on and on and on.

Furthermore, the loans are not technically loans in some states, because there's a check. And if a check bounces, more severe penalties apply than those for unrepaid loans. Borrowing $300, for instance, an Indiana woman paid a $30 fee and wrote a check for $330. When the check bounced, her bank and the payday loan establishment charged $80 in fees. Then the lender took her to court, won triple damages of $990, lawyer's fees of $150, and $60 in court costs. The total charge on the $300 loan: $1,310.

Con artists have also enticed the working poor with false promises of outright grants from foundations; all people have to do, the mailings promise, is pay $19.95 to $49.95 for a list of foundation names and addresses, then write heart-rending letters. "There are literally hundreds of private foundations that are anxious to donate money by mail to people who have genuine reasons for needing the money," says one solicitation. "Many foundations are not concerned with what you wish to use the money for as long as it is something legal . . . to pay off bills, go on vacation, meet emergency need or to buy anything that you might need." This absurd assertion has swamped foundations large and small with desperate pleas for cash to repair houses, pay medical bills, and pay off debt. In 2001 an Ohio judge sentenced one operator to five years in prison for bilking people out of at least $500,000 this way. A New Jersey man was raking in $30,000 a week, a prosecutor charged.

Another marvelous setting for scams is the workplace. Korean restaurants in Los Angeles have come under scrutiny for their inventive ways of swindling waiters and cooks, almost all of whom are Korean or Latino, said Roy Hong, head of Korean Immigrant Workers Advocate. Many are paid a flat monthly wage, which is customary in South Korea, and have to work up to twelve hours a day, six days a week, violating state wage laws. Unlike the federal minimum wage of $5.15 an hour, California's minimum of $6.75 applies to waiters, so many restaurateurs cook the books by faking time cards to show employees working shorter shifts.

Some restaurants also file W-2s that exaggerate the amount of tips paid to workers, a way of transferring part of the tax burden from the business to the employee. When a customer puts a $20 meal on a credit card and adds a $2 tip, for example, the owner pays the worker the $2 tip but tells the IRS that $3 went for the tip and $19 for the meal. (Businesses, as well as individuals, get audited more frequently when their incomes are under $25,000.)

In campaigning for Korean workers, the association has uncovered a pernicious scheme in the custodial business. Korean mom-and-pop janitorial contractors in Los Angeles offer their newly arrived compatriots a tempting deal. Eager for jobs, devoid of English, and frightened that their illegal status may be discovered, the recent immigrants are enticed by the proposition that they can become subcontractors making $1,000 or more a month cleaning commercial buildings where dentists and doctors, lawyers and executives keep their offices. All they have to do, the contractor explains, is put up two and a half months' wages as a contracting fee.

Many Koreans come to the United States with extensive family ties for pooling money and cushioning financial hardship. So the up-front funds can usually be scraped together. "They give away the last bit of their savings in the hope that they too can start a janitorial company," Roy Hong noted. The immigrants usually work at night, cleaning the offices, and everything goes along nicely for a few months. But then the contractor may delay a wage, saying he hasn't yet been paid by the building management. "The next thing you know, you're owed several thousand dollars, and you wonder what happened," Roy explained. Finally, "three or four months later," he said, "the contractor shows up. 'You're out of here. Give me the key.'

" 'What did I do?'

" 'There's been too many complaints.' "

And the next "subcontractor" is offered a tempting deal, if he'll just put up two and a half months' wages.

Behind respectable facades, some major institutions also have their way with the poor. Few banks want depositors who keep low balances, so in states where no laws require otherwise, banks set high minimums and charge prohibitive fees. Many impoverished neighborhoods have no branches at all. This forces low-income families into the expensive check-cashing services, whose outlets have multiplied across the country.

Even where state law requires "lifeline" accounts for the poor, they are rarely advertised because banks tend to lose money on them. Branch officers often don't know about them, and most potential depositors don't either. The best-kept financial secret in New York is the state requirement that banks offer accounts with a $25 minimum opening deposit, a one-cent minimum balance, and eight free withdrawals a month for a $3 monthly fee. Most depositors are kept ignorant of such terms, and major banks report few people opening those accounts.

One reason may be that many workers prefer to earn under the table and keep their finances unrecorded. Others may believe folklore they've heard about unscrupulous banks. "We have our little methods of stashing stuff," said Wendy Waxler, a single mother who had just moved off welfare to a job. "What I plan on doing is getting a safe. It won't draw interest. But at the same time, if the bank go bankrupt, I still have money! You know, I know how they do that money exchange with the bank. It's your money but it's being bought by somebody. It's some kind of system they go through, so when you get there and you say I want all my money, you can't get it right away, you have to wait a certain amount of days so they can get it back. That's what I was told. It's some kind of money something exchange of hands."

Wendy was wrong about the waiting period, but her suspicions were understandable. At the confluence of private industry and government, American society devises numerous techniques of separating the working poor from their meager cash. State lotteries do a booming business at the corner stores in poor parts of town as people pray for the right number to come up and deliver them from hardship. Businesses large and small practice American consumer culture's universal deception: the sweet-sounding come-on that doesn't quite resemble the fine print. Everything is strictly legal; it's just that you have to listen and read carefully before signing, and you have to be a little savvy about the ways of the commercial world. In Debra Hall's case, the enticement was a cellular phone that she got for her daughter, who was in her early twenties. It seemed ridiculously cheap. "It was easy to get," she recalled. "I didn't have the credit, and they still gave it to me. The contract, she just filled it out and I signed it. I didn't take time to read it. . . . The lady made it sound so good. It was gonna be $9 a month. That turned out to be a tale." Debra had somehow missed a digit. "It was $89 a month. I got tricked into a three-year contract. They give you like two thousand minutes. My calls over the weekend were supposed to be free. They weren't. It ended up costing me. I done made two payments toward them. They called me, threatened to take me to court, but they accepted I made two payments. I told the man I feel like I got ripped off."

By contrast, Ann Brash did read her contract when she took over a lease on a Jeep Cherokee. She knew the terms were unfavorable, but she felt forced into an unwanted choice. Ten years earlier, a divorce had plunged her and her two children into poverty and temporary homelessness. Child support payments plus a pittance as a freelance copy editor brought her about $10,000 a year until she landed a full-time editing job at $23,000. She simply needed a reliable vehicle to get to work through the snows of New Hampshire.

"I have a Toyota," she said. "Something's wrong with the starter, and one front panel in the door is pretty lacy with rust. I don't think it's going to pass inspection. . . . Something's wrong with the front end at the moment. I know the brakes need to be redone." She had no savings, no credit, no money to make the repairs. Her teenage children, Sandy and Sally, offered to give up their driver's licenses for a year to cut the insurance premium, hoping that she could replace the car with the money saved.

Then, "a car fell into my lap," she said. "A nice young man in Plainfield wouldn't continue leasing his Jeep. He got married and had too many expenses. He had put quite a bit down on it, and I think there were fifteen months left on the lease, and the [car dealership's] chief person called me and said, 'Would you like to take over his lease for him? It won't require any down payment or anything like that.' So that's what I've done. Did it last week. Seems a little silly to be driving this gas-guzzling huge yuppie car."

The lease ran $293 a month, which was barely manageable for her, and at the end of the lease loomed a crisis. If she wanted to keep the car, she would have to come up with $17,000; if not, she'd have to pay 15 cents a mile over the 36,000 she was allotted, or $2,500 for the nearly 53,000 miles on the odometer. "So, because I hadn't $2,500 to pull out of my pocket, I needed to buy the thing," she said. "My credit is awful." Having defaulted on $18,000 in student loans and $12,000 in credit card debt, she could get a car loan only by enlisting a couple from her church as co-signers. Even at that, the interest rate would have been 24 percent; it dropped to 19 when the man agreed to put his name first as the owner. Payments were $394.45 a month, and they would last until the Cherokee was likely to collapse into a heap of junk.

High interest may be the most ubiquitous trap for low-wage workers. Married, Ann was in the middle class, with all the perks of easy credit. Divorced, she sank rapidly, and for a while, the only barriers between her and utter destitution were four thin pieces of plastic: one from Discover, another from Citibank, and two from Sears. As the balances ran up, she restricted the use of her cards to essentials such as car repairs or purchases that she could justify as contributions to her children's physical health and intellectual well-being: a set of cross-country skis, a computer for Sandy, who later won full financial aid at Dartmouth. "Credit cards went for things like a bicycle," she insisted, "not for potato chips or little Barbie dolls, but things like books, for things that would make them larger and their lives larger, that would contribute to their growing."

The current moment always chafed against the uncertain future. "Christmas was always huge in gift giving," she confessed, "because I thought there may not be a next year."

"Each year you said we can't do it again," added Sandy as he stared at his laptop in the living room.

Ann's relatives were critical of her. "If we decided to splurge and get a box of raspberries in the middle of the winter, that would be just unforgivable, because we didn't have the means to do that," she said. "We shouldn't have those kinds of choices. And I often hear people say, 'Well, look at them, I think they're on welfare. They have food stamps. What are they doing with a television?' I know from the everyday grind of not knowing what's going to happen next that people need some way to relieve that pressure and that pain—and it is pain. Some of us can do it in healthy ways, like putting cross-country skis on a credit card—and that's not very responsible, but it's pretty healthy." She laughed, but not merrily.

The real price was reflected in those bills with the snowballing balances. Since her credit rating was not exactly AAA, she was being charged up to 23.999 percent interest. What's more, while she was faithfully paying the finance charge and minimum almost every month, she did not always get her salary in time to meet the deadline; as a result, she gradually realized, the card companies were adding late fees to her principal, then charging the exorbitant interest on that ever-growing principal. Long after she stopped using the cards, the balance continued to rise.

This has become a chronic problem across the country as lenders search credit records for minor delinquencies to label them "subprime." If you're in that category you get charged higher fees and interest, but you may not know it, because few states require lenders to reveal the score that determines a consumer's credit rating, even when the borrower sees his credit report. The score, running from a low of 375 to a high of 900, is based on five factors: punctuality of payment, the amount of debt, how long credit has been used (the longer the better), how much new credit has been requested (the less the better), and whether the borrower uses a mixture of credit (mortgages and auto loans are preferred over credit cards). Often, the lenders get the facts wrong, of course, and it's to their advantage. Subprime lending grew from about $37 billion to $370 billion from 1994 to 1999, with major banks among the culprits, according to *Consumer Reports*. In the 1990s, the magazine reported, lenders "relaxed the old standards of sound lending by luring consumers into debt waters well over their head, but they didn't relax the old strict standards of loan repayment. The result: Easy-money lenders point fingers at the subprime class they helped create, then punish those borrowers with significantly higher interest rates and fees. College students—and now even 16-year-olds—are a new target for subprime lenders."

Sandy Brash, an Ivy League student with no money at all, "gets an offer a day, at least," said his mother. Because of the aggressive soliciting and the easy credit, even teenagers were declaring bankruptcy, a financial counselor told Ann. She found the notion of bankruptcy abhorrent. She sat one day at the dining room table in her shabby, $400-a-month apartment, her head in her hands, compiling the modest figures for her tax return and tracking her expenses. On a pad of white lined paper, she had written lists of numbers, none of them very large. "I don't know," she said. "I don't even feel like trying; I feel that hopeless. There's no way out of this." Many people get out by declaring bankruptcy, I said. "It sounds like taking welfare, and I don't want to do it," she retorted. "I just want to pay what I owe." Her voice rose onto a high note of anxious melancholy. "But I can't do it with these kinds of rates. I knew that it was gonna take me about an extra thousand dollars a year to get the kids by over those growing years, but I just couldn't find a way around it. And so I did it. And I knew I'd have to pay the piper. So. There it is."

In one respect, Ann was typical of the low-wage working people I spoke with across the country—in New Hampshire towns, North Carolina fields, and Los Angeles housing projects. They were white and black, Latino and Asian, native-born and newly arrived in America, and they were not gripped by rage. Ann did not point a finger of blame. She did not make sweeping criticisms of society at large. "I got myself into this, I made the choices," she said plainly. "In spite of the fact that the credit card companies are taking advantage of people, that they're really awful in charging such awful interest rates, I made the choice of using them. I haven't used them in a couple of years. And plus I can't answer the phone." She did not answer the phone because she hated to hear the bill collectors. "They have all kinds of tones of voices," she said. They left alarming messages on the answering machine, like, "Call this number immediately."

Always when she talked this way she then apologized for "complaining." But I was an instigator in her complaints, I suppose, for I kept asking questions. What does this feel like? What do you think about? How foreign does the zone along the edge of poverty seem to someone who grew up in middle-class comfort? "Nobody really wants to know that sometimes $2 is a significant amount, and $25 always is tremendous," she said, as if this condition still amazed her as well. "Tell me it's not true for ordinary, everyday people. Is it the same? I mean, normal life"—she gave a despairing laugh—"before life was like this. I can't remember. I can't remember what it was like. I mean, every day and every night when I'm trying to fall asleep, there's this worry hanging. Is the car gonna make it through because I haven't maintained it properly? How am I gonna get this? I know I have to do this. How am I gonna get it done? How am I gonna stretch to get these bills paid? If one extra thing happens—."

In May, three months before her car lease expired, her ex-husband's $100-a-week child support payments were scheduled to end because Sally would turn eighteen. It was a deadline of sorts, and Ann finally conceded that bankruptcy had to be considered. It went against her grain, but she couldn't make the numbers add up another way. She then discovered that she was too poor to declare bankruptcy; she would need $700 for the lawyer and $200 as a filing fee. She went to a financial counselor instead.

The counselor was accustomed to working with credit card companies to lower the interest rate to zero if the principal could be paid off in regular installments. But Ann turned out to be too poor for that option as well; looking at her low income, her expenses, and her complete lack of assets, the counselor told her that she would not be able to make the payments. So he advised her to stop paying her credit card bills, pay the rent and electricity first, save the money for bankruptcy, and file when she had enough. Gritting her teeth to "put the moral question aside," as she described it, she stopped paying the credit card bills in March, took sums out of her food money, saved for seven months, and finally in October had pulled together the $900 required to file. It was no cause for celebration. "I take home about $860 every two weeks," she explained. "One half of the biweekly check goes to rent, the other half to the car. Then there are utilities and transportation costs to get back and forth to work. I can't replace underwear. We're not having Christmas this year, though we will try to have a meal. I'm sorry, I don't mean to complain."

On the surface, it seems odd that an interest rate can be determined by the condition of an apartment, which in turn can generate illness and medical bills, which may then translate into a poor credit rating, which limits the quality of an automobile that can be purchased, which jeopardizes a worker's reliability in getting to work, which limits promotions and restricts the wage, which confines a family to the dilapidated apartment. Such are the interlocking deficits of poverty, one reinforcing the other until an entire structure of want has been built. Such was the prison of Lisa Brooks.

She was only twenty-four, but a blemish of weariness tainted her youthful face, and her blond hair was stringy with the carelessness of stress. She worked hard and well as a caretaker at a halfway house for mentally ill adults. She was good with them, kind and firm, but she was paid only $8.21 an hour, which put her and her four children a couple of thousand dollars a year below the federal poverty line.

She lived in a rough section of Newport, New Hampshire, in the kind of housing shown by recent studies to cause and exacerbate asthma in children. Lisa had never noticed any mold, mites, mouse droppings, or roaches, which have been linked to asthma. But she did notice that her nine-year-old son, Nicholas, got worse after they moved into a damp, drafty apartment in an old wooden house on Beech Street.

Nicholas, home with his blind grandmother, had sudden trouble breathing on two occasions. She called 911, and each time an ambulance whisked him to a hospital, once to Claremont and once to New London. In each emergency room, he was treated with oxygen and steroids. But the family's health insurance, for which Lisa paid $97 every two weeks, refused to cover the ambulance charges of $240 and $250, arguing that the doctor had never obtained the proper authorization. Lisa did not understand the insurance rules and procedures and did not know how to appeal. "I fought with the doctor's office and the insurance company," she complained, "and they still said no matter what, I had to pay for it."

She could not pay immediately or all at once, for she operated close to the edge of insolvency. So the charges went onto her credit report. When she tried to move to decent housing by applying for a loan to buy a mobile home, she was denied because her credit record showed the overdue ambulance bills. When she tried to buy a more reliable car, which she needed to get to work, she was also denied. So when her 1989 Dodge Caravan developed fatal electrical problems, she had no choice but to go to a used-car lot that didn't do credit checks but charged her 15.747 percent interest. She paid $5,800 for a 1995 Plymouth Neon that had 82,000 miles, a bad alternator, and other troubles that cost $100 to $200 a month to repair.

On the day Lisa told me about her high-interest loan, I happened to receive an unsolicited offer from my insurance company of an auto loan at 7.5 percent, less than half of her rate. I didn't need the loan, and that's why my rate was so low. In a free market economy, people are like corporations issuing bonds: the less secure they are financially, the more interest they have to pay when they borrow.

Poor people and investment bankers have one thing in common: They both expend considerable energy thinking about money. They have to juggle, predict, and plan, and every decision has magnitude. "If you are starving, you become interested in food. If you are struggling to pay the bills, money becomes tragically important," observed Sebastian Junger, who had the experience before his best-seller, *The Perfect Storm*, suddenly made him a millionaire. Many of those for whom money is tragically important make their choices with enormous care, scouring the papers for sales, clipping coupons, perusing secondhand stores with a canny eye for bargains. Others, however, allow their cash to hemorrhage, never knowing the benefits of saving because they have never had enough to save.

They are caught between America's hedonism and its dictum that the poor are supposed to sacrifice, suffer, and certainly not purchase any fun for themselves. So Ann Brash gets raised eyebrows when she buys raspberries, and many others come under criticism for such indulgences as cable TV. The monthly cable bills cause acid indigestion in some people who do anti-poverty work, and the harshest critics seem to be those who were once poor themselves.

If you sit with a group of dedicated men and women who are trying to help impoverished families, you often notice that one or two among them have apparently been licensed to pronounce stern judgment on their clients' profligate spending. Invariably, the faultfinders display their credentials: a childhood on welfare, an unwed pregnancy, an unhappy intimacy with the culture of hopelessness. Their previous poverty confers an authenticity that commands respect. Having found their way out of the quagmire, they cannot stand to see those left behind, who remind them of themselves, wasting their chance.

So it was that Nancy Szeto spoke up in a discussion at Valley Regional Hospital in Claremont, New Hampshire. Nancy was the streetwise case manager at Partners in Health, a clinic and medical program that served a poor white population abandoned by closing textile mills and shoe factories. She had grown up in the projects in South Holyoke, Massachusetts, and knew all the tricks of staying alive by selling food stamps, stealing off clotheslines, "shopping" by eating quickly off the shelves of supermarkets. She listened for a few minutes to her colleagues' polite analysis of medical problems and services, then cut through the niceties.

"If they're gonna get any money from the state, they should be forced to go through budget counseling," she declared. "I see so many people spending $150 on a phone bill, and all of them have $90 on a cable bill."

"And they all have call waiting," added a caseworker, her tongue loosened by Nancy's outburst.

The others chimed in with stories and complaints. The principal of an elementary school told of trying to call the home of a little girl who was sick only to discover that the phone had been disconnected. "The girl said, 'Yeah, we couldn't afford both the cable bill and the phone bill,' " the principal told the group. The others nodded knowingly.

"They don't have milk, but they do have cable," said Brenda St. Laurence, a home visitor in a program for young mothers at risk. Her clients seemed to love her sweet toughness, which they took as affection unlike anything they had ever received. Brenda applied her lessons from a working-class childhood of frugal self-help and self-denial, of her parents' pride in the hand-me-downs and the hand-sewn clothes and the refusal to take welfare or food stamps. Her formula for survival consisted of good choices and hard work. "We're imposing our values on their priority," she declared without apology. Her clients wouldn't buy health insurance because the expense seemed overwhelming, she complained, but they would buy $200 VCRs and television sets.

"It's instant gratification and an escape," one of her colleagues remarked.

Yes, and why not? some might ask. There are worse ways than television to escape, and why should the poor not share in that vast common ground created by American TV? It is worth remembering that not many decades ago, a welfare recipient wasn't allowed to have the unwarranted luxury of a telephone. The prohibition succumbed to the argument that a phone facilitated job searches, not to mention summoning help for a sick or injured child.

Many middle-class anti-poverty workers feel no right to dictate that the poor shall not purchase middle-class pleasures. It strikes some aid-givers as condescending across class and sometimes cultural and racial lines. The inhibition seems less common among the formerly poor who are now providing assistance, and who often cite good reasons to second-guess the spending habits of their clients—people who are fleeced by corporate and freelance rip-off artists and also fleece themselves by ill-conceived buying. Having seen recovering addicts and alcoholics squander money, for example, some drug and alcohol treatment programs require working residents of halfway houses to turn over their wages for deposit in escrow accounts.

Brenda couldn't make her young mothers do that, but she tried to guide them. "I make them write a list before going to the grocery store," she explained. It was a frustrating effort. "Money saved for bills goes for sodas, cigarettes. They all have pets."

By contrast, the families she admired were those often seen by the principal: working poor parents too proud to use the free lunches for which their children qualified. "They will pack a good, nutritious lunch for their kids," the principal said. "They won't send the Twinkies. They'll send a nice sandwich, a piece of fruit."

That kind of quiet good sense is always less memorable than excess, so the anecdotes around the table may or may not have been representative. The profligate were the ones who stood out to Nancy, who remembered a man requesting help to pay for prescription drugs. Pharmaceutical companies are willing to donate medicine that is nearly outdated, and she routinely worked overtime on the intricate paperwork needed to make the case in situations of particular need. But when she learned that this man had contracted to bring every available television channel into the comfort of his living room, she blew. "I said I'm not gonna waste any time working on his $40 medicine bill if he's gonna spend $90 a month on cable."

Nancy would have liked Leetha Butler, a grandmother who sat smoking in a cool breeze on the concrete patio behind her apartment. This was Benning Terrace, a poor, largely black section of Washington, D.C. Outside the recreation center, just after a July midnight not long before, her daughter Diane had been killed in a drive-by shooting, leaving Leetha with the three grandchildren, four, eight, and sixteen. The circumstance forced her to hone her expertise in saving money, and she was a font of unsolicited advice to her neighbors. If people were hired to run seminars on the subject, which they should be, Leetha would have been the most venerable professor.

Because she drew Social Security, she got less in welfare than her daughter had—$379 compared with $500 a month. Her daughter had received $400 in food stamps; Leetha got $180. She and her husband, now deceased, had worked as custodians, and then she cooked at the Paradise Restaurant. She had no pension.

"It's not tight with me, because I'm an old country woman who knows how to be economy," she declared out of syntax and puffed on her cigarette. Her résumé may have read country woman because she came from Mississippi forty years ago, but she had the cunning of a field commander who knew when to feint and advance and pull back as she played the needs and wishes of her grandchildren. "They don't want for nothin'," she said proudly. They were not allowed to go to the ice cream truck when it cruised temptingly through the neighborhood; it was cheaper to keep ice cream, cookies, candy, and soda at home. She watched for the sales, of course, and could recite the prices of ketchup and Coke in the Safeway, Giant, and Shoppers Warehouse. "I get the papers on a Wednesday and get me a pad and write them down. Coke is $1.89 a box. When they have it on sale for 69 cents, I buy two or three cases. Kmart has ketchup and mustard, 69 cents a bottle. The cheapest you can buy it at Safeway is $1.23." When roast beef was on sale, she bought a lot of it. "I dice it up and use it for stew beef. I dice it up and make pepper steak. When sales be, I buy in quantity. I don't have a car, but I gets around. I get on that iron horse—the bus." If she bought more than she could carry, she paid some fellow $5 to bring her home.

"I went to the thrift store Sunday, and I bought four sets of sheets with pillowcases, four mattress covers, eight coffee cups, and a single bed, and all of that come to $43 and something. My neighbor, she used to go to the store every day, and I said, 'You're just wasting money.' " Leetha Butler would tell anyone who would listen how to do it.

Anti-poverty workers often wish that schools would give required courses in responsible budgeting, but sometimes the opposite occurs. A school in Washington, D.C., preparing fourth-graders from poor families for the Stanford 9 Achievement Test, used a workbook containing this exercise:

> Victor loved money above all things. He had few friends. He never spent any of his money having fun. He never gave any money away to people who were in need. *He just worked very hard and saved. Needless to say, Victor was often unhappy.* [emphasis added]
>
> Dorian was completely different. He liked to have fun. He liked to go to movies and plays. He worked hard, but money wasn't very important to him. Whenever anyone asked to borrow some money, he was happy to help out.

Having confused thrift with stinginess, hard work with misery, and extravagance with generosity and happiness, the exercise asked students to choose the best description of the difference between Victor and Dorian. The correct answer: "D. Dorian helped others and Victor didn't." Teaching children charity shouldn't require denigrating hard work and saving. You don't have to idolize money to need some of it, as the families of these children knew, and if you don't have any, it does take on a certain importance.

Barter is a frequent answer to the lack of cash. Sometimes it looks like a simple favor, as when Marquita Barnes, one of Leetha Butler's neighbors, got her car fixed for a minimal price from a mechanic friend, or lent her car to another friend who did some shopping for her. She and another woman traded day care for the other's kids, and no money changed hands. In other cases, the swaps become explicit. Nancy Szeto worked in a doctor's office in exchange for her hysterectomy. "Lynn," a middle-aged librarian, retained bartering habits from her dirt-poor childhood in Tennessee, and so did her schoolteacher husband, who came out of poverty in Eastern Europe.

"I have a friend who is a better seamstress than I," said Lynn, "and if she will sew sometimes for me, I will clean her house." Her husband used his amateur carpentry skills to make cupboards, bookcases, and the like out of wood scraps he picked up from behind a cabinetmaker's shop. He bartered a kitchen cupboard for a blueberry pie from "a lady that makes the world's best blueberry pies," Lynn said. "We barter for repair of the car sometimes." And her nephew built them a computer in exchange for bookcases in his office.

Lynn lamented the decline of such homespun, marketable know-how. "I have actually made all my clothing in some years," she noted. "I have grown and canned all the vegetables that we have had, he has rebuilt or built every house that we have had, and I have never had anyone in my house to repair any kind of appliance or anything." They had adjusted very tentatively to their rise into the middle-class. "It's just now in our late fifties that we have given ourselves certain luxuries," she said. Such as? "Such as, we paid $8 for a bottle of wine at Christmas, and we shared that. We still have a little bit left, here it is in January. I had a little glass last night." Her thrift made her proud, though it grew out of fear of destitution. "It doesn't matter how much money you make, it's how you spend it," she declared. "And it goes for millionaires to the most poverty stricken people in this country. And I think this is an American problem . . . this advertising, you got to have this, you got to have the newest, the latest, the best, and so on—and that is, I think, an American problem."

Overspending is certainly not the exclusive province of the poor. Tom Wolfe, capturing the opposite side of Horatio Alger's America, deftly caricatures the foibles of the affluent. *"I'm already going broke on a million dollars a year!"* the bond trader screams to himself in *The Bonfire of the Vanities:*

> The appalling figures came popping up into his brain. Last year his income had been $980,000. But he had to pay out $21,000 a month for the $1.8 million loan he had taken out to buy the apartment. What was $21,000 a month to someone making a million a year? That was the way he had thought of it at the time—and in fact, it was merely a *crushing, grinding burden*—that was all! It came to $252,000 a year. . . . So, considering the taxes, it required $420,000 in income to pay the $252,000. Of the $560,000 remaining of his income last year, $44,000 was required for the apartment's monthly maintenance fees; $116,000 for the house on Old Drover's Mooring Lane in Southampton ($84,000 for mortgage payment and interest, $18,000 for heat, utilities, insurance, and repairs, $6,000 for lawn and hedge cutting, $8,000 for taxes). Entertaining at home and in restaurants had come to $37,000. This was a modest sum compared to what other people spent; for example, Campbell's birthday party in Southampton had had only one carnival ride (plus, of course, the obligatory ponies and the magician) and had cost less than $4,000. The Taliaferro School, including the bus service, cost $9,400 for the year. The tab for furniture and clothes had come to about $65,000. . . . The servants (Bonita, Miss Lyons, Lucille the cleaning woman, and Hobie the handyman in Southampton) came to $62,000 a year. That left only $226,200, or $18,850 a month, for additional taxes and this and that . . . garage rent for two cars ($840 a month), household food ($1,500 a month), club dues (about $250 a month)—the abysmal truth was that he had spent *more* than $980,000 last year. Well, obviously he could cut down here and there-but not nearly enough—*if the worst happened!*

In real life, the numbers were lower for Willie and Sarah Goodell, but the pattern was similar. They were barely out of their teens, with three small children and their own missed childhoods to make up for. Both of them had inherited destructive behaviors from their upbringing—he drinking, she violence—and were busily reenacting them in their young adulthood.

They lived upstairs in Sarah's grandmother's beaten-up house. As if the weathered building had no purpose but to fade and sag, it stood sadly among the tightly crisscrossed streets of old homes in the center of Claremont, New Hampshire. The grandmother had no money to repair the place, so nothing much worked: the shower, the washer and dryer, the kitchen sink. Windows were broken, and the living room had no carpet—only bare linoleum—but plenty of toys were stacked along the wall, and a tall rack of music CDs adorned a cabinet containing a stereo and a large television set. The two oldest children, ages three years and eighteen months, wore no clothes, only diapers.

Like many New England mill towns, all that is left of Claremont's quaintness are the pretty sounding names: Sugar River, and streets called Summer and Pleasant and Pearl. Most of the decent jobs in mills and factories have disappeared, leaving a gritty struggle to find work that barely pays a living wage. Willie and Sarah, who lived on Pearl Street, were luckier than most because Willie got a job through Sarah's stepfather installing sheet metal roofs on candy factories and pharmaceutical plants being built in Massachusetts. Although it took him two and a half hours to drive each way every day, he could make $13 to $20 an hour, which added up to $31,000 in his best year. The trouble was, they spent it all, scratching little pleasures out of a constant, grinding, and unsatisfying chore of buying: $50 a week on cigarettes alone; clothes, shoes, CDs here and there; almost every dinner out at McDonald's, Pizza Hut, or Taco Bell. They had no bank account.

Willie was lanky, mild, easy, with glasses and a mop of light brown hair. He often wore a slight smile that made him look a bit lost, as if he had suddenly awakened to find himself in a mysterious mess. His kids were hellions, and Cody, the three-year-old, already had wild anger in his eyes, already shouted with a rage that sounded as deep as a man's. He hit his younger sister, who in turn hit the baby. Cody actually looked like a good buddy of Willie's, and sure enough, turned out to be the buddy's son. But Willie was an honorable man, and he adopted his wife's firstborn.

Sarah had short, spiky, reddish hair; a ring through her right ear; and another through her right eyebrow. Her face was very pale and often sullen, her pasty complexion betraying her preference to stay inside, usually in bed, rather than take her restless kids into the country daylight to run off their energy. She spoke in a morose and despairing tone, almost a whine.

"I got molested twice as a child," she told me the first time we talked. "When my mom and dad broke up and my dad moved out, my mom decided that she wanted to be a kid again 'cause she had me when she was eighteen. She went to bars quite a bit. I was nine years old, and I stayed home by myself. So that was real hard. I was in foster homes, group homes. I was molested by an uncle and a family friend. I have a lot of mental health problems because of my upbringing. That's why I can't work. I suffer from severe anxiety, panic, post-traumatic stress syndrome, all kinds of different stuff. I have a severe drug phobia, too, so I go to see counselors, but I can't take any medication." She lit a Marlboro with a lighter. Nicotine was a drug she didn't fear.

Sarah also went to bars quite a bit, because she also needed to be a kid, she explained. By twenty-one her marriage to Willie would collapse and she would have four children by three fathers. She fed the kids junk food and a constant stream of inconsistency, one moment allowing them to run wild, the next scolding them angrily for the same behavior. Threats of punishment—being deprived of a trip to rent a movie, being sentenced to bed—came and went like blowing leaves, creating no consequence.

Brenda, the home visitor, worried about the dangerous conditions. I saw them too while the couple was still together. Cody turned on an electric fan one day, stuck his fingers close to the blades, and received a mild rebuke. He climbed onto the sill of a window without a screen. Willie said firmly, "Get out of the window," and Cody ignored him with impunity. Brenda once arrived at the house to find Sarah asleep and Kayla, at eighteen months, chewing on a cigarette and putting a Bic lighter in her mouth. She played in the dirty toilet while Cody pulled his chair up to the stove with the burners lit. I saw Kayla hit the baby in the face with a sneaker and pick up a plastic bench, ready to slam it onto the baby's head. Cody screamed, and Willie stopped her. But less serious behavior seemed to get more serious scolding: Kayla was permitted to eat cheese while walking around the living room, and then got a harsh reprimand for the natural result of dropping cheese all over the living room floor. Neither Willie nor Sarah nor the kids seemed to know how to play; their few expensive toys were mostly just dragged noisily around the house. Willie's idea of a fun Saturday outing, after his license was suspended for drunken driving, was to walk with the children to Wal-Mart. Brenda's agency and the state's protective services tried unsuccessfully to get a judge to remove the children from the home.

Sarah's marriage was stormy while it lasted. Having grown up watching her mother hit her stepfather, she explained, she did the same to Willie. "I beat the hell out of him. He goes through about four pairs of glasses a year." Since she could stand a few paces back from herself and see clearly what she was doing, I asked, couldn't she change? She answered in a small voice, "I feel absolutely helpless."

To avoid her violence, Willie bought her off. "I know I could put money in the bank," he said, "but what's easier, puttin' money in the bank or havin' a mellow home life? Really." With a wan smile, he looked over at Sarah. They had just kept a month's accounting for me, and Willie and Sarah both thought they could have cut a lot of their spending if they'd tried. "Six hundred of it," Willie estimated. What would that have done to their lives? "It would have been terrible," he said. "You tell him," he suggested to Sarah, who kept silent. "She can't—you know, with her problems and stuff, it seems like, being depressed all the time, if she's not spending money she's not happy."

But buying a couple of CDs didn't make her happy for long. "For the day," she said.

"Till she's out of the store," he countered.

Their routine living expenses were not exorbitant. They included $300 a month rent to Sarah's grandmother, about $100 for the use of her phone, and nothing for electricity and cable TV. But Willie's long commute usually cost several hundred dollars a month in gas, except when he hitched a ride with fellow workers, as he had to do after his license was suspended. The couple paid $220 a month for a car they couldn't afford to insure, about $200 a month on laundry because their appliances didn't work, and $200 a month to eat out because the gas company wouldn't turn on their gas until they paid $400 in overdue bills. Also, Sarah rarely felt emotionally well enough to cook, and Willie was too exhausted when he got home from a fourteen-hour day.

Furthermore, they liked to spoil themselves sometimes. "We're both young," Willie explained, "and because neither one of us really had everything when we were kids, I suppose we do sometimes go overboard with birthdays and Christmas and stuff."

Their accounting, from mid-April to mid-May, showed that they had added enough outflow to their rent, car payments, and other recurring bills to use up almost all of the $2,500 Willie had earned.

Groceries (includes diapers and cigarettes)	$467.19
Movie rentals	$53.93
Eating out	$214.45
Miscellaneous	$785.09

The groceries included expensive items, such as $3.99 a day for Lunchables, the only kind of lunch that Cody would not hurl around the room of his preschool. The Miscellaneous category comprised fifty-two entries, most of whose details neither Sarah nor Willie could remember a month after listing them. They ranged from $2 and $5 for instantly forgotten things to $161 for concert tickets (to hear Ozzy Osbourne), a $52 outfit for a wedding, and numerous presents at $45 and $50 for birthdays, weddings, and one of those occasions cleverly invented by the manufacturers of nonessential items: Mother's Day.

Their main effort at economizing came at Willie's expense. Instead of smoking Camels, his favorite, he agreed to smoke Marlboros at $4 a carton less. Cutting out smoking altogether did not make it onto the agenda. Forgoing restaurants, prepared foods, and junky snacks seemed an impossible sacrifice, and Sarah angrily spurned advice on this point from Brenda the home visitor. "Her plans on a budget are: You eat hamburger and mashed potatoes for the week and stuff like that, and that's just not the way I want to live," Sarah scoffed. "I like to be able to eat what *I* like."

Even if Sarah and Willie had been models of frugality, their lives would still have been shackled to a heavy history of debt. From leaner days before he'd landed his roofing job, Willie owed $700 on a phone bill, $5,000 on a repossessed car, and $10,000 in medical pills. He could not get a phone; she could, only because her phone debts were run up before she became legally responsible at age eighteen. Eventually, she would probably have to try a ruse employed by some parents in this situation: open telephone accounts under a child's name and Social Security number.

Willie's medical bills were incurred in a fashion typical of working people without health insurance. He could not afford to go to the dentist, his teeth were decaying, and he was on the road working construction jobs. Whenever an abscess developed, he went to the nearest emergency room for painkillers and antibiotics. The law requires hospital emergency rooms to treat everyone, covered or not, but they can then send bills, which are usually whoppers. The charges were all beyond Willie's reach, and they ruined his credit rating.

"Poor," Sarah said in describing their socio-economic level, and then laughed a high-pitched, nervous giggle.

"We'd put ourselves poor," Willie echoed, "but I know if we were smart people, we could be very well off. Sometimes I bring home $700 a week. I know I could be very well off. But, you know, neither one of us can just sit home and say, OK, this is what we've got for dinner, and that's it." He smiled sadly. "If we had $10 in our pocket and we were sick and tired of sitting in the house, we'd go out and spend $10 on ice cream and supper. I guess it's easier to make life easier by doing something that costs money."

Sarah offered her definition of being poor: "We don't have any money saved. We don't really have a home we can call our own."

"It's our own fault," said Willie. "I'm not blaming it on anybody else."

Willie's earnings from working with sheet metal were high enough to put his family above the federal poverty line but low enough to get them some benefits. The children were eligible for SCHIP, the federally funded State Children's Health Insurance Program, and Sarah got milk, cereal, peanut butter, baby formula, and other foods from WIC, the Special Supplemental Nutrition Program for Women, Infants, and Children. Some years, when they filed their income tax return, they received not only a refund of taxes withheld, but the additional Earned Income Tax Credit.

One year, they used part of their check from the IRS to get tattoos. "It's like we're still kids ourselves," she said, "so we've got to act like kids once in a while." Willie got a wizard etched on his arm. Sarah pulled her shirt up in back to show hers: a heart made of thorns.

NOTES

NOTES

THE DEVELOPMENT OF WHITE IDENTITY: "I'M NOT ETHNIC, I'M JUST NORMAL"

Beverly Daniel Tatum

(1954–)

Beverly Daniel Tatum earned her B.A. from Wesleyan, her M.A. from Hartford Seminary, and M.A./Ph.D. from the University of Michigan. This scholar, professor, author, is also an expert on race relations and currently the ninth President of Spelman College in Atlanta, Georgia.

I often begin the classes and workshops I lead by asking participants to reflect on their own social class and ethnic background in small discussion groups. The first question I pose is one that most people of color answer without hesitation: "What is your class and ethnic background?" White participants, however, often pause before responding. On one such occasion a young White woman quickly described herself as middle-class but seemed stumped as to how to describe herself ethnically. Finally, she said, "I'm just normal!" What did she mean? She explained that she did not identify with any particular ethnic heritage, and that she was a lot like the other people who lived in her very homogeneous White middle-class community. But her choice of words was telling. If she is just normal, are those who are different from her "just abnormal"?

Like many White people, this young woman had never really considered her own racial and ethnic group membership. For her, Whiteness was simply the unexamined norm. Because they represent the societal norm, Whites can easily reach adulthood without thinking much about their racial group. For example, one White teacher who was taking a professional development course on racism with me wrote in one of her papers: "I am thirty-five years old and I never really started thinking about race too much until now, and that makes me feel uncomfortable. . . . I just think for some reason I didn't know. No one taught us." There is a lot of silence about race in White communities, and as a consequence Whites tend to think of racial identity as something that other people have, not something that is salient for them. But when, for whatever reason, the silence is broken, a process of racial identity development for Whites begins to unfold.

Counseling psychologist Janet Helms has described this process of development for Whites in her book Black and White Racial Identity Development: Theory, Research, and Practice. She assumes, as do I, that in a race-conscious society, racial group membership has psychological implications. The messages we receive about assumed superiority or inferiority shape our perceptions of reality and influence our interactions with others. While the task

Reprinted from *Why Are All the Black Kids Sitting Together in the Cafeteria?: A Psychologist Explains the Development of Racial Identity* (1997), by permission of the author.

for people of color is to resist negative societal messages and develop an empowered sense of self in the face of a racist society, Helms says the task for Whites is to develop a positive White identity based in reality, not on assumed superiority. In order to do that each person must become aware of his or her Whiteness, accept it as personally and socially significant, and learn to feel good about it, not in the sense of a Klan member's "White pride," but in the context of a commitment to a just society.

It comes as a surprise to some White people to think about their race in this way. "Of course White people feel good about being White," they say. But that is not my experience with my students or with the people who come to my workshops. Most of the White people I talk to either have not thought about their race and so don't feel anything, or have thought about it and felt guilt and shame. These feelings of guilt and shame are part of the hidden costs of racism.

How can White people achieve a healthy sense of White identity? Helms's model is instructive. For Whites, there are two major developmental tasks in this process, the abandonment of individual racism and the recognition of and opposition to institutional and cultural racism. These tasks occur over six stages: *contact, disintegration, reintegration, pseudo-independent, immersion/emersion,* and *autonomy.*

Abandoning Racism

At the contact stage, the first step in the process, Whites pay little attention to the significance of their racial identity. As exemplified by the "I'm just normal" comment, individuals at this point of development rarely describe themselves as White. If they have lived, worked, or gone to school in predominantly White settings, they may simply think of themselves as being part of the racial norm and take this for granted without conscious consideration of their White privilege, the systematically conferred advantages they receive simply because they are White.

While they have been breathing the "smog" and have internalized many of the prevailing societal stereotypes of people of color, they typically are unaware of this socialization process. They often perceive themselves as colorblind, completely free of prejudice, unaware of their own assumptions about other racial groups. In addition, they usually think of racism as the prejudiced behaviors of individuals rather than as an institutionalized system of advantage benefiting Whites in subtle as well as blatant ways. Peggy McIntosh speaks for many Whites at the contact level when she writes, "I was taught to recognize racism only in individual acts of meanness by members of my group, never in invisible systems conferring unsought racial dominance on my group from birth."

While some Whites may grow up in families where they are encouraged to embrace the ideology of White superiority (children of Klan members, for example), for many Whites this early stage of racial identity development represents the passive absorption of subtly communicated messages. Robert Carter, another racial identity researcher, illustrates this point when he quotes a forty-four-year-old White male who grew up in upstate New York, where he had limited direct contact with Blacks.

> There was no one to compare ourselves to. As you would drive through other neighborhoods, I think there was a clear message of difference or even superiority. The neighborhoods were poorer, and it was probably subtle, I don't remember my parents being bigoted, although by today's standards they clearly were. I think there was probably a message of superiority. The underlying messages were subtle. No one ever came out and said, White people are this and Black people are like this. I think the underlying message is that White people are generally good and they're like us, us and them.

These messages may go unchallenged and unexamined for a long time.

However, the next level, disintegration, is marked by a growing awareness of racism and White privilege as a result of personal encounters in which the social significance of race is made visible. For some White people, disintegration occurs when they develop a close friendship or a romantic relationship with a person of color. The White person then sees firsthand how racism can operate. For example, one female college student described her experiences shopping with a Puerto Rican roommate. She couldn't help noticing how her Latina friend was followed around in stores and was asked for more identification than Whites when writing checks: She also saw how her friend's Black boyfriend was frequently asked to show his college ID when he visited their residence hall, while young White men came and went without being questioned. For other White people, disintegration may result from seeing racist incidents such as the police beating of Rodney King or participating in an "unlearning racism" workshop. Certainly being in a classroom where the social consequences of racial group membership are explicitly discussed as part of the course content is likely to trigger the process.

Once the silence is broken, the cycle of racism becomes increasingly visible. For example, in my class I show a very powerful video, *Ethnic Notions,* on the dehumanizing images of African Americans in the popular culture from before the Civil War through the twentieth century. The video links the nineteenth-century caricatures of Black physical features, commonly published racial epithets, and the early cinematic portrayals of stupid but happy "darkies," menacing Black "savages," and heavyset, caretaking "mammies," to their updated forms in today's media. After seeing this film, students can't help but notice the pervasiveness of racial stereotyping on television each night. The same programs they used to find entertaining now offend them. They start to notice the racism in the everyday language of family and friends. For example, one White student reported that when she asked her roommate to get her a glass of water, the White roommate jokingly replied, "Do I look Black to you?" Although I had never heard of this expression, it was very familiar to the student. Yet, before then, she had never recognized the association of Blackness with servitude, and the assumed superiority of Whiteness being conveyed in the remark.

This new awareness is characterized by discomfort. The uncomfortable emotions of guilt, shame, and anger are often related to a new awareness of one's personal prejudices or the prejudices within one's family. The following excerpts from the journals of two White students illustrate this point:

> Today was the first class on racism. . . . Before today I didn't think I was exposed to any form of racism. Well, except for my father. He is about as prejudiced as they come.
>
> It really bothers me that stereotypes exist because it is from them that I originally became uninformed. My grandmother makes all kinds of decisions based on stereotypes—who to hire, who to help out. When I was growing up, the only Black people that I knew were adults [household help], but I admired them just as much as any other adult. When I expressed these feelings to my parents, I was always told that the Black people that I knew were the exceptions and that the rest of the race were different. I, too, was taught to be afraid.

Others' parents were silent on the subject of racism, simply accepting the status quo.

Those whose parents were actively antiracist may feel less guilt, but often still feel unprepared for addressing racism outside the family, a point highlighted by the comments of this young woman:

> Talking with other class members, I realized how exceptional my parents were. Not only were they not overtly racist but they also tried to keep society's subtle racism from reaching me. Basically I grew up believing that racism was no longer an issue and all people should be treated as equals. Unfortunately, my parents were not being very realistic as society's racism did begin to reach me. They did not teach me how to support and defend their views once I was interacting in a society without them as a buffer.

At the disintegration stage, White individuals begin to see how much their lives and the lives of people of color have been affected by racism in our society. The societal inequities they now notice directly contradict the idea of an American meritocracy, a concept that has typically been an integral part of their belief system. The cognitive dissonance that results is part of the discomfort which is experienced at this point in the process of development. Responses to this discomfort may include denying the validity of the information that is being presented, or psychologically or physically withdrawing from it. The logic is, "If I don't read about racism, talk about racism, watch those documentaries or special news programs, or spend time with those people of color, I won't have to feel uncomfortable." (In the case of my students, this is usually not an option. By the time they have to deal with these emotional responses, it is too late to drop the course.)

If the individual remains engaged, he or she can turn the discomfort into action. Once they have an awareness of the cycle of racism, many people are angered by it and want to interrupt it. Often action comes in the form of educating others—pointing out the stereotypes as they watch television, interrupting the racial jokes, writing letters to the editor, sharing articles with friends and family. Like new converts, people experiencing disintegration can be quite zealous in their efforts. A White woman in her forties who participated in an antiracist professional development course for educators described herself at this stage:

> What it was like for me when I was taking the course [one year ago] and just afterwards, hell, because this dissonance stuff doesn't feel all that great. And trying to put it in a perspective and figure out what to do with it is very hard. . . . I was on the band wagon so I'm not going to be quiet about it. So there was dissonance everywhere. Personally, I remember going home for Thanksgiving, the first Thanksgiving [while taking the course], back to our families . . . and turning to my brother-in-law and saying, "I really don't want you to say that in front of me—I don't want to hear that joke—I am not interested." . . . At every turn it seemed like there, I was *responsible* for saying something. . . . My husband, who I think is a very good, a very liberal person, but who really hasn't been through [this], saying, "You know I think you're taking yourself too seriously here and where is your sense of humor? You have lost your sense of humor." And my saying, "It isn't funny; you don't understand, it just isn't funny to me." Not that he would ever tell a racial joke, but there were these things that would come up and he would just sort of look back and say, "I don't understand where you're coming from now." So there was a lot of dissonance. . . . I don't think anybody was too comfortable with me for a while.

My college students have similar experiences with family members and friends. Though they want to step off the cycle of racism, the message from the surrounding White community seems to be, "Get back on!" A very poignant example of this was shared with me by a young White man from a very privileged background. He wrote:

> I realized that it was possible to simply go through life totally oblivious to the entire situation or, even if one realizes it, one can totally repress it. It is easy to fade into the woodwork, run with the rest of

> society, and never have to deal with these problems. So many people I know from home are like this. They have simply accepted what society has taught them with little, if any, question. My father is a prime example of this. . . . It has caused much friction in our relationship, and he often tells me as a father he has failed in raising me correctly. Most of my high school friends will never deal with these issues and propagate them on to their own children. It's easy to see how the cycle continues. I don't think I could ever justify within myself simply turning my back on the problem. I finally realized that my position in all of these dominant groups gives me power to make change occur. . . . It is an unfortunate result often though that I feel alienated from friends and family. It's often played off as a mere stage that I'm going through. I obviously can't tell if it's merely a stage, but I know that they say this to take the attention off of the truth of what I'm saying. By belittling me, they take the power out of my argument. It's very depressing that being compassionate and considerate are seen as only phases that people go through. I don't want it to be a phase for me, but as obvious as this may sound, I look at my environment and often wonder how it will not be.

The social pressure from friends and acquaintances to collude, to not notice racism, can be quite powerful.

But it is very difficult to stop noticing something once it has been pointed out. The conflict between noticing and not noticing generates internal tension, and there is a great desire to relieve it. Relief often comes through what Helms calls reintegration. At this stage, the previous feelings of guilt or denial may be transformed into fear and anger directed toward people of color. The logic is, "If there is a problem with racism, then you people of color must have done something to cause it. And if you would just change your behavior, the problem would go away." The elegance of this argument is that it relieves the White person of all responsibility for social change.

I am sometimes asked if it is absolutely necessary to go through this phase. Must one blame the victim? Although it is not inevitable, most White people who speak up against racism will attest to the temptation they sometimes feel to slip back into collusion and silence. Because the pressure to ignore racism and to accept the socially sanctioned stereotypes is so strong, and the system of advantage so seductive, many White people get stuck in reintegration thinking. The psychological tension experienced at this stage is clearly expressed by Connie, a White woman of Italian ancestry who took my course on the psychology of racism. After reading about the stages of White identity development, she wrote:

> There was a time when I never considered myself a color. I never described myself as a "White, Italian female" until I got to college and noticed that people of color always described themselves by their

> color/race. While taking this class, I have begun to understand that being White makes a difference. I never thought about it before, but there are many privileges to being White. In my personal life, I cannot say that I have ever felt that I have had the advantage over a Black person, but I am aware that my race has the advantage.
>
> I am feeling really guilty lately about that. I find myself thinking: "I didn't mean to be White, I really didn't mean it." I am starting to feel angry toward my race for ever using this advantage toward personal gains. But at the same time I resent the minority groups. I mean, it's not my fault that society has deemed us "superior." I don't feel any better than a Black person. But it really doesn't matter because I am a member of the dominant race. . . . I can't help it . . . and I sometimes get angry and feel like I'm being attacked.
>
> I guess my anger toward a minority group would enter me into the next stage of Reintegration where I am once again starting to blame the victim. This is all very trying for me and it has been on my mind a lot. I really would like to be able to reach the last stage . . . where I can accept being White without hostility and anger. That is really hard to do.

"But I'm an Individual!"

Another source of the discomfort and anger that Whites often experience in this phase stems from the frustration of being seen as a group member, rather than as an individual. People of color learn early in life that they are seen by others as members of a group. For Whites, thinking of oneself only as an individual is a legacy of White privilege. As McIntosh writes, "I can swear, or dress in second hand clothes, or not answer letters, without having people attribute these choices to the bad morals, the poverty, or the illiteracy of my race. . . . I can do well in a challenging situation without being called a credit to my race. . . . I am never asked to speak for all the people of my racial group." In short, she and other Whites are perceived as individuals most of the time.

The view of oneself as an individual is very compatible with the dominant ideology of rugged individualism and the American myth of meritocracy. Understanding racism as a system of advantage that structurally benefits Whites and disadvantages people of color on the basis of group membership threatens not only beliefs about society but also beliefs about one's own life accomplishments. For example, organizational consultant Nancie Zane writes that senior White male managers "were clearly invested in the notion that their hard work, ingenuity and skills had won them their senior-level positions." As others talked about the systemic racist and sexist barriers to their own achievement, "white men heard it as a condemnation that they somehow didn't 'deserve' their position." If viewing oneself as a group member threatens one's self-definition, making the paradigm shift from individual to group member will be painful.

In the case of White men, both maleness and Whiteness are normative, so acknowledging group status may be particularly difficult. Those White women who have explored their subordinate gender identity have made at least some movement away from the notion of a strictly individual self-definition and may find it easier to grasp the significance of their racial group membership. However, as McIntosh and others have pointed out, understanding one form of oppression does not guarantee recognition of another.

Those Whites who are highly identified with a particular subordinate identity may also struggle with claiming Whiteness as a meaningful group category because they feel far from the White male norm. For example, Jewish people of European ancestry sometimes do not think of themselves as White because for them the term means White Christian. Also, in Nazi Germany, Jews were defined as a distinct, non-Aryan racial group. In the context of an anti-Jewish culture, the salient identity may be the targeted Jewish identity. However, in terms of U.S. racial ideology, Jews of European ancestry are also the beneficiaries of White racial privilege. My White Jewish students often struggle with the tension between being targeted and receiving privilege. In this case, as in others, the reality of multiple identities complicates the process of coming to terms with one particular dimension of identity. For example, one student wrote:

> I am constantly afraid that people will see my assertion of my Jewish identity as a denial of whiteness, as a way of escaping the acknowledgment of white privilege. I feel I am both part of and not part of whiteness. I am struggling to be more aware of my white privilege . . . but I will not do so at the cost of having my Jewishness erased.

Similarly, White lesbians sometimes find it hard to claim privileged status as Whites when they are so targeted by homophobia and heterosexism, often at the hands of other Whites.

These complexities notwithstanding, when White men and women begin to understand that they are viewed as members of a dominant racial group not only by other Whites but also by people of color, they are sometimes troubled, even angered, to learn that simply because of their group status they are viewed with suspicion by many people of color. "I'm an individual, view me as an individual!" For example, in a racially mixed group of educators participating in an antiracist professional development course, a Black man commented about using his "radar" to determine if the group would be a safe place for him. Many of the White people in the room, who believed that their very presence in the course was proof of their trustworthiness, were upset by the comment, initially unprepared to acknowledge the invisible legacy of racism that accompanied any and every interaction they had with people of color. The White people in the course found some comfort in reading Lois Stalvey's memoir, *The Education of a WASP,* in which she described her own responses to the ways Black people tested her trustworthiness. She writes,

> I could never resent the tests as some white people have told me they do. . . . But to me, the longest tests have always indicated the deepest hurts. We whites would have to be naive to expect that hundreds of years of humiliation can be forgotten the moment we wish it to be. At times, the most poignant part of the test is that black people have enough trust left to give it. Testing implies we might pass the test. It is safer and easier for a black person to turn his back on us. If he does not gamble on our sincerity, he cannot be hurt if we prove false. Testing shows an optimism I doubt I could duplicate if I were black.

Sometimes poorly organized antiracism workshops or other educational experiences can create a scenario that places participants at risk for getting stuck in their anger. Effective consciousness-raising about racism must also point the way toward constructive action. When people don't have the tools for moving forward, they tend to return to what is familiar, often becoming more vigorous in their defense of the racial status quo than they were initially.

As we have seen, many White people experience themselves as powerless, even in the face of privilege. But the fact is that we all have a sphere of influence, some domain in which we exercise some level of power and control. The task for each of us, White and of color, is to identify what our own sphere of influence is (however large or small) and to consider how it might be used to interrupt the cycle of racism.

Defining a Positive White Identity

As a White person's understanding of the complexity of institutional racism in our society deepens, the less likely he or she is to resort to explanations that blame the victim. Instead, deepening awareness usually leads to a commitment to unlearn one's racism, and marks the emergence of the pseudo-independent stage.

Sometimes epitomized by the "guilty White liberal" persona, the pseudo-independent individual has an intellectual understanding of racism as a system of advantage, but doesn't quite know what to do about it. Self-conscious and guilty about one's own Whiteness, the individual often desires to escape it by associating with people of color. Ruth Frankenberg, author of *White Women, Race Matters: The Social Construction of Whiteness,* describes the confusing emotions of this process in an autobiographical essay. "I viewed my racial privilege as total. I remember months when I was terrified to speak in gatherings that were primarily of color, since I feared that anything I did say would be marked by my whiteness, my racial privilege (which in my mind meant the same)." When her friends of color were making casual conversation—chatting about their mothers, for example—she would worry that anything she might say about her own mother would somehow reveal her race privilege, and by the time she had sorted it out mentally, the topic of conversation would have changed. She writes, "In that silence, I tried to 'pass' (as what? as racially unmarked? as exceptional? as the one white girl who could 'hang'?)."

Similarly, a student of mine writes:

> One of the major and probably most difficult steps in identity development is obtaining or finding the consciousness of what it means to be White. I definitely remember many a time that I wished I was not White, ashamed of what I and others have done to the other racial groups in the world. . . . I wanted to pretend I was Black, live with them, celebrate their culture, and deny my Whiteness completely. Basically, I wanted to escape the responsibility that came with identifying myself as "White."

How successful these efforts to escape Whiteness via people of color will be depends in part on the racial identity development of the people of color involved. Remember the Black students at the cafeteria table? If they are in the encounter or immersion/emersion stages, they are not likely to be interested in cultivating White friendships. If a White person reaches out to a Black person and is rebuffed, it may cause the White person to retreat into "blame the victim" thinking. However, even if these efforts to build interracial relationships are successful, the White individual must eventually confront the reality of his or her own Whiteness.

We all must be able to embrace who we are in terms of our racial and cultural heritage, not in terms of assumed superiority or inferiority, but as an integral part of our daily experience in which we can take pride. But, as we see in these examples, for many White people who at this stage have come to understand the everyday reality of racism, Whiteness is still experienced as a source of shame rather than as a source of pride.

Recognizing the need to find a more positive self-definition is a hallmark of the next phase of White racial identity development, the immersion/emersion stage. Bob, a White male student in my racism class, clearly articulated this need.

> I'm finding that this idea of White identity is more important than I thought. Yet White identity seems very hard to pin hole. I seem to have an idea and feel myself understanding what I need to do and why and then something presents itself that throws me into mass confusion. I feel that I need some resources that will help me through the process of finding White identity.

The resource Bob needs most at this point are not people of color, but other Whites who are further along in the process and can help show him the way.

It is at just this point that White individuals intensify their efforts to see their Whiteness in a positive light. Just as Cross describes the period of Black redefinition as a time for Black people to seek new ways of thinking about Blackness, ways that take them beyond the role of victim, White people must seek new ways of thinking about Whiteness, ways that take them beyond the role of victimizer.

The Search for White Allies and the Restoration of Hope

In fact, another role does exist. There is a history of White protest against racism, a history of Whites who have resisted the role of oppressor and who have been allies to people of color. Unfortunately these Whites are often invisible to us. While the names of active racists are easily recalled—past and present Klan leaders and Southern segregationists, for example—the names of White allies are often unknown. I have had the experience of addressing roomfuls of classroom teachers who have been unable to name even one White person who has worked against racism without some prompting from me. If they can't do it, it is likely that their students can't either.

Those who have studied or lived through the Civil Rights era (many of my students have not) may know the names of Viola Liuzzo, James Reeb, or Michael Schwerner, White civil rights workers who were killed for their antiracist efforts. But most people don't want to be martyrs. There is a need to know about White allies who spoke up, who worked for social change, who resisted racism and lived to tell about it. How did these White allies break free from the confines of the racist socialization they surely experienced to claim this identity for themselves? These are the voices that many White people at this stage in the process are hungry to hear.

Biographies of or autobiographies by White individuals who have been engaged in antiracist activities can be very helpful. For example, there is *A Season of Justice,* the autobiography of Morris Dees, the executive director of the Southern Poverty Law Center and a vigorous anti-Klan litigator. There is *Outside the Magic Circle,* the oral history of Virginia Foster Durr, a Southern belle turned civil rights activist. And there is *The Education of a WASP,* the story of Lois Stalvey, a mother struggling to create a nonracist environment for her children. Such books can be an antidote to the feelings of isolation and loneliness that White people often feel at this point. There is comfort in knowing that others have traveled this terrain.

One of the consequences of racism in our society is that those who oppose racism are often marginalized, and as a result, their stories are not readily accessed. Yet having access to these stories makes a difference to those Whites who are looking for ways to be agents of change. White people who are doing this work need to make their stories known to serve as guides for others.

In my class I try to address the lack of knowledge of White role models by providing concrete examples of such people. In addition to assigning reading material, my strategy has been to invite a local White antiracist activist, Andrea Ayvazian, to my class to speak about her own personal journey toward an awareness of racism and her development as a White ally. Students typically ask questions that reflect their fears about social isolation at this phase of development. "Did you lose friends when you started to speak up?" "My boyfriend makes a lot of racist comments. What can I do?" "What do you say to your father at Thanksgiving when he tells those jokes?" These are not just the questions of late adolescents. The mature White teachers I work with ask the same things.

My White students, who often comment about how depressing it is to study racism, typically say that the opportunity to talk with this ally gave them renewed hope. Through her example, they see that the role of the ally is not to help victims of racism, but to speak up against systems of oppression and to challenge other Whites to do the same. One point that Andrea emphasizes in her speaking and writing is the idea that "allies need allies," others who will support their efforts to swim against the tide of cultural and institutional racism. This point was especially helpful for one young woman who had been struggling with feelings of isolation. She wrote:

> About being an ally, a positive role model: . . . it enhanced my positive feelings about the difference each individual (me!) can make. I don't need to feel helpless when there is so much I can do. I still can see how easily things can back-up and start getting depressing, but I can also see how it is possible to keep going strong and powerful. One of the most important points she made was the necessity of a support group/system; people to remind me of what I have done, why I should keep going, of why I'm making a difference, why I shouldn't feel helpless. I think our class started to help me with those issues, as soon as I started to let it, and now I've found similar supports in friends and family. They're out there, it's just finding and establishing them—it really is a necessity. Without support, it would be too easy to give up, burn-out, become helpless again. In any endeavor support is important, but when the forces against you are so prevalent and deep-rooted as racism is in this society, it is the only way to keep moving forward.

Participation in White consciousness-raising groups organized specifically for the purpose of examining one's own racism are another way to "keep moving forward." At Mount Holyoke College such a group, White Women Against Racism, was formed following the 1992 acquittal of the Los Angeles police officers involved in the beating of Rodney King. There are similar groups with different names operating formally and informally in local communities around the country. Support groups of this nature help to combat the social isolation that antiracist Whites often experience, and provide places to forge new identities.

I am sometimes asked why such groups need to be made up of Whites only. To many Whites it seems inconceivable that there would be any value in participating in all-White discussions of racism. While of course there is value in cross-racial dialogue, all-White support groups serve a unique function. Particularly when Whites are trying to work through their feelings of guilt and shame, separate groups give White people the "space to speak with honesty and candor rarely possible in racially-mixed groups." Even when Whites feel comfortable sharing these feelings with people of color, frankly, people of color don't necessarily want to hear about it. The following comment, written by a Black woman in my class, illustrates this dilemma:

> Many times in class I feel uncomfortable when White students use the term Black because even if they aren't aware of it they say it with all or at least a lot of the negative connotations they've been taught goes along with Black. Sometimes it just causes a stinging feeling inside of me. Sometimes I get real tired of hearing White people talk about the conditions of Black people. I think it's an important thing for them to talk about, but still I don't always like being around when they do it. I also get tired of hearing them talk about how hard it is for them, though I understand it, and most times I am very willing to listen and be open, but sometimes I can't. Right now I can't.

Though a White person may need to describe the racist things a parent or spouse has said or done, to tell the story to a person of color may reopen that person's wounds. Listening to those stories and problem-solving about them is a job that White people can do for each other.

It is at this stage of redefining Whiteness, immersion/emersion, that the feelings of guilt and shame start to fade. Reflecting on her own White identity development, sociologist Becky Thompson chronicles this process:

> [I understood] that I didn't have to recreate the wheel in my own life. I began to actively seek writing by white women who have historically stood up against racism—Elly Bulkin, Lillian Smith, Sara Evans, Angelina Grimke, Ruth Frankenberg, Helen Joseph, Melanie Kaye/Kantrowitz, Tillie Olsen, Minnie Bruce Pratt, Ruth Seid, Mab Segrest, and others.

She also realized that she needed antiracist White people in her daily life with whom she could share stories and whom she could trust to give her honest feedback. Her experience in a White antiracism group helped her to stop feeling bad because she was White. She writes, "I started seeing ways to channel my energies without trying to leave a piece of my identity behind."

The last stage, autonomy, represents the culmination of the White racial developmental process. At this point, a person incorporates the newly defined view of Whiteness as part of a personal identity. The positive feelings associated with this redefinition energize the person's efforts to confront racism and oppression in daily life. Clayton Alderfer, a White man with many years of personal and professional experience, describes the thinking that characterizes this stage. "We have a more complete awareness of ourselves and of others to the degree that we neither negate the uniqueness of each person, regardless of that person's group memberships nor deny the ever-present effects of group memberships for each individual."

While autonomy might be described as racial self-actualization, racial identity development never really ends. The person at this level is continually open to new information and new ways of thinking about racial and cultural variables. Helms describes each of the six stages as representing patterns of thinking that predominate at particular points of development. But even when active antiracist thinking predominates, there may still be particular situations that trigger old modes of responding. Whites, like people of color, continue to be works in progress.

A major benefit of this racial identity development process is increased effectiveness in multiracial settings. The White person who has worked through his or her own racial identity process has a deep understanding of racism and an appreciation and respect for the identity struggles of people of color. When we see strong, mutually respectful relationships between people of color and Whites, we are usually looking at the tangible results of both people's identity processes. If we want to promote positive cross-group relations, we need to help young White people engage in the kind of dialogue that precipitates this kind of identity development just as we need to help youth of color achieve an empowered sense of racial and ethnic identity.

Though the process of examining their racial identity can be uncomfortable and even frightening for Whites, those who persist in the struggle are rewarded with an increasingly multiracial and multicultural existence. In our still quite segregated society, this "borderland" is unfamiliar to many Whites and may be hard to envision. Becky Thompson has experienced it, and she writes: "We need to talk about what living in this borderland feels like, how we get there, what sustains us, and how we benefit from it. For me, this place of existence is tremendously exciting, invigorating, and life-affirming." Though it can also be "complicated and lonely," it is also liberating, opening doors to new communities, creating possibilities for more authentic connections with people of color, and in the process, strengthening the coalitions necessary for genuine social change.

NOTES

NOTES

A SITUATIONIST PERSPECTIVE ON THE PSYCHOLOGY OF EVIL: UNDERSTANDING HOW GOOD PEOPLE ARE TRANSFORMED INTO PERPETRATORS

Philip G. Zimbardo

(1933–)

Philip G. Zimbardo is a psychologist and former professor at Stanford University. He graduated from Yale University and Brooklyn College. Currently he teaches at Palo Alto University. He has served as President of the American Psychological Association.

I endorse the application of a situationist perspective to the ways in which the antisocial behavior of individuals and the violence sanctioned by nations can be best understood, treated, and prevented. This view, which has both influenced and been informed by a body of social-psychological research and theory, contrasts with the traditional perspective that explains evil behavior in dispositional terms: Internal determinants of antisocial behavior locate evil within individual predispositions—genetic "bad seeds," personality traits, psychopathological risk factors, and other organismic variables. The situationist approach is to the dispositional as public health models of disease are to medical models. Following basic principles of Lewinian theory, the situationist perspective propels external determinants of behavior to the foreground, well beyond the status as merely extenuating background circumstances. Unique to this situationist approach is the use of experimental laboratory and field research to demonstrate vital phenomena, that other approaches only analyze verbally or rely on archival or correlational data for answers. The basic paradigm presented in this chapter illustrates the relative ease with which ordinary, "good" men and women can be induced into behaving in "evil" ways by turning on or off one or another social situational variable.

I begin the chapter with a series of "oldies but goodies"—my laboratory and field studies on deindividuation, aggression, vandalism, and the Stanford prison experiment, along with a process analysis of Milgram's obedience studies, and Bandura's analysis of "moral disengagement." My analysis is extended to the evil of inaction by considering bystander failures of helping those in distress. This body of research demonstrates the underrecognized power of social situations to alter the mental representations and behavior of individuals, groups, and nations. Finally, I explore extreme instances of "evil" behavior for their dispositional or situational foundations: torturers, death-squad violence workers, and terrorist suicide bombers.

Evil can be defined as intentionally behaving, or causing others to act, in ways that demean, dehumanize, harm, destroy, or kill innocent people. This behaviorally focused definition makes the individual or group responsible for

Reprinted from *The Social Psychology of Good and Evil,* edited by Arthur G. Miller (2005), by permission of Guilford Press.

purposeful, motivated actions that have a range of negative consequences for other people. The definition excludes accidental or unintended harmful outcomes, as well as the broader, generic forms of institutional evil, such as poverty, prejudice, or destruction of the environment by agents of corporate greed. However, it does include corporate forms of wrongdoing, such as the marketing and selling of products with known disease-causing, death-dealing properties (e.g., cigarette manufacturers or other substance/drug dealers). The definition also extends beyond the proximal agent of aggression, as studied in research on interpersonal violence, to encompass those in distal positions of authority whose orders or plans are carried out by functionaries. Such agents include military commanders and national leaders, such as Hitler, Stalin, Mao, Pol Pot, Idi Amin, and others whom history has identified as tyrants for their complicity in the deaths of untold millions of innocent people.

History will also have to decide on the evil status of President George W. Bush's role in declaring a pre-emptive, aggressive war against Iraq in March 2003, with dubious justification, that resulted in widespread death, injury, destruction, and enduring chaos. We might also consider a simpler definition of evil, proposed by my colleague, Irving Sarnoff: "Evil is knowing better but doing worse."

We live in a world cloaked in the evils of civil and international wars, of terrorism (home-grown and exported), homicides, rapes, domestic and child abuse, and countless other forms of devastation. The same human mind that creates the most beautiful works of art and extraordinary marvels of technology is equally responsible for the perversion of its own perfection. This most dynamic organ in the universe has served as a seemingly endless source of ever viler torture chambers and instruments of horror in earlier centuries, the "bestial machinery" unleashed on Chinese citizens by Japanese soldiers in their rape of Nanking (see Chang, 1997), and the recent demonstration of "creative evil" in the destruction of the World Trade Center by "weaponizing" commercial airlines. We continue to ask, *why*? Why and how is it possible for such deeds to continue to occur? How can the unimaginable become so readily imagined? These are the same questions that have been asked by generations before ours.

I wish I had answers to these profound questions about human existence and human nature. Here I can offer modest versions of possible answers. My concern centers around how good, ordinary people can be recruited, induced, seduced into behaving in ways that could be classified as evil. In contrast to the traditional approach of trying to identify "evil people" to account for the evil in our midst, I focus on trying to outline some of the central conditions that are involved in the transformation of good people into perpetrators of evil.

Locating Evil within Particular People: The Rush to the Dispositional

"Who is responsible for evil in the world, given that there is an all-powerful, omniscient God who is also all-Good?" That conundrum began the intellectual scaffolding of the Inquisition in the 16th and 17th centuries in Europe. As revealed in *Malleus Maleficarum*, the handbook of the German Inquisitors from the Roman Catholic Church, the inquiry concluded that "the Devil" was the source of all evil. However, these theologians argued the Devil works his evil through intermediaries, lesser demons, and, of course, human witches. So the hunt for evil focused on those marginalized people who looked or acted differently from ordinary people, who might qualify, under rigorous examination of conscience and torture, as "witches," and then put them to death. The victims were mostly women who could be readily exploited without sources of defense, especially when they had resources that could be confiscated. An analysis of this legacy of institutionalized violence against women is detailed by historian Anne Barstow (1994) in *Witchcraze*. Paradoxically, this early effort of the Inquisition to understand the origins of evil and develop interventions to cope with it instead fomented new forms of evil that fulfill all facets of my definition. The phenomenon of the Inquisition exemplifies the notion of simplifying the complex problem of widespread evil by identifying *individuals* who might be the guilty parties and then making them "pay" for their evil deeds.

Most traditional psychiatry as well as psychodynamic theory also locate the source of individual violence and antisocial behavior within the psyches of disturbed people, often tracing it back to early roots in unresolved infantile conflicts. Like genetic views of pathology, such psychological approaches seek to link behaviors society judges as pathological to pathological origins—be they defective genes, "bad seeds," or premorbid personality structures. However, this view overlooks the fact that the same violent outcomes can be generated by very different types of people, all of whom give no hint of evil impulses. My colleagues and I (Lee, Zimbardo, & Bertholf, 1977) interviewed and tested 19 inmates in California prisons who had all recently been convicted of homicide. Ten of these killers had a long history of violence, showed lack of impulse control (on the Minnesota Multiphasic Personality Inventory), were decidedly masculine in sexual identity, and generally extraverted. The other murderers were totally different. They had never committed any criminal offense prior to the homicide—their murders were totally unexpected, given their mild manner and gentle disposition. Their problem was an *excessive* impulse control that inhibited their expression of any feelings. Their sexual identity was feminine or androgynous, and the majority were shy. These "shy sudden murderers" killed just as violently as did the habitual criminals, and their victims died just as surely, but it would have been impossible to predict this outcome from any prior knowledge of their personalities, which were so different from the more obvious habitual criminals.

The concept of an authoritarian personality syndrome was developed by a team of psychologists (Adorno, Frenkel-Brunswick, Levinson, & Sanford, 1950) after World War II who were trying to make sense of the Holocaust and the broad appeal of fascism and Hitler. Their dispositional bias led them to focus on identifying a set of personality factors that might underlie the fascist mentality. However, they over-looked the host of processes operating at political, economic, societal, and historical levels, all of which influenced and directed so many millions of individuals into a constrained behavioral channel of hating Jews and other minority groups, while endorsing and even applauding the views and policies of their dictator.

This tendency to explain observed behavior by reference to internal dispositional factors while ignoring or minimizing the impact of situational variables has been termed the fundamental attribution error (FAE) by my colleague Lee Ross (1977). We are all subject to this dual bias of overutilizing dispositional analyses and underutilizing situational explanations when faced with ambiguous causal scenarios we want to understand. We succumb to this effect because our educational institutions, social and professional training programs, and societal agencies are all geared toward a focus on individual, dispositional orientations. Dispositional analyses are a central operating feature of cultures that are based on individualistic rather than collectivist values (see Triandis, 1994). Thus, it is individuals who are lauded with praise and fame and wealth for achievement and are honored for their uniqueness, but it is also individuals who are blamed for the ills of society. Our legal, medical, educational, and religious systems all are founded on principles of individualism.

Dispositional analyses of antisocial, or non-normative, behaviors typically include strategies for behavior modification, whereby deviant individuals learn to conform better to social norms, or facilities for excluding them from society via imprisonment, exile, or execution. Locating evil within selected individuals or groups carries with it the "social virtue" of taking society "off the hook" as blameworthy; societal structures and political decision making are exonerated from bearing any burden of the more fundamental circumstances that create racism, sexism, elitism, poverty, and marginal existence for some citizens. Furthermore, this dispositional orientation to understanding evil implies a simplistic, binary world of good people, like us, and bad people, like them. That clear-cut dichotomy is divided by a manufactured line that separates good and evil. We then take comfort in the illusion that such a line constrains crossovers in either direction. We could never imagine being like *them*, of doing their unthinkable dirty deeds, and do not admit them into our company because they are so essentially different as to be unchangeable. This extreme position also means we forfeit the motivation to understand how they came to engage in what we view as evil behavior. I find it helpful to remind myself of the geopolitical analysis of the Russian novelist Alexander Solzhenitsyn, a victim of persecution by the Soviet KGB, that the line between good and evil lies in the center of every human heart.

The Transformation of Good People into Agents of Destruction

My bias is admittedly more toward situational analyses of behavior and comes from my training as an experimental social psychologist as well as from having grown up in poverty, in a New York City ghetto of the South Bronx. I believe that dispositional orientations are more likely to correlate with affluence: The rich want to take full credit for their success, whereas the situationists hail more from the lower classes who want to explain the obvious dysfunctional lifestyles of those around them in terms of external circumstances rather than internal failures. I am primarily concerned with understanding the psychological and social dynamics involved when an ordinary, "good" person begins to act in antisocial ways and, in the extreme, behaves destructively toward the property or person of others. I saw, firsthand, my childhood friends go through such transformations, and I wondered how and why they changed so drastically and whether I could also change like that (e.g., they were bullied, failed in school, parents fought all the time, nothing to look forward to). I was similarly fascinated with the tale of the behavioral transformation of Robert Louis Stevenson's good Dr. Jekyll into the murderous Mr. Hyde. What was in his chemical formula that could have such an immediate and profound impact? Even as a child, I wondered if there were other ways to induce such changes, since my friends did not have access to his elixir of evil before they did such bad things to other people. I would later discover that social psychology had recipes for such transformations.

Our mission is to understand better how virtually anyone could be recruited to engage in evil deeds that deprive other human beings of their dignity, humanity, and life. The dispositional analysis has the comforting side effect of enabling those who have not yet done wrong to righteously assert, "Not *me*, I am different from those kinds of people who did that evil deed!" By positing a "me-us-them" distinction, we live with the illusion of moral superiority firmly entrenched in the pluralistic ignorance that comes from not recognizing the set of situational and structural circumstances that empowered others—like ourselves—to engage in deeds that they too once thought were alien to their nature. We take false pride in believing that "I am not that kind of person."

I argue that the human mind is so marvelous that it can adapt to virtually any known environmental circumstance in order to survive, to create, and to destroy, as necessary. We are not born with tendencies toward good or evil but with mental templates to do *either*. What I mean is that we have the potential to be better or worse than anyone who has existed in the past, to be more creative and more destructive, to make the world a better place or a worse place than before. It is only through the recognition that no one of us is an island, that we all share the human condition, that humility takes precedence over unfounded pride in acknowledging our vulnerability to situational forces. If we want to develop mechanisms for combating such malevolent transformations, then it seems essential to learn to appreciate the extent to which ordinary people can be seduced or initiated into the performance of evil deeds. We need to focus on discovering the mechanisms among the causal factors that influence so many to do so much bad, to commit so much evil throughout the globe. (See also the breadth of ideas presented by Baumeister, 1997; Darley, 1992; Staub, 1989; Waller, 2002.)

The Milgram Obedience Experiments

The most obvious power of the experimental demonstration by Stanley Milgram (1974) of blind obedience to authority lies in the unexpectedly high rates of such compliance, with the majority—two-thirds—of the subjects "going all the way" in shocking a victim with apparently lethal consequences. His finding was indeed shocking to most of those who read about it or saw his movie version of the study, because it revealed that a variety of ordinary American citizens could so readily be led to engage in "electrocuting a nice stranger." But the more significant importance of his research comes from what he did after that initial classic study with Yale College undergraduates. Milgram conducted 18 experimental variations on more than a *thousand* subjects from a variety of backgrounds, ages, both genders, and all educational levels. In each of these studies he varied one social-psychological variable and observed its impact on the extent of obedience to the unjust authority's pressure to continue to shock the "learner-victim." He was able to demonstrate that compliance rates of those who delivered the maximum 450 volts to the hapless victim could soar to 90% or could be reduced to less than 10% by introducing a single variable into the compliance recipe.

Milgram found that obedience was maximized when subjects first observed peers behaving obediently; it was dramatically reduced when peers rebelled or when the victim acted like a masochist asking to be shocked. What is especially interesting to me about this last result are the data Milgram provides on the predictions of his outcome by 40 psychiatrists who were given the basic description of the classic experiment. Their average estimate of the percentage of U.S. citizens who would give the full 450 volts was fewer than 1%. Only sadists would engage in such sadistic behavior, they believed. In a sense, this is the comparison level for appreciating the enormity of Milgram's finding. These experts on human behavior were *totally* wrong because they ignored the situational determinants of behavior in the procedural description of the experiment and overrelied on the dispositional perspective that comes from their professional training. Their error is a classic instance of the FAE at work. In fact, in this research, the average person does *not* behave like a sadist when an apparently masochistic victim encourages him or her to do so.

Milgram's intention was to provide a paradigm in which it was possible to quantify "evil" by the number of buttons a subject pushed on a shock generator, which allegedly delivered shocks to a mild-mannered confederate, playing the role of the pupil or learner, while the subject enacted the teacher role. Some of the procedures in this research paradigm that seduced many ordinary citizens to engage in evil offer parallels to compliance strategies used by "influence professionals" in real-world settings, such as salespeople, cult recruiters, and our national leaders (see Cialdini, 2001).

Ten Ingredients in the Situationist's Recipe for Behavioral Transformations

Among the influence principles in Milgram's paradigm for getting ordinary people to do things they originally believed they would not do are the following:

1. Presenting an acceptable justification, or rationale, for engaging in the undesirable action, such as wanting to help people improve their memory by judicious use of punishment strategies. In experiments this justification is known as the "cover story" because it is intended to cover up the procedures that follow, which might not make sense on their own. The real-world equivalent of the cover story is an ideology, such as "national security," that often provides the nice big lie for instituting a host of bad, illegal, and immoral policies.
2. Arranging some form of contractual obligation, verbal or written, to enact the behavior.
3. Giving participants meaningful roles to play (e.g., teacher, student) that carry with them previously learned positive values and response scripts.
4. Presenting basic rules to be followed, which seem to make sense prior to their actual use, but then can be arbitrarily used to justify mindless compliance. "Failure to respond must be treated as an error" was a Milgram rule for shock omissions as well as for false commissions. But then what happens when the learner complains of a heart condition, wants to quit, then screams, followed by a thud and silence? The learner's apparent inability to respond to the teacher's testing due to death or unconsciousness must be continually challenged by further shocks, since omission equals commission. The proceedings do not make sense at all: How could the teacher be helping to improve the memory of a learner who is incapacitated or dead? All too many participants stopped engaging in such basic, obvious critical thinking endeavors as their confusion and stress mounted.
5. Altering the semantics of the act and action: from hurting victims to helping learners by punishing them.
6. Creating opportunities for diffusion of responsibility for negative outcomes; others will be responsible, or it will not be evident that the actor will be held liable.
7. Starting the path toward the ultimate evil act with a small, insignificant first step (only 15 volts).
8. Increasing each level of aggression in gradual steps that do not seem like noticeable differences (only 30 volts).

9. Gradually changing the nature of the influence authority from "just" to "unjust," from reasonable and rational to unreasonable and irrational.
10. Making the "exit costs" high and the process of exiting difficult by not permitting usual forms of verbal dissent to qualify as behavioral disobedience.

Such procedures are utilized across varied influence situations, in which those in authority want others to do their bidding but know that few would engage in the "end game" final solution without first being properly prepared psychologically to do the "unthinkable." I would encourage readers to engage in the thought exercise of applying these compliance principles to the tactics used by the Bush administration to cajole Americans into endorsing the preemptive invasion of Iraq (discussed further later in the chapter).

Lord of the Flies and the Psychology of Deindividuation

William Golding's (1954) Noble prize-winning novel of the transformation of good British choir boys into murderous beasts centers on the point of change in mental state and behavior that follows a change in physical appearance. Painting themselves, changing their outward appearance, made it possible for some of Golding's characters to disinhibit previously restrained impulses to kill a pig for food. Once that alien deed of killing another creature was accomplished, they could then continue on to kill, with pleasure, both animals and people alike. Was Golding describing a psychologically valid principle in his use of external appearance as catalyst to dramatic changes in internal and behavioral processes? That is the question I answered with a set of experiments and field studies on the psychology of deindividuation (Zimbardo, 1970).

The basic procedure involved having young women deliver a series of painful electric shocks to each of two other young women whom they could see and hear in a one-way mirror before them. Half were randomly assigned to a condition of anonymity, or deindividuation, half to one of uniqueness, or individuation. The appearance of the four college student subjects in each deindividuation group was concealed, and they were given identifying numbers in place of their names. The comparison individuation subjects in the four-woman groups were called by their names and made to feel unique. They were asked to make the same responses of shocking each of two female "victims"—all with a suitable cover story, the big lie that they never questioned.

The results were clear: Women in the deindividuation condition delivered twice as much shock to both victims as did the women in the individuated comparison condition. Moreover, the deindividuated subjects shocked both victims, the one previously rated as pleasant and the other as unpleasant, more over the course of the 20 trials, whereas the individuated subjects shocked the pleasant woman less over time than they did the unpleasant one. One important conclusion flows from this research and its various replications and extensions, some using military personnel: Anything that makes a person feel anonymous, as if no one knows who he or she is, creates the potential for that person to act in evil ways—if the situation gives permission for violence.

Halloween Disguises and Aggression in Children

Outside the laboratory, *masks* may be used to create the anonymity needed to disinhibit typically restrained behavior. For example, people mask themselves at Carnival rituals in many Catholic countries. Children in the United States don masks and costumes for Mardi Gras and Halloween parties. Bringing the laboratory to the party, so to speak, Fraser (1974) arranged for elementary school children to go to a special, experimental Halloween party given by their teacher. There were many games to play and for each game won, tokens were earned that could be exchanged for gifts at the end of the party. Half the games were nonaggressive in nature, and half were matched in content but involved aggression: Physical confrontations between two children were necessary to reach the goal and win the contest. The experimental design was a within-subject (A-B-A) format: in the first phase the games were played without costumes; then the costumes arrived and were worn as the games continued; finally, the costumes were removed and the games went on for the third phase (each phase lasted about an hour). The data are striking testimony to the power of anonymity. Aggression increased significantly as soon as the costumes were worn, more than doubling from the initial base level average. When the costumes were removed, aggression dropped back well below the initial base rate. Equally interesting was the second result: that aggression had negative instrumental consequences on winning tokens—that is, it costs money to be aggressive—but that cost did not matter when the children were anonymous in their costumes. The least number of tokens won occurred during the costumed anonymity phase, when aggression was highest.

Cultural Wisdom of Changing Warriors' Appearances

Let us leave the laboratory and the fun and games of children's parties to enter the real world, where these issues of anonymity and violence may take on life-and-death significance. Some societies go to war without having the young male warriors change their appearance, whereas others always include ritual transformations of appearance by painting or masking the warriors (as in *Lord of the Flies*). Does that change in external appearance make a difference in how warring enemies are treated? After reading my Nebraska Symposium chapter, Harvard anthropologist John Watson (1973) posed a research question, then went to the human area files to find the answer, then published the data: (1) the societies that did or did not change appearance of warriors prior to going to war; and (2) the extent to which they killed, tortured, or mutilated their victims. The results are striking confirmation of the prediction that anonymity promotes destructive behavior, when permission is also given to behave in aggressive ways that are ordinarily prohibited. Of the 23 societies for which these two data sets were present, the majority (12 of 15, 80%) of societies in which warriors changed their appearance were those noted as most destructive, whereas only one of the eight societies in which the warriors did *not* change appearance before going to battle was noted as destructive. Cultural wisdom dictates that when old men want usually peaceful young men to harm and kill other young men like themselves in a war, it is easier to do so if they first change their appearance by putting on uniforms or masks or painting their faces. With that anonymity in place, out goes their usual internal focus of compassion and concern for others.

The Theoretical Model of Deindividuation and Bandura's Model of Moral Disengagement

The psychological mechanisms involved in getting good people to do evil are embodied in two theoretical models, the first elaborated by me (Zimbardo, 1970) and modified by input from subsequent variants on my deindividuation conceptions, notably by Diener (1980). The second is Bandura's model of moral disengagement (1998, 2003), which specifies the conditions under which anyone can be led to act immorally, even those who usually ascribe to high levels of morality.

Bandura's model outlines how it is possible to morally disengage from destructive conduct by using a set of cognitive mechanisms that alter (1) one's perception of the reprehensible conduct (e.g., by engaging in moral justifications, making palliative comparisons, using euphemistic labeling for one's conduct); (2) one's sense of the detrimental effects of that conduct (e.g., by minimizing, ignoring, or misconstruing the consequences); (3) one's sense of responsibility for the link between reprehensible conduct and the detrimental effects (e.g., by displacing or diffusing responsibility); and (4) one's view of the victim (e.g., by dehumanizing him or her, attributing the blame for the outcome to the victim).

Dehumanization in Action: "Animals" by Any Other Name Are College Students

A remarkable experiment by Bandura, Underwood, and Fromson (1975) reveals how easy it is to induce intelligent college students to accept a dehumanizing label of other people and then to act aggressively based on that stereotyped term. Four participants were led to believe they were overhearing the research assistant tell the experimenter that the students from another college were present to start the study in which they were to deliver electric shocks of varying intensity to the participants (according to the dictates of a reasonable cover story). In one of the three randomly assigned conditions, the subjects overheard the assistant say to the experimenter that the other students seemed "nice"; in a second condition, they heard the other students described as "animals"; in the third group, the assistant did not label the students in the alleged other group.

The dependent variable of shock intensity clearly reflected this situational manipulation. The subjects gave the highest levels of shock to those labeled in the dehumanizing way as "animals," and their shock level increased linearly over the 10 trials. Those labeled "nice" were given the least shock, whereas the unlabelled group fell in the middle of these two extremes. Thus, a single word—*animals*—was sufficient to incite intelligent college students to treat those so labeled as if they deserved to be harmed. On the plus side, the labeling effect resulted in others being treated with greater respect if someone in authority labeled them positively. The graphed data is also of interest: On the first trial there is no difference across the three experimental treatments in the level of shock administered, but with each successive opportunity, the shock levels diverge. Those shocking the so-called "animals" shock them more and more over time, a result comparable to the escalating shock level of the deindividuated female students in my earlier study. That rise in aggressive responding over time, with practice, or with experience belies a self-reinforcing effect of aggressive or violent responding: It is experienced as increasingly pleasurable.

What my model adds to the mix of what is needed to get good people to engage in evil deeds is a focus on the role of cognitive controls that usually guide behavior in socially desirable and personally acceptable ways. The shift from good to evil behavior can be accomplished by knocking out these control processes, blocking them, minimizing them, or reorienting them. Doing so suspends conscience, self-awareness, sense of personal responsibility, obligation, commitment, liability, morality, and analyses in terms of costs-benefits of given actions. The two general strategies for accomplishing this objective are (1) reducing cues of social accountability of the actor (i.e., "No one knows who I am, nor cares to know"), and (2) reducing concerns for self-evaluation by the actor. The first eliminates concerns for social evaluation and social approval by conveying a sense of anonymity to the actor and diffusing personal responsibility across others in the situation. The second strategy stops self-monitoring and consistency monitoring by relying on tactics that alter states of consciousness (e.g., via drugs, arousing strong emotions or hyper-intense actions, creating a highly focused present-time orientation wherein there is no concern for past or future), and by projecting responsibility outside the self and onto others.

My research and that of other social psychologists (see Prentice-Dunn & Rogers, 1983) on deindividuation differs from the paradigm in Milgram's studies in that there is no authority figure present, urging the subject to obey. Rather, the situation is created in such a way that subjects act in accordance to paths made available to them, without thinking through the meaning or consequences of those actions. Their actions are not cognitively guided, as they are typically, but directed by the actions of others in proximity to them or by their strongly aroused emotional states and situationally available cues, such as the presence of weapons.

Environmental Anonymity Breeds Vandalism

It is possible for certain environments to convey a sense of anonymity on those who live in, or pass through, their midst. The people living in such environments do not have a sense of community. Vandalism and graffiti may be interpreted as an individual's attempt for public notoriety in a society that deindividuates him or her.

I conducted a simple field study to demonstrate the ecological differences between places ruled by anonymity versus those conveying a sense of community. I abandoned used but good-condition cars in the Bronx, New York City, and in Palo Alto, California, one block away from New York University and Stanford University, respectively. License plates were removed and hoods raised slightly to serve as ethological "releaser cues" for the potential vandals' attack behavior. It worked swiftly in the Bronx, as we watched and filmed from a vantage point across the street. Within 10 minutes of officially beginning this study, the first vandals surfaced. This parade of vandals continued for 2 days, by which time there was nothing of value left to strip; then they simply began destroying the remains. In 48 hours we recorded 23 separate "destructive contacts" by individuals or groups, who either took something from the abandoned vehicle or did something to wreck it. Curiously, only one of these episodes involved adolescents; the rest of the vandals were adults, many well dressed and many driving cars, so that they might qualify as, at least, lower middle class. Anonymity can make brazen vandals of us all. But what about the fate of the abandoned car in Palo Alto? Our time-lapse film revealed that no one vandalized any part of the car over a 5-day period. When we removed the car, three local residents called the police to say that an abandoned car was being stolen (the local police had been notified of our field study). That is one definition of "community," where people care about what happens on their turf, even to the person or property of strangers, with the reciprocal assumption that they would also care about them.

I now feel that any environmental or societal conditions that contribute to making some members of society feel that they are anonymous—that no one knows or cares who they are, that no one recognizes their individuality and thus their humanity—makes them potential assassins and vandals, a danger to my person and my property—and yours (Zimbardo, 1976).

The Faces of the "Enemy": Propaganda Images Condition Us to Kill Abstractions

We need to add a few more operational principles to our arsenal of variables that trigger the commission of evil acts by men and women who are ordinarily good people. We can learn about some of these principles by considering how nations prepare their young men (admittedly, women are now members of the armed forces in many countries, but it is primarily the men who are sent into combat zones) to engage in deadly wars, and how they prepare citizens to support the risks of going to war, especially a war of aggression. This difficult transformation is accomplished by a special form of cognitive conditioning. Images of "The Enemy" are created by national propaganda to prepare the minds of soldiers and citizens alike to hate those who fit the new category of "your enemy." This mental conditioning is a soldier's most potent weapon, for without it, he could probably never fire his weapon to kill another young man in the cross-hairs of his gun sight. A fascinating account of how this "hostile imagination" is created in the minds of soldiers and their families is presented in *Faces of the Enemy* by Sam Keen (1986; see also his companion video). Archetypal images of the enemy are created by propaganda fashioned by the governments of most nations against those judged to be the dangerous "them"—the outsiders who are also "our" enemies. These visual images create a consensual societal paranoia that is focused on the enemy who would do harm to the women, children, homes, and god of the soldier's nation, way of life, and so forth. Keen's analysis of this propaganda on a worldwide scale reveals that there are a select number of attributes utilized by "homo hostilis" to invent an evil enemy in the minds of good members of righteous tribes. The enemy is aggressive, faceless, a rapist, godless, barbarian, greedy, criminal, a torturer, harbinger of death, a dehumanized animal, or just an abstraction. Finally, there is the enemy as worthy, heroic opponent to be crushed in mortal combat—as in the video game of the same name.

Ordinary Men Murder Ordinary Men, Women, and Children: Jewish Enemies

One of the clearest illustrations of my fundamental theme of how ordinary people can be transformed into engaging in evil deeds that are alien to their past history and to their moral development comes from the analysis of British historian Christopher Browning. In *Ordinary Men: Reserve Police Battalion 101 and the Final Solution in Poland* (1992) he recounts that in March 1942 about 80% of all victims of the Holocaust were still alive, but a mere 11 months later about 80% were dead. In this short period of time, the *Endlösung* (Hitler's "Final Solution") was galvanized by means of an intense wave of mass mobile murder squads in Poland. This genocide required mobilization of a large-scale killing machine at the same time as able-bodied soldiers were needed on the Russian front. Since most Polish Jews lived in small towns and not the large cities, the question that Browning raised about the German High Command was "where had they found the manpower during this pivotal year of the war for such an astounding logistical achievement in mass murder?" (p. xvi).

His answer came from archives of Nazi war crimes, in the form of the activities of Reserve Battalion 101, a unit of about 500 men from Hamburg, Germany. They were elderly family men, too old to be drafted into the army, from working-class and lower middle-class backgrounds, with no military or police experience, just raw recruits sent to Poland without warning of, or any training in, their secret mission: the total extermination of all Jews living in the remote villages of Poland. In just 4 months they had shot to death at point blank range at least 38,000 Jews and had deported another 45,000 to the concentration camp at Treblinka. Initially, their commander told them that this was a difficult mission which must be obeyed by the battalion, but any individual could refuse to execute these men, women, and children. Records indicate that at first about half the men refused, letting the others commit the mass murder. But over time, social modeling processes took their toll, as did any guilt-induced persuasion by buddies who did the killing, until by the end, up to 90% of the men in Battalion 101 had participated in the shootings, even proudly taking photographs of their up-close and personal slaughter of Jews.

Browning makes clear that there was no special selection of these men, only that they were as "ordinary" as could be imagined—until they were put into a situation in which they had "official" permission, even encouragement, to act sadistically and brutishly against those arbitrarily labeled, as "the enemy."

Let us go from the abstract to the personal for a moment: Imagine you witnessed your own father shooting to death a helpless mother and her infant child, and then imagine his answer to your question, "Why did you do it, Daddy?"

The War on Iraq: A Spurious Creation of Evil Terrorists and Infusion of National Fears

Fast forward to our time, our nation, our citizenry, and the fears of terrorism instilled by the destruction of the World Trade Center towers since that unforgettable day of September 11, 2001. The initial press and official reaction was to label the perpetrators of this horrific deed as "hijackers," "murderers," "criminals." Soon the label changed to "terrorists" and their deeds described as "evil." *Evil* became the coin of the realm, used repeatedly by the media as fed by the administration, and with an ever-widening net of inclusiveness. Osama bin Laden, the mastermind of 9/11, was the first culprit designated as evil. But when he proved elusive, escaping from the war zone in Afghanistan, it became necessary for the administration's war on terrorism campaign to put a new face and a new place on terrorism. Of course, terrorism works its generation of fear and anxiety by its very facelessness and nonlocal ubiquity. Several countries were labeled by our president as the "axis of evil," with the leader of one of those countries, Iraq, designated as so evil that he, Saddam Hussein, had to be removed from power by all means necessary.

A propaganda campaign was created to justify a preemptive war against Saddam Hussein's regime by identifying the clear and imminent threat to the national security of the United States posed by the alleged weapons of mass destruction (WMD) this evil leader had at his disposal. Then a link was erected between him and the terrorist networks to whom, allegedly, he would sell or gift these WMD. Over time, many Americans began to believe the falsehoods that Saddam Hussein was involved in the 9/11 terrorist attacks, was in complicity with Osama bin Laden, and had ready and operational an arsenal of deadly weapons that threatened U.S. security and well-being. Magazine images, newspaper accounts, and vivid TV stories contributed to the "evilization" of Saddam Hussein over the course of a year.

The vulnerability to terrorism that Americans continued to experience on deep, personal levels—in part, sustained and magnified by the administration's issuance of repeated (false) alarms of imminent terrorist attacks on the homeland—was relieved by the action of officially going to war. The public and Congress strongly supported a symmetrical war of "shock and awe"—to rid Iraq of the feared WMD and destroy Hussein's evil menace. Thus, for the first time in its history, the United States endorsed what the majority believed to be a justified aggressive war that has already cost billions of dollars, untold thousands of deaths (soldiers *and* civilians), totally destroyed a nation, weakened the United Nations, and will enmesh the United States in a prolonged, Vietnam-like, "no exit" scenario for years to come.

When no WMD were uncovered, despite the alleged best intelligence reports and aerial photos of them presented by the Secretary of State to the United Nations, collective cognitive dissonance reduction seeped in to maintain the belief that it was still a "necessary" and "good" war against evil (Festinger, 1957). After many months of an all-out, desperately intense search of every part of Iraq, American troops and intelligence forces have not unearthed a single WMD! So the original reason for going to war is being played down and is being replaced by the mantra that Iraq is the new front in our worldwide fight against terrorism, thus it is good we are in control of the destiny of Iraq. But who cares what the truth really is regarding the deceptive reasons for going to war, if the United States is now safer and the president is a commander-in-chief of decisive action—as his image crafters have carefully depicted him in the media. This national mind control experiment deserves careful documenting by unbiased social historians for the current and future generations to appreciate the power of images, words, and framing that can lead a democratic nation to support *and even relish* the unthinkable evil of an aggressive war.

The Socialization of Evil: How the "Nazi Hate Primers" Prepared and Conditioned the Minds of German Youth to Hate Jews

The second broad class of operational principles by which otherwise good people can be recruited into evil is through education/socialization processes that are sanctioned by the government in power, enacted within school programs, and supported by parents and teachers. A prime example is the way in which German children in the 1930s and 1940s were systematically indoctrinated to hate Jews, to view them as the all-purpose enemy of the new (post-World War I) German nation. Space limitations do not allow full documentation of this process, but I touch on several examples of one way in which governments are responsible for sanctioning evil.

In Germany, as the Nazi party rose to power in 1933, no target of Nazification took higher priority than the reeducation of Germany's youth. Hitler wrote: "I will have no intellectual training. Knowledge is ruin to my young men. A violently active, dominating, brutal youth—that is what I am after" (*The New Order*, 1989, pp. 101–102). To teach the youth about geography and race, special primers were created and ordered to be read starting in the first grade of elementary school (see *The New Order*, 1989). These "hate primers" were brightly colored comic books that contrasted the beautiful blond Aryans with the despicably ugly caricatured Jew. They sold in the hundreds of thousands. One was titled *Trust No Fox in the Green Meadows and No Jew on His Oath*. What is most insidious about this kind of hate conditioning is that the misinformation was presented as facts to be learned and tested upon, or from which to practice penmanship. In the copy of the *Trust No Fox* text that I reviewed, a series of cartoons illustrates all the ways in which Jews supposedly deceive Aryans, get rich and fat from dominating them, and are lascivious, mean, and without compassion for the plight of the poor and the elderly Aryans.

The final scenarios depict the retribution of Aryan children when they expel Jewish teachers and children from their school, so that "proper discipline and order" could then be taught. Initially, Jews were prohibited from community areas, like public parks, then expelled altogether from Germany. The sign in the cartoon reads, ominously, "One-way street." Indeed, it was a unidirectional street that led eventually to the death camps and crematoria that were the centerpiece of Hitler's Final Solution: the genocide of the Jews. Thus, this institutionalized evil was spread pervasively and insidiously through a perverted educational system that turned away from the types of critical thinking exercises that open students' minds to new ideas and toward thinking uncritically and close-mindedly about those targeted as the enemy of the people. By controlling education and the propaganda media, any national leader could produce the fantastic scenarios depicted in George Orwell's (1981) frightening novel *1984*.

The institutionalized evil that Orwell vividly portrays in his fictional account of state dominance over individuals goes beyond the novelist's imagination when its prophetic vision is carried into operational validity by powerful cult leaders or by agencies and departments within the current national administration of the United States. Previously I have outlined the direct parallels between the mind control strategies and tactics Orwell attributes to "The Party" and those that Reverend Jim Jones used in dominating the members of his religious/political cult, Peoples Temple (Zimbardo, 2003a). Jones orchestrated the suicide/murders of more than 900 U.S. citizens in the jungles of Guyana 25 years ago, perhaps as the grand finale of his experiment in institutionalized mind control. I learned from former members of this group that not only did Jones read *1984*, he talked about it often and even had a song commissioned by the church's singer, entitled "1984 Is Coming," that everyone had to sing at some services. I will leave it to the reader to explore the similarities between the mind control practices in *1984* and those being practiced on U.S. citizens in the past few years (see Zimbardo, 2003b).

The Stanford Prison Experiment: A Crucible of Human Nature Where Good Boys Encountered an Evil Place

Framing the issues we have been considering as, in essence, who wins when good boys are put in an evil place casts it as a neo-Greek tragedy scenario, wherein "the situation" stands in for the externally imposed forces of "the gods and destiny." As such, we can anticipate an outcome unfavorable to humanity. In more mundane psychological terms, this research on the Stanford prison experiment synthesized many of the processes and variables outlined earlier: those of place and person anonymity that contribute to the deindividuation of the people involved, the dehumanization of victims, giving some actors (guards) permission to control others (prisoners), and placing it all within a unique setting (the prison) that most societies throughout the world acknowledge provides some form of institutionally approved sanctions for evil through the extreme differentials in control and power fostered in prison environments.

In 1971, I designed a dramatic experiment that would extend over a 2-week period to provide our research participants with sufficient time for them to become fully engaged in their experimentally assigned roles of either guards or prisoners. Having participants live in a simulated prison setting day and night, if prisoners, or work there for long 8-hour shifts, if guards, would also allow sufficient time for situational norms to develop and patterns of social interaction to emerge, change, and crystallize. The second feature of this study was to ensure that all research participants would be as normal as possible initially, healthy both physically and mentally, and without any history of involvement in drugs or crime or violence. This baseline was essential to establish if we were to untangle the situational versus dispositional knot: What the situation elicited from this collection of similar, interchangeable young men versus what was emitted by the research participants based on the unique dispositions they brought into the experiment. The third feature of the study was the novelty of the prisoner and guard roles: Participants had no prior training in how to play the randomly assigned roles. Each subject's prior societal learning of the meaning of prisons and the behavioral scripts associated with the oppositional roles of prisoner and guard was the sole source of guidance. The fourth feature was to create an experimental setting that came as close to a *functional simulation* of the psychology of imprisonment as possible. The details of how we went about creating a mindset comparable to that of real prisoners and guards are given in several of the articles I wrote about the study (see Zimbardo, 1975; Zimbardo, Haney, Banks, & Jaffe, 1973).

Central to this mind set were the oppositional issues of power and powerlessness, dominance and submission, freedom and servitude, control and rebellion, identity and anonymity, coercive rules and restrictive roles. In general, these social-psychological constructs were operationalized by putting all subjects in appropriate uniforms, using assorted props (e.g., handcuffs, police clubs, whistles, signs on doors and halls), replacing corridor hall doors with prison bars to create prison cells, using windowless and clock-less cells that afforded no clues as to time of day, applying institutional rules that removed/substituted individual names with numbers (prisoners) or titles for staff (Mr. Correctional Officer, Warden, Superintendent), and that gave guards control power over prisoners.

Subjects were recruited from among nearly 100 men between the ages of 18 and 30 who answered our advertisements in the local city newspaper. They were given a background evaluation that consisted of a battery of five psychological tests, personal history, and in-depth interviews. The 24 who were evaluated as most normal and healthiest in every respect were randomly assigned, half to the role of prisoner and half to that of guard. The student-prisoners underwent a realistic surprise arrest by officers from the Palo Alto Police Department, who cooperated with our plan. The arresting officer proceeded with a formal arrest, taking the "felons" to the police station for booking, after which each prisoner was brought to our prison in the reconstructed basement of our psychology department.

The prisoner's uniform was a smock/dress with a prison ID number. The guards wore military-style uniforms and silver-reflecting sunglasses to enhance anonymity. At any one time there were nine prisoners on "the yard," three to a cell, and three guards working 8-hour shifts. Data were collected via systematic video recordings, secret audio recordings of conversations of prisoners in their cells, interviews and tests at various times during the study, postexperiment reports, and direct, concealed observations.

For a detailed chronology and fuller account of the behavioral reactions that followed, readers are referred to the above references, to Zimbardo, Maslach, and Haney (1999), and to our new website: *www.prisonexp.org*. For current purposes, let me simply summarize that the negative situational forces overwhelmed the positive dispositional tendencies. The Evil Situation triumphed over the Good People. Our projected 2-week experiment had to be terminated after only 6 days because of the pathology we were witnessing. Pacifistic young men were behaving sadistically in their role as guards, inflicting humiliation and pain and suffering on other young men who had the inferior status of prisoner. Some "guards" even reported enjoying doing so. Many of the intelligent, healthy college students who were occupying the role of prisoner showed signs of "emotional breakdown" (i.e., stress disorders) so extreme that five of them had to be removed from the experiment within that first week. The prisoners who adapted better to the situation were those who mindlessly followed orders and who allowed the guards to dehumanize and degrade them ever more with each passing day and night. The only personality variable that had any significant predictive value was that of *F*-scale authoritarianism: The higher the score, the more days the prisoner survived in this totally authoritarian environment.

I terminated the experiment not only because of the escalating level of violence and degradation by the guards against the prisoners that was apparent when viewing the videotapes of their interactions, but also because I was made aware of the transformation that I was undergoing personally (see the analysis by Christina Maslach of how she intervened to help bring light to that dark place and end the study; in Zimbardo et al., 1999). I had become a Prison Superintendent in addition to my role as Principal Investigator. I began to talk, walk, and act like a rigid institutional authority figure more concerned about the security of "my prison" than the needs of the young men entrusted to my care as a psychological researcher. In a sense, I consider the extent to which I was transformed to be the most profound measure of the power of this situation. We held extended debriefing sessions of guards and prisoners at the end of the study and conducted periodic checkups over many years. Fortunately, there were no lasting negative consequences of this powerful experience.

Before moving on, I would like to share parts of a letter sent to me recently (e-mail communication, October 18, 2002) by a young psychology student, recently discharged from military service. It outlines some of the direct parallels between the aversive aspects of our simulated prison many years ago and current despicable practices still taking place in some military boot-camp training. It also points up the positive effects that research and education can have:

> I am a 19-year-old student of psychology [who watched] the slide show of your prison experiment. Not too far into it, I was almost in tears. . . . I joined the United States Marine Corps, pursuing a childhood dream. To make a long story short, I had become the victim of repeated illegal physical and mental abuse. An investigation showed I suffered more than 40 unprovoked beatings. Eventually, as much as I fought it, I became suicidal, thus received a discharge from boot camp. . . .
>
> The point I am trying to make is that the manner in which your guards carried about their duties and the way that military drill instructors do is unbelievable. I was amazed at all the parallels of your guards and one particular D.I. who comes to mind. I was treated much the same way, and even worse, in some cases.

One incident that stands out was the time, in an effort to break platoon solidarity, I was forced to sit in the middle of my squad bay (living quarters) and shout to the other recruits "If you guys would have moved faster, we wouldn't be doing this for hours," referencing every single recruit who was holding over his head a very heavy foot locker. The event was very similar to the prisoners saying #819 was a bad prisoner. After my incident, and after I was home safe some months later, all I could think about was how much I wanted to go back to show the other recruits that as much as the D. I.s told the platoon that I was a bad recruit, I wasn't.

Other behaviors come to mind, like the push-ups we did for punishment, the shaved heads, not having any identity other than being addressed as, and referring to other people as, "Recruit So-and-So"—which replicates your study. The point of it all is that even though your experiment was conducted 31 years ago, my reading the study has helped me gain an understanding I was previously unable to gain before, even after therapy and counseling. What you have demonstrated really gave me insight into something I've been dealing with for almost a year now. Although, it is certainly not an excuse for their behavior, I now can understand the rationale behind the D. I.'s actions as far as being sadistic and power hungry.

The Failure of the Social Experiment of the U.S. Correctional System

As much joy that such personal reactions bring to someone whose vision has always been for psychological research to make a difference in people's lives, I have been saddened by the lack of impact the Stanford prison experiment has had on the correctional system in the United States. When Craig Haney and I recently did a retrospective analysis of our study, with contrasting views of U.S. and California correctional policies over the past 30 years, our conclusions were disheartening (Haney & Zimbardo, 1998). Prisons continue to be failed social experiments that rely on a dispositional model of punishment and isolation of offenders. Gone is any sense of the modifiable situational determinants of crime or of basic rehabilitation practices that might reduce persistently high rates of recidivism. The United States is now the prison center of the universe, with more than 2 million citizens incarcerated, *greater than any other nation*, and growing. Our analysis revealed that prison conditions had significantly worsened in the decades since our study, as a consequence of the politicization of prisons, with politicians, prosecutors, DAs, and other officials taking a hard line on crime as a means of currying favor of an electorate made fearful of crime by media exaggerations. Misguided policies about sentencing for crack cocaine use and sale and the "Three Strikes" rulings have put a disproportionately large number of African American and Hispanic men behind bars for long sentences. There are now more African American men wasting away in the nation's prison system than fulfilling their potentials in our higher educational system.

The Evil of Inaction

Our usual take on evil focuses on violent, destructive actions, but *non*action can also become a form of evil, when assistance, dissent, and disobedience are needed. Social psychologists heeded the alarm when the infamous Kitty Genovese case made national headlines. As she was being stalked, stabbed, and eventually murdered, 39 people in a housing complex heard her screams and did nothing to help. It seemed obvious that this was a prime example of the callousness of New Yorkers, as many media accounts reported. A counter to this dispositional analysis came in the form of a series of classic studies by Latané and Darley (1970) on bystander intervention. One key finding was that people are less likely to help when they are in a group, when they perceive that others are available who could help, than when those people are alone. The presence of others diffuses the sense of personal responsibility of any individual.

A powerful demonstration of the failure to help strangers in distress was staged by Darley and Batson (1973). Imagine you are a theology student on your way to deliver the sermon of the Good Samaritan in order to have it videotaped for a psychology study on effective communication. Further imagine that as you are heading from the psychology department to the video taping center, you pass a stranger huddled up in an alley in dire distress. Are there any conditions that you could conceive that would not make you stop to be that Good Samaritan? What about "time press"? Would it make a difference to you if you were late for your date to give that sermon? I bet you would like to believe it would not make a difference, that you would stop and help no matter what the circumstances. Right? Remember, you are a theology student, thinking about helping a stranger in distress, which is amply rewarded in the Biblical tale.

The researchers randomly assigned students of the Princeton Theological Seminary to three conditions that varied in how much time they thought they had between receiving their assignment from the researchers and getting to the communication department to tape their Good Samaritan speeches. The conclusion: Do not be a victim in distress when people are late and in a hurry, because 90% of them are likely to pass you by, giving you no help at all! The more time the seminarians believed they had, the more likely they were to stop and help. So the situational variable of *time press* accounted for the major variance in extending or withholding help, without any need to resort to dispositional explanations about theology students being callous or cynical or indifferent, as Kitty Genovese's nonhelpers were assumed to be—another instance of the FAE, one that needs to be reversed.

The Worst of the Apples in the Evil Barrel: Torturers and Executioners?

There is little debate but that the systematic torture by men and women of their fellow men and women represents one of the darkest sides of human nature. Surely, my colleagues and I reasoned, here was a place where dispositional evil would be manifest among torturers who did their dirty deeds daily, for years, in Brazil as policemen sanctioned by the government to extract confessions through torturing so-called enemies of the state. We began by focusing solely on the torturers, trying to understand both their psyches and the ways they were shaped by their circumstances, but we had to expand our analytical net to capture their comrades-in-arms who chose, or were assigned to, another branch of violence work—death-squad executioners. They shared a "common enemy": men, women, and children who, though citizens of their state, even neighbors, were declared by "the authorities" to be threats to the country's national security. Some had to be eliminated efficiently, whereas those who might hold secret information had to be made to yield it up and confess to their treason.

In carrying out this mission, these torturers could rely, in part, on the "creative evil" embodied in the torture devices and techniques that had been refined over centuries since the Inquisition by officials of The Church and, later, of the National State. But our current-day torturers added a measure of improvisation to accommodate the particular resistances and resiliencies of the enemy standing before them, claiming innocence, refusing to acknowledge their culpability, or not succumbing to intimidation. It took time and emerging insights into exploitable human weaknesses for these torturers to become adept at their craft, in contrast to the task of the death-squad executioners, who, wearing hoods for anonymity and sporting good guns and group support, could dispatch their duty to country swiftly and impersonally. For the torturer, it could never be "just business." Torture always involves a personal relationship, essential for understanding what kind of torture to employ, what intensity of torture to use on this person at this time: wrong kind or too little, no confession; too much, and the victim dies before confessing. In either case, the torturer fails to deliver the goods. Learning to select the right kind and degree of torture that yields up the desired information makes rewards abound and praise flow from the superiors.

What kind of men could do such deeds? Did they need to rely on sadistic impulses and a history of sociopathic life experiences to rip and tear flesh of fellow beings day in and day out for years on end? Were these violence workers a breed apart from the rest of humanity—bad seeds, bad tree trunks, bad flowers? Or, is it conceivable that they were programmed to carry out their deplorable deeds by means of some identifiable and replicable training processes? Could a set of external conditions—that is, situational variables—that contributed to the making of these torturers and killers be identified? If their evil deeds were not traceable to inner defects but attributable to outer forces acting upon them—the political, economic, social, historical, and experiential components of their police training—then we might be able to generalize, across cultures and settings, those principles responsible for this remarkable transformation. Martha Huggins, Mika Haritos-Fatouros, and I interviewed several dozen of these violence workers in depth and recently published a summary of our methods and findings (Huggins, Haritos-Fatouros, & Zimbardo, 2002). Mika had done a similar, earlier study of torturers trained by the Greek military junta, and our results were largely congruent with hers (Haritos-Fatouros, 2003).

We learned that sadists are *selected out* of the training process by trainers because they are not controllable, get off on the pleasure of inflicting pain, and thus do not sustain the focus on the goal of confession extraction. From all the evidence we could muster, these violence workers were not unusual or deviant in any way prior to practicing this new role, nor were there any persisting deviant tendencies or pathologies among any of them in the years following their work as torturers and executioners. Their transformation was entirely understandable as a consequence of (1) the training they were given to play this new role, (2) group camaraderie, (3) acceptance of the national security ideology, and (4) the belief in socialist-communists as enemies of their state. They were also influenced by being made to feel special—above and better than peers in public service—by the secrecy of their duties and by the constant pressure to produce desired results regardless of fatigue or personal problems. We report many detailed case studies that document the ordinariness of these men engaged in the most heinous of deeds, sanctioned by their government at that time in history, but reproducible at this time in any nation whose obsession with national security and fears of terrorism permit suspension of basic individual freedoms.

Suicide Bombers: Senseless Fanatics or Martyrs for a Cause?

Not surprisingly, what holds true for the Brazilian violence workers is comparable to the nature of the transformation of young Palestinians from students to suicide bombers killing Israelis. Recent media accounts converge on the findings from more systematic analyses of the process of becoming a suicidal killer (see Atran, 2003; Bennet, 2003; Hoffman, 2003; Merari, 1990, 2002; Myer, 2003). There have been more than 95 suicide bombings by Palestinians against Israelis since September, 2000. Originally, and most frequently, the bombers were young men, but recently a half dozen women have joined the ranks of suicidal bombers. What has been declared as senseless, mindless murder by those attacked and by outside observers is anything but to those intimately involved. It was mistakenly believed that it was poor, desperate, socially isolated, illiterate young people with no career and no future who adopted this fatalistic role. That stereotype has been shattered by the actual portraits of these young men and women, many of whom were students with hopes for a better future, intelligent and attractive youth, connected with their family and community.

Ariel Merari, an Israeli psychologist who has studied this phenomenon for many years, outlines the common steps on the path to these explosive deaths. Senior members of an extremist group first identify particular young people who appear to have an intense patriotic fervor, based on their declarations at public rallies against Israel or their support of some Islamic cause or Palestinian action. These individuals are invited to discuss how serious they are in their love of their country and their hatred of Israel. They are then asked to commit to being trained in how to put their hatred into action. Those who make the commitment are put into a small group of three to five similar youth who are at varying stages of "progress" toward becoming agents of death. They learn the tricks of the trade from elders: bomb making, disguise, selecting and timing targets. Then they publicize their private commitment by making a videotape on which they declare themselves to be "living martyrs" for Islam and for the love of Allah. In one hand they hold the Koran, a rifle in the other, their head-band declaring their new status. This video binds them to the final deed, since it is sent home to the family of the recruit before they execute the final plan. The recruits also realize that not only will they earn a place beside Allah, but their relatives will also be entitled to a high place in heaven because of their martyrdom. A sizable financial incentive is bestowed on their family as a gift for their sacrifice.

Their photo is emblazoned on posters that will be put on walls everywhere in the community the moment they succeed in their mission. They will be immortalized as inspirational models. To stifle concerns about the pain from wounds inflicted by exploding nails and other bomb parts, they are told that before the first drop of their blood touches the ground, they will already be seated at the side of Allah, feeling no pain, only pleasure. An ultimate incentive for the young males is the promise of heavenly bliss with scores of virgins in the next life. They become heroes and heroines, modeling self-sacrifice to the next cadre of young suicide bombers.

We can see that this program utilizes a variety of social-psychological and motivational principles in turning collective hatred and general frenzy into a dedicated, seriously calculated program of indoctrination and training for individuals to become youthful "living martyrs." It is neither mindless nor senseless, only a very different mind set and with different sensibilities than we have been used to witnessing among young adults in our country. A recent television program on female suicide bombers went so far as to describe them in terms more akin to the girl next door than to alien fanatics. Indeed, that very normalcy is what is so frightening about the emergence of this new social phenomena—that so many intelligent young people could be persuaded to envision and welcome their lives ending in a suicidal explosive blast.

To counteract the powerful tactics of these recruiting agents requires the provision of meaningful, life-affirming alternatives to this next generation. It requires new national leadership that is willing and able to explore every negotiating strategy that could lead to peace instead of death. It requires these young people across national boundaries to openly share their values, their education, and their resources and to explore their commonalities, not highlight their differences. The suicide, the murder, of any young person is a gash in the fabric of the human connection that we elders from every nation must unite to prevent. To encourage the sacrifice of youth for the sake of advancing ideologies of the old might be considered a form of evil from a more cosmic perspective that transcends local politics and expedient strategies.

Conclusions

It is a truism in psychology that personality and situations interact to generate behavior, as do cultural and societal influences. However, I have tried to show in my research over the past 30 years that situations exert more power over human actions than has been generally acknowledged by most psychologists or recognized by the general public. Along with a hardy band of experimental social psychologists, I have conducted research demonstrations designed, in part, to provide a corrective balance to the pervasive fundamental attribution error. Nevertheless, the traditional dispositional perspective continues to dominate Anglo-American psychology fueled by reliance on the individualist orientation central in our institutions of medicine, education, psychiatry, law, and religion. Acknowledging the power of situational forces does not excuse the behaviors evoked in response to their operation. Rather, it provides a knowledge base that shifts attention away from simplistic "blaming the victim" mentality and ineffective individualistic treatments designed to change the evil doer, toward more profound attempts to discover causal networks that should be modified. Sensitivity to situational determinants of behavior also affords "risk alerts" that allow us to avoid or modify prospective situations of vulnerability.

Please consider this Zimbardo homily that captures the essence of the difference between dispositional and situational orientations: "While a few bad apples might spoil the barrel (filled with good fruit/people), a barrel filled with vinegar will *always* transform sweet cucumbers into sour pickles—regardless of the best intentions, resilience, and genetic nature of those cucumbers." So, does it make more sense to spend our resources on attempts to identify, isolate, and destroy the few bad apples or to learn how vinegar works so that we can teach cucumbers how to avoid undesirable vinegar barrels?

My situational sermon has several related dimensions. First, we should be aware that a range of apparently simple situational factors can impact our behavior more compellingly than we would expect or predict. The research outlined here, along with that of my colleagues presented in this volume, points to the influential force of numerous variables: role playing, rules, presence of others, emergent group norms, group identity, uniforms, anonymity, social modeling, authority presence, symbols of power, time pressures, semantic framing, stereotypical images and labels, among others.

Second, the situationist approach redefines heroism. When the majority of ordinary people can be overcome by such pressures toward compliance and conformity, the minority who resist should be considered *heroic.* Acknowledging the special nature of this resistance means that we should learn from their example by studying *how* they have been able to rise above such compelling pressures. That suggestion is coupled with another that encourages the development of an essential but ignored domain of psychology—heroes and heroism.

Third, the situationist approach should, in my view, encourage us all to share a profound sense of personal humility when trying to understand those "unthinkable," "unimaginable," "senseless" acts of evil. Instead of immediately embracing the high moral ground that distances us good folks from those bad ones and gives short shrift to analyses of causal factors in the situations that form the context of the evil acts, the situational approach gives all others the benefit of "attributional charity." This means that any deed, for good or evil, that any human being has ever performed or committed, you and I could also perform or commit—given the same situational forces. If so, it becomes imperative to constrain our immediate moral outrage that seeks vengeance against wrongdoers and turn our efforts toward uncovering the causal factors that could have led them in that aberrant direction.

The obvious current instantiation of these principles is the rush to characterize terrorists and suicide bombers as "evil" people, instead of working to understand the nature of the psychological, social, economic, and political conditions that have fostered such generalized hatred of an enemy nation, including our own, that young people are willing to sacrifice their lives and murder other human beings. The "war on terrorism" can never be won solely by the current administration's plans to find and destroy terrorists—since any  individual, anywhere, at any time, can become an active terrorist. It is only by understanding the *situational determinants of terrorism* that programs can be developed to win the hearts and minds of potential terrorists away from destruction and toward creation—not a simple task, but an essential one that requires implementation of social-psychological perspectives and methods in a comprehensive, long-term plan of attitude, value, and behavior change.

REFERENCES

Adorno, T. W., Frenkel-Brunswick, E., Levenson, D. J., & Sanford, R. N. (1950). *The authoritarian personality.* New York: Harper & Row.

Atran, S. (2003, May 5), Who wants to be a martyr? *The New York Times,* p. A23.

Bandura, A. (1998). Mechanisms of moral disengagement. In W. Reich (Ed.), *Origins of terrorism: Psychologies, ideologies, theologies, states of mind* (pp. 161–191). New York: Cambridge University Press.

Bandura, A. (2003). The role of selective moral disengagement in terrorism and counterterrorism. In F. M. Mogahaddam & A. J. Marsella (Eds.), *Understanding terrorism* (pp. 121–150). Washington, DC: American Psychological Association.

Bandura, A., Underwood, B., & Fromson, M. E. (1975). Disinhibition of aggression through diffusion of responsibility and dehumanization of victims. *Journal of Personality and Social Psychology, 9*, 253–269.

Barstow, A. L. (1994). *Witchcraze: A new history of the European witch hunts.* New York: HarperCollins.

Baumeister, R. F. (1997). *Evil: Inside human cruelty and violence.* New York: Freeman.

Bennet, J. (2003, May 30). A scholar of English who clung to the veil. *The New York Times*, pp. A1, A14.

Browning, C. R. (1992). *Ordinary men: Reserve police battalion 101 and the final solution in Poland.* New York: HarperPerennial.

Chang, I. (1997). *The rape of Nanking: The forgotten holocaust of World War II.* New York: Basic Books.

Cialdini, R. B. (2001). *Influence: Science and practice* (4th ed.). Boston: Allyn & Bacon.

Darley, J. M. (1992). Social organization for the production of evil. *Psychological Inquiry 3*, 199–218.

Darley, J. M., & Batson, D. (1973). From Jerusalem to Jericho: A study of situational and dispositional variables in helping behavior. *Journal of Personality and Social Psychology, 27*, 100–108.

Diener, E. (1980). Deindividuation: The absence of self-awareness and self-regulation in group members. In P. B. Paulus (Ed.), *The psychology of group influence* (pp. 209–243). Hillsdale, NJ: Erlbaum.

Festinger, L. (1957). *A theory of cognitive dissonance.* Palo Alto, CA: Stanford University Press.

Fraser, S. C. (1974). *Deindividuation: Effects of anonymity on aggression in children.* Unpublished manuscript, University of Southern California, Los Angeles.

Golding, W. (1954). *Lord of the flies.* New York: Capricorn Books.

Haney, C., & Zimbardo, P. G. (1998). The past and future of U.S. prison policy: Twenty-five years after the Stanford Prison Experiment. *American Psychologist, 53*, 709–727.

Haritos-Fatouros, M. (2003). *The psychological origins of institutionalized torture.* London: Routledge.

Hoffman, B. (2003, June). The logic of suicide terrorism. *The Atlantic Monthly*, 40–47.

Huggins, M., Haritos-Fatouros, M., & Zimbardo, P. G. (2002). *Violence workers: Police torturers and murderers reconstruct Brazilian atrocities.* Berkeley: University of California Press.

Keen, S. (1986). *Faces of the enemy: Reflections of the hostile imagination.* New York: HarperCollins.

Kramer, H., & Sprenger, J. (1971). *The malleus maleficarum.* New York: Dover. (Original work published 1486.)

Latané, B., & Darley, J. M. (1970). *The unresponsive bystander: Why doesn't he help?* New York: Appleton-Century-Crofts.

Lee, M., Zimbardo, P. G., & Bertholf, M. (1977). Shy murderers. *Psychology Today, 11,* 69–70, 76, 148.

Merari, A. (1990). The readiness to kill and die: Suicidal terrorism in the Middle East. In W. Reich (Ed.), *Origins of terrorism: Psychologies, theologies, states of mind* (pp. 192–200). New York: Cambridge University Press.

Merari, A. (2002, October). *Suicide terrorism.* Paper presented at the First Conference of the National Center for Disaster Psychology and Terrorism, Palo Alto, CA.

Milgram, S. (1974). *Obedience to authority.* New York: Harper & Row.

Myer, G. (2003, May 30). A young man radicalized by his months in jail. *The New York Times,* pp. A1, A14.

The new order (The Third Reich). (1989). Alexandria, VA: Time Life Books.

Orwell, G. (1981). *1984.* New York: Signet.

Prentice-Dunn, S., & Rogers, R. W. (1983). Deindividuation and aggression. In R. G. Geen & E. I. Donnerstein (Eds.), *Aggression: Theoretical and empirical reviews—issues in research* (Vol. 2, pp. 155–171). New York: Academic Press.

Ross, L. (1977). The intuitive psychologist and his shortcomings. In L. Berkowitz (Ed.), *Advances in experimental social psychology* (Vol. 10, pp. 173–220). New York: Academic Press.

Staub, E. (1989). *The roots of evil: The origins of genocide and other group violence.* New York: Cambridge University Press.

Waller, J. (2002). *Becoming evil: How ordinary people commit genocide and mass killing.* New York: Oxford University Press.

Watson, R. I., Jr. (1973). Investigation into deindividuation using a cross-cultural survey technique. *Journal of Personality and Social Psychology, 25,* 342–345.

Zimbardo, P. G. (1970). The human choice: Individuation, reason, and order versus deindividuation, impulse, and chaos. In W. J. Arnold & D. Levine (Eds.), *1969 Nebraska Symposium on Motivation* (pp. 237–307). Lincoln: University of Nebraska Press.

Zimbardo, P. G. (1975). On transforming experimental research into advocacy for social change. In M. Deutsch & H. Hornstein (Eds.), *Applying social psychology: implications for research, practice, and training* (pp. 33–66). Hillsdale, NJ: Erlbaum.

Zimbardo, P. G. (1976). Making sense of senseless vandalism. In E. P. Hollander & R. G. Hunt (Eds.), *Current perspectives in social psychology* (4th ed., pp. 129–134). Oxford, UK: Oxford University Press.

Zimbardo, P. G. (2003a). Mind control in Orwell's *1984*: Fictional concepts become operational realities in Jim Jones' jungle experiment. In M. Nussbaum, J. Goldsmith, & A. Gleason (Eds.), *1984: Orwell and our future.* Princeton: Princeton University Press.

Zimbardo, P. G. (2003b). Phantom menace: Is Washington terrorizing us more than Al Qaeda? *Psychology Today, 36*, pp. 34–36.

Zimbardo, P. G., Haney, C., Banks, C., & Jaffe, D. (1973, April 8). The mind is a formidable jailer: A Pirandellian prison. *The New York Times Magazine*, pp. 38 ff.

Zimbardo, P. G., Maslach, C., & Haney, C. (1999). Reflections on the Stanford Prison Experiment: Genesis, transformation, consequences. In T. Blass (Ed.), *Obedience to authority: Current perspectives on the Milgram Paradigm* (pp. 193–237). Mahwah, NJ: Erlbaum.

NOTES

APPENDIX

Digital Nation

List practical advice you ~~took~~ from Lights piece

Bauerlein and Light [illegible] might want the same thing from you. What is it?

Is it easier for you to take advice from Light or Bauerlein?

the two groups of sophomores.
indeed a single word, was a key
successful transitions repeatedly
ores who had experienced diffi-
vhen prompted.
o had a great first year typically
e, that they had to think about
e management, and time allo-
ast, sophomores who struggled
n any way.
year students find it a real chal-
ppy personally and effective in
nage their time well are often
rst arrive. It isn't easy for every
eavy demands of most college
igh school, reinforce the value
rnative of feeling overwhelmed
gned in college courses. When
ew arrivals, this idea of learn-
ink it is a wise one. The dis-
tes into a distinction between
le.

Activities

netimes, but what I do
l have been for me back
ealize it until I go home
afternoon. I forget how
0 P.M. and wake up at
A.M. and waking up at
And you're going from
he library, to meals, to
ent.

advice, I pass on some of
ourage them to take full
urge them to *get involved*
can be paid employment
h other students, or per-
sees understand this, but
ll, and some are nervous

rs who
habits
ademic
n't such
ourses—
rom me?
wn expe-

t work
material
It was a
couldn't

ot get off
his enor-
one sub-
k. Then I
week. So
to do with
spend a lit-

om high school
o certain behav-
, making superb
ngly similar stu-

f colleagues from
o groups of soph-
t year in all ways,
The interviewers'
ved freshman, had
ollege. They hoped

s (2001), Harvard Uni-

to find a few important differences between
They quickly discovered that one difference,
factor. Sophomores who had made the most
brought up this word on their own. Sophom
culty hardly ever mentioned the word, even

The critical word is *time*. Sophomores wh
talked about realizing, when they got to colle
how to spend their time. They mentioned ti
cation, and time as a scarce resource. In contr
during their first year rarely referred to time i

Several advisors have told me that some first-
lenge to allocate their time so they are both ha
their academic work. Students who learn to m
those who work hard on this topic when they fi
student. It requires systematic effort. But the h
courses, compared with what students faced in h
of making such an effort. It certainly beats the alte
when suddenly facing the amount of reading assi
seniors are asked what advice they would offer n
ing to manage time is a common response. I th
tinction in attitudes toward managing time transl
new students who prosper and those who strug

Balancing Academics and Othe

A sophomore told Buchanan and her colleagues:

> Everything here is so fast paced. I forget so
> here in a day is what an exciting month woul
> home. It's really intense. And I think I don't r
> for vacations and sleep until one o'clock in the
> in high school I used to go to bed at 10:3
> 8:00 A.M. Here you're going to bed at 1:00
> 8:30—I have a class at nine every morning.
> class, to study group, to my part-time job in t
> friends, to performance. It's been a big adjustm

Each year when new students come to me for
what I have learned from their predecessors: I en
advantage of the university community. Above all, I
in depth in at least one activity other than courses. I
if they need to earn money. It can be an activity wi
haps athletics or volunteer work. Many of my advi
a few need convincing. New students want to do w

when they first arrive. For a few students, their idea of life at college is to sit in classes for twelve to fifteen hours each week and spend the rest of their time studying alone in their rooms.

Some of these students are not very happy. There is a risk they will spend too much time alone. Whenever I see this pattern developing, I raise the issue. Their response is nearly always the same: "My academic work is my priority, and doing other things will hurt my academic work."

Thanks to findings from an extensive survey of Harvard undergraduates directed by Thomas Angelo, I and other advisors now know how to answer such students. We now have concrete data on how outside-of-class activities relate to academic success. The big finding is that a substantial commitment to one or two activities other than coursework—for as much as twenty hours per week—has little or no relationship to grades. But such commitments *do* have a strong relationship to overall satisfaction with college life. More involvement is strongly correlated with higher satisfaction.

Here is a brief overview of students' outside-of-class commitments. These are findings for just one campus. The situation on other campuses may differ somewhat, yet I expect the main relationships, which point to a strong conclusion, will hold up.

First let's consider *paid work*. More than half of all Harvard undergraduates work part time for money, regardless of their academic focus at college. More women work than men. Older students work more than younger students.

They work at an enormous variety of jobs. The most common by far is administrative/clerical, followed by research/data analysis. Women are more likely to have clerical jobs than men. Men are more likely to have custodial jobs than women. The most common time commitment for students who work is between seven and twelve hours per week.

A steadily increasing number of undergraduates work in computing and technology. Many do this for their own learning, separate from paid employment. And for a growing number (now approaching 55 percent), their task on the job is either to help develop new technologies or new applications of existing technologies or to help others on campus apply technology to their work.

There is no significant relationship between paid work and grades. Students who work a lot, a little, or not at all show similar patterns of grades. The grade distributions of students whose jobs have flexible schedules are almost identical to those with less flexible schedules.

Students who work and those who don't work express identical levels of satisfaction with their overall college experience. Workers' ratings of the "overall quality of their courses" are similar to those of nonworkers. Workers' ratings of "overall satisfaction with the challenge level of courses," are similar to those of nonworkers. Responses are also similar for "overall satisfaction with relationships with friends," and "satisfaction with romances."

Two striking findings pop up when students are asked to describe their satisfaction with work experiences. First, on average, the more hours per week a student works, the happier he or she is with work experience as an integral part of college. Second, three-fourths of all working students say that working has a positive effect on their overall satisfaction with college. Only 6 percent think work has a negative effect. Women are even more likely than men to report that work has a positive effect.

What about *extracurricular activities*—outside-of-class commitments not including paid work or intercollegiate athletics? For these the participation rate is 80 percent: 86 percent of women and 76 percent of men. Part of this gender difference is due to men's heavier commitments to intercollegiate athletic teams. This gap has shrunk dramatically in the last ten years as women increasingly participate in intercollegiate sports.

Seventy percent of all students are involved in two or more activities, and 14 percent are involved in four or five. Of those participating in any extracurricular activities, 68 percent invest more than six hours per week on average, and 34 percent spend more than twelve hours per week.

As with paid work, there is no significant relationship between participating in extracurricular activities and academic performance. Students who participate and those who don't have similar grade distributions. Even students with heavy involvement do not have significantly lower grades than those who are less involved.

Another type of out-of-class involvement is *volunteer work*. In any one semester, 25 percent of all undergraduates are involved in volunteering. More than 65 percent of all students do volunteer work at some point during college. Women volunteer somewhat more than men, and upperclassmen are significantly more likely to volunteer than first-year students. Students who work for money somehow find time to do volunteer work more often than those who don't work for money.

Volunteers typically spend between three and six hours per week at their activity. The average is just over five hours. Of the volunteers, 46 percent work with children and teens, 13 percent with the homeless and the poor, 9 percent with handicapped people, and 10 percent with senior citizens.

Why do students volunteer? They report that they "enjoy helping others," or they "want to give something back," or they "want to make the world a better place." Of students now volunteering, 96 percent plan to continue doing so in the future.

As with paid work and extracurricular activities, there is no significant relationship between volunteering and grades. On average, students who do volunteer work have slightly higher grades than those who don't. When asked how volunteering affects their grades, students report no negative impact whatever. When asked how volunteering affects their social life and overall satisfaction with college, students report that on balance it has a positive effect on both.

With the exception of *intercollegiate athletics*, no extracurricular activity is associated with lower grades. Intercollegiate athletes at our campus have slightly lower grades on average than non-athletes. From explorations on other campuses, I believe this finding is widely true. Among athletes, there is also a modest but clear negative relationship between hours spent on sports and grades. It is important to mention one fascinating trade-off here. While varsity athletes have slightly lower grades than average, they also are, as a group, among the happiest students on campus. They have many friends and feel closely bonded to the college.

lower grades but happier

To summarize, two main findings stand out. If we aggregate all the nonacademic commitments of students, adding up total hours spent on paid employment, extracurricular activities, volunteer work, and athletics, *there is no significant relationship between level of involvement and grades. Yet there is a clear relationship between participation and satisfaction with college.* Students involved in some outside-of-classroom activities are far happier with their college experience than the few who are not involved.

Participating in the Arts

> My engagement with the theater, not on the acting side, but on the technical side and choreography, has had an impact on me that I wouldn't have predicted when I arrived as a freshman. It has helped me to establish unexpected connections between what I do at the Dramatic Society, or the Experimental Theater, and academic work. I am a History and Literature concentrator. One example came up when we discussed two recent plays by Edward Albee, and how their organizational structure is so different from plays written in the nineteenth century. I had worked hard on producing an Albee play at the Experimental, and it was such a pleasure to share insights about that play with my class.
>
> I don't want this to sound too arrogant, but I think because of my work with drama here I might have actually known more about Albee's writing structure than my instructor, good as she is. After all, I lived it, brooded about it, and had to actually produce it on stage. I think this is what some people mean when they talk about different activities "dovetailing." For me, it all came together thanks to my theater work.
>
> Not every band member became my friend. In fact, I don't especially love many of them. But within a week, since we practiced several times, I found myself making about half a dozen friends. We have stayed close throughout our years here. Between those friends and unexpectedly feeling part of this community the moment I put on my band uniform, it changed my entire sense of well-being.

Many students make a substantial commitment to one or more activities in the arts. Artistic activities are enormously popular at many colleges. Students engage with the arts even more, in sheer numbers, than with athletics and with politics. This is true at nearly every college I have visited. Second to volunteer work, it is the most popular area for students' outside-of-class activities.

If we define the arts broadly to include music, singing groups, orchestra, chamber music, dance, and dramatic productions, nearly half of all undergraduates at Harvard participate at some time during their college years. If we include writing, directing, producing, and doing tech work for programs of music, theater, and dance, the proportion rises to over half. When undergraduates track how they spend their time, about 35 percent find that engagement with the arts is the activity that takes the biggest hunk of their outside-of-class time. This includes planning, tryouts, rehearsals, and actual performances.

Students are enthusiastic about "the incredibly active arts scene" on campus—and I have found similar enthusiasm on many campuses. They characterize the arts as an important source of both pleasure and learning. Since certain kinds of involvement in the arts offer any student at any college the opportunity to build connections between academic work and extracurricular interests, it is worth discussing why students find engagement with arts activities so special.

First, for many students they serve the classic function of sheer pleasure. This pleasure has nothing to do with connecting, say, music outside of class with the formal study of music in classes. It is done for its own sake. Something that takes an undergraduate's mind away from intense academic work. Hundreds of students report that singing or acting or directing or dancing or playing a musical instrument is simply fulfilling, a joy, a release, a "very different kind of creative activity from writing a research paper."

fragment!

A second reason given by students builds more specifically on how the arts can help to make connections between in-class academic work and outside-of-class activities. A remarkably large number of interviewees mention connections between their own pleasure in the arts and their formal classroom work. Directing, or acting in, or "tech-ing for" a play by Anton Chekhov or Arthur Miller helps students develop insights that transfer to academic work. Their experience with drama leads them to think more deeply about writing, about history, about psychology, about physical environments, about literature in specific contexts, than some might from just reading a play for a class. Similarly, understanding the context and background of music that a member of the orchestra is performing, complete with the context of the composer's life and perhaps the composer's culture, gives many students insights to enrich their academic work. Connections emerge, sometimes unexpectedly. Not for all students, but for some.

A third finding is that a significant fraction of students who participate in the arts report learning certain things about themselves. Sometimes what they learn is unexpected. And sometimes what they learn shapes what classes they choose, their excitement about these classes, and occasionally even what careers they decide to pursue after they graduate. More than a few students report in their interviews that a combination of engagement with the arts and formal academic work shaped their "next steps" in life.

This idea of the arts connecting to classwork is a recurring theme. Some students report that a certain kind of performing, such as drama or singing, opened their eyes to new possibilities for their own future work—possibilities they simply had not thought of before. One example is a young man who tried out for and joined one of the *a capella* singing groups in his first year. He knew he had a good singing voice, yet he was hesitant to perform publicly. By participating in the singing group, he not only overcame his hesitancy, he came to genuinely relish this public performance. He stayed with the group for the next three years, and senior year he became its president. In his senior year he applied to graduate schools of public policy and public administration. He was now considering a career in elective politics. It was performing with the singing group that had given him new personal confidence.

A fourth reason students find arts activities so engaging is that such activities offer special opportunities to interact with, and ideally to learn from, fellow students who come from backgrounds unlike their own. Some of the best interactions, and the most powerful learning experiences, occur when students work together to achieve a common goal. Often at college this happens around a common academic pursuit. But activities in the arts offer a remarkably similar opportunity—a chance to work with people who may be different in countless ways, including academic interests, yet share a commitment to producing a superb play, concert, or ballet performance.

A number of students bring up this point with special enthusiasm. They say that working with others in the arts, more than any other specific activity, has enabled them to benefit from, and learn from, their extraordinarily diverse and talented fellow students. The result is that these students report a high level of engagement, and satisfaction, with their overall college experience.

Even more impressive numbers of students say that by participating in arts groups, especially in the performing arts, they learn about themselves—their strengths, their weaknesses, their interests. And especially how to integrate active commitment to the arts with the college's intense academic demands. In coursework, the task is to do a professor's readings and assignments. You work hard, and you learn a lot about physics, or history, or economics, or literature, but not necessarily so much about yourself. If learning about yourself is an integral part of education, engaging with the arts offers a critical and unique opportunity.

Getting Help When Needed

> I can't expect the faculty to read my mind, so in the end it really is up to me to take charge of this. My message to other students is simple. Unending help is available, but you have to ask for it. I learned an important lesson. Don't keep academic problems a secret. Unfortunately, it took me far too long to learn it. I hope others with my dilemma figure this out more quickly.

Why do some students perform significantly less well than expected? Reflecting on three questions may help students understand their own situation, and may help their advisors know how to help them. First, are there certain problems that are not unique to any one student, but that are shared by others who are also having academic trouble? Second, what can advisors do to help students who are struggling? Third, what can the students do to help themselves?

While interviewing students, we searched for patterns of adjusting to college, and choices students make, that lead talented people to struggle. We turned up two symptoms of students in trouble and four possible explanations for that trouble. I am confident they characterize many campuses across the country.

(2) Symptoms of Trouble

It is easy enough to identify certain students about whom faculty and advisors should be concerned—those with distressingly low grades. But they are just the tip of the iceberg. There are two other symptoms that, while less easy to identify, may well be predictive of troubling outcomes.

One symptom, a warning flag, is that a student feels a sense of isolation from the rest of the college community. A handful of undergraduates may relish such isolation, but only a handful. With a bit of effort, an advisor can spot isolated students. They are not involved in any extracurricular activities. They are not members of a study group in any of their courses. And they deal with their low grades by going from classroom to dorm room, closing their door, and studying, studying, and then studying some more, nearly always alone. If their grades don't improve as the year progresses, they don't change their behavior pattern. They just do more of the same, stay up later and later at night, or, in a few cases, simply give up on their coursework.

The second symptom is unwillingness to seek help. Many students show little hesitancy in seeking help from a professor, a departmental advisor, a teaching fellow, or a residence hall advisor. Most universities and colleges have their own organizations designed to provide help.

Yet more than a few students are hesitant to ask for help. And if a student who is having trouble does not seek help and avoids sharing problems with an advisor or professor or teaching fellow, it's hard to give help. Our interviews with forty sophomores who were struggling drove home this point sharply. Of the twenty students who were struggling yet were able to share their problems and to seek help from one of these many sources, all, *without exception*, were able to work at developing strategies to improve their academic performance.

Is asking for help good?

But most of the twenty who were unable to share their problems remained distressingly isolated. They became caught in a downward spiral of poor grades and lack of engagement with other people at the college. It was far harder for them, struggling alone, to turn their situation around.

As the interviews revealed this repeated pattern, my colleagues began to work on concrete suggestions for reaching out to students, even to those students who might be initially resistant to getting help. We met with some success. Four particular sources of potential trouble, and suggestions for helping students to help themselves, emerged from this work.

Reasons for Academic Trouble

One source of trouble is poor management of time. Several of the sophomores with poor grades were studying so inefficiently that they themselves were taken aback when they described their study habits to our interviewers. The single biggest trouble with time use for nearly all students who struggle is their pattern of studying in a series of short bursts. Instead of spending sustained periods of time engaging with their coursework, they squeeze in twenty-five minutes between two classes. They stop by the library to read for thirty minutes on the way to dinner. They begin writing long essays, or working on problem sets, for the next day's classes after coming home from a full evening with a drama group, or sports practice, or singing rehearsal. They are tired before they start, and a long night lies ahead.

This failure to dig in and engage with one piece of work in depth for hours at a time is hurting these students enormously. But the way they organize their time never seems to include longer stretches for serious engagement. Anyone who does much writing knows how difficult it is to do effective and serious writing when the hard work is forced into ten minutes here and fifteen minutes there. This sort of time allocation simply does not enable most people to produce excellent written material. And while this may be obvious to most faculty members, interviews reveal that for a large proportion of students in academic trouble, it is not so obvious at all.

A second source of trouble is that many students who struggle continue to organize their work in college the same way they did in high school. For the lucky ones, this works. For others, especially those who were academic stars in high school but at schools that made only modest demands upon them, this strategy can lead to big problems.

Some students have great difficulty developing new study skills. It is just too easy to continue, locked in, using old patterns. One crucial skill that students must constantly refine is "critical thinking": the ability to synthesize arguments and evidence from multiple sources, sources that often disagree. Nearly all of the students who were having academic difficulty pointed out that their high schools did not demand much of this type of thinking, but that at college it is a crucial skill.

Compounding the problem for students who are struggling academically is their observation that most of their fellow students make the adjustment from high school to college without much difficulty. Watching their friends and classmates and roommates develop certain skills that elude them is maddening. A first-year student described the frustration:

> All four of us in my rooming group are taking economics. I would say we are all about equally smart, I know we have similar SAT scores, and we discuss the material sometimes in the evening. Yet they were getting A's and I kept getting C's. I just couldn't figure out why.
>
> Finally, it was driving me nuts, so I went for help. My resident advisor asked if she could see my notes from that class. She looked them over carefully, and then asked me a few questions based on those notes. She helped me to realize that I was great on "giving back the facts," but not so good at all at extending those facts to new situations. Yet here at college, all the questions on exams are about new situations. This is unlike my high school, where all the questions involved simply spitting back the basics.
>
> There is no point in blaming the high school. It just took someone here to help me refocus how I study. Now I understand what the goal of the whole enterprise here actually is. I still am not getting A's, but at least solid B+'s. I don't know what would have happened if I hadn't asked for help and had just continued using that old high school style.

A third source of trouble for some students is their selection of courses. Nearly without exception, students who are struggling, or who are dissatisfied with their academic performance, are taking nothing but large, introductory courses. When asked why they made these choices, nearly every student offers the same response: "to get my requirements out of the way." Clearly, a few students arrive at college each year with the belief that making the most of their experience here involves a sequence of steps. Step one: get all the requirements out of the way. Step two: choose a concentration or major. Step three: take advanced courses in the concentration, while saving electives, the "good stuff," for junior and senior year.

Adopting a strategy of getting the required courses out of the way may work fine for some students. But nearly all students who were in trouble reported that they had chosen this strategy. Since many of the basic required courses have large enrollments, they make it possible for any student to become distressingly anonymous. No professor with a class of hundreds of students pretends to be able to get to know each student well. This is a special dilemma at any large university. Students who choose their courses in this way may rarely engage seriously with a faculty member throughout their first year at college. It is important to stress that this characterization applies to only a small number of students. Yet for this small number, even if it is just 5 to 10 percent of all students, the quality of their academic experience is diminished.

Another disadvantage of using freshman year to simply "get the requirements out of the way" is that students may not find courses that truly engage them, that excite them. The result is that by the end of freshman year (or by sophomore year at many colleges), when it is time to choose a concentration, a student may not yet have been "turned on" by any discipline. The majority of students who followed this strategy of "getting the requirements out of the way" when choosing courses in freshman year regretted having done so.

A fourth source of trouble is a particular study habit shared by almost all students who are struggling academically: they always study alone. Students point out that those who always study alone are isolating themselves from a key benefit of college—the opportunity to learn from fellow students. Fortunately, studying with other students is a suggestion that is relatively easy for a faculty member or an advisor to make to any student. I hope students who read this will decide for themselves to work cooperatively, at least some of the time. 

This idea of working cooperatively outside of classes may be new to many students. Indeed, it is new to many faculty members, who went to college when students' working together outside of classes was forbidden, was considered cheating.

Choosing Living Arrangements

With whom should I live? On a residential campus, nearly every student must answer this question. And the decisions students make play a critical part in how they experience college. Thinking through this decision in a careful, systematic way will be an investment that yields high dividends.

A South Asian senior talked about this issue with interviewer Anna Fincke:

> Freshman year we had a big mixture. We were six people: Jewish from New York, Jewish from Boston, WASP from Orange County, California, another Indian from Florida, Chinese from California, and me. It was a real mixture in terms of racial background, economic background, and interests. We had all different concentrations: engineering, economics, biology, biochemistry, physics, and social studies. We all wanted to become different things: aerospace engineer, lawyer, doctor, businessman.
>
> We became such a family. That's been one of my most valuable experiences here. I got sick in March and they treated me like my mother would. One guy woke me up every two hours to give me medicine. They were running all over the place, talking to my teachers. And they didn't think twice.
>
> We were really a family. We had a big common room, and we would spend a lot of time with each other, laughing, making jokes. We still have reunions. It was a very meaningful experience. Diversity was central to it all.
>
> The guy from Orange County was conservative, traditional, came from a WASPy family. We butted heads, so to speak. Politically, we'd be battling. He had some religious right leanings. I'm pretty liberal. We would argue or debate. I really like him as a person. It's good to consider someone my good friend who has such divergent views.

> Enlightenment about other cultures doesn't often come in an epiphany like that.

The first people new students meet, the first day on campus, are their roommates or suitemates. These roommates are assigned by the college; students do not choose their own roommates for first year. At Harvard, first-year students usually live in groups of between two and four. Often, because of the architecture of the first-year dormitories, two groups of suitemates push open a door, keep it open, and informally become a larger "living group" of four or six or eight.

The next group of people new students meet, while they are moving in, are other first-year students who are simultaneously arriving and moving into their entry. At Harvard each student lives in an entry. An entry consists of a dormitory door that leads to a group of rooms and suites, which typically house a total of between fifteen and twenty-five students. This group of students in an entry is assigned to a proctor, usually a graduate student who lives in that entry. This proctor, when all goes as it should, invites all students in the entry to gatherings. These gatherings may focus on simply getting acquainted, or sharing general information, or holiday and birthday celebrations. Sometimes they focus on discussion of academic topics, such as helping students think about how to choose academic majors and concentrations.

Harvard has had such living arrangements for many years. Almost without exception, students describe their first-year rooming experiences as setting a tone for their interactions with other students from backgrounds different from their own. A majority of rooming groups include some ethnic diversity. And every undergraduate lives in an entry that has substantial ethnic diversity. As a result, from the moment a student arrives and puts down the suitcases, the abstraction of a "diverse undergraduate community" comes alive as he or she immediately sees, interacts with, and begins to go to meals with students from a broad range of ethnic and racial backgrounds.

The tone has been set. And this immediate exposure of every newcomer to people from different backgrounds—from that moment of arrival, to the first meals together, to the first dormitory entry meeting, to all the Freshman Week activities—is what nearly all students characterize as the single most critical, positive first step. It is critical for helping each student feel part of a community. A community with fellow first-year students who look different, and bring different interests and perspectives to campus, and with whom the student will be living, day in and day out, for an entire year. This tone and spirit inevitably become a natural part of college life.

Why do students bring this up over and over as such a big deal? For two reasons. First, they believe the college is sending a message, loud and clear:

the message that living with a diverse group of classmates, day and night, weekdays and weekends, *from the outset*, is a standard, important, and, we all hope, enjoyable aspect of coming to this college.

The second reason so many students consider this first-year roommate planning so important is that whether or not any particular undergraduate chooses to continue to live with his or her first-year roommates in ensuing years, an overwhelming majority describe the first-year living experience as a positive one. And the learning that flows from ethnic diversity is repeatedly characterized as an important component of that experience.

As a result, the most frequent suggestion from students is to continue to embed diversity, in a planned, purposeful way, into first-year living arrangements. Doing so sends a message about an idea the college leadership considers important. It leads to surprises. Sometimes it leads to stresses, but usually those stresses are worked through and result in significant learning. In some cases, it leads to lasting friendships that students might never have made otherwise.

Evidence that students respond positively to this policy of embedding diversity into first-year living arrangements comes from their choices of roommates for future years. Interviewer Shu-Ling Chen has found that after freshman year, when they have entirely free choice of roommates, students often decide to live with a remarkable array of friends. For example, several students described to Chen, in late spring of their first year, the living groups they had chosen for sophomore year:

A white man planned to live with another white man, a man from Russia, a Haitian man, two Asian-American women, a black woman, and a Lebanese woman.

A Hispanic man planned to live with "two blacks, six whites, a Pakistani from London, and me."

Another Hispanic man was going to live with one other Latino, three whites, two blacks, and an Asian-American.

A Chinese-American woman planned to live with fourteen others: one other Asian-American, one black, one Hawaiian, one deeply religious Jew, and ten other whites.

A conclusion seems clear. When given an opportunity to choose whom to live with as an upperclassman, a large fraction of undergraduates choose a diverse set of friends and roommates. They report that their choices are influenced in large measure by first-year experiences with their roommates and dormitory neighbors. The assignment of first-year roommates and neighbors shapes whom they meet and whom they come to know. Their strong suggestion to those who design first-year living patterns—it is close to unanimous—is to keep in mind that initial living arrangements can and do shape all future social interactions, especially inter-ethnic social interactions.

NOTES